APOCALYPSE AGAINST EMPIRE

APOCALYPSE AGAINST EMPIRE

Theologies of Resistance in Early Judaism

Anathea E. Portier-Young

WILLIAM B. EERDMANS PUBLISHING COMPANY
GRAND RAPIDS, MICHIGAN / CAMBRIDGE, U.K.

Published 2011 by
Wm. B. Eerdmans Publishing Co.
2140 Oak Industrial Drive N.E., Grand Rapids, Michigan 49505 /
P.O. Box 163, Cambridge CB3 9PU U.K.

Printed in the United States of America

17 16 15 14 13 12 11   7 6 5 4 3 2 1

Library of Congress Cataloging-in-Publication Data

Portier-Young, Anathea, 1973-
Apocalypse against empire: theologies of resistance in early Judaism /
Anathea E. Portier-Young.
p.   cm.
Includes bibliographical references.
ISBN 978-0-8028-6598-4 (pbk.: alk. paper)
1. Resistance (Philosophy)   2. Jews — History — 586 B.C.–70 A.D.
3. Bible. O.T. Former prophets — History of Biblical events.
4. Ethiopic book of Enoch — Criticism, interpretation, etc.
5. Judaism — Social aspects — Israel.   6. Maccabees.
7. Military history in the Bible.   8. Palestine — History, Military.
I. Title.

B105.R47.P67   2011
296.3'82 — dc22

2010022222

www.eerdmans.com

To Jim Crenshaw,
my teacher, colleague, and friend

Contents

Contents

Contents

Foreword

The last half century has seen intense, if sporadic, study of early Jewish apocalyptic literature. Much of this study has been literary. We have attained a clearer grasp of the apocalyptic genre and of the traditional associations of apocalyptic symbolism. We have also made important advances in the sociological study of apocalypticism, inspired in part by Paul Hanson's groundbreaking study, *The Dawn of Apocalyptic* (Fortress Press, 1975) and the lively debate it stimulated, but also by the broader interest in apocalypticism as a social phenomenon at the end of the twentieth century. Scholars have long recognized that apocalyptic literature originated as resistance literature, even if was sometimes co-opted for other purposes in the course of history. We must admit, however, that the study of the social function of apocalyptic writings has lagged somewhat in relation to literary and historico-traditional studies.

Anathea Portier-Young bids fair to redress this situation in this sweeping and learned work. She breaks new ground in two important respects.

First, she has read widely in the theoretical literature on the subjects of imperial power and resistance thereto. As a result, she brings to this subject a degree of sophistication that has been lacking in previous biblical scholarship on the subject. She sees the exercise of power as a complex phenomenon, sometimes mediated by brute force but often by symbolism and ritual. Equally, resistance is not simplistic rejection but may involve selective appropriation or subversion of the ideology of the dominant power. Both the exercise of power and resistance are processes of negotiation, and each may take a range of forms.

Second, Portier-Young has immersed herself in the study of the Seleucid empire in a way that biblical scholars seldom do. Not since the early work of Martin Hengel have we seen such a thick description of Seleucid history and politics in the context of biblical scholarship. Building on the work of such scholars as John Ma, she views the Seleucid empire in terms of its strategies of domination. This enables her to shed new light on the perennially debated motives of Antiochus Epiphanes in his persecution of the Judeans. Portier-Young views his actions through the lens of *Realpolitik*, the strategy of a pragmatic ruler intent on asserting and maintaining his own power. Epiphanes was no madman but, rather, a cynical and brutal pragmatist.

The theoretical studies and the in-depth historical background of this book establish the context for the early Jewish apocalyptic writings. Apocalyptic literature has often been stereotyped as otherworldly. Portier-Young makes a persuasive case that it is deeply immersed in political reality and cannot be properly understood without seeing it against the foil of Hellenistic imperial rule.

This book makes an important contribution to the study of Judea under Seleucid rule and to the social context of apocalyptic literature, but it also does more than that. The use of state terror Portier-Young describes here is in no way peculiar to the Seleucid empire. It is an important phenomenon in the world we live in. Equally, the diverse strategies of resistance that she describes are still employed in the modern world. It is an uncomfortable reality that modern America is most often perceived as empire in the tradition of the Seleucids. Portier-Young's sympathetic account of the various strategies of resistance should help us understand the motives of people who resist imperial domination and are often labeled as terrorists. But it also shows that recourse to violence is not the only strategy of resistance that is sanctioned and modeled by the scriptures we have inherited from ancient Judaism.

JOHN J. COLLINS
Holmes Professor of Old Testament
Yale

Preface

In 2004 I completed my dissertation, "Theologies of Resistance in Daniel, the Apocalypse of Weeks, the Book of Dreams, and the Testament of Moses," under the direction of James Crenshaw at Duke University. I thank Jim for granting me the freedom to dream up my own project, for directing me with gentle grace, and for modeling intellectual courage, precision, and care. I offer special thanks, once again, to the other members of my committee, Richard Hays, Eric Meyers, and Ed Sanders.

In that earlier project I offered a literary and theological analysis of four resistant responses to Seleucid domination in Judea. I was especially interested in the intersection of theology, hermeneutics, and ethics, in the use of Israel's war traditions, and in understanding why two of the texts I studied advocated armed revolt while two advocated martyrdom. I thought I would come away with a clear sense of their differences. Instead I came away impressed by how much these four texts had in common. They functioned *as resistance literature* in remarkably similar ways, owing in large part, it seemed, to their common genre, historical apocalypse (or, in the case of *Testament of Moses,* an apocalyptic testament that shared many generic features with the historical apocalypses). This conclusion left me with a new set of questions about the genre and the circumstances in which it arose. I have taken them up in this book.

A few years ago I sent my dissertation to John Collins, who sent back a reader's report with copious guidance on how to make this a better book. He challenged me to define resistance, to engage the work of James C. Scott, and to weigh in on emerging debates in the study of Enochic Judaism. He asked me to say more about what, exactly, these writers and their contemporaries were resisting, especially if some of the apocalypses dated earlier than Antiochus's persecution in 167 BCE. The questions seemed straightforward, and I naively thought I could turn it around in a few months. As I dug deeper, I realized there was a lot to work out. I am grateful to John for the challenges and for the encouragement. Pursuing these questions has not only improved the book but has made me a better scholar.

The book you hold in your hands has (heavily) revised versions of three chapters from my dissertation (chs. 7, 9, and 10 of the present book). It also has seven new chapters, including all of Parts One (ch. 1) and Two (chs. 2–6) as well as chapter 8.

When I voiced my bold hope to Michael Thomson that this book "fly to press," I didn't dare to expect it could happen. To the incredibly supportive team at Eerdmans who gave this book wings, I offer profuse thanks: Michael Thomson, Linda Bieze, Jon Pott, Allen Myers, David Cottingham, and Jenny Hoffman.

I owe thanks also to Hindy Najman, for your encouragement and grace.

As I was preparing my manuscript for press I had the pleasure of reading Richard Horsley's *Revolt of the Scribes: Resistance and Apocalyptic Origins* (Minneapolis: Fortress, 2010). Part One of Horsley's book covers much the same ground as my own book. Yet it would have been disingenuous to insert references to Horsley's book throughout this manuscript. Instead, I offer a few words here. My hope is that whoever is interested in this subject will read both books. Horsley's thesis and my own are very similar — I take this as a good sign! Starting from the observation that the surviving "apocalyptic" texts from ancient Judea all "focus on imperial rule and the opposition to it," Horsley insists on "a more historical approach," specifically calling for "critical attention to the political-economic-religious structure and dynamics within Judean society in the broader context of conflict with the dominant empires." I could not agree more, and my reader will find just such critical attention in Part Two. But our approaches, and our accounts of that history, also differ in significant ways, and that impacts our conclusions. Moreover, in shifting the focus to history, Horsley aims to shift the focus away from genre and away from "apocalypticism." Questioning the distinctiveness of the apocalyptic worldview and discarding the genre label "historical apocalypse," Horsley prefers to analyze the extant texts apart from constructed genre expectations. I believe this is a mistake. I argue that the characteristic features of the genre historical apocalypse, including such elements as the prophetic review of history, narrative frame, angelic mediation, and revered human recipient of revelation, all play a crucial role in how the text functions as resistant discourse and how the text presents its program of resistance. This is consistent in each of the texts I study in this volume and tells us a great deal about the nascent genre. Reading Horsley's book makes me all the more excited to think about future work on the history and development of the genre apocalypse. I thank Horsley for bringing a new surge of energy to the questions of empire, resistance, and apocalyptic.

I completed several chapters in Parts One and Two during a year-long sabbatical in 2008-09. I owe a tremendous debt of gratitude to my colleagues in the Catholic Biblical Association of America, who supported my work for six months of that sabbatical through a Young Scholars' Fellowship. The great gift of the sabbatical was not only the chance to "get it done" but also to remember why I love my research. Every day of my sabbatical I gave thanks for each of you, and I continue to do so.

Duke University supported me during my sabbatical as well, and I thank Dean Greg Jones, the office of Academic Affairs, our library staff, and others at the University for vital support at this time and throughout my years at Duke.

As the project grew (and grew) Jon Berquist, Greg Carey, John Collins, Joel Marcus, Bill Portier, Bonnie Portier, Phil Portier, and Lauren Winner all read and commented on multiple chapters and assorted parts, often on very short notice. They gave encouragement when I most needed it and also helped me see weaknesses and ways to remedy them. I incorporated as many of your suggestions as I could. I offer very deep gratitude to each of you.

Many colleagues at Duke and elsewhere have been conversation partners as I explored new ways of thinking and tested ideas. I have learned more from you than I can say. I owe special thanks to my colleagues in Old Testament, Ellen Davis and Stephen Chapman, for your mentoring, support, and example.

The students in my courses on Daniel and Apocalyptic Literature and Early Jewish Apocalypses created the forum where I worked out many of the ideas in this book. You are a treasure.

Anne Weston provided invaluable editorial assistance, first as a colleague and then as a friend. From teaching me about comma splices and restrictive clauses to fixing my dashes, hyphens, and multiform footnotes, Anne's light but careful touch graces every page. As the project neared its conclusion Anne worked at lightning speed. There aren't enough honeycomb-filled chocolate bars in the world to convey my thanks for the gift of your patience, time, and expertise.

To Judith Heyhoe, for help with indexes, thank you!

I thank Sean Burrus, Jay Forth, Tyler Garrard, Jill Hicks, Logan Kruck, Mindy Makant, Dan Rhodes, Candice Ryals, Denise Thorpe, and Jess Wong (quite a team!) for your cheerful help in tracking down references, adding to my piles of folders (you may not have thought I would read them all, but I really did), and assembling the bibliography. I thank Diane Decker for helping them and me with photocopies, scans, printing, and logistics. Even more, I thank Diane for daily moral support, friendship, cheerleading, and the big thermometer-chart that got me to the end.

So many friends have loved and supported me and my family along the way. I cannot name everyone here. I thank you. I am incredibly fortunate to count you in my life.

Preface

Finally, I thank my family. My mom and dad, Bonnie and Bill Portier, knew when to encourage and when to remind. That was tricky. You did great! You bless me so much. During the past two years my husband Steve has repeatedly made time and space for me to write. I don't know how. This book would not have happened without Steve's support. I am truly grateful. No one has wanted this book to end as much as I have, but my son Sebastian comes close. Sebastian, I thank you for your patience and understanding. To you alone of my readers I say, close this book immediately! Let's get back to our adventures! And let's start planning for a book we'll write together one day . . .

Abbreviations

Ancient Authors

Arist.	Aristotle
Jos.	Josephus
Polyb.	Polybius
Diod.	Diodorus
Vell. Pat.	Velleius Paterculus
Xen.	Xenophon

Primary Sources

1 En.	*1 Enoch*
A.J.	Josephus *Antiquitates judaicae* (Jewish Antiquities)
Ad Nic.	Isocrates, *Ad Nicoclem* (To Nicocles)
Aem.	Plutarch *Aemilius Paulus*
Ages.	Xenophon *Agesilaeus*
Anab.	Arrian *Anabasis*
Anach.	Lucian *Anacharsis*
B.J.	Josephus *Bellum judaicum* (Jewish War)
Exod. Rab.	*Exodus Rabbah*
Flacc.	Philo *In Flaccum* (Against Flaccus)
Ill.	Appian *Illyriaca* (Illyrian Wars)
In Dan.	Jerome *In Danielem*
Jub.	*Jubilees*
L.A.B.	*Liber antiquitatum biblicarum* (Pseudo-Philo)
LXX	Septuagint
Mac.	Appian *Macedonian Affairs*
OG	Old Greek
Or.	Dio Chrysostom *Orationes*

Pol.	Aristotle *Politica* (Politics)
PV	Aeschylus *Prometheus Vinctus* (Prometheus Bound)
Resp.	Plato *Respublica* (Republic)
Sib. Or.	*Sibylline Oracles*
Syr.	Appian *Syriaca* (Syrian Wars)
Tg. Isa.	*Targum Isaiah*
T. Mos.	*Testament of Moses*

Secondary Sources

AJA	*American Journal of Archaeology*
AJSR	*Association for Jewish Studies Review*
BASOR	*Bulletin of the American Schools of Oriental Research*
BibInt	*Biblical Interpretation*
BDB	F. Brown, S. R. Driver, and C. A. Briggs. *A Hebrew and English Lexicon of the Old Testament.* Oxford, 1907
BTB	*Biblical Theology Bulletin*
CBQ	*Catholic Biblical Quarterly*
CBQMS	Catholic Biblical Quarterly Monograph Series
CCSL	Corpus Christianorum: Series latina. Turnhout, 1953-
CEJL	Commentaries on Early Jewish Literature
CT	Cuneiform Texts from Babylonian Tablets in the British Museum. London, 1896-
C. Ord. Ptol.	*Corpus des ordonnances des Ptolémées*
EA	*Epigraphica Anatolica*
FOTL	Forms of Old Testament Literature
HeyJ	*Heythrop Journal*
HTR	*Harvard Theological Review*
HUCA	*Hebrew Union College Annual*
ICC	International Critical Commentary
IEJ	*Israel Exploration Journal*
IJAHS	*International Journal of African Historical Studies*
JAAR	*Journal of the American Academy of Religion*
JANESCU	*Journal of the Ancient Near Eastern Society of Columbia University*
JBL	*Journal of Biblical Literature*
JCS	*Journal of Cuneiform Studies*
JJS	*Journal of Jewish Studies*
JRE	*Journal of Religious Ethics*
JSJ	*Journal for the Study of Judaism in the Persian, Hellenistic, and Roman Periods*
JSOT	*Journal for the Study of the Old Testament*

JSP	*Journal for the Study of the Pseudepigrapha*
LSJ	H. G. Liddell, R. Scott, H. S. Jones. *A Greek-English Lexicon.* 9th ed. with revised supplement. Oxford, 1996
Neot	*Neotestamentica*
NIB	*The New Interpreter's Bible*
NIDOTTE	*New International Dictionary of Old Testament Theology and Exegesis.* Edited by W. A. VanGemeren. 5 vols. Grand Rapids, 1997
NTS	*New Testament Studies*
PL	Patrologia latina [= Patrologiae cursus completus: Series latina]. Edited by J.-P. Migne. 217 vols. Paris, 1844-64
PRSt	*Perspectives in Religious Studies*
RB	*Revue biblique*
REJ	*Revue des études juives*
RevPhil	*Revue de philologie*
RevQ	*Revue de Qumran*
RIDA	*Revue Internationale des Droits de l'Antiquité*
SBL	Society of Biblical Literature
SBLSCS	Society of Biblical Literature Septuagint and Cognate Studies
SBLSP	*Society of Biblical Literature Seminar Papers*
SEG	*Supplementum Epigraphicum Graecum*
SIFC	*Studi Italiani di Filologia Classica*
TDNT	*Theological Dictionary of the New Testament.* Edited by G. Kittel and G. Friedrich. Translated by G. W. Bromiley. 10 vols. Grand Rapids, 1964-76
TDOT	*Theological Dictionary of the Old Testament.* Edited by G. J. Botterweck and H. Ringgren. Translated by J. T. Willis, G. W. Bromiley, and D. E. Green. 15 vols. Grand Rapids, 1974-2006
USQR	*Union Seminary Quarterly Review*
VT	*Vetus Testamentum*
WBC	Word Biblical Commentary
ZNW	*Zeitschrift für die neutestamentliche Wissenschaft und die Kunde der älteren Kirche*
ZPE	*Zeitschrift für Papyrologie und Epigraphik*

Introduction

In 167 BCE the Seleucid king Antiochus IV Epiphanes issued an edict that
sought to annul the ancestral laws of Judea, proscribing traditional Jewish religion and mandating new religious practice in its place. According to
2 Maccabees, 22,000 Seleucid troops already occupied the city of Jerusalem, and
had already massacred and enslaved thousands among its population. Now
they would kill any who did not comply with the king's edict. Many Judeans did
comply with Antiochus's program of terror. In so doing they saved their lives
and the lives of their families. Others resisted. They resisted by remaining faithful to the law of Moses, circumcising their children, reading the scrolls, and refusing to eat pork or sacrifice to other gods. They resisted by preaching and
teaching, praying, fasting, and dying. These first martyrs of the Jewish faith
have inspired generations of Jews and Christians who have told and retold (and
relived) their stories of courage and faithfulness. Others resisted with arms,
fighting in self-defense and to reclaim their temple and city, ultimately expel-
ling the occupying Seleucid troops from Judea. They succeeded in establishing
Judea as a semi-independent nation-state after over four hundred years of colonial rule. Each year Jews around the world celebrate this accomplishment during the festival of Hanukkah.

The reign of Antiochus marked a turning point in the history of Judaism
for another reason that, though rarely remarked upon, is no less momentous.
For during this period emerged a new literary genre, the historical apocalypse,
and with it an apocalyptic worldview and consciousness that would become
enormously influential in the history of Judaism and Christianity alike.[1] Why

---

1. Elements of that worldview and consciousness were already taking shape perhaps a century earlier, as evidenced by the Book of the Watchers (*1 En.* 1–36), commonly considered the first
extant apocalypse of the "heavenly journey" type. The two subgenres are closely related. While

this genre at this moment? What is the relationship between apocalypse and empire?

I argue that the first Jewish apocalypses emerged as a literature of resistance to empire. Empire claimed the power to order the world. It exercised this power through force, but also through propaganda and ideology. Empire manipulated and co-opted hegemonic social institutions to express and reinforce its values and cosmology. Resisting imperial domination required challenging not only the physical means of coercion, but also empire's claims about knowledge and the world. The first apocalypses did precisely this.

In examining *how* they resisted empire, this book corrects a common set of misperceptions about apocalypticism and about Judaism in this vital period. It is often thought that early apocalyptic literature represents a flight from reality into fantasy, leading to radical detachment from the world or a disavowal of the visible, embodied realm. It has been imagined that the pseudonymous writers of the apocalypses hid their identities in order to avoid retaliation for their radical critique, or that they belonged to fringe sectarian groups with little connection to mainstream Judaism or centers of influence in Judean society. Nothing could be further from the truth. The early apocalyptic visionaries numbered among Judea's elite. During the persecution they did not hide, but urged public preaching, aiming to convert a wide audience to their message of faithfulness and hope. And they did not flee painful and even devastating realities, but engaged them head on.

This book is divided into three parts, moving through theory, history, and texts to arrive at an understanding of apocalyptic theology and praxis at this crucial juncture in Judean and Jewish history. Part One (ch. 1), "Theorizing Resistance," lays out a framework for understanding the meaning of resistance, for identifying and analyzing its objects, domination and hegemony, and for understanding the literary genre apocalypse as resistant counterdiscourse. I lay out this framework at the book's beginning so that it can inform the analysis in subsequent chapters. Yet I risk losing the energy of readers drawn more to the drama of history and ancient text than to theory. I invite readers less inclined toward theory to read the conclusion of chapter one and proceed to Parts Two and Three.

Part Two, "Seleucid Domination in Judea" (chs. 2–6), traces the history of Hellenistic rule in Judea, with special attention to the era of Seleucid rule from 200 BCE to the persecution in 167 BCE. What was happening in Judea at this

---

my primary focus is on the first historical apocalypses, namely Daniel, the Apocalypse of Weeks (*1 En.* 93:1-10 + 91:11-17), and the Book of Dreams (*1 En.* 83–90), I also give attention to the Book of the Watchers, which deeply influenced both the Apocalypse of Weeks and the Book of Dreams.

time had never happened before. These conditions formed the matrix in which the first apocalypses took shape. A common narrative for this period has painted the early years of Seleucid rule as beneficent and peaceful, suddenly interrupted in 167 BCE by the inexplicable and murderous ravings of a mad king. Another explanation characterizes the conflict as a clash of cultures between Judaism and Hellenism. Locating events in Judea in a wider imperial context, I offer a more nuanced account. I examine the violence of conquest and the stressors of imperial rule in Judea from the very beginning of Hellenistic rule and Seleucid domination. I document interaction between ruler and ruled, and offer new lenses for viewing the encounter between Judaism and Hellenism. I then identify the logic that ultimately led to Antiochus's edict and persecution of Judeans. He aimed to re-create his own empire through the reconquest, de-creation, and re-creation of Judea. Judea's conquest was carried out not only by force but through a program of state terror. The persecution was not something wholly discontinuous after all, but continued a program of terror already well underway. Understanding the logic of Antiochus's program of terror and de-creation, we perceive not only what the apocalyptic writers were resisting, but how they resisted. Trauma stopped time. With visions of a unified past, present, and future, the historical apocalypses put time back together. With vivid symbols they asserted the integrity of a world that had threatened to shatter. They answered terror with radical visions of hope.

Part Three (chs. 7–10), "Apocalyptic Theologies of Resistance," treats in detail the three extant historical apocalypses written in Judea during Antiochus's reign, namely Daniel (ch. 7), the Apocalypse of Weeks (*1 En.* 93:1-10 + 91:11-17; ch. 9), and the Book of Dreams (*1 En.* 83–90; ch. 10). Chapter 8 introduces the two Enochic texts by addressing the relationship between Enochic authority in the early Enochic writings and Israel's other scriptural traditions as well as the epistemological and cosmological claims of the Hellenistic ruling powers. As resistant discourse, each apocalypse countered the totalizing narrative of the Seleucid empire with an even grander total vision of history, cosmos, and the reign of God. But their resistance did not stop at the level of discourse or belief. Vision and praxis shaped one another. From each apocalyptic discourse emerged a program of radical, embodied resistance rooted in covenant theology and shaped by models from Israel's scriptures as well as new revelatory paradigms. I examine each text in turn, giving careful attention to the creative interplay between theology, hermeneutics, and ethics, or, put another way, between the framework of belief, practices of reading, and the shaping of resistant action.

PART ONE

THEORIZING RESISTANCE

CHAPTER 1

Theorizing Resistance

Theology or Theologies of Resistance?

In the title of this book I borrow and modify a phrase from Rainer Albertz's *History of Israelite Religion in the Old Testament Period*. In a section titled "Late prophetic and apocalyptic theology of resistance," Albertz identifies in the Hellenistic period "a new apocalyptic theology of resistance" that grows naturally out of the "revolutionary force intrinsic to Yahweh religion from its beginnings."[1] This theology emerges among those who are deeply aware of and also challenged by "sometimes painful political contradictions in the reality of Hellenistic Israel, at home and abroad."[2] That is, for Albertz, the experience of the contradiction between the claims of Yahwism and the claims of the Hellenistic rulers catalyzes the growth of a new theology that equips its adherents for the work of political and, later, social resistance.[3] The key to this theology is its extension and transformation of liberation traditions into an "eschatological religion of redemption."[4]

Albertz's formulation of a singular "apocalyptic theology of resistance" un-

---

1. Rainer Albertz, *A History of Israelite Religion in the Old Testament Period,* vol. 2: *From the Exile to the Maccabees,* trans. John Bowden (Louisville: Westminster John Knox, 1994), p. 564. Originally published as *Religionsgeschichte Israels in alttestamentlicher Zeit* (Göttingen: Vandenhoeck & Ruprecht, 1992).

2. Albertz, *History of Israelite Religion,* p. 564. "Israel" must be understood here not in a localized sense, but as a theological identity.

3. Albertz, *History of Israelite Religion,* pp. 594-95. For Albertz, a theology of social resistance finds expression in the Epistle of Enoch, during the period of Maccabean rule. Prior to this period (up until 160 BCE), he asserts that "the theme of social conflict plays no role at all" (p. 565).

4. Albertz, *History of Israelite Religion,* p. 564.

3

derscores the theological common ground between such works as Daniel, the Apocalypse of Weeks, and the Book of Dreams, drawing particular attention to what is theologically *new* in this group of works, namely elements of a shared apocalyptic worldview. In this chapter, I explain why this apocalyptic vision of the world was especially suited for the work of resistance to the Hellenistic rulers in the period following Alexander's conquest of Judea in 332 BCE, particularly at the point, beginning in 167 BCE, when Antiochus IV Epiphanes sought to annul the very covenantal basis of the Jewish religion. During the persecution, competing demands for absolute loyalty rested on competing claims to absolute power and competing visions and constructions of reality. The apocalyptic worldview envisioned a radical relocation of power and in this way redefined the possible and the real, thus clarifying the context for action and empowering the work of resistance. The apocalypses studied in this volume hold this view in common.

Yet we should not so quickly assume that this common ground spells one theology. Albertz himself notes the patent theological differences between Daniel and the Animal Apocalypse (contained within the Book of Dreams): "The theological struggle which became visible between the Hebrew book of Daniel and 1 Enoch 85–90 makes it clear that the dispute over the proper way to assess the painful present and the right alternatives of action for the future was fought out in the Maccabaean period essentially on the ground of apocalyptic theology."[5] As Albertz notes here, theology, interpretation (in this case of the present circumstances), and right action are inextricably intertwined. In our sources we find not one apocalyptic theology of resistance (nor can we posit one, unitary "apocalyptic theology" as such), but multiple theologies of resistance. Moreover, while 1 and 2 Maccabees do not give us unmediated access to the theology of resisters, we nonetheless find evidence in these texts of alternate, nonapocalyptic theologies of resistance at work during this period.[6]

---

5. Albertz, *History of Israelite Religion*, p. 594. For a recent study of the theology of the Animal Apocalypse, see Daniel Assefa, *L'Apocalypse des animaux (1 Hen 85–90): une propagande militaire? Approches narrative, historico-critique, perspectives théologiques* (Leiden: Brill, 2007), pp. 239-327. Assefa summarizes the distinctive features of its theology under the following points: (1) return from exile does not indicate divine forgiveness; (2) rule of angels; (3) strict emphasis on sanctity and purity, not only of the tabernacle but also of the camp and Jerusalem; (4) God builds a city-sanctuary in the place of Jerusalem and the second temple; (5) Israel's history is situated within human history and culminates in a final convergence; (6) panoramic view of biblical history; (7) presenting history as future emphasizes expectation for events yet to come; (8) exemplary role of Enoch as a just intercessor who is transformed by the revelation of mysteries (pp. 321-23).

6. Second Maccabees also displays elements of what would be described as an apocalyptic worldview, including the belief in otherworldly agents whose actions directly impinge upon this-worldly lived realities.

Conceptualizing Resistance

Forms of Resistance

Many studies of resistance proceed without defining the term, instead describing its forms, the conditions in which they take shape, and their relationship to systems of domination. An obvious, and extreme, form of resistance that frequently attracts scholarly attention (as it does in this study) is the revolt, rebellion, or revolution.[7] In their introduction to the edited volume *Contesting Power: Resistance and Everyday Social Relations in South Asia,* Douglas Haynes and Gyan Prakash identify a tendency in earlier scholarship on resistance to focus on these obvious, extreme, and often violent forms of resistance.[8] James C. Scott notes a parallel tendency in studies of peasantry, in which "much attention has been devoted to organized, large-scale, protest movements that appear, if only momentarily, to pose a threat to the state."[9]

Yet while revolt or organized protest movements occur relatively infrequently, the phenomenon of resistance is widespread. In *Weapons of the Weak,* Scott calls attention to forms of "everyday" resistance that are less dramatic, if more frequent, and harder for the historian to spot.[10] Scott is interested in the forms of resistance by which members of an oppressed or weaker group can gain or maintain privileges, goods, rights, and freedoms in a system in which they have little ascribed power. As examples of these forms he offers "foot dragging, dissimulation, desertion, false compliance, pilfering, feigned ignorance, slander, arson, [and] sabotage."[11] Scott's resisters are not interested in overthrow of government structures, nor do they agitate openly for social change. Yet they do struggle, not only to secure and maintain a way of life but also to

7. This has been true in the field of history more broadly as well as in the study of biblical history, including other studies of Jewish responses to the persecution of Antiochus. Crane Brinton's *The Anatomy of Revolution,* rev. ed. (New York: Vintage, 1965) informed Daniel Harrington's study *The Maccabean Revolt: Anatomy of a Biblical Revolution* (Wilmington, DE: Michael Glazier, 1988).

8. Douglas Haynes and Gyan Prakash, "Introduction: The Entanglement of Power and Resistance," in *Contesting Power: Resistance and Everyday Social Relations in South Asia,* ed. Douglas Haynes and Gyan Prakash (Berkeley: University of California Press, 1991), pp. 1-22, 1.

9. James C. Scott, *Weapons of the Weak: Everyday Forms of Peasant Resistance* (New Haven: Yale University Press, 1985), p. xv.

10. For examples of earlier scholarship moving in a similar direction, see Allen Isaacman and Barbara Isaacman, "Resistance and Collaboration in Southern and Central Africa, c. 1850-1920," *IJAHS* 10 (1977): 31-62; and Allen Isaacman, Michael Stephen, Yussuf Adam, Maria João Homen, Eugenio Macamo, and Augustinho Pililão, "'Cotton Is the Mother of Poverty': Peasant Resistance to Forced Cotton Production in Mozambique, 1938-1961," *IJAHS* 13 (1980): 581-615.

11. Scott, *Weapons of the Weak,* p. xvi.

name their world and narrate who they are. Of the people in the pseudonymous village of Sedaka, where Scott conducted his fieldwork, Scott writes: "The
struggle between rich and poor in Sedaka is not merely a struggle over work,
property rights, grain, and cash. It is also a struggle over the appropriation of
symbols, a struggle over how the past and present shall be understood and labeled, a struggle to identify causes and assess blame, a contentious effort to give
partisan meaning to local history."[12] Thus, while their ambitions may seem
modest by comparison with their revolutionary counterparts, Scott takes great
pains to demonstrate that they have not simply swallowed whole the hegemonic discourse of their oppressors.[13] They have their own discourse, too, and
they fight — quietly, audible only to one another — to assert its validity.[14]

In Search of a Definition

The two poles of armed revolt and silent foot-dragging mark endpoints on a
spectrum of resistance. Goals range from overthrow or replacement of structures of domination to maintenance of threatened structures of security. What
do they share? I consider three definitions of resistance, highlighting elements
in each that will be useful for analyzing Jewish responses to Hellenistic rule in
general and to Antiochus's persecution in particular.

Resistance Limits Power

A very simple definition comes from J. M. Barbalet, who, in his essay "Power
and Resistance," emphasizes the necessary relationship between resistance and
power.[15] Barbalet accepts and expounds Max Weber's understanding of power
as "the probability that one actor within a social relationship will be in a position to carry out his own will despite resistance, regardless of the basis on
which this probability rests."[16] In light of this definition, and drawing on the

12. Scott, *Weapons of the Weak*, p. xvii.
13. I will take up below Scott's engagement with the work of Gramsci on the question of
hegemony. See esp. Scott, *Weapons of the Weak*, pp. 314-46; and Antonio Gramsci, *Selections from
the Prison Notebooks*, ed. and trans. Quintin Hoare and Geoffrey Nowell Smith (London: Lawrence & Wishart, 1971).
14. Scott, *Weapons of the Weak*, p. 331: "The imaginative capacity of subordinate groups to
reverse and/or negate dominant ideologies is so widespread — if not universal — that it might
be considered part and parcel of their standard cultural and religious equipment."
15. J. M. Barbalet, "Power and Resistance," *British Journal of Sociology* 4 (1985): 531-48.
Barbalet writes, "There can be no adequate understanding of power and power relations without the concept of 'resistance'" (p. 532).
16. Barbalet, "Power and Resistance," p. 532, citing Max Weber, *Economy and Society,*

work of Barry Hindess on the limitations of power in social contexts,[17] Barbalet develops a concept of resistance as "those factors which in limiting the exercise of power contribute to the outcome of the power relation."[18] While this definition is essentially a formal one, Barbalet insists on the necessity of analyzing the social relations in any given context.[19]

Barbalet's emphasis on the necessary structural relation between resistance and power provides a helpful starting point for understanding resistance in the present study. Each of the texts I examine participates in a radical relocation of ultimate power, countering imperial claims to ultimate power by asserting God's power and power given by God to the faithful. The apocalyptic writings take great pains to demonstrate the limits of temporal power (e.g., Dan 2 and 7; *1 En.* 89:59–90:25).[20] They do not deny the power of the empires, but they portray this power as partial, contingent, and finite. Those who exercise it are subject to the greater power of God and held accountable through divine judgment. The narration of the supernatural attack on Heliodorus in 2 Maccabees 3:25-28 conveys the same message: despite his magnificent retinue and bodyguard, the imperial agent Heliodorus is rendered helpless (ἀβοήθητον) in the face of God's sovereign power (δυναστείαν). While the narratives of 1 Maccabees do not portray this power through the appearance of heavenly beings, yet Heaven (the book's primary title for God) is the acknowledged source of strength and victory (1 Macc 3:19, 50-53). Recollections of miraculous deliverance at the Red Sea and during Sennacherib's siege of Jerusalem (as in 2 Kgs 19:35, Judas here attributes this deliverance to an angel who slaughters 185,000

---

ed. Guenther Roth and Claus Wittich; trans. Ephraim Fischoff (Berkeley: University of California Press, 1978), p. 53; trans. of *Wirtschaft und Gesellschaft: Grundriss der verstehenden Soziologie,* 4th ed., ed. Johannes Winckelmann (Tübingen: J. C. B. Mohr [Siebeck], 1956).

17. Barry Hindess, "Power, Interests and the Outcome of Struggles," *Sociology* 16, no. 4 (1982): 498-511.

18. Barbalet, "Power and Resistance," p. 539.

19. Barbalet, "Power and Resistance," p. 546. Cf. the critical assessment of Daniel Miller, Michael Rowlands, and Christopher Tilley, who note that scholars increasingly recognize that "the sociological traditions of the 19th century, stemming from Marx, Freud, Comte, Weber and Nietzsche, have specific preoccupations that cannot be universalized. There is a need for a more radical recontextualization of social theory than has hitherto been the case." In the process, "concepts such as domination and resistance will be invested with new contents depending on the situation being investigated." Introduction to *Domination and Resistance,* ed. Daniel Miller, Michael Rowlands, and Christopher Tilley (London: Unwin Hyman, 1989), p. 3.

20. Albertz notes ways in which the Book of the Watchers counters claims for the divinization of Hellenistic rulers through the symbolic equation of the successor kings with the demonic and bastard offspring of the fallen watchers (*History of Israelite Religion,* pp. 578-84). He writes, "The author of I Enoch 6–11 wants to make it possible for his audience to see rationally that the deification of power, violence and economic exploitation in the Hellenistic rule of the world must necessarily soon come to an end" (p. 580).

Assyrian soldiers) instill confidence in God's power over the great empires (1 Macc 4:9; 7:41). By contrast to the power that Heaven confers on the faithful from generation to generation (2:61), the ephemeral persecutor will return to dust (2:63). In each of these texts the relocation of ultimate power from earth to heaven makes it possible both to imagine and engage in effective resistance.

Intentions and Actions

A second definition comes from Klaas van Walraven and Jon Abbink, who emphasize intention and action in their understanding of resistance. They define resistance as "intentions and concrete actions taken to oppose others and refuse to accept their ideas, actions, or positions for a variety of reasons, the most common being the perception of the position, claims, or actions taken by others as unjust, illegitimate, or intolerable attempts at domination."[21] Their emphasis on perceptions of injustice may owe to Barrington Moore Jr.'s influential study *Injustice: The Social Bases of Obedience and Revolt.*[22] Moore attends to what he considers to be the tragic and vast "human capacity to withstand suffering and abuse," in light of which it becomes all the more important to examine "under what conditions and why do human beings cease to put up with it."[23] These questions are relevant for the present study as well. Attention to the difficult conditions of Judeans under Seleucid rule prior to the persecution by Antiochus IV Epiphanes, which I analyze in chapters 2–5, illuminates the multiple sources of strain on this population while also helping us to understand why resistance took the forms it did when it did. While our evidence for radical resistance in the years preceding the persecution is more limited, it is important to recognize that such resistance did exist (see, e.g., Dan 11:14). Yet the larger scale and broader spectrum of resistance during the years of the persecution focus our attention more narrowly on the persecution itself as — for those who resisted — an intolerable challenge to the religion, way of life, and identity of Judeans who worshiped Yhwh.

Indeed, for Van Walraven and Abbink, resistance is defined not by its forms, whether violent or nonviolent, "radical" or "everyday," but rather by its intentions to defend that which is threatened, whether ideals, power structures,

---

21. Klaas van Walraven and Jon Abbink, "Rethinking Resistance in African History: An Introduction," in *Rethinking Resistance: Revolt and Violence in African History,* ed. Jon Abbink, Mirjam de Bruijn, and Klaas van Walraven (Leiden: Brill, 2003), pp. 1-40, 8.

22. Barrington Moore Jr., *Injustice: The Social Bases of Obedience and Revolt* (White Plains, NY: M. E. Sharpe, 1978). Moore asserts a pre-social (biologically encoded) "natural morality" that makes it possible to generalize about the relationship between the perception of injustice, the response of moral outrage, and consequent revolutionary actions (p. 7).

23. Moore, *Injustice,* p. 13.

or "sociopolitical arrangements."[24] Helpful in their definition are the link between intention and action and the prominent place they give to the rejection of hegemonic ideas (on which, see further below). Both of these elements are key to Jewish resistance to Antiochus's persecution. Yet Van Walraven and Abbink conceive too narrowly the motivations for resistance. Curious is their omission of defending a way of life, which must encompass more than "sociopolitical arrangements," as well as the recognition that ideals take embodied form in religious, cultural, and social practices. I return to this question in the discussion of domination later in this chapter.

Contesting Hegemony and Domination

Barbalet's focus on limiting power and influencing outcomes helpfully illuminates structural and functional dimensions of resistance. Haynes and Prakash place a similar emphasis on the effects of resistance, but narrow the field slightly from considerations of power in general to focus on hegemony and domination.[25] Unlike Van Walraven and Abbink, they do not view intention as a necessary component of resistance. They offer the following definition: "Resistance, we would argue, should be defined as those behaviours and cultural practices by subordinate groups that contest hegemonic social formations, that threaten to unravel the strategies of domination; 'consciousness' need not be essential to its constitution."[26] In this definition, domination, its strategies, and the hegemony that reinforces it provide the conditions for and objects of resistance. The terms "hegemonic" and "domination" invoke the conceptual categories of Antonio Gramsci (hegemony) and Karl Marx, Weber, and Louis Althusser (domination). The references to "cultural practices" and "strategies of domination" also invoke the work of Pierre Bourdieu.[27] I return to each of these concepts below. In the view of these theorists, domination is a feature of everyday life, such that within particular social settings it is the norm, rather than the exception. In such settings hegemony shapes the contours of perceived

24. Van Walraven and Abbink, "Rethinking Resistance in African History," p. 8.

25. Power remains for them an important consideration. Following Timothy Mitchell's critique of Scott's understanding of hegemony (Timothy Mitchell, "Everyday Metaphors of Power," *Theory and Society* 19 [1990]: 545-77; see further below), they note that a more sophisticated notion of "contradictory consciousness" in the experience of hegemony facilitates a "reformulation of the concept of everyday resistance so that it recognizes how such struggles commonly occur not outside but inside the field of power" (Haynes and Prakash, "Introduction," p. 11).

26. Haynes and Prakash, "Introduction," p. 3.

27. Pierre Bourdieu, *Outline of a Theory of Practice*, trans. Richard Nice (Cambridge: Cambridge University Press, 1977). Originally published as *Esquisse d'une théorie de la pratique, précédé de trois études d'ethnologie kabyle* (Geneva: Librairie Droz, 1972).

reality. For these reasons, Haynes and Prakash wish to move away from a view that sees resistance "as a response to a radical dislocation in the nature of the social order." Like Scott (and influenced by his work), they argue that resistance belongs equally to the realm of the everyday and commonplace, where no "unusual threat" is perceived to exist.[28]

Finally, their use of the term "consciousness" in their definition is meant in the very limited sense of "conscious ideologies of opposition."[29] For Haynes and Prakash the *intention* to resist is not a necessary prerequisite for resistance itself.[30] As they explain, "seemingly innocuous behaviours can have unintended yet profound consequences for the objectives of the dominant or the shape of a social order."[31] By this understanding, resistance is measured solely in terms of its limiting or transformative effects on relations, structures, and strategies of domination.

For the present study, what is helpful in this definition is its recognition of the social dimensions and context of resistance and its effects on structures and strategies of domination. I do not, however, follow Haynes and Prakash in rejecting the role of consciousness or intention. In the texts studied in this volume, consciousness — powerfully expressed in the Book of Dreams' imagery of "open eyes" — is always in view, and is absolutely necessary for right action. In Daniel and *1 Enoch* resistance flows from particular claims for knowledge and understanding. In many sources for this period it flows also from a commitment of the will to serve God alone and to remain faithful to the demands of covenant. The very burden of the apocalypses is to demonstrate and persuade that this radical epistemology and commitment of the will is not only a necessary precondition for right action but must in fact result in radical resistance. While I do not deny that unintended actions can defeat strategies of domination and, even more, work powerful transformations in the very structures of domination, I do not identify unintended actions as "resistance," and they will not be a focus in the present study.

Summary

What can we conclude from this survey of definitions of resistance? Daniel Miller, Michael Rowlands, and Christopher Tilley emphasize the shifting nature

---

28. Haynes and Prakash, "Introduction," p. 3.

29. Haynes and Prakash, "Introduction," p. 4.

30. I will return below to a discussion of the idea of "consciousness" in the sense used by Gramsci, but that is not the sense in which the term is used here. Haynes and Prakash do use the word in this sense later in the essay with reference to "contradictory consciousness," an important concept in their critique of Scott ("Introduction," p. 11).

31. Haynes and Prakash, "Introduction," p. 3.

of the very concept of resistance, cautioning against efforts to arrive at "absolute and unchanging definitions."[32] Rather than suggesting a definition that will be universally valid, I lift up instead three major points that provide a conceptual framework for the understanding of resistance I adopt in the present study.

1. Domination, its strategies, and the hegemony that reinforces it provide the conditions for and objects of resistance.
2. Acts of resistance proceed from the intention to limit, oppose, reject, or transform hegemonic institutions (and cosmologies — see discussion of hegemony below) as well as systems, strategies, and acts of domination.
3. Resistance is effective action. It limits power and influences outcomes, where power is understood as an agent's ability to carry out his or her will.

Hegemony and Domination:
The Conditions and Objects of Resistance

I have stated above that domination and hegemony provide the conditions and objects of resistance. Yet as with resistance itself, it is difficult to arrive at concise definitions of these concepts. Nonetheless, attention to these concepts will help us to articulate both the conditions and objects of resistance for the writers of the earliest apocalypses, as well as their strategies of resistance to each.

Hegemony

Timothy Mitchell summarizes Gramsci's concept of hegemony as "non-violent forms of control exercised through the whole range of dominant cultural institutions and social practices, from schooling, museums, and political parties to religious practice, architectural forms, and the mass media."[33] A key to this definition is the emphasis on "non-violent forms of control." In examining resistance to Antiochus's persecution and to the Hellenistic empires more generally, we need to look at responses not only to the violent forms of physical coercion

32. Miller, Rowlands, and Tilley, introduction to *Domination and Resistance*, p. 3. In their view, the concepts of resistance and domination alike are only useful in their application, i.e., in "substantive analysis" of specific situations (p. 4). They suggest moreover that this conceptual fluidity "should be regarded as something productive rather than an unfortunate flaw in social analysis" (p. 4).

33. Mitchell, "Everyday Metaphors of Power," p. 553. See further Joseph Femia, *Gramsci's Political Thought: Hegemony, Consciousness, and the Revolutionary Process* (Oxford: Oxford University Press, 1981).

and control exercised through killing, torture, enslavement, plunder, and the policing actions of the imperial armies and military garrison, but also responses to more subtle forms of control conveyed through cultural institutions (including gymnasia and games), systems of patronage (see, e.g., Dan 11:32, 39), social networks, and the structured practices of everyday life.

While Mitchell's summary highlights the media and mechanisms of hegemony, Miller emphasizes its cosmological dimension.[34] That is, hegemony asserts as normative and universal what are in fact particular and contingent ways of perceiving the world, mapping the universe and humanity's place in it, and defining poles of opposition. This cosmology demarcates inside from outside, center from periphery, normal from aberrant. Its logic legitimates claims about truth and morality, but this very logic can become so invisible as to resist questioning.[35] Bourdieu names this invisible logic *doxa*, "the sum total of the theses tacitly posited on the hither side of all inquiry."[36] To the extent that this logic becomes internalized, the merely possible appears necessary, the contingent appears absolute, and ways of ordering human life that have taken shape through time appear to be part of "nature."[37] For Bourdieu, this internalized *doxa* limits the range of thought and action: "When, owing to the quasi-perfect fit between the objective structures and the internalized structures which results from the logic of simple reproduction, the established cosmological and political order is perceived not as arbitrary, i.e., as one possible order among others, but as a self-evident and natural order which goes without saying and therefore goes unquestioned, the agents' aspirations have the same limits as the objective conditions of which they are the product."[38] Periods of rapid change, including experiences of intensive cultural contact and crisis, open up possibilities for challenging this *doxa*, for naming what was previously unnamed and thinking beyond the previously thinkable in order to answer hegemony with new, resistant counterdiscourse that articulates new parameters for thought and action.[39]

Indeed, articulating and promulgating counterdiscourse are primary forms of resistance to hegemony.[40] The teaching function of Daniel's *maśkîlîm*,

34. Daniel Miller, "The Limits of Dominance," in *Domination and Resistance*, ed. Daniel Miller, Michael Rowlands, and Christopher Tilley (London: Unwin Hyman, 1989), pp. 63-79, 64.

35. Miller, "Limits of Dominance," p. 66.

36. Bourdieu, *Outline of a Theory of Practice*, p. 168.

37. Bourdieu, *Outline of a Theory of Practice*, pp. 78-79.

38. Bourdieu, *Outline of a Theory of Practice*, p. 166.

39. Bourdieu, *Outline of a Theory of Practice*, p. 166. Richard Terdiman, *Discourse/Counter-Discourse: The Theory and Practice of Symbolic Resistance in Nineteenth Century France* (Ithaca, NY: Cornell University Press, 1985), p. 59.

40. Other forms include religious practices that testify to a competing account of reality, on which see further below.

or "wise teachers," which I discuss in chapter 7, presents a key example of resistant counterdiscourse, as do the witnessing of the chosen righteous in the Apocalypse of Weeks and the prophetic role of the sighted lambs in the Book of Dreams (discussed in chs. 9 and 10 respectively). In each case articulating and promulgating resistant discourse accompanies other forms of resistance, including embodied practices such as fasting (Daniel), prayer (Daniel, Book of Dreams), fighting (Book of Dreams), or the acceptance of martyrdom (Daniel). Like the counterdiscourses they accompany, these embodied practices testify to the radical relocation of power from earth to heaven and from empire, king, and army to God, angels, one like a human being, and God's people (e.g., the people of the holy ones of the most high in Daniel, the chosen righteous in the Apocalypse of Weeks).

In addition to the forms of resistant counterdiscourse advocated and envisioned by these texts, the texts themselves also articulate and serve as counterdiscourse. To this end they employ a variety of discursive strategies. One form of counterdiscourse answers myth with myth, as in the Book of the Watchers, the Book of Dreams, or Daniel 7. Another form reveals an alternative cosmology in the form of a narrated heavenly journey (Book of the Watchers; see ch. 8). Still another form turns to history as a means of revealing the contingency of present realities, as in the historical reviews of Daniel, the Apocalypse of Weeks, and the Book of Dreams. Even the syntax of Daniel's apocalyptic visions destabilizes the very logic and coherence of a social reality some believed to be structured and governed by the empire.[41] The book of Daniel foretells the downfall of the persecutor Antiochus IV in halting, jumbled phrases: "And in a torrent will be his end, a war decreed, great devastation, until an end" (9:26b).[42] As Jin Hee Han puts it, "The book of Daniel proceeds to conceptualize a linguistic system in order to shed light on a full array of characteristics of an instrument that would help to drive a wedge between the world it describes and the world it deconstructs. Apocalyptic language, thus born and raised, is ready to produce a radically revised perspective on reality."[43] This revised perspective also relies heavily on traditional discourses, especially those of Israel's prior

---

41. I similarly argue that the sequence of language choices in Daniel is a key strategy in the book's articulation of resistant counterdiscourse. See Anathea Portier-Young, "Languages of Identity and Obligation: Daniel as Bilingual Book," *VT* 60, no. 1 (2010): 98-115.

42. Terdiman discusses Mallarmé's reflections on syntax, which Terdiman describes as "the elemental characteristic of socially instituted intelligibility in any discourse" (*Discourse/Counter-Discourse*, p. 333). Even here the author of Daniel, like Mallarmé, pushes the limits of syntax but does not abandon it all together, for a discourse without syntax produces no intelligibility and thus no comprehension or meaning.

43. Jin Hee Han, *Daniel's Spiel: Apocalyptic Literacy in the Book of Daniel* (Lanham, MD: University Press of America, 2008), p. 98.

scriptural traditions, as I discuss in Part Three. These traditions provided fruitful material for conceptualizing resistance to the Hellenistic empires in general and the measures of Antiochus IV in particular.[44]

The very binary nature of the hegemonic construction of reality noted above (inside/outside, center/periphery, good/bad, civilized/barbaric, normal/aberrant) also creates the possibility for resistance to hegemony through critical inversion, wherein categories are retained but the hierarchy of values or assignment of value is turned upside down.[45] This inversion is most effectively achieved by recasting myths and revalorizing symbols. A frequently touted example of the latter is the Christian transformation of the cross from an instrument of torture and symbol of imperial coercive power into a symbol of nonviolence, self-giving, and divine redemptive power.[46] As Klaus Koch observes, the

44. In his study of Galilean and Judean resistance to the Roman Empire in the first and second centuries CE, Richard A. Horsley asserts that "a principal reason that Galileans and Judeans proved so persistent in rebellion against Roman imperial rule was the prominence of resistance to oppressive alien rule in Israelite tradition." Richard A. Horsley, *Jesus and Empire: The Kingdom of God and the New World Disorder* (Minneapolis: Fortress, 2003), p. 37. For a sustained exploration of resistance to empire in Israel's traditions, see the essays in Richard A. Horsley, ed., *In the Shadow of Empire: Reclaiming the Bible as a History of Faithful Resistance* (Louisville: Westminster John Knox, 2008) by Norman K. Gottwald, "Early Israel as an Anti-Imperial Community," pp. 9-24; Walter Brueggemann, "Faith in the Empire," pp. 25-40; and Jon L. Berquist, "Resistance and Accommodation in the Persian Empire," pp. 41-58.

45. David Sánchez traces the inversion of imperial myths in Rev 12 and in later appropriation of its imagery in the Americas. Referring to the "dragon slayer myth," Sánchez writes: "Subjects of the empire were well aware of the power of this mythical motif and understood that effective diatribes against emperor and empire could begin only with a critique of this foundational myth." *From Patmos to the Barrio: Subverting Imperial Myths* (Minneapolis: Fortress, 2008), p. 13.

46. See, e.g., Michael Gorman, *Cruciformity: Paul's Narrative Spirituality of the Cross* (Grand Rapids: Eerdmans, 2001), p. 395; Neil Elliott, "Strategies of Resistance and Hidden Transcripts in the Pauline Communities," in *Hidden Transcripts and the Arts of Resistance: Applying the Work of James C. Scott to Jesus and Paul*, ed. Richard A. Horsley (Atlanta: Society of Biblical Literature, 2004), pp. 97-122, 118-19; Neil Elliott, "The Anti-imperial Message of the Cross," in *Paul and Empire: Religion and Power in Roman Imperial Society*, ed. Richard A. Horsley (Harrisburg, PA: Trinity Press International, 1997), pp. 167-83. Elliott emphasizes ways in which Paul's understanding of the cross is "informed by the symbolism of Jewish apocalyptic mythology" (p. 176). Note that in 1 Cor 1:17-25 Paul expresses the reversal in terms of honor and shame (cf. Gal 6:14). Elaine Scarry argues that torture reads pain as power in *The Body in Pain: The Making and Unmaking of the World* (Oxford: Oxford University Press, 1985), p. 28. In her discussion of the cross, she asserts that "the weapon becomes the primary sign and summary of the entire religion precisely because the entire religion is at its very heart an alteration in the reading of this sign. . . . The central work of the Christian story is the fundamental restructuring and redirecting of the referential activity of the generic sign of the weapon." In this restructuring, the pain the empire inflicts no longer signifies its power. Moreover, by telling the story in which "God is both omnipotent and in pain" (p. 214), "the altered relation in the Christian Scripture between

use of "mythical images rich in symbolism" is one of the distinguishing features of apocalyptic discourse.[47] In the earliest Jewish apocalypses (as in the early Christian apocalypse Revelation), this use of "mythical images rich in symbolism" owes much to the writers' interests in exposing and countering the mythologies that fund imperial hegemony. Critical inversion is one strategy for shaping the countermythologies that make it possible to reimagine a world governed not by empires, but by God.

The Book of the Watchers provides key examples of such critical inversion strategies. In merging structures and motifs from Greek, Babylonian, and Israelite traditions, it creates a new mythology that inverts motifs from Greek and Babylonian religious traditions. The mythic framework and symbolic thought world of the Book of the Watchers are vitally important for the Apocalypse of Weeks and Book of Dreams. Moreover, understanding the discursive strategies of resistance employed in this first extant Jewish apocalypse illuminates the development of discursive strategies of resistance in later apocalyptic literature. For these reasons, I consider here three examples of critical inversion in the Book of the Watchers.

1. The Book of the Watchers adapts elements of the Greek Prometheus myth, assimilating the role of the titan and culture hero Prometheus to two of its characters, 'Asa'el (and the fallen watchers more generally) and Enoch, both of whom cross the boundary between earth and heaven to transmit knowledge to humankind.[48] Both Prometheus and the fallen watchers, 'Asa'el among them, are condemned for excessive, indeed inappropriate, "love" of humankind.[49] As

---

the body of the believer and the object of belief subverts this severed relation between pain and power, assuring that sentience and authority reside at a single location and thus cannot be achieved at each other's expense" (p. 219). Mitchell B. Merbach builds on Scarry's insights in his analysis of the cross in medieval Christian art, *The Thief, the Cross, and the Wheel: Pain and the Spectacle of Punishment in Medieval and Renaissance Europe* (Chicago: University of Chicago Press, 1999), pp. 198-217. Of course, the Christian symbol of the cross is itself susceptible to inversions and revalorizations, sometimes reinstating the violence of the empire. See the fine collection of essays in Marit Trelstad, ed., *Cross Examinations: Readings on the Meaning of the Cross Today* (Minneapolis: Fortress, 2006).

47. Klaus Koch, *The Rediscovery of Apocalyptic: A Polemical Work on a Neglected Area of Biblical Studies and Its Damaging Effects on Theology and Philosophy* (London: SCM, 1972), p. 26. Originally published as *Ratlos vor der Apokalyptik* (Gütersloh: Gütersloh Verlagshaus Gerd Mohn, 1970). He comments: "The picture language of the apocalypses is so noticeable and so curious that it stands out clearly from the normal framework of the literature of the time and suggests a particular linguistic training, perhaps even a particular mentality" (p. 27).

48. See George W. E. Nickelsburg, "Apocalyptic and Myth in 1 Enoch 6–11," *JBL* 96, no. 3 (1977): 383-405, esp. 399-404.

49. Prometheus's chains will teach him "to stop his way of loving humankind" (φιλανθρώπου δὲ παύεσθαι τρόπου *PV* 11; line numbers correspond to Aeschylus, *Prometheus Bound*, ed. and trans. with introduction and commentary by A. J. Podlecki [Oxford: Aris and

in the Prometheus myth, so in the Book of the Watchers the high god punishes the one who transmits stolen knowledge to humans by having him bound in a deserted place and subjected to physical torment (1 En. 10:4-5). These structural parallels allow for a series of inversions. While Prometheus, "the patron of suffering [hu]mankind,"[50] was portrayed by Aeschylus as a noble benefactor whose teachings bettered human existence and even saved humans from extinction (PV 231-36), 'Asa'el is portrayed in the Book of the Watchers as the one "who has taught all iniquity on the earth" (1 En. 9:6). The consequences of the watchers' transgressions threaten the earth and humankind. By contrast, in the Book of the Watchers it is God who intervenes so that "all humankind may not perish" as well as for the healing of the earth (1 En. 10:7).

The inversion delivers an epistemological and theological critique.[51] The

---

Phillips, 2005]); he names his crime as "loving mortals too much" (τὴν λίαν φιλότητα βροτῶν 123; cf. 30, 543-44). On the theme of *"Prometheus philanthrôpos,"* see Podlecki's introduction to Aeschylus, *Prometheus Bound* (2005), pp. 16-27. Yet in *PV* it is Zeus's lust for Io that more closely parallels the fallen watchers' transgressive sexual desire for human women, prompting the chorus to reflect on the wisdom of marrying one's "own kind" (καθ' ἑαυτὸν 890) and proclaiming "nor would I be the bride of any god come out of heaven" (μηδὲ πλαθείην γαμέτᾳ τινὶ τῶν ἐξ οὐρανοῦ 897). Translation is that of James Scully in Aeschylus, *Prometheus Bound,* trans. James Scully with introduction and notes by C. John Herington (New York: Oxford University Press, 1975).

50. C. John Herington, introduction to Aeschylus, *Prometheus Bound* (1975), p. 11.

51. Few scholars would dispute that the Book of the Watchers is sharp in its critique. Yet its complex composition history and the multiple traditions it engages make it impossible to pin down one target for all its layers, or even for its "final form." Its rich symbolism speaks into many moments and settings and addresses multiple, shifting concerns. While Nickelsburg has called attention to a likely critique of the Diadochoi in chs. 6–11 ("Apocalyptic and Myth"), David Suter has argued that chs. 6–16 take aim at an internal threat, namely a corrupt priestly group that has violated purity laws concerning marriage. David Suter, "Fallen Angel, Fallen Priest: The Problem of Family Purity in 1 Enoch," *HUCA* 50 (1979): 115-35. Suter's suggestion relies in part on the reconstructions of the growth of "apocalyptic" from within a movement that exhibited "growing dissatisfaction with the priestly establishment in Jerusalem" (p. 134) as argued in the works of Otto Plöger (*Theocracy and Eschatology,* trans. S. Rudman [Oxford: Blackwell, 1968]; originally published as *Theokratie und Eschatologie* [Neukirchen: Neukirchener Verlag, 1959]) and Paul D. Hanson (*The Dawn of Apocalyptic: The Historical and Sociological Roots of Jewish Apocalyptic Eschatology* [Philadelphia: Fortress, 1975]) (both are cited in Suter, "Fallen Angel," p. 134n52). Yet the sociological models used by Plöger and Hanson have rightly been challenged, most notably in the work of Stephen L. Cook, *Prophecy and Apocalypticism: The Postexilic Social Setting* (Minneapolis: Fortress, 1995). This does not invalidate all of Suter's arguments. The reference to the watchers' abandoning the heavenly sanctuary (1 En. 12:4) and violating ordained boundaries certainly suggests priestly concerns. See also David Suter, "Revisiting Fallen Angel, Fallen Priest," *Henoch* 24 (2002): 137-42. William Loader suggests that the critique of "forbidden mixing" in 1 En. 12–16 may extend beyond inner-priestly critique to a critique of marriage with Gentile women more generally, with a special concern for the knowledge they bring from their native cultures. *Enoch, Levi, and Jubilees on Sexuality: Attitudes toward*

content of the watchers' stolen knowledge in the Book of the Watchers can be identified with various cultural legacies from Babylonian and Greek traditions, including military technologies, metallurgy, cosmetology, herbology, sorcery, and astronomy (*1 En.* 8:1-3), all valued in Greek and Babylonian traditions. In the Book of the Watchers these are degraded as the false teachings of fallen watchers (*1 En.* 9:6; 13:2; 16:3).[52] At the same time, the role of transmitter of salvific knowledge is transferred to Enoch, a human being. The knowledge he carries across heaven's threshold (i.e., the revealed wisdom transmitted through the Enochic literature) is preserved not among the Greeks but among the Jewish tradents of the Enoch traditions. Knowledge is power, and knowledge claims underwrite power. By condemning as false and demonic various forms of knowledge associated with Babylonian and Greek traditions — including the knowledge of warfare and methods of prognostication that played a crucial role in military campaigns and other affairs of state[53] — and by elevating Enochic revealed wisdom, the Book of the Watchers begins to deconstruct the very epistemological claims of the Hellenistic empires and assert in their place a knowledge that reveals the universal sovereignty of the one God.

2. Prometheus played an important role in the Greek myth of titanomachy,

---

Sexuality in the Early Enoch Literature, the Aramaic Levi Document, and the Book of Jubilees (Grand Rapids: Eerdmans, 2007), pp. 43, 46-49.

52. As Nickelsburg points out ("Apocalyptic and Myth," p. 400), several of these types of knowledge were associated with the teachings of Prometheus. See also Podlecki, introduction to Aeschylus, *Prometheus Bound* (2005), p. 25. Examples from *PV* include astronomy (ll. 454-58), mantic arts (484-99), metals (500-503), chariotry (465-66), and healing arts (478-83). At the same time, the treatment of these forms of knowledge in the Book of the Watchers is not dependent on or interacting with *solely* Greek traditions. The fact that multiple fallen angels, associated with the stars, are mediators of the knowledges in question suggests a strong connection to Babylonian learning as well. For the relation of the study of metals, herbs, and sorcery to astronomy in Babylonian thought and scholarship, see Erica Reiner, "Astral Magic in Babylonia," *Transactions of the American Philosophical Society* 85, no. 4 (1995): i-150.

53. Francesca Rochberg, *The Heavenly Writing: Divination, Horoscopy, and Astronomy in Mesopotamian Culture* (Cambridge: Cambridge University Press, 2004), pp. 76-77, 221-26. Rochberg notes that in the classic compendium *enuma anu enlil* the apodoses were concerned with the "health and life of the body politic," both agricultural and political, with political concerns including the "king's military campaigns, diplomatic relations, [and the] downfall of kingdoms" (pp. 76-77). She notes that the scribal office of *tupshar enuma anu enlil* reemerged in Seleucid Babylonia (p. 228). Though its social roles and location had changed considerably (most notably moving from palace to temple), traditional associations would have remained strong (pp. 233, 295). On Alexander's regard for Babylonian prognostication, see Robartus van der Spek, "Darius III, Alexander the Great, and Babylonian Scholarship," in *A Persian Perspective: Essays in Memory of Heleen Sancisi-Weerdenburg*, ed. Wouder Henkelman and Amélie Kuhrt (Leiden: Nederlands Instituut voor het nabije Oosten, 2003), pp. 289-346.

or the war between the Olympian gods and the titans (a generation of gods older than the Olympians) that would give the Olympians rule in heaven and confine the titans to Tartaros.[54] Closely related to the titanomachy was the myth of gigantomachy, in which the earth (Gaia), angered by the imprisonment of the defeated titans, roused her children the giants to challenge the rule established by the Olympians through their earlier victory. By the fifth century BCE, the two myths were frequently merged, paving the way for creative adaptation of elements from both traditions in the Book of the Watchers.[55]

The gigantomachy served as political myth, allegorically portraying Greek victory over "barbarian" enemies.[56] In the symbolism of the gigantomachy, giants represent "uncivilized" peoples, distinguished above all by their violence.[57] David Castriota argues that by the fifth century BCE "the violence and disorder of the giants and other monsters had already come to appear as the antithesis of the human values of moderation, virtue, and piety considered essential to civilized life."[58] The defeat of the giants by the Olympian gods served as "the ultimate mythic paradigm for the defense of law and *sophrosyne* [moderation or self-control] and the punishment of *hubris.*"[59] At the political level, the myth thus provided a paradigm for conceiving the victory of "Greeks," symbolically identified with the Olympians they worshiped, over excessive, disorderly "bar-

54. On the influence of the titanomachy on Jewish traditions, including *1 Enoch,* see Jan M. Bremmer, "Remember the Titans!" in *The Fall of the Angels,* ed. Christoph Auffarth and Loren Stuckenbruck (Leiden: Brill, 2004), pp. 35-61. Prometheus himself was a titan, but in the great combat he allied himself with the Olympian gods.

55. On the merger or confusion of the two traditions, see Bremmer, "Remember the Titans!" p. 54. See also Eduard Fraenkel, "The Giants in the Poem of Naevius," *The Journal of Roman Studies* 44 (1954): 14-17. In this fragmentary poem from the third century BCE, the designations *Titani* and *Gigantes* are employed in synonymous parallelism.

56. For analysis of how this mythology functioned in monumental art, see David Castriota, *Myth, Ethos, and Actuality: Official Art in Fifth Century Athens* (Madison: University of Wisconsin Press, 1992); and Françoise-Hélène Massa-Pairault, *La gigantomachie de Pergame ou l'image du monde* (Athens: École française d'Athènes, 2007). While the altar at Pergamon postdates the Book of the Watchers, it testifies to the enduring legacy of the gigantomachy as political myth in the Hellenistic era. For a study of the classical gigantomachy tradition that gives special attention to its religious and cultic associations, see Francis Vian, *La guerre des géants: Le mythe avant l'époque hellénistique* (Paris: Librairie C. Klincksieck, 1952).

57. Cf. Richard T. Neer's analysis of the North frieze of the Siphnian treasury at Delphi (dating to the sixth century BCE): "Siphnian North expresses the difference between gods and giants — the difference between order and impiety — as a difference of fighting style." Richard T. Neer, "Framing the Gift: The Siphnian Treasury at Delphi and the Politics of Public Art," in *The Cultures within Ancient Greek Culture: Contact, Conflict, Collaboration,* ed. Carol Dougherty and Leslie Kurke (Cambridge: Cambridge University Press, 2003), pp. 129-52, 143.

58. Castriota, *Myth, Ethos, and Actuality,* p. 139. See also Ken Dowden, *The Uses of Greek Mythology* (London: Routledge, 2005), pp. 58, 96, 112-14.

59. Castriota, *Myth, Ethos, and Actuality,* p. 139.

barians."[60] In the Hellenistic period, the conquests of the Hellenistic kings and the spread of their culture, religion, and forms of "civilization" could be conceived as a reenactment of and participation in the gigantomachy myth and the political and cultural ideals it enshrined.[61]

Drawing heavily on native Israelite traditions, especially those found in Genesis 6:1-4, *1 Enoch* 6–11 reverses this allegory in its own elaborated mythology, suggesting an identification between the giants and the Hellenistic rulers themselves.[62] In a variation on the theme of gigantomachy, the watchers who have abandoned their place in heaven to live among and have intercourse with human women beget monstrous children, giants characterized above all by their brutality and voracious appetites. First they devour "the labor of all human beings," until humans no longer have food to feed them (*1 En.* 7:3). Then they devour people (7:4). Finally, they begin to devour one another (7:5).[63] In a

60. Susan A. Stephens, *Seeing Double: Intercultural Poetics in Ptolemaic Alexandria* (Berkeley: University of California Press, 2003), p. 64. She notes that in classical Greek art the defeat of the giants "signaled iconographically the civilizing influence of the Greek city-states and their individual or collective defeat of the irrational, uncivilized worlds that preceded them." See also Edith Hall, *Inventing the Barbarian: Greek Self-Definition through Tragedy* (Oxford: Oxford University Press, 1991), pp. 53, 68, 102.

61. This development goes *against* the grain of one of the most famous renderings of the gigantomachy, namely the west *metopes* of Pheidias's Parthenon frieze. Here, as Castriota has demonstrated, the aim was not to legitimate empire, which would violate Athenian democratic ideals, but rather to deny empire and lift up instead the ideal of *symmachia* (*Myth, Ethos, and Actuality,* pp. 194-98). It is precisely in the transition from *symmachia* (the allied city-state model) to empire, and in efforts, like those of the Diadochoi Antigonus and Demetrius, to yoke *symmachia* to imperial ambitions, that the "Greeks" become susceptible to the critique through inversion that I describe here.

62. For the argument that the fallen watchers and giants in the Book of the Watchers symbolize, at one level, the Diadochoi and their successors, see Nickelsburg, "Apocalyptic and Myth," pp. 383-405. Albertz also finds that in the battle of "mutual extermination" fought by the giants "anyone could recognize the battles of the Diadochi and the never-ending chain of Syrian wars" (*History of Israelite Religion,* p. 579). In ch. 2 I treat the violent legacy of the Hellenistic kings in greater detail. A later Jewish corpus uses the same myth to convey a polemic against Alexander and his successors: in the Sibylline oracles Alexander and his descendants are identified as "from the race of Cronos, the progeny of bastards and slaves" (*Sib. Or.* 3.383). Alexander is called "savage, stranger to justice" (3.390; cf. 11.216) and the "bastard of the son of Cronos" who "lay waste the cities of many articulate men" (11.198). The Diadochoi are "kings who are devourers of the people and overbearing and faithless." Translations are those of John J. Collins, "Sibylline Oracles," *Old Testament Pseudepigrapha,* vol. 1, *Apocalyptic Literature and Testaments,* ed. James H. Charlesworth (New York: Doubleday, 1983), pp. 317-472. The verses from book 3 date to the late first century BCE, while the verses from book 11 date to the turn of the era (Collins, "Sibylline Oracles," pp. 358, 432).

63. Cf. Greg Carey's reading of Rev 17:16: "We cannot readily account for how Revelation at once identifies Babylon with the Beast, then depicts the devastation of the one by the other. That the Empire devours its own self, however, seems evident." "The Book of Revelation as

pointed inversion of Gaia's outrage against the Olympians, in the Book of the Watchers the ravaged earth accuses the *giants* before the heavenly court (7:6). Inverting the ideals of moderation/self-control *(sophrosyne)*, law, and order, they are the portrait of excess, lawlessness, and disorder. Their appetites know no limits, exhausting food supplies, violating the sacred boundaries that mark life from death (their final crime: "they drank the blood," 7:5), devastating humanity, and eventually consuming one another. Gabriel receives the commission to destroy them, yet in a radical twist on the traditional gigantomachy myth, their destruction will come about through their very lack of self-control: he will "send them against one another in a war of destruction" (10:9).

This critical inversion retains the polarities and value structures of inside/outside, civilized/uncivilized, ordered/violent, moderate/excessive. But in refracting the myth through native Israelite traditions regarding Enoch, the "sons of God," and the mighty warriors found in Genesis 5–6, and by symbolically recasting the role of the giants in both myths, *1 Enoch* 6–11 implicitly assigns the negative value of each pair to the "Greeks" or, more accurately, the warring rulers, generals, and armies of the Hellenistic empires.[64] This critical inversion is closely linked with the inversion of the Prometheus myth, noted above. That is, the unceasing violence and devastating appetite of the Hellenistic rulers and their armies suggest that they, not the people they have conquered, are the mythic "giants." The corollary to this identification is that they are also uncivilized. The culture and knowledge they bear, as noted above, are not civilizing, as they and others imagine, but destructive and death-dealing.

3. A third example of inversion draws on Babylonian traditions. Babylonian astral magic identified the stars as heavenly mediators. A line from a cultic prayer to the Yoke star portrays this role by means of a tightly structured chiasm that foregrounds the messenger role while underscoring the reciprocity between human and divine made possible by the star's mediation:

išapparkunūši ilu ana amēli amēlu ana ili
The god sends you to a human, and human to the god.[65]

In this latter role, sent from human to god, stars could carry prayers from the human realm to the divine realm, conveying the extent of human suffering and presenting petitions to the gods.[66] In this intercessory role, "stars are [hu]man's

---

Counter-Imperial Script," in *In the Shadow of Empire: Reclaiming the Bible as a History of Faithful Resistance,* ed. Richard A. Horsley (Louisville: Westminster John Knox, 2008), pp. 157-82, 167.

64. Elsewhere in the Book of the Watchers the giants provide an etiology for diseases and evil spirits (*1 En.* 15:6–16:1).

65. Reiner, *Astral Magic in Babylonia,* p. 15.

66. Reiner, *Astral Magic in Babylonia,* p. 16.

medium of communication with the divine."[67] In the prayer quoted above, the verbal root *šapāru,* "to send a message" or "to write," not only underscores the mediatorial function of the star as messenger but also evokes the correlation between stars and writing.[68] Other prayers address the stars as divine judges *(ilū dajānī).* They rendered verdicts or decrees, sometimes in the form of dreams (cf. the decree of the heavenly watchers delivered to Nebuchadnezzar in his dream in Dan 4:17), at other times through omens.[69]

    1 Enoch 12–16 inverts key features of this cosmic relationship between humanity, God, and divinely appointed heavenly mediators by means of a partial correlation between the watchers and stars.[70] Like the stars, the watchers are to mediate between humans and God. Yet in abandoning their heavenly sanctuary (*1 En.* 12:4, 15:3) they have also forsaken their proper role as mediators. God now assigns this role to Enoch, "righteous scribe" (12:4), who will convey the verdict to the watchers. They are condemned to "make perpetual petition" (12:6), with no hope of mercy (14:4), while 'Asa'el is denied even the possibility of petition (13:2). When Enoch conveys the message to the watchers, they ask him to write and convey their petition for them, which he does (13:4-7). The rebuke he carries to them in response denies them any possibility of serving as intermediaries in the future, for they will never again ascend to heaven (14:5). Not only will their own petition be forever refused, but they cannot intercede for the children

    67. Reiner, *Astral Magic in Babylonia,* p. 15.

    68. See Rochberg, *Heavenly Writing,* pp. 1-2 and passim. For a semiological account of the relation between writing and creation, destiny, and divination in Mesopotamia, see Zainab Bahrani, *The Graven Image: Representation in Babylonia and Assyria* (Philadelphia: University of Pennsylvania Press, 2003), pp. 96-120, 202-10.

    69. Reiner, *Astral Magic in Babylonia,* pp. 68-73.

    70. Their precise relationship is ambiguously constructed in the earliest Enochic booklets (see *1 En.* 18:12-16; 21:1-5; 75:1; 80:1, 6-8; 82:4, 9-20). George W. E. Nickelsburg notes that "when 18:15 speaks of 'transgressing' stars, it is alluding to a variation on the myth of the rebellion of the watchers." *1 Enoch 1: A Commentary on the Book of 1 Enoch, Chapters 1–36, 81–108,* Hermeneia (Minneapolis: Fortress, 2001), p. 288. Stars symbolize the watchers in the allegory of the Animal Apocalypse (*1 En.* 86:1, 3). In Babylonian prayer, the stars are addressed as "You who see the entire world" (*hā'iṭ kibrāti,* CT 23 36; Reiner, *Astral Magic in Babylonia,* p. 17). The verb to see, *barû,* can also mean "watch over." The Babylonian god Shamash was also identified as the "one who sees," and the *bārû* priesthood who served him derived their name from this root (Reiner, *Astral Magic in Babylonia,* p. 65). For a suggested connection between the "watchers" and the *bārû* priests, see Siam Bhayro, "Daniel's 'Watchers' in Enochic Exegesis of Genesis 6:1-4," in *Jewish Ways of Reading the Bible,* ed. George Brooke (Oxford: Oxford University Press, 2000), pp. 58-66, esp. 63-64. In keeping with the inversion described here, the Book of the Watchers transfers many characteristics of Enmeduranki, the legendary founder of the *bārû* priesthood, to Enoch. See James C. VanderKam, *Enoch and the Growth of an Apocalyptic Tradition,* CBQMS 16 (Washington, DC: Catholic Biblical Association of America, 1984), pp. 43-45, 56-70; and Andrei A. Orlov, *The Enoch-Metatron Tradition* (Tübingen: Mohr Siebeck, 2005), pp. 23-76.

they love, the giants (14:6-7). Enoch must proclaim to them the irony of the inversion: "You should petition in behalf of humans, and not humans in behalf of you" (15:2).

The emphasis on the mediating function of the watchers, linked with their heavenly temple service, appears at first glance to be only loosely connected with the critique, described above, of the Hellenistic rulers, their armies and ideology of conquest, and the culture they represent. The references to the heavenly sanctuary suggest instead an interest in those who have responsibility for the temple cult in Jerusalem.[71] Yet these concerns are closely intertwined. As I discuss in the following chapter, priests within the Jerusalem establishment worked closely with the imperial administration and derived at least a portion of their authority from this source. Recognizing this connection, Patrick Tiller suggests that the Book of the Watchers "reflects an anti-imperial stance that rejects not only the foreign rulers, but also their local, priestly representatives."[72] Local cultic leaders who have allied themselves closely with the imperial administration, whether through nontraditional marriages or other forms of alliance and patronage, have, according to the Book of the Watchers, abandoned their proper mediating role between God and God's people. By combining inverted elements from Babylonian and Greek traditions with native traditions that highlight purity concerns and (abandoned) temple service, the book's composers symbolically locate the practices of local religious authorities within the broader hegemonic system and hold them accountable alongside the Hellenistic rulers with whom they now appear to be complicit.

These three examples of critical inversion in the Book of the Watchers illustrate one set of discursive strategies for constructing resistant counterdiscourse in the face of imperial hegemony. Yet just as hegemony contains within itself tools for its own inversion, it is also able to assimilate and transform ideas and forces that oppose it.[73] For this reason, Raymond Williams cautions against viewing hegemony as a fixed system or structure. Rather, hegemony is a dynamic process, continually retooled and reinvented in the face of resistance and coun-

71. At the same time, other features suggest an identification of the watchers (and not only the giants, as posited above) with the Hellenistic rulers, including the forms of knowledge they bring, their superhuman stature and might (see ch. 2), their outsider status, and their transgressive desire (here reading sexual desire as a symbol for the desire enacted through conquest and imperial exploitation). They are not simply stand-ins for Hellenistic rulers or for priests, but supple symbolic vehicles for critique of a complex and shifting target.

72. Patrick Tiller, "The Sociological Settings of the Components of 1 Enoch," in *The Early Enoch Literature*, ed. Gabriele Boccaccini and John J. Collins (Leiden: Brill, 2007), p. 252.

73. See especially Richard Terdiman, *Discourse/Counter-Discourse*, passim. Terdiman describes this process as "slippage," and refers to the "absorptive capacity" of established discourses (p. 13), which constantly infect subversive discourses with harmonizing stability, sameness, and inertia (p. 14).

terclaims.[74] This observation alerts us to the fact that the objects of resistance for the writers of the earliest apocalypses are dynamic, multifaceted, and evershifting. They responded with a similar dynamism, as evidenced by the complex layering of polemical traditions within the Book of the Watchers itself and by the complex composition history of Daniel and *1 Enoch* as a whole.

Domination and dominio

What is the relationship between hegemony and domination? While some thinkers do not sharply distinguish the two, Gramsci's concept of *dominio* helps us to clarify their relationship. For Gramsci, the nonviolent forms of control he identifies as hegemony can overlap and interlock with but also be distinguished from forms of rule *(dominio)* "expressed in directly political forms and in times of crisis by direct or effective coercion."[75] Through these directly political and physically coercive forms of rule the empire acts on the bodies of its subjects, claiming a sovereign power over their bodies not only in matters of life and death but also in the structured and structuring practices of daily life.[76]

Michel Foucault examines an extreme form of the latter in his study of "docile" bodies regulated and shaped by the bio-power of the state to further a state's economic and political ends.[77] According to Foucault, a state's coercive discipline, exercised in schools, military, and other institutional settings, both increases the body's potential (e.g., for labor, production, reproduction, and military service) and confines the exercise of that potential within the structures of the domination system.[78] It will be important to keep this process in mind when we consider the significance of Jason's building a gymnasium and establishing an ephebate in Jerusalem in 175 BCE (see ch. 3).

Yet the sovereign state does not only exercise its power through structures of discipline and order. Carl Schmitt defines sovereignty as the power to define

74. Raymond Williams, *Marxism and Literature* (Oxford: Oxford University Press, 1977), pp. 109-13. Williams writes, "A lived hegemony is always a process. It is not, except analytically, a system or a structure. It is a realized complex of experiences, relationships, and activities, with specific and changing pressures and limits. . . . It has continually to be renewed, recreated, defended, and modified. It is also continually resisted, limited, altered, challenged by pressures not at all its own" (p. 112).

75. Williams, *Marxism and Literature,* p. 108.

76. Cf. Catherine M. Bell's discussion of the "Ritual Body" in *Ritual Theory, Ritual Practice* (Oxford: Oxford University Press, 1992), pp. 94-117.

77. Michel Foucault, *Discipline and Punish: The Birth of the Prison,* trans. Alan Sheridan (New York: Pantheon, 1978; 2nd ed. New York: Vintage, 1995), pp. 127-69; originally published in French as *Surveiller et punir: naissance de la prison* (Paris: Gallimard, 1975).

78. Foucault, *Discipline and Punish,* p. 137.

the "state of exception."[79] That is, the sovereign is the one who can say when the rules do not apply, all the while keeping the rules in place. Giorgio Agamben merges Foucault's concept of "docile bodies" as the bio-power that fuels the state with Schmitt's understanding of sovereignty.[80] Though Agamben writes about the modern state, he correlates modern sovereignty with ancient conceptions of *imperium*. In both, he identifies the power over life and death, or "bare life" (rendering Walter Benjamin's phrase *bloßes Leben*), as "the original — if concealed — nucleus of sovereign power."[81] In Agamben's formulation, sovereign power draws bare life into the civic life of the *polis,* bringing bodies under the regulating discipline of the state while also subjecting them to its arbitrary power over life and death.[82] As a result, bare life becomes "the one place for both the organization of State power and emancipation from it."[83] That is, the vulnerable body becomes the locus of resistance for those who would deny the sovereign power of the king.

The *dominio* of the Hellenistic kings claimed such a sovereignty over the lives and deaths of their subjects. Prior to the persecution of Jews under Antiochus IV Epiphanes, this *dominio* expressed itself through conquest, killing and maiming, slavery, intimidating displays of martial power, and the policing presence and actions of imperial agents, as well as through economic redistribution achieved through ordinary systems of taxation and tribute and extraordinary acts of plunder (see further chs. 2–5). These forms of *dominio* were oppressive, to be sure, and, as noted above, they occasioned a critical response in the Book of the Watchers. But they did not seek overtly to negate Jewish theological claims for the sovereignty of their God.

By contrast, Antiochus IV's persecution of the Jews made a totalitarian claim on his Judean subjects that not only denied God's sovereignty but, as some Jews perceived (Dan 8:11-12; 11:36), directly attacked it. His decrees took aim at the body of the believer. Through embodied practices of circumcision, sacrifice and other forms of worship, ritual purity, Sabbath, and diet, ancient Jews pro-

79. Carl Schmitt, *Political Theology: Four Chapters on the Concept of Sovereignty* (Chicago: University of Chicago Press, 2005).

80. Giorgio Agamben, *Homo Sacer: Sovereign Power and Bare Life,* trans. Daniel Heller-Roazen (Stanford, CA: Stanford University Press, 1998), pp. 3-12. Originally published as *Homo Sacer: Il potere sovrano e la nuda vita* (Torino: Einaudi, 1995).

81. He continues: "Placing biological life at the center of its calculations, the modern State therefore does nothing other than bring to light the secret tie uniting power and bare life, thereby reaffirming the bond (derived from a tenacious correspondence between the modern and the archaic which one encounters in the most diverse spheres) between modern power and the most immemorial of the *arcana imperii."* Agamben, *Homo Sacer,* p. 6.

82. Agamben, *Homo Sacer,* pp. 4, 9. This too will be relevant for understanding the impact of Jason's reforms in 175 BCE, which included establishing Jerusalem as a *polis.*

83. Agamben, *Homo Sacer,* p. 9.

claimed and enacted the sovereignty of God in every sphere of life. By outlawing these very practices, compelling alternative practices, and punishing noncompliance with torture and death, Antiochus IV sought to negate God's claim over the very bodies of Jews, asserting in its place his own sole sovereignty.

According to 1 Maccabees, it was in the face of compulsory sacrifice that Mattathias's "zeal for the law" led to the first act of armed resistance to Antiochus IV's decrees (1 Macc 1:15-26). Others endured torture and martyrdom as a way to deny Antiochus's claim over their bodies and the bodies of their children, holding fast to practices of infant circumcision, Sabbath, and *kashrut* even in the face of pain and death (2 Macc 6:9–7:42). By producing "absolute pain," to use the words of Elaine Scarry, Antiochus sought to create "the fiction of absolute power."[84] The martyrs negated the fiction of Antiochus's sovereign power by denying the ultimacy of pain and death alike. Judith Perkins examines similar resistance through martyrdom in her analysis of suffering and power in the early church. In this later period, she writes, "Martyrs' deaths . . . display not the power of the Roman state but rather the power of the Christian community's reordered beliefs about pain and death."[85] The same is true for the Jewish martyrs memorialized in 2 Maccabees. The scribe and elder Eleazar submits to torture rather than eat sacrificial pork or even publicly pretend to have done so. In his refusal he denies the king the power to overrule the embodied practices commanded by God (2 Macc 6:23). Moments before dying he asserts, "Although I could have escaped death, I am not only enduring terrible pain in my body from this scourging, but also suffering it with joy in my soul" (2 Macc 6:30 NAB). His joy in his own death would leave an example "for the whole nation" (2 Macc 6:31 NAB).[86] The seven brothers and mother who die martyrs' deaths at Antiochus's hands similarly reveal the power of "reordered beliefs about pain and death." Even as they watched each other's horrific sufferings and suffered themselves, each in turn proclaimed the power of the creator God (2 Macc 7:22-23, 28) to piece together the dismembered body, to raise the dead to life, and to restore a community ripped apart by violence (2 Macc 7:9, 11, 14, 23, 29).[87] The martyrs' embrace of their own deaths asserts that death is not the limit of human exis-

---

84. Scarry, *Body in Pain*, p. 27.

85. Judith Perkins, *The Suffering Self: Pain and Narrative Representation in the Early Christian Era* (London: Routledge, 2003), p. 119.

86. Elizabeth A. Castelli asserts that "martyrdom requires audience." *Martyrdom and Memory: Early Christian Culture Making* (New York: Columbia University Press, 2007), p. 34. She discusses martyrdom as spectacle on pp. 104-33. The martyr story places the experiences of violence and suffering within a broader, meaningful narrative "that invokes notions of justice and the right ordering of the cosmos" (p. 34).

87. Perkins, *The Suffering Self*, p. 119, emphasizes that it is not just the individual body but also the social body of the community that is reimaged as receiving life beyond death.

tence. For them, Antiochus's power to inflict bodily pain and death (2 Macc 7:16) is cancelled out by the greater lifegiving, restoring, and salvific power of God, and will be answered with divine judgment against the earthly sovereign (2 Macc 7:17, 19, 35-36). A theology affirming God's power and providence as creator and restorer of life and as guarantor of justice thus counteracts the *dominio* or coercive rule of Antiochus and its totalitarian claim over the bodies of his Judean subjects and enables the resistant action of the martyrs.

Gramsci's notion of *dominio* as directly political and sometimes coercive forms of rule brings us close to contemporary usage of the term domination.[88] In line with Gramsci's understanding of *dominio*, the concept of domination is sometimes limited to political, economic, or physically coercive forms of social control.[89] Others understand domination in a broader and more complicated sense that includes hegemony.[90] Scott emphasizes social hierarchies in his definition of domination as "systemic forms of social subordination."[91] I understand domination as the social and ideological structures that create and maintain conditions of subordination as well as particular strategies and actions that aim to establish, maintain, or augment these structures.

Finally, it is important to note here, with Miller, that in complex social systems domination may operate through "several different and often competing hierarchical classifications."[92] That is, there is not one ladder from bottom to top, not one system of subordination only, but multiple systems of authority, legitimation, and control that impinge on one another in various complex ways. This multiplicity cautions us against formulating too simplistic a view of the context and objects of resistance (cf. the discussion of the Book of the Watchers above). This insight also draws our attention to the existence of multiple and competing sources of authority that may either reinforce or deconstruct systems of domination.[93] Competing claims for the location and legiti-

88. For a succinct survey of different approaches to domination, see Miller, Rowlands, and Tilley, introduction to *Domination and Resistance*, pp. 3-17.

89. Miller, "Limits of Dominance," p. 64.

90. Cf. Miller's definition of dominance as "the condition in which a set of ideas or practices, usually favourable to a particular minority within a society, appear to hold sway over the whole of that society and act to reproduce the same condition. Dominance may be exercised through sufficient coercive force as to be independent of the acquiescence of the dominated population, but more commonly it relates to principles of ideology and underlying discourses which structure both the construction of the subject and the subsequent acknowledgement by that subject of at least some of the legitimation claims made by the dominant group." "Limits of Dominance," p. 63.

91. James C. Scott, *Domination and the Arts of Resistance: Hidden Transcripts* (New Haven: Yale University Press, 1990), p. 2.

92. Miller, "Limits of Dominance," p. 64.

93. Miller, "Limits of Dominance," p. 68.

mation of power and knowledge make it possible for resisters not only to limit the exercise of power within a given system, but also to contest the cosmologies that authorize the system itself. This type of resistance is not grounded in the inversion of hegemonic categories, but in the assertion of alternative cosmologies (2 Macc 7:22-23, 28 invokes God's role as Creator; for a discussion of the Book of the Watchers' alternative cosmology, see ch. 8).[94]

Resistance to the Hellenistic Empires: Key Studies

Having established a conceptual framework for understanding resistance, hegemony, and domination in the present study, I turn now to survey a few key works of scholarship on ancient Near Eastern resistance to the Hellenistic empires.[95] While not all their conclusions (or assumptions) have withstood the test of time, some of their insights may inform our discussion of resistance to Antiochus's persecution.

A key discursive strategy of resistance shared by Daniel, the Apocalypse of Weeks, and the Book of Dreams is the historical review, cast in the form of prophetic prediction, that at the same time interprets past and present, asserts the transience and finitude of temporal powers, affirms God's governance of time and the outworking of God's plan in history, and gives hope for a transformed future. Two passages in Daniel, namely Daniel 2:31-45 (the interpretation of Nebuchadnezzar's dream of the statue) and 7:1-14 (the succession of beastly kingdoms followed by the grant of rule to one like a human being) present this prophetic review of history and vision of the future in a sequence of five kingdoms. In these passages the first four kingdoms imply a succession of known imperial powers from the past and present (presented, within the narrative, as

---

94. Both strategies may operate side by side, as they do in the Book of the Watchers.

95. While I limit my attention here to the Hellenistic empires, classic studies of resistance to the Roman Empire include Harald Fuchs, *Der geistige Widerstand gegen Rom in der antiken Welt* (Berlin: Walter de Gruyter, 1938); and Ramsay MacMullen, *Enemies of the Roman Order: Treason, Unrest, and Alienation in the Empire* (Cambridge, MA: Harvard University Press, 1966). MacMullen demonstrates that those who opposed Rome were neither members of oppressed classes nor marginal figures in Roman society, but belonged to the ruling elite (p. vii). As he notes, "The foes of the monarch rise from the midst of his friends" (p. viii; cf. 243). This insight will be important for our consideration of the social matrix of the apocalyptic literature of resistance studied in this volume. Recent treatments of resistance to the Roman empire can be found in two collected volumes: Kurt Raaflaub, Adalberto Giovannini, and Denis van Berchem, eds., *Opposition et resistances à l'Empire d'Auguste à Trajan: neuf exposés suivis de discussions,* Entretiens sur l'antiquité classique 33 (Vandoeuvres-Genève: Fondation Hardt, 1987); and Toru Yuge and Masaoki Doi, eds., *Forms of Control and Subordination in Antiquity* (Leiden: Brill, 1988).

present and future), while the fifth is presented as a future just kingdom categorically distinct from the first four (uncut stone, Dan 2; like a human being, Dan 7).[96] In a now classic article, "The Theory of the Four Monarchies: Opposition History under the Roman Empire," Joseph Ward Swain called attention to parallels between these passages and a passage attributed to one Aemilius Sura in the writings of the Roman historian Velleius Paterculus.[97] Though Velleius wrote in the early decades of the first century CE, Swain dates the quoted passage between 189 and 171 BCE.[98] Sura's historiographic fragment traces world power in a succession of five empires (Assyria, Media, Persia, Macedonia, Rome). Swain argues that the core of Sura's list would have originated in Seleucid Asia Minor, and he suggests ways such a list could have functioned in various contexts to rouse opposition to Seleucid rule.[99]

David Flusser argues that a similar schema expressed opposition to Seleucid (i.e., Macedonian) rule in a source used by the fourth Sibylline oracle. Based on evidence from later Zoroastrian texts, Flusser posits an ancient Persian tradition of four ages, with the fourth age being a time of "the evil sovereignty of wicked demons."[100] He argues that at some time prior to the composition of Daniel 2, the four ages came to be aligned with a sequence of empires,

96. For David Flusser, the reason for the distinction is that "the idea of the four empires was already fully developed by then and their number could not be changed." "The Four Empires in the Fourth Sibyl and in the Book of Daniel," *Israel Oriental Studies* 2 (1978): 148-75, 157. Yet he does not state on what authority it could not be changed, or why. Other textual clues suggest, contra Flusser, that the different symbolism used for the four known world empires, on the one hand, and the one that will succeed them, on the other, signals that they (not only the symbols that represent them) are fundamentally different in kind. Sharon Pace argues that in Dan 2 the uncut stone can be taken "as symbolizing God's power, forming a dynamic contrast to the pretensions of empires, symbolized by the statue." Sharon Pace, *Daniel,* Smyth & Helwys Bible Commentary (Macon, GA: Smyth & Helwys, 2008), p. 69. In Dan 7 the disjuncture is more forceful still, answering the succession of beastly, mutated, and finite kingdoms with the eternal rule of one like a human being. The rapacity of the monstrous empires, signaled in part by a ravenous appetite for flesh (7:5, 7), contrasts sharply with the "humane" rule that follows from the judgment of the heavenly court and the "giving of justice" (cf. Psalm 72:1 MT) to the holy ones of the most high (7:10-14, 17-18, 22).

97. Joseph Ward Swain, "The Theory of the Four Monarchies: Opposition History under the Roman Empire," *Classical Philology* 35, no. 1 (1940): 1-21. Swain notes that the quotation of Sura is typically viewed as a gloss, and not original to Velleius Paterculus (p. 2).

98. For an opposing view, see Doron Mendels, "The Five Empires: A Note on a Propagandistic *Topos*," *American Journal of Philology* 102 (1981): 330-37. Mendels sees no warrant for such an early date for Aemilius Sura (who is otherwise unknown to history) and his fragment. He dates Roman use of the "four plus one" *topos* (with Rome as the "plus one," or fifth kingdom) to the end of the first century BCE, "when Rome started to interfere intensively in the regions which belonged to the first three empires of the *topos*" (p. 335).

99. Swain, "Theory," pp. 7-8.

100. Flusser, "Four Empires," p. 173.

specifically the first four empires in the list already noted above: Assyria, Media, Persia, and Macedonia. In this identification, "Macedonian rule [and by extension the age of the Seleucid empire] became the period of final wickedness before heavenly vengeance and salvation, and so the new concept became political as well as eschatological and served in the Book of Daniel and probably also in the ancient source of the fourth Sibyl and elsewhere as an ideological weapon of the East against the West."[101] Flusser's reconstruction of an ancient Avestan source must remain hypothetical. Nonetheless, his analysis, like Swain's, helpfully places Daniel's visionary report of a succession of empires in the broader context of ancient Near Eastern resistance to Hellenistic rule. By suggesting a link between the *historiographic* account of a sequence of empires and the *theological* understanding of time in the Zoroastrian traditions, Flusser highlights the political dimension of particular theologies of time.[102] As in the sources Flusser examines, so in Daniel, the review of history serves multiple purposes: it critiques the ruling powers of the present age, characterizing their rule as evil, demonic, monstrous, or exceptionally destructive; by claiming knowledge of past, present, and future, it claims a greater power than that available to current temporal rulers and assures its audience of divine providence; it projects an end to current rule, countering imperial claims to ultimacy; and it frames hope for the faithful in terms of justice, reversal, and a good age to come. While we cannot identify the exact sources on which the composers of Daniel 2 and 7 drew as they adapted such a schema of empires and ages, Flusser's arguments help us to recognize that these writers likely drew on *topoi* known from other Near Eastern traditions, possibly merging elements of a Zoroastrian theology of time with ideas of time and history already present in native Israelite traditions. As Flusser notes, similar understandings of time appear in the Apocalypse of Weeks.[103] These insights suggest that the apocalyptic review of history may have had its roots in ancient Near Eastern traditions of resistance to Macedonian/Seleucid rule and was fundamental to the way in which these early Jewish apocalypses functioned as resistance literature.[104]

An earlier work by Samuel Eddy emphasizes a different aspect of ancient

101. Flusser, "Four Empires," p. 173.

102. See also John Collins, "Temporality and Politics in Jewish Apocalyptic Literature," in *Apocalyptic in History and Tradition*, ed. Christopher Rowland and John Barton (London: Sheffield Academic Press, 2002), pp. 26-43.

103. Flusser, "Four Empires," p. 162.

104. For a contrasting view, see Josef Wiesehöfer, "Vom 'oberen Asien' zur 'gesamten bewohnten Welt': Die hellenistisch-römische Weltreiche-Theorie," in *Europa, Tausendjähriges Reich und Neue Welt: Zwei Jahrtausende Geschichte und Utopie in der Rezeption des Danielbuches*, ed. Mariano Delgado, Klaus Koch, and Edgar Marsch (Stuttgart: Universitätsverlag Freiburg Schweiz, 2003), pp. 66-81.

Near Eastern resistance to Hellenistic rule. In the influential study *The King Is Dead: Studies in the Near Eastern Resistance to Hellenism,* Eddy sought to uncover "evidence for opposition to Hellenistic imperialism" and to identify its forms, causes, and effects as well as the "ways it was advocated and justified."[105] He concludes that, throughout the ancient Near East, resistance to the Hellenistic empires was almost always grounded in a theology of kingship.[106] In Jewish traditions, this theology of kingship was closely linked to the exercise of justice,[107] a theme clearly evident in Daniel 7 (cf. *1 En.* 90:24-25). For Persians, so Eddy argues, earthly kingship belonged to the human representative of the god Ahura Mazda (whom Eddy calls an "imperial deity"), who ordered the world and ordained the Persian state as its ruler.[108] After Alexander's defeat of the Persian empire, the cosmic battle between Ahura Mazda and the demonic Angra Mainyu ("destructive spirit") could be understood in political terms, with Alexander in the role of Angra Mainyu and the "Greeks" in the role of the *daevas,* or "false gods."[109] In the linking of cosmic battles and temporal politics, Eddy finds parallels between Persian and Jewish theologies of resistance, noting also that each "developed a rigidly henotheistic belief and an eschatology which saw human and divine affairs moving inexorably towards the predetermined divine and universal victory."[110]

While Persia had a robust theology of resistance to Hellenistic rule, Eddy finds that Babylonian and Elamite resistance was slight, owing in part to their polytheistic beliefs and the ways these were linked to understandings of human kingship.[111] Within this belief system, human rulers did not represent one god only. In a given time, a god might be associated with a particular place, typically a city. During that time, the human ruler of that place could be understood as the earthly mediator of the god's rule. But human kingship, like divine king-

---

105. Samuel K. Eddy, *The King Is Dead: Studies in the Near Eastern Resistance to Hellenism, 334-31 B.C.* (Lincoln: University of Nebraska Press, 1961), p. vii. In his conclusion Eddy identifies four kinds of resistance, namely "passive, militant, messianic, and proselytic" (pp. 335-39). The first type circulated legends of ancient, native heroes to create and maintain a sense of local identity. His analysis of resistance through stories of native heroes sheds light on the prominence of such ancient figures as Daniel and Enoch in the narrative portions of the texts studied in the present volume. Eddy's second category included armed revolt, and was frequently accompanied by the third. He finds in the Maccabees an example of the fourth category as well.

106. Eddy, *King Is Dead,* p. vii.

107. Eddy, *King Is Dead,* p. 192.

108. Eddy, *King Is Dead,* p. 9.

109. Eddy, *King Is Dead,* p. 31.

110. Eddy, *King Is Dead,* p. 42.

111. Eddy, *King Is Dead,* p. 132. It would be a mistake, however, to move from these localized observations to generalizing conclusions about an inherent relationship between monotheism and resistance or polytheism and accommodation.

ship, was conditional, and the rise and fall of earthly kings and empires could reflect shifts in power among the gods in heaven.[112] This very idea of conditional kingship holds a central place in Daniel's theo-politics as well (and appears in earlier Israelite traditions), even though Daniel affirms the existence of only one, sovereign God who was not bound by place and did not share the vulnerability of Babylon's gods.

Eddy's study of resistance in Babylon and Elam yields another important parallel for the texts studied in this volume. Although the Babylonians and Elamites were not quick to resist Hellenistic rule, Eddy observes that assaults on their native temples, introduction of Hellenistic motifs into temple worship, and imperial efforts to access temple treasuries triggered strong, even militant resistance in these regions, just as it did in Judea.[113] In each case of resistance that Eddy studies, he concludes that local cults played a key role in creating and sustaining a sense of unity that was a necessary component of resistance to Hellenistic imperial rule.[114]

James C. Scott, the Hidden Transcript, and Apocalyptic Pseudonymity

The studies of Swain, Flusser, and Eddy predate contemporary theoretical discussions of domination and resistance reviewed earlier in this chapter. In recent years, discussions of domination and resistance in the ancient world have taken a more theoretical turn. The work of one theorist in particular now holds a prominent place. In the field of biblical studies, political scientist James C. Scott's theory of the hidden transcript, or "offstage dissent to the official tran-

---

112. Eddy, *King Is Dead*, p. 102.

113. Eddy, *King Is Dead*, pp. 133-36, 145. G. W. Bowersock similarly emphasizes the centrality of temples in his study of resistance to Roman rule in a later period, noting that local priests were well positioned to influence popular opinion and so galvanize resistance. "The Mechanics of Subversion in the Roman Provinces," in *Opposition et resistances à l'Empire d'Auguste à Trajan: neuf exposés suivis de discussions,* ed. Kurt Raaflaub, Adalberto Giovannini, and Denis van Berchem, Entretiens sur l'antiquité classique 33 (Vandoeuvres-Genève: Fondation Hardt, 1987), pp. 291-317, 297. As in 2 Macc, so in the sources Bowersock studies, miracles played an important role (p. 298). Bowersock concludes (p. 315): "And so at the center of provincial subversion stood the local temples, revealed to have been far more vital than many have thought." In the discussion that follows the essay, Adalberto Giovannini adds examples of the same phenomenon in the Hellenistic period, concluding, "It seems indeed that these indigenous sanctuaries knew how to preserve a high degree of autonomy through the ages; they fiercely defended their privileges under the Roman empire, just as they had done against the Hellenistic kings" (discussion in *Opposition et resistances,* p. 319; my translation from French).

114. Eddy, *King Is Dead*, p. 333.

script of power relations,"[115] has now become a standard feature in treatments of resistance to empire, and for that reason merits a closer look here.[116]

Scott's theory of the hidden transcript begins from the recognition that, in stable systems of domination and subordination, power relations play out in a form of public theater. In this drama, dominant and dominated each has a scripted part to play. Their public speech and gesture generate a transcript of power relations in which the dominant appear honorable, beneficent, and just, while the dominated appear subservient, deferential, and grateful.[117] Offstage, a

115. Scott, *Domination and the Arts of Resistance*, p. xi.

116. Curiously, Scott's work has made a far greater splash in studies of New Testament than in studies of Hebrew Bible/Old Testament and ancient Judaism. Two Semeia Studies volumes have given a central place to Scott's concept of the hidden transcript: Richard A. Horsley, ed., *Oral Performance, Popular Tradition, and Hidden Transcript in Q* (Atlanta: Society of Biblical Literature, 2006); and Richard A. Horsley, ed., *Hidden Transcripts and the Arts of Resistance: Applying the Work of James C. Scott to Jesus and Paul* (Atlanta: Society of Biblical Literature, 2004). Richard Horsley also utilizes the concept in his study *Jesus and Empire: The Kingdom of God and the New World Disorder* (Minneapolis: Fortress, 2003), pp. 53-54; as does Neil Elliott in *The Arrogance of Nations: Reading Romans in the Shadow of Empire* (Minneapolis: Fortress, 2008). Other examples (the list is by no means exhaustive) include David Reed, "Rethinking John's Social Setting: Hidden Transcript, Anti-Language, and the Negotiation of the Empire," *BTB* 36 (2006): 93-106; and Monya A. Stubbs, "Subjection, Reflection, Resistance: An African American Reading of the Three-Dimensional Process of Empowerment in Romans 13 and the Free Market Economy," in *Navigating Romans through Cultures: Challenging Readings by Charting a New Course*, ed. Yeo Khiok-khng (K.K.) (London: Continuum, 2004), pp. 171-97. Danna Nolan Fewell and David Valeta both use the concept to analyze the stories in Dan 1–6: Danna Nolan Fewell, *The Children of Israel: Reading the Bible for the Sake of Our Children* (Nashville: Abingdon, 2003), pp. 117-30; David Valeta, "Polyglossia and Parody: Language in Daniel 1–6," in *Bakhtin and Genre Theory in Biblical Studies*, ed. Roland Boer (Atlanta: Society of Biblical Literature, 2007), pp. 91-108. Gerald O. West applies Scott's theories to the field of biblical studies more broadly. See, e.g., Gerald O. West, "Gauging the Grain in a More Nuanced and Literary Manner: A Cautionary Tale Concerning the Contribution of the Social Sciences to Biblical Interpretation," in *Rethinking Contexts, Rereading Texts: Contributions from the Social Sciences to Biblical Interpretation*, ed. M. Daniel Carroll R. (London: Continuum, 2000), pp. 75-105; and Gerald O. West, "And the Dumb Do Speak: Articulating Incipient Readings of the Bible in Marginalized Communities," in *The Bible in Ethics: The Second Sheffield Colloquium*, ed. John William Rogerson, Margaret Davies, and M. Daniel Carroll R. (London: Continuum, 1995), pp. 174-92. Outside the field of biblical studies, see Daniel Boyarin, *Dying for God: Martyrdom and the Making of Christianity and Judaism* (Stanford: Stanford University Press, 1999); and Shadi Bartsch, *Actors in the Audience: Theatricality and Doublespeak from Nero to Hadrian* (Cambridge, MA: Harvard University Press, 1998).

117. E.g., Scott, *Weapons of the Weak*, pp. 169-78. In American pop culture the scripting of gratitude has been memorialized in a line from the movie *Animal House*, where the fraternity inductee voluntarily submits to a ritual paddling while responding to each blow with the phrase "Thank you, Sir, may I have another?" As the ritual progresses, the phrase is spoken as a statement rather than a question, reinforcing the apparent inevitability of the script and the power relations it encodes. The counterintuitive script reveals and ritualizes the interrelationship between systems of patronage and violent discipline, portrayed also in Dan 2.

different drama unfolds. In private, protected by the closed circle of their own class, the actors say what they really think: dominant and dominated each derides the other behind his or her back. While Scott calls attention to the hidden transcripts of the dominant and dominated alike, he and the majority of those who engage his ideas give greatest attention to the hidden transcript of the dominated. In private, the dominated dream out loud; they sing and tell stories of reversal; they paint pictures of another kind of life.

Actors rarely voice this hidden transcript on the public stage — to do so is risky, to self and others. But occasionally a dominated individual or group is pushed to the limit. No longer willing to act out a humiliating public script of accommodation and subservience, they say no out loud, sometimes pairing words with actions.[118] At times a people are ready to rise up, even to declare war: they make the hidden transcript public as part of their effort to transform the social order that binds them. But such an outright declaration of opposition to the dominant powers invites reprisal, and is rarely entered into lightly. Where there is little hope of reversal, such a revelation can undermine an intricate and dearly bought system of survival and even advantage.

More frequently, the hidden transcript finds its way onstage through an infra-politics of anonymity, ambiguity, and disguise.[119] Anonymous speech forms such as rumor, gossip, and folktales encode messages of resistance to be shared among those who have ears to hear.[120] Songs of courage, hope, anger, or sorrow carrying promises of retribution and reward can be sung out loud in the presence of the master while those who sing them deny that they carry any meaning at all.[121] No one knows who wrote them; no one will vouch for what they really mean.[122] These special forms of speech make it possible publicly to communicate the hidden transcript, thinly veiling from the powerful its message of resistance while strengthening the weak in their resolve to resist.

For Scott these forms of speech are "somewhat analogous" to the silent sabotage he analyzed in his groundbreaking study *Weapons of the Weak: Everyday Forms of Peasant Resistance.*[123] Just as the foot-dragger will not publicly acknowledge her foot-dragging, neither will the person who has started a rumor own up to it.[124] She must remain anonymous. She must be able publicly to

118. Scott, *Domination and the Arts of Resistance*, pp. 7-9, 41, 221-22.

119. Scott, *Domination and the Arts of Resistance*, pp. xiii, 18-20.

120. Cf. Daniel L. Smith's treatment of "Folklore of Hope" in *The Religion of the Landless: The Social Context of the Babylonian Exile* (Bloomington, IN: Meyer-Stone, 1989), pp. 153-78.

121. Scott, *Domination and the Arts of Resistance*, p. 158.

122. Scott, *Domination and the Arts of Resistance*, p. 161.

123. Scott, *Domination and the Arts of Resistance*, p. xiii.

124. Scott describes an indirect method by which the women workers of Sedaka "let it be known" to the farmers who employed them that they were unhappy with new technologies that

deny the power and meaning of her own speech, or even privately to disown it, even though its power is real. A rumor, like foot-dragging, can cost a landowner — or a king — time and money. By the very threat of loss, it will also convey dissatisfaction on the part of workers (or subjects), and an attendant need for redress, new terms, or better treatment, at the risk of greater loss to the landowner (or king) in the future. Such practices typically threaten not to overthrow, but to cost.[125] They allow the powerful the opportunity to meet unvoiced demands while also maintaining appearances of generosity, fairness, and, most importantly, power.[126] The gossip, like the foot-dragger, may publicly acknowledge the authority of her oppressor. She may still bow and scrape, using the sanitized rhetoric of the public transcript to call forth justice. Yet both parties know that the public transcript is an act. And both parties are, to varying degrees, interested in keeping up appearances.[127]

Scott's theory is compelling. But not all actors, or writers, wish to keep up appearances. Some are convinced that appearances are fatally deceptive. We have in the literary genre apocalypse a pseudonymous speech form that strives to strip away appearances. At this juncture we must ask whether apocalyptic discourse has any relation to Scott's system of public and hidden transcripts. Does the apocalyptic dualism between the visible and invisible correspond in some way to Scott's idea of the public and hidden transcript? Do the composers of apocalypses who conceal their identity within the pseudonymous attribution of authorship to a noteworthy figure from the past choose this device for the same reasons that the peasant in Sedaka begins a rumor only to deny it publicly? While the parallels are tantalizing, to both questions I answer "no." Ultimately, something very different is at work in the apocalyptic literature of resistance studied in the present volume, as I explain below.

I insisted above that not only domination but also hegemony provide the conditions and objects of resistance for our authors. Yet Scott's theory wrongly minimizes the role of hegemony as Gramsci understands it. While Scott helps us to recognize the many, sometimes less obvious forms resistance can take, the fundamental linking of consciousness and resistant action in our texts requires that we move beyond Scott's theory as we work to understand apocalyptic resistance to empire. I begin with a critique of Scott's understanding of hegemony, then discuss the function of pseudonymity as a discursive strategy

---

threatened their livelihood and might strike. By using this indirect method of communication rather than publicly refusing to work, they retained the option of abandoning the boycott if the farmers did not give in (*Weapons of the Weak*, pp. 248-55).

125. Cf. Scott, *Domination and the Arts of Resistance*, pp. 142-47.

126. Bourdieu, *Outline of a Theory of Practice*, p. 41.

127. Scott, *Weapons of the Weak*, p. 282.

of resistance to empire in our texts. I argue that the composers and tradents of these early apocalyptic writings recognized the power of hegemonic discourse and sought to counter it with an equally totalizing discourse of their own.[128] The imperial domination system could most easily perpetuate itself by rendering the structures of domination invisible. Apocalyptic writings rendered them visible and characterized them as monstrous or demonic precisely to enable full-fledged resistance of the mind, spirit, and body. Similarly, the device of pseudonymity served not to hide the person or community who composed the apocalypse, but rather to assert that they were not the originators of this counterdiscourse. The guarantee of their revelation stood upon the givenness of tradition: the plan of God was embedded in creation, fixed for all time, and handed down in the unitary witness of a great figure from long ago. By positing the contingency of their own discourse, these writers were able to assert the parallel contingency of the imperial domination system, undercutting its claims to ultimacy and depriving it of the power to assign meaning within the world.

Practice versus Belief?

For Scott public acquiescence to the demands of the domination system need not correspond to acceptance in the realm of belief. Scott seeks to refute the Marxist understanding of false consciousness (he refers specifically to Gramsci and Georg Lukacs), which posits that through religion, education, media, and culture, elites are able to control symbol systems within a culture, replicating an ideology that supports their own interests while symbolically imprisoning the weak.[129] Paraphrasing Gramsci (in order to disagree with him), Scott writes: "By creating and disseminating a universe of discourse and the concepts to go with it, by defining the standards of what is true, beautiful, moral, fair, and legitimate, they build a symbolic climate that prevents subordinate classes from

---

128. Cf. the analysis of rap as a totalizing discourse (with the recognition that as such a discourse it exceeds academic analysis) in Toby Daspit and John A. Weaver, "Rap (in) the Academy," in *Imagining the Academy: Higher Education and Popular Culture*, ed. Susan Edgerton (New York: RoutledgeFalmer, 2005), pp. 89-114. As Daspit and Weaver recognize, to identify a discourse as totalizing is neither to discredit it nor to reduce it to something monolithic. In their understanding, "a totalizing discourse contains moments of romance and resistance in it, but it is more. A totalizing discourse is a self-contained system of affective experiences and inventions about the world but not hermetically sealed. It contains seeds of radical change but also kernels of dominance and repression. More important, a totalizing discourse is heteroglossic" (p. 98).

129. See especially Scott, *Weapons of the Weak*, pp. 314-18, with a proleptic summary of his argument on p. 317.

thinking their way free."[130] For Gramsci, those without power may be free to act in radical ways, but not so to think.[131]

Scott insists, to the contrary, that it is in the realm of action that dominated classes are most constrained, while it is in the realm of belief and interpretation that they are most free.[132] He writes, "It is more accurate to consider subordinate classes *less* constrained at the level of thought and ideology, since they can in secluded settings speak with comparative safety, and *more* constrained at the level of political action and struggle, where the daily exercise of power sharply limits the options available to them."[133] Citing examples of utopian beliefs, he denies the claim that subordinate groups are not able to imagine a different social or world order.[134] Yet, as I discuss below, by Scott's own logic, the covert, anonymous, and ambiguous speech forms that convey these alternate visions of reality reveal that these forms do not seek to challenge or transform the current world order at all. They are to remain in the realm of fantasy, leaving the "real" world untouched. But how free is an imagination that does not imagine the power of its visions to reshape perceptions of the possible and so transform the real?

As Timothy Mitchell has noted, Scott's theory here rests on a false dualism. For Scott, mind and body, thought and action, reside in two separate domains. Persuasion compels the former. Coercion compels the latter. It is possible, in this view, for the body to submit to coercion, while the mind remains entirely free. For Scott the hidden transcript reveals that while behavioral constraints outwardly conform practices to the demands of the domination system, subordinate individuals and groups retain freedom in the realm of ideas and beliefs. Yet Scott does not allow for the ways in which practices shape consciousness.[135] As Mitchell states, "These practices are inseparable from the shaping of ideas: they are the source of identity, loyalty and emotion."[136] They embed themselves in the structure of daily life and in its rationale.[137]

Mitchell observes that the distinction between power that acts on behavior and power that acts (or does not act) on consciousness accompanies a host of

---

130. Scott, *Weapons of the Weak*, p. 39.

131. Scott, *Weapons of the Weak*, p. 322.

132. Scott, *Weapons of the Weak*, p. 322; cf. 331; *Domination and the Arts of Resistance*, p. 91.

133. Scott, *Domination and the Arts of Resistance*, p. 91.

134. Scott, *Domination and the Arts of Resistance*, pp. 81, 166-72.

135. See the discussion of embodied practices above.

136. Mitchell, "Everyday Metaphors of Power," p. 558.

137. Bourdieu, *Outline of a Theory of Practice*, p. 95: "As an acquired system of generative schemes objectively adjusted to the particular conditions in which it is constituted, the habitus engenders all the thoughts, all the perceptions, and all the actions consistent with those conditions, and no others."

false oppositions: "material versus ideological, actions versus words, observable versus hidden, coerced versus free, base versus superstructure, body versus spirit."[138] Scott wants to claim that power operates in the material, public sphere, compelling behavior but not assent. Mitchell observes that this understanding of power is linked to an understanding of the person, staking out a preserve of "self-formed and autonomous personhood" in the midst of the domination system.[139]

Contra Scott, Mitchell asserts that the very idea that mind and body or belief and practice might operate independently of one another is a product of the domination system and serves to maintain and perpetuate structures of domination. In this system, structures of power take on the appearance of something ideal, nonparticular, transcendent, and metaphysical.[140] Metaphysical structures look unassailable; they cannot be challenged in deed or in thought. But as Mitchell argues, and as our writers understood, there is no "nonphysical framework" for belief. As I noted above, the veiled and unveiling discourse of apocalyptic literature that is at the same time secret and disclosure, obscure and transparent, tantalizes the critic with its parallels to Scott's theory of the hidden and public transcript. What is remarkable about the apocalypses, however, is *not* their claim that there is an invisible, hidden world distinct from the visible world. It is their exposure of the hidden structures of false power and assertion of a more potent invisible power. It is their insistence that both of these invisible powers impact the material and visible realm in dramatic fashion. Moreover, against the myth of autonomy, to which I return below, apocalypses recognize that the visible is always conditioned by the invisible. The thesis of apocalyptic literature is that hidden realities ineluctably shape the visible, and therefore must be revealed: revelation of hidden things provides the necessary basis for action. Apocalyptic discourse grounds itself not in false dualism between consciousness and behavior but in recognition of the mutual interdependence of belief and practice, mind and body, awareness and action.

Anonymity or Pseudonymity

Scott on Anonymity

I asked above whether the composers of apocalypses chose the device of pseudonymity for the same reasons that govern the choice of anonymity in

---

138. Mitchell, "Everyday Metaphors of Power," p. 562.
139. Mitchell, "Everyday Metaphors of Power," p. 563.
140. Mitchell, "Everyday Metaphors of Power," p. 569.

public iterations of the hidden transcript analyzed by Scott. I turn to that question here. Although Scott's treatment of anonymity is not systematic, he appears to see it functioning in three ways: (1) It discourages open acts of rebellion, (2) it protects its users from loss or harm,[141] and (3) it allows a subversive message to circulate more freely.[142] I consider each in turn, testing the degree to which each does or does not apply to the apocalyptic writers studied here. I argue that while the first two do not in fact apply to our texts, the third helpfully shifts our focus from speaker to spoken. By focusing on the discourse itself, rather than the writer, we are able to distinguish apocalyptic pseudonymity from anonymity.

1. *Anonymity discourages open acts of rebellion.* Scott's treatment of anonymous resistant speech forms includes a discussion of the anonymous expression of utopian beliefs, through which subordinate groups "imagine both the reversal and negation of their domination." He includes among these beliefs the "millennial theme of a world turned upside down," noting that its open expression frequently incites subordinate groups to (unsuccessful) acts of rebellion.[143] In his view, anonymity and such devices of ambiguation as double-speak, metaphor, and allusion function precisely to *prevent* such acts: "Utopian thought of this kind has typically been cast in disguised or allegorical forms in part because its open declaration would be considered revolutionary."[144] By refusing an open declaration of reversal, the speaker, writer, or artist stops short of revolution and signals to the audience that it is not (yet) time for open, public acts of resistance. The anonymous speech act thereby leaves the structures of domination and subordination fully intact.

By contrast, the analysis of Daniel, the Apocalypse of Weeks, and the Book of Dreams in chapters 7, 9, and 10 shows that these writers believe that the time for open, public resistance is not in the distant future; it is at the moment of their writing, and the moment of their reading. The device of pseudonymity they each employ can explain the restraint exercised in an earlier period. Daniel himself is told to "keep these words secret: seal the scroll until the end time" (Dan 12:4; cf. *T. Mos.* 1:16-17; 10:11-12), while in the Apocalypse of Weeks it is not until the end of the seventh week that the chosen are chosen to witness, to uproot structures of violence and deceit, and to enact justice (*1 En.* 93:10; 91:11).

141. It "minimizes the risks its practitioners run." Scott, *Domination and the Arts of Resistance*, p. 200.

142. While Scott does not say this, the refusal of discursive authority also entails a refusal to be one's own interpreter and disambiguate a polyvalent discourse for an audience not "in the know." This refusal makes it more difficult for dominant powers to neutralize the counterdiscourse through assimilation into the dominant discourse.

143. Scott, *Domination and the Arts of Resistance*, pp. 80-81; see further pp. 166-72.

144. Scott, *Domination and the Arts of Resistance*, p. 81.

But these works do not encourage continued restraint in the present hour. Rather, if the scroll is now being read, it stands to reason that the seal has been broken and wisdom has been given: the end time, the hour of witnessing, the seventh week is now. Whatever means they envision, these writers share a certainty that the current structures of domination and subordination will — in the immediate future — be shattered (Dan 2), uprooted (the Apocalypse of Weeks), and replaced with a just order (e.g., Dan 7:13-14, 22, 27; *1 En.* 90:28-38; 91:12-17; cf. *T. Mos.* 10:1).

2. *Anonymity protects its users from loss or harm.* Through most of his discussion of anonymity (and the concomitant use of ambiguous and allusive modes of expression) Scott lays primary emphasis on issues of safety and danger.[145] In this understanding, the motive for anonymity — and for its refusal to challenge systems of domination — is fear of reprisal. He introduces his discussion as follows:

> A subordinate conceals the hidden transcript from powerholders largely because he fears retaliation. If, however, it is possible to declare the hidden transcript while disguising the identity of the persons declaring it, much of the fear is dissipated. Recognizing this, subordinate groups have developed a large arsenal of techniques that serve to shield their identity while facilitating open criticism, threats, and attacks. Prominent techniques that accomplish this purpose include spirit possession, gossip, aggression through magic, rumor, anonymous threats and violence, the anonymous letter, and anonymous mass defiance.[146]

Paul D. Hanson expresses precisely this understanding of apocalyptic pseudonymity in his seminal study *The Dawn of Apocalyptic.* While he recognizes the apocalyptic writers' expectation that God will intervene to "overturn existing powers and structures," he understands that articulating such a radical vision is risky. He thus speaks of "the anonymity or pseudonymity whereby the writer hid his identity for fear of retaliation by the authorities."[147] But while anonymity may serve such a purpose for some apocalyptic writers in later periods, the writers studied here had no desire to avoid retaliation by the authorities, as I show in subsequent chapters.[148] Like Eleazar who found joy in his torture and death, the heroes of Daniel do not shun death but embrace martyrdom in the

---

145. E.g., Scott, *Domination and the Arts of Resistance,* pp. 164-65.

146. Scott, *Domination and the Arts of Resistance,* p. 140.

147. Paul D. Hanson, *The Dawn of Apocalyptic: The Historical and Sociological Roots of Jewish Apocalyptic Eschatology,* rev. ed. (Philadelphia: Fortress, 1979), p. 252.

148. See also John J. Collins, *The Apocalyptic Imagination: An Introduction to Jewish Apocalyptic Literature,* 2nd ed. (Grand Rapids: Eerdmans, 1998), p. 39.

face of persecution. The militant action envisioned in the Apocalypse of Weeks and the Book of Dreams similarly engages the powers directly and openly. None of the apocalyptic writings examined in this study acquiesce to a culture of repression and fear. They seek rather to embolden the faithful for active and open resistance.

3. *Anonymity allows a subversive message to circulate more freely.* Scott also recognizes that one might choose anonymity, disguise, or indirection in order to protect not the speaker, but the spoken. Regarding the prophecies of Joachim de Fiore, he writes, "It was the veiling that permitted the prophecies to be disseminated in this public fashion at all."[149] In his discussion of "world-upside-down prints," an anonymous art form that uses imagery of inversion to critique structures of domination, he similarly asserts that this form of reply to the dominant transcript "must be evasive if it is to be public at all."[150] That is, anonymity enables a work to evade censorship.[151] The writer or artist whose identity remains obscure is much harder to silence. Alive and free, she is able to continue producing new speech or art forms conveying the message of resistance. Meanwhile, because those who circulate the anonymous speech or art form do not claim authorship, they are, in theory, not subject to the penalties reserved for those who do. The message circulates more freely because the fear of reprisal is diminished.

This understanding of anonymity helpfully shifts the focus from speaker to spoken. Moreover, by highlighting the ways anonymous speech forms circulate, sometimes growing and changing in the process, Scott calls our attention to the ways such speech forms, though claimed by none, can belong to many. This insight pushes us past understandings of anonymity and its functions to a consideration of the distinctive practice of *pseudonymous* attribution. Anonymity may well function, in various settings, to restrain and protect. But it does not do so for the writings studied here for the simple reason that they are not anonymous, but pseudonymous. They do not withhold the authors' names, but provide them.[152] The names they give are Daniel and Enoch.[153]

---

149. Scott, *Domination and the Arts of Resistance*, p. 171.

150. Scott, *Domination and the Arts of Resistance*, p. 172.

151. See, e.g., Richard Wrigley, "Censorship and Anonymity in Eighteenth-Century French Art Criticism," *Oxford Art Journal* 6, no. 2 (1983): 7-28.

152. That is, while they withhold their *own* names, they assign authorship of their work to a figure from the past, whose name they are eager to provide. On authorship, see further below.

153. In subsequent chapters I discuss the ways each of these figures, and others within the same works, serve as examples and role models for the tradents and audiences of Dan and 1 En., just as the narrative situation of the revealer-hero could function typologically in relation to events in the writer's day. The Roman consul Publius Valerius Publicola and his historical setting served such a function for Alexander Hamilton, John Jay, and James Madison, who in 1787-

Pseudonymity and Contingency

It is commonly recognized in studies of pseudepigrapha that attributing authorship to a revered figure from the past lends authority to a written work.[154] But it does not function only in this way. As Hindy Najman has argued, pseudonymity also signals participation in an existing discourse.[155] To understand this function of pseudonymity, it is helpful to understand the position and function of authorship in relation to discourse and power. Foucault understands power as a "complex, strategic situation" in which "discourse is at once the struggle for domination and the means by which the struggle is waged."[156] In this struggle, the author holds a central role, and is a key to the strategy a writer employs in the textual bid for power. For Foucault, the author is not a person but a principle, not the originator of discourse but a means for its characterization.[157] Authorship — or what we are more accustomed to thinking of as the attribution of authorship, in this case to Daniel or Enoch — classifies and differentiates

---

1788 published the Federalist Papers as a series of articles in the New York *Independent Journal* under the pseudonym Publius. Publicola co-led the revolution that replaced the Roman monarchy with the Roman Republic in 509 BCE. See Livy *History of Rome* II, and Plutarch *Life of Publicola,* in his *Parallel Lives.* Plutarch pairs his biography of Publicola with that of Solon. See further Monica Affortunati and Barbara Scardigli, "Aspects of Plutarch's Life of Publicola," in *Plutarch and the Historical Tradition,* ed. Philip A. Stadter (London: Routledge, 1992), pp. 109-31. For a critical edition of the Federalist Papers and commentary, see J. R. Pole, ed., *The Federalist* (Indianapolis: Hackett, 2005). On Publius, see Albert Furtwangler, *The Authority of Publius: A Reading of the Federalist Papers* (Ithaca, NY: Cornell University Press, 1984).

154. See the discussion of "Attribution and Authoritativeness" in Jed Wyrick, *The Ascension of Authorship: Attribution and Canon Formation in Jewish, Hellenistic, and Christian Traditions* (Cambridge, MA: Harvard University Press, 2004), pp. 105-10. For an astute analysis of authority-conferring strategies in the one ancient apocalypse that does not employ pseudepigraphy, see Greg Carey, *Elusive Apocalypse: Reading Authority in the Revelation to John* (Macon, GA: Mercer University Press, 1999).

155. Hindy Najman, *Seconding Sinai: The Development of Mosaic Discourse in Second Temple Judaism* (Leiden: Brill, 2003), p. 10. In a study of 1 Tim, Deborah Krause examines how not only the pseudonymous author but also the pseudonymous addressee position the text and its readers within an existing discourse. Her insight is helpful for our consideration in later chapters of the role of Methuselah and the function of direct address in *1 En.* Deborah Krause, *1 Timothy* (London: T. & T. Clark, 2004), pp. 4-8 and passim.

156. Josué V. Harari, "Critical Factions/Critical Fictions," *Textual Strategies: Perspectives in Post-Structuralist Criticism,* ed. Josué Harari (Ithaca, NY: Cornell University Press, 1979), pp. 17-72, 42. For the texts studied here, I want to quarrel with the formula "struggle for domination." Yet I also want this phrase to speak a cautionary word in my own analysis, reminding me and my reader how easily and often visions of justice give birth to new structures of domination. For the danger this poses within biblical studies itself, see Elisabeth Schüssler Fiorenza, *The Power of the Word: Scripture and the Rhetoric of Empire* (Philadelphia: Fortress, 2007), pp. 91-95.

157. Harari, "Critical Factions/Critical Fictions," p. 42.

texts, enabling the contrast between one text, and the set of truth-claims it makes, and another.[158] The function of the author is to introduce "principles of reality, truth, noncontradiction, causality, order."[159] Asserting common authorship for a group of texts not only allows them to authenticate and explain each other but mandates that they do so.

How does the apocalyptic practice of pseudepigraphy relate to Foucault's concept of the author function? Each apocalypse studied here is attributed to an ancient figure known from earlier traditions. Each figure has a narrated history and an associated body of tradition already known to the audience. The composer situates her work within this discourse. She makes a deliberate choice not to identify herself as author. By choosing to claim only the authority of the pseudonymous hero (and the heavenly sources from which that hero's revelation proceeds), she claims *no* authority for the self embedded within existing structures of domination. Instead, she locates authority within a tradition of revelatory discourse that testifies to an alternative source of power and alternative vision of reality. Within this narrative of revelation all other claims to authority, including the authorizing claims of imperial discourse, are rendered derivative, contingent, or invalid.

The false dualism between matter and spirit, behavior and consciousness critiqued above is not Scott's creation. It is a creation of domination systems, of empire, whose power works not only by coercion, not only by limiting options, but also by "creating truths and subjects and sites of apparent autonomy."[160] The capacity to imagine that one's mind, spirit, or will remains free even in the face of coercion serves imperial interests by masking the scope of imperial domination. It occludes hegemony and denies that coercion is really limiting after all. The object of resistance fades from view, so that resistance itself seems unnecessary, costly, inappropriate. The determinism of the apocalyptic texts studied in this volume works in part to deconstruct this illusion of autonomy.[161] The actors in these apocalyptic texts still make choices — life-and-death choices, ramifying to eternity — as do the audiences for whom they

---

158. Michel Foucault, "What Is an Author?" trans. by Josué Harari, in *Textual Strategies: Perspectives in Post-Structuralist Criticism,* ed. Josué Harari (Ithaca, NY: Cornell University Press, 1979), pp. 141-60, 147. The essay originally appeared in French as "Qu'est-ce qu'un auteur?" *Bulletin de la société française de philosophie* 63, no. 3 (1969): 73-104.

159. Harari, "Critical Factions/Critical Fictions," p. 42.

160. Mitchell, "Everyday Metaphors of Power," p. 564.

161. I take this as one example of the "relationship between apocalyptic form (knowledge through vision and symbolic mythical expression) and the content of the thought" posited by Paolo Sacchi, *Jewish Apocalyptic and Its History,* trans. William J. Short (Sheffield: Sheffield Academic Press, 1996), p. 17. The English text is a translation of Paolo Sacchi, *L'apocalittica giudaica e la sua storia* (Brescia: Paideia, 1990).

are intended. If this were not so these hortatory works would not have been written at all. But their writers seek to demonstrate that the truths of the empire are not true, and the subjects of the empire, both those who act as its representatives and those who submit to its authority, are not in fact autonomous. The givenness of tradition invoked by pseudonymous attribution authorizes a view of reality *differently* constructed from that of the empire, challenging the myth of autonomy by revealing the radical contingency of self and empires alike.

Williams argues that a writer's autonomy is limited by the social production of the "contents of consciousness."[162] Yet the shaping force of imperial *doxa* does not leave the subjects of empire forever shackled by its projection of power and vision of the real. The earliest apocalyptic writers recognize that a key question is not whether one's consciousness will be so shaped, but by what — by what practices and liturgies, by what traditions, by what discourse, syntax, myths, and symbols. The choice to write pseudonymously affirms the limits of autonomy by affirming the dynamic processes that shape consciousness and so form the parameters for action. At the same time, it aims to shape those processes by positioning writer and reader alike within a particular tradition, privileging an ancient and also living, organic discourse that displaces that of the empire. Each of these writers identifies this discourse with a specific authorial figure or figures from the past, while also incorporating, creatively adapting, and entering into dialogue with a broad range of scriptural traditions. The reader enters into this discourse by identifying with the pseudonymous author as well as the addressee, whether Enoch and Methuselah in *1 Enoch* or Daniel in the book that bears his name. Through direct address, these writers draw the reader into this reality, laying upon each reader the authoritative claim of a living tradition and identifying the reader as a participant in that tradition. The apocalyptic texts studied in this volume each outline a program of resistance by means of new revelation; each offers a new vision that shatters the illusions manufactured by the empire and its supporters. Yet the authority each claims is an ancient one. The tradition in which each participates proclaims that, before the empire was, God revealed what is and what would be. Before the empire was, God established order and justice. Before the empire was, God chose the righteous ones who must now reject its claims to ultimacy and resist its violence and deceit. Ancient traditions and new revelation together shape the consciousness of writer and reader alike, making it possible to envision and enact a program of resistance to empire.

162. Williams, *Marxism and Literature*, p. 193.

Conclusion

A survey of definitions of resistance yielded the following key points: (1) The conditions and objects of resistance are domination, its strategies, and the hegemony that reinforces it. (2) Acts of resistance aim to limit, oppose, reject, or transform hegemonic institutions and cosmologies as well as systems, strategies, and acts of domination. (3) Resistance is effective action.

The paired concepts of domination and hegemony illuminate the ways in which the early Jewish apocalypses and related forms could function as a literature of resistance to empire, especially in the face of persecution. In Part Three, I give sustained attention to the ways three such texts, Daniel, the Apocalypse of Weeks, and the Book of Dreams, envision and advocate multiple forms of resistant action that refuses to submit to the coercive power of Antiochus and his representatives, denying his sovereignty over their bodies and holding fast to practices that testify instead to the sovereign power of God.

But the writers of these texts are not interested in resistant action only. They are committed to the articulation and promulgation of resistant discourse that unthinks the logic of empire and asserts in its place an alternative vision of reality. Our writers insist on the interdependence of belief and practice, mind and body, awareness and action. They understand that because hidden realities shape visible realities, they must be revealed. They counter imperial hegemony by exposing it, making visible the hidden logic and structures of domination in order to enable full-fledged resistance in mind, spirit, and body. They also reveal the hidden power and providence of God, relocating ultimate power from earth to heaven and asserting the conditional, finite, and partial nature of temporal rule. This revealed knowledge provides the necessary basis for the resistant action they advocate.

The apocalyptic texts studied in this volume share key discursive strategies of resistance. Their use of "mythical images rich in symbolism" exposes and counters imperial mythologies, sometimes through a strategy of critical inversion that enables readers to reimagine a world governed not by empires, but by God. Alternative symbol-making, like alternative syntax, disrupts the logic of imperial hegemony and introduces other ways of seeing and speaking the real. The apocalyptic claim to heavenly knowledge similarly relativizes and declares false the knowledge claims that underwrite imperial power. The device of pseudonymity stakes the guarantee of this revelation upon the givenness of tradition and the plan of God embedded in creation, fixed for all time, and handed down within a community of faithful. Apocalyptic determinism reveals the contingency of self and empire, deconstructing a myth of autonomy that serves imperial interests.

Scholars typically divide ancient Jewish apocalypses into two major generic subcategories: those containing a review of history (in the form of *ex eventu* prophecy), also known as historical apocalypses, and those containing an otherworldly journey.[163] The apocalypses studied in this volume provide our first examples of the genre historical apocalypse. The preceding analysis revealed that theologies of time can have political dimensions, and considered the possibility that the apocalyptic review of history may have developed out of a matrix of ancient Near Eastern literature of resistance to the Hellenistic empires. The writers of Daniel, the Apocalypse of Weeks, and the Book of Dreams use the apocalyptic review of history to critique ruling powers by exposing their character (as demonic, monstrous, violent, destructive, or rapacious), revealing their transience, and asserting that they are subject to the greater power of God and accountable to divine judgment. By affirming God's governance of time and the outworking of God's plan in history they give their readers hope for justice, reversal, and a transformed future. While none of the apocalyptic texts written in response to Antiochus's persecution contains an otherworldly journey, the Enochic Book of the Watchers provides our first example of this type of apocalypse. The preceding discussion of the cosmological dimensions of hegemony clarifies the ways in which Enoch's tour of the cosmos framed a different form of apocalyptic counterdiscourse, to which I return in chapter 8.

Not all apocalypses articulate a discourse or program of resistance to empire. But the fact that in our earliest extant Jewish apocalypses so many of the distinctive formal features of the genre apocalypse served precisely this purpose suggests that renewed attention to the ways these early apocalypses respond to their imperial context will shed further light on the origins of the genre itself as a literature of resistance.

Having established a conceptual framework for understanding resistance in the earliest apocalypses, I investigate its conditions and objects. Moving now from theory to story, in Part Two I examine historical events and conditions in Judea from the beginnings of Hellenistic rule through the period of persecution by Antiochus IV Epiphanes.

---

163. See John J. Collins, "The Jewish Apocalypses," *Semeia* 14 (1979): 21-59, 22-28. Collins notes that the *Apocalypse of Abraham* is the only ancient Jewish apocalypse to combine the two features.

PART TWO

SELEUCID DOMINATION IN JUDEA

CHAPTER 2

Hellenistic Rule in Judea:
Setting the Stage for Resistance

The Beginnings of Hellenistic Rule

Alexander, the Successors, and the Ideology of Conquest

Alexander the Great conquered Judea in 332 BCE, during his successful campaign for control of the territories previously consolidated under the rule of the Persian Empire. Military conquest was the origin and basis of his rule, and would be the basis for that of his Successors (the *diadochoi*) as well.[1] These victorious generals inherited not only the fragments of Alexander's broken empire but also his ideology of conquest. From his death in 323 until the year 281, the Successors fought to establish their kingship and the boundaries of their kingdoms.[2] First Maccabees assesses the activities of Alexander and his Successors from the perspective of a Jewish author in the second or first century BCE (1 Macc 1:1-9 NAB):

> After Alexander the Macedonian, Philip's son, who came from the land of Kittim, had defeated Darius, king of the Persians and Medes, he became king in his place, having first ruled in Greece. 2He fought many campaigns, cap-

1. See Peter Green, *Alexander to Actium: The Historic Evolution of the Hellenistic Age* (Berkeley: University of California Press, 1990), p. 187. See also Dov Gera, *Judaea and Mediterranean Politics, 219-161 B.C.E.* (Leiden: Brill, 1998), p. 7; and M. M. Austin, "Hellenistic Kings, War and the Economy," *Classical Quarterly* 36 (1986): 450-66, 457, who writes, "In every case for which we have specific evidence, the title and status of a *basileus* was acquired in a military context after a victory in battle." He offers as examples Alexander (after victory over Darius III at Gaugamela), Demetrius (victory over Ptolemy at Cyprus, 306 BCE), and Attalus (after defeat of Antiochus Hierax, 238/7 BCE).

2. David Braund, "After Alexander: The Emergence of the Hellenistic World, 323-281," in *A Companion to the Hellenistic World,* ed. Andrew Erskine (Oxford: Blackwell, 2003), pp. 19-34.

tured fortresses, and put kings to death. ₃He advanced to the ends of the earth, gathering plunder from many nations; the earth fell silent before him, and his heart became proud and arrogant. ₄He collected a very strong army and conquered provinces, nations, and rulers, and they became his tributaries. ₅But after all this he took to his bed, realizing that he was going to die. ₆He therefore summoned his officers, the nobles, who had been brought up with him from his youth, to divide his kingdom among them while he was still alive. ₇Alexander had reigned twelve years when he died. ₈So his officers took over his kingdom, each in his own territory, ₉and after his death they all put on royal crowns, and so did their sons after them for many years, causing much distress over the earth.

Jonathan Goldstein identifies this passage as a "scene-setting sentence" typically found at the beginning and at major transition points of biblical books.[3] Such a sentence informs the reader about time, space, and characters.[4] This scene-setting passage functions above all to establish a stereotyped characterization of the Hellenistic kings. Alexander is militaristic, gaining kingship through conquest; he is a man of plunder, power, and pride.[5] The generals who succeeded Alexander and the dynasties they established continued in the militaristic vein of Alexander, multiplying evils on the earth (ἐπλήθυναν κακὰ ἐν τῇ γῇ 1:9) as they founded and supported their empires through wars of conquest.[6] For the writer of 1 Maccabees, the king who would ultimately persecute the Jews was a sinful offshoot of the same militaristic, rapacious, and prideful stock as the kings who preceded him (1 Macc 1:10).

These Hellenistic kings were military leaders first and foremost;[7] they warred constantly.[8] According to M. M. Austin, "The vast majority of [the Hellenistic] kings fought conspicuously at the head of their troops. . . . It remained true of all subsequent kings except for the Ptolemies after Ptolemy IV."[9] Victory

---

3. Jonathan A. Goldstein, *I Maccabees: A New Translation with Introduction and Commentary,* Anchor Bible 41 (Garden City, NY: Doubleday, 1976), p. 190.

4. Goldstein, *I Maccabees,* p. 190.

5. Cf. the judgment of Klaus Koch: "Die griechische Unterwerfung dieser Völker wurde mit brutaler Härte durchgefuhrt." "Daniel und Henoch — Apokalyptik im antiken Judentum," in *Apokalyptik und kein Ende?* ed. Bernd Schipper and Georg Plasger (Göttingen: Vandenhoeck & Ruprecht, 2007), pp. 31-50, 33.

6. The language of filling the earth with evil echoes the traditions preserved in Genesis 6 and the Book of the Watchers, perhaps signaling an awareness of the use of the watcher myths to characterize the *diadochoi.*

7. Austin, "Hellenistic Kings," pp. 456-58, 464.

8. Susan Sherwin-White and Amélie Kuhrt, *From Samarkhand to Sardis: A New Approach to the Seleucid Empire* (Berkeley: University of California Press, 1993), p. 129.

9. Austin, "Hellenistic Kings," p. 458.

in war was the basis for kingship. The king's heroism and success on the battle-field inspired the loyalty of his troops; it also guaranteed their pay.[10] According to Dov Gera, "All of Alexander's heirs were dependent on their armies. The glory of victory and the resulting war plunder were important elements in pre-serving the army's loyalty to their commander-in-chief, and Hellenistic kings were judged in accordance with their behavior and accomplishments on the battlefield. Rulers could not survive without their armies, and it is difficult to visualize the Hellenistic world without the military campaigns of the *Diadochi* and their heirs."[11] Indeed, conquest was more than ideology: it was a primary tool for economic gain, and so fueled the imperial economy.[12] According to Su-san Sherwin-White and Amélie Kuhrt, the successor kings "dominate[d] by military conquest and military force," establishing administrative structures de-signed to extract resources from the conquered territories.[13] Created by con-quest, these empires were maintained by "military constraint (armies, colonies, military expeditions, garrisons), which permit[ted] the levy of tribute and ser-vice from the subjugated peoples."[14]

For these reasons, the militaristic image — and reality — of the king as brave and mighty warrior was a core component of the Successors' royal ideolo-gies.[15] Such ideology was perpetuated through imperial iconography (e.g., coins and statues), architecture, legend, and the ruler cult,[16] all of which portrayed a "superman dimension to the military basis of their power."[17] The iconography of Seleucid coins illustrates ways in which this ideology was perpetuated through a monetary system designed in part to facilitate payment of tribute from subject peoples to the empire, thus undergirding the imperial system of economic exploitation. In addition, it facilitated payment to soldiers in the Seleucid army, thus perpetuating the military machine of conquest and con-straint that made the exaction of tribute possible.[18] Jan Zahle writes of the ideo-

10. Sherwin-White and Kuhrt indicate that from the time of Seleucus I onward mutiny commonly resulted from failure to pay soldiers' wages (*From Samarkhand to Sardis*, p. 58).

11. Gera, *Judaea and Mediterranean Politics*, p. 7.

12. Austin goes further, pointing out the economic motives driving both Alexander's con-quest and the wars of the Successors ("Hellenistic Kings," passim).

13. Sherwin-White and Kuhrt, *From Samarkhand to Sardis*, p. 40.

14. Sherwin-White and Kuhrt, *From Samarkhand to Sardis*, p. 40.

15. Sherwin-White and Kuhrt, *From Samarkhand to Sardis*, pp. 28, 129.

16. On the ruler cult and iconography, see Paul Zanker, *The Power of Images in the Age of Augustus*, trans. Alan Shapiro (Ann Arbor: University of Michigan Press, 1990).

17. Sherwin-White and Kuhrt, *From Samarkhand to Sardis*, p. 114.

18. I say "in part," acknowledging C. J. Howgego's argument that coinage also served as a unit of exchange. "Why Did Ancient States Strike Coins?" *Numismatic Chronicle* 150 (1990): 1-25. I use the example of coinage here for the reasons just stated, but further because coins con-stitute our most abundant evidence for such propaganda. R. A. Hadley reminds us that the

logical function of the imagery on Seleucid coins as follows:[19] "The significance of the motifs was rather political and ideological and everything served to convey a message to the subjects. The names of the kings, their portraits and their Greek gods on the coins of the state all advertise the firm control or claim of the king in question. The fact that the Diadochi were conquerors and needed instruments to legitimate their individual rule explains this new development."[20]

Seleucus I provides an example that is both illustrative and, for the Seleucid dynasty, paradigmatic. Austin observes that of the Seleucid rulers, Seleucus I stood out for his "lasting reputation as the founder of an empire and an undefeated conqueror."[21] In his numismatic iconography, he selected motifs that would reinforce the image of king as mighty conqueror, favored by the gods, and perhaps even divine. These motifs included images of Athena, goddess of war, Zeus, god of thunder and ruler of the Greek pantheon, and Apollo, whose appearance to Seleucus in a dream presaged his military victory and rise to kingship.[22] They also included portraits of the emperor (or his predecessor Alexander) with the attributes of Heracles and Dionysus. The former, "mythical ancestor of the Macedonian royal house,"[23] was famous for his strength, while the latter was associated with Alexander's conquest of Asia, as far as India, and Seleucus's subsequent mastery of the same region.[24]

A well-known coin type minted by Seleucus I at Persepolis and Susa illus-

---

coinage complemented "oral, written, and artistic propaganda of which Seleucus availed himself frequently and which was so commonly employed by the other Successors." "Royal Propaganda of Seleucus I and Lysimachus," *Journal of Hellenic Studies* 94 (1974): 50-65, 54.

19. It is worth noting here the connection between coin and conquest for Alexander and his Successors. Coins could not be struck without bullion, which could be mined, but could also be gained through conquest. According to Howgego, the acquisition of large amounts of bullion as booty in the conquest of the Persian empire "lay behind the massive coinages of Alexander" ("Why Did Ancient States Strike Coins?" p. 5). Thus the very minting of coins testified to the military might of the conquering king and to the wealth acquired through conquest.

20. Jan Zahle, "Religious Motifs on Seleucid Coins," in *Religion and Religious Practice in the Seleucid Kingdom*, ed. Per Bilde, Troels Engberg-Pedersen, Lise Hannestad, and Jan Zahle (Aarhus: Aarhus University Press, 1990), pp. 125-35, 127. Zahle argues that the religious motifs on Hellenistic coins always had political connotations (p. 130). The Seleucids sought to construct a common identity grounded in the ruler cult, portraits of the king, and the king's gods, but largely failed because the images chosen did not reflect the religious beliefs of the diverse subject peoples until the second century BCE (p. 133).

21. M. M. Austin, "The Seleukids and Asia," in *A Companion to the Hellenistic World*, ed. Andrew Erskine (Oxford: Blackwell, 2003), pp. 121-33, 132.

22. Hadley, "Royal Propaganda," pp. 53, 58.

23. Arthur Houghton and Catherine Lorber, *Seleucid Coins: A Comprehensive Catalogue, Part I: Seleucus through Antiochus III*, vol. 1 (New York: The American Numismatic Society, 2002), p. 5.

24. Hadley, "Royal Propaganda," p. 56.

trates the royal-military ideology.[25] The coin bears on its obverse a portrait of either Seleucus or Alexander wearing the leopard-skin helmet of Dionysus, adorned with the horns and ears of a bull.[26] Hadley observes that these "Dionysiac symbols would be a fitting device with which to celebrate the completion of [Seleucus's] conquests."[27] Moreover, the taurine features, especially the horns, symbolized military might and were common motifs on Seleucus's coins. In addition to coins featuring horned bulls pawing the ground in excitement, many coins featured the motif of horns adorning the heads of war horses, war elephants,[28] and even the emperor himself.[29] Each such image emphasized the military might of the empire and the victories of its king.[30] Appian preserved a legend that linked these taurine motifs with Seleucus's superhuman

25. Houghton and Lorber identify the type as "Nike crowning trophy" (*Seleucid Coins,* pp. 71-72, 77-78). Images of four examples of the type can be found on plate 61 (nos. 1022-25) in Arthur Houghton, *Coins of the Seleucid Empire from the Collection of Arthur Houghton* (New York: The American Numismatic Society, 1983). See also Edward T. Newell, *The Coinage of the Eastern Seleucid Mints: From Seleucus I to Antiochus III,* Numismatic Studies I (New York: The American Numismatic Society, 1938), nos. 300-302 (description), p. 113, plate XXIII, nos. 6-9.

26. The identity of the king is debated. R. A. Hadley argues that the portrait is of Alexander, not Seleucus. "Seleucus, Dionysus, or Alexander?" *Numismatic Chronicle* 14 (1974): 9-13. Seleucus minted coins bearing Alexander's image in order to emphasize the continuity of his military success, his kingship, and his empire with Alexander's.

27. Hadley, "Royal Propaganda," p. 56.

28. The horned elephants frequently pull a quadriga bearing the goddess Athena, who holds a shield and spear. For examples, see Houghton, *Coins of the Seleucid Empire,* nos. 914-18, 921-26, 929-31, 1280-82, all minted during the reign of Seleucus I (the last three examples were minted during the joint reign of Seleucus I and Antiochus I in Bactra; see Houghton, *Coins of the Seleucid Empire,* p. 118). See also Houghton and Lorber, *Seleucid Coins,* pp. 57-62.

29. For examples of bulls on the reverse of coins of Seleucus I, see Houghton, *Coins of the Seleucid Empire,* nos. 9, 10 (Seleucis), 927, 928, 932, 933, 942, 943, 944, 946 (Babylonia). For the image of the horned and bridled horse, see Houghton, *Coins of the Seleucid Empire,* nos. 917, 968. See discussion in Houghton and Lorber, *Seleucid Coins,* p. 7. The bridle and horns combine to indicate that the horse is a warhorse. For images of horned elephants see previous note. According to Houghton and Lorber, "Seleucus was later portrayed with bull's horns both on a statue erected at Antioch, and on posthumous portrait coins" (p. 6). Reference to the statue is found in Libanius, *Or.* 11.93. Houghton and Lorber indicate further that "conspicuous coins with the horned portrait of Seleucus were minted at Sardis and at a Bactrian mint (see cat. nos. 322-23, 469, 471-72)" (p. 6n20).

30. Cf. the remarks of Robert Fleischer regarding the coins of Ptolemy I and Seleucus I: "These Diadochs were shown as energetic, physically strong men about whom stories were told that they tamed lions, wild boars and bulls with only their hands.... The heirs of Alexander had to legitimize their rule. They showed their leadership qualities, their successful actions. The divine pedigrees, which were rapidly constructed (Seleucus I a son of Apollo, etc.) were not considered sufficient." "Hellenistic Royal Iconography on Coins," in *Aspects of Hellenistic Kingship,* ed. Per Bilde, Troels Engberg-Pedersen, Lise Hannestad, and Jan Zahle (Aarhus: Aarhus University Press, 1996), pp. 28-40, 31.

size and strength, his devotion to the gods, and his association with Alexander (*Syr.* 9.57). Appian reported that Seleucus "was of such a large and powerful frame that once when a wild bull was brought for sacrifice to Alexander and broke loose from his ropes, Seleucus held him alone, with nothing but his hands, for which reason his statues are ornamented with horns."[31] The numismatic portrait featuring the horned helmet of Dionysus similarly linked Seleucus to his conquering predecessor Alexander and combined a message of piety with one of power and victory.

The theme of victory is continued and augmented on the coin's reverse, which shows Nike (Victory) lifting a laurel wreath or victory crown to place it on a war trophy. The trophy consists of a full suit of armor, comprising "a helmet, cuirass (a breast- and back-plate) with leather straps and skirt, and a star-adorned shield."[32] The trophy is mounted on a tree, with foliage sprouting from its base. The image of Victory is flanked by the inscriptions ΣΕΛΕΥΚΩΣ ("Seleucus") and ΒΑΣΙΛΕΩΣ ("king"). The paired image and inscriptions equate victory crown and royal crown, basing the claim to kingship on military victory.[33] This royal ideology of Seleucus as victorious king was perpetuated further through his title "Nikator" ("Victor"), a name which, according to Appian, he owed to his military successes (*Syr.* 9.57). After his death Seleucus would be divinized as an incarnation of Zeus Nikator, laying the foundation for a ruler cult that would remain forever wedded to the military persona of the powerful warrior-king.[34]

Caught in the Battle for Domination

The need for such royal-military ideology reminds us that the Hellenistic kings continued to challenge *one another* for dominance, warring for control over regions that each king claimed as part of his rightful and conquered territory. The land of Judea fell in such contested territory, claimed by both Seleucus I and Ptolemy I and their successors as well. In 301 Ptolemy I claimed sovereignty over the region of Coele-Syria as part of his spear-won land. Seleucus I dis-

---

31. Appian, *The Foreign Wars*, trans. Horace White (New York: Macmillan, 1899).

32. "Tetradrachm of Seleucus I [Iran, excavated at Pasargadae] (1974.105.9)," n.p. [Cited 23 April, 2008]. Online: http://www.metmuseum.org/toah/ho/04/wam/ho_1974.105.9.htm

33. Cf. Hadley's remark that the images of Nike "are a sure indication that Seleucus sought to publicise his recent military successes." Such publicity was necessary, according to Hadley, to maintain morale in the face of challenges from Antigonus and his son Demetrius ("Royal Propaganda," p. 53).

34. Hadley underscores the role of the coinage and other propaganda in laying this foundation ("Royal Propaganda," p. 65).

puted this claim, asserting his own right to the territory. Although the Ptolemies maintained control of the region for a century, the warrior kings of the Ptolemaic and Seleucid dynasties never ceased to battle and jockey for dominion over Coele-Syria.[35] As a result, inhabitants of Coele-Syria, including the Judeans, suffered through no fewer than six "Syrian wars" waged on their land by the Ptolemies and Seleucids between the years 274 and 168 BCE. By contrast with the two centuries of Persian rule that preceded it, the Hellenistic era was a time of almost ceaseless violence for Judeans.[36]

The Transition to Seleucid Rule

Seleucid rule over Judeans began in 200 BCE, at the conclusion of the Fifth Syrian War, when Antiochus III finally defeated the Egyptian armies to claim sovereignty over Phoenicia and Palestine.[37] In this Fifth Syrian War, key religious and civic leaders among the Judeans gave their allegiance and support to Antiochus III, helping to oust the Egyptian garrison from the citadel in Jerusalem and providing needed provisions to the Seleucid army.[38] Two documents preserved in Josephus's *Antiquitates judaicae*, likely issued by Antiochus III between 200 and 199 BCE, are, in the words of Elias Bickerman, "the corner-stone for any reconstruction of the fate of Seleucid Jerusalem."[39]

The Letter to Ptolemy

The first, a letter to Ptolemy, *strategos* (governor) of Coele-Syria and Phoenicia, documents the alliance between Jewish leaders and Antiochus III and outlines

---

35. Austin ("Hellenistic Kings," p. 461) observes that even after the Seleucids gained control of the region in 200, "The Ptolemies never relinquished their claim to the lost territories, as the reign of Cleopatra VII was to show as late as the 30s B.C."

36. Daniel 11:2-29 describes the prolonged struggle between the Ptolemies and Seleucids, referring to them as "the King of the South" and "the King of the North" respectively.

37. On the strategic and economic importance of this region, see Gera, *Judaea and Mediterranean Politics*, p. 9; and Austin, "Hellenistic Kings," p. 461.

38. See discussion in James Ellis Taylor, "Seleucid Rule in Palestine" (Ph.D. diss., Duke University, 1979), pp. 56-58.

39. Elias Bickerman, *The God of the Maccabees: Studies on the Meaning and Origin of the Maccabean Revolt*, trans. Horst Moehring (Leiden: Brill, 1979), p. 33. Originally published as *Der Gott der Makkabäer: Untersuchungen über Sinn und Ursprung der makkabäischen Erhebung* (Berlin: Schocken Verlag, 1937). Bickerman argued persuasively for the authenticity of these documents in two essays, "La charte séleucide de Jérusalem," *REJ* 100 (1935): 4-35; and "Une proclamation séleucide relative au temple de Jérusalem," *Syria* 25 (1946-48): 67-85.

privileges to be granted to these leaders and to the people as a whole in return for their support (*A.J.* 12.138-144).[40] A summary of these privileges follows:[41]

1. The king will furnish a one-time contribution in-kind for temple sacrifices and offerings, worth 20,000 silver drachmas.[42]
2. The king authorizes the reconstruction and restoration of the temple, and grants tax exemption for transported building materials.[43]
3. The people *(ethnos)* have the right to govern themselves in accordance with their ancestral laws (142).[44]
4. Community leaders and cultic functionaries, including members of the *gerousia* (a council of elders), the priests, the temple scribes, and the temple singers, will be exempt from taxation (142). The nature and extent of the taxes in question are not specified, but are presumably similar to the taxes described in the letter of Demetrius preserved in 1 Maccabees 10:25-45, including a tax on the land's produce (10:30), a cattle tax (10:33), a crown tax (10:29; cf. 11:35), and a tax on temple revenue (10:44).[45]
5. Current inhabitants of Jerusalem and those returning before the end of the

40. Taylor suggests that this Ptolemy transferred his allegiance from Egypt to Seleucia during the Fifth Syrian War ("Seleucid Rule in Palestine," pp. 125-26). Yet for precisely this reason he was ineffective in controlling soldiers in his territory, who were seizing for themselves the homes of local inhabitants, perhaps also enslaving those they evicted (p. 137).

41. For a recent brief analysis of this document in relation to Seleucid economic practices and structure, see G. G. Aperghis, *The Seleukid Royal Economy: The Finances and Financial Administration of the Seleukid Empire* (Cambridge: Cambridge University Press, 2004), pp. 166-68.

42. I agree with Taylor that this is the plain sense of the text, rather than understanding, with Bickerman ("La charte séleucide," p. 12), an annual cash contribution. Taylor, "Seleucid Rule in Palestine," pp. 76-80.

43. Cf. Sir 50:1-4, which attributes repair of the temple to the leadership of the high priest Simon II. On Simon's role, see further Taylor, "Seleucid Rule in Palestine," pp. 82-83; and Victor Tcherikover, *Hellenistic Civilization and the Jews,* trans. S. Applebaum (Philadelphia: Jewish Publication Society, 1959); repr. with a pref. by John J. Collins (Peabody, MA: Hendrickson, 1999), p. 88. For evidence of Seleucid taxation of imports, see Taylor, "Seleucid Rule in Palestine," p. 84.

44. Cf. the letter of Antiochus III to his *strategos* Zeuxis regarding the settlement of two thousand Jewish families from Mesopotamia to Asia Minor (ca. 210): they are to use "their own laws" (νόμοις . . . τοῖς ἰδίοις *A.J.* 12.147). See discussion of this document in Getzel Cohen, *The Seleucid Colonies: Studies in Founding, Administration and Organization* (Wiesbaden: Frank Steiner Verlag GMBH, 1978), pp. 5-9. Cohen suggests that this provision "assured both the loyalty and the demographic integrity of the colonists and hence the stability of the colony" (p. 35).

45. As Goldstein notes (*I Maccabees,* p. 407), the taxation rate cited in Demetrius's letter (a third of the grain and half of the fruit of trees, 10:30) is unusually high. According to Taylor, the usual rate levied by the Seleucids was closer to one tenth ("Seleucid Rule in Palestine," p. 102n88). Goldstein speculates that the high rate cited in Demetrius's letter may have been a punitive levy instituted at the time of the expedition of Apollonius the Mysarch under Antiochus IV Epiphanes (*I Maccabees,* p. 212).

year will be exempt from taxes for three years, in order to facilitate economic recovery from the war (143).[46]

6. Enslaved war captives will be liberated, along with their families, and their property will be returned to them (144).

As Bickerman notes, "These provisions, in principle, are by no means extraordinary."[47] They are minimal measures intended to secure loyalty and help Jerusalem and its inhabitants recover from the effects of occupation and war.[48] John Ellis Taylor compares these concessions and modes of assistance with those Antiochus III granted to Lysimacheia and Sardis under similar circumstances. He arrives at two conclusions: (1) Antiochus conferred substantial material benefits on the religious and civic leaders in Jerusalem, including lifelong tax exemption. (2) By contrast, the provisions pertaining to the general populace of Jerusalem "appear rather unimpressive" and "commonplace."[49] The letter confers no material benefits on Judeans living outside Jerusalem itself.

The civic and religious leaders singled out for privilege in Antiochus's letter, namely members of the *gerousia*, priests, temple scribes, and temple singers, appear to have exerted significant influence on Antiochus III's policies in Palestine, securing not only material benefits for themselves, but also the provision of generous resources for restoring and improving the temple.[50] These leaders also appear to have had a strong hand in drafting the second document, an official decree, or *programma*, from the king, that immediately follows the letter to Ptolemy in Josephus's *Antiquitates judaicae*.[51]

The Programma

This decree, or *programma*, focuses more narrowly on the Jerusalem temple and attendant issues of purity within the city. The decree contains three sets of

46. Taylor clarifies that the expression ἕως τοῦ Ὑπερβερεταίου μηνός probably means through the end of the last month of the Macedonian year ("Seleucid Rule in Palestine," p. 96).

47. Bickerman, *God of the Maccabees*, p. 33. Cf. Aperghis's observation that, absent relief for Judean farmers, "Antiochos' gesture does not appear to have been quite so generous" (*Seleukid Royal Economy*, p. 168).

48. Because the Jews now form part of the tax base of the Seleucid empire, their economic recovery will lead to increased revenue for the Seleucids. For Aperghis, "Antiochos' decisions regarding the Jews were probably based on short-term political and financial considerations" (*Seleukid Royal Economy*, p. 168). Privileges to the ruling class would build loyalty; tax relief and repair to the temple would stimulate economic recovery.

49. Taylor, "Seleucid Rule in Palestine," pp. 104, 106.

50. Taylor, "Seleucid Rule in Palestine," p. 169.

51. Bickerman, "Une proclamation séleucide," p. 84.

restrictions followed by a penalty clause. The restrictions concern human access to the temple, animals and animal products permitted in the city, and animals permitted for sacrifice. A brief summary of each restriction follows:

1. No foreigner (μηδενὶ . . . ἀλλοφύλῳ) is permitted to enter the temple precincts (εἰς τὸν περίβολον εἰσιέναι τοῦ ἱεροῦ 12.145).
2. The meat and skins of animals forbidden to the Jews/Judeans (πάντων τῶν ἀπηγορευμένων ζῴων τοῖς Ἰουδαίοις) may not be brought into the city, nor may such animals be raised, or nourished (τρέφειν), within the city (12.146).[52]
3. Jews/Judeans may only offer "ancestral sacrifices" (12.146).

The first restriction confirms priestly regulations regarding access to the temple sanctuary, reinforcing the compromised boundaries of Jerusalem's most sacred space and reasserting its purity and holiness. After forbidding foreigners to enter the sanctuary, the decree explains that, according to ancestral law (κατὰ τὸν πάτριον νόμον), only Jews/Judeans who have purified themselves may enter the sanctuary. This explanation links the new decree with ancient tradition, reinforces priestly distinctions between pure and impure, and extends that distinction to mark off Jew/Judean from foreigner. While the distinction between Judean and foreigner may not be as clear as the decree would imply, the *point* of the distinction is quite clear. As a colony under foreign occupation, Judea will assert its distinct identity through recourse to ancestral law. That law calls the Jews to be a holy people, set apart. The priests mediate between this holy people and God through their service in the sacred space of the temple. By protecting that space from the intrusion of unauthorized (foreign) individuals, the decree emphasizes the holiness of God and those who serve God and enshrines both traditional conceptions of holiness and current practices of temple worship as primary loci of distinctive Jewish identity.[53]

The second set of restrictions moves beyond the boundaries of the temple and its worship life to the boundaries of the city (τὴν πόλιν). In this context, the city becomes a metonym for the social body of the Jewish people; its

52. William Whiston translates the Greek phrase reproduced here "any animal which is forbidden to the Jews to eat." *The Works of Flavius Josephus* (Edinburgh: Thomas Nelson and Peter Brown, 1828). Certainly that is the sense of the Levitical dietary laws that the decree (or Josephus's edition of the decree) alludes to. But the decree is noteworthy precisely because it goes beyond the emphasis on eating — restricting what enters the human body — to restrict also what enters the social body, as represented metonymically by temple and city.

53. Jacob Milgrom describes the purity system as "a symbolic system reminding Israel of the divine imperative to reject death and choose life." *Leviticus: A Book of Ritual and Ethics: A Continental Commentary* (Minneapolis: Fortress, 2004), p. 13.

boundaries mirror the prescribed boundaries of the human (Jewish) body.[54] Levitical laws mandated the purity of the sanctuary and those who served it; they also charged the people as a whole to be holy. The call to holiness included the maintenance of purity through observance of dietary laws (Lev 11; cf. Deut 14). Just as a common meal could imitate the sacred meal offered and celebrated in the temple, so the sanctity of the body could imitate that of the temple itself. In similar fashion, just as restricted access to the temple could emphasize and protect the sanctity of that space, so observance of the dietary laws provided an opportunity for Judeans to emphasize and protect the sacred boundaries of their own bodies. By allowing only the foods permitted by God to pass through these boundaries and enter into the body, Jews/Judeans honored the particularity of their unique identity as God's people and observed the call to holiness in their daily life. As Mary Douglas puts it, "Observance of the dietary rules would thus have been a meaningful part of the great liturgical act of recognition and worship which culminated in the sacrifice in the Temple."[55]

Indeed, since the groundbreaking work of Mary Douglas, scholars have also recognized that the Levitical classification of animals as pure (permitted) and impure (forbidden) relates to the maintenance of categories and distinctions within creation. The priestly worldview insisted that God's will for the ordering of human life was inseparably bound up with God's will for the ordering of creation. God's people acknowledged the sanctity and sovereign power of God by respecting and maintaining this order. For Douglas, then, God's people maintain their holiness by "keeping distinct the categories of creation." Holiness is also wholeness, or "unity, integrity, perfection of the individual and of the kind."[56] Animals that do not neatly fit into one category, but instead have characteristics of multiple categories or kinds, are forbidden for consumption.

The *programma* reminds its readers that these animals are forbidden to the Jews. But it also goes a step further in forbidding anyone to carry the flesh or skin of these animals into the city of Jerusalem.[57] Scholars have found this in-

54. Compare Mary Douglas's discussion of the camp in *Purity and Danger: An Analysis of Concepts of Pollution and Taboo* (London: Routledge, 2002), p. 64. On bodily boundaries and the social body, see Jon Berquist, *Controlling Corporeality: The Body and the Household in Ancient Israel* (New Brunswick, NJ: Rutgers University Press, 2002). Berquist writes that "for ancient Israel, the body was always a unit in and of itself while at the same time being a building block of larger social units that operated according to the same rules" (p. 59). See also Alice Keefe, "Rapes of Women/Wars of Men," *Semeia* 61 (1993): 70-98, esp. 85. In distinction to the approach taken here, Keefe is interested in ways in which biblical narrative portrays the human body as a metonym for the social body.

55. Douglas, *Purity and Danger*, p. 71.

56. Douglas, *Purity and Danger*, p. 67.

57. Jerusalem is not named. Josephus introduces the *programma* as pertaining to the temple; context makes it clear that the Jerusalem temple is intended. "The city" would then refer to

novation and the one that follows it puzzling. Tcherikover has gone so far as to assert that either (a) Josephus has mangled his text, or (b) the word *polis* here means not city but only the part of the city closest to the temple.[58] Tcherikover offers two arguments to support the latter conclusion. First, he suggests that, for the prohibition of foreign access to the temple to succeed, the *programma* would need to have been displayed near the entrance to the temple precincts. From that location, the prohibition regarding the transport of animal meat and skin would hardly reach the notice of those entering the gates of the city itself. While this may be so, there was presumably nothing to prevent such a document from being posted in multiple locations. If in fact it was only displayed near the entrance to the temple precincts, its presumed inefficacy need not negate the intentions of the document's framers.[59] Whether or not the prohibition successfully regulated the transport of animal meat and skin, its symbolic claims were nonetheless efficacious, marking the city as sacred space.

Second, Tcherikover discerns a parallelism between the first restriction contained in the *programma,* addressing *human* access to the temple, and the second restriction, addressing *animal* access. Yet the possible existence of such a parallelism does not require that "the temple precincts" in one line mean the same as "the city" in the next. Rather, the parallelism moves outward, from sacred space to common space, and in so doing asserts that the common space of Jerusalem is also holy.

As noted above, the *programma* reflects a context in which the city serves as a metonym for the social body, and its boundaries mirror those of the human (Jewish) body.[60] This understanding clarifies the innovative prohibitions contained in this second set of restrictions. Observance of dietary laws could serve in this period as a distinctive marker of particular Jewish identity (see examples in Jdt and 2 Macc). A close connection already existed between daily meals and temple sacrifices, connecting temple with body and daily life with worship life.[61] Tcherikover correctly notes that "the composer of the document . . . is

---

Jerusalem. But see the discussion below of Tcherikover's proposal that "the city" refers only to the part of the city closest to the temple. Lexically speaking, *polis* means city, not "area surrounding a temple." The document used a very precise phrase to describe the perimeter of the temple grounds themselves (τὸν περίβολον . . . τοῦ ἱεροῦ); presumably similar precision could have been employed to designate the area around the temple perimeter.

58. Tcherikover, *Hellenistic Civilization*, p. 86.

59. As in the modern world, the fact that a resolution or law is obscure, unenforced, or unenforceable does not negate the intentions, often quite serious, of those who promoted, drafted, passed, or ratified it.

60. Such an understanding would be consistent with the priestly/Levitical worldview that saw a close connection between the purity of the people and that of the land/space they inhabited.

61. Milgrom notes that according to Lev 17:3-7 "all meat for the table had initially to be sanctified on the altar" (*Leviticus*, p. 14).

thinking of animals from the cultic point of view."[62] The *programma* now goes a step further to view the city itself — and even the commercial transactions that take place within it — from this same point of view, asserting its identity as a "Jewish" city, a holy city, dedicated to the worship of the god of the Jews. Although foreign individuals could be prevented from entering the temple, in the imperial situation, they could not be prevented from entering the city. But the document protects the city's purity through its symbolic claims: forbidden foods will not pass through the boundaries of the city, just as they may not pass through the boundaries of the body, and just as they may not be offered in sacrifice to the God of the Jews. Not even the skins of impure animals may be brought in, whether for clothing and furnishings that would touch the human body, or for any other purpose — they would render the city impure.[63]

The prohibition against feeding, raising, or nourishing these animals within the city makes similar symbolic claims.[64] Within the holy city, the food of Jerusalem should not pass into the bodies of impure animals. Presuming that, as Bickerman suggests, Jewish leaders played a strong role in drafting the document (cf. 2 Macc 4:11), the prohibition may also encode a subtle act of resistance in the face of Seleucid occupation: while Judeans could not prevent the Seleucid military from bringing (or riding) horses and supply animals into Jerusalem, they could potentially, on religious grounds, limit the presence and activity of these animals within the city walls.

The third restriction pertains to cultic sacrifices. Like the first set of restrictions, this one also establishes a strong link with tradition: only "ancestral" (προγονικοῖς) sacrifices are permissible (12.146). The earlier reference to "the ancestral law" (12.145), understood to be binding in matters of purity, provides the contextual framework for identifying proper sacrifices as well, establishing a connection between sacred (biblical) text, tradition, and cultic practice.[65] The sacrifices are also "necessary" (δεῖ) for worship of "the god" (12.146). The verb

---

62. Tcherikover, *Hellenistic Civilization*, p. 86.

63. Gera provides bibliography on recent treatments of potentially similar prohibitions in Qumran texts, including the Temple Scroll and 4Q Halakhic Letter (*Judaea and Mediterranean Politics*, p. 34n109).

64. Taylor takes τρέφειν to mean "breeding" ("Seleucid Rule in Palestine," p. 105). Tcherikover similarly takes it to mean "rearing" (*Hellenistic Civilization*, p. 85). This is certainly semantically plausible. In this context, however, and given that the primary meaning of τρέφω pertains to the provision of nourishment, attention to the particular symbolic value of food and bodily boundaries is warranted.

65. The text does not specify to whom this final restriction applies, nor the physical scope. The main verb, ἐπιτέτραπται, is impersonal, and there is no dative clause to indicate to whom "it is permitted." In light of the document's interest in protecting the purity of the city, we might reasonably conclude that the document prohibits anyone from offering "new" or "foreign" sacrifices anywhere within the city of Jerusalem.

used here to describe the act of sacrifice, καλλιερεῖν, connotes sacrificing in a manner that brings about good omens or good favor.[66] In this way, the *programma* links the future well-being and prosperity of Jerusalem and its inhabitants with adherence to the law and the continuation of traditional worship practices. The converse is implied: the introduction of "new" or "foreign" worship practices would result in loss of divine favor for Jerusalem and its inhabitants; loss of divine favor would lead to disaster. Finally, the decree carries stiff penalties: any who violate its provisions must pay a fine of three thousand silver drachmas to the priests (12.146).

Peaceful Coexistence?

Taylor suggests that the privileges granted in these two documents created the conditions for a "peaceful coexistence" between the Seleucid empire and Judeans that lasted until the time of the persecution of the Jews by Antiochus IV Epiphanes.[67] Erich Gruen similarly proposes that "those benefactions set the tone for three decades of cordial collaboration between the Seleucid regime and the Jewish nation."[68] Yet the very ideology of benefaction underscores a deep-seated tension regarding the basis and limits of local self-governance. Does the authority and validity of the ancestral laws derive from God or from the emperor? John Ma notes the dual function of the *programma*: it "validates the content of the local customs, by endorsing them, investing them with royal authority, and protecting them. At the same time, the royal performative utterance, by repeating the local rules and substituting its own efficacy for theirs, ensures the supremacy and ubiquity of royal form and authority over local sources of legitimacy. This manoeuvre is typical of the way 'empires of domination' function: tolerating local autonomy but redefining it in terms of central authority, through administrative speech-acts."[69] Through both the letter to Ptolemy and the *programma*, Antiochus claims that the Jewish ancestral laws and customs derive their ultimate authority not from their god Yhwh, but from the Seleucid empire. According to imperial logic, the only freedoms they possess are granted by the king. Freedom is not absolute, but conditional: it comes at a cost, and can always be revoked.

Moreover, a closer look at the evidence reveals a high number of stressors

---

66. LSJ, 867.

67. Taylor, "Seleucid Rule in Palestine," pp. 56, 107.

68. Erich S. Gruen, "Hellenism and Persecution: Antiochus IV and the Jews," in *Hellenistic History and Culture*, ed. Peter Green (Berkeley: University of California Press, 1993), pp. 238-64, 240.

69. John Ma, "Seleukids and Speech-Acts: Performative Utterances, Legitimacy and Negotiation in the World of the Maccabees," *Scripta Classica Israelica* 19 (2000): 71-112, 89.

on Jerusalem and Judea, their population, governing infrastructure, and economy during this transition period, as well as multiple sites of internal division. Fuller consideration of these stressors and divisions will help to reveal tensions both between Judeans and the Seleucids and within the Judean community, setting the stage for analysis of the multiple forms of resistance that arose prior to and during the persecution of Jews by Antiochus IV Epiphanes.

Stressors and Divisions

First, before, during, and after the Fifth Syrian War, Jerusalem lacked political autonomy.[70] Judeans were subject to the rule of two foreign empires.[71] The stresses of colonial rule are manifold, and were certainly felt by Judeans in this period. As Berquist notes, in the imperial system, colonies "serve to support and finance the imperial power and its expansion."[72] Marked above all by the "asymmetrical distribution of resources and power," an empire sustains itself by continually extracting resources — material and human — from the colonies it controls, by conquest, taxation, and even slavery.[73] Moreover, an empire exerts its power and control not only in political and economic life but also in "intellectual, emotional, psychological, spiritual, cultural, and religious arenas."[74] These forms of control

70. John Hayes and Sara Mandell point out that grants of *autonomia* to city-states under Ptolemaic and Seleucid rule in this period guaranteed "nominal freedom" only. *The Jewish People in Classical Antiquity: From Alexander to Bar Kochba* (Louisville: Westminster John Knox, 1998), p. 16. See also Green, "Alexander and the Successor Kingdoms," p. 40, and discussion in ch. 6.

71. Martin Hengel's assertion that "Jewish judgments on the foreign state and its rulers in the early Hellenistic period are still overwhelmingly positive" rests on analysis of texts such as Dan 1–6, Tobit, Esther, and Sirach that in fact show serious ambivalence toward and critique of foreign monarchs, as Hengel himself notes. *Judaism and Hellenism: Studies in Their Encounter in Palestine during the Early Hellenistic Period* (Philadelphia: Fortress, 1974), 1:29. What's more, these texts form part of a public transcript, and do not provide a complete picture of Jewish attitudes toward the kingdoms that ruled them. On ambivalence and resistance, see Homi K. Bhabha's engagement with the ideas of Frantz Fanon in *Location of Culture* (London: Routledge, 1994), pp. 86-91.

72. Jon Berquist, "Postcolonialism and Imperial Motives for Canonization," *Semeia* 75 (1996): 16.

73. Berquist, "Postcolonialism," pp. 16-17. With regard to Ptolemaic imperial administration, Green ("Alexander and the Successor Kingdoms," p. 39) observes that "every department, from the state treasury to the ministry of justice, had as its prime objective the increasing of the king's power and revenues." John Ma similarly describes the Seleucid imperial apparatus ("roads, garrisons, governors, and officials") as "structures of control" designed "to carry out the extraction of surplus from the local communities." "Kings," in *Companion to the Hellenistic World*, ed. Andrew Erskine (Oxford: Blackwell, 2003), pp. 177-95, 183.

74. Joerg Rieger, "Christian Theology and Empires," in *Empire: The Christian Tradition: New Readings of Classical Theologians*, ed. Kwok Pui-lan, Don H. Compier, and Joerg Rieger (Minneapolis: Fortress, 2007), pp. 1-13, 3. According to Cohen, "The *purpose* of the various colo-

are more subtle, but no less potent. Recognizing these multiple spheres of influence, Joerg Rieger defines empire as "massive concentrations of power which permeate all aspects of life and which cannot be controlled by any one actor alone."[75]

Empire's pervasive reach was already keenly felt during the Ptolemaic period, as the Zenon papyri show.[76] The Ptolemies, according to Tcherikover, "strove . . . to introduce the Egyptian bureaucratic regime into Palestine," including a policy of "strict official surveillance over the life of the private individual."[77] Egyptian presence and rule thus exerted significant control over daily life and governance. As Daniel Smith-Christopher observes, Jewish literature from this period shows "a heightened consciousness of a people not in control of their own lives."[78]

The Egyptian military garrison housed in the citadel in Jerusalem was a daily reminder to Judeans of the coercive power of the Ptolemaic empire both beyond their borders and in the heart of their holy city. The burden of occupation was both psychological and material. Soldiers stationed in Jerusalem would have required housing, service, and food from the local population, displacing families from their homes and ancestral lands, enslaving local inhabitants, and constituting a significant drain on the community's food supply.[79]

The material support provided to the Seleucids during the war itself was an

---

nizing programs [of the Hellenistic empires] was military, economic, or political, not cultural" (*The Seleucid Colonies*, p. 69). Yet this does not negate the influence of empire in all spheres of life; the cultural legacy of Hellenism could be seen in every part of the Hellenistic world, as Cohen admits.

75. Rieger, "Christian Theology and Empires," p. 3. Rieger develops this definition in his book *Christ and Empire: From Paul to Postcolonial Times* (Minneapolis: Fortress, 2007). A major thesis of the book of Daniel is that one actor, namely God, does in fact control all empires.

76. According to Hayes and Mandell, the Judean temple state "was subject to the system of heavy taxation, royal monopolies, and land lease policy that the Ptolemies maintained" (*Jewish People in Classical Antiquity*, p. 32), and was "being exploited to the fullest through both taxation and trade" (p. 34). The practice of tax-farming led to an increased tax burden, generating ill-will among the general populace; it also created division and animosity between wealthy families who competed for the privilege of collecting taxes (p. 35). For the Zenon papyri, see editions of W. Spiegelberg, ed., *Die Demotischen Urkunden des Zenon-Archivs*, Dem. Stud. 8, Nos. 1-25 (Leipzig: Hinrichs, 1929); C. C. Edgar, ed., *Zenon Papyri, Catalogue général des antiquités égyptiennes du Musée du Caire*, 5 vols. (Cairo: Imprimerie de l'Institut français d'archéologie orientale, 1925-1940); M. Norsa, G. Vitelli, V. Bartoletti, et al., eds., *Papiri greci e latini*, 15 vols. (Florence: Pubblicazioni della Società Italiana per la ricerca dei papiri greci e latini in Egitto, 1912-1979); P. W. Pestman, ed., *Greek and Demotic Texts from the Zenon Archive* (Leiden: Brill, 1980).

77. Tcherikover, *Hellenistic Civilization*, pp. 88, 62.

78. Daniel Smith-Christopher, "Daniel," *NIB*, vol. 7 (Nashville: Abingdon, 1996), p. 32.

79. Hengel suggests that "probably the Graeco-Macedonian military settlers tried to make the Semitic peasants who worked their lots of land into their slaves." The practice of enslaving "the semi-free population" of Syria and Phoenicia was, according to Hengel, widespread in the Ptolemaic period. Laws were enacted to prevent the practice, but the law would not be needed if it were not happening in the first place (*Judaism and Hellenism*, 1:42). See further n. 100 below.

additional burden. Bickerman notes that ancient armies could not be sustained on transported foodstuffs, but relied on sustenance from the regions in which they campaigned.[80] The size of the army and elephant corps Jerusalem provisioned can be estimated from reports of the battle of Panion, fought 93 miles north of Jerusalem at the source of the Jordan River in 200 BCE. According to Bezalel Bar-Kochva, Antiochus III mobilized "all available troops" to fight in this decisive battle; he estimates the size of the Seleucid army that fought at Panion at "several tens of thousands."[81] He arrives at a more exact figure of more than 70,000 soldiers based on the description in Daniel 11:13 and figures for the earlier battle of Raphia.[82] In addition to the soldiers, Antiochus III deployed a herd of 150 elephants.[83] In light of these figures, it is important to recognize that the "abundance of provisions" (ἄφθονον δὲ τὴν χορηγίαν 12.138; cf. 12.133) given by the Judeans to Antiochus's soldiers and elephants was no small gift.[84] Elephants, for example, consume roughly 5 percent of their body weight every day.[85] The elephants deployed by Antiochus III were Asian elephants of the subspecies known as Indian elephants *(elephas maximus indicus)*.[86] Mature elephants of this species weigh between 6,600 and 11,000 pounds.[87] One of Antiochus's elephants would accordingly consume between 330 and 550 pounds of vegetation daily. Even if the Judeans had provisioned only a portion of Antiochus's army and herd

80. Bickerman, "La charte séleucide," p. 9. He adds, "L'aide des villes était dans ces conditions extrêmement précieuse" (p. 9).

81. Bezalel Bar-Kochva, *The Seleucid Army: Organization and Tactics* (Cambridge: Cambridge University Press, 1976), p. 19.

82. Bar-Kochva, *Seleucid Army,* p. 18.

83. Bar-Kochva, *Seleucid Army,* p. 80, citing Polyb. 11.34.10. See also Polybius's treatment of Zeno's account in 16.18-19.

84. Various scholars interpret the verse to mean that the Judeans provisioned the entire army and the entire herd of elephants following the battle of Panion. See, e.g., Hayes and Mandell, *Jewish People in Classical Antiquity,* p. 39.

85. This figure is for fresh vegetation. The dry fodder equivalent would be approximately 1.25 percent of body weight. New studies indicate that these are conservative estimates. Raman Sukumar concludes that elephants "consume between 1.5% and 2.0% of their body weight as dry forage each day," translating to 6 percent to 8 percent of their body weight in fresh vegetation. *The Living Elephants: Evolutionary Ecology, Behavior, and Conservation* (Oxford: Oxford University Press, 2003), pp. 196-99. Averaging to 7 percent, a single mature elephant would thus consume between 462 and 770 lbs. of fresh vegetation daily, or between 115.5 and 192.5 lbs. of dry fodder. According to Sukumar, elephants "spend anywhere between about 40% and 75% of their time in feeding," i.e., between 9.6 and 18 hours per day, depending on the season (p. 198).

86. On the tactical use of elephants by the Seleucids, see Bar-Kochva, *Seleucid Army,* pp. 75-83. On the species used by both the Seleucids and Ptolemies, see Michael Charles, "Elephants at Raphia: Reinterpreting Polybius 5.84-5," *Classical Quarterly* 57 (2007): 306-11.

87. D. Ciszek, "Elephas maximus" (1999), Animal Diversity Web. Accessed April 2, 2008, at http://animaldiversity.ummz.umich.edu/site/accounts/information/Elephas_maximus.html.

over a short span of time, this support would have been a serious drain on local food supplies needed for humans and livestock. The burden of provision would have fallen most heavily on farmers in the Judean countryside.[88]

While the transition to Seleucid rule was welcomed and aided by many Judeans, a change in empire added further stressors, including the stress of rapid political change.[89] Moreover, a change of empire did not eliminate the imperial situation itself — taxes once paid to the Ptolemies would now be paid to the Seleucids.[90] At the war's end, Judeans were still subjects, and still lacked political autonomy.[91] Although the Seleucids and Judeans had driven the Egyptians from the Jerusalem citadel, the citadel itself remained, and could potentially be occupied by Seleucid forces (2 Macc 4:28). If, as Tcherikover suggests, the Seleucids allowed a higher degree of *autonomia* (civic freedom) to their subjects, preferring to make only occasional visits to the cities they ruled, yet they retained the power to intervene "whenever there was need."[92] Recent evidence indicates, however, that the Seleucids were not so hands-off: according to Sherwin-White and Kuhrt, the Seleucid bureaucratic machine was "as complex and developed as that of Ptolemaic Egypt."[93]

Second, the people and land of Judea experienced significant hardship during the war itself. Josephus writes that "the Judeans . . . suffered many hardships,

88. See further Angelos Chaniotis, *War in the Hellenistic World* (Oxford: Blackwell, 2005), pp. 121-29, 140-41. J. A. Thorne provides estimates for the quantity of grain required to feed an army close in size to Antiochus's. "Warfare and Agriculture: The Economic Impact of Devastation in Classical Greece," *Greek, Roman, and Byzantine Studies* 42 (2001): 225-53, 249-50.

89. On rapid change, see Albert Baumgarten, *The Flourishing of Jewish Sects in the Maccabean Era: An Interpretation* (Leiden: Brill, 1997), pp. 26-33, 57, 70-73. Referring to the Maccabean era, he writes: "The flourishing of sectarianism, to use a slightly crude analogy, is a case of collective national religious, political or social indigestion in the aftermath of rapid change, when the old and the new are still coexisting in an odd but ultimately unstable equilibrium . . . when the old world has been jigged out of place for a sufficient number of sensitive people, and is now inadequate to deal with the situation, alternative, hence competing, new orders emerge, each appealing for allegiance" (pp. 70-71).

90. As Hengel notes, the Seleucids not only adopted the system of taxation introduced by the Ptolemies, but, after the initial period of tax exemption, "exploited the country still more" (*Judaism and Hellenism,* 1:23). According to Fergus Millar, "The Seleucid state, like most ancient states, was primarily a system for extracting taxes and forming armies." "The Problem of Hellenistic Syria," in *Hellenism in the East: The Interaction of Greek and Non-Greek Civilizations from Syria to Central Asia after Alexander,* ed. A. Kuhrt and S. Sherwin-White (Berkeley: University of California Press, 1987), pp. 129-30.

91. Austin writes, "There is no reason to suppose that Seleukid rule was in the first instance anything but an imposition on the peoples of the empire. Even communities that outwardly professed loyalty saw them as outsiders" ("Seleukids and Asia," p. 123).

92. Tcherikover is careful to point out that under Seleucid rule subject peoples "enjoyed a certain degree of home-rule and obeyed their national leaders" (*Hellenistic Civilization,* p. 88).

93. Sherwin-White and Kuhrt, *From Samarkhand to Sardis,* p. 48.

and their land was ruined" (Τοὺς γὰρ Ἰουδαίους . . . ἔτυχεν αὐτούς τε πολλὰ ταλαιπωρῆσαι τῆς γῆς αὐτῶν κακουμένης *A.J.* 12.129). According to Taylor, Jerusalem "was seized three times by Ptolemaic and Seleucid forces" and "suffered extensively" in the war.[94] Josephus likens Jerusalem and the rest of the Coele-Syrian region during this period to a ship in a storm, tossed on both sides (12.130). Battles fought in and around Jerusalem caused death and injury as well as damage to public buildings, homes, places of business, and fields. Antiochus's letter states that the city had been destroyed, or ruined (κατεφθαρμένην), on account of the battles. This is consistent with evidence from other towns subjugated by Antiochus III, as analyzed by Sherwin-White and Kuhrt, who summarize their findings this way: "The impact of the army on territories newly subjugated, or in the process of being conquered, was horrendous and brutal . . . pillage, destruction, mass enslavement were the norms of war."[95]

The allocation of funds for temple repairs indicates that the temple itself was damaged, perhaps even looted.[96] As Schiffman notes, the temple "served as the governmental center of the Jews to the extent to which the Jewish community operated as an autonomous unit within the Ptolemaic and Seleucid empires."[97] Damage to the temple had serious practical consequences for religious and administrative life in Judea, and would present a visible reminder of the extent to which the politics and struggles of the Ptolemaic and Seleucid empires constrained Judean autonomy and self-governance. Moreover, the temple symbolized and mediated God's power, providence, and presence; as such it was "a symbol for the unity of the populace" as people of God.[98] Just as rebuilding, re-

---

94. Taylor, "Seleucid Rule in Palestine," p. 57, following Polyb. 16.39.3-5 and Jos. *A.J.* 12. Bickerman describes Jerusalem in the years 202-200 as "le théâtre des operations militaires" ("La charte séleucide," p. 11).

95. Sherwin-White and Kuhrt, *From Samarkhand to Sardis*, p. 58. See also pp. 201-2. Inscriptions from Labraunda and Amyzon dating from the reign of Antiochus III show that his campaigns in Anatolia and elsewhere were "rough . . . for the communities involved," demonstrating "the awful realities of the local effects of this warfare" (p. 202).

96. Sherwin-White and Kuhrt explain that "the enormous problem of keeping troops under control vis-à-vis the local populations, whether in billeting or in campaigns, and of curbing looting of sanctuaries and violence against them, is only too clear from the growing documentation of royal officials' orders prohibiting and trying to redress violations and dealing with the aftermath" (*From Samarkhand to Sardis*, p. 59).

97. Lawrence H. Schiffman, *From Text to Tradition: A History of Second Temple and Rabbinic Judaism* (Hoboken: Ktav, 1991), pp. 67-68.

98. Jon Berquist, *Judaism in Persia's Shadow: A Social and Historical Approach* (Minneapolis: Fortress, 1995), p. 147. Doron Mendels similarly asserts that the temple "was a center for the preservation of the traditional culture and religion. The Temple symbolized the continuity of the Jewish people since the reign of King Solomon." It also embodies the particularity or uniqueness of the Jewish people. *The Rise and Fall of Jewish Nationalism* (New York: Doubleday, 1992), p. 138. Brian S. Osborne links awareness of national identity with the creation of distinc-

pair, and rededication could unify the people in confidence and hope in God's power, mercy, and presence among them (cf. Sir 50:1-24),[99] so damage to or defilement of the temple could symbolize a beaten and fractured people and elicit a theological crisis, as it had in 587 and would again in 167.

Antiochus's letter also speaks of the scattering of the city's inhabitants. Under Ptolemaic rule and during the war some families were taken captive and enslaved; others fled.[100] Their homes and land were confiscated.[101] Under the new

---

tive "place," i.e., "the nurturing of a collective memory and social cohesion through the representation of national narratives in symbolic places, monumental forms, and performance. Taken together, these constitute the geography of identity." "Landscapes, Memory, Monuments, and Commemoration: Putting Identity in Its Place," *Canadian Ethnic Studies Journal* 33, no. 3 (2001): 39-187, 40. Osborne (p. 53) notes that monuments can serve not only "as passive visual statements contributing to social cohesion" but also "as active elements in a public discourse of redefinition." Moreover, "The ritualized performance of commemoration [in public places of memory] communicates shared values in order to reduce internal tensions" (p. 59).

99. Sirach's praise of the high priest Simon emphasizes his work in repairing and rebuilding the temple, protecting it with walls, and leading worship there. According to Sirach, he "made the court of the sanctuary glorious" (50:11 NRSV), unified the people in worship, and brought God's blessing upon them. In these ways he "save[d] his people from ruin" (50:4 NRSV).

100. According to Hengel, slave trade flourished under Ptolemaic rule (*Judaism and Hellenism*, 1:41). For a list of sources, see Hengel, *Judaism and Hellenism*, 2:32-33n323. See also Jos. *A.J.* 12.20-33, which narrates the negotiated release of Judean captives in Egypt under the reign of Ptolemy Philadelphus. *Antiquitates Judaicae* 12.29 suggests that soldiers sold slaves independently of imperial policy as a way to increase their profits from campaigning. Austin ("Hellenistic Kings," p. 465) calls attention to the labor force the captives provided: "The Ptolemies used their Syrian wars to make vast hauls of captives whom they then imported to Egypt to augment their military or working manpower." Presumably, during war, the sale of captives would have helped finance the campaign itself. Aperghis cites the later example of Nicanor's expectation that the sale of Judean captives during the Maccabean war would yield 2000 talents in revenue for the Seleucids (reported in 2 Macc 8:10 and Jos. *A.J.* 12.299). He comments that "captives were an important element of plunder in warfare" (*Seleukid Royal Economy*, p. 173). On the other hand, Roger S. Bagnall and Peter Derow note that "the Ptolemies in general tried to minimize the Greek tendency to enslave non-Greek peoples, since in Syria and in Egypt the latter formed a class of peasants producing rent and taxes on royal land and private estates, and the loss of their manpower was a serious threat." *Greek Historical Documents: The Hellenistic Period* (Chico, CA: Scholars Press, 1981), p. 95. An edict, or *prostagma*, of Ptolemy II Philadelphus dating to ca. 260 BCE regulates and limits the sale of native slaves in Syria and Phoenicia, but the very need for such tight regulation suggests a widespread practice (*C. Ord. Ptol.* 21-22; Rainer Papyrus Inv. 24,552). William Westermann writes, "It is clear, however, that the Ptolemaic government had become cognizant of the fact that there was a considerable body of σώματα λαϊκὰ ἐλεύθερα in Syria-Phoenicia who were being employed by the inhabitants of Syria-Phoenicia in slave services who had not been registered as slaves." "Enslaved Persons Who Are Free," *American Journal of Philology* 59, no. 1 (1938): 1-30, 3. Westermann further argues that the fictionalized account in Jos., referred to above, is based on a source that borrows directly from the Rainer *prostagma* (p. 22). English translation of this document is provided in Bagnall and Derow, *Greek Historical Documents*, pp. 95-96.

101. Tcherikover suggests that the Ptolemies would have claimed royal rights to various

regime, who would oversee the promised liberation of slaves and return of an-cestral lands? How would the new policies be enforced? It is difficult to imagine that the *strategos* Ptolemy, weak as he was, would be able to enforce a policy of liberation and land return for those enslaved locally.[102] To the contrary, records indicate that elsewhere in the region of Coele-Syria and Phoenicia Ptolemy struggled to curb ongoing practices of land seizure by the Seleucid soldiers un-der his command.[103] Moreover, no royal proclamation would guarantee the wholesale liberation and return of Judeans who had been exported in the slave trade.[104] For those who did return to their homes, Antiochus's policies of liber-ation, return of land, and tax relief would not erase experiences of violence, rape, shaming, and other hardships associated with slavery, flight, and land sei-zure. Finally, the scattering of the city's inhabitants was a strain not only for in-dividual households, but for the larger community as well, dissolving social unity and introducing new forms of fear, isolation, and instability.

A third form of stress is evident in the internal divisions among the inhab-itants of Jerusalem and its environs. Before, during, and after the war, Judeans were divided in their allegiances — some supported the Seleucids, others sup-ported the Ptolemies.[105] These divisions no doubt existed both among the gen-eral populace and among community leaders.[106] In time of war, this could

---

landholdings throughout Palestine, and could assign or lease these to royal officials and other tenants (*Hellenistic Civilization*, p. 67). These royal lands may have constituted "the lion's share of the country's area" (p. 72).

102. Gera sees Ptolemy as having strong support and influence in the region because he in-herited the position and connections from his father (*Judaea and Mediterranean Politics*, p. 33). But this view doesn't take into consideration the effect of Ptolemy's defection, as described in Taylor.

103. Ptolemy's petitions can be found in T. Fischer, "Zur Seleukideninschrift von Hafzibah," *Zeitschrift für Papyrologie und Epigraphik* 33 (1979): 131-38. See extensive discussion in Taylor, "Seleucid Rule in Palestine," pp. 108-68, esp. 136-37. See also brief treatment in Millar, "Problem of Hellenistic Syria," pp. 120-21. On the dating of the petitions (between 201 and 195 BCE), see Hannah Cotton and Michael Wörrle, "Seleukos IV to Heliodoros: A New Dossier of Royal Correspondence from Israel," *Zeitschrift für Papyrologie und Epigraphik* 159 (2007): 191-205, 194.

104. Angelos Chaniotis, *War in the Hellenistic World* (Oxford: Blackwell, 2005), p. 125: "In addition to the casualties of battles, slaves and free persons were frequently captured in the countryside. . . . If they were sold abroad, as frequently happened . . . they were lost forever."

105. Jerome writes: *Pugnantibus contra se Magno Antiocho et ducibus Ptolemaei, in medio Judaea posita in contraria studia scindebatur: Aliis Antiocho, aliis Ptolemaeo faventibus* (*In Dan.* 11.13-14, PL 25.08, col. 0562C). Polybius comments on the frequency with which Syrians shifted their political allegiances: ἴσως μὲν οὖν εἰώθασι πάντες περὶ τοὺς τοιούτους καιροὺς ἁρμόζεσθαί πως ἀεὶ πρὸς τὸ παρόν· μάλιστα δὲ τὸ κατ' ἐκείνους τοὺς τόπους γένος τῶν ἀνθρώπων εὐφυὲς καὶ πρόχειρον πρὸς τὰς ἐκ τοῦ καιροῦ χάριτας (5.86.9). See further Austin, "Seleukids and Asia," p. 124.

106. Gera argues against the view that the aristocracy supported the Seleucids while the

mean a community divided not only within itself but also against itself.[107] After the war, those leaders who had allied themselves with the Seleucids were confirmed in positions of authority and privilege within the Jerusalem community. Leaders who supported the Ptolemies were disenfranchised.[108] They might now choose to leave, accept a position of lower status within the community, fight to regain influence, or work to integrate into the current pro-Seleucid leading class.

In addition to these divisions of loyalty and their repercussions, the letter of Antiochus also reveals a significant gap in the distribution of privileges between the ruling elite and lower classes. Members of the Jerusalem leadership who allied themselves with Antiochus III were richly rewarded for their support of his campaign. These included the *gerousia*, a governing body composed of elders, or "heads of leading families,"[109] as well as priests, temple scribes, and temple singers. The general populace, by contrast, did not fare so well, as Taylor has shown.[110] The sharp contrast between the lifelong tax exemption promised to the ruling class and the three-year exemption and subsequent tax reduction granted to other residents of Jerusalem highlights the unequal distribution of privilege. Inhabitants of the Judean countryside who were not also members of the ruling class received no tax relief at all.[111] The meager relief measures offered

---

"masses" supported the Ptolemies. He also argues against the notion that there were "factions which consistently supported either the Ptolemaic or the Seleucid dynasty." Rather, loyalties were governed by expediency (*Judaea and Mediterranean Politics*, pp. 18-19).

107. Hayes and Mandell, *Jewish People in Classical Antiquity*, pp. 18, 19-21, 30-31, 39, and 47. For Hayes and Mandell this factionalism polarized the Jewish community in Palestine, and led to civil strife during the Fifth Syrian War (pp. 31, 47).

108. Schiffman, *From Text to Tradition*, p. 72.

109. This formulation is from Taylor, "Seleucid Rule in Palestine," p. 65. According to Hayes and Mandell, the *gerousia* originated in the Persian period, when it consisted of "rulers of Judean districts, heads of major families, and wealthy nobles." They emphasize that "the *gerousia* was an aristocratic, not a democratically elected, body" (*Jewish People in Classical Antiquity*, p. 32).

110. Paolo Sacchi identifies this period as one of rapid development and favorable economic conditions in Palestine, adducing as evidence "the very numerous deposits in the Temple, which became the object of the Seleucids' greed." *The History of the Second Temple Period* (Sheffield: Sheffield Academic Press, 2000), p. 220. Yet many of these deposits were no doubt made by members of the leading class who were the beneficiaries of Antiochus's largesse. Moreover, members of the lower classes may well have made voluntary contributions to the temple even during times of financial hardship. Seth Schwartz notes that the wealth of the temple treasury derived mainly from voluntary contributions, even though the "economy was probably functioning not far above subsistence level." *Imperialism and Jewish Society, 200 B.C.E. to 640 C.E.* (Princeton: Princeton University Press, 2001), p. 62.

111. Aperghis writes, "There is not a single tax concession in Antiochos' letter for the rest of the population of Judaea, unless a few of the members of the Jewish ruling classes, who benefited from the head-taxes exemption, happened to reside in the countryside. Indeed it is very

to the general public suggest that, for the majority, the process of rebuilding and recovery would be slow and difficult. Indeed, Martin Hengel describes this period as a time of economic recession throughout the eastern Mediterranean region.[112] Under such conditions, the unequal distribution of privilege would prove to be a source of tension both within the Jerusalem community (see, for example, the Epistle of Enoch, including the Apocalypse of Weeks) and between inhabitants of the city and inhabitants of the surrounding countryside.[113]

To some extent, provisions for the restoration of the temple and support of worship would aid in the process of unification and confer a significant measure of confidence and hope on many among the general populace, paving the way for economic recovery in subtle but tangible ways.[114] According to G. G. Aperghis, "by repairing [the temple], and in particular its commercial porticoes (τάς τε στοὰς) . . . the economy of Judaea could be stimulated."[115] Indeed, the large sums of money deposited in the temple treasury in the decades following the war suggest such a connection.[116] For Seth Schwartz, these deposits, the bulk of which would have been brought to the temple as voluntary offerings, demonstrate "the symbolic power of the Temple."[117] Yet precisely because of this symbolic power, deposits need not have reflected economic recovery so much as the *hope* for recovery. The presence of such large sums in a time of economic hardship testifies to the hope placed in the Jerusalem cult, perhaps even the hope that a well-supported and flourishing cult would bring about God's renewed favor for the struggling city and the people of Judea. Yet neither the splendor of the temple and its newly invigorated worship life nor the wealth of its treasury would suffice to ease all the hardships of a ravaged and divided people.

In fact the provisions outlined in Antiochus's *programma* for the safe-

---

probable that Judaea would continue to pay tribute, assessed on its towns and villages, as well as head taxes and transaction taxes" (*Seleukid Royal Economy*, p. 167).

112. "An economic recession set in from the second century, as it did throughout the eastern Mediterranean. The confusion of war, with the conquest of Palestine by Antiochus III, the high Seleucid war damages to Rome which meant a heavy burden of taxation, and finally the Maccabean war of liberation followed by the Hasmonean war of conquest, did not favour future developments" (Hengel, *Judaism and Hellenism*, 1:47).

113. Hengel comments on this division, noting that "the preliminaries to the Maccabean revolt . . . consist principally in partisan struggles in Jerusalem itself. . . . Hellenistic cultural influence, too, was limited for the most part to the capital. Thus the old opposition between city and the people of the land (ʿam hā-āreṣ) reached a new climax" (*Judaism and Hellenism*, 1:53).

114. Cf. Sir 50:1-24.

115. Aperghis, *Seleukid Royal Economy*, p. 168.

116. Indeed, 1 and 2 Macc, Dan, and Jos. all indicate that, in the decades that follow the war, the temple treasury accumulated large enough sums of money to attract the attention of Seleucid rulers in need of funds. See, e.g., 1 Macc 1:20-23; 2 Macc 5:15-16, 21.

117. Schwartz, *Imperialism and Jewish Society*, p. 62.

guarding of the purity of the temple cult, with attendant financial benefits for the priests themselves, may have *exacerbated* tensions and divisions among the people as a whole. To understand how this is so we must recognize that in addition to the religious, administrative, and economic functions noted above, the temple also served important social regulatory functions. According to Jon Berquist, "Temple ideology establishes sacred space and sacred activity, which then separates the populace by differentiating between those who participate in such sacred occasions and those who do not. The temple creates social boundaries and in effect splits the world into those who worship and those who do not."[118] The resulting insider/outsider dynamic "produces a social and religious hierarchy."[119] Berquist notes that the elite of Jerusalem would have had greatest access to the temple for geographic, social, and financial reasons — these elites would have been the insiders. Those lacking the same geographic proximity, social status, and/or financial means could easily be relegated to outsider status. By reinforcing and perhaps tightening restrictions regarding access to the temple itself and allowing for closer regulation of worship practice, the *programma* may have reinforced and even increased already existing social divisions in Judea. Schwartz makes similar observations regarding Antiochus's letter to Ptolemy, which, he argues, "demonstrat[es] the hierocratic character of Judaea."[120] It also *reinforces* these same hierocratic structures. Thus, while the letter and *programma* of Antiochus III confer (or confirm) a measure of self-rule and self-determination to Judeans under the leadership of the *gerousia,* the high priest, and other temple officials, they also reinforce boundaries and divisions within the population, marking as outside those who do not have the means to participate fully in the official worship and administrative life of Jerusalem as well as those who elect not to worship in the same way.[121]

Moreover, provisions regarding the temple and its leadership are closely linked to the provision for self-governance in accordance with the ancestral laws (κατὰ τοὺς πατρίους νόμους).[122] While each served a crucial mediatory function between God and God's people, they were also primary sites for the

---

118. Berquist, *Judaism in Persia's Shadow,* p. 149.

119. Berquist, *Judaism in Persia's Shadow,* p. 150.

120. Schwartz, *Imperialism and Jewish Society,* p. 54.

121. Bickerman describes the political structure in Judea as an "aristocratic regime" in which "the priestly aristocracy takes its place alongside the secular aristocracy" ("La charte séleucide," pp. 32-33). He emphasizes that Antiochus III confirmed the privileged status of the ruling elite (p. 35).

122. Schwartz writes, "The term 'ancestral laws' implies that imperial support for the temple and the Torah were closely bound together, for it is overwhelmingly likely that concealed behind this standard Hellenistic administrative jargon are the laws of the Torah" (*Imperialism and Jewish Society,* p. 55).

exercise of power, and were implicated in the imperial project.[123] Schwartz emphasizes in his study *Imperialism and Jewish Society* that the authority of these laws "rests not simply, and initially perhaps not at all, on the consensus of the Jews, but on the might of the imperial and native rulers of Palestine."[124] The fact that priests held the authority to interpret these laws illustrates the close tie between temple and laws. But the extent to which priests (including the high priest) were also agents of the empire underscores the dependence in this period of both temple and the laws on the authorizing power of the empire.[125]

The preceding analysis revealed a significant number of stressors on the city, land, and inhabitants of Jerusalem at the dawn of Seleucid hegemony over Judea. These included lack of political autonomy, imperial exploitation, military occupation, rapid political change, the ravages of war, personal and economic hardship, internal division, and unequal distribution of privilege. In the face of these stressors, temple and ancestral laws occupy a complex position: authorized by the empire, they are also primary sites of mediation between the Jewish people and the God they recognize as ultimate sovereign. As such, they have the potential to both unify and divide the people of Judea. Some would find in the Jerusalem temple and the ancestral laws avenues to greater participation in the imperial power structure. Others would ultimately perceive a conflict of sovereignties, and fight to wrest both away from imperial control. While both temple and ancestral laws would continue to bear the stamp of the colonizing powers, they were vital resources not only for "self-governance" but also for self-definition in relation to the ruling powers.

Ancestral Laws, Scripture, and Invented Tradition

What were these ancestral laws? Most scholars are quick to identify the ancestral laws with the Torah of Moses.[126] While Tcherikover agrees with this identi-

---

123. Schwartz, *Imperialism and Jewish Society*, p. 58: "The Temple and the Torah were thus not only the main mediators between Israel and its God, but also among the prime (though not the only) repositories of power in Hellenistic and Roman Jewish Palestine, nodal points, like the temples of Egypt and the city oligarchies of Ionia and Caria, in imperial and native royal control of the native population of the country."

124. Schwartz, *Imperialism and Jewish Society*, p. 56.

125. Schwartz, *Imperialism and Jewish Society*, p. 56. In Josephus's account of the persecution of the Jews under Antiochus IV, the ancestral laws are contrasted with the king's laws (*A.J.* 12.240). While the king here authorizes governance according to the ancestral laws, the Jews were able to recognize that the laws rested on an authority external to the empire itself.

126. Schwartz writes, "It would not be an exaggeration to say that the Torah was the constitution of the Jews in Palestine" (*Imperialism and Jewish Society*, p. 56). Taylor writes, "This reference to the ancestral laws of the Jews can hardly refer to anything other than the traditional laws

fication, he helps to complicate it, asking whether only written Torah or also oral traditions would have been intended. He points out, for example, that nothing in the Mosaic Torah (i.e., the Pentateuch) assigns to a high priest the governing position he holds at this time in Jerusalem, nor can the Mosaic Torah alone account for all of the cultic and administrative practices that Antiochus III intends to confirm in this document. Tcherikover asserts, "There is no doubt that the concept of 'ancestral laws,' where it concerns the Jews, is much broader than the law of Moses, and includes, not only the elements of Jewish religion, but the maintenance of political institutions, the form of the regime, the methods of social organization, and the like."[127]

Tcherikover is certainly right, but it will be necessary for us to complicate this picture still further, to consider not only the place of Mosaic Torah in relation to oral traditions intended to interpret or supplement this law, but also other written and oral traditions backed by competing claims to ancestral (and divine) authority. That is, the generic authorization of self-governance according to "ancestral laws" masks the possibility that the scope and content of these laws were not universally agreed upon by Jews in this period. The literary evidence suggests that not all Jews would have agreed on the content and limits of authoritative tradition.[128] In light of this fact, we must also consider that there may have been disagreement as to (1) whether written Mosaic Torah was agreed to be the primary source for ancestral laws; (2) whether other written or oral traditions might have held equal or greater status as a source of ancestral laws; and (3) whether current social, political, and religious norms or practices were perceived to be in accordance with ancestral laws, whatever these were understood to be.

It will help to view the ancestral laws as part of a tradition that is not a "fixed tablet" but rather constantly in the process of being articulated and performed.[129] For this reason, while the idea of "ancestral laws" and their concomitant authority for the community may be fairly fixed in this period, their *contents* — and their meaning — may be more fluid. This makes the ancestral laws

of Moses contained in the Torah" ("Seleucid Rule in Palestine," p. 85). He adds, "The Jews continued to govern themselves according to these traditional laws until the reign of Antiochus IV when these and other privileges were revoked" (pp. 85-86). Bickerman similarly identifies these laws with the Pentateuch ("La charte séleucide," p. 27).

127. Tcherikover, *Hellenistic Civilization,* p. 83.

128. Cf. the remark of John M. G. Barclay, "Using and Refusing: Jewish Identity Strategies under the Hegemony of Hellenism," in *Ethos und Identität: Einheit und Vielfalt des Judentums in hellenistisch-römischer Zeit,* ed. Matthias Konradt and Ulrike Steinert (Paderborn: Ferdinand Schöningh, 2002), pp. 13-25, 19: "Even the claim merely to 'maintain tradition' is itself partisan and contestable, as any reading of Jubilees, Josephus, and the Dead Sea Scrolls can testify."

129. Bhabha, *Location of Culture,* p. 3.

an important site of contest as well as an important resource for the ongoing negotiation, construction, and articulation of Jewish identity, practice, and belief in the midst of the colonial situation. Bhabha writes of the repeated invention of tradition in this way:

> The social articulation of difference, from the minority perspective, is a complex, on-going negotiation that seeks to authorize cultural hybridities that emerge in moments of historical transformation. The "right" to signify from the periphery of authorized power and privilege does not depend on the persistence of tradition; it is resourced by the power of tradition to be reinscribed through the conditions of contingency and contradictoriness that attend upon the lives of those who are "in the minority." The recognition that tradition bestows is a partial form of identification. In restaging the past it introduces other, incommensurable cultural temporalities into the invention of tradition. This process estranges any immediate access to an originary identity or a "received tradition."[130]

Bhabha calls our attention to the fact that tradition — in this case "ancestral law," though we will soon turn our attention to other traditions — is not simply inherited or received, but is actively produced in an ongoing process of negotiation that both uses and invents the past as a resource for constructing identity and meaning in the present.[131] The active production of tradition is an imaginative and creative process. In a similar vein, Stephen Weitzman has emphasized the vital role of imagination and creativity in what he calls the "cultural persistence" of Judaism in the Second Temple period, especially in the face of threats from imperial powers.[132]

Such threats took the form of repeated wars and finally reconquest in 200 BCE. Within a few decades they would take the form of conquest again, culminating in persecution. The transition to Seleucid hegemony — with its opportunities (for a few) and burdens (for the majority) — constituted a new present, a new situation, that brought to the fore questions of identity, meaning, and even survival. The events leading up to the persecution by Antiochus and the persecution itself would bring them to a crisis. In this crisis the invention of

130. Bhabha, *Location of Culture*, p. 3.

131. John Thiel, *Senses of Tradition: Continuity and Development in Catholic Faith* (Oxford: Oxford University Press, 2000), includes the category of "Incipient Development" among the four senses of tradition he identifies. He argues for an appreciation of novel elements ("incipiently developing belief and practice") in continuity with the senses he identifies as "literal" and "development-in-continuity" (p. 134). Thiel's work provides a (Christian) theological framework for understanding the processes of invention of tradition described here.

132. Steven Weitzman, *Surviving Sacrilege: Cultural Persistence in Jewish Antiquity* (Cambridge, MA: Harvard University Press, 2005), pp. 6, 8-11, and passim.

tradition would reorient, draw new boundaries, and stake out new claims for identity, meaning, and value, but would do so always in relation to construc- tions of the past.[133] That is, invented traditions are marked both by creativity and by claims to continuity with the past; as such they are "responses to novel situations which take the form of reference to old situations."[134]

Eric Hobsbawm further explains this connection to the past as follows: "'Invented tradition' is taken to mean a set of practices, normally governed by overtly or tacitly accepted rules and of a ritual or symbolic nature, which seek to inculcate certain values and norms of behavior by repetition, which auto- matically implies continuity with the past. In fact, where possible, they nor- mally attempt to establish continuity with a suitable historic past."[135] While Hobsbawm is primarily interested in practices, we can equally apply his under- standing to textual and oral traditions.[136] Unfortunately, the attention we can give to oral traditions from this period, both in relation to the "ancestral laws" and in relation to other authoritative traditions, is severely limited by the na- ture of our sources: the deposit of tradition comes to us not in the form of sound recordings, but only through written documents. For this reason the present study is limited mainly to the use and construction of tradition in tex- tual form. I focus on texts for another reason as well.

William Schniedewind has shown that in the ancient world writing had its origins in the exercise of royal power and was a prerogative of kings.[137] He de- scribes the process by which the written word comes to occupy "its eventual place as sacred text and the standard for religious orthodoxy" both through the interac- tions between textuality and orality and through the increasing authority ac- corded to texts (by contrast with the authority of oral tradition and teaching).[138]

133. "Invention" can be understood both in its archaic sense of "finding" what is already there and in its modern sense of "producing or creating with the imagination."

134. Eric Hobsbawm, "Introduction: Inventing Traditions," in *The Invention of Tradition*, ed. Eric Hobsbawm and Terence Ranger (Cambridge: Cambridge University Press, 1983), pp. 1- 14, 2. Hobsbawm is interested not only (and not primarily) in texts, but in symbolic and ritual practices.

135. Hobsbawm, "Introduction: Inventing Traditions," p. 1. Tessa Rajak describes the "in- vention of tradition" by the Hasmoneans, though she does not refer to Hobsbawm and Ranger's edited volume by the same name. Tessa Rajak, "Hasmonean Kingship and the Invention of Tra- dition," in *Aspects of Hellenistic Kingship*, ed. Per Bilde, Troels Engberg-Pedersen, Lise Hannestad, and Jan Zahle (Aarhus: Aarhus University Press, 1996), pp. 99-116.

136. On the relation between the two in this period, see Richard Horsley, *Scribes, Visionar- ies, and the Politics of Second Temple Judea* (Louisville: Westminster John Knox, 2007).

137. William Schniedewind, *How the Bible Became a Book* (Cambridge: Cambridge Univer- sity Press, 2004). See also Donald Polaski, "*Mene, Mene, Tekel, Parsin:* Writing and Resistance in Daniel 5 and 6," *JBL* 123 (2004): 649-69.

138. Schniedewind, *How the Bible Became a Book*, pp. 212-13.

He remarks that "textual authority" was "a road built by the government with the support of social and religious elites."[139] But to the extent that God is imagined as king, royal prerogative is also divine prerogative. Writing thus becomes an avenue for asserting divine will and authority, whether in concert with temporal authority (e.g., the *programma* discussed above) or in opposition to it. Divinely authored and authorized text (i.e., scripture) thus has the capacity to challenge ruling powers not (only) from below, but from above. In this period the use and invention of scriptural tradition will be a crucial resource for the construction of Jewish identity, practice, and belief in relation to the colonizing powers, both asserting divine sovereignty over imperial powers and providing divine authorization for resistance when those powers threatened the peace, well-being, and even survival of the Jewish people. As such, the use and invention of scriptural tradition would also become a primary locus and means of resistance to oppression and persecution during the reign of Antiochus IV Epiphanes.

---

139. Schniedewind, *How the Bible Became a Book,* p. 213.

CHAPTER 3

Interaction and Identity
in Seleucid Judea: 188-173 BCE

The Broader Context:
The Seleucid Empire under Roman Hegemony

The same Antiochus III who claimed victory over Ptolemy V's general Scopas
in the battle of Panion, ca. 200 BCE — and with that victory control over Judea
— faced bitter defeat at the hands of Rome some ten years later, as the two empires battled for control of Greece. Rome's victory over Antiochus at the Battle
of Magnesia (190 BCE) was followed by a series of naval battles in which Rome
again proved victorious. Negotiations between the two powers concluded in
the year 188 with the Treaty of Apamea.[1] The terms were severe, limiting
Seleucid activity in Europe and Asia Minor, transferring control of territories
and cities in these regions to Rome (who in turn transferred them to their client, the Attalid king Eumenes II of Pergamon), dismantling Antiochus's elephant corps, reducing his naval fleet to ten warships, and requiring indemnities of 540,000 *modii* of corn and 15,000 talents of silver.[2] Of the latter, 3000
were to be paid up front, while the remaining 12,000 were to be paid in equal
installments over a period of twelve years.[3] According to Dov Gera, the repara-
tions "were aimed to ensure that Antiochus would suffer from a continued

---

1. For a detailed analysis of the terms of the treaty, see Dov Gera, *Judaea and Mediterranean
Politics, 219-161 B.C.E.* (Leiden: Brill, 1998), pp. 90-99.
2. A *modius* is a dry measure equaling 8.615 l. R. P. Duncan-Jones, "The Choenix, the
Artaba, and the Modius," *ZPE* 21 (1976): 43-52, 43.
3. The terms of the treaty are recorded in Polyb. 21.42.1-26. See also Livy 38.38.11-17. In 1998
John Hayes and Sara Mandell could write that, "when correlated in terms of changing monetary
values," this was "the largest war indemnity ever imposed in recorded history from the past up
till today." *The Jewish People in Classical Antiquity: From Alexander to Bar Kochba* (Louisville:
Westminster John Knox, 1998), p. 46.

shortage of money, which would, in turn, adversely affect his ability to manage the affairs of the kingdom."[4] By these economic, military, and territorial demands Rome was able to weaken the Seleucid kingdom and neutralize its threat to Rome while simultaneously broadening Rome's reach and strengthening its hold in the Mediterranean and Near Eastern world. Rome further stipulated that Antiochus send twenty hostages to Rome, to be replaced every three years, a measure designed both to ensure compliance and to weaken Seleucid power networks by removing high-ranking officials and members of the royal family from their spheres of influence within the Seleucid empire.[5] One such hostage would be the future king Antiochus IV, to whom our attention will turn below.

Domination and Interaction in Seleucid Judea

These economic and political pressures form part of the backdrop for events in Judea in the years that follow. The weakened Seleucid kingdom was now a client of Rome. As John Hayes and Sara Mandell have observed, its king "was no longer totally free to exercise his sovereignty with impunity even in that part of his kingdom that he was permitted to control."[6] Yet it would be wrong to see the Seleucid kingdom as suddenly hobbled by the rope of Rome. Although they would not directly challenge Rome again, Antiochus III and his heirs continued to pursue their ambitions for expansion, now focusing their efforts on territories not yet claimed by Rome. The royal treasury strained under the burden of paying war indemnities.[7] Under these circumstances, Seleucid ambitions for expansion would require both Antiochus III and his sons and successors, Seleucus IV (who reigned from 187 to 175 BCE) and Antiochus IV (who reigned from 175 to 164 BCE), to identify new sources of revenue within the boundaries

---

4. Gera, *Judaea and Mediterranean Politics*, p. 93.

5. Polybius 21.42.22.

6. Hayes and Mandell, *Jewish People in Classical Antiquity*, p. 16.

7. Note, however, that Georges Le Rider has revised earlier assessments of the kind of burden these indemnities posed for the Seleucids. He concludes that the indemnities were onerous ("une charge irritante") but hardly as debilitating as scholars previously thought. "Les ressources financières de Séleucos IV (187-175) et le paiement de l'indemnité aux Romains," in *Essays in Honour of Robert Carson and Kenneth Jenkins*, ed. Martin Price, Andrew Burnett, and Roger Bland (London: Spink, 1993), pp. 49-67, 62. For a closer look at Seleucid finances under Antiochus IV, see Georges Le Rider, "Un essai de réforme monétaire sous Antiochos IV en 173/2? Remarques sur l'idée d'une pénurie d'argent dans les Etats hellénistiques au II⁰ siècle," in *Recherches récentes sur le monde hellénistique: Actes du colloque international organisé à l'occasion du 60ᵉ anniversaire de Pierre Ducrey (Lausanne, 20-21 novembre 1998)*, ed. Regula Frei-Stolba and Kristine Gex (Berlin: Peter Lang, 2001), pp. 269-79.

of their own empire.[8] Antiochus III died in his effort to extract funds from a temple of Bel/Zeus in Elam (in southwest Iran).[9] According to 2 Maccabees, Seleucus IV turned his attention to the temple in Jerusalem, sending his minister Heliodorus to appropriate the needed funds (2 Macc 3:4–4:1; cf. Dan 11:20). Robert Doran has called this episode "a historically minor event" and "an isolated incident which does not influence further historical developments."[10] Yet close analysis of this event within the broader context of Seleucid imperial administration of the province of Coele-Syria and Phoenicia reveals that the episode has historical significance after all. It testifies to important shifts in regional and civic government, as first the fiscal administration of Jerusalem's temple and eventually the conduct of its worship came under the purview of Seleucid imperial control, violating an earlier agreement that protected the temple from foreign intruders and ultimately asserting power over Judean religious praxis.[11] It also reveals heightened tensions within the Jerusalem aristocracy and sheds light on the complex interactions between Judean elites and the Seleucid imperial government, both of which would play a role in the events that precipitated the persecution. A newly published dossier of royal correspondence from Seleucus IV to Heliodorus and certain regional officials helps us situate this event in the broader imperial context.[12]

The Heliodorus Stele

The dossier survives on a fragmentary stele published by Hannah Cotton and Michael Wörrle. Based on its contents, they surmise that the stele would have

8. Seleucus IV apparently did not make all of his scheduled payments to Rome, for when Antiochus IV took the throne in 175, there was still a balance remaining, which Antiochus himself did not settle until 173 BCE (Livy 42.6). See further discussion below.

9. Diodorus 28.3, 29.15; Strabo 16.1.18; Susan M. Sherwin-White and Amélie Kuhrt, *From Samarkhand to Sardis: A New Approach to the Seleucid Empire* (Berkeley: University of California Press, 1993), p. 215.

10. Robert Doran, *Temple Propaganda: The Purpose and Character of 2 Maccabees* (Washington, DC: Catholic Biblical Association of America, 1981), p. 51. By contrast to its purported lack of historical significance, Doran highlights the passage's literary importance. Daniel R. Schwartz similarly suggests that as far as plot, were it removed "the Heliodorus story would never have been missed." *2 Maccabees*, CEJL (Berlin: Walter de Gruyter, 2008), p. 4.

11. See the discussion in the preceding chapter of the *programma* issued perhaps a few decades earlier and preserved in Josephus's *Antiquities,* which stated that no foreigner (μηδένι . . . ἀλλοφύλῳ) is permitted to enter the temple precincts (εἰς τὸν περίβολον εἰσιέναι τοῦ ἱεροῦ 12.145).

12. Hannah Cotton and Michael Wörrle, "Seleukos IV to Heliodoros: A New Dossier of Royal Correspondence from Israel," *ZPE* 159 (2007): 191-205. The minimally reconstructed text is transliterated on p. 192, with translation on p. 193. Commentary follows. I thank Eibert Tigchelaar for calling my attention to this dossier.

been displayed "in a sanctuary in a *polis* or a village of Seleucid Palestine."[13] The stele reads like a monumental email forwarded from one recipient to another, with the original message appearing at the bottom and each subsequent message appearing above the one that precedes it. Each time the message is forwarded, a date is recorded. The date, given in Seleucid years, communicates imperial control over the demarcation of time. As John Ma notes, imposing Seleucid time in this fashion is an act of "symbolical violence, as real as the military violence which characterized the empire."[14] Antiochus I established the Seleucid Era as a measure of time by continuing the regnal dating of his father Seleucus I. As a result, "royal time now had continuity and was *Seleucid*, not an individual king's."[15] Seleucid dating makes a claim for the empire itself: it is that which endures. All that precedes the Seleucid empire is erased from memory; it is not to be marked or measured. All past, all present, all future unfolds from the empire's beginning. The ordering of human life in time is now guaranteed by the structures of empire and depends on the empire for its stability. It is in the face of just such claims that the historical apocalypses studied in this volume give so much attention to questions of time, the unfolding of history, the succession of finite temporal powers, and a past and future that extend beyond the "ends" of measured and measurable time. For our writers, God, not Seleucus or Antiochus, establishes times and seasons.

The control over time asserted by Seleucid royal dating was only one way the stele communicated and enacted imperial power. The most important part of the document, the *prostagma* from Seleucus himself, addressed to his "brother" Heliodorus (ll. 13-28), is located at the stele's base. The familial language by which Seleucus addresses his subordinate naturalizes administrative hierarchies within the imperial domination system; they are as inevitable as the blood ties between brothers. The *prostagma* further expands the reach of the imperial administration, confirming the appointment of one Olympiodorus as the official responsible for bringing the administration of sanctuaries within the province of Coele-Syria and Phoenicia into line with administrative practices elsewhere in the Seleucid empire. From their position at the bottom of the stele, the king's commands and the language that testifies to his beneficence provide a visible foundation for the bureaucratic edifice of imperial power and patronage that now circumvallates the sanctuaries of Coele-Syria and Phoenicia.

13. Cotton and Wörrle, "Seleukos IV to Heliodoros," p. 192.

14. John Ma, *Antiochos III and the Cities of Western Asia Minor* (Oxford: Oxford University Press, 1999), p. 148.

15. Susan Sherwin-White, "Seleucid Babylonia: A Case Study for the Installation and Development of Greek Rule," in *Hellenism in the East: The Interaction of Greek and Non-Greek Civilizations from Syria to Central Asia after Alexander,* ed. Amélie Kuhrt and Susan Sherwin-White (Berkeley: University of California Press, 1987), pp. 1-31, 27.

Above the *prostagma*, one finds evidence of this bureaucratic edifice in the form of a letter from Heliodorus to Dorumenes (ll. 7-11), dated to the month of Gorpiaios in year 134 of the Seleucid Era, or mid-summer of 178 BCE (l. 12).[16] The letter introduces the *prostagma* and concludes with the short and understated advisement: "You will do well to follow the instructions" (ll. 10-11).[17] Above this letter appears yet another (ll. 1-5), from Dorumenes to his subordinate Diophanes, presumably a local official, dated within the same month (l. 6). By means of this introductory letter, Dorumenes enters the *prostagma* into public record (κατακεχώρισται τὸ ἀντίγραφον l. 3). His wordy conclusion echoes that of Heliodorus, reminding the stele's public audience that compliance to this perhaps unpopular decree was not optional, and its details were not negotiable: "You will therefore do well to ensure that each thing is accomplished in accordance with the instructions" (ll. 3-5).

The letters of Heliodorus and Dorumenes reveal the chain of command responsible for executing and enforcing the king's decree. By publishing these letters along with the *prostagma* — in stone, a medium that aims for permanence — local officials display and reinforce this administrative structure for the public. James Young writes that "monuments have long sought to provide a naturalizing locus for memory, in which a state's triumphs and martyrs, its ideals and founding myths, are cast as naturally true as the landscape in which they stand. These are the monument's sustaining illusions, the principles of its seeming longevity and power. But in fact . . . neither the monument nor its meaning is really everlasting. Both a monument and its significance are constructed in particular times and places, contingent on the political, historical, and aesthetic realities of the moment."[18] Seleucus's *prostagma* and the letters that accompany it, engraved on stone and erected in a Palestinian *polis* or village, render the empire's administrative apparatus as part of the local landscape, frozen in cold stone to project this new instrument of control as something inevitable, unchanging and unyielding, continuous with what had always been "from the beginning" (ἐξ ἀρχῆς l. 23). The imagined permanence of stone matches that of the empire itself. Yet, like the stele's present, fragmentary form, a closer consideration of the contents and consequences of the decree suggests instead the fragility of the imperial apparatus.

While the stele's fragmentary state — a testament to its final contingency — withholds from us full details, the extant portions identify the primary sub-

16. Cotton and Wörrle discuss whether this Dorumenes might be the father of Ptolemaios in 2 Macc 4:43-50 and 1 Macc 3:32-39, but find the evidence inconclusive ("Seleukos IV to Heliodoros," pp. 200-201).

17. From one administrator to another, *verbum sat.*

18. James E. Young, "Memory and Counter-Memory: The End of the Monument in Germany," *Harvard Design Magazine* 9 (1999): 6-13, 6.

ject of the decree and reveal features of the rhetorical strategy employed by the king in presenting his policy to its intended public audience.[19] This intended audience would have most likely been local, literate elites involved in various aspects of leadership in the communities affected.

The king indicates that in the other satrapies of his empire he has from the beginning of his reign ([ἐ]ξ ἀρχῆς l. 23) taken measures to ensure that local sanctuaries "receive the traditional honors with the care befitting them" (τὰς πατρίο[υς] κομίζηται τιμὰς μετὰ τῆς ἁρμοζούσης θεραπ[είας] ll. 21-22, Cotton and Wörrle's translation). Yet what Seleucus IV has accomplished elsewhere in his empire, he has not accomplished in Coele-Syria and Phoenicia, the satrapy or province that included Judea. To remedy this deficit, Seleucus now appoints Olympiodorus as royal official responsible for care of the sanctuaries of Coele-Syria and Phoenicia (ll. 23-25, 27).

A closer look at the language of the *prostagma* illuminates its rhetorical strategies. The language of "traditional honors" (οἱ πάτριοι τιμαί) quoted above reminds us of the "traditional" or "ancestral" laws referred to in l. 142 of the letter to Ptolemy discussed in the previous chapter. This stereotypical language seeks to legitimate the new imperial policy by aligning it with local religious traditions, suggesting that the policy would aim at preserving traditional practices of worship for the purpose of ensuring the ongoing good will of the gods. Yet the reference to τιμαί also evokes the financial apparatus housed within local sanctuaries, likely denoting both the flow of offerings from worshipers into the sanctuary and from the sanctuary to the king. These offerings had more than monetary value: they served as currency in the public exchange of honor by which Judeans and other inhabitants of Coele-Syria and Phoenicia participated in highly scripted ritualizations of beneficence and gratitude. Like τιμαί, the phrase Cotton and Wörrle have translated "with the care befitting them" also has a dual meaning, with θεραπεία suggesting on the one hand the worship that would take place in the sanctuaries and on the other the care (i.e., maintenance and repair) of the temples themselves, without which such worship could not continue. Taken together, these two short phrases aim to persuade readers of the necessary interdependence of local temple administration and imperial oversight. Their pairing hints that, while tighter oversight would result in reduced autonomy and a heavier financial burden, it would be accompanied by necessary provisions for the upkeep of the local sanctuaries.

The argument for interdependence is a key to the ideology of empire, and is especially important in the transition beyond conquest to successful long-term rule.[20] Jack Goldstone and John Haldon point out that "a crucial element

19. Cotton and Wörrle, "Seleukos IV to Heliodoros," p. 196.

20. John Ma emphasizes the ideological component of Seleucid imperial rule: "Empire is

in the longer-term success of a state formation is a degree of acceptance of that state as normatively desirable, especially by elites, but even by the broader populace from which it draws its resources."[21] Such acceptance emerges from the crafting of "increasingly complex relationships of reciprocity, consensus, and interdependence with leading elements of conquered groups or previous political formations."[22] In the year 178 BCE, the province of Coele-Syria and Phoenicia was still a relatively new acquisition for the Seleucid empire. The rhetoric of the new policy aimed to promote an ideology of interdependence that would strengthen imperial structures of domination, all the while cloaking them with language of piety and providence.[23]

The king states from the outset that his primary concern is for the safety, peace of mind, and even prosperity of his subjects (ll. 14-19). He wants them to live free of anxiety (ἀδεῶς l. 17). A pious king knows that none of these can be achieved "without the goodwill of the gods" (ll. 18-20). While the rhetoric of these first lines emphasizes the king's piety and providential care (πρόνοια) for his subjects, it first heightens the very fear it purports to remove. The logic behind the king's rhetoric is as follows: If the king's policy is not enacted, the local sanctuaries will not receive their proper care. If the sanctuaries do not receive proper care, the gods will be displeased. If the gods are displeased, the people have no hope of prosperity or even safety. The king relies on the logic of fear to sell the people a very expensive insurance policy; purchase is mandatory.[24]

Cotton and Wörrle surmise, "Seleukos IV was aware of and disapproved the lack of control over the sanctuaries in the satrapy of Koilē Syria and Phoinikē."[25] Based on the fragmentary evidence of the stele, we cannot say whether the control in question, or in the language of the empire, "oversight," extended to worship itself or was limited to financial matters. But economic

---

based on the components of conquest — violence and military compulsion, as made clear by Antiochos' confidence that most cities will give in to these means; but at the same time, also requires consent or at least quiescence, and the illusion or representation of power — in other words, ideological means" (*Antiochos III*, p. 9). Hence the need to analyze both *dominio* and hegemony, as discussed in ch. 1.

21. Jack A. Goldstone and John F. Haldon, "Ancient States, Empires, and Exploitation: Problems and Perspectives," in *The Dynamics of Ancient Empires: State Power from Assyria to Byzantium*, ed. Ian Morris and Walter Scheidel (Oxford: Oxford University Press, 2009), pp. 3-29, 11.

22. Goldstone and Haldon, "Ancient States," p. 12.

23. Goldstone and Haldon discuss the formation of "a network of royal and spiritual patronage" that could provide "a rationale for the prevailing political institutions and social-economic relations" ("Ancient States," p. 12).

24. On terror as a Seleucid technique of power, see Ma, *Antiochos III*, p. 111; and ch. 5 in the present book.

25. Cotton and Wörrle, "Seleukos IV to Heliodoros," p. 198.

motives clearly occupy a central position. I noted above that Seleucus IV needed to identify new sources of revenue within his empire in order to meet the ongoing financial demands of war indemnities to Rome and still finance Seleucid ambitions for expansion. According to the terms of the treaty of Apamea, Seleucus should have continued to pay indemnities for two more years. Yet evidence from Livy (42.6.7) suggests that at some point, perhaps already, he had ceased making the annual payments (whether due to a lack of sufficient funds or for other reasons we cannot say for sure). What is certain is that Seleucus sought new sources of income, and he looked to the sanctuaries of Coele-Syria and Phoenicia to provide them. To the extent that local temples served as important economic centers, they could provide financial data not available elsewhere, serve as bases for financial oversight of the broader region, and provide the king with additional sources of income out of their own revenues.[26] Cotton and Wörrle summarize the aim of the policy this way: "Behind the euphemistic ἁρμόζουσα θεραπεία a harsh reality is likely to be lurking — above all the appointment of a new officer for the specific purpose of exercising close control, in the interests of the royal administration, over the assets, revenues and liabilities of the sanctuaries in the satrapy."[27] This "strict bureaucratic control" aimed above all at "more efficient fiscal exploitation."[28]

At the same time, whether or not Olympiodorus had any interest in the conduct of worship at the various sanctuaries, both the pious language of the *prostagma* and its practical ramifications testify to an ideology and structure of domination that locates cultic life within the purview of the empire.[29] Goldstone and Haldon observe a similar dynamic at work in the Assyrian and Persian empires, in which rulers "became actively involved in the dominant cults

26. Goldstone and Haldon note that states that are unable to maintain sufficient control by "primary surplus distribution," such as taxation, must turn to secondary modes of "surplus *redistribution*" ("Ancient States," p. 14). Sanctuaries are an important site of redistribution. See Marty E. Stevens, *Temples, Tithes, and Taxes: The Temple and the Economic Life of Ancient Israel* (Peabody, MA: Hendrickson, 2006), pp. 113, 128-35.

27. Cotton and Wörrle, "Seleukos IV to Heliodoros," p. 198. Cf. John Ma's methodological remarks concerning the analysis of such public decrees: "The way to study this language and these documents without believing that they are the whole story is to bear in mind the pervasive violence and structures of exploitation that the Hellenistic empires lived off, and which form the general context in which the civic decrees were produced" (*Antiochos III*, p. 22).

28. Cotton and Wörrle, "Seleukos IV to Heliodoros," p. 203.

29. Cf. Ma's assessment of Seleucid involvement in the administration of sanctuaries in Asia Minor: the evidence implies "an active, attentive administration endowed with strong capacities for control and involvement." A very close parallel to the *prostagma* discussed here is Antiochus III's *prostagma* appointing one Nicanor over the sanctuaries of Asia Minor. Ma calls the decision to display publicly the latter *prostagma* "a complex message about imperial power" (*Antiochos III*, p. 147).

of conquered territories, which were then assimilated into a broader network of divine relationships, participation in which guaranteed both continuing divine support and therefore political and institutional stability."[30] This last point is precisely the claim Seleucus makes in his appeal to safety, security, and prosperity. The apocalyptic texts studied in Part Three will counter this claim, and the ideology that would assimilate the cult of Jerusalem into the project of empire, by exposing the impious and exploitative practices of the empires and the ruling elites who knowingly collaborated with them.

Heliodorus's Incursion into the Jerusalem Temple: 2 Maccabees 3:1–4:6

The newly discovered dossier allows us to place the events described in 2 Maccabees 3:1–4:6 in the wider context of this Seleucid bid for heightened control of the financial administration of sanctuaries in the province of Coele-Syria and Phoenicia. Cotton and Wörrle even suggest that the new policy toward sanctuaries would have been one in "a series of measures" initiated in the region by Seleucus IV at this time, perhaps on the occasion of Ptolemy son of Thraseas's ceasing to hold the position of *strategos*. Such measures may have aimed at restructuring the provincial government to render its workings more manageable or more efficient.[31] In light of the date of the dossier, we can now date Heliodorus's incursion into the Jerusalem temple between the summer of 178 BCE, the date when the new policy was promulgated, and the death of Seleucus IV in 175 BCE.[32]

Let us look at this episode in greater detail. Second Maccabees 3 opens with an idyllic view of Seleucus IV's policies toward the Jerusalem cult, paired with an equally idyllic view of conditions in Jerusalem ("utter peace" μετὰ πάσης εἰρήνης; "the laws were maintained/observed to the highest degree" τῶν νόμων ὅτι κάλλιστα συντηρουμένων 3:1).[33] The narrator informs us that the kings had previously lavished gifts on the temple (3:2), and Seleucus IV himself funded the sacrificial cult in its entirety (3:3).[34] Into this harmonious relationship en-

---

30. Goldstone and Haldon, "Ancient States," p. 13.

31. Cotton and Wörrle, "Seleukos IV to Heliodoros," p. 199. This is the same Ptolemy who governed the province under Ptolemy V, during Ptolemaic rule, and under Antiochus III, under early Seleucid rule. The date of Ptolemy's exit from regional power is unknown.

32. Cotton and Wörrle, "Seleukos IV to Heliodoros," p. 203.

33. Jan Willem van Henten recognizes the role of this idyllic beginning in the larger narrative pattern of 2 Macc. *The Maccabean Martyrs as Saviours of the Jewish People: A Study of 2 and 4 Maccabees* (Leiden: Brill, 1997), pp. 26-34.

34. According to Ma, subject peoples frequently told "non-realistic" narratives that obscured conditions of conquest and domination and emphasized instead royal beneficence. While

ters the meddling Simon,[35] an individual from the priestly ranks of the family of Bilgah whose position is here identified as "temple administrator" (προστάτης τοῦ ἱεροῦ 3:4). Frustrated in his attempts to control the local market,[36] he now seeks leverage by which to expand his political influence. According to 2 Maccabees (the composer of which I hereafter call the "epitomator"),[37] Simon sees in the temple treasury his ladder to success. He reveals to the king its vast wealth, and proposes that the king bring the temple under royal control (ἐξουσία) in order to allocate these funds as the king sees fit. In this account, 2 Maccabees attributes to Simon, not Seleucus IV, all initiative for the imperial bid for control of the Jerusalem temple that would soon manifest itself so offensively in the actions of Heliodorus.

This attribution occupies an important structural position in relation to one of the book's major theological premises: when the people follow the laws,

---

these narratives internalized and diffused imperial ideology, they were also a way for subjects to represent themselves not as dominated, but as dignified participants in an exchange economy. Such a representation contributed to "strong self-identity, the tenacity of their values and sense of autonomy," out of which seeds of resistance could grow (*Antiochos III*, p. 228; see also 239). Here Ma's analysis sounds similar to the work of James C. Scott (see ch. 1). While 2 Macc postdates the period of direct Seleucid rule, its narrative serves, superficially at least, to construct a more "honorable" and autonomous past for the now independent Judeans.

35. Second Maccabees shares a pattern Mario Liverani has identified in the Hittite Edict of Telepinu and which he finds to be characteristic of all "edicts of 'reform.'" This stylized, narrative pattern portrays a period of harmony disrupted by internal strife and remedied by a king whose reforms restore "the ancient model." See Mario Liverani, *Myth and Politics in Ancient Near Eastern Historiography*, ed. and intro. Zainab Bahrani and Marc Van De Mieroop (Ithaca, NY: Cornell University Press, 2004), pp. 27-52. While 2 Macc serves rhetorical aims different from those of the Edict of Telepinu, Liverani's analysis helps us to appreciate the ways this pattern asserted the conservatism of a novel regime by projecting continuity with an idealized past.

36. For a different understanding of ἀγορονομίας in this verse, see Gregg Gardner, "Jewish Leadership and Hellenistic Civic Benefaction in the Second Century B.C.E.," *JBL* 126 (2007): 327-43, 331-32.

37. Following two prefaced letters (2 Macc 1:1–2:18), an unnamed author explains that the historical account that comprises the remainder of the book abridges the five-volume history of Jason of Cyrene (2:19-32); this epitomator is an artist who paints the house that another person has designed and built (2:29). Schwartz (*2 Maccabees*, p. 25) and Van Henten (*Maccabean Martyrs*, p. 20) prefer to call this person not "epitomator" but "author." I would endorse this designation in its sense of "artful composer of a literary work." The epitomator's chosen image of a painter certainly emphasizes, among other things, the artistic and interpretive character of the composition, which clearly has an integrity and purpose of its own. However, in light of the discussion of "author function" in ch. 1, I want to recognize here the complex view of authorship projected by the epitomator, who does not give his or her own name but instead asserts a close literary relationship to the work of Jason of Cyrene and, for the most part, deliberately refrains from distinguishing his or her authorial and narratival voice from Jason's.

God protects them and protects the temple.[38] When the people forsake the laws, God punishes them, and ceases to protect the temple (see 5:17-20 for the clearest articulation of this view).[39] The epitomator wished to show that the cause of the persecution was the people's infidelity to the ancestral laws. Simon himself does not lead the people directly down the path of infidelity. But his ambition and *modus operandi* establish a pattern soon followed by Jason, brother of Onias, whom the narrator introduces in the same breath as Antiochus IV Epiphanes (4:7). For Jason, the path to success is paved with "Greek ways" (4:10; see further the discussion of "Judaism versus Hellenism?" below). For the epitomator, the exchange of ancestral traditions for Greek ways spells disaster (4:16). He explains: "To flout the divine laws is no light thing, as the subsequent period will make clear" (4:17). According to the epitomator's theology, the Seleucid turn from benevolent monarchy to oppressive regime serves the purposes of God, who will chastise the people for their sins through the actions of Antiochus IV Epiphanes (5:17-18; cf. 4:38).[40]

In light of this theology, we see that imperial rule *per se* was not problematic for the epitomator.[41] It was a mark of God's total power that God could provide for the people's needs — and the needs of the temple — through the benevolence of a monarch such as Seleucus IV. At the same time, God did not require such a monarch to protect and maintain his city and temple. The emphasis on divine ἐξουσία in 3:24 relativizes the power of the earthly king in relation to the power of "the one whose dwelling is in heaven" (3:39). For the author of 2 Maccabees, it is not the Seleucid monarch at all who guarantees safety and security, but God, who protects the city and temple from those who would harm them (3:39). The epitomator conveys the same point in the story of the

38. The logic is similar to that of the king's rhetoric, examined above, but a detriangulation has occurred, such that here the Seleucid king does not serve as a mediator protecting against divine displeasure. Structurally, the ancestral laws occupy the position in which Seleucus's *prostagma* had stood. For 2 Macc, security has nothing to do with obedience to the Seleucid monarch, and everything to do with obedience to the laws of God.

39. See Jonathan A. Goldstein, *II Maccabees: A New Translation with Introduction and Commentary,* Anchor Bible 41A (New York: Doubleday, 1983), pp. 12-13; Doran, *Temple Propaganda,* p. 75.

40. Beate Ego discusses the function of "pedagogical punishment," an understanding of divine justice operative in 2 Macc alongside the "'measure for measure' principle." "God's Justice: The 'Measure for Measure' Principle in 2 Maccabees," in *The Books of the Maccabees; History, Theology, Ideology: Papers of the Second International Conference on the Deuterocanonical Books, Pápa, Hungary, 9-11 June, 2005,* ed. Géza G. Xeravits and József Zsengellér (Leiden: Brill, 2007), pp. 141-54.

41. Cf. Robert Doran, "Independence or Co-Existence: The Responses of 1 and 2 Maccabees to Seleucid Hegemony," *SBLSP* (1999): 94-103. Doran speculates that the epitomator's portrait of "coexistence with an imperial power" may reflect elements of a compositional setting in which Rome had begun to serve as the new imperial patron (p. 103).

martyred brothers and mother that occupies the book's center and serves as a narrative hinge marking the end of God's anger and inaugurating the reversal of the people's suffering. The fifth brother begins his speech to Antiochus by noting the king's power among human beings (ἐξουσίαν ἐν ἀνθρώποις ἔχων 7:16). Yet he immediately counters the king's power by marking its limit, reminding him that he is mortal, perishable, destructible (φθαρτὸς ὢν 7:16). As Antiochus will see, and as his own death will reveal to others (φανερὰν τοῦ θεοῦ πᾶσιν τὴν δύναμιν ἐνδεικνύμενος 9:8), the greater power (τὸ μεγαλεῖον αὐτοῦ κράτος 7:17) belongs to God (cf. 9:12; 15:4-5).[42] The brother assures Antiochus that God has not forsaken the people of Judea (7:16). God need not work through the Seleucid king to provide for God's people or the temple.

Reading the Sources Together

Juxtaposing the evidence of 2 Maccabees with that of the newly discovered stele alerts us to ways in which the epitomator's theological framework shapes the history presented in the book, just as the imperial ideology of interdependence shapes the rhetoric of Seleucus IV's *prostagma*. Behind them both lies a complex network of interactions and negotiations. On the one hand, 2 Maccabees likely preserves important historical insight into the disastrous consequences of local priestly elites' jockeying for power and influence. On the other hand, we cannot follow 2 Maccabees in attributing to Simon or any other Judean sole or even primary responsibility for initiating the imperial policy of increased administrative control over the Jerusalem sanctuary. This policy was initiated by the king himself as part of a broader effort to bring the administration of sanctuaries in Coele-Syria and Phoenicia in line with the administration of sanctuaries elsewhere in the Seleucid empire. I highlighted above the ways language of reciprocity and interdependence reinforced imperial hegemony. At the same time, the narrative in 2 Maccabees reveals that such reciprocity was not entirely a fiction. In the view of classicist John Ma, language of reciprocity served the cities' interests as much as the king's, "converting straight domination into interaction."[43] From the standpoint of the imperial administration, the purpose

---

42. On the account of Antiochus's death in 2 Macc, see Doron Mendels, "A Note on the Tradition of Antiochus IV's Death," *IEJ* 31 (1981): 53-56, who argues that the account draws on a Babylonian tradition associated with Nabonidus; and Daniel R. Schwartz, "Why Did Antiochus Have to Fall (II Maccabees 9:7)?" in *Heavenly Tablets: Interpretation, Identity and Tradition in Ancient Judaism*, ed. Lynn LiDonnici and Andrea Lieber (Leiden: Brill, 2007), pp. 257-64, who establishes that the author draws also on Isa 14 and 40:12, wishing to evoke Isaiah's contrast between human and divine.

43. Ma, *Antiochos III*, p. 10. He similarly writes, "The fact that the image of cordiality and

of the *prostagma* was both to increase imperial revenues and to promote structures and ideologies of interdependence that would strengthen imperial hegemony. Yet a king's effort to strengthen control in this way calls attention to the agency of the local populace and its leaders. The account in 2 Maccabees similarly highlights the interactive dynamics of consent and collaboration.[44] As I noted above, these dynamics are complex. Local cults played an important role in regional administration but also in preserving local traditions and shaping communal identity. Behind the interdependence Seleucus sought to establish was also a measure of independence, and we are reminded of Samuel Eddy's observation that local sanctuaries were key loci of resistance to Seleucid rule, not only in Judea but in Babylonia and Elam as well (see ch. 1).[45]

In the case of Jerusalem, Seleucus's new policy seems to have had a series of unintended and unanticipated effects. Rather than promoting an ideology of cohesion, the measure seems to have intensified the internal divisions identified in the previous chapter. Other factors heightened these tensions as well. Influential families — Tobiads, Oniads, Simonites — vied for power, status, and privileges (the Hasmoneans would soon enter the fray). Each had a different vision for Judea's future. As in an earlier period, rifts again developed between supporters of the Seleucid government and supporters of the Ptolemies (2 Macc 4:2). Peter Schäfer identifies three factors contributing to the new factionalism: "the frustration of the hopes raised when power changed hands, the internal power struggle between the Tobiads and the Oniads and, above all, the simple fact that the financial burden placed upon the Seleucid state would certainly have left its mark on Jerusalem, and little would have remained of Antiochus III's tax concessions."[46] In a community whose elites imitated their Hellenistic overlords in their continued struggle for power, the new policy of imperial oversight of sanctuaries created new opportunities to negotiate privileges, purchase offices, and propose reforms. These opportunities invited ambitious leaders to seek their own interests above those of the people they ostensi-

---

benevolence presented by the cities [via public honors for the king] is a construct does not mean that it should be condemned as non-factual" (p. 38). Ma also takes pains to demonstrate that the cities were not "abject and defenseless," but "capable of resistance, whether physical or ideological" (p. 10; see also 244).

44. Cf. Ma, *Antiochos III*, p. 104.

45. Jerusalem fits among the cities described by Ma as "simultaneously self-governing (the necessary condition for their political existence) and subordinate to the king. . . . They were self-governing, because the king by 'giving back' their constitution or their laws had granted their continuing existence as political communities; they were formally subordinate to a king, as we can tell from open signs of the king's legal authority and rights" (*Antiochos III*, pp. 153-54).

46. Peter Schäfer, *The History of the Jews in the Greco-Roman World*, rev. ed. (London: Routledge, 2003), pp. 33-34.

bly served, and quickly pitted powerful men against each other (4:1-4), leading to murderous strife (4:3) and the creation of still more political factions.

In spite of these internal divisions, according to 2 Maccabees, the high priest and "mixed multitude" (τοῦ πλήθους παμμιγῆ) of Jerusalem had united in supplication before God to prevent Heliodorus from appropriating the temple funds (3:16-21), as the deposits were sacrosanct and could not be taken by the king's agent (3:12). On this occasion, divine intervention averted the crisis (3:24-30). Yet the move to bring the Jerusalem cult more directly into the Seleucid imperial orbit raised a separate question for the future, to which different Judeans would respond in different ways. To what extent would heightened imperial oversight lead to the Jerusalem cult's being "assimilated into a broader network of divine relationships," as Goldstone and Haldon suggest typically followed? When more than money, status, and privilege was at stake, would local cult leaders support or oppose this kind of assimilation? I return to these questions below.

This analysis yields several insights: (1) Rather than viewing Heliodorus's incursion into the Jerusalem temple as an isolated attempt at temple robbery instigated by a meddlesome temple official, we must view Heliodorus's actions as one component of an imperial policy of increased financial oversight of local sanctuaries and perhaps part of an even broader initiative to restructure provincial government in Coele-Syria and Phoenicia. (2) We recognize that 2 Maccabees' idyllic projection of "utter peace" and perfect lawfulness into the period preceding Heliodorus's incursion into the temple is a narrative device that introduces and supports the epitomator's theological premise that God protected the people when they were faithful and punished them when they were not. (3) From the preceding point we learn to be cautious about treating this projection of absolute harmony between the Seleucid empire and its Judean subjects as a historically accurate description of the sociopolitical climate prior to the ascension of Antiochus IV Epiphanes. (4) We can appreciate the ways in which imperial policy exacerbated internal divisions within the Judean community at this time. (5) And we can recognize the contributing role of Judean internal strife in the events leading up to the persecution, without minimizing the role of the Seleucid kings and Seleucid imperial structures of domination.

Judaism versus Hellenism?

After the Heliodorus episode and the intrigue that followed in its wake, 2 Maccabees narrates the death of Seleucus IV and the ascension of Antiochus IV Epiphanes. The year is now 175 BCE, eight years prior to Antiochus's persecution of the Jews in Judea. Upon introducing Antiochus IV, the epitomator immediately recounts Jason's purchase of the high priesthood (the office was, prior to Jason's purchase of it, occupied by his brother Onias III[47]), followed by a description of what have commonly been characterized as Jason's "Hellenizing reforms" (4:7-10).[48] It is at this juncture that 2 Maccabees introduces the term "Hellenism" or "Greek way of life" (Ἑλληνισμός 4:13), a seeming foil to the "Judaism" or "Judean/Jewish way of life" (Ἰουδαϊσμός) for which, the epitomator tells us, the book's heroes were willing to fight and die (2:21; 8:1; 14:38).[49] Although the two terms do not appear together in our sources for the events that precipitated the persecution and revolt, scholars have counterposed these terms to assert a fundamental opposition between Judaism and Hellenism at the heart of Jewish resistance to the measures of Antiochus some seven years later.[50]

Yet while it became a commonplace in discussions of the persecution and revolt to assert that the Maccabees fought against Hellenism, Erich Gruen has called the supposed opposition between Judaism and Hellenism in this period "artificial."[51] He writes, "'Judaism' and 'Hellenism' were neither competing systems nor incompatible concepts. It would be erroneous to assume that Hellenization entailed encroachment upon Jewish traditions and erosion of Jewish beliefs. Jews did not face a choice of either assimilation or resistance to Greek culture."[52] But the issue is more complex than Gruen lets on. On the one hand, the opposition between Judaism and Hellenism is a construct employed to particular literary effect in 2 Maccabees and in contemporary scholarship.[53]

---

47. On the identification of Onias (whether III or IV), see Schwartz, 2 Maccabees, p. 187. For an extended treatment of his tenure as high priest, see James C. VanderKam, From Joshua to Caiaphas: High Priests after the Exile (Minneapolis: Fortress, 2004), pp. 188-97.

48. On Jason's tenure as high priest, see VanderKam, From Joshua to Caiaphas, pp. 197-203.

49. Judith Lieu emphasizes the "embodied, political" dimension of Ἰουδαϊσμός for the epitomator. "Not Hellenes but Philistines? The Maccabees and Josephus Defining the 'Other,'" JJS 53, no. 2 (2002): 246-63, 251.

50. A sensitive treatment of the question can be found in John J. Collins, Jewish Cult and Hellenistic Culture: Essays on the Jewish Encounter with Hellenism and Roman Rule (Leiden: Brill, 2005), pp. 21-43.

51. Erich S. Gruen, Heritage and Hellenism: The Reinvention of Jewish Tradition (Berkeley: University of California Press, 1998), p. xix. On the relationship between Judaism and Hellenism more generally, see the seminal work of Martin Hengel, Judaism and Hellenism: Studies in Their Encounter in Palestine during the Early Hellenistic Period, 2 vols. (Philadelphia: Fortress, 1974); as well as more recent treatments by Lee I. Levine, Judaism and Hellenism in Antiquity: Conflict or Confluence (Seattle: University of Washington Press, 1998); and Collins, Jewish Cult and Hellenistic Culture.

52. Gruen, Heritage and Hellenism, p. xiv. See also his essay "Hellenism and Persecution: Antiochus IV and the Jews," in Hellenistic History and Culture, ed. Peter Green (Berkeley: University of California Press, 1993), pp. 238-74, esp. 257-60.

53. Judith Lieu, "Not Hellenes," p. 247.

At the same time, it also names a real tension that comes to a crisis in the time of the persecution. That said, it cannot account for the persecution, nor can it serve as a summary of the issues at stake during the persecution — it is one element only.

Jason's Hellenizing Reforms

A closer examination of the passage in 2 Maccabees reveals the complex negotiations of cultural, ethnic, and religious identity elicited by Jason's Hellenizing reforms. Second Maccabees 4:7-17 narrates the ambition and subsequent Hellenizing activities and measures of the "Reformers," beginning with Jason. We learn that Jason, an Oniad by birth, purchases from the king the office of high priest as well as three privileges: (1) the privilege to establish a gymnasium in Jerusalem;[54] (2) the privilege to establish an ephebate;[55] and (3) the privilege to enroll members of the Jerusalem elite as citizens of Antioch (4:9).[56] These privileges would establish Jason as an exemplary statesman and benefactor (according to Hellenistic norms), committed to the prosperity and defense of his city.[57]

54. Victor Tcherikover views the *gymnasion* and *ephebeion* as constitutional reform (reshaping process and definitions concerning who could become a citizen). *Hellenistic Civilization and the Jews*, trans. S. Applebaum (Philadelphia: Jewish Publication Society, 1959; repr. with a pref. by John J. Collins, Peabody, MA: Hendrickson, 1999), pp. 163-69. See also Hengel, *Judaism and Hellenism*, 1:74; and Schäfer, *History of the Jews*, pp. 36-37. Robert Doran argues to the contrary that this measure aimed solely at educational reform. "Jason's Gymnasion," in *Of Scribes and Scrolls: Studies on the Hebrew Bible, Intertestamental Judaism, and Christian Origins Presented to John Strugnell on the Occasion of His Sixtieth Birthday*, ed. Harold W. Attridge, John J. Collins, and Thomas H. Tobin, SJ (Lanham, MD: University Press of America, 1990), pp. 99-109.

55. Angelos Chaniotis defines *ephebeia* as "the training of age-classes of young men (usually between 18 and 20) under the supervision of the state authorities." *War in the Hellenistic World: A Social and Cultural History* (Oxford: Blackwell, 2005), p. 47.

56. The latter privilege seems to have entailed renaming Jerusalem in honor of the king. Goldstein suggests that Jason's requests were "a response to the invitation of Antiochus IV to the subject populations of his empire that they should join his Antiochene republic and become Antiochene citizens" (*II Maccabees*, p. 85). Goldstein argues elsewhere that Antiochus developed a "policy of voluntary civic Hellenization" as a method, learned from the Romans during his years among them as a hostage, of fostering loyalty in subject peoples. *I Maccabees: A New Translation with Introduction and Commentary*, Anchor Bible 41 (Garden City, NY: Doubleday, 1976), pp. 105-21. Unfortunately, we don't have definitive evidence of such a policy. Schwartz argues instead that the text refers to the establishment of a new *polis* within Jerusalem called "Antioch-in-Jerusalem" (2 *Maccabees*, pp. 530-32), while Tcherikover argues that "the new city was identical with Jerusalem" (*Hellenistic Civilization*, p. 165).

57. On euergetism and the role of gymnasiarch, see Chaniotis, *War in the Hellenistic World*, pp. 30-37.

Yet the accounts in 1 and 2 Maccabees hardly pass a favorable judgment on Jason's actions. The epitomator accuses Jason of having set aside or made light of (παρώσας) previously negotiated royal benefactions, "dissolving the established principles of civic government, and establishing new customs contrary to the law" (2 Macc 4:11). First Maccabees appears to summarize the same events when it declares that "lawless" ones (υἱοὶ παράνομοι 1:11) among the people were empowered by the king to enact the "ordinances of the nations" (τὰ δικαιώματα τῶν ἐθνῶν 1:13). These statements have led some scholars to conclude that Jason's measures did away with the privilege of governance according to ancestral laws granted by Antiochus III's letter to Ptolemy (see ch. 2).[58] While the rhetoric in both passages is strong, I believe that a more subtle point is being made. The verb παρωθέω means neither "abrogate" nor "annul," but more precisely "push aside," "make light of," or "reject."[59] In the six occurrences of the verb in Josephus's works, for example (the verb occurs nowhere else in the biblical corpus), it refers to denigration, lowering of status, or removal from a previous position of influence or authority.[60] Seen in this light, the statement in 2 Maccabees need not mean that Jason did away with the Judean right of governance according to the ancestral laws. The epitomator complains rather that he "demoted" the earlier benefactions by seeking new ones and similarly "demoted" the ancestral laws by introducing new structures and principles of governance that were not consistent with them. The epigraphic record confirms that such a new civic constitution need not have abrogated the privilege of living according to one's own laws. In an inscription from Phrygia dating shortly after 188 BCE (and therefore perhaps a decade or so prior to Jason's reforms), the Attalid king Eumenes II of Pergamon responds favorably to the petition of his subjects the Toriaians that "a *polis* constitution (πολιτείαν) be granted to you, and your own laws (νόμους ἰδίους), and a gymnasium, and as many things as are consistent with those" (ll. 9-11).[61] The right to live according to their own laws is emphasized again later in the letter, where the king states that he grants both to the letter's primary addressees and to the local population (καὶ ὑμῖν καὶ

58. E.g., Tcherikover, *Hellenistic Civilization*, p. 164.

59. LSJ, 1344.

60. *A.J.* 16.86, 192, 280, 295, 305; *B.J.* 1.209.

61. Translation is that of Roger S. Bagnall and Peter Derow, *The Hellenistic Period: Sources in Translation* (Oxford: Blackwell, 2004), p. 80, §43. The inscription was originally published by Lloyd Jonnes and Marijana Ricl, "A New Royal Inscription from Phrygia Paroreios: Eumenes II Grants Tyriaion the Status of a Polis," *EA* 29 (1997): 1-29. The petition arose in light of the transfer of Tyriaion from Seleucid to Attalid control effected by the treaty of Apamea (see ll. 21-22; Jonnes and Ricl, "New Royal Inscription," pp. 6-7, 13). On further points of contact between this inscription and Jason's reforms, see Nigel M. Kennell, "New Light on 2 Maccabees 4:7-15," *JJS* 56, no. 1 (2005): 10-24.

τοῖς μεθ᾽ ὑμῶν συνοικοῦσιν ἐν χωρίοις ll. 26-27) the right "to use your own laws" (νόμοις τε χρῆσθαι ἰδίοις ll. 27-28).[62] In a similar fashion, Jason's reforms did not do away with the earlier privilege of following ancestral customs and laws.[63] Rather, they publicly recognized and displayed new structures and principles of governance alongside the former ones. They also introduced new avenues to power through the embrace and imitation of the cultural legacies of the Hellenistic conquerors.

In particular, the gymnasium and ephebate would make available to the young male members of Jerusalem's upper classes a new educational institution drawn from the cultural heritage of their Greco-Macedonian rulers.[64] This institution trained young citizens in Greek culture, philosophy, and mores, forming them for political involvement in the life of the *polis* and shaping their communal identity.[65] More importantly, throughout the empire the gymnasium and ephebate also trained and formed young bodies for military service.[66] Typical exercises of the gymnasium variously included wrestling, running, and hand-to-hand combat skills as well as weapons training such as javelin throwing and archery.[67] We do not know for certain the specific exercises conducted at the Jerusalem gymnasium, yet it is clear that Judean bodies formerly marked by circumcision and habituated to the embodied practices of Jewish faith

62. In technical terms, this was a grant of *autonomia* (Jonnes and Ricl, "New Royal Inscription," pp. 15, 21). Eumenes further indicates that if the Toriaians cannot agree on the content of the laws, he will provide ones suitable to them (ἐπιτηδείους l. 31).

63. But see the remarks of Kennell, who suggests that Jason adopted a prefabricated bundle of laws akin to the ones offered to the Toriaians by Eumenes ("New Light," p. 17). I do not see sufficient evidence for this, despite the statements in 1 and 2 Macc.

64. Philip of Macedon had used athletic games to project his own "Greekness" prior to his conquest of Greece. See Donald G. Kyle, *Sport and Spectacle in the Ancient World* (Oxford: Blackwell, 2007), pp. 232-34.

65. Chaniotis, *War in the Hellenistic World*, p. 49. But see Robert Doran, "Jewish Education in the Seleucid Period," in *Second Temple Studies III: Studies in Politics, Class and Material Culture*, ed. Philip R. Davies and John M. Halligan (London: Sheffield Academic Press, 2002), pp. 116-32, 126-31, who rightly reminds us how little we know about the curriculum of Jason's gymnasium.

66. Philippe Gauthier and Miltiades B. Hatzopoulos, *La loi gymnasiarchique de Beroia* (Athens: Centre de recherches de l'antiquité grecque et romaine, 1993), p. 103; cf. 65. See also Kyle, *Sport and Spectacle*, p. 245; Chaniotis, *War in the Hellenistic World*, p. 47; Jonnes and Ricl, "New Royal Inscription," p. 15. For a later period, see Zahra Newby, *Greek Athletics in the Roman World: Victory and Virtue* (Oxford: Oxford University Press, 2005), esp. pp. 143-68. In her discussion of Sparta, Newby writes, "Ephebic education in general . . . seems always to have been associated with training for warfare" (p. 155).

67. Gauthier and Hatzopoulos, *La loi gymnasiarchique*, p. 72; Chaniotis, *War in the Hellenistic World*, pp. 49-50. See also Robert Doran, "The High Cost of a Good Education," in *Hellenism in the Land of Israel*, ed. John J. Collins and Gregory E. Sterling (Notre Dame: University of Notre Dame Press, 2001), pp. 94-115, 95-96.

would now be visibly reshaped by participation in its structured athletic practices. Those practices inculcated virtues, chief among them obedience and discipline.[68] As Angelos Chaniotis has observed, "The cardinal virtue of ephebic education is *eutaxia*, 'discipline,' the virtue that permits the introduction of young people to ordered life."[69]

Indeed, an inscription from Beroia in ancient Macedonia, roughly contemporary with Jason's gymnasium, reveals that gymnasia were tightly structured institutions with clearly defined administrative hierarchies and a strict code of obedience and discipline, including provisions for corporal punishment (by flogging) and/or fines for those who flouted the rules.[70] There were also rewards for those who respected the rules and exemplified other virtues of the gymnasium. The inscription from Beroia provides guidelines for three contests to be judged at the annual festival of the Hermaia:[71] one for physical fitness

---

68. See, e.g., Nigel Kennell, *The Gymnasium of Virtue: Education and Culture in Ancient Sparta* (Chapel Hill: University of North Carolina Press, 1995).

69. Chaniotis, *War in the Hellenistic World*, p. 51. John Ma observes that *eutaxia* is the virtue most emphasized among groups occupying a liminal status, whose potential for disorder the society perceives as a danger to itself. Such groups included not only ephebes but also garrisoned soldiers occupying a conquered city. "'Oversexed, Overpaid and Over Here': A Response to Angelos Chaniotis," in *Army and Power in the Ancient World,* ed. Angelos Chaniotis and Peter Ducrey (Stuttgart: Franz Steiner Verlag, 2002), pp. 115-22, 115. See also Giovanni Salmeri, "Empire and Collective Mentality: The Transformation of *eutaxia* from the Fifth Century BC to the Second Century AD," in *The Province Strikes Back: Imperial Dynamics in the Eastern Mediterranean*, ed. Björn Forsén and Giovanni Salmeri (Helsinki: The Finnish Institute at Athens, 2008), pp. 137-55, 142-43. Salmeri argues that *eutaxia* "came to denote orderliness, the 'discipline' of campaigning armies and especially of the garrisons sent by the kings to keep the Hellenistic cities under control" (p. 142). Salmeri also discusses the role of *eutaxia* in politics and ethics, noting especially its connection with "*homonoia* (concord) and *kosmos politeias* (civic order)" as well as *nomos* (law) (pp. 138-40, 150).

70. *SEG* 27.261. The inscription, dated between 200 and 170 BCE, provides our most detailed information about the conduct of a gymnasium in this period. Full text and commentary can be found in Gauthier and Hatzopoulos, *La loi gymnasiarchique*. On corporal punishments and fines, see Gauthier and Hatzopoulos, *La loi gymnasiarchique,* pp. 65-68. On the date, see further Miltiades B. Hatzopoulos, "Quaestiones Macedonicae: lois, decrets, et epistates dans les cités Macedoniennes," *Tekmeria* 8 (2003): 27-60. Bagnall and Derow provide an English translation (*Hellenistic Period*, pp. 133-38, §78). The same contests are described in an inscription concerning the gymnasium at Samos (*IG* XII.6.1 179-84, cited in Chaniotis, *War in the Hellenistic World*, p. 51).

71. The Hermaia honored the god Hermes, whom Gauthier and Hatzopoulos call "le dieu par excellence du gymnasie" (*La loi gymnasiarchique*, p. 95; see 95n4 for extensive bibliography). Nick Fisher writes: "Evidence from many other Hellenistic cities reveals the Hermaia as the major annual festival of any self-respecting *gymnasion*." Aeschines, *Against Timarchos*, trans. with intro. and comm. Nick Fisher, Clarendon Ancient History (Oxford: Oxford University Press, 2001), p. 132.

(εὐεξία), with victory awarded to the most physically fit; a second for "good discipline" or "right ordering" (εὐταξία), with victory awarded to the individual under thirty years of age judged to be "the most well-behaved"; and a third for "hard training" (φιλοπονία, literally "love of labor" or "industry"), with victory awarded to the individual under thirty judged to have trained the hardest in the preceding year.[72] The virtues inculcated in these contests and in the activities by which young men trained for them were a crucial part of their formation for citizenship. As discussed in chapter 1, these disciplines formed minds and bodies for service to the state, furthering its economic and political ends by increasing the body's potential (for labor, production, military service) and the drive to achieve while also conditioning the mind and spirit in the habits of obedience. At the same time, shaping young Judeans as citizen soldiers along this model could create a strong sense of local autonomy, enabling Jerusalem's upper classes "to achieve productive ends of their own"[73] and apparently equipping them with the skills, disciplines, knowledge, and drive to reestablish *autonomia* when it was later taken away by Antiochus IV.[74] I discussed the problematic of perceived autonomy in chapter 1. The epitomator, like the apocalyptic writers, understood that there was no absolute freedom, and laws were never strictly of one's own making — they emerged from the givenness of tradition and claimed the authority of God, king, or both. But the ordering principles of the gymnasium emerged from a different tradition than that of Israel's scriptures, and if they inculcated habits of obedience, the question would have been raised, obedience to what, and to whom? By introducing the gymnasium into Jerusalem, Jason introduced new hierarchies, a school of virtues, and principles of order that had no apparent connection to the cosmic order established by Israel's God or the sacred ordering of human life set forth in Judea's ancestral laws.

The disparity between these two systems of order took visible form in the bodies and habits of dress of the young Jews who enrolled in the gymnasium. As Donald Kyle has noted, ancient athletics were communicative events, performance and spectacle "by which cultural orders (i.e., values, norms, status re-

---

72. See further Nigel B. Crowther, "Euexia, Eutaxia, Philoponia: The Contests of the Greek *gymnasion*," *ZPE* 85 (1983): 301-4; and Gauthier and Hatzopoulos, *La loi gymnasiarchique*, pp. 102-5.

73. Arthur W. Frank, "For a Sociology of the Body: An Analytical Review," in *The Body: Social Process and Cultural Theory*, ed. Mike Featherstone, Mike Hepworth, and Bryan S. Turner (London: Sage, 1991), pp. 36-102, 58.

74. I cannot claim with any certainty that leaders of the successful Maccabean revolt had ever trained at the gymnasium. But it stands to reason that some of the young Judeans who had trained there would eventually have fought for Judea against the Seleucid army. This no doubt also occurred when Jason assaulted the city in 169 or 168 BCE, on which see ch. 4.

lationships) [we]re formulated, communicated, and reformulated."[75] In this spectacle, bodies were fully on display: as the name "gymnasium" suggests, exercises and competitions were conducted in the nude.[76] The athlete's naked body communicated important information about his culture and identity.[77] As such, this "absence of a costume was itself a costume."[78] Nigel Crowther explains how the athlete's nudity provided a mark of distinction between "Greek" and "barbarian":[79] "Whatever the original reason for nudity in athletics, the Greeks, as Solon is made to explain in the *Anacharsis* of Lucian, were proud of their bodies, their lack of flab, their tan; it was nudity which separated them from barbarians, from whom they wished to be distinguished."[80] The athlete's nakedness, then, gave physical proof of discipline, strength, and endurance. These virtues not only shaped his body, but were constitutive elements of his cultural and ethnic identity.[81]

75. Kyle, *Sport and Spectacle*, p. 17.

76. Gymnasium, or γυμνάσιον, derives from the adjective γυμνός, meaning "naked." Note however that Lester Grabbe disputes that athletes in the Jerusalem gymnasium would have exercised in the nude. "The Hellenistic City of Jerusalem," in *Jews in the Hellenistic and Roman Cities*, ed. John R. Bartlett (London: Routledge, 2002), pp. 6-21, 12-13.

77. Cf. Kyle, *Sport and Spectacle*, p. 18.

78. Kyle, *Sport and Spectacle*, p. 118, discussing mandatory nudity at the Olympic games. See further Larissa Bonfante, "Nudity as Costume in Classical Art," *AJA* 93 (1989): 543-70, esp. 551-52. Bonfante argues that nudity was above all the "costume" of the Greek citizen.

79. Bonfante observes that "as it developed, Greek nudity came to mark a contrast between Greek and non-Greek" ("Nudity," p. 544). She traces this development, noting also a break from earlier Greek associations between nudity and shame, leading to "a definition of [male nudity] as heroic, divine, athletic, and youthful" (pp. 547, 549).

80. Nigel B. Crowther, *Athletika: Studies on the Olympic Games and Greek Athletics*, Nikephoros 11 (Hildesheim: Weidmann, 2004), p. 140. Concerning both skin-tone and flabbiness, see also Xen. *Ages.* 1.28, cited in Bonfante, "Nudity," p. 555n77. Thucydides contrasts Greek athletic nudity (which, he reports, originated among the Spartans) with the "barbarian" style of wearing a belt or loincloth during exercise (1.6.5), while both Herodotus and Plato's Socrates observe that among "barbarians" it is shameful for a man to be seen naked (1.10.3; *Resp.* 452c). Nakedness is frequently (though not always — see Song of Songs) related to shame in the Hebrew Bible (Mic 1:11; Isa 20:2-4; Ezek 16:39; 23:29; Hos 2:3; 2 Chron 28:15; cf. Amos 2:16, where nakedness symbolizes a warrior's unexpected transformation from powerful to vulnerable). Johanna Stiebert calls attention to Deut 25:11, where the link between nakedness and shame is lexically encoded in the *hapax legomenon* מְבֻשִׁים, signifying male genitalia (cf. the Greek noun αἰδοῖα). *The Construction of Shame in the Hebrew Bible: The Prophetic Contribution* (London: Sheffield Academic Press, 2002), p. 122. Stiebert also notes the opposition to public nudity in the Community Rule of Qumran (1QS VII.12-15): "Whoever walks about naked in front of his fellow, without needing to, shall be punished for six months." Translation is that of Florentino García Martínez and Eibert Tigchelaar, *The Dead Sea Scrolls Study Edition*, vol. 1 (Leiden: Brill, 2000), p. 87. Does this prohibition arise as a reaction to the practices of the gymnasium in Jerusalem?

81. Bonfante discusses the ways in which the image of the naked young male as represented in the kouros statue "embodied the *arete* or glory of an aristocratic youth, who was *kalos-*

The athlete prepared for training and competition by anointing his body with olive oil. The inscription from Beroia reveals the signal importance of anointing the body as not only practical preparation for exercise, but also a ritual marker of belonging.[82] Because oil was costly, selected individuals would have the honor of providing it for the use of others;[83] sometimes it was even provided as a royal benefaction.[84] This oil could also have sacred connotations: it was considered sacred to the goddess Athena, for which reason amphorae of olive oil were awarded to victors in the Panathenaea festival games held in her honor.[85] As is well known, the practice of anointing with oil (not the whole body, but typically the head) frequently had a sacred character in Israel's traditions as well.[86] With these traditions in mind, the ritualistic practice of anointing the body for athletic activity highlights a tension between the embodied practices of Jewish faith and those of the gymnasium. The epitomator's account of the gymnasium contains an implicit reference to the oil, condemning its use in the gymnasium as "contrary to law" (2 Macc 4:14). According to the epitomator, at "the signal of the discus" (τὴν τοῦ δίσκου πρόσκλησιν) the young priests abandoned their sac-

---

kagathos, 'beautiful and noble'" ("Nudity," pp. 544, 550). Nudity, then, was a marker not only of ethnic, cultural, and civic identity, but also of class.

82. Gauthier and Hatzopoulos, "La loi gymnasiarchique," pp. 57-58. Cf. David Sansone, *Greek Athletics and the Genesis of Sport* (Berkeley: University of California Press, 1992), p. 95. On the religious and ritual associations of Greek athletic nudity in general, see Bonfante, "Nudity," pp. 551-53. Drawing on the work of Pierre Vidal-Naquet, Bonfante links the "sacred quality of nudity" with the role of the ephebate in "the initiation of youths" ("Nudity," p. 551). See Pierre Vidal-Naquet, *The Black Hunter: Forms of Thought and Forms of Society in the Greek World*, trans. Andrew Szegedy-Maszak (Baltimore: Johns Hopkins University Press, 1986), pp. 106-28. Bonfante believes that the religious and ritual associations are transformed into civic ones ("Nudity," p. 556), yet subsuming a rite's religious functions into civic ones does not eliminate its sacred character.

83. See Bagnall and Derow, *Hellenistic Period*, p. 79 (inscription from Chios, c. 188 BCE); p. 131 (inscription from Samos, c. 240); pp. 136-37 (inscription from Beroia, discussed above). Lin Foxhall estimates that 25-50 ml. of olive oil would be used per person per visit to the gymnasium. *Olive Cultivation in Ancient Greece: Seeking the Ancient Economy* (Oxford: Oxford University Press, 2007), p. 92.

84. Eumenes II provides the oil for the Toriaians. See discussion in Jonnes and Ricl, "New Royal Inscription," p. 24.

85. Lucian, *Anach*. 9; Kyle, *Sport and Spectacle*, pp. 153, 155-60. The sacred character of the gymnasium is suggested by the legislation in the Beroia inscription: anyone who steals from the gymnasium is to be charged with temple-robbery. For a reading of modern gyms in relation to the Jerusalem temple, and vice versa, see Stephen D. Moore, *God's Gym: Divine Male Bodies of the Bible* (London: Routledge, 1996), pp. 103-7.

86. Note however that anointing with oil had different meanings in different settings; we should avoid "illegitimate totality transfer" (James Barr, *The Semantics of Biblical Language* [London: Oxford University Press, 1961], p. 218) even as we seek to understand the significance this practice would have had in second-century Jerusalem.

rifices and rushed to the palaestra. The epitomator describes their purpose as μετέχειν τῆς ἐν παλαίστρη παρανόμου χορηγίας (4:14). Nigel Kennell notes that the "call of the discus" that so distracted the young priests was not an athletic event but a signal that was given for the distribution of oil that would initiate the day's activities in the gymnasium.[87] The priests rushed from their sacrificial duties in order to receive their portion of oil, anoint themselves, and begin their daily exercise. The epitomator's description of their intent has two meanings, revolving around the dual meaning of the word χορηγία: the young priests rush to have a share of the *supplies* of the palaestra (i.e., the oil);[88] by doing so they also rush to participate in the *offices* of the palaestra, for which they have abandoned the duties of the office of priesthood. The epitomator's double meaning economically characterizes both as "contrary to law."

While the practice of anointing with oil highlighted a tension between the praxis of the Jewish faith and that of the gymnasium, to these young priests it seems to have been unproblematic. Yet they were keenly aware of a different tension, related to a particular physical marker of Jewish identity: circumcision.[89] In most settings this marker was hidden; it rarely communicated Jewish identity in public.[90] In the gymnasium, however, the whole body was on display. Just as the oiled and muscular naked male body communicated and performed "Greekness," so in this period and setting the circumcised penis communicated and performed "Jewishness."[91] According to 1 Maccabees, in the context of the gymnasium, for some athletes the mark of circumcision that symbolized their belonging to the covenant people became an embarrassment. It was overly, or wrongly, particular. That is to say, it marked a particular identity different from the one most associated with power and status in the Hellenistic world. It was inconsistent with the ideal of the "Greek" male body, and for this reason was perceived as an obstacle to civic advancement.[92] To remove this obstacle, 1 Maccabees reports, "They made for themselves foreskins, and abandoned the holy covenant. They yoked themselves to the nations and sold themselves to do evil/labor" (τὸ πονηρόν 1:15). This dramatic imagery inverts

87. Kennell, "New Light," p. 18.

88. This was a usual term for the distribution of oil. See the epigraphic evidence examined in Kennell, "New Light," pp. 18-19.

89. Note, however, that Jews were not the only people in the ancient Near East who practiced circumcision. See Jack M. Sasson, "Circumcision in the Ancient Near East," *JBL* 85 (1966): 473-76.

90. Cf. Shaye Cohen, *The Beginnings of Jewishness: Boundaries, Varieties, Uncertainties* (Berkeley: University of California Press, 1999), pp. 47, 49.

91. See Cohen, *Beginnings of Jewishness*, pp. 39-49.

92. On idealized representations of the youthful Greek penis in classical painting and sculpture, see Bonfante, "Nudity," pp. 551-52n48.

traditional associations between the ideal Greek body and the nobility of citizenship, as well as the athletic virtue of φιλοπονία, and declares instead that the young Judeans who imitate the Greeks have willingly made themselves beasts of burden and even slaves to the empire. They have traded the glory of the covenant for a life of shameful toil.

There were less dramatic manifestations of submission to the empire through imitation of its ideals. Outside the gymnasium, it was a simple matter for Judeans to imitate Greekness through the fashions they wore. "Fashion," Nickolas Pappas observes, communicates "social like-mindedness."[93] Following Jason's reforms, changes in the fashions of young Judeans symbolized the diverse ways in which communal identity formerly shaped by native religious traditions and practices was now increasingly being shaped by traditions and practices drawn from the culture of Judea's conquerors. Karen Hanson emphasizes the way fashion embodies subjectivity.[94] The epitomator captures the new subjectivity of Judean elites in the image of the broad-brimmed Greek hat, or *petasos.*

Because it was originally a traveling hat, the *petasos* was associated with Hermes, the Greek god of travelers who was also the deity most closely linked with the activities of the gymnasium.[95] Hermes, known as "Lord of Contests," was "an archetype of the ephebe, or young male citizen on the cusp of manhood."[96] Hermes was associated not only with the athletic activities of the gymnasium, but with all aspects of ephebic formation. As Thomas Scanlon observes, "Hermes . . . is important as a deity of the transmission of social values, of 'education' very broadly conceived by the Greeks as *paideia,* more properly translated as 'formation' or 'upbringing.'"[97] Wearing the fashionable sun-hat known for its association with Hermes may have been a way that young ephebes of Jerusalem identified themselves to one another outside the walls of the gymnasium, publicly signaling their common belonging and formation.[98]

93. Nickolas Pappas, "Fashion Seen as Something Imitative and Foreign," *British Journal of Aesthetics* 48, no. 1 (2008): 1-19, 3.

94. Karen Hanson, "Dressing Down, Dressing Up: The Philosophical Fear of Fashion," in *Aesthetics in Feminist Perspective,* ed. Hilde S. Hein and Carolyn Korsmeyer (Bloomington: Indiana University Press, 1993), pp. 229-42.

95. Heracles and Eros were also closely linked to the gymnasium. See Newby, *Greek Athletics,* p. 119; Jennifer Lynn Larson, *Ancient Greek Cults: A Guide* (London: Routledge, 2007), pp. 147-48. On the *petasos,* see Chryssoula Saatsoglou-Paliadeli, "Aspects of Ancient Macedonian Costume," *Journal of Hellenic Studies* 113 (1993): 122-47, 129-30; and Larissa Bonfante, *Etruscan Dress* (Baltimore: Johns Hopkins University Press, 2003), pp. 68-69.

96. Larson, *Ancient Greek Cults,* pp. 147-48.

97. Thomas F. Scanlon, *Eros and Greek Athletics* (Oxford: Oxford University Press, 2002), pp. 5-6.

98. It also communicated a common desire to be like the "Greeks" and gain the benefits of

To the epitomator, it was a symbol of their subjection. Jason was now "submitting" (ὑποτάσσων) the "strongest" youths of Jerusalem to the *petasos* (2 Macc 4:12).[99] They wore upon their heads the very symbol of their embrace of foreign values and subordination to an alien order and hegemony.[100]

This hegemonic order was also writ large in the new constitution of the city itself. As noted above, the third privilege for which Jason petitioned Antiochus IV was that of enrolling members of the Jerusalem elite as citizens of "Antioch." To the content of education, the shaping of bodies, and the outward marks of another culture would be added a new civic identity. This new identity for place and for people would displace an identity grounded in the traditions and practices of Yahwism.[101] This new identity, moreover, bears the name of the Seleucid king, and makes of what was formerly called Jerusalem a nominal copy of the Seleucid capital, Antioch. Inclusion in the list of citizens would carry both costs and privileges, drawing Jerusalem's Hellenized elite deep within the system of local and imperial patronage and benefaction.

Victor Tcherikover has emphasized the ways in which these reforms "deepened the gulf between the wealthy urban population" and the rural peasantry.[102] Participation in the new institutions would have been limited to those with means. Yet the epitomator highlights a different issue: the measures embody "a height" or "extreme of Hellenism" (ἀκμή τις Ἑλληνισμοῦ) and "inroads of foreignness" (πρόσβασις ἀλλοφυλισμοῦ 4:13).[103] The latter expres-

---

adopting "Greek" ways. Arthur Frank discusses Jean Baudrillard's ideas about desire and consumption: "Desire can only operate on objects by turning them into signs. The commodity is less a real thing than it is a sign itself, because it is the sign we desire" (Frank, "For a Sociology of the Body," p. 64).

99. Goldstein calls attention to the nuance of the final verb in this verse, ἤγαγεν: though it can simply be rendered causally, in the sense that "he *led* them" (in procession), the verb also means "to educate" (*II Maccabees*, p. 229). The cognate noun form ἀγωγάς, which, as Goldstein notes, can refer to "educational curriculum," occurs in the epitomator's subsequent condemnation of Jason and his cohort's desire to imitate Greek ways (4:16). This wordplay heightens the metonymic function of the hat as a symbol of Greek education and imperial domination. See also Kennell ("New Light," pp. 19-21), who emphasizes the "military overtones" of the verb ὑποτάσσω (p. 21).

100. Cf. Zeph 1:8. On fashion as imitation and the trope of the foreign fashion model in classical and modern philosophy, see Pappas, "Fashion." On hegemony, cf. the statement of Elias Bickerman: "When the native people participated in the athletic contests, they were accepted into the ruling class, and they acknowledged the hegemony of the Greek way of life." *The God of the Maccabees: Studies on the Meaning and Origin of the Maccabean Revolt*, trans. Horst Moehring (Leiden: Brill, 1979), p. 39.

101. Cf. Benedict Anderson's discussion of censuses in *Imagined Communities: Reflections on the Origin and Spread of Nationalism* (London: Verso, 1983), pp. 164-70.

102. Tcherikover, *Hellenistic Civilization*, p. 169.

103. Martha Himmelfarb is right to assert that "for 2 Maccabees, *Hellenismos* is defined by

sion, which might also be translated "access" or "approach of foreign ways," alludes to the way in which adopting Greek culture, manners, and markers of
identity could give greater access to avenues of power.[104] If one element of the
population saw it as an intrusion, another saw it as a path to success. For the
author of 2 Maccabees this embrace of Hellenism signaled impiety.[105] Jason is
characterized first and foremost as "impious" (ἀσεβοῦς), and therefore a false
priest (4:13). The epitomator here establishes a conflict between extreme Hellenism, as I will call it, and traditional Jewish piety (cf. 1 Macc 1:15, examined
above). Moreover, the impiety of the high priest has serious consequences. He
sets an example for other members of the priesthood. They in turn neglect
their mediatory role in the temple cult. Thus the ambition of one man has
consequences for the entire community of Jerusalem; the path to power and
status among the "Greeks" is a path away from right relationship with God.
The epitomator illustrates the conflict in the following verse: as a result of Jason's wicked embrace of extreme Hellenism, other priests have followed suit.
Those set apart for service to God and God's people and ordained as protec-
tors and teachers of sacred tradition have abandoned the sacrifices to attend
the games. They prefer wrestling to worship (2 Macc 4:14). Changed practices
signal a changed value system. The priests have replaced old (Jewish) values
with new (Greek) ones; they count as nothing the honors of their ancestral
tradition, and consider "Greek glories" (Ἑλληνικὰς δόξας) most precious
(4:15). The epitomator is quick to point out that the ambitions of Jason and his
followers betrayed them: they did not gain the power they sought. Instead, in a
fitting reversal, the Greeks whom they so admired and sought to imitate became their enemies (πολεμίους) and punishers (4:16; cf. 1 Macc 1:15). The
epitomator understands this punishment as the consequence of their impiety
(ἀσεβεῖν), and in particular their neglect of the laws of God (τοὺς θείους
νόμους 2 Macc 4:17).

Cultural Encounter in the Hellenistic Empires

It cannot be doubted that Jason's reforms accelerated a cultural shift among the
Jerusalem elites that had serious consequences for religious and civic life in
Judea, and I return to this below. Yet both the binary construction of Judaism
and Hellenism and the portrayal of the persecution and resistance to it as a bat-

---

the gymnasium and the behavior associated with it" and has nothing to do with religious reforms. "Judaism and Hellenism in 2 Maccabees," *Poetics Today* 19, no. 1 (1998): 19-40, 24.

104. Cf. Collins, *Jewish Cult and Hellenistic Culture*, p. 31.

105. Cf. Andrea Spatafora, "Hellénisme et Judaïsme: Rencontre ou Confrontation: Étude
de 1 M 1,11-15, 2 M 4,7-20 et Sg 1,16–2,24," *Science et Esprit* 56, no. 1 (2004): 81-102, 98.

tle between the two rest on false assumptions about culture and identity.[106] As I noted above, the constructed opposition between Judaism and Hellenism names a real tension that does indeed have something to do with the persecution and resistance to it. But the relationship is not a simple one. The Hellenistic kings, Antiochus IV included, were not cultural evangelists, and those who resisted Antiochus's edict were not culture-warriors. Rather, they fought and died for the law of God. While Hellenistic cultural institutions did not directly jeopardize God's law, they were nonetheless vehicles of power in the imperial domination system. When Antiochus IV made the unprecedented move to attack the divine law and kill those faithful to its precepts, the institutions and practices that symbolized and conferred power within the imperial domination system became symbols of imperial hubris and Jewish apostasy. To better understand this process, we must first consider the relationship between "Greek ways" and native traditions, practices, and beliefs in the Hellenistic empires more broadly.

I asserted above that the Hellenistic kings were not cultural evangelists. Yet many have made such a claim. Wendy Kasinec and Michael Polushin represent a common view when they suggest that Alexander's imperial ambitions and military success were driven in part by his "conceit in the superiority of Greek society," while his founding of cities throughout the regions he conquered "reflected the belief that the Hellenistic city formed the basis of a superior culture and civilization."[107] Founding cities would remain a key strategy of the rulers who followed Alexander, and we have already discussed Jason's "founding" and renaming Jerusalem as a Hellenistic city in 175 BCE. Yet if the city was a basis for Hellenistic culture and civilization, the founding of such cities in the territories conquered by Alexander and ruled by his successors did not necessarily signal a

106. Jonathan Friedman deconstructs the very concept of culture(s): "Our construction of them, our reification of their cultures, is a highly reductionist project whose rationalization has been and is the concept of culture itself, i.e., the assumption that the world is made up of cultures, and that culture is a fundamental unit of understanding or even analysis. Culture, instead, might be seen as an enormous interplay of interpretations of a given social reality, in which the anthropologist has the last word." "Notes on Culture and Identity in Imperial Worlds," in *Religion and Religious Practices in the Seleucid Kingdom,* ed. Per Bilde, Troels Engberg-Pedersen, Lise Hannestad, and Jan Zahle (Aarhus, Denmark: Aarhus University Press, 1990), pp. 14-39, 22. As an alternative to such a reductionist view, Friedman (drawing on the work of Fredrik Barth, on which see further below) calls attention to the "multiple voices already present in society, which are positioned according to relations of power and authority" and suggests that culture be seen as a product of "multiple and socially situated acts of attribution of meaning to the world" ("Notes on Culture and Identity," p. 23).

107. Wendy F. Kasinec and Michael A. Polushin, introduction to *Expanding Empires: Cultural Interaction and Exchange in World Societies from Ancient to Early Modern Times,* ed. Wendy F. Kasinec and Michael A. Polushin (Wilmington, DE: Scholarly Resource Books, 2002), pp. xi-xxii, xi.

program of "world hellenisation" to match Alexander's goals of world domination. To the contrary, Susan Sherwin-White and Amélie Kuhrt argue that "in the hellenistic period, there is every reason to suppose that 'hellenisation' is an adjunct, not an aim, of imperialism."[108] In other words, there was no programmatic, empire-wide attempt to replace local traditions with Greek ones.[109] The establishment of cities (as well as colonies, or *katoikiai*) served primarily economic and secondarily military needs of the empire.[110] The building of gymnasia has also been adduced as evidence for Hellenic cultural evangelism. Yet frequently, as was the case in Jerusalem and among the Toriaians, the impulse to build a gymnasium came not from the king, but from local elites. Moreover, in colonial settings Greek institutions such as the gymnasium served first and foremost for the edification and formation of the Greco-Macedonian settlers themselves: they reinforced their Greek identity and helped secure their continuing loyalty.[111] Getzel Cohen notes that the gymnasium, more than any other institution, "typified life for the Greco-Macedonian throughout the Hellenistic diaspora" and served as "the repository of Hellenic culture and the training ground for entry into the social, political, and military life of the Hellenistic East."[112] Developing and sustaining a "Greek atmosphere" and way of life was crucial for maintaining morale among settlers; it also served an important role

108. Sherwin-White and Kuhrt, *From Samarkhand to Sardis,* p. 142. They conclude: "There was no global hellenising crusade" (p. 145). Getzel Cohen reaches a similar conclusion: "Hellenisation *per se* did not play any part in their scheme." Hellenization was rather a natural process, "not one actively fostered by the kings." *The Seleucid Colonies: Studies in Founding, Administration and Organization* (Wiesbaden: Frank Steiner Verlag GMBH, 1978), p. 88.

109. Sherwin-White and Kuhrt acknowledge that "the idea of 'hellenisation' as in part a directed process 'from above' is not totally implausible," but they see this happening in particular times and places only, and only at certain levels of society (*From Samarkhand to Sardis,* pp. 186-87).

110. G. G. Aperghis, *The Seleukid Royal Economy: The Finances and Financial Administration of the Seleukid Empire* (Cambridge: Cambridge University Press, 2004), pp. 89-99. Aperghis argues that "the primary motive for Seleukid city-building was not political or military, but economic, the desire to open up relatively undeveloped land to economic exploitation" (p. 99). He allows military and political considerations as secondary motives. See also Michel Austin, "The Seleukids and Asia," in *A Companion to the Hellenistic World,* ed. Andrew Erskine (Oxford: Blackwell, 2003), pp. 121-33, 130.

111. Cohen, *Seleucid Colonies,* p. 69. For this reason, Joseph Sievers wonders whether the soldiers in the Akra would have been "promoters of the construction project" for Jason's gymnasium. "Jerusalem, the Akra, and Josephus," in *Josephus and the History of the Greco-Roman Period: Essays in Honor of Morton Smith,* ed. Fausto Parente and Joseph Sievers (Leiden: Brill, 1994), pp. 195-209, 203. As he notes, "They would certainly have claimed access" to the gymnasium once it was built (p. 202).

112. Cohen, *Seleucid Colonies,* p. 36. Cohen notes that gymnasia provided formal education, lectures, exhibits, libraries, paramilitary and military training, public assemblies, feasts, and trials, and served as a religious center for the royal cult.

in perpetuating political, military, and religious structures essential to the successful administration of the empire.[113]

But if Macedonian settlers used such institutions to preserve their "Greek" identity in ways that sometimes set them apart from native populations, Alexander and his successor dynasts also recognized that they could not be effective rulers if they had no ties to the native populations they ruled.[114] Alexander forged these ties in various ways. After defeating the Achaemenid (Persian) empire, Alexander compelled ninety-two of his ranking officers, themselves Macedonians, to marry women from the local Persian population.[115] Alexander himself adopted Persian styles of dress and cultural practices, even allowing his new subjects to bow to him as a god, as they had once bowed down before their Persian rulers.[116] His successor, Seleucus I, claimed continuity not only with the Persian empire, but with the Babylonian as well, calling himself King of Babylon and occupying the Achaemenid palaces in Babylon before establishing capitals at Seleucia on the Tigris and later at Antioch on the Orontes.[117] In addition, at various times male members of the Seleucid royal family continued the practice of marrying women from the local Iranian elite, beginning with Seleucus I's marriage to Apame. Their son and future king Antiochus I and the Seleucid dynasty itself were consequently half-Macedonian and half-Iranian.[118] Antiochus III's marriage to the daughter of the Iranian King Mithridates served similar political aims.[119]

Like the Persians before them, the Seleucids also respected local traditions, including religion.[120] They assimilated Achaemenid styles (including art and

113. Cohen, *Seleucid Colonies*, p. 36.

114. Pierre Briant, "The Seleucid Kingdom and the Achaemenid Empire," in *Religion and Religious Practice in the Seleucid Kingdom*, ed. Bilde, Engberg-Pedersen, Hannestad, and Zahle, pp. 40-65, 55: "All the Successors, once installed in their areas of rule, had to face the problem of creating ties of collaboration with the local élites and their government."

115. Kasinec and Polushin, introduction to *Expanding Empires*, pp. xi-xii.

116. Kasinec and Polushin, introduction to *Expanding Empires*, pp. xii-xiii, xxi n10.

117. Briant notes that Seleucus's choice of Babylon for his capital signaled continuity with the Achaemenids ("Seleucid Kingdom," p. 47). At the same time, "Seleucus and his successors presented themselves as successors to the Babylonian dynasties with all its rights and obligations in relation to the local population, and above all their élites" (p. 57). For a list of other capitals, see Sherwin-White and Kuhrt, *From Samarkhand to Sardis*, p. 38. Austin offers an opposing view, arguing that "no Seleukid ruler ever contemplated linking himself to the Persian past." He contrasts the Seleukids with the dynasties of Pontus and Kommagene ("Seleukids and Asia," p. 128). Yet this may be a question of emphasis and degree.

118. From this and other evidence Sherwin-White and Kuhrt conclude that "the Seleucid ruling group was not an impermeable, unchanging élite rigidly marking itself off from the 'ruled' along purely ethnic lines" (*From Samarkhand to Sardis*, p. 124).

119. Sherwin-White and Kuhrt, *From Samarkhand to Sardis*, p. 38.

120. Austin, "Seleukids and Asia," p. 128; Erich S. Gruen, "Seleucid Royal Ideology," *SBLSP* 38 (1999): 24-53, 35-36.

architecture) and practices, including the celebration of a Persian religious festival by the Seleucid army.[121] For John Ma, this respect for the local and particular was part of a unifying strategy: "Diversity was subsumed within an imperial discourse where local multiplicity could be made to speak of unity and dominance."[122] That is to say, Hellenistic kings attempted to interact with subjects in different locales according to their own political and religious idioms, precisely in order to foster unity and strengthen their control in a diverse empire. This created a dynamic process of interaction, in which "local communities changed," but so did the kings.[123]

We see that the encounter between Hellenism and the cultures of the ancient Near Eastern world is from the start a complex phenomenon. Moreover, it is never simply a matter of one culture imposed on another, or even the encounter of two cultures. First, the cultures that we would identify as Hellenistic or Jewish are always already hybrid, always already the result of the encounters of multiple peoples and traditions.[124] The Greeks and Macedonians emerge out of a history of encounter, borrowing, and interaction, as do the Persians, as do the Jews. As anthropologist Eric Wolf observes, "Human populations construct their culture in interaction with each other, and not in isolation."[125] Second, this kind of interaction occurs not only prior to the encounter of Greeks and

---

121. Sherwin-White and Kuhrt, *From Samarkhand to Sardis*, p. 75.

122. John Ma, "Kings," in *A Companion to the Hellenistic World*, ed. Andrew Erskine (Oxford: Blackwell, 2003), pp. 177-95, 179.

123. Ma, "Kings," p. 182.

124. Sherwin-White and Kuhrt call attention to the "complicated inheritance from previous empires" (*From Samarkhand to Sardis*, p. 144). Moreover, as Pnina Werbner writes, "Culture as an analytic concept is always hybrid . . . , since it can be understood properly only as the historically negotiated creation of more or less coherent symbolic and social worlds." "Introduction: The Dialectics of Cultural Hybridity," in *Debating Cultural Hybridity: Multi-Cultural Identities and the Politics of Anti-Racism*, ed. Pnina Werbner and Tariq Modood (London: Zed Books, 1997), p. 15. On the construction of a coherent Hellenic identity out of originally diverse population groups and cultural elements, see the influential study of Jonathan Hall, *Hellenicity: Between Ethnicity and Culture* (Chicago: University of Chicago Press, 1999). Hall traces the construction and consciousness of Greek/Hellenic identity and its transformation from ethnic identity (based on fictive kinship) to cultural identity. Relevant to the present discussion of the encounter between Greek and Jewish culture, Hall gives examples of "Greek" cultural borrowing from ancient Near Eastern cultures (and even Semitic languages) as early as the eighth century BCE (pp. 106-7). He cites W. Burkert, *The Orientalizing Revolution: Near Eastern Influence on Greek Culture in the Early Archaic Age*, trans. M. E. Pinder and W. Burkert (Cambridge, MA: Harvard University Press, 1992). He argues that this influence does not make Greek culture less "Greek," but by the same token the influence of Greek culture did not negate the particularity of cultures of colonized peoples.

125. Eric R. Wolf, *Europe and the People without History* (Berkeley: University of California Press, 1982), p. ix.

Jews (i.e., in their interactions and recombinations with other population groups), but also in their encounters with one another.[126] They are now in some measure "mutually constituted," connected and interdependent, so that in their encounters with one another, there is give and take, and mutual transformation.[127] In these interactions emerge new identities, new traditions and practices, new worlds of meaning and value.[128]

Distinctive Identities

Yet even as we recognize the hybridity of these two worlds, we also see that a boundary, however porous and even mobile, persists between them.[129] Hellenic culture continues to be identified as such, even as it is reshaped in the encounter with other cultures. The ruling elite of the Hellenistic empires retain and continue to assert their identity as ethnic Macedonians and Greeks.[130] At the same time, the Jews remain a distinctive population group recognized as such by their Hellenistic rulers.[131] A modern definition of an "ethnic community"

126. Cf. Tcherikover, *Hellenistic Civilization,* p. 115.

127. Catherine Hall, "Histories, Empires and the Post-Colonial Moment," in *The Post-Colonial Question: Common Skies, Divided Horizons,* ed. Iain Chambers and Lidia Curti (London: Routledge, 1996), pp. 65-77, 70.

128. See Hans Rudolf-Wicker, "From Complex Culture to Cultural Complexity," in *Debating Cultural Hybridity: Multi-Cultural Identities and the Politics of Anti-Racism,* ed. Pnina Werbner and Tariq Modood (London: Zed Books, 1997), p. 40: "Because meanings are negotiated directly in (political, social and economic) practice, integration in analytical terms can no longer be described as the change from one cultural system to another. Instead, integration becomes a social field of interaction in itself, wherein processes of creolisation occur with increasing frequency to produce culture in the form of new habits, and from which emerge the categories of a new public sphere."

129. See Fredrik Barth, introduction to *Ethnic Groups and Boundaries: The Social Organization of Cultural Difference,* ed. Fredrik Barth (Bergen: Universitetsforlaget, 1969; repr., Long Grove, IL: Waveland, 1998), pp. 9-38, 14: "Continuity of ethnic units . . . depends on the maintenance of a boundary. The cultural features that signal the boundary may change, and the cultural characteristics of the members may likewise be transformed, indeed, even the organizational form of the group may change — yet the fact of continuing dichotomization between members and outsiders allows us to specify the nature of continuity, and investigate the changing cultural form and content." Barth states plainly that *boundary,* not *cultural content,* defines an ethnic group (p. 15).

130. Ma, "Kings," pp. 187-89.

131. On the identification of Jews as an "ethnic entity" in Greek and Roman sources, see John M. G. Barclay, *Jews in the Mediterranean Diaspora: From Alexander to Trajan (323 BCE–117 BCE)* (Berkeley: University of California Press, 1996), pp. 407-8. See also David Goodblatt, "From Judeans to Israel: Names of Jewish States in Antiquity," *JSJ* 29, no. 1 (1998): 1-36, 5, who defines *ethnos* as "a culturally homogenous group of people concentrated in a given terri-

can help us to understand how the Jews could remain a distinctive group in the face of their encounters with Hellenistic culture.[132] John Hutchinson and Anthony Smith define an "ethnic community" as "a named human population with myths of common ancestry, shared historical memories, one or more elements of common culture, a link with a homeland and a sense of solidarity among at least some of its members."[133] The Jews (or Judeans) of the second century clearly fit this definition. Their encounters with Hellenism and resulting hybrid culture do not negate their particular myths of ancestry, attachment

---

tory." I wish to acknowledge here Shaye Cohen's argument that one should not translate Ἰουδαῖοι as "Jews," but rather as "Judaeans," until middle or late second century BCE when it takes on more of a religious meaning and less of an "ethnic-geographic" meaning, to use Cohen's term (*Beginnings of Jewishness*, p. 70). Yet Cohen's distinguishing of three meanings of Ἰουδαῖοι, one a matter of geography and birth, one religious and cultural, and one political, does not account for overlap, i.e., the possibility that the same term can have signaled group belonging in a way that comprised more than one of these categories at a time. Theories of ethnicity have come to acknowledge that an ethnic group can be defined according to different diagnostic criteria at different times. This means that an ethnic community might be identified by geographic boundaries and common government in one period, and by "religious" criteria in another. Alternatively, the same name, in this case Ἰουδαῖοι, might identify a group for whom the criteria of belonging are contested at any one moment in time, or at the very least differently defined by different groups or individuals in the same period, some emphasizing one set of criteria (such as homeland and/or ancestry and kinship), others emphasizing another (such as circumcision, diet, and/or monotheistic worship of Yhwh). Finally, the diagnostic criteria that are determined by a group to mark off its boundaries of belonging are not the whole of what it means to belong to the group. They are simply that: diagnostic criteria. Cohen has identified a shift in boundaries, noting in particular the new possibility of converts to "Judaism" that apparently develops in the second century BCE. Yet it is important to recognize that boundary does not equal the sum of what it contains. We must acknowledge the degree to which religious belief and practices were an important component of the self-definitions of the ethnic group known to us as Ἰουδαῖοι prior to the Maccabean period, just as attachment to the homeland remained (and remains) an important feature for many Diaspora Jews after the second century BCE (with regard to the latter point, see Steve Mason, "Jews, Judaeans, Judaizing, Judaism: Problems of Categorization in Ancient History," *JSJ* 38 [2007]: 457-512; Mason identifies problems with Cohen's approach but argues that because *Ioudaios* is always an ethnic, and not a religious, designation in the ancient world, the translation "Judaean" is to be preferred). Moreover, even as the door opened for converts, the criterion of ancestry or kinship did not become irrelevant. The myths of common ancestry preserved in the ancestral narratives of the Hebrew Bible remained an important unifying element, and could be "claimed" by converts in a variety of ways. See Barclay, *Jews in the Mediterranean Diaspora*, pp. 408-13.

132. In contemporary literature on ethnicity, "Jews" tend to be regarded as a classic example of an *ethnie* or ethnic community. See, e.g., Anthony D. Smith, "Chosen Peoples: Why Ethnic Groups Survive," *Ethnic and Racial Studies* 15, no. 3 (1992): 440-49.

133. John Hutchinson and Anthony Smith, introduction to *Ethnicity*, Oxford Readers, ed. John Hutchinson and Anthony Smith (Oxford: Oxford University Press, 1996), p. 6.

to place, shared cultural and historical memories, distinctive practices, and other features of their shared identity.[134] What is important to note is that, while "elements of common culture" are a component of ethnic identity, "culture" and "ethnic community" or "ethnic group" are not coterminous. Culture may become "hybridized" even as the boundary between two (or more) groups remains firm. As Fredrik Barth observes, "Most of the cultural matter that at any time is associated with a human population is *not* constrained by this boundary; it can vary, be learnt, and change without any critical relation to the boundary maintenance of the ethnic group."[135] That is to say, the exchange and transformation of Jewish and Hellenic culture through cultural and imperial encounter do not necessarily signal the dissolution of either distinctive (ethnic) identity as such.[136]

Barth argues that it is not the entire content of a culture that marks its particular ethnic identity (in this case Jewish and Greek/"Hellenic"),[137] but only certain diacritical markers or criteria perceived or defined as relevant by those ascribing ethnic identity (whether from within or without).[138] For this reason he observes that the "drastic reduction of cultural differences between ethnic groups" that emerges in situations of cultural encounter and even influence "does not correlate in any simple way with a reduction in the organizational relevance of ethnic identities, or a breakdown in boundary-maintaining processes."[139] We will need to consider that the content, markers, and boundaries of what it means to be "Greek" and what it means to be "Jewish" will be defined and demarcated differently at different moments and in different places (and by

134. Aijaz Ahmad, "The Politics of Literary Postcoloniality," *Race and Class* 36, no. 3 (1995): 1-20, 14, 16. Cited in Werbner, "Introduction: The Dialectics of Cultural Hybridity," p. 21.

135. Barth, introduction to *Ethnic Groups and Boundaries*, p. 38.

136. Hall describes the resilience of Hellenic identity even in the face of intentional cultural mixing: "It has sometimes been suggested that Alexander wished to promote an almost biological miscegenation of populations, forging a new 'hybrid' Graeco-Makedonian-Persian élite by encouraging and even coercing intermarriage between his officers and the indigenous women of Asia. Whether or not this was his intention, Hellenicity refused to melt in the new cauldron of the Hellenistic world" (*Hellenicity*, pp. 220-21). Fergus Millar says of the Jewish reception of Greek elements: "The culture of Judaea and Jerusalem thus exhibits a profound continuity with the pre-Greek past and an equally undeniable absorption of Greek elements." "The Problem of Hellenistic Syria," in *Hellenism in the East: The Interaction of Greek and Non-Greek Civilizations from Syria to Central Asia after Alexander*, ed. Amélie Kuhrt and Susan Sherwin-White (Berkeley: University of California Press, 1987), pp. 110-33, 110.

137. On the relation between Greek identity and "Hellenism as a cultural phenomenon" in this period, Friedman writes, "It might be argued that Hellenism was a kind of textualization of Greek identity, an institutionalization of a corpus of knowledge and practices by a people who already experienced a distance to their identity" ("Notes on Culture and Identity," pp. 37-38).

138. Barth, introduction to *Ethnic Groups and Boundaries*, pp. 15, 35.

139. Barth, introduction to *Ethnic Groups and Boundaries*, pp. 32-33.

different individuals and groups), sometimes broadly overlapping, at other times more clearly opposed or exclusive.[140]

John M. G. Barclay, in his essay "Using and Refusing: Jewish Identity Strategies under the Hegemony of Hellenism," describes this process as one of negotiation.[141] He characterizes Jews under Hellenistic rule as negotiators of culture who consciously employ strategies of both adaptation (or fusion) and resistance.[142] He further locates these negotiations within arenas of power, attending to the realities of empires and their armies, local politics, economics, and social status, both within the local community and within broader networks.[143] The result of these negotiations is a "continuous process of self-refashioning" in which Jewish identity and its authorizing traditions are continually reconstructed and redefined.[144]

The texts studied in this volume clearly exhibit this process of negotiation. None reject Hellenism outright.[145] As early as the third century BCE the author(s) of the Book of Watchers helped to construct a new tradition (rooted, of course, in already existing traditions and at the same time claiming greater antiquity than the Mosaic traditions; see ch. 8) that emphasized divine order and rejected key elements of the cultural legacy associated with the Hellenistic kings while at the same time appropriating material from this same cultural repertoire (see ch. 1).[146] Other Jews writing in this era could be critical of the imperial powers but advocate neither wholesale rejection of Hellenistic culture nor

140. Jonathan Hall points out that core-periphery models of acculturation sometimes fail "to take account of the fact that the nature, intensity and perceptions of encounters between Greek and indigenous populations varied significantly from area to area" (*Hellenicity*, p. 121). For an example of significant variation even within one period and region, see Hall's discussion of cultural and ethnic identities in Ptolemaic Egypt (pp. 222-23).

141. John M. G. Barclay, "Using and Refusing: Jewish Identity Strategies under the Hegemony of Hellenism," in *Ethos und Identität: Einheit und Vielfalt des Judentums in hellenistisch-römischer Zeit*, ed. Matthias Konradt and Ulrike Steinert (Paderborn: Ferdinand Schöningh, 2002), pp. 13-25.

142. Barclay, "Using and Refusing," pp. 16-17.

143. Barclay, "Using and Refusing," pp. 17-18.

144. Barclay, "Using and Refusing," pp. 18, 15.

145. Seth Schwartz argues that the search for opposition to Hellenism in literature of this period is "largely misguided"; he calls for "a more subtle search for cultural reorientation." *Imperialism and Jewish Society, 200 B.C.E. to 640 C.E.* (Princeton: Princeton University Press, 2001), p. 31. For much of the literature, I agree with Schwartz, though it is clear that the trope of Judaism versus Hellenism did some work for our authors, as I argue below.

146. David Jackson identifies in the Book of the Watchers an overarching pattern of regularity and deviance, the former corresponding to the divinely established order and the latter exemplifying sin and evil. Jackson further identifies three paradigms of deviance in the Book of the Watchers — ethnic, cultural, and cosmic. *Enochic Judaism: Three Defining Paradigm Exemplars* (London: T. & T. Clark, 2004).

of the imperial powers themselves.[147] We also saw in chapter 2 that at the turn of the century, elite Jews in Jerusalem sought to carve out a moderate accommodationist position that cooperated with the Seleucid empire in the political realm but at the same time claimed a high level of continuity with ancestral traditions and identified both the city of Jerusalem and the Jerusalem cult as key loci of Jewish identity.[148]

Asserting a Threatened Identity

Yet, as discussed above, in the years preceding the persecution by Antiochus IV, some members of the Jewish elite in Jerusalem sought to refashion not only their own identities but also that of Jerusalem to conform more closely with Hellenistic cultural practices and ideals in order to gain attendant economic, political, and social advantages both locally and within the broader network of the Seleucid empire. The same desire for economic, political, and social advantages would lead yet again to the sale of the high priesthood in 172 BCE (2 Macc 4:24; see ch. 4), and would culminate in violence. As far as we know, up to this point the cult had remained a preserve of particular Jewish identity.[149] Yet Seleucid policy had brought temple administration under the purview of the empire. If at first this meant only (!) access to revenues and the sale of the high priesthood, it would open the door to imperial efforts to impose dramatic changes in the operation of the cult itself.

Indeed, these changes, and the persecution that accompanied them, would create a new moment of threat and as a result elicit new constructions of Jewish identity. Those resisting religious assimilation in the face of threatening impe-

---

147. Philip R. Davies identifies in Daniel "an unresolved tension between qualified approval [of imperial powers] and outright condemnation, between obedience and resistance, between co-operation and opposition." "Daniel in the Lion's Den," in *Images of Empire*, ed. Loveday Alexander (Sheffield: Sheffield Academic Press, 1991), pp. 160-78, 161. Chapters 1–6 provide models of selective cooperation and resistance. In response to radically new circumstances (the persecution), chs. 7–12 call only for resistance. As a whole, the Hebrew and Aramaic book of Daniel seeks to persuade those who have in the recent past occupied an accommodationist stance toward the Seleucid regime to abandon strategies of cooperation for outright resistance and rejection of the current empire. See Anathea Portier-Young, "Languages of Identity and Obligation: Daniel as Bilingual Book," *VT* 60, no. 1 (2010): 98-115.

148. Those who assisted in the framing of the *programma* issued by Antiochus III exemplify Jews who sought to accommodate the ruling power while also claiming ties to ancestral traditions, including (and perhaps especially) ancestral religion.

149. Lester Grabbe, "The Jews and Hellenization: Hengel and His Critics," in *Second Temple Studies III: Studies in Politics, Class, and Material Culture,* ed. Philip R. Davies and John M. Halligan (London: Sheffield Academic Press, 2002), pp. 52-66, 66.

rial encounter, especially the persecution, would invest places, traditions, symbols, and practices of the past with new meaning and value while also forging a new tradition, new symbols, and a new identity. Emphasis on elements of a particular "Jewish" identity thus served as a cornerstone for resistance, particularly in the face of a persecution that sought to erase the very traditions, practices, and identity markers that formed such a core component of Jewish identity in this period. From this perspective, it would appear that asserting and (re)defining particular Jewish identity as distinct and separate from Hellenistic "culture" and identity emerges most strongly as a response to perceptions of threat originating with the Hellenistic imperial powers and those who support them.

As I noted above, in the years following the persecution (and perhaps to some extent during the persecution, though we cannot know this for certain), the crisis came to be defined by some as a conflict between "Hellenism" and "Judaism," partly owing to causal connections drawn between the actions of the "Hellenizers" or "Reformers" (our modern terms) and those of Antiochus IV, and partly owing to interpretations of Antiochus's persecution as a program of forced Hellenization. I argued that the Hellenistic kings never sought simply to Hellenize the world they conquered, and we should thus be cautious of attributing to Antiochus's persecution motives of cultural (or religious) evangelism. Yet John Ma has shown that Hellenistic kings and other ruling elites could deploy "Greekness" as a marker of differential status and tool of dominance.[150] Ma indicates that while Hellenistic kings typically sought, for strategic reasons, to situate their own claims to power within local "traditions of legitimacy," they could also play "ethno-power games."[151] The rules of these games equated "Greek" (i.e., "Hellenic" or "Macedonian") with power. In these ethno-power games, respect for and interaction with local, non-Greek traditions and mores could be offered as privileges bestowed on subject peoples, reinforcing the structures of imperial power while also promoting a myth of autonomy. At the same time, such outward signs of Greekness as language, style of dress, public architecture, and religious iconography could readily become symbolic assertions of power and domination. Thus, for Ma, "The background to interaction remained the awareness of the king's foreignness, and Greekness, shared by ruler and ruled and sometimes explicitly stated. . . . The details show the deftness, and the symbolical violence, which the kings could deploy to make domination visible."[152]

150. In this regard, Gruen's assessment that "the actions of Antiochus IV Epiphanes in Judaea . . . far from representing Seleucid ideology of rule . . . were at drastic variance with it," appears not to be entirely accurate ("Seleucid Royal Ideology," p. 47).

151. Ma, "Kings," p. 188.

152. Ma, "Kings," p. 188. As one example, Ma demonstrates that Alexander rejected continuity with local tradition in favor of rupture when he established himself as king in Sardis. By

With this awareness in view, we can see how resistance to the empire and rejection of its militarism, structures of exploitation, and/or claims to sovereignty could and did (in particular circumstances) entail concomitant rejection of elements of Hellenism — in particular those elements of Hellenistic culture and markers of Hellenistic identity that were deployed as symbols of power over the Jews and tools for their domination.[153] "Hellenism" could then become a trope for the structures and symbols of imperial power and domination that revoked the Jews' freedom to live according to their traditions, denied the sovereignty of their god, and threatened the lives of those Jews who would remain faithful to their ancestral religion. As such it was to be resisted by those who believed that Jewish identity was defined by its particularity, including the particularity of its religious tradition and worship of Yhwh. Yet it was never the case that second-century Jews — even those who resisted Antiochus's persecution — rejected all things Greek. I stated above that Jewish, like Hellenistic, was always already hybrid. This did not make it less Jewish.[154] Those who resisted the "Hellenizers" and later the persecution could reject the level of intentional Hellenization advocated by Jason and the other "Reformers." They could reject Greek symbols and tools of domination, and they could reject the empire itself. Yet they would inevitably retain in varying degrees aspects of the hybrid identity and hybrid culture that resulted from their ongoing interaction with Hellenistic culture.

---

constructing a shrine to Zeus Olympios, the patron deity of the Macedonians, in the Lydian palace on the acropolis of Sardis, he publicly associated his kingship with Macedonian ethnicity and the authorizing patronage of the Macedonian god (p. 189).

153. Cf. Grabbe, "Jews and Hellenization," p. 62.

154. Cf. the remarks of Grabbe: "To be 'Hellenized' did not mean to cease to be a Jew." Regarding Jason he says, "The fact that some Jews may have judged him an apostate is irrelevant to the question of his own self-designation or Jewish identity" ("Jews and Hellenization," p. 65). Doran writes in a similar vein: "Rather than use the framework of the sources — Jason is a nasty Hellenizer, Judas Maccabeus a pious Torah observer — I want to allow Jason and Judas to coexist in Jerusalem as Judeans" ("The High Cost of a Good Education," p. 111).

CHAPTER 4

Re-creating the Empire: The Sixth Syrian War, Jason's Revolt, and the Reconquest of Jerusalem

Between the years 170 and 168 BCE the Seleucid and Ptolemaic empires engaged one another in the so-called Sixth Syrian War. Like all of the Syrian wars, its objective was control of the strategically located and resource-rich province of Coele-Syria and Phoenicia, to which Judea belonged.[1] Roman intervention ended the war and dictated new terms in the regional balance of power. The final vision of the book of Daniel reveals and interprets these Seleucid interactions with the Ptolemaic and Roman empires as part of the "invisible" realities shaping conditions in Judea in the years immediately preceding the persecution (Dan 10–12).[2] Like Daniel, the epitomator conveys a collective awareness of these dynamics in the form of a vision report (2 Macc 5:2-4). This near-forty-day vision of cavalry charging through the air above Jerusalem immediately fol-

---

1. On the region's strategic and economic importance, see Heinz Heinen, "The Syrian-Egyptian Wars and the New Kingdoms of Asia-Minor," in *The Cambridge Ancient History*, vol. 7, pt. 1, *The Hellenistic World*, ed. A. E. Astin, F. W. Walbank, M. W. Fredriksen, and R. M. Ogilvie (Cambridge: Cambridge University Press, 1984), pp. 412-45, 440-44; Édouard Will, "The Succession to Alexander," in *The Cambridge Ancient History*, vol. 7, pt. 1, *The Hellenistic World*, ed. A. E. Astin, F. W. Walbank, M. W. Fredriksen, and R. M. Ogilvie, pp. 23-61, 41; and Getzel M. Cohen, *The Hellenistic Settlements in Syria, the Red Sea Basin, and North Africa* (Berkeley: University of California Press, 2006), pp. 32-33. On the terminology for the region, see pp. 35-41.

2. Our sources also allow us to glimpse some of the interactions with Judea's neighbors in the province of Coele-Syria and Phoenicia. This part of the story deserves more attention than it receives here or in much of the secondary literature. New epigraphic evidence continues to enrich our understanding of the region, but a comprehensive history of the province in the Ptolemaic and Seleucid periods remains a desideratum. For an important treatment of one region within the province, see John Grainger, *Hellenistic Phoenicia* (Oxford: Clarendon, 1991). Helpful perspective on the interactions between cities and the royal administration in the neighboring region of Syria can be found in John Grainger, *The Cities of Seleukid Syria* (Oxford: Oxford University Press, 1990).

lows the report that Antiochus IV was campaigning in Egypt (5:1). Positioned in this way, the vision evokes the distant battles being waged between the Seleucid and Egyptian armies, making visible these hidden realities and asserting their immediate relevance for the people of Jerusalem. These battles were being fought "over" Jerusalem inasmuch as the city was part of the disputed territory of Coele-Syria and Phoenicia. The vision report further testifies to a belief in supernatural armies whose battles both mirrored those on earth and affected their outcomes. War was "in the air" as surely as it was "on the ground." Again like Daniel, the epitomator believed that both dimensions had serious consequences for the people of Judea.[3]

Alongside these battles, 2 Maccabees recounts a series of incidents that reveal both the increasing encroachment of imperial power in the internal affairs of Judea in this period and early stirrings of resistance, including Jason's revolt in the year 169 or 168 BCE. What happened next defies easy telling. Following Jason's revolt, Antiochus slaughtered many thousands of Jerusalemites and sold many thousands into slavery. He reconquered Judea's capital, inaugurating a regime of terror that would culminate in the religious persecution of 167 BCE. As stated above, international imperial politics form the context for Antiochus's interventions in Judea during this period, and this claim in itself is not new. But the link between Antiochus's international agenda and his actions in Judea has not been properly understood. Neither has the severity of Antiochus's interventions or the logic that guided them.

Lacking precedent for some of his actions, particularly the persecution (see further chs. 5 and 6), scholars have proposed various explanations. Two of them require mentioning here, as they receive attention later in this chapter: (1) Antiochus referred to himself as Epiphanes, or "[god] Manifest." Some of his behaviors led observers to invent a different nickname, substituting one letter and calling the king not Epiphanes but Epimanes, "Madman." Perhaps, some scholars have suggested, he really was insane, and his actions had no rational basis.[4] (2) If he was not entirely insane, perhaps he was enraged, venting shame and fury on a city of scapegoats after a humiliating defeat in Egypt. Both of these explanations abandon the attempt to discover the logic in Antiochus's policies in Judea.

In this and the following chapters, I argue that, while resistance rendered

3. Without interpretation, the meaning of the vision — like the outcomes and consequences of the battles being fought far away — remained unclear. The people therefore "asked" (God) that the epiphany portend for the good (2 Macc 5:4).

4. For a list of proponents and opponents of this position, see Christian Habicht, "The Seleucids and Their Rivals," in *The Cambridge Ancient History,* vol. 8, *Rome and the Mediterranean to 133 BCE,* ed. A. E. Astin, F. W. Walbank, M. W. Fredriksen, and R. M. Ogilvie (Cambridge: Cambridge University Press, 2000), pp. 324-87, 345n74.

Antiochus's actions in Judea ineffective, those actions were nonetheless guided by logic.[5] The logic was that of the re-creation of empire through reconquest. As I explain in chapters 5 and 6, it was also the logic of repression and control, unmaking and making a world through techniques of state terror. This twisted logic justified a rule that repudiated justice, aiming at creation through destruction, order through terror, and glory through shaming. The apocalyptic writers whose works I turn to in Part Three sought to expose and counter this logic.

Preparing for War

I noted earlier that at some point during his reign — we are not certain why or when — Seleucus IV had ceased paying scheduled war indemnities to Rome. His successor Antiochus IV inherited the debt. Not wishing to make an enemy of Rome, Antiochus paid the outstanding balance in 173 BCE, perhaps finally eliminating this longstanding drain on Seleucid imperial funds (Livy 42.6.7).[6]

5. My aim in this chapter and the ones that follow is not to offer an exhaustive reconstruction of events and circumstances surrounding the persecution, but rather to highlight features relevant for understanding the conditions and objects of resistance for the texts studied in this volume, with special attention to Seleucid hegemony and domination. Detailed scholarly reconstructions can be found in Elias Bickerman, *The God of the Maccabees: Studies on the Meaning and Origin of the Maccabean Revolt*, trans. Horst Moehring (Leiden: Brill, 1979), originally published as *Der Gott der Makkabäer: Untersuchungen über Sinn und Ursprung der makkabäischen Erhebung* (Berlin: Schocken Verlag, 1937); Victor Tcherikover, *Hellenistic Civilization and the Jews*, trans. S. Applebaum (Philadelphia: Jewish Publication Society, 1959; repr. with a preface by John J. Collins, Peabody, MA: Hendrickson, 1999); Klaus Bringmann, *Hellenistische Reform und Religionsverfolgung in Judäa: Eine Untersuchung zur jüdisch-hellenistischen Geschichte (175-163 v. Chr.)* (Göttingen: Vandenhoeck & Ruprecht, 1983); Jonathan A. Goldstein, *I Maccabees: A New Translation with Introduction and Commentary*, Anchor Bible 41 (Garden City, NY: Doubleday, 1976), pp. 104-74. An account aimed at a wider audience can be found in Daniel Harrington, *The Maccabean Revolt: Anatomy of a Biblical Revolution* (Wilmington, DE: Michael Glazier, 1988). For chronologies of the events, see Goldstein, *I Maccabees*, pp. 161-73; and Bickerman, *God of the Maccabees*, pp. 6-8, 101-11. Major primary sources for the historical reconstruction of these events include Daniel and 1 and 2 Maccabees.

6. According to the original terms of the treaty, the final payment to Rome would have been due during the reign of Seleucus IV, in 177 BCE. Yet according to Livy 42.6 that payment was delayed until 173. Two years after he succeeded to the throne, Antiochus IV made payment to Rome via a delegation led by Apollonius, who offered apologies for the delay along with a gift of costly gold vases weighing five hundred Roman pounds (the Roman pound was approximately 324 grams; see Michael Hewsom Crawford, *Roman Republican Coinage* [Cambridge: Cambridge University Press, 1974], pp. 590-92). Whether or not this was the final payment is still open for debate. According to Livy, Apollonius apologized that the *stipendium* had not been paid, and stated that he had brought it in full (*omne*). But whether *stipendium* refers here to the

But Antiochus was now preparing for war with the Ptolemaic empire, whose ruling family, the Lagids, sought to reclaim the province of Coele-Syria and Phoenicia (Polyb. 28.20.9). To defend his claim to the province, Antiochus planned a preemptive strike against Egypt. A successful campaign would require a strong navy. To this end, as Antiochus began moving his troops southward, he was also building ships. Traveling through the contested province of Coele-Syria and Phoenicia, he was able not only to assess and strengthen loyalties in the province,[7] but also to take advantage of Phoenician naval technology for building and outfitting his fleet.[8] The Seleucids had taken advantage of Phoenician shipbuilding at least once before, in 191 BCE, when Antiochus III sought to rebuild his own tattered navy after a crushing defeat by the Romans and their ally Eumenes II off the coast of the Seleucid seaport Corycus (Livy 37.8).[9] While the treaty of Apamea placed severe restrictions on Seleucid naval

entire debt or only an annual installment is unclear. According to 2 Maccabees, Antiochus was still struggling to make payments of tribute to Rome in 165 BCE (2 Macc 8:10, 36). See further Daniel R. Schwartz, *2 Maccabees,* CEJL (Berlin: Walter de Gruyter, 2008), pp. 544-45. Regardless of whether the indemnities continued so late into Antiochus's reign, the passage in Livy calls our attention to the structures of Roman domination and patronage to which Antiochus himself was subject. As John D. Grainger puts it, after Magnesia and Apamea "Rome was clearly the one and only superpower in the known world"; see *The Roman War of Antiochos the Great* (Leiden: Brill, 2002), p. 351. Yet Grainger reads Apollonius's apology as "ironic," noting that Rome had never complained about the delay. Based on earlier arguments set forth by E. Paltiel ("The Treaty of Apamea and the Later Seleucids," *Antichthon* 13 [1979]: 30-41), he maintains that the treaty would have been binding only on Antiochus III, such that "Seleukos IV and Antiochos IV were thus quite at liberty to recruit where they wished, to build ships and collect elephants, or to fail to implement the details of the treaty" (*Roman War,* p. 353). Against this view, see M. Gwyn Morgan, "The Perils of Schematism: Polybius, Antiochus Epiphanes, and the 'Day of Eleusis,'" *Historia: Zeitschrift für Alte Geschichte* 39, no. 1 (1990): 37-76, 48. Dov Gera calls attention to a later passage in Livy (42.29.5-6) that highlights Antiochus's independent agency at this time. Even as he dispensed with the obligation of indemnities and mollified the Romans with vases, he was rebuilding his navy and preparing for war against Egypt. *Judaea and Mediterranean Politics, 219-161 B.C.E.* (Leiden: Brill, 1998), pp. 119-21. Morgan emphasizes, however, that Antiochus gave Rome no reason to doubt his protestations of loyalty ("Perils," p. 51).

7. Peter Franz Mittag, *Antiochos IV. Epiphanes: Eine politische Biographie* (Berlin: Akademie Verlag, 2006), p. 155.

8. On Phoenician naval technology, see María Eugenia Aubet, *The Phoenicians and the West: Politics, Colonies, and Trade,* trans. Mary Turton (Cambridge: Cambridge University Press, 2001), pp. 166-82. On ancient shipbuilding technology more broadly, with excellent bibliography, see Seán McGrail, "Sea Transport, Part 1: Ships and Navigation," in *The Oxford Handbook of Engineering and Technology in the Classical World,* ed. John Peter Oleson (Oxford: Oxford University Press, 2008), pp. 606-37. On Hellenistic naval technology and the conduct of war, see Philip de Souza, "Greek Warfare and Fortification," in *The Oxford Handbook of Engineering and Technology in the Classical World,* ed. John Peter Oleson (Oxford: Oxford University Press, 2008), pp. 673-90.

9. At various times, the other Hellenistic empires also availed themselves of Phoenician

activity, nearly twenty years later Antiochus IV was ready to reassert Seleucid naval power to defend his claim to Coele-Syria and Phoenicia.

The central hub of Phoenician shipbuilding was the city of Tyre.[10] In 173 or 172 BCE, Antiochus IV staged a visit to Tyre during their quadrennial games in honor of the Greek god Heracles, who was locally identified with the Phoenician deity Melqart.[11] The involvement of Antiochus (and, as was likely, some of his own army) in the Tyrian games allowed him to make a public show of Seleucid wealth and might, rouse the morale of his troops, and engage local inhabitants in the spirit of competition and spectacle that was such a central component of the Hellenistic ideology of war.[12] The event had more than local significance. It was widely publicized, and a delegation of citizens from Antioch-in-Jerusalem represented their city as spectators to the games (2 Macc 4:19).[13] Jason had sent these delegates with a contribution for the sacrifices to

---

shipbuilding, as well as timber from Lebanon (Diod. 18.59; 18.63.6; 19.58.2). These natural and human resources were one reason the Hellenistic kings fought each other for control of Coele-Syria and Phoenicia. See James Ellis Taylor, "Seleucid Rule in Palestine" (Ph.D. diss., Duke University, 1979), p. 8.

10. Aubet, *Phoenicians*, p. 175.

11. For the date, see Mittag, *Antiochos IV. Epiphanes*, p. 154. On the identification of Heracles and Melqart, see Corinne Bonnet, *Melqart: Cultes et mythes de l'Héraclès tyrien en Méditerranée* (Leuven: Peeters, 1988). The association with the local deity Melqart may have called to mind for Judean observers traditions in Israel's Scriptures concerning the classical prophet Elijah's opposition to the cult of Baal practiced by Jezebel (herself from Sidon, 1 Kgs 16:31) and Ahab in the northern kingdom, even though this Baal and Melqart were likely not identical (on which question, see Mark S. Smith, *The Early History of God: Yahweh and the Other Deities in Ancient Israel,* 2nd ed. [Grand Rapids: Eerdmans, 2002], pp. 68-71). Quadrennial: the word in 2 Maccabees would literally be rendered "quinquennial," but the counting system was inclusive, such that English usage demands the translation "quadrennial." See Jonathan A. Goldstein, *II Maccabees: A New Translation with Introduction and Commentary,* Anchor Bible 41A (New York: Doubleday, 1983), pp. 521-22; Schwartz, *2 Maccabees,* p. 226.

12. Mittag writes: "Die Teilnahme an den lokalen Kultfeiern in Tyros demonstrierte die Verbundenheit des Königs mit der Stadt und diente der Sicherung der seleukidischen Herrschaft" (*Antiochos IV. Epiphanes,* p. 155). Cf. this rationale for state-sponsored spectacles in Argentina in 1979: "Public performances, sport events, civil-military parades, and cultural competitions are in themselves very important means to influence the population, and these resources must be used permanently in the fight against subversion." Antonius C. G. M. Robben, *Political Violence and Trauma in Argentina* (Philadelphia: University of Pennsylvania Press, 2005), p. 311, quoting CJE (Comando en Jefe del Ejército) 1979 anexo 9:7.

13. See Robert Doran, "The High Cost of a Good Education," in *Hellenism in the Land of Israel,* ed. John J. Collins and Gregory E. Sterling (Notre Dame: University of Notre Dame Press, 2001), pp. 94-115, 108-9. Getzel Cohen argues that these were not native Jerusalemites, but rather Phoenician colonists who had settled in Jerusalem. "The 'Antiochenes in Jerusalem.' Again," in *Pursuing the Text: Studies in Honor of Ben Zion Wacholder on the Occasion of His Seventieth Birthday,* ed. John C. Reeves and John Kampen (Sheffield: Sheffield Academic Press, 1994), pp. 243-59, 252. But the epitomator's interest in the delegates' desire to use the money for a purpose

Heracles that would have formed a central part of the festivities. The epitomator takes pains to communicate that while Jason had not hesitated to involve his envoys in the cult of Heracles, the delegates themselves judged it "unfitting."[14] They conveyed the money to Antiochus on condition that it not be used for sacrifices. It was allocated instead for the building of warships (4:20). The anecdote sheds light on strategies of negotiation between participation in Hellenistic cultural forms and fidelity to native religious praxis. The solution — contributing funds to the imperial war chest — highlights just how fraught those negotiations could be.

According to the epitomator, after the games in Tyre, Antiochus's tour of Coele-Syria and Phoenicia brought him to Judea, where he visited the newly "founded" city of Antioch-in-Jerusalem. He was received in a grand and lavish (μεγαλομερῶς) torch-lit procession by Jason and "the city"; the citizens of Antioch-in-Jerusalem greeted their royal benefactor with shouts of acclaim (4:22). This, too, was a kind of spectacle. Such processions, as Angelos Chaniotis argues, were "a complex propagandistic enterprise conveying more than one message: legitimacy of rule, divine protection, affluence, and power."[15] But there were multiple actors in the performance, and the local leadership also had a stake in its successful execution. Like the games at Tyre, the carefully orchestrated procession that marked the king's visit to Jerusalem was a spectacular drama that conveyed a message of beneficence and loyalty, publicly performing an exchange of honors that would provide a foundation for continued mutual support as Jason pursued his ambitions in Judea and as Antiochus prepared for war abroad.

But despite his show of support for the king, Jason would soon lose his foothold in Jerusalem. In fact, Jason's earlier purchase of Jerusalem's high priesthood (4:7-9) had set a precedent that would precipitate his fall from power (4:26).[16] Jason had gained the high-priestly office by promising to increase Judea's annual tribute to its Seleucid king to 360 talents; he also provided 80 talents of "other revenue" and 150 talents for the privileges concerning the gymnasium, ephebate, and citizen rolls (4:8-9). As Antiochus continued his

---

they deemed more fitting (καθήκειν) than sacrifice to Heracles suggests that the epitomator thought they were not Phoenician but Jewish.

14. Lester Grabbe speculates that Jason himself likely did not intend the money for sacrifices to Heracles. "The Hellenistic City of Jerusalem," in *Jews in the Hellenistic and Roman Cities*, ed. John Bartlett (London: Routledge, 2002), pp. 6-21, 12.

15. Angelos Chaniotis, *War in the Hellenistic World: A Social and Cultural History* (Oxford: Blackwell, 2005), p. 74.

16. The epitomator records this irony as yet another example of fitting reversal. Cf. James C. VanderKam, *From Joshua to Caiaphas: High Priests after the Exile* (Minneapolis: Fortress, 2004), p. 203.

preparations for war, he welcomed further promises of increased revenue to fund the invasion he planned.[17] In 172 BCE, Jason sent Menelaus, brother of the (former?) temple administrator Simon (3:4), to pay the annual tribute to Antiochus IV (4:23). Menelaus, however, promised to pay Antiochus an additional 300 talents of silver in exchange for the high priestly office for himself (4:24). While the epitomator does not specify whether this was a promised increase to the annual tribute or another type of payment, the verb εὐτάκτει ("to pay regularly" 4:27) suggests that it was meant to be a recurring payment. If in fact the recurring payment was an increase in annual tribute — a burden born by the Judean people, not its high priestly leader — Menelaus's promise nearly doubled that tribute from 360 to 660 talents (4:24). Recalling that the annual indemnity owed to Rome by the Seleucid king, who commanded the resources of an entire empire, had been 1000 talents, this sum appears to be an enormous, indeed impossible burden for the comparatively tiny Judea to bear.[18] Antiochus did not foresee that Menelaus would be unable to raise the promised funds. Instead, he accepted his offer and transferred the high priesthood to Menelaus (4:24-27).[19]

The office of high priest had been sold once before. But by appointing Menelaus, Antiochus violated traditional Jewish cultic practice in another way. James VanderKam observes that "Menelaus is the first recorded high priest in the Second-Temple period to belong to a different family than the one directly descended from Joshua, the first high priest."[20] Ambition, greed, and the convergence of local and imperial politics had already made of Judea's most sacred office a saleable commodity. Now with Menelaus's appointment, the centuries-old tradition of a hereditary (and Zadokite) high priesthood in Judea came to an end.[21] It was a major step in Seleucid encroachment into the operation of the cult itself. It coincided with an increased and unsustainable financial burden on the people of Judea.

17. On budgetary aspects of Hellenistic warfare, see Chaniotis, *War in the Hellenistic World*, pp. 115-21.

18. Mittag calls the 300 talents alone an "enorme Summe" (*Antiochos IV. Epiphanes*, p. 248).

19. For the career of Menelaus and an assessment of the evidence for his role in events to follow, including the drafting and promulgation of Antiochus's edict of 167 BCE, see Mittag, *Antiochos IV. Epiphanes*, pp. 247-77.

20. VanderKam, *From Joshua to Caiaphas*, p. 203. Fergus Millar speculates that the office may have been subject to royal appointment for some time already, with attendant opportunities for disagreement about who should occupy the office. "The Background to the Maccabean Revolution: Reflections on Martin Hengel's 'Judaism and Hellenism,'" *JJS* 29, no. 1 (1978): 1-21, 8.

21. Note, however, that Josephus identifies Menelaus as a brother of Jason, and therefore also an Oniad directly descended from Joshua (*A.J.* 12.238).

The Akra

Unsurprisingly, Menelaus failed to deliver the promised funds to Antiochus, despite the repeated demands of the king's agent Sostratus, commander of the citadel in Jerusalem (4:27-28). This latter detail, which the epitomator provides almost incidentally, calls attention to the visible and invisible structures and strategies of Seleucid domination in the years preceding the persecution. The Seleucids had a military presence at the heart of Jerusalem, perhaps close to the temple itself (1 Macc 13:52), though its exact location is a matter of debate.[22] Our Greek sources call this citadel the Akra. Lee I. Levine notes that "the Akra seems to have had an enormous impact on the city not only militarily, but also physically, politically, and socially."[23] It was first and foremost a mechanism of control.[24] Under the Hellenistic empires, one measure of a city's freedom was the presence or absence of a garrison; the words *autonomos* (αὐτόνομος, "possessing civic freedom") and "ungarrisoned" (ἀφρούρητος) could be virtually synonymous (e.g., Diod. 15.38.2).[25] In this vein, Polybius characterizes the motivations of the allied council of Corinth when they declared war on the Aetolians in 220 BCE: they desired freedom to follow their own laws (πολιτείαις καὶ νόμοις χρωμένους τοῖς πατρίοις), freedom from paying tribute (ἀφορολόγητους), and freedom from military occupation (ἀφρούρητους 4.25.7).[26] The Akra reminded the inhabitants of Jerusalem and the surrounding countryside that, despite the privileges granted by Antiochus III, Judea was not fully *autonomos*. As a tangible testament to imperial domination over and within Judea, the physical structure of the Akra visibly competed with the temple as a locus of governance, power,

---

22. On its location, see Bezalel Bar-Kochva, *Judas Maccabeus: The Jewish Struggle against the Seleucids* (Cambridge: Cambridge University Press, 1989), pp. 445-64. Lee I. Levine posits two successive fortresses in Jerusalem, one dating to the Ptolemaic period and also referred to in the present verse, and another built by Antiochus in 168 BCE. *Jerusalem: Portrait of the City in the Second Temple Period (538 B.C.E.–70 C.E.)* (Philadelphia: Jewish Publication Society, 2002), pp. 76-77, based on 1 Macc 1:33-36. But Bar-Kochva demonstrates the likely continuity of the earlier and later fortresses (*Judas Maccabeus*, pp. 462-65). On its functions, see Joseph Sievers, "Jerusalem, the Akra, and Josephus," in *Josephus and the History of the Greco-Roman Period: Essays in Memory of Morton Smith*, ed. Joseph Sievers and Fausto Parente (Leiden: Brill, 1994), pp. 195-209, 202-9.

23. Levine, *Jerusalem*, p. 75.

24. Chaniotis, *War in the Hellenistic World*, p. 88; Bar-Kochva, *Judas Maccabeus*, p. 465; Grainger, *Cities of Seleukid Syria*, 62, 67. Cf. Nigel Pollard, *Soldiers, Cities, and Civilians in Roman Syria* (Ann Arbor: University of Michigan Press, 2000), p. 37.

25. Angelos Chaniotis, "Foreign Soldiers — Native Girls? Constructing and Crossing Boundaries in Hellenistic Cities with Foreign Garrisons," in *Army and Power in the Ancient World*, ed. Angelos Chaniotis and Peter Ducrey (Stuttgart: Franz Steiner Verlag, 2002), pp. 99-114, 101.

26. For the same triad of freedoms, see also Polyb. 4.84.3; 18.46.5, 15; cf. 15.18.11; 15.24.2.

and meaning-making.[27] These twin loci of power, in Joseph Sievers's words, "[gave] Jerusalem at times the character of a divided city."[28] The fortifications of the Akra and the armed, policing presence of its soldiers were a daily reminder that Seleucid power rested on the might of its military. The threat of violence always lurked beneath a strained and superficial peace.[29]

There were economic and social ramifications as well.[30] Sievers has demonstrated that the Seleucid Akra in Jerusalem would have controlled a portion of the countryside and derived revenues from it.[31] The impact on the inhabitants of Judea was significant.[32] The land controlled by the soldiers in the Akra would have formerly belonged to native residents. As Victor Tcherikover observes, maintaining a self-sufficient garrison in the Akra "meant confiscation of the agricultural property of the citizens, the introduction of new settlers into their homes, deeds of violence and rape upon the former inhabitants, the imposition of taxes upon them and sometimes even their expulsion from the town."[33] The book of Daniel describes the role of the Seleucid king in establishing this type of military settlement, also known as a *katoikia*, and the system of royal patronage on which it was founded: "He will cause people of a foreign god to occupy walled-fortresses. He will heap rewards on all who endorse him, letting them rule over the many, dividing land for a price" (Dan 11:39). While the precise nature of governance exercised from the Akra is unclear, it is clear that the Akra was an important link between local power structures and those of the empire, just as it linked local and imperial economies. In John Ma's words, such garrisons "were a direct and vital part of imperial administration, by providing the local means for structures of control and extraction."[34] The

27. Bar-Kochva describes the Akra as "symbolizing Seleucid sovereignty over the country" (*Judas Maccabeus*, p. 458).

28. Sievers, "Jerusalem," p. 208. Cf. John Ma, "'Oversexed, Overpaid and Over Here': A Response to Angelos Chaniotis," in *Army and Power in the Ancient World*, ed. Angelos Chaniotis and Peter Ducrey (Stuttgart: Franz Steiner Verlag, 2002), pp. 115-22, 115. Ma emphasizes that the situation of occupation is not a unidirectional experience of imperial power, but a constant negotiation.

29. Chaniotis comments on the anxieties caused by the presence of a garrison, "since they could revolt or become the object of attacks." Their presence thus reminded inhabitants of a potential for violence that could never be fully predicted (*War in the Hellenistic World*, p. 89).

30. Chaniotis, *War in the Hellenistic World*, p. 26; cf. 29.

31. Sievers, "Jerusalem," pp. 205-7. Kenneth Hoglund asserts that the inhabitants of the Akra would have been economically "well-off." "The Material Culture of the Seleucid Period in Palestine: Social and Economic Observations," in *Second Temple Studies III: Studies in Politics, Class and Material Culture*, ed. Philip R. Davies and John M. Halligan (London: Sheffield Academic Press, 2002), pp. 67-73, 73.

32. Cf. Chaniotis, *War in the Hellenistic World*, pp. 92, 121-29.

33. Tcherikover, *Hellenistic Civilization*, p. 189. Cf. Jos. A.J. 12.151-53, 159.

34. Ma, "'Oversexed,'" p. 117.

fact that Sostratus, the commander of this military garrison, was responsible for collecting tribute from the high priest Menelaus testifies to the interweaving of military, economic, and even religious forms of domination in Seleucid Judea.[35]

Sacrilege and Riot

Sostratus's demands were ineffective: money that did not exist could not be paid. Summoned now before the king to account for his delinquency, Menelaus resorted to theft and bribery. But it was no longer a matter of money only. Menelaus stole "some wrought gold objects belonging to the temple" (χρυσώματά τινα τῶν τοῦ ἱεροῦ 2 Macc 4:32). Some of these he gave as a bribe to the king's official Andronicus; others he had already sold abroad for cash (4:32). While the epitomator gives little detail as to the nature of the stolen objects — were they ornaments, votives, perhaps vessels or tools for sacrifice? — these were not items on deposit, but property of the temple itself. Onias's outrage and legal action against Menelaus (4:33) suggest that the objects were considered sacred, and Menelaus had crossed a line. Indeed, Onias knew that the accusation was a serious matter: he took measures to protect his life before publicly denouncing Menelaus's actions (4:33). Onias's fears were well founded. According to the epitomator, Menelaus orchestrated the murder of the former high priest at the hands of the same man Menelaus had earlier bribed (4:34).[36] As VanderKam has noted, the murder of Onias "made a deep impression" on writers in this period, including the writer(s) of Daniel (9:26; possibly 11:22) and perhaps the Animal Apocalypse (1 En. 90:8).[37] When Gabriel foretells this moment to Daniel, he identifies the death of Onias III as a turning point in Judean history that marks the shift from rebuilding after the exile to destruction at the hands of Antiochus IV:[38] after an "anointed one" is cut down, "a prince's people will come and wreak destruction on the city and the holy place" (Dan 9:26). That destruction had not yet come, but the situation in Jerusalem was now fraught with danger.

Violence soon erupted on a much larger scale. Menelaus had appointed his brother Lysimachus to serve as deputy high priest (τῆς ἀρχιερωσύνης διάδοχον) during his absence from the city (2 Macc 4:29), and the two brothers

---

35. Sievers highlights economic dimensions of the Akra's function ("Jerusalem," pp. 202-4).

36. Note that Gera regards the account of Onias's murder as a fiction (*Judaea and Mediterranean Politics*, p. 129).

37. VanderKam, *From Joshua to Caiaphas*, p. 208.

38. VanderKam, *From Joshua to Caiaphas*, p. 207.

apparently colluded in temple robbery (4:39). The epitomator thus reports that Lysimachus had also stolen wrought gold objects from the temple, and had done so more than once (4:39). His sacrilege provoked rioting in Jerusalem, to which he responded with a force of 3000 troops (4:40-42). The people of Jerusalem attacked and routed Lysimachus's troops, even though, according to the epitomator, the crowd was armed only with stones, pieces of wood and, curiously, fistfuls of ashes (ἐκ τῆς παρακειμένης σποδοῦ 4:41). Daniel R. Schwartz explains this unusual detail by reference to the sacrificial cult: the epitomator wants "to suggest to us that the wood and ashes were from the altar, it itself being mobilized, as it were, to defend its sanctity against the crimes of Menelaus and his stand-in."[39] Ashes were also a sign of mortality, contrasting with the divinity of God (e.g., Gen 18:27; Job 42:6). Rolling or sitting in dust or throwing ashes on one's head were acts of mourning, repentance, and petition, embodied reminders of the human condition before God.[40] Within the symbolic world of 2 Maccabees, wielding ashes against Lysimachus's troops thus focused attention on the crime of sacrilege and reasserted the order of creation.[41] By covering with ashes the bodies of those who served Lysimachus, the crowd reminded themselves and the soldiers they fought of their position in the created order, dependent for all things not on Lysimachus, Menelaus, or Antiochus, but on God. The detail highlights the connection between one of the first major (recorded) outbreaks of resistance in Jerusalem in this period — here resistance not to Antiochus's actions, but to those of his appointed Judean administrators — and the experience or perception of threat to the cult.[42] Yet the crowd's actions suggest that tensions were already high, and this first recorded act of violent resistance in Jerusalem marked a turning point, or, in Tcherikover's words, "a mass awakening."[43] Commenting on the collective action of crowds in twentieth-century Argentina, Miguel Bonasso describes crowds as "hinges where years of history are compressed, and where one sees history turning a page to start a new chapter."[44] In this case, the rioting crowd killed Lysimachus

---

39. Schwartz, *2 Maccabees*, p. 242.

40. E.g., Jer 6:26; Ezek 27:30; Jon 3:6; Dan 9:3; cf. 2 Macc 10:25.

41. Ashes have a similar symbolic function in the epitomator's report of Antiochus's execution of Menelaus (2 Macc 13:4-8). For the crime of sacrilege, he is brought to the top of a tower in Beroea, fifty cubits in height and filled with ashes, and he is pushed in, with no hope of escape. The epitomator views this as fitting punishment for his "many sins against the altar whose fire and ashes were pure" (13:8).

42. Daniel 11:14 alludes to an earlier uprising just prior to Antiochus III's victory over Ptolemy V at Panion.

43. Tcherikover, *Hellenistic Civilization*, p. 173. He adds, "The plundering of the Temple plate made good material for religious propaganda among the masses."

44. Miguel Bonasso, *Recuerdo de la Muerte* (Mexico City: Editiones Era, 1984), p. 361, cited in Robben, *Political Violence*, p. x.

and wounded many of his soldiers (2 Macc 4:42). After the riot, Jerusalem's council of elders, the *gerousia,* brought charges before the king against Menelaus (4:43). Resorting once more to bribery, he gained acquittal for himself and death for his accusers (4:43-48).[45] His murderous tenure as high priest continued. The stage was now set for civil war and even revolt.

Civil War and Revolt

While Menelaus continued to ingratiate himself with Seleucid officials, the former high priest Jason was gathering troops in the Transjordanian territory of Ammanitis, where he had fled in 172 after losing his office to Menelaus (4:26). The region had a history of opposition to the Seleucids: it was here that, during the reign of Seleucus IV, the Tobiad Hyrcanus had settled, built a fortress, and apparently established an independent kingdom (*A.J.* 12.229). According to Josephus, Hyrcanus had supported the Ptolemies, and was supported by them in turn. After the death of Seleucus IV, when Antiochus IV ascended the Seleucid throne, Hyrcanus took his own life to avoid capture by the Seleucid army (12.236). Now, while the same Antiochus fought against the Ptolemies in Egypt, rumor of the Seleucid king's death spurred Jason the Oniad to make a bid for control of Jerusalem. In 169 or perhaps 168 BCE, emboldened by the false report that Antiochus IV had died, Jason mustered from this region 1000 troops and marched with them against the city (2 Macc 5:5).[46]

Jason's actions initiated a civil war.[47] Menelaus was unprepared for the attack; he retreated into the Akra as Jason's army forced their way past the city walls (5:5). But while Menelaus apparently had the support of the Seleucid garrison, Josephus reports that for a time Jason enjoyed support from Jerusalem's inhabitants (*A.J.* 12.240). Although we must be cautious in using Josephus as a source for these events,[48] Jason may well have retained the support of some who

45. For these events we rely almost solely on the testimony of 2 Maccabees. For a discussion of its historical merits here, see Schwartz, *2 Maccabees,* p. 212. John J. Collins notes that "while the account in 2 Maccabees may be distorted, it remains the only account we have." "Cult and Culture: The Limits of Hellenization in Judea," in *Hellenism in the Land of Israel,* ed. John J. Collins and Gregory E. Sterling (Notre Dame: University of Notre Dame Press, 2001), pp. 38-61, 46.

46. For a discussion of the date, see Schwartz, *2 Maccabees,* pp. 533-36. Schwartz favors the date 168 BCE, following 2 Maccabees rather than 1 Maccabees.

47. Tcherikover, *Hellenistic Civilization,* pp. 175-203. It is not necessary to follow Tcherikover's reconstruction in all its details (on which, see further below) to recognize the validity and importance of this insight.

48. Millar offers this assessment of Josephus's account: "The whole context is muddled, and we do not reach good evidence until Antiochus IV's letter of Spring 164 B.C." ("Background," p. 17).

enjoyed his patronage during his tenure as high priest, including those who participated in the activities of the gymnasium he founded. Similarly, those who hoped an Oniad would again be high priest may have welcomed his return to Jerusalem.[49] Moreover, recent events — including the riot against Lysimachus — had revealed deep and deadly tensions within the city. Menelaus's sharp dealings with the *gerousia* likely fanned the flames of public opposition to his administration. But if Jason had support from the people of Jerusalem, he did not keep it.[50] The epitomator reports that he "mercilessly slaughtered his own citizens" (2 Macc 5:6). These likely included troops who fought on behalf of Menelaus. Whether they also included unarmed civilians we do not know. The epitomator states only that they were ὁμοεθνῶν: Jason fought against and killed his own people (5:6). In the midst of such chaos, he was unable to keep the advantage and failed to take control of the city (5:7). He fled once more to Ammanitis (5:7), and remained a fugitive until the day of his death (5:8-10).

While I have suggested that those who fought against Jason likely included troops loyal to Menelaus (and/or to the king who had appointed him), Tcherikover posits the existence of a third group, "opponents of the king" but also "enemies of the Hellenizers" (i.e., enemies of Jason and his supporters), who drove Jason from Jerusalem and subsequently gained control of the city.[51] In

---

49. Cf. Gera, *Judaea and Mediterranean Politics*, p. 160. According to the epitomator, Lysimachus had commanded a force three times the size of Jason's, and they were put to flight by the people of Jerusalem. Goldstein speculates that "mere probability would indicate that Jason's relatively small force must have had help from within Jerusalem before it could capture the city" (*II Maccabees*, p. 249). VanderKam similarly remarks that "the low number given for Jason's troops implies that he had expected more help from within Jerusalem" (*From Joshua to Caiaphas*, p. 210).

50. No doubt many were unsure where to place their loyalties, while others refused to take sides for reasons both pragmatic and principled. One imagines that most of the population endeavored to stay out of the way. This likely put Jason at a disadvantage. Antonius C. G. M. Robben discusses anxiety experienced by combatants in civil wars regarding civilians who refuse to commit to a "side": the uncommitted introduce an unknown variable into the calculus of control, often spelling "defeat by default." "The Fear of Indifference: Combatants' Anxieties about the Political Identity of Civilians during Argentina's Dirty War," in *Societies of Fear: The Legacies of Civil War, Violence, and Terror in Latin America*, ed. Kees Koonings and Dirk Kruijt (New York: Zed Books, 1999), pp. 125-40, 126.

51. Tcherikover, *Hellenistic Civilization*, p. 188. VanderKam considers a similar reconstruction, specifying that Onias IV may have staged a coup after Jason's failed revolt. While VanderKam remains cautious in his conclusions, he notes that "it has the potential for providing a satisfactory explanation for why Antiochus reacted as he did in 167 BCE, two years after he had taken the city: A man with a hereditary claim to the high priesthood (Onias IV) had ousted Menelaus. In view of the troubles he had encountered before in Jerusalem, Antiochus determined to attack the problem at the root and drive out both Onias IV and the traditional Jewish practices with which he was associated" (*From Joshua to Caiaphas*, p. 221).

Tcherikover's view, the existence of this third party is necessary because "if we suppose that it was Menelaus [who drove Jason from Jerusalem and thereafter retained control of the city], the entire course of subsequent events ceases to be comprehensible. Antiochus, seeing in the happenings at Jerusalem a rebellion against his royal authority, came to put it down with a strong hand; but had Menelaus regained control of the city in the meantime, there would have been no occasion for such extreme measures, for with Menelaus' assistance the city would have returned to its previous allegiance to Syria."[52] It seems likely enough that Jason's opponents had varied allegiances and reasons for resisting his assault on the city. We would be mistaken to imagine with Josephus a population neatly arrayed in two camps, one supporting the king and his appointee, the other supporting Jason (*A.J.* 12.239). At the same time, we do not need to posit a third party in control of Jerusalem after Jason's retreat to make sense of Antiochus's actions.

Tcherikover's argument presumes that the sole or primary purpose of Antiochus's reprisals was to put down a rebellion in progress. Tcherikover therefore infers that because Antiochus intervened in the way that he did a state of active rebellion must have continued *after* Jason's expulsion, even though no direct evidence supports this inference.[53] Second Maccabees, our most reliable source for these events, reports that Jason's revolt had ended by the time Antiochus and his army arrived on the scene, and mentions no further revolt until that of the Maccabees. Such silence may be apologetic: even with regard to Jason's revolt, the epitomator allows only that Antiochus *thought* Judea was rebelling (2 Macc 5:11). Schwartz observes that while Antiochus probably had reliable intelligence concerning the rebellion, "it is of cardinal importance for our author that we understand that the king's notion, although perhaps reasonable, was in fact a mistaken inference."[54]

Despite the epitomator's apparent apologetic concern, the detail calls our attention to an important element in the structures of revolt and reprisal. It was enough for the king to think, or even decide, that there had been a rebellion. The king did not need actual proof of rebellion, nor did it matter if the state of rebellion ended quickly or continued for a longer period. Antiochus needed only a pretext for intervention. Thus, the city may or may not have continued to rebel after Jason's final expulsion, and Menelaus may or may not have been supplanted as high priest in the period between Jason's revolt and Antiochus's repri-

---

52. Tcherikover, *Hellenistic Civilization*, p. 187.

53. He also presumes that, were Menelaus in office during this period, Antiochus could have relied on Menelaus's influence to assure the loyalty of Jerusalem's inhabitants. Setting aside the question of Menelaus's actual influence on Jerusalem's inhabitants, the analysis below will demonstrate that loyalty as such was not Antiochus's primary concern. He was concerned with the amplification of Seleucid power through the diminution of Judean autonomy.

54. Schwartz, 2 *Maccabees*, p. 257.

sals against Jerusalem. Whatever the case, it is sure that Menelaus's ability to manipulate and even govern the populace was compromised. But in Antiochus's calculations, these details were almost irrelevant, because regardless of who subsequently had "control" of Jerusalem, the king stood to gain from a show of power in Judea, specifically through the reconquest of its capital. By providing a pretext for reconquest, Jason's failed revolt presented Antiochus with a critical and no doubt welcome opportunity to reassert Seleucid imperial claims to Coele-Syria and Phoenicia and consolidate his power in the region.

In order to understand how the revolt could function in this way, it is first necessary to clarify how a civil war in Jerusalem could have been construed as rebellion against the king's authority. Antiochus had removed Jason from the office of high priest and installed in his place Menelaus, who now served at the king's pleasure. In challenging Menelaus's authority and attempting to regain control of the city for himself, Jason challenged the sovereignty of Antiochus, who, contrary to rumor, was still very much alive. Moreover, Jason had not only challenged the king's official, he likely also attacked the king's army. While the epitomator reports only Jason's slaughter of native Judeans, the soldiers who defended the walls of Jerusalem were most likely a combined force of native Judeans and Seleucid soldiers of the Akra. These would have sworn their loyalties to the king and the commanders who served him.[55] Finally, the Akra itself belonged to the king, and Jason had attacked the city that bore the king's own name. As far as Antiochus was concerned, Judea had rebelled.

Antiochus IV had begun the Sixth Syrian War precisely to secure his claim to the spear-won province of Coele-Syria and Phoenicia. To this end he conducted not one, but two campaigns in Egypt, the first in 169 BCE, the second in 168 BCE. Judea was a strategic part of the contested province,[56] and Jason's assault on its capital city gave the king an opportunity to secure his holdings and assert his power within the disputed region. Our sources make it difficult to ascertain whether Jason's revolt occurred at the conclusion of Antiochus's first or second Egyptian campaign. While Schwartz makes a strong case for dating the revolt to the conclusion of the first campaign,[57] many discussions of Antiochus's reprisals against Jerusalem set these within the context of the famous

---

55. Chaniotis describes some of the mechanisms for deepening the loyalties of garrisoned soldiers to their king, including participation in the ruler cult ("Foreign Soldiers," p. 107).

56. Robert Doran, "The First Book of Maccabees," *NIB*, vol. 4 (Nashville: Abingdon, 1996), pp. 1-178, 36.

57. Daniel R. Schwartz, "Antiochus IV Epiphanes in Jerusalem," in *Historical Perspectives from the Hasmoneans to Bar Kokhba in Light of the Dead Sea Scrolls: Proceedings of the Fourth International Symposium of the Orion Center for the Study of the Dead Sea Scrolls and Associated Literature, 27-31 January, 1999*, ed. David Goodblatt, Avital Pinnick, and Daniel R. Schwartz (Leiden: Brill, 2001), pp. 45-56.

"Day of Eleusis" that marked the end of Antiochus's second Egyptian campaign, and for the sake of argument I work from this chronology. The date of the revolt does not materially affect the argument presented here concerning the structures of revolt and reprisal (on which, see further below).

Antiochus IV, Rome, and the Plan of God

A brief account of the Egyptian campaigns brings the broader context into focus. It also confronts us with another reason commonly adduced for the severity of Antiochus's reprisals against Judea, namely his presumed humiliation in Egypt. Antiochus fought successfully against Egypt in 169 BCE, first near Pelusium and then progressing further into Egypt's heartland.[58] According to one tradition, on reaching the old capital at Memphis he staged his own coronation as king of Upper Egypt (cf. 1 Macc 1:16).[59] Yet he failed to take Alexandria, the true seat of Ptolemaic power, and withdrew from Egypt that same year.[60] Antiochus launched a second Egyptian campaign in 168 BCE.[61] At the Lagids' request, the Roman Senate intervened, sending the legate C. Popillius Laenas (a former and future consul, whom Polybius here calls a *strategos*) to demand Antiochus's final withdrawal from Egypt. In the eyes of many historians this has appeared as a severe and humiliating loss for Antiochus. Walter Otto argues that it precipitated his descent into madness.[62] While Otto Mørkholm's judgment is far more restrained, he nonetheless speculates that "to Antiochus the Roman intervention must have been bitter," and "a grave affront to his dignity."[63]

The Evidence of Polybius

This view appears to be supported by Polybius's dramatic characterization of Antiochus's reaction at the moment of his withdrawal from Egypt, but closer

58. For Antiochus's first campaign in Egypt, see Otto Mørkholm, *Antiochus IV of Syria* (Copenhagen: Gyldendal, 1966), pp. 64-87; Mittag, *Antiochos IV. Epiphanes*, pp. 159-81; Gera, *Judaea and Mediterranean Politics*, pp. 131-53.

59. On evidence for the coronation in particular, see Mittag, *Antiochos IV. Epiphanes*, pp. 171-75. Against this tradition, see Mørkholm, *Antiochus IV*, pp. 81-84.

60. Gera, *Judaea and Mediterranean Politics*, p. 142; Mørkholm, *Antiochus IV*, p. 86. For different accounts of why Antiochus withdrew, see Gera, *Judaea and Mediterranean Politics*, pp. 145-48; Morgan, "Perils," pp. 59-64.

61. See Mørkholm, *Antiochus IV*, pp. 88-101; Mittag, *Antiochos IV. Epiphanes*, pp. 209-23.

62. Walter Otto, "Zur Geschichte der Zeit des 6. Ptolemäers," *Abhandlungen der Bayerischen Akademie der Wissenschaften* 11 (1934): 84.

63. Mørkholm, *Antiochus IV*, pp. 95-96.

scrutiny challenges this interpretation. According to Polybius, Antiochus complies with the Senate's wishes βαρυνόμενος καὶ στενῶν (29.27.8), a phrase often understood as attributing to Antiochus an intense emotional reaction to the Roman intervention, such that he withdraws "groaning and in bitterness of heart."[64] Another possible translation would emphasize not an emotional response but the constraining effect of the Roman intervention: Antiochus withdrew from Egypt because he was "weighed down/disabled [i.e., by Roman authority and circumstances in Egypt] and in narrow straits."[65] Such a translation may be less dramatic, but makes good sense in light of the phrase that follows, which explains Antiochus's compliance by reporting his reasoned assessment of his limited options at the time of his withdrawal: εἴκων δὲ τοῖς καιροῖς κατὰ τὸ παρόν, "yielding to present circumstances" (cf. Polyb. 1.88.11-12, 16.24.4). Peter Green characterizes Antiochus's response this way: "Antiochus may have been nicknamed *Epimanēs* ("Madman") by his own people, a parody of what he called himself on coins, *Theos Epiphanēs* ("God Manifest"), but he could be discreet enough when he chose. He bowed to the inevitable."[66]

The reality was that, even in the absence of Roman intervention, Antiochus's prospects of conquering the Ptolemaic empire were not good. Whether this was truly his goal remains unclear.[67] As noted above, the ostensible purpose of the two Egyptian campaigns was first and foremost to secure Antiochus's claim to the contested province of Coele-Syria and Phoenicia. Despite his mandated withdrawal from Egypt, and indeed at the moment of his mandated withdrawal, he had succeeded in obtaining this goal. In fact, Rome's intervention made his claim to the disputed province all the more secure, for on this question the Romans settled the Sixth Syrian War in Antiochus's favor. That is, though they required his withdrawal from Egypt, they nonetheless con-

64. Translation is that of Edwyn R. Bevan, *The House of Seleucus*, vol. 2 (London: E. Arnold, 1902), p. 145, cited by Morgan, "Perils," p. 70n137.

65. The form στενῶν can be analyzed as a present active participle of either στενόω, "to straiten, confine, contract," "to be in difficulty," or στένω, "to moan, sigh, groan" (LSJ, 1639).

66. Peter Green, *Alexander to Actium: The Historical Evolution of the Hellenistic Age* (Berkeley: University of California Press, 1990), pp. 431-32. Habicht's judgment is similar: "His compliance, painful as it must have been, shows wisdom and restraint and effectively disproves the allegations that he was unbalanced" ("Seleucids and Their Rivals," p. 344). Though Green views favorably Morgan's argument (laid out in "Perils"; see further below) that Antiochus may have welcomed the Roman intervention, he still adopts the view that the events were a source of humiliation for Antiochus (*Alexander to Actium*, pp. 432; 843n180).

67. See Morgan, "Perils," p. 53. For the view that Antiochus fought the Lagids not only for control of Coele-Syria and Phoenicia, but for control of the Ptolemaic empire itself, see Erich Gruen, "Hellenism and Persecution: Antiochus IV and the Jews," in *Hellenistic History and Culture*, ed. Peter Green (Berkeley: University of California Press, 1993), pp. 238-74, 244; Goldstein, *II Maccabees*, p. 253.

firmed the Seleucid claim to Coele-Syria and Phoenicia. Any further challenge to this claim would constitute a challenge to Roman authority. Moreover, by his preemptive strike, Antiochus had turned the tables on his southern rivals, shifting their position from an offensive one to a defensive one. Prior to the war, the Lagids had plans for northern expansion. But the war with Antiochus forced them to defend their heartland, and they were now beholden to Rome for ending the Seleucid threat to their kingdom. By the war's end, Antiochus's campaigns had considerably weakened the Ptolemaic empire, and he had grown wealthier at his rivals' expense. Though he was certainly constrained by the Roman intervention, it is unclear that he had grounds for complaint, let alone for groaning and bitterness.[68]

A consideration of its rhetorical and narrative function elsewhere in Polybius's histories further clarifies the meaning of the phrase βαρυνόμενος καὶ στενῶν in Polybius's account of Antiochus's encounter with Popillius Laenas. As M. Gwyn Morgan has observed, Polybius uses the identical phrase in one other passage, in his account of Philip V of Macedon's withdrawal from the cities of Thrace in 187 BCE, also mandated by Rome (Polyb. 23.8.1).[69] The similarity between the two contexts suggests that the phrase is somewhat stereotyped. In Philip's case, Polybius makes it clear that Philip V wished to give the appearance of total submission, "setting all things straight" in order to give no hint of alienation between himself and Rome even as he prepared in secret for war: διωρθώσατο δὲ καὶ τἄλλα πάντα, περὶ ὧν οἱ Ῥωμαῖοι προσεπέταττον, βουλόμενος ἐκείνοις μὲν μηδεμίαν ἔμφασιν ποιεῖν ἀλλοτριότητος (23.8.2). He saw his withdrawal as a necessary but temporary show of compliance, and he continued to plan for the attainment of his own goals despite but also in light of Rome's assertion of power. Given Philip's goals (as expressed by Polybius), it would have made little sense for Philip to make a public show of his dissatisfaction: any "groaning" would alert Rome that things were not as "straight" as they appeared.[70] The same would have been true for Antiochus, whatever his plans for the future.[71] Seen in this light, it appears all the more likely that Polybius did

68. Cf. Erich Gruen, *The Hellenistic World and the Coming of Rome* (Berkeley: University of California Press, 1984), pp. 659-60. He remarks: "Outside of Egypt, the effects of Eleusis were indiscernible" (p. 660).

69. Morgan, "Perils," p. 71. While Morgan does not explore alternate (i.e., nonemotive) meanings for Polybius's phrase, he nonetheless concludes, based on his analysis of the historical situation, that "whatever emotion the 'Day of Eleusis' aroused in the royal bosom, it was not . . . resentment" (p. 53).

70. Cf. the judgment of Green: "Philip may have been headstrong and ambitious, with the temper of his ancestor Pyrrhus, but he had a very firm grasp on logistical realities" (*Alexander to Actium*, p. 287).

71. While acknowledging that Polybius's descriptions of Antiochus contain "strange things," including "lack of tact," Tcherikover also highlights Polybius's portrayal of Antiochus's

not intend the phrase to convey an emotional response but rather a judgment of the practical constraints imposed by Roman intervention. Rhetorically, the phrase highlights the constraints operating in international politics, with special emphasis on the sometimes irresistible force of Roman power; both of these are major themes in Polybius's histories.[72]

This analysis suggests that we should not so hastily assume that Antiochus was humiliated by the Roman intervention at Eleusis, despite the interpretation given to this event by later historians. Peter Franz Mittag argues to the contrary that the "Day of Eleusis" need not have caused Antiochus to lose face at all.[73] While we do not know how Antiochus narrated his final withdrawal from Egypt, Mittag suggests that Antiochus could well have highlighted various positive outcomes, portraying the two Egyptian campaigns as a "great success."[74] Morgan likewise observes that Antiochus's "gains outweighed losses."[75] Rome's demands may even have saved him from future embarrassment, for "the Romans' intervention extricated Antiochus from a war he could neither justify nor win."[76] The greatest gain, as noted above, was that Rome had thrown its weight firmly behind Antiochus's claim to Coele-Syria and Phoenicia, the same spear-won territory Antiochus had invaded Egypt to defend. By this measure, Antiochus's campaigns were indeed successful. Morgan writes that

> by ending Lagid threats to the area, [the Romans] granted to the king the objective for which he had originally gone to war. Moreover, the Seleucid left Egypt with an undefeated army and a massive haul of booty, both paraded at Daphne in 166. And finally, there was no talk of the Treaty of Apamea, of any breaches of its terms, or of any other sanctions against Antiochus. The king, in short, was made to disgorge some ill-gotten gains and suffered minor dents in his amour-propre, but he came away from Eleusis with his primary

---

"cautious attitude to Rome which testifies to his shrewd judgment in the field of international politics" and provides "evidence that he was a ruler with realistic and logical political aspirations" (*Hellenistic Civilization*, pp. 176-77). Habicht similarly finds his response to be evidence of "wisdom and restraint," and characterizes Antiochus as a "king of flawless loyalty to Rome" ("Seleucids and Their Rivals," p. 344).

72. On "constraints on international behavior" in Polybius, see Arthur M. Eckstein, *Moral Vision in the Histories of Polybius* (Berkeley: University of California Press, 1995), p. 196, citing Rudolf von Scala, *Die Studien des Polybios* (Stuttgart: Kohlhammer, 1890), pp. 299-324. See, e.g., Polyb. 5.86.9. On Rome as an irresistible force in Polybius, see Green, *Alexander to Actium*, pp. 271, 284, 449. Eckstein demonstrates that Polybius's attitude toward Rome is not finally neatly pro-Roman. Rather, he thematizes the "problem of Roman power" (*Moral Vision*, p. 197).

73. Mittag, *Antiochos IV. Epiphanes*, pp. 222-23.

74. Mittag, *Antiochos IV. Epiphanes*, p. 222.

75. Morgan, "Perils," p. 72. Cf. Mittag, *Antiochos IV. Epiphanes*, p. 222.

76. Morgan, "Perils," p. 72.

objective achieved, a substantial profit, and the continued friendship of the Romans.[77]

These positive outcomes indicate that even though Antiochus had not succeeded in making the Ptolemaic empire his own, and even though he continued to acknowledge the superior might and authority of Rome, he left Egypt in a position not of weakness and humiliation, but of strength.

The Evidence of Daniel

These conclusions notwithstanding, as I noted above, Antiochus's presumed humiliation at the hands of Rome on the famous "Day of Eleusis" has sometimes been adduced by biblical scholars to explain the severity of Antiochus's subsequent actions in Judea. While this interpretation has found support in a passage from Daniel's final vision (Dan 11:30-31), I argue that this passage does not in fact provide evidence for Antiochus's alleged emotional response to the Roman intervention, but instead serves to place Antiochus's brutal edict of persecution within the broader context of God's own plan for Jerusalem and for God's people. We must therefore look elsewhere for an explanation of the severity of Antiochus's actions.

The final vision of Daniel links Antiochus's response to the Roman intervention (symbolically represented in the vision by "ships of the Kittim") with his subsequent actions in Judea, which I discuss in detail in chapters 5 and 6. The passage contains a clear reference to the persecution in 167 BCE, and, in its phrase "ones who forsake a holy covenant," a likely reference to "Hellenizers," perhaps supporters of Jason: "Ships of the Kittim will come against him, and he will turn coward. He will pronounce doom (וְזָעַם) against a holy covenant, taking action, and he will give renewed attention to ones who forsake a holy covenant. His forces will rise up and violate the sanctuary, the walled-fortress. They will halt the daily sacrifice and set up a desolating abomination" (11:30-31). The verb וְזָעַם, which I have translated "he will pronounce doom," has often been translated as an expression of Antiochus's rage. NRSV translates the verb "he shall be enraged"; NAB "he shall direct his rage"; and NJPS "raging." All of these interpretations have the support of LXX, which renders the verb ὀργισθήσεται, "he will become angry." As I noted above, the close proximity of this verb to the report of Antiochus's confrontation with Rome and "cowardly" retreat from Egypt leads scholars to detect a causal link between this purported rage against the covenant and Antiochus's presumed experience of humiliation. John J. Collins, for example, states that "the severity of the punishment was un-

77. Morgan, "Perils," p. 72.

doubtedly influenced by the fact that the king had been humiliated in Egypt by the Roman legate, Popilius Laenas. This humiliation is clearly linked to the fury of the king in Daniel 11:30: 'Ships of the Kittim will come against him and he will be intimidated. He will return and rage against the holy covenant.'"[78]

It is not clear, however, that "rage" is the most obvious meaning of זעם in this context. Etymologically, the root appears to be connected with speech.[79] The verb, which occurs thirteen times in the Hebrew scriptures, typically refers to "indignant" or "angry" speech that is also efficacious, namely cursing or pronouncing doom.[80] Thus it has the meaning "curse" in Numbers 23:7, 8 (x2) and Proverbs 24:24. It expresses divine judgment for wrongs committed in Psalm 7:12, and "wrath" against God's enemies (who have, in the prophet's view, given God cause for their punishment) in Isaiah 66:14 and Malachi 1:4, while in Micah 6:10 the *qal* passive participle is used to characterize unjust measures that have elicited a pronouncement of divine judgment on those who use them (see Mic 6:11-13). While no wrong is named in Proverbs 22:14, there too it refers to a negative fate pronounced by God. In similar fashion, the related noun זעם comes to express divine wrath, including instances where that wrath actualizes a divine decree (Dan 8:19; 11:36). While the visions of Daniel do not explicitly attribute this wrath to judgment for crimes committed, the majority of the twenty-two occurrences of this noun in the Hebrew scriptures make this connection clear, such that the meaning "wrath" in those instances must be understood in relation to that of "decreed punishment" or "doom."[81] Finally, the verb occurs in Zechariah 1:12, in a reference to God's judgment against Jerusalem, the seventy-year curse that the interpreting angel promises will be lifted in the time of restoration. In chapter 7, I examine in greater detail the importance of

---

78. Collins, "Cult and Culture," p. 49. He later adds, "Jerusalem had incurred his wrath by seeming to rebel at the moment of his humiliation. . . . It is not impossible that in his anger and wounded pride he took unprecedented measures against what he perceived as a strange and alien people" (p. 51). Collins offers ample evidence for the humiliation of Antiochus, including the passage from Polybius examined above, Diod. 31.2 and Livy 45.12.3-6 ("Cult and Culture," p. 59n59). Morgan analyzes each of these passages, noting that "in Polybius' and Diodorus' opinion, the Romans had not meant to humiliate the king. For his part, Livy attributes the gesture to Popillius Laenas' customary asperitas animi" ("Perils," p. 69). On the later sources that do insist on a Roman effort to intimidate Antiochus, see Morgan, "Perils," p. 69n131.

79. Cf. Bertil Wiklander, "זעם *zāʿam;* זעם *zaʿam*," *TDOT* 4:106-11, 107.

80. Proverbs 25:23 is an exception, describing the "wrathful face" of one who has been a victim of "secret speech." The comparison to a north wind that produces rain suggests nonetheless that the "wrathful face" will itself eventuate in a form of efficacious speech; the "wrathful face" would then be a metonym for the act of cursing.

81. E.g., Nah 1:6 (guilt specified in 1:3); Zeph 3:8; Ezek 21:36 (31) (guilt specified in 21:35 [30]); 22:24 (guilt specified in 22:25); 22:31; Lam 2:6 (guilt specified in 2:14); etc. Cf. Wiklander, "זעם *zāʿam;* זעם *zaʿam*," *TDOT* 4:110.

this seventy-year curse for Daniel (Dan 9:2, 24). Gabriel explains to Daniel that the seventy years decreed for Jerusalem's desolation are in fact seventy weeks of years, such that this decree of destruction culminates in Antiochus's actions against the holy city and temple before reaching its end (9:24-27). Moreover, the angel's revelations to Daniel indicate that the divinely decreed wrath of Daniel 8:19 and 11:36 coincides with and includes the decreed wrath of Antiochus in 11:30. The root's apparent etymological sense of efficacious speech suggests that וְזָעַם in 11:30 should be taken to refer not to Antiochus's emotional state, but to his edict (on which see further below), and for this reason I have translated the verb "he will pronounce doom."[82] By utilizing the same root to refer both to Antiochus's edict and to God's decreed timetable for the desolation of Jerusalem, the writer of Daniel circumscribes Antiochus's actions within the foreordained plan of God, emphasizing divine foreknowledge and permission of the desolation but also the decreed end to wrath and the suffering it brings.

Revolt and the Re-creation of Empire

I argued above against explaining the severity of Antiochus's reprisals against Jerusalem by reference to his presumed humiliation at the hands of Rome, for it is not clear that he was humiliated at all, nor does evidence from Daniel provide insight into his state of mind at this time. I also argued that his intervention in Jerusalem did not necessitate the inference of ongoing conditions of rebellion. Instead, as I explain further below, Antiochus's reprisals against Jerusalem followed the logic of reconquest and even state terror. In this understanding, as I stated above, Jason's revolt provided Antiochus with an opportunity to assert and solidify Seleucid control of Judea.

Whether Jason's revolt and the first round of reprisals occurred in 169 or 168 BCE (i.e., between the two Egyptian campaigns or at their conclusion), the revolt's significance should nonetheless be understood in light of the Sixth Syrian War and its reported objective to secure Antiochus's claim to the province of Coele-Syria and Phoenicia.[83] The basis for Antiochus's claim to the province

---

82. Wiklander's assessment of the verb's meaning in this passage is similar to my own: "The purpose of the verb is to identify the person who inaugurated the period of desolation or malediction that the religious policies of the Seleucids spelled for faithful Jews" ("זָעַם za'am; זַעַם za'am," TDOT 4:107-8). Wiklander's choice of the word "malediction" underscores the connotation of efficacious speech.

83. F. W. Walbank observes: "It was important to [a Hellenistic king's] status and his renown that he should control territory, in which he could exercise his kingship (and from which he could draw revenues and recruit troops); and claims to territory were never lightly relinquished. Conquest was the strongest title to land, as Polybius (XXVIII.1.6) records of Antio-

was that it was "spear-won": as discussed in chapter 3, his father Antiochus III had conquered the region in the Fifth Syrian War. Whether this claim was still contested by Egypt, as it would have been in 169 BCE, or had already been settled on the international stage, as in 168 BCE, it would be important for Antiochus to reassert his power within the province itself. Jason's revolt provided Antiochus with an opportunity to reconquer one of the region's major civic centers — a city to which he had only a few years before granted the status of *polis* (or *politeuma*) and the right to train its citizens for war.[84] Jerusalem's reconquest promised significant material benefits for Antiochus, as suggested by 1 Maccabees 1:21-23 and 2 Maccabees 5:16 and 21. But there were other, more important benefits, both practical and symbolic.

In chapter 2, I identified conquest as a core component of Hellenistic ideology of empire. In this ideology, conquest gave visible and palpable proof of imperial power, even revealing the king as a god. Vincent Gabrielsen has argued that, for the Hellenistic kings, conquest equaled creation, including creation of the empire itself.[85] It was impossible for these kings to continually conquer new lands. Antiochus himself was well aware, especially by 168 BCE, that he would conquer neither the Ptolemaic nor the Roman empires.[86] But the Hellenistic kings, Antiochus included, could continually re-create their empires and so assert their power and even divinity by reconquering their provincial subjects. Gabrielsen characterizes the primary mechanism for this process of imperial re-creation as "the perpetuation of 'creation' of the empire by means of its recurrent 're-creation'; the quasi-ritualized re-enactment of conquest by means of separate acts of re-conquest of imperial components. Almost unexceptionally, such a regularly occurring re-enactment was set in motion by the 'provincial' challenge *par excellence:* revolt."[87] In Gabrielsen's analysis, revolt was

---

chus IV who, at the outset of the Sixth Syrian War, was determined to maintain his hold on Coele-Syria and Phoenicia, since he 'regarded possession through warfare as the surest claim and the best.'" "Monarchies and Monarchic Ideas," in *The Cambridge Ancient History*, vol. 7, part 1, *The Hellenistic World*, ed. A. E. Astin, F. W. Walbank, M. W. Fredriksen, and R. M. Ogilvie (Cambridge: Cambridge University Press, 1984), pp. 62-100, 66.

84. Schwartz, *2 Maccabees*, p. 257. See further Schwartz, "Antiochus IV Epiphanes in Jerusalem," pp. 53-55.

85. Vincent Gabrielsen, "Provincial Challenges to the Imperial Centre in Achaemenid and Seleucid Asia Minor," in *The Province Strikes Back: Imperial Dynamics in the Eastern Mediterranean*, ed. Björn Forsén and Giovanni Salmeri (Helsinki: Foundation of the Finnish Institute at Athens, 2008), pp. 15-44, 23.

86. Discussing a seeming equilibrium between the Ptolemaic and Seleucid empires, Heinen writes, "In general, each of the two rivals was too strong to be destroyed by the other, in other words, neither of the two dynasties was normally in a position to eliminate the other and to incorporate its territory in its own empire by 'unification'" ("Syrian-Egyptian Wars," p. 445).

87. Gabrielsen, "Provincial Challenges," p. 23.

hardly an anomaly (cf. 2 Macc 4:30). It was a regular occurrence and even a "dominant feature" of the Hellenistic empires. Nor was revolt a great irritant to the Hellenistic kings. They were well aware of revolt's unique capacity to integrate the empire, enabling kings to consolidate power within their borders and reassert their own system of order.[88] If they publicly denounced revolt, they privately welcomed it. Sometimes, as Gabrielsen shows, they went so far as to instigate it.[89] Seen in this light, revolt emerges as an "energizing force" and "structural necessity of empire," yielding "a system of political control and readjustment over the very units that produced it."[90]

Revolt, then, provided an opportunity for reconquest that enabled the re-creation of empire. Indeed, as Gabrielsen argues, imperial responses to revolt were "functionally indistinguishable from campaigns of conquest — in fact, any time a part of the empire revolted, the scene was set for a reenactment of conquest."[91] Antiochus's reprisals against Jerusalem must be understood in these terms. According to the epitomator, following Jason's revolt he and his army visited Jerusalem, where they meted swift and brutal punishment to the city and its inhabitants for their earlier insubordination, killing 40,000 and selling 40,000 into slavery (5:12-14). If these details are not sufficient to make the point, the epitomator confirms that Antiochus's reprisals took the form of reconquest, stating that Antiochus dealt with the people of Jerusalem not as citizens or subjects but as "captives of the spear" (δοριάλωτον 5:11), enemies newly conquered. Jonathan Goldstein explains the significance of this detail: "In the Hellenistic and Roman world, a conqueror had absolute power over the conquered, but it was considered illegal and immoral to massacre and despoil those who had surrendered without a fight. However, persons or cities captured through combat were completely at the mercy of the conqueror."[92] From this moment, not only the empire but the conquered city would be re-created according to the will of Antiochus. The unity and vitality of the Seleucid empire were predicated on the raw power of the king; by diminishing Jerusalem's *autonomia* he would magnify his own glory. Moreover, as conqueror Antiochus aimed also to be creator, source, and sole sovereign: he intended the people of Jerusalem to enjoy only those freedoms he had granted. To ensure that this was so, he would first take their freedoms away; later he could again pose as benefactor and protector. Antiochus's methods of reconquest were thus calculated to shatter the people's sense of autonomy and will to resist, so that all will and all freedom would derive from his own regime and person. To this end he relied

88. Gabrielsen, "Provincial Challenges," pp. 23, 25, 28.
89. Gabrielsen, "Provincial Challenges," pp. 23, 29.
90. Gabrielsen, "Provincial Challenges," p. 23.
91. Gabrielsen, "Provincial Challenges," p. 24.
92. Goldstein, *II Maccabees*, p. 257.

not only on the shock tactics of large-scale massacre and captivity, but also on more subtle strategies of repression and state terror, as I explain in chapter 5.

Thus far I have considered the cycle of revolt and reconquest in largely structural terms, considering the benefits to the empire of the integrative and unifying mechanisms of repression. Yet buried within and supporting these structures lie horrors that the apocalyptic writers and even the epitomator took great pains to reveal. Chapters 5 and 6 attend not only to the logic but also to the experience, effects, and interpretation of reconquest and state terror in Jerusalem, before pressing forward through these horrors to outline the beginnings of resistance.

CHAPTER 5

Seleucid State Terror

In the preceding chapter I argued that Antiochus's reprisals following Jason's revolt aimed at the re-creation of empire through the reconquest of Jerusalem and Judea. I also suggested that his actions were governed by the logic of repression and control. According to the narratives in 1 and 2 Maccabees, the primary mechanism for Judea's reconquest was not simple force, but rather state terror. Antiochus sought through a program of terror to dismantle the order of life and undermine security in Judea, replacing existing order and security with his own. The writers of the historical apocalypses studied in this volume answered terror with visions of hope, providence, and the promise of justice. They resisted fragmentation by reasserting the ground of identity and the continuity of past, present, and future. This chapter examines in detail the logic and techniques of Seleucid state terror in Judea from the first round of reprisals following Jason's revolt (in 169 or 168 BCE) through the mission of Apollonius in 167 BCE, as well as early forms of resistance to Antiochus's program of terror attested in our sources. Chapter 6 continues the examination of Seleucid state terror by analyzing the edict and subsequent persecution.[1]

1. I rely heavily in this and the next chapter on the accounts of 1 and 2 Macc. In neither case do we have unmediated access to "what really happened." Numbers appear to be rounded and inflated; other details may well be embellished. Each book has its own guiding interests and aims that necessarily color its account (see further comments in the Epilogue). At the same time, numerous studies have documented the historical value of these sources. On the historical value of the testimony of 1 Macc, see John R. Bartlett, *1 Maccabees* (Sheffield: Sheffield Academic Press, 1998), pp. 101-2. Bartlett characterizes the writer of 1 Macc as a "responsible historian" who "offers a comparatively balanced picture of the political concerns of the Seleucids and the Romans." He concludes that "the modern historian must treat the ancient historian of 1 Maccabees with great respect" (p. 102). On the historical value of the testimony of 2 Macc, see Daniel R. Schwartz, *2 Maccabees*, CEJL (Berlin: Walter de Gruyter, 2008), pp. 38-56. Schwartz concludes that 2 Macc "is so often confirmable that we must follow it, all things being equal,

The Logic of State Terror

The *prostagma* of Seleucus IV examined in chapter 3 emphasized a royal providence that would grant to the king's subjects security, safety, and freedom from fear. Yet I noted there how the ideology of the *prostagma* in fact created the fear it purported to relieve. I also noted in chapter 4 the fear and anxiety created by the presence of the Seleucid garrison in the Akra of Jerusalem. In fact, not simply fear, but terror was a mechanism of control regularly employed by the Hellenistic kings (e.g., Polyb. 21.41.2; cf. *A.J.* 13.388; 15.326).[2] John Ma writes: "Violence, destruction, and depredation played their part in the techniques of power used by the Seleukids, creating the atmosphere of terror, φόβος, instrumental in the conquering royal progress and essential to the image of royal might. . . . The terror inspired by royal violence forms the backdrop for the discursive interaction between ruler and subject . . . ; it informs and problematizes the royal claim to benevolence and protection."[3] Fear, anxiety, and even terror had always formed part of the context for Judean interaction with the Seleucid empire, even when Judeans gave their support to Antiochus III, received the privilege from him of self-governance, and received benefactions from Antiochus III and Seleucus IV to support the cult of Yhwh in Jerusalem.

But a distinction must be made between anxiety, fear, and terror. All three arise from the perception of threat, whether real or imagined. Anxiety arises when the exact nature or timing of the threat is unknown.[4] As threat takes concrete, identifiable form, the response can be named fear.[5] Effects of fear include feelings of weakness and vulnerability, powerlessness concerning the future, and a distorted sense of reality.[6] Terror is something more. Psychologically, terror strikes at one's core, bringing the self "to the verge of shattering."[7] But, as

---

even when it cannot be confirmed. This is particularly the case for the period that preceded the Hasmonean revolt, a period that drew only minimal attention from the dynastic historian who produced 1 Maccabees" (p. 42). He adds that "2 Maccabees stands today, alongside 1 Maccabees, as a firm foundation for the construction of the history of the period with which it deals" (p. 44). While further evidence may give cause for revision, I build my reconstruction on the evidence of these sources.

2. John Ma, *Antiochos III and the Cities of Western Asia Minor* (Oxford: Oxford University Press, 1999), p. 111.

3. Ma, *Antiochos III*, p. 111.

4. Sofia Salimovich, Elizabeth Lira, and Eugenia Weinstein, "Victims of Fear: The Social Psychology of Repression," in *Fear at the Edge: State Terror and Resistance in Latin America*, ed. Juan E. Corradi, Patricia Weiss Fagen, and Manuel Antonio Garretón (Berkeley: University of California Press, 1992), pp. 72-89, 73.

5. Salimovich, Lira, and Weinstein, "Victims of Fear," p. 73.

6. Salimovich, Lira, and Weinstein, "Victims of Fear," pp. 74-75.

7. Yolanda Gampel, "Reflections on the Prevalence of the Uncanny in Social Violence," in

noted above, terror is not only a psychological or physiological response. It is also "a social fact and a cultural construction" that mediates and strengthens imperial hegemony.[8]

Like anxiety and fear, terror can be employed by the state as a mechanism for social control. Jeffrey A. Sluka defines state terror as "the use or threat of violence by the state or its agents or supporters, particularly against civilian individuals and populations, as a means of political intimidation and control (i.e., a means of repression)."[9] Such terror thus operates on both individual and social levels. Typically, state terror targets an entire population or group within a population, whether through unpredictable, selective acts of terror, or through acts of massive brutality out of all proportion to any claimed offense.[10] Terror aims to transform the world of its targets, destroying networks of trust and frameworks for meaning.

According to 1 and 2 Maccabees, in the wake of Jason's revolt Antiochus terrorized the population of Jerusalem and Judea through massacre, abduction, home invasion, and plunder of the temple, as well as through the spectacular display of imperial might. His soldiers built up the Akra that served as a base of military operations for Seleucid troops, while simultaneously setting fire to the city, destroying homes, and leveling city walls. These acts of terror were designed to shatter the illusion of Judean *autonomia*, rob the populace of its will to resist, and create a lasting atmosphere of deep insecurity.

Cultures Under Siege: Collective Violence and Trauma, ed. Antonius C. G. M. Robben and Marcelo M. Suárez-Orozco (Cambridge: Cambridge University Press, 2000), pp. 48-69, 51.

8. Michael Taussig, "Culture of Terror — Space of Death: Roger Casement's Putumayo Report and the Explanation of Torture," *Comparative Studies in Society and History* 26 (1984): 467-97, 468.

9. Jeffrey A. Sluka, "Introduction: State Terror and Anthropology," in *Death Squad: The Anthropology of State Terror,* ed. Jeffrey A. Sluka (Philadelphia: University of Pennsylvania Press, 2000), pp. 1-45, 2. Rudolph J. Rummel's corpus on democide provides a sobering overview of state terror in the twentieth century, with an emphasis on those regimes that, by his estimates, have committed the greatest number of murders. See *Lethal Politics: Soviet Genocides and Mass Murders 1917-1987* (Rutgers, NJ: Transaction Publishers, 1990); *China's Bloody Century: Genocide and Mass Murder since 1900* (Rutgers, NJ: Transaction Publishers, 1991); *Democide: Nazi Genocide and Mass Murder* (Rutgers, NJ: Transaction Publishers, 1992); and the summary volume *Death by Government* (New Brunswick, NJ: Transaction Publishers, 1994).

10. Raymond D. Duvall and Michael Stohl, "Governance by Terror," in *The Politics of Terrorism,* ed. Michael Stohl, 3rd ed. (New York: M. Dekker, 1988), pp. 231-71, 238: "We would emphasize the *unpredictability of violence for members of some identity group* as the primary means through which violence terrorizes witnesses" (italics original).

Massacre

The reprisals began with a massacre of Jerusalem's inhabitants. The epitomator reports that in three days, Antiochus's soldiers killed old and young, men and women, children and babies — 40,000 in all — and sold as many into slavery (2 Macc 5:12-14). We need not posit the historical accuracy of these numbers to recognize the impact of such a massacre.[11] It would have aimed to shatter all hope of independence and create a climate of terror and insecurity among survivors who witnessed its horrors and lived through its painful aftermath. The people of Jerusalem had shown that they were not "docile bodies" grateful to assume their assigned position in service to the empire. Antiochus responded to Jason's challenge to his sovereignty by imposing the state of exception (see ch. 1). Because he was king, the rules of the game were that he could suspend the rules at any moment.[12] He now did so. He suspended all semblance of contractual rule, interaction, and mutuality. He abandoned rhetoric of benefactions, privileges, and protections. He did not attempt to single out and bring to justice those who had participated in the rebellion. The king's power — specifically, the power of his army — stood outside the law and systems of justice.[13] Moreover, by rendering the scope, forms, and timing of his retaliation impossible to predict (according to 1 Macc 1:29, further retribution followed two years later), he would convey to the people of Jerusalem the omnipotence of the empire and the helplessness of its subjects. He would communicate to the people of Judea, even to the wealthiest and most powerful inhabitants of the city of Jerusalem, that all freedom was his to give and take away, all justice his to grant or

11. Joseph Sievers observes that "the number of victims seems grossly exaggerated." *The Hasmoneans and Their Supporters: From Mattathias to the Death of John Hyrcanus I* (Atlanta: Scholars Press, 1990), p. 17n67. Brian McGing cautions that estimates of population and death counts derived from ancient literary sources are "extremely unreliable." "Population and Proselytism: How Many Jews Were There in the Ancient World?" in *Jews in the Hellenistic and Roman Cities*, ed. John R. Bartlett (London: Routledge, 2002), pp. 88-106, 98. While McGing estimates a maximum population for ancient Jerusalem at 70,000-100,000 persons (p. 106), more recent estimates are far more conservative. Oded Lipschits estimates between 1250 and 1500 people in Jerusalem in the Persian and early Hellenistic periods, with significant subsequent growth in the Hasmonean period. "Persian Period Finds from Jerusalem: Facts and Interpretations," *The Journal of Hebrew Scriptures* 9, article 20 (2009): 1-30. Israel Finkelstein has proposed even more conservative estimates for the Persian and early Hellenistic periods, but documents a substantial increase by the Seleucid period, yielding 42,000 people in the whole of Judea by the time of the Maccabean revolt. "The Territorial Extent and Demography of Yehud/Judea in the Persian and Early Hellenistic Periods," *RB* 117, no. 1 (2010): 39-54, 50.

12. Cf. Edelberto Torres-Rivas, "Epilogue: Notes of Terror, Violence, Fear and Democracy," in *Societies of Fear: The Legacies of Civil War, Violence, and Terror in Latin America*, ed. Kees Koonings and Dirk Kruijt (New York: Zed Books, 1999), pp. 285-300, 292.

13. On the link between state terror and militarism, see Sluka, "Introduction," p. 7.

refuse.[14] If their lives were sometimes his to protect or to improve, it was only because they were also his to command and kill.

The epitomator reports Antiochus's actions in poetic verse (2 Macc 5:13):

ἐγίνοντο δὲ νέων καὶ πρεσβυτέρων ἀναιρέσεις
γυναικῶν καὶ τέκνων ἀφανισμός
παρθένων τε καὶ νηπίων σφαγαί[15]

Of young and old, there were murders
Of women and children, disappearance
Of young women and infants, slaughters.

The verse identifies the victims of Antiochus's slaughters and abductions, revealing the enormity of indiscriminate murders as well as the many familial and social ties that were irreparably cut. Jason himself had fled the city. No doubt some of his troops fled with him. From the king's perspective, it did not matter. Antiochus was not hunting down insurgents. Nor did he limit his retaliation to the adult men and ephebes who would have rallied to the city's defense. He terrorized an entire city in order first to unmake and then to remake the city as his own creation, enforcing upon it an order determined solely by his will and might.[16] To create a feeling of helplessness and powerlessness in Judea, Antiochus's soldiers entered its capital city by force and killed and enslaved many of its inhabitants, showing that walls and soldiers were no defense against

14. According to Livy 33.38.5-7, Antiochus IV's father, Antiochus III, had made this principle clear to the people of Smyrna and Lampsacus in 196 BCE. They in turn recognized that freedom so granted was not true freedom and not to be trusted: *nec ui tantum terrebat, sed per legatos leniter adloquendo castigandoque temeritatem ac pertinaciam spem conabatur facere breui quod peterent habituros, sed cum satis et ipsis et omnibus aliis appareret ab rege impetratam eos libertatem, non per occasionem raptam habere. aduersus quae respondebatur nihil neque mirari neque suscensere Antiochum debere, si spem libertatis differri non satis aequo animo paterentur.*

15. I follow here the critical text of Robert Hanhart, ed., *Septuaginta: Vetus Testamentum Graecum* vol. IX.2, *Maccabaeorum Liber II* (Göttingen: Vandenhoeck & Ruprecht, 1976). The textual variants for this verse do not alter the conclusions drawn here or later in this chapter.

16. On order and terror, see Sluka, "Introduction," p. 22. Rudolph J. Rummel documents a strong correlation between totalitarianism and state violence: "As the arbitrary power of a regime increases massively, that is, as we move from democratic through authoritarian to totalitarian regimes, the amount of killing jumps by huge multiples." *Death by Government*, p. 17. The killing Rummel documents includes governmental killing of a state's own subjects: "The more power a government has, the more it can act arbitrarily according to the whims and desires of the elite, and the more it will make war on others and murder its foreign and domestic subjects" (pp. 1-2). This state murder is what Rummel calls "democide," or "the murder of any person or people by a government, including genocide, politicide, and mass murder" (p. 31). Democide is to be distinguished from killing in war (p. 25): "Killing people with weapons in their hands is not democide" (p. 38).

his army. These tactics of terror made victims of the most vulnerable and defenseless, elderly and infants alike. Soldiers took women and children as slaves. They killed babies, and with them hope for the future. They killed even young virgins, prized captives in time of war.[17] In so doing they would curtail the city's power to reproduce, and reproduce itself,[18] again reminding the people of Jerusalem of one of the empire's great lies, that the privilege of life was granted by the king alone, just as he alone possessed the power to create.

Murder in the Home

The epitomator reports that while the soldiers mercilessly cut down everyone they encountered, the slaughters did not end in the street. They also killed people in their homes (2 Macc. 5:12). Like the murders, the invasion of homes would render atrocity, death, and horror the new normal, creating an environment in which the violence of the empire was always in view and always to be feared, and creating the conditions of a common life not simply at death's threshold but permeated by the horrifying experience of death. Edelberto Torres-Rivas describes this as a "trivialization of horror," in which "a politically insecure existence — a situation in which the condition of citizen is unpredictable in its durability, together with a certain perception of danger resulting from probable threats — ends up constituting a general socio-political syndrome that is not adequately described by the word 'insecurity.' To this condition of insecurity resulting from direct threat, one must add the intimate reaction produced by the mere information received of deaths repeated on a massive scale, taking place in our midst."[19] Antiochus's invasion and brutal capture of the city itself had already created a sense of insecurity and terror, proving that the city's defenses were (for now) no defense against the Seleucid king.[20] By committing murder in the houses of Jerusalem, Antiochus went a step further, transforming spaces of intimacy, solace, and safety into places of violence, death, and vulnerability.

I discussed in chapter 2 the importance of boundaries — of the body, sacred space, the city itself — in maintaining holiness and ordering human life in accordance with the laws of Yhwh set forth in Israel's sacred traditions and embodied in Jewish religious praxis and daily life. Home invasion violated spatial, social, and personal boundaries. Antonius C. G. M. Robben describes

17. Susan Niditch, "War, Women, and Defilement in Numbers 31," *Semeia* 61 (1993): 39-58.
18. Cf. Robert Doran, "The First Book of Maccabees," *NIB*, vol. 4 (Nashville: Abingdon, 1996), pp. 1-178, 36.
19. Torres-Rivas, "Epilogue," p. 291.
20. Cf. Salimovich, Lira, and Weinstein, "Victims of Fear," p. 76.

the damaging psychological and social effects of similar practices of home invasion in Argentina in the 1970s: "The violation of home by the State, and the invasion of the inner by the outer reality, shattered ego and superego boundaries. Political violence was directed at the cultural and psychological divisions between public and domestic, family and community, even at the passage between life and death."[21] In similar fashion, by violating and erasing boundaries Antiochus began to unmake the order God had ordained for Israel, and in so doing to replace security with horror. Murder in the home made this horror nearly inescapable, as cosmos reverted to chaos. In her analysis of horror, Julia Kristeva describes the experience of being in the presence of a corpse as a moment of falling into a space where boundaries are erased and the world breaks down.[22] Kristeva plays on the etymological link between "cadaver" and the Latin verb *cadere*, "to fall," but while the etymology identifies the deceased as "fallen," in Kristeva's reflections it is not the dead body that falls but the living person witnessing death's horror. The presence within the home of a murdered corpse symbolically collapses all boundaries, breaking down not only the structures of public and private life but also the division between life and death. In Kristeva's words, the corpse is "a border that has encroached upon everything," "death infecting life."[23] Kristeva recognizes that these boundaries of life and death are closely linked to those of purity and impurity.[24] In his study of the book of Leviticus, Jacob Milgrom demonstrates that the boundary between life and death is in fact the overarching principle that governs Israel's purity laws and system of holiness.[25] By violating these boundaries Antiochus worked to dismantle the existing symbolic, social, and psychological foundations — and by extension the religious foundations, from which none of these can be separated — of security, identity, order, and meaning for the people of Jerusalem, to create in their city and homes a "space of death

21. Antonius C. G. M. Robben, "The Assault on Basic Trust: Disappearance, Protest, and Reburial in Argentina," in *Cultures Under Siege: Collective Violence and Trauma,* ed. Antonius C. G. M. Robben and Marcelo M. Suárez-Orozco (Cambridge: Cambridge University Press, 2000), pp. 70-101, 70. Sluka notes that "the dirty war in Argentina [has] become synonymous with modern reigns of terror and [has] stimulated the anthropology of state terror" ("Introduction," p. 14). Thus anthropological studies of state terror in Argentina are at the forefront of scholarly investigation of this phenomenon more broadly and provide an important resource for understanding the dynamics of state terror in the ancient world as well. See further Sluka, "Introduction," pp. 20-22.

22. Julia Kristeva, *Powers of Horror: An Essay on Abjection,* trans. Leon S. Roudiez (New York: Columbia University Press, 1982), pp. 3-4.

23. Kristeva, *Powers of Horror,* pp. 3-4.

24. Kristeva, *Powers of Horror,* pp. 2-4.

25. Jacob Milgrom, *Leviticus: A Book of Ritual and Ethics* (Minneapolis: Fortress, 2004), pp. 12-13, 99, 114, 134, 180, and passim.

where reality is up for grabs," and to impose upon this formless void an alternate and unholy world order of his own making.[26]

Abduction

While murder in the home sought to undermine psychological and even religious foundations of security and render meaningless the very architecture of social life in Jerusalem, Antiochus further terrorized the people of Jerusalem through abduction.[27] As I noted above, the epitomator states that Antiochus's soldiers abducted into slavery as many people as they killed. The poetic lament chooses the wrenching vocabulary of "disappearance." Women and children vanished from the city, never to be seen again.

Antiochus's economic motives for abduction are clear.[28] Slave trade and slave labor were core components of the Hellenistic economy, and healthy war captives could command a price between 100 and 300 drachmas each.[29] The epitomator reports that during the Maccabean revolt the Seleucid general Nicanor expected to raise 2000 talents from the sale of Judean slaves in the markets of Phoenicia, at the price of 90 slaves for one talent, or 67 drachmas each (2 Macc 8:10-11).[30] While the anticipated price reported in 2 Maccabees is unusually low, the overall financial gain for Antiochus would still have been high. But though Antiochus would have derived substantial economic profit from the sale of Judean slaves, the event has even greater significance as an act of power and terror.

By selling a large segment of the population into slavery, Antiochus ne-

26. The quoted phrase is that of Taussig, "Culture of Terror," p. 471. In Taussig's analysis the colonial "space of death" is characterized and accomplished by an "epistemic murk" brought about through misinformation and the imposition of categories that do not comport with sensible reality but nonetheless transform sensory experience, creating terror even when the object of terror is absent or imagined (p. 494).

27. According to Livy, around this time (at the conclusion of his successful Macedonian campaign in 167 BCE) L. Aemilius Paullus sold into slavery 150,000 residents of seventy Epirot towns as punishment for supporting Rome's enemy and in order to raise capital to reward his troops. They also plundered the towns and razed their walls (Livy 45.34).

28. These are highlighted by William Linn Westermann, *The Slave Systems of Greek and Roman Antiquity* (Philadelphia: American Philosophical Society, 1955), p. 29.

29. On slave trade and war, see Angelos Chaniotis, *War in the Hellenistic World: A Social and Cultural History* (Oxford: Blackwell, 2005), pp. 129-37; on price, p. 136. See also Vincent Gabrielsen, "Piracy and the Slave Trade," in *A Companion to the Hellenistic World*, ed. Andrew Erskine (Oxford: Blackwell, 2003), pp. 389-404.

30. An attic talent was 6000 drachmas. See the comments of Schwartz, *2 Maccabees*, pp. 333-34, who speculates that Nicanor's increased supply would have driven down prices.

gated existing structures of social order and imposed his own. In the imposed social order, he was master and Judeans were slaves.[31] Those sold into slavery experienced a "social death," alienated from their birthplace, families, community, and social structures of meaning and no doubt forced to violate core cultural and religious values associated with holiness, purity, honor, and shame.[32] To whatever extent Jason had aimed through his reforms to assimilate Jerusalem's elite to an ideal of "Greek" citizenship, Antiochus now issued a definitive refutation of this ambition. He made it known that Judeans could be sold as slaves. Therefore they were not citizens, and they were not "Greek."[33] Moreover, by imperial design Judean captives would no longer be "Judean" either. In the social death of slavery they were to become blank tablets on which the empire could write its own meanings.[34]

Captivity and enslavement were also transactions in the ancient economy of honor and shame. This exchange accorded dishonor to those enslaved (and to Judeans generally, who were all potential slaves) and honor to the master, Antiochus.[35] As trophies of war, the degraded bodies of Judean captives also conferred glory on the Seleucid soldiers who captured them. As the captives were transported and sold elsewhere in the Near Eastern and Mediterranean world — whether in the Phoenician markets of their own province, elsewhere in the Seleucid empire, in Egypt, or in lands controlled by the Romans — they would symbolically communicate the military successes of the Seleucid empire and the might and mastery of its king. The dispersal of enslaved Judeans would broadcast Seleucid hegemony within the Seleucid empire and beyond, enacting and symbolizing the empire's sovereignty over the bodies and wills of its subjects.

31. Cf. Orlando Patterson, *Slavery and Social Death: A Comparative Study* (Cambridge, MA: Harvard University Press, 1982), p. 42.

32. See Patterson, *Slavery and Social Death*, p. 38. For contemporary associations between slavery and shame, see Jud 8:22-23.

33. On the parallel distinctions between citizen and noncitizen, Greek and non-Greek, free and potential slave, see Patterson, *Slavery and Social Death*, p. 30.

34. I by no means intend to deny the agency of captives, or to reduce the meaning and symbolic power of their embodied experience, but rather to highlight the way in which Antiochus aimed to communicate Seleucid power through their subjugated bodies. The embodied experience of captives was conditioned by but also exceeded the meanings attributed by Antiochus's violence. See the sophisticated treatment of these issues in the context of twentieth-century Northern Ireland in Allen Feldman, *Formations of Violence: The Narrative of the Body and Political Terror in Northern Ireland* (Chicago: University of Chicago Press, 1991), pp. 79-81. Feldman writes, "The attempt through violence to inscribe symbolic time and space (ethnohistory and ethnic space) onto the register of the body is a fundamental suppression of historicity. . . . Yet in this process by which ideological time and imagined space are duplicated in matter, the body acquires its own clandestine history of alterity" (p. 80). See also Elaine Scarry, *The Body in Pain: The Making and Unmaking of the World* (Oxford: Oxford University Press, 1985), pp. 110-13.

35. Patterson, *Slavery and Social Death*, pp. 78-79.

Abduction was also an act of terror. Like Jerusalem's murdered children, those who were abducted and sold into slavery were the victims of Seleucid terror, but not its targets.[36] The targets were those left behind in Jerusalem and Judea.[37] As an act of terror, abduction aimed to traumatize bereft individuals and erode the social fabric of the communities of Jerusalem and the rest of Judea.[38] Among the traumatic effects of disappearance were not only loss but also the prolongation of fear and doubt concerning the fate of loved ones. This uncertainty was a source of hope but also of great psychological and social strain. Those who had seen their loved ones cut down knew they had died, and could mourn and hopefully bury their dead. But the fate of the disappeared would remain unknown. Those who were left standing in a city full of corpses but had not found their own family members among the dead would nurse both hope and fear. The very existence of hope made this fear (not for self, but for loved ones) the more palpable. As Torres-Rivas observes, "The modality of the 'disappeared' is even more cruel than public assassination, since it raises the perception of danger by placing it in an imaginary world, unsure but probable, created by the possibility that the disappeared person is still alive."[39] Antiochus's act of terror through abduction added a new chapter to a long history of enslavement and deportation. A community already aware of its dispersion — both by events in the distant past, memorialized in its traditions of history and lament, and by more recent events, including the capture and sale of its inhabitants in the Fifth Syrian War three decades previously — would feel a cumulative effect as it was once again ripped apart.[40] Yet the very traditions that recorded this history of enslavement and deportation would also provide a deep wellspring of hope and rich resources for resistance through its testimony to the past actions of Israel's God on behalf of God's enslaved people, through its attribution of ultimate agency and meaning-making to God, rather than the

36. Eugene Victor Walter identifies a triangular relationship between terrorist, victim, and target in his seminal study *Terror and Resistance: A Study of Political Violence* (New York: Oxford University Press, 1969), p. 9.

37. It was also an act of intimidation and repression directed at Judea's neighbors in the province, including Samaria and Phoenicia, who would be warned of the consequences of insubordination on any scale.

38. Cf. Antonius C. G. M. Robben, "State Terror in the Netherworld: Disappearance and Reburial in Argentina," in *Death, Mourning, and Burial: A Cross-Cultural Reader*, ed. Antonius C. G. M. Robben (Oxford: Blackwell, 2004), pp. 134-48. The mass disappearance perpetrated by Antiochus is different from the serial selective disappearances perpetrated in Argentina. Nonetheless, common elements of state terror through abduction, the traumatic loss of family members, and subsequent resistant response warrant exploration of further parallels.

39. Torres-Rivas, "Epilogue," p. 292.

40. Cf. Antonius C. G. M. Robben, *Political Violence and Trauma in Argentina* (Philadelphia: University of Pennsylvania Press, 2005), p. 166.

king, and through its promises for justice, liberation, restoration, and a transformed order in the future.

Plundering the Temple

In addition to the slaughters, home invasions, and disappearances, the epitomator reports that, in the company of the high priest Menelaus, Antiochus entered and plundered from the temple furniture and decorations, implements of sacrificial worship, and votive offerings worth a total of 1800 talents (2 Macc 5:15-16, 21).[41] Although the chronologies differ, 1 Maccabees may provide more detail concerning the same event.[42] According to 1 Maccabees, Antiochus stole the golden altar, lampstand, table, cups and bowls, censers, the curtain, the crown, ornaments from the temple façade, silver and gold, and all the "hidden" stores of wealth that he could find (1 Macc 1:21-24).[43] As with the abductions, Antiochus's economic motives are clear, but we must also understand his actions as an assertion of power.

As I discussed in chapter 2, some thirty years earlier the king's father Antiochus III had affirmed by royal fiat that no foreigner (μηδενὶ . . . ἀλλοφύλῳ) would be allowed to enter the Jerusalem temple precincts (εἰς τὸν περίβολον εἰσιέναι τοῦ ἱεροῦ A.J. 12.145). Now king and high priest colluded in violating the temple's sacred boundary, deliberately taking away what had earlier been granted. The king's entry into the temple directly challenged Jewish conceptions concerning the holiness of God, God's people, sacred space, and the conduct of worship by which God had ordered all of reality, from the structure of the cosmos to the practices of daily life. The public display of Menelaus's coop-

41. Two biblical passages emphasize the value of the items used in building Yhwh's sanctuary, first with reference to the wilderness tabernacle (Ex 38:24-31), and later with reference to the first temple (1 Chron 29:3-9).

42. The chronology of this event in relation to Jason's rebellion, the murder of civilians in Jerusalem, other instances of temple robbery, and the mission of Apollonius is far from clear in our sources, and there is little consensus among scholars. See discussions in Daniel R. Schwartz, "Antiochus IV Epiphanes in Jerusalem," in *Historical Perspectives from the Hasmoneans to Bar Kokhba in Light of the Dead Sea Scrolls: Proceedings of the Fourth International Symposium of the Orion Center for the Study of the Dead Sea Scrolls and Associated Literature, 27-31 January, 1999,* ed. David Goodblatt, Avital Pinnick, and Daniel R. Schwartz (Leiden: Brill, 2001), pp. 45-56; Klaus Bringmann, *Hellenistische Reform und Religionsverfolgung in Judäa: Eine Untersuchung zur jüdisch-hellenistischen Geschichte (175-163 v. Chr.)* (Göttingen: Vandenhoeck & Ruprecht, 1983), pp. 32-40.

43. According to Jonathan A. Goldstein, *I Maccabees: A New Translation with Introduction and Commentary,* Anchor Bible 41 (Garden City, NY: Doubleday, 1976), p. 210, "hidden" here means "on deposit."

eration sent a message to the people of Jerusalem: although Menelaus was the ordained leader of the cult of Yhwh, he served the king. Where the laws of God contravened the commands of the king, Menelaus would choose the latter. By conscripting the cooperation of the high priest, Antiochus suggested to the people that they had no recourse: the minister appointed to mediate their petitions to God and God's will to them not only found nothing objectionable in Antiochus's actions and failed to oppose them (cf. Jer 27:18), he also participated in them.

The catalogue of items stolen is also significant. We cannot know for certain whether the list is historically reliable in its details. If we assume the list is historically reliable, we gain from it a clearer picture of Antiochus's motives and techniques of repression. Even if we view the list as a stylized report, it nonetheless reveals cultural and theological meanings attached to Antiochus's sacrilege.

In the ancient Near East, conquerors often abducted a city's cultic image(s) as an assertion of power over the conquered people and their god(s). A cultic image represented the deity in the strong sense, marking and effecting the deity's presence in the temple and the protection this presence afforded. By abducting a city's cultic image(s), a conqueror removed the effective symbol(s) of divine presence and protection. As Zainab Bahrani writes, "Taking the cult statue of an enemy land was not an act of barbaric plunder, but one of taking the enemy's source of divine power into captivity, and thus suppressing its power. Similarly, the deportation of royal monuments was an act of magical and psychological warfare."[44] While Israel's sacred traditions expressly forbade the representation of their God through graven images, various cultic objects symbolized and mediated God's presence in the Jerusalem temple. Like the theft of cultic statues, Antiochus's theft of Jerusalem's cultic objects similarly aimed to suppress and deny the power and protection of Judea's God. This act of psychological warfare communicated to Judeans that they were powerless and defenseless before the might of their Seleucid king. Like the temple itself, the cultic objects also symbolized God's creation and mediated divine providence. By their theft Antiochus continued his program of de-creation.

The altar, table, cups, bowls, and censers were all necessary for the conduct of worship in the temple. Worship not only brought God's people before the presence of God, bridging human and divine, earth and heaven, it was also a way in which God's people could "participat[e] in the divine ordering of the world."[45] Through their participation in the temple cult, Judeans also acknowl-

---

44. Zainab Bahrani, "Assault and Abduction: The Fate of the Royal Image in the Ancient Near East," *Art History* 18, no. 3 (1995): 363-82, 378.

45. Jon D. Levenson, *Creation and the Persistence of Evil: The Jewish Drama of Divine Omnipotence* (San Francisco: Harper & Row, 1988; repr. Princeton: Princeton University Press, 1994), p. 91.

edged God's sovereignty by fulfilling God's commands. Without altar, table, vessels, and censers, God's people in Jerusalem could not offer animal sacrifice, cereal offerings, libations, or incense to Yhwh. While artisans could surely furnish the temple anew, as they had apparently done more than once in the past (2 Chron 24:12-13; 29:19), Antiochus's theft of the objects necessary for worship ruptured the relationship between the people of Judea and their God, rendering impossible certain forms of obedience to divine law (cf. 2 Chron 13:11) and depriving Judeans of the mediation of the temple cult.

Over four centuries earlier, the Babylonian king Nebuchadnezzar had also carried away implements of worship and "all the treasures from the Lord's house."[46] Antiochus's actions recapitulated this earlier act of sacrilege, a connection highlighted by the opening verses of the book of Daniel (Dan 1:1-2). Similarly, Robert Doran notes that "1 Maccabees perceives the events it tells as another reenactment of the events of the Hebrew Scriptures."[47] Yet the catalogue of plundered objects in 1 Maccabees does not simply repeat lists from earlier accounts. Among other differences, Antiochus stole two items conspicuously absent from earlier lists: the lampstand and the curtain. Each had richly symbolic meaning in Israel's cultic life.

The lampstand symbolized light and illumination (cf. Num 8:2-3), motifs related to divine wisdom and revelation (Dan 2:22-23; cf. 5:5). In form, however, it represented a fruit tree in flower (Ex 25:33-34; 37:19-20). Carol Meyers links this tree symbolism to themes of life and creation: "The sacred quality of trees lies in the fact of their embodiment of the life principle. . . . Since the ultimate source of this life that renews is found within divine creation, trees become imbued with the divine power that has deigned to impart life and regeneration within the mundane sphere."[48] Meyers examines associations with fertility and eternal life as well as the motif of "the divinity revealed in the tree," linking the latter with the cosmic tree (cf. Dan 4:10-12; 1 En. 24:4–25:7).[49] She concludes that the lampstand was not only a symbol of life but also a symbol and assur-

46. 2 Kgs 24:13; 25:13-17; 2 Chron 36:7, 10, 18; cf. Isa 39:6; 2 Kgs 20:17.

47. Doran, "First Book of Maccabees," p. 19.

48. Carol Meyers, *The Tabernacle Menorah: A Synthetic Study of a Symbol from the Biblical Cult* (Missoula, MT: Scholars Press, 1976), p. 95.

49. Meyers, *Tabernacle Menorah*, p. 143. In Proverbs 3:18, Wisdom is described as a tree of life. Meyers does not explore connections with Wisdom as tree of life in her dissertation, but the multiplex associations of Wisdom as animating force within creation, means to long life and good name, mode of revelation, and mediator of divine presence suggest significant parallels and overlap in the function and meaning of the tabernacle lampstand and that of the image of Wisdom as tree of life. On the trees of life and wisdom in the Book of the Watchers, see Kelley Coblentz Bautch, *A Study of the Geography of 1 Enoch 17–19: "No One Has Seen What I Have Seen"* (Leiden: Brill, 2003), pp. 122-25, 207-9, 219. The Book of the Watchers envisions that the tree of life will be transplanted to the site of the temple (25:5).

ance of God's sustaining presence.[50] Antiochus's theft of the lampstand thus removed from Jerusalem a preeminent cultic symbol of divine sustaining presence and creative source of life, effecting a symbolic de-creation.

The curtain's theft had a similar symbolic meaning. While the curtain would have been woven from the finest materials available — according to the instructions in Exodus, it was to be made of blue, purple, and crimson yarns and fine linen (Ex 26:31; 36:35; cf. 2 Chron 3:14) — for Antiochus the curtain likely had more symbolic than monetary value, perhaps serving as a trophy. In Israel's sacred traditions, the curtain had once screened off the ark of the covenant (Ex 40:3) that symbolized divine presence and Israel's call to obedience (25:8). The curtain was even used to cover the ark during Israel's wilderness wanderings (Num 4:5). But the curtain was not simply a screen or a covering. It was a divider. Division or separation was fundamental to Israel's understanding of God's work in creation, the ordering of space and time, and the identity of God's chosen people as a people "set apart" (Lev 20:24-25). In creating the cosmos, God divided (וַיַּבְדֵּל) light from darkness (Gen 1:4), formed a dome to separate (מַבְדִּיל) waters above from waters below (1:6-7), and ordained lights in the sky to divide (לְהַבְדִּיל) day from night, marking the divisions of time (1:14) and maintaining the division (וּלֲהַבְדִּיל) of light and darkness (1:18). In Israel's scriptures, the verb בדל next appears in the description of the curtain's function in Exodus 26:33; there it evokes for the reader the account of creation in Genesis 1. Just as God created the firmament to divide waters above from waters below and celestial bodies to mark and maintain the divisions of time, so God's appointed artisans would make the curtain to divide (וְהִבְדִּילָה) holy space from most holy space (Ex 26:33).[51] The curtain was thus a symbol of God's ordering of the cosmos, marking in space the divisions between what was profane, what was holy, and what was most holy. Its theft aimed symbolically to negate these divisions, making of ordered space an undifferentiated chaos.

Creation symbolism was not limited to the lampstand and curtain. On the basis of a comparison of the creation narrative of Genesis 1 and the report of the construction of the tabernacle in the book of Exodus as well as a consideration of such texts as Isaiah 65:17-18 and Psalm 78:69, Jon Levenson has argued that Israel's traditions witness to a fundamental homology between the Jerusalem temple and the created cosmos.[52]

The narrative of the design and construction of the tabernacle and its fur-

---

50. Meyers, *Tabernacle Menorah,* p. 180.

51. Cf. Ezek 42:20, where the ideal temple's outer wall functions to separate holy space from profane space. The root is also used to express the priestly role of distinguishing between what is pure and impure (Lev 10:10; 11:47).

52. Gen 1:3, 6, 9, 11, 15, 20, 24, 30-31; Ex 39:32, 42; 40:16. Levenson, *Creation and the Persistence of Evil,* p. 84.

nishings in Exodus provides a paradigm for understanding Israel's sacred space as a mirror and map of creation. God fills the artisan Bezalel with divine spirit (רוח אלהים), ability, intelligence, and knowledge in every kind of craft, such that he can conceive of designs in order to make, or do (עשה), and so participate in divine creative work (Ex 31:3; 35:31).[53] Animated by the divine spirit, Bezalel, Oholiab, and their team of craftsmen design and make the tabernacle and its furniture, shaping through divinely imparted wisdom the cultic space that both mirrors God's cosmos and mediates God's presence to the people.[54] The artisans carry out their work in accordance with God's commands (36:1). According to the Chronicler, the temple and its furnishings were designed through similar inspiration and were likewise executed according to God's commands (1 Chron 28:19; 29:19; 2 Chron 4:7).

In both Genesis and Exodus, formulaic language emphasizes the perfect correspondence between divine command and creative act, such that "the temple and the world both result from the perfect realization of divine commandments."[55] From his analysis of these and other correspondences, Levenson concludes: "Collectively, the function of these correspondences is to underscore the depiction of the sanctuary as a world, that is, an ordered, supportive, and obedient environment, and a depiction of the world as a sanctuary, that is, a place where the reign of God is visible and unchallenged, and his holiness is palpable, unthreatened, and pervasive."[56] Antiochus challenged this claim for Yhwh's absolute sovereignty. By plundering the visible monument and map of God's sovereignty over creation he denied the power of God and declared himself both ruler and creator in God's stead. The epitomator attributes Antiochus's plunder of the temple to delusions of pride: Antiochus had risen to such heights of arrogance that he imagined he could alter creation itself, turning earth into ocean and sea into dry land. The world he designed was thus one of inversions, in which a human could sail on land and walk on water (2 Macc 5:21). As I noted in chapter 1, apocalyptic discourse could set things "straight" by effecting a double inversion that would turn an upside-down world right-side-up again. By inverting the symbols, structures, and values of

---

53. This word "to make" or "do" is often used in describing God's own creative activity (e.g., Gen 2:4; 2 Kgs 19:15; Isa 45:12). Levenson calls attention to the echo of Gen 1:2 in the phrase רוח אלהים at Ex 31:3 and 35:31 (*Creation and the Persistence of Evil*, p. 84), although he is mistaken that the phrase does not occur anywhere between these passages: it occurs also at Gen 41:38.

54. The position of the command concerning the sabbaths in Ex 31:13-17 connects the sacred ordering of space and time, revealing the common principles that structure each dimension of the cosmos. See also Ex 35.

55. Levenson, *Creation and the Persistence of Evil*, p. 84.

56. Levenson, *Creation and the Persistence of Evil*, p. 86.

the empire, the writers of the apocalypses reasserted what they perceived to be true created order.

The revelation of hidden reality was another way of exposing and countering imperial hegemony. In the exilic period, the profaning of the temple had occasioned a theological crisis for God's people, prompting the faithful to ask whether and how God would remain with them if the temple cult was not functioning properly. Israel's sacred traditions answered this question in multiple ways. One stream of thought that would be exemplified in later Jewish apocalyptic traditions came to understand the earthly temple as a copy of the heavenly temple, by which human, earthly worship imitated and participated in angelic, heavenly worship.[57] In this view, the cessation or corruption of worship in the earthly sphere and the violation of the earthly sanctuary did not automatically signal the unmaking of God's creation, for the heavenly temple and its worship perdured. Nonetheless, the correspondences between the earthly and heavenly realms were powerful, and a threat in one sphere could also constitute a threat in the other. According to Daniel's second vision, Antiochus's arrogance would lead him to challenge not only the earthly but also the heavenly realm (Dan 8:10-12). But the apocalyptic seers revealed the limit of Antiochus's power. Though he would overturn even the heavenly sanctuary (8:11), holiness would finally be vindicated (8:14), and heavenly worship, like earthly worship, would be restored. The famous scene of judgment against the fourth beast in Daniel's first vision reveals that worship in heaven had not ceased after all, for the angels were ministering (יְשַׁמְּשׁוּנֵּהּ) before the heavenly throne (7:10). This scene of judgment asserted the absolute sovereignty of God, promising justice and vindication for the faithful and an end to the oppressive regime. It also demonstrated the limits of Antiochus's power on earth and heaven, reassuring the faithful that there had been no interruption in the provident care of God and no challenge to the created order, for service before God's heavenly throne had not ceased.

Jerusalem's Shame

First Maccabees follows the description of Antiochus's sacrilege with a lament, echoing those sung over Jerusalem and the temple following their destruction by Nebuchadnezzar in 587 BCE (1 Macc 1:25-28; cf. 1:36-40).[58] The lament's final

---

57. See Jonathan Klawans, *Purity, Sacrifice, and the Temple: Symbolism and Supersessionism in the Study of Ancient Judaism* (Oxford: Oxford University Press, 2006), pp. 128-42.

58. Doron Mendels, *The Rise and Fall of Jewish Nationalism* (New York: Doubleday, 1992), p. 123.

verse emphasizes that Antiochus's actions were a source of shame for the house of Jacob (1:28; see also 1:40). Shame was a powerful mechanism of social control, well known and often used in the ancient Near Eastern and Mediterranean worlds.[59] Stephen Pattison calls shame "an indispensable and necessary part of the socio-emotional architecture of any social order."[60] Shaming can be used to shape attitudes and behaviors and create conformity within a social group.[61] Precisely for this reason, it can be exploited "for purposes of power and control."[62] Yet, as Pattison points out, the effects of shaming are sometimes ambivalent and unpredictable.[63] Among the inhabitants of Jerusalem, some were able to limit and transform the shaming effects of Antiochus's actions, and so resist his program of repression, by reframing the honor-shame relationship, such that the social system in which honor and shame were accorded was one dictated and shaped not by Antiochus but rather by Israel's sacred traditions, those who preserved them, and, above all, by God.

Those who worshiped Yhwh effected this reframing through acts of lament and confession. Thus, while the portrayal of public and universal (ἐν παντὶ τόπῳ 1:25) mourning conveys the depth of the community's suffering (1:25-27), it also reveals a source of their strength in the face of terror and shame.[64] By its

59. See David D. Gilmore, ed., *Honor and Shame and the Unity of the Mediterranean* (Washington, DC: American Anthropological Association, 1987); J. G. Peristiany, ed., *Honour and Shame: The Values of Mediterranean Society* (Chicago: University of Chicago Press, 1966); Victor H. Matthews, "Honor and Shame in Gender-Related Legal Situations in the Hebrew Bible," in *Gender and Law in the Hebrew Bible and the Ancient Near East,* ed. Victor H. Matthews and Tikva Frymer-Kensky (London: T. & T. Clark, 2004), pp. 97-112; Lyn Bechtel, "Shame as a Sanction of Social Control in Biblical Israel: Judicial, Political, and Social Shaming," *JSOT* 16, no. 49 (1991): 47-76; Johanna Stiebert, *The Construction of Shame in the Hebrew Bible: The Prophetic Contribution* (London; Sheffield Academic Press, 2002). Citing the dissertation of Lyn Bechtel Huber ("The Biblical Experience of Shame/Shaming: The Social Experience of Shame/Shaming in Biblical Israel in Relation to Its Use as Religious Metaphor" [Ph.D. diss., Drew University, 1983], p. 93), Stiebert calls attention to the shaming practices used in ancient Near Eastern "psychological warfare" (*Construction of Shame,* p. 50n40).

60. Stephen Pattison, *Shame: Theory, Therapy, Theology* (Cambridge: Cambridge University Press, 2000), p. 131. Pattison suggests locating shame within the "metaphorical ecology of pollution and defilement" (p. 90), which also points the way to reintegration through rituals of cleansing and purification (p. 149; but see also 160). Pattison's approach illuminates the connection between the defiled temple, the shame of Jerusalem's inhabitants, and the ritual purification that holds such a prominent place in the narratives of 1 and 2 Maccabees (1 Macc 4:36-59; 2 Macc 1:18; 10:1-9). First Maccabees 4:58 highlights the people's joy at this removal of the "disgrace of nations" (ὀνειδισμὸς ἐθνῶν; cf. 2 Macc 1:27).

61. Pattison, *Shame,* p. 152. See also Bechtel, "Shame as a Sanction," p. 53.

62. Pattison, *Shame,* p. 131. Bechtel, "Shame as a Sanction," p. 53, identifies shame "as an important means of dominating others and manipulating social status."

63. Pattison, *Shame,* pp. 151, 153.

64. My reading contrasts with that of Joseph Sievers, *The Hasmoneans and Their Sup-*

public recognition of shared past and present, lament leads the way forward to a common future.[65] The inhabitants of Jerusalem would approach that future in part through traditional practices of communal confession, a key ritual of reintegration that invited God to remove shame and restore honor.[66] As I discuss in chapter 7, the book of Daniel prescribes precisely this confessing response, modeled by Daniel himself, as part of the book's program of resistance (Dan 9:3-20). Reframed within the practices of confession, Jerusalem's shame would not serve Antiochus's program of repression and control, but would lead rather to restoration of right relationship between the people of Judea and their God.

To this end, in Daniel's prayer, parallel syntactic constructions frame the attribution of shame within the confession of divine justice:

לְךָ אֲדֹנָי הַצְּדָקָה
וְלָנוּ בֹּשֶׁת הַפָּנִים

Yours, Lord, is justice
Ours is shame of face. (9:7)

The prayer acknowledges God's "just acts" (צִדְקֹתֶךָ) again in 9:16. According to the prayer, God is the one who has brought about Jerusalem's ruin and the desolation of its temple; its inhabitants only experience shame in relation to God's just claims on them. Yet the language of shame and confession of justice is also matched by the confession of divine mercy and compassion. The prayer repeats the phrase "ours is shame of face," connecting shame with a history of sin against the Lord at the highest levels of Judean leadership as well as in the more intimate spaces of family life (9:8). But now the prayer shifts its emphasis from justice to mercy, naming God as sovereign lord and confessing rebellion not against any earthly king, be he Nebuchadnezzar or Antiochus, but against God:

---

porters, p. 22, who tentatively classifies this passage under the rubric of "non-reaction" or "paralysis" and characterizes the sorrow it describes as "dismay, lament, and mourning without knowing what to do or not do." It is true that sometimes people just cry, shout, and scream, shake and fall, with no meaning beyond the pain, loss, and fear their sounds and motions express. Yet individual and communal lament are responses drawn from and patterned on Israel's religious traditions. Familiar forms and practices of mourning were an active, engaged response to crisis that also provided a framework of meaning that could direct future action.

65. Cf. Andrew C. Cohen, *Death Rituals, Ideology, and the Development of Early Mesopotamian Kingship: Toward a New Understanding of Iraq's Royal Cemetery at Ur* (Leiden: Brill, 2005). Cohen, pp. 20-21, argues that the language and practices of mourning can be strategic and disruptive, providing an avenue for social action.

66. On the need for rituals of reintegration after shaming, see Pattison, *Shame,* pp. 149, 151.

לַאדֹנָי אֱלֹהֵינוּ הָרַחֲמִים וְהַסְּלִחוֹת
כִּי מָרַדְנוּ בּוֹ

To the Lord our God belong compassion and repeated forgiveness,
Because we rose in revolt against you. (9:9)

Toward the prayer's conclusion, Daniel begs God to shine God's face once more on the defiled sanctuary, grounding his plea in an appeal to "the Lord's own sake" (9:17) and the fact that the city and people are called by God's name (9:18-19). In this way the prayer reveals God's honor, not Antiochus's, as the foil to Jerusalem's shame and the source of hope for the restoration of the city, temple, and people. Though their shame is made known in the desolation of city and temple, it results from nothing other than a ruptured relationship with their just God. That is, Antiochus does not cause the rupture: the rift between Judeans and their God precedes the sanctuary's desolation at Antiochus's hands, and does not result from it. Finally, the God of justice is also the God of mercy, and will demonstrate God's honor by restoring the people, the temple, and the city, for they are called not by the name of Antiochus, but of God.

Apollonius's Mission

First and 2 Maccabees report that after plundering the temple, Antiochus appointed new officials to police the region and administer its finances (1 Macc 1:29; 2 Macc 5:22-24), perhaps instituting a new tax structure and other financial reforms.[67] Echoing the language used in Exodus to describe the taskmasters in Egypt (Ex 1:11), the epitomator calls these officials "Ministers of Oppressing the People" (ἐπιστάτας τοῦ κακοῦν τὸ γένος 2 Macc 5:22), implicitly comparing the Seleucid occupation of Judea with Egypt's enslavement of the Hebrews.[68] Not only Judea but also Samaria was affected (5:23), although our sources re-

---

67. Otto Mørkholm, *Antiochus IV of Syria* (Copenhagen: Gyldendal, 1966), pp. 145-46. Mørkholm writes that "the status of the Judaean temple state was completely transformed by a series of administrative measures" (p. 145). He interprets Apollonius's title "chief tribute collector" (ἄρχοντα φορολογίας) in 1 Macc 1:29 as a clue that the new tax system ratified in 1 Macc 10:30, namely a "proportional land-tax levied directly on agricultural production and collected by royal agents," was introduced under Apollonius at this time as "a punitive measure intended to curb the resist[a]nce to the king and his High Priest." Cf. Dov Gera, *Judaea and Mediterranean Politics, 219-161 B.C.E.* (Leiden: Brill, 1998), p. 225.

68. Jonathan A. Goldstein observes that the epitomator "writes as if the men's chief function and title was 'official in charge of maltreatment.'" *II Maccabees*, Anchor Bible 41A (New York: Doubleday, 1983), p. 261. Schwartz, *2 Maccabees*, pp. 263-64, identifies here the deliberate echo of Ex 1:11.

main focused on events in Jerusalem. There Antiochus stationed the exceptionally "barbaric" or "savage" (βαρβαρώτερον) Philip, a Phrygian by birth (τὸ μὲν γένος Φρύγα) who may have commanded a group of mercenaries from the same region (5:22).[69]

The repeated noun "people" (γένος) here underscores the contrast between the Judean populace and their nonnative oppressors. In addition, the emphatic comparative form βαρβαρώτερον echoes the reference to "the barbarian multitudes" (τὰ βάρβαρα πλήθη) in the epitomator's introduction, where their expulsion from Jerusalem is key to the defense of "the Judean way of life" or "Judaism" (τοῦ Ἰουδαϊσμοῦ), a term first introduced in that verse (2:21).[70] These repetitions and echoes signal to the reader that the measures that follow, especially the edict of Antiochus, which I treat in chapter 6, will constitute an unprecedented external threat to the collective identity and security of the Judean people and their common way of life. This external threat was compounded by the actions of the Judean high priest Menelaus, whom the epitomator judges more harshly for betraying his own people (5:23). Yet, while our sources suggest a complex interplay of international, imperial, regional, and local interests at work in the events that follow, they assign primary responsibility to Antiochus and those he commanded.[71]

According to the epitomator, in addition to reinforcing the bureaucratic apparatus of oppression, in 167 BCE Antiochus sent the military commander Apollonius to occupy the city with 22,000 mercenary troops (5:24).[72] Robert Doran suggests that sending troops to Jerusalem was consistent with Antiochus's need to fortify his southern border against further threats from Egypt.[73] This is certainly true, and underscores the strategic importance of Jerusalem and Judea in the face of ongoing conflict and negotiation between the Seleucids and Ptolemies. Antiochus planned to strengthen his control in this region not only by repositioning his troops, but also by continuing the conquest and subjugation of Jerusalem.

Apollonius and his army arrived with instructions to conduct a second

69. Victor Tcherikover, *Hellenistic Civilization and the Jews,* trans. S. Applebaum (Philadelphia: Jewish Publication Society, 1959; repr. with a pref. by John J. Collins, Peabody, MA: Hendrickson, 1999), p. 188. For the meaning "savage," see Goldstein, *II Maccabees,* p. 192.

70. Note also the contrast between the Seleucid officials whose office is "to injure" or "oppress" (τοῦ κακοῦν) the people (2 Macc 5:22) and the heroes who bravely defend (τοῖς . . . ἀνδραγαθήσασιν) the Judean way of life (2:21).

71. See the discussion in Peter Franz Mittag, *Antiochos IV. Epiphanes: Eine politische Biographie* (Berlin: Akademie Verlag, 2006), pp. 256-68.

72. For the timing, see Gera, *Judaea and Mediterranean Politics,* p. 224, who speculates that Apollonius probably arrived in early summer.

73. Doran, "First Book of Maccabees," p. 36.

round of slaughter and deportation (5:24).[74] Apollonius did not advertise his intentions. According to 1 Maccabees, when he first arrived he spoke in peaceful terms, winning trust before suddenly attacking the city and dealing a severe blow to its population (1 Macc 1:30).[75] His soldiers took spoils from the city, set it on fire, and tore down its houses and walls (1:31). Beyond the traumatic loss of life and home, the leveling of houses represented a negation and dismantling of family and household structures at the heart of Jerusalem's social life. The dismantling of social architecture from within was matched by the removal of the city's outer architecture of protection, denying the city its right and means of self-defense. The destruction of walls communicated a city's total subjugation. It could also communicate its destruction.[76] For Dio Chrysostom (*Or.* 48.9) and Pausanius (10.4.1), a city without walls was not a city at all.[77]

The epitomator adds the further detail that Apollonius waited until the sabbath, then staged a military parade which he gruesomely transformed into a massacre of its spectators. His soldiers then fell upon the rest of the city (2 Macc 5:25-26). Victor Tcherikover interprets Apollonius's trickery as a sign that he did not expect to gain control of the city by direct means. From this he infers that Jerusalem was being held by a group of insurgents. The brutal assault would then be understood as retaliation for a second, current revolt that took

74. Although the subject is not named in the verse, commentators agree that Antiochus must be the one issuing the command, as he is at 5:22 and 6:1. Schwartz speculates that the epitomator inserted the mention of Menelaus in 5:23, interrupting a chain of verbs that originally all shared Antiochus as their expressed subject (2 *Maccabees*, pp. 264-65).

75. Livy reports that Paullus accomplished the massive plunder and abductions of seventy Epirot towns in 167 BCE by means of a similar ruse, first sending soldiers to announce to the towns that Rome had decided to grant them independence and remove their garrisons (Livy 45.34). Plutarch (*Aem.* 29) and Appian (*Ill.* 9-10) narrate the ruse differently, but all agree that Paullus assured the townspeople of his peaceful intent as a way of putting them off guard.

76. Getzel Cohen writes that in the Hellenistic world "the 'destruction' of a city could take a number of forms: the physical destruction of the acropolis or buildings in the city; the demolition of parts or all of its walls, or the deprivation of its rights as an independent, corporate body." *The Hellenistic Settlements in Europe, the Islands, and Asia Minor* (Berkeley: University of California Press, 1995), p. 186. See also p. 185n2. For a review of key ancient sources, see Louis Robert, review of Franz Georg Maier, *Griechische Mauerbauinschriften*, in *Gnomon* 42 (1970): 579-603, 597-98. Discussing Josephus's account of the destruction of Hellenistic cities by Alexander Jannaeus almost a century later, Aryeh Kasher observes that "the Hellenists felt it proper to claim that, as the political status and sovereignty of a *polis* were symbolized by its walls, the razing of those walls by the Hasmonaean conquerors could be equated to the destruction of the entire *polis*." *Jews and Hellenistic Cities in Eretz-Israel: Relations of the Jews in Eretz-Israel with the Hellenistic Cities during the Second Temple Period (332 BCE-70 CE)* (Tübingen: J. C. B. Mohr [Paul Siebeck], 1990), p. 163.

77. Cited in Richard Billows, "Cities," in *A Companion to the Hellenistic World*, ed. Andrew Erskine (Oxford: Blackwell, 2003), pp. 196-215, 197.

place between the revolts of Jason and the Maccabees: "Although the renewal of the rising is nowhere referred to, it cannot be doubted, for according to all our sources Apollonius . . . was compelled to capture the city by trickery on a Sabbath, a sign that once again it was not in the hands of the Syrian forces. Apollonius had received from Antiochus the assignment of putting an end once and for all to the danger threatening the peace of the kingdom from the rebellious Jews."[78] Daniel Schwartz supports Tcherikover's hypothesis.[79] As I noted in the previous chapter, such a revolt is certainly possible but is not necessary for understanding the logic that governed the actions of Antiochus and his agents. It is unlikely that after the earlier reprisals Apollonius believed he and his troops needed to resort to a ruse to enter Jerusalem and kill its men, even if the city was still exhibiting signs of unrest. Apollonius was not "compelled" to act in this way but chose to do so. His act of deception would have aimed to undermine patterns of relationship and structures of trust that made life in Jerusalem predictable and secure, compounding in the Judeans a deep sense of insecurity, unpredictability, and fear that would create the need for the new order and security the Seleucid occupation would ostensibly provide.[80] The psychological assault was matched by a physical one, as the demolition of houses and walls deconstructed familiar architecture of safety and security and focused attention on the alternative and alien structure of the Akra, a storehouse of weapons, provisions, and plunder (1 Macc 1:36) which Apollonius now fortified with a "great strong wall and strong towers" (1:33).

Erich Gruen aptly characterizes Apollonius's mission: he was sent "to terrorize the populace of Jerusalem."[81] New acts of terror did not require new reasons, for the goals of domination and repression remained the same. Each new act of terror and violence built on the ones that preceded it, with cumulative effects designed to destabilize and debilitate the Judean social body. Robben describes similar cumulative effects in his study of political violence in Argentina: "The social traumas from the past became vessels of suffering whose posttraumatic effects increased with every new violent act. . . . Every violent act car-

78. Tcherikover, *Hellenistic Civilization*, p. 188. See also John J. Collins, *Daniel, First Maccabees, Second Maccabees, with an Excursus on the Apocalyptic Genre* (Wilmington, DE: Michael Glazier, 1981), p. 301.

79. Schwartz, *2 Maccabees*, p. 251; "Antiochus IV Epiphanes in Jerusalem," pp. 53-55. Schwartz argues that our sources would have suppressed references to further revolt out of a desire to portray the Judean people as compliant with their Seleucid rulers.

80. Cf. Robben, *Political Violence*, p. 211. When an act of violence is unexpected and the reason for it is not apparent, the trauma is heightened. State terror therefore uses arbitrary, unpredictable, or unexpected acts of violence to instill fear and uncertainty.

81. Erich S. Gruen, "Hellenism and Persecution: Antiochus IV and the Jews," in *Hellenistic History and Culture*, ed. Peter Green (Berkeley: University of California Press, 1993), pp. 239-64, 247.

ried an emotional price. . . . The various social traumas reinforced one another, as one was interpreted as a duplication of the other. The trauma of the afflicted group became therefore a layered, oversaturated phenomenon. . . ."[82] In such a context, the seemingly arbitrary and unpredictable sequence and severity of brutalities served to heighten anxiety and magnify the effects of trauma, as Antiochus and his agents continued their program of terror in Jerusalem.

Parade Turned Massacre

According to the epitomator, Apollonius began his particular mission of terror with a military parade. Military parades in the Greco-Roman world evolved in part from religious processions, wherein a victorious general might bring an offering to a deity's temple.[83] They were also crafted displays of power meant to stir the emotions of their participants and spectators, creating and manipulating a sense of collective identity mixed with awe and fear of the conquering empire. Richard Beacham writes of such military parades as follows: "The primary expressive element of a parade is, of course, the ranks of marchers, who . . . are simultaneously the 'performers' as well as a highly effective living scenic device, whose controlled and coordinated movement and sounds can stimulate a powerful emotional response in the spectators. . . . The event is also defined and the emotional response to it informed by a motivating purpose: in the case of the triumph, to celebrate an entire panoply of entities — the gods, the state, the conquering general, his soldiers, the captured plunder, and the victory."[84] A year later, in 166 BCE, Antiochus would stage his greatest military parade at Daphne, a suburb of his own capital city Antioch, as a "demonstration of power" and "celebration of victory" after his Egyptian campaigns (Polyb. 30.25-6; Diod. 31.16.2).[85] Like the parade at Daphne, Apollonius's parade in Jerusalem was also a "demonstration of power" and "celebration of victory," albeit on a smaller scale. Yet the different context and motivating purpose, to borrow Beacham's phrase, gave his parade a very different meaning.

82. Robben, *Political Violence*, p. 166.

83. Alison Futrell, *The Roman Games: A Sourcebook* (Oxford: Blackwell, 2006), 1. She notes that the procession "convey[ed] the worshipers, the officiants, and their implements of worship to the sacred space of the altar or temple." The procession would then be followed by sacrifice and games.

84. Richard C. Beacham, *Spectacle Entertainments of Early Imperial Rome* (New Haven: Yale University Press, 1999), p. 40.

85. Brian McGing, "Subjection and Resistance: To the Death of Mithridates," in *A Companion to the Hellenistic World,* ed. Andrew Erskine (Oxford: Blackwell, 2003), pp. 71-89, 74. See further Andrew Bell, *Spectacular Power in the Greek and Roman City* (Oxford: Oxford University Press, 2004), pp. 140-43.

Though many of those on parade at Daphne would be mercenaries from other regions, one conceit of the victory parade was that the soldiers had left the field of battle and returned home, ceremonially reentering civic space and life and bringing with them captives and spoil of war.[86] Parades concealed death from view and instead vaunted power, wealth, glory, the reach of empire, and the health of the human military body as well as the imperial social body it symbolized and protected.[87] Through the pretense of conflict's absence a military parade showcased the containment and control of its own violence, focusing attention on the means, proof, and agents of order, stability, and prosperity secured through war. In this way the projection of power, victory, and wealth also projected civic peace through imperial (and in Rome's case, republican) order.[88]

Understanding the military parade in this way highlights the ambiguity of the display in Jerusalem, even before spectacle turned to slaughter. According to the triumphal conceit, the army of Apollonius and the absent king they represented entered Jerusalem as victors coming home, reminding those who already lived there that Jerusalem had taken the name of its king and belonged to him; his soldiers were there to stay.[89] This act of displacement served to alienate the people of Jerusalem from their home, transforming familiar space into foreign territory.

I have noted that the procession was a display of power and control. It was

---

86. Note however that Paullus's procession and games at Amphipolis preceded his triumphal procession in Rome (Livy 45.40). Staging such a procession abroad was unusual, and contributed to Paullus's reputation among the Greeks as a Roman truly skilled in the art of spectacle (45.32).

87. Guy Debord emphasizes what is hidden by spectacle in *Comments on the Society of the Spectacle,* trans. Malcolm Imrie, 2nd ed. (London: Verso, 1998), pp. 12-13, 60-62.

88. The Roman triumph served as an important model for Antiochus's own military parades. In his classic treatment of the origins of the Roman triumph, H. S. Versnel locates the origins of the practice in a merging of Dionysian traditions from Asia Minor with Jupiter traditions from Etruria and Rome. These connections may help to explain the significance of the Dionysiac procession soon to follow in Jerusalem. See H. S. Versnel, *Triumphus: An Inquiry into the Origin, Development and Meaning of the Roman Triumph* (Leiden: Brill, 1970). For sophisticated recent treatments of the Roman triumphal procession, see Mary Beard, *The Roman Triumph* (Cambridge, MA: Harvard University Press, 2007); and Egon Flaig, *Ritualisierte Politik: Zeichen, Gesten, und Herrschaft im Alten Rom* (Göttingen: Vandenhoeck & Ruprecht, 2003), pp. 32-48.

89. Cf. n. 86 above. Aemilius Paullus's triumphal procession and games at Amphipolis provide a contemporary parallel for staging a parade on provincial soil. See Futrell, *Roman Games,* pp. 9-10. By staging games Aemilius Paullus was also participating in the economy of benefaction, on which see Claire Holleran, "The Development of Public Entertainment Venues in Rome and Italy," in *Bread and Circuses: Euergetism and Municipal Patronage in Roman Italy,* ed. Kathryn Lomas and Tim Cornell (London: Routledge, 2003), pp. 46-50.

also a farce. The Judeans already knew that they were not to identify with the conquerors but with the conquered. Their own treasures were the spoil and their own people had already been taken captive; they must have been aware that it could happen again at any time. No one returned safely to their homes. Home was instead the battlefield. The display of soldiers' hyper-militarized bodies emphasized the reality of foreign occupation. Fully armored and armed (ἐξοπλησίαν), the soldiers wore, wielded, and marched as signs of Seleucid strength and Judean subjugation.

Just as Apollonius's parade transformed familiar space into foreign territory, it also intervened in the structure of time. Antiochus's edict, still to come, would continue and deepen this pattern of intervention. The Jewish sabbath laws replicated the pattern of God's creative activity in the human cycle of labor and rest. Time was structured by the activity, rest, and plan of God and marked by the cessation of human effort and striving that signaled radical trust in divine providence (cf. Ex 16). By staging his parade on the sabbath, Apollonius demonstrated a knowledge of Jewish religious observances: when better to have a parade than on a day when no one was working? Armed with this knowledge, Apollonius also used it to undermine trust in divine providence and to replace the divinely ordained cycle of creation, labor, and rest with a different way of marking time.

H. S. Versnel has argued that triumphal processions in the Greco-Roman world originated in the merging of new year's festival traditions from Asia Minor and Italy associated with the gods Dionysus and Jupiter respectively.[90] The key difference, as Versnel observed, is that new year's festivals are fixed in time, while triumphal processions occur irregularly, commemorating the specific, "historical" human accomplishments of military victory. Yet the very relationship between the two suggests that the military procession makes a claim for the meaning of an empire's military power and victories. New year's festivals affirmed the ordering of time and seasons, celebrating the very cycles of life and death, growth and harvest that assured the stability and continuity of human existence on earth. The transfer of formal elements of the new year procession to the triumphal procession suggests that military victory accomplishes the same stability and continuity. Polybius reports that in the procession at Daphne in 166 BCE Antiochus included representations of night and day, earth and heaven, dawn and midday (Polyb. 30.25.15), arranging the elements of time and space within the ordered display of imperial might. I discussed in the preceding chapter the ways in which conquest re-created the empire. The temporary (and sometimes permanent) identification of the victorious general or king with the creating and conquering deity merges human conqueror with creator. A trium-

90. Versnel, *Triumphus*, pp. 288-99.

phal procession gave public ceremonial form to the celebration of empire's creation and the military commander who created it.[91] Time's cycle symbolically began again in the ritualistic celebration of conquest. Though not a formal triumph, Apollonius's parade nonetheless marked both space and time with his own creative stamp as well as that of Antiochus and his gods.

Finally, by its visibility the parade created a spectacle that drew attention away from God's ordering of space, time, and human life (cf. 2 Macc 8:27) and focused it instead on the ordered formation of Apollonius's army (cf. 15:20, 6:21) and the imperial regime it served and represented. Yet as soon as its audience gathered to take in the spectacle the ordered formation erupted into a scene of destruction, turning Jerusalem's streets into a deadly arena.

The link between the military parade and the arena was well established in this period. In contemporary Roman and Hellenistic celebrations of military victory, triumphal parades were followed by the celebration of votive games, or what the Romans called *ludi extraordinarii*.[92] These included athletic contests, long familiar to the Greeks, as well as more violent entertainments such as gladiatorial games and staged hunts. Andrew Bell comments on Antiochus's penchant for such displays, noting that this first Hellenistic king to stage Roman-style gladiatorial games and animal killings *(venationes)* in a city of the east recognized "the significance of giving his audience spectacles of violence and death."[93] According to Athenaeus, the parade at Daphne was followed by thirty days of games, combining traditional Greek games with gladiatorial combat and animal hunts.[94] In the spectacle of a game, such displays of violence evoked a strange "merriment and wonder" while also communicating the king's "control of an awful instrumentality of bloodshed."[95] Livy describes the novelty of Antiochus's gladiatorial games, showing that Antiochus understood the dissonance of violence in the civic arena (Livy 41.20). The king who "surpassed [literally, conquered] former [or better] kings in the magnificence of every kind of public show" (*spectaculorum quoque omnis generis magnificentia superiores reges uicit* 41.20; cf. Dan 7:20) also understood how to manipulate his subjects through spectacle:

---

91. Note that in republican Rome a triumph had to be approved by vote of the Senate. Livy reports in great detail the animated senatorial debate over the authorization of Aemilius Paullus's triumph (45.35-39).

92. Beacham, *Spectacle Entertainments*, p. 2.

93. Bell, *Spectacular Power*, p. 148. For Bell, Antiochus ranks with Pericles, Caesar, and Pompey as individuals "willfully striving to make of themselves an attractive and memorable aesthetic phenomenon" (p. 12). Futrell (*Roman Games*, p. 3) notes that the Romans themselves first staged *venationes* only two decades previously in 187 BCE, as part of the votive games following the triumphal procession of Marcus Fulvius Nobilior (Livy 39.22).

94. *Philosopher's Banquet* 5.194-95, cited in Futrell, *Roman Games*, p. 11.

95. Bell, *Spectacular Power*, p. 150.

[He presented] a gladiatorial exhibition, after the Roman fashion, which was at first received with greater terror than pleasure on the part of men who were unused to such sights; then by frequent repetitions, by sometimes allowing the fighters to go only as far as wounding one another, sometimes permitting them to fight without giving quarter, he made the sight familiar and even pleasing, and he roused in many of the young men a joy in arms. And so, while at first he had been accustomed to summon gladiators from Rome, procuring them by large fees, finally he could find a sufficient supply at home.[96]

Antiochus acclimated audiences in his capital city, including young men at arms, to the spectacle of violence and the ludic "joy" of killing for sport. Violent games created drama, suspense, and relief as conflict unfolded and met its resolution before the spectators' eyes. Spectators eventually became participants.

Although at the time of Apollonius's mission in 167 BCE Antiochus had not yet staged his parade and games at Daphne, he already understood the relation between conquest and spectacle, as did his general Apollonius. That same year, in celebration of the Roman conquest of Macedonia, the Roman general L. Aemilius Paullus was advertising widely his own lavish victory parade and games at Amphipolis, inviting kings and dignitaries from the Hellenistic empires to witness the proofs of Rome's power and glory (Livy 45.32).[97] In narrating this event, Livy attributes to Paullus a famous saying that asserts the connection between conquest and spectacle: "The man who knows how to conquer in war is the same man who knows how to draw up a banquet and put on games" (45.32).[98] Paullus's command of the theater of power made a strong impression on Antiochus, who, according to Polybius, strove to emulate and compete with Paullus in his own display at Daphne (Polyb. 30.25.1).[99]

Apollonius's procession into Jerusalem linked conquest and spectacle in a different way. The parade did not celebrate a completed conquest but continued to enact it, turning the ordered display of military power into a horrifying game of death with every spectator its participant.[100] The epitomator's keen sense of irony and just punishment likely colors the report that Apollonius's

96. Livy 41.20, translated in Futrell, *Roman Games*, p. 10.

97. Amphipolis, the Macedonian city that hosted the procession and games, was now one of four Roman capitals in the newly conquered and divided region (Livy 45.29; Strabo 7 fr. 47). See also Klaus Bringmann, *A History of the Roman Republic* (Cambridge: Polity, 2007), p. 99.

98. *et conuiuium instruere et ludos parare eiusdem esse, qui uincere bello sciret.*

99. See further Jonathan C. Edmondson, "The Cultural Politics of Public Spectacle in Rome and the Greek East, 167-166 BCE," in *The Art of Ancient Spectacle*, ed. Bettina Bergmann and Christine Kondoleon (New Haven: Yale University Press, 1999), pp. 77-95.

100. On the contrast between triumphal and circus processions, see Beacham, *Spectacle Entertainments*, p. 42.

soldiers first ran through those who had come to watch the spectacle (2 Macc 5:26). The occupying soldiers then raced (εἰσδραμὼν) into the city to level its population (5:25-26). The participle εἰσδραμὼν evokes associations with the *dromos*, the foot race or running track that was a key feature of celebratory games in the Hellenistic world.[101] The entertainments that had so powerfully attracted the young men of Jerusalem that priests neglected their duties in the temple thus foreshadowed and, in the epitomator's view, invited Apollonius's deadly incursion (cf. 4:14-17).

The detail of public parade turned ludic massacre highlights the imperial staging and manipulation of spectacle, or visible show, to announce and create its power, while at the same time revealing the spectacle as dark and deadly farce. Those who imagined that the imperial show (τὴν θεωρίαν 5:26) was real and worth watching lost their lives. More horrifying spectacles were still to come in the form of tortures and public executions.[102] Unlike the parade, in which violence was carefully hidden and controlled, these spectacles made a visible show of imperial violence in order to assert imperial control over life and death, hiding from view the possibility, or the reality, of life outside and beyond the limits of imperial power. For modern theorist Guy Debord, spectacle negates life by convincing others that *this* projected form is *all* there is: "Understood on its own terms, the spectacle proclaims the predominance of appearances and asserts that all human life, which is to say all social life, is mere appearance. But any critique capable of apprehending the spectacle's essential

101. See Nigel Crowther, "More on 'dromos' as a Technical Term in Greek Sport," *Nikephoros* 6 (1993): 33-37; and Waldo E. Sweet, *Sport and Recreation in Ancient Greece: A Sourcebook* (Oxford: Oxford University Press, 1987), pp. 27-36. The *hoplitodromos*, or hoplite race, was run in partial armor (Sweet, *Sport and Recreation*, p. 31).

102. Execution and spectacle were united elsewhere in the Greco-Roman world as well. According to Valerius Maximus, in 168 or 167 BCE Paullus staged dramatic public executions of foreign soldiers who had deserted from his army during the war with Macedon (2.7.14). He used elephants as the means of execution (cf. 3 Macc 4:11, 5:1–6:21). Their massive size would have made them easily visible to spectators, while their "strangeness" would have heightened the terror of *morituri* and spectators alike. The spectacle was intended to deter (or as Valerius puts it, to crush) insubordination and strengthen military discipline through fear and through the shared experience of witnessing the gruesome punishment. Valerius offers this report and commentary: *et L. Paulus Perse rege superato eiusdem generis et culpae homines elephantis proterendos substravit, utilissimo quidem exemplo, si tamen acta excellentissimorum virorum humiliter aestimare sine insolentiae reprehensione permittitur: aspero enim et absciso castigationis genere militaris disciplina indiget, quia vires armis constant, quae ubi a recto tenore desciverint, oppressa sunt, nisi opprimantur.* According to Alison Futrell, some have linked the execution with the games at Amphipolis. She observes that "this combination of spectacular celebration of Roman conquest and public execution would set a pattern to be followed for centuries." *Blood in the Arena: The Spectacle of Roman Power* (Austin: University of Texas Press, 1997), pp. 28-29.

character must expose it as a visible negation of life — and as a negation of life that has *invented a visual form for itself*."[103]

Exposing the Spectacle, Answering Terror

The writers of the apocalypses would insist on revealing the imperial spectacles, and the empires themselves, as a visible negation of life. By insisting on empire's contingency, they aimed to show that its visible forms were neither necessary, nor eternal, nor truthful, but invented, finite, and deceptive. They would also redirect the gaze of the faithful from the disordered and disordering gleam of imperial arms to the ordering brilliance of the eternal divine throne (e.g., Dan 7:9-10; *1 En.* 90:20) and future temple (*1 En.* 90:28; 91:13), as well as to the books of truth that recorded and revealed judgment for the oppressing empires and deliverance for the faithful.[104]

Into the Wilderness

In addition, the epitomator redirects the gaze from the imperial spectacle of urban slaughter to a small group who fled to the wilderness, highlighting another form of resistance to the empire that would prepare the way for revolt as well as martyrdom. After the report of Apollonius's parade and massacre, the epitomator introduces the book's first heroes, momentarily focusing attention on Judas Maccabeus and his company of ten. They decline the scripted roles of spectator and participant in the imperial show, and withdraw instead to the wilderness (εἰς τὴν ἔρημον 2 Macc 5:27).

The wilderness setting held symbolic importance in Israel's sacred traditions. During the period of forced labor in Egypt, Moses fled to the wilderness (to Midian, Ex 2:15) after killing an Egyptian man who had struck one of the Hebrew slaves (2:11-15). There, in or beyond the wilderness (אַחַר הַמִּדְבָּר MT; ὑπὸ τὴν ἔρημον LXX Ex 3:1), on Mount Horeb, God declared to Moses that God had seen and heard and knew the suffering of God's people (Ex 3:7), and called Moses to lead and deliver them out of Egypt (3:10). In the wilderness, at Mount Sinai, God revealed the divine self to the liberated people of Israel, and there established with them the covenant that would define and shape their common life with God.

---

103. Guy Debord, *Society of the Spectacle* (1967), §10 in *The Visual Culture Reader*, ed. Nicholas Mirzoeff (London: Routledge, 1998), p. 142.

104. Dan 7:10; 12:1; *1 En.* 89:62-64, 70-71, 76-77; 90:17, 20; 93:2. Cf. *T. Mos.* 10:1, 3, 7. *T. Mos.* emphasizes the visibility of God and God's kingdom in the time of deliverance: "Then his kingdom will appear throughout his whole creation" (10:1); "in full view will he come" (10:7).

The author of 1 Maccabees also tells of flight into the wilderness, after reporting the edict of Antiochus, which I explore in detail in the chapter that follows. At Modein, Mattathias summons "all who are zealous for the law and who stand by the covenant" to go out with him from the city (1 Macc 2:27) into the mountains (2:28). According to 1 Maccabees, "many who were seeking righteousness and judgment [or justice] went down into the wilderness to live there" (2:29).

For each of these authors, and no doubt for those who fled there, wilderness was a place "outside," beyond the city and beyond the reach of the political machinery of empire and its local collaborators. Unlike the city of Jerusalem, the wilderness of Judea did not bear the stamp of Antiochus's policies of terror. Life in the wilderness was not structured by royal decree, royal punishment, or royal enticement, but by the precepts of the God who desired the freedom of God's people and commanded their holiness. In the face of terrors (Ex 14:10) Moses had instructed the people whom he led from Egypt into the wilderness, "Do not be afraid, stand firm, and see the deliverance that the Lord will accomplish for you today. . . . The Lord will fight for you and you have only to keep still" (14:13-14 NRSV). By analogy with the era of the exodus from Egypt, the retreat to the wilderness of Judea marked the beginning of a new deliverance for God's people. For the authors of 1 and 2 Maccabees, it was a key moment in the narrative of resistance to Antiochus, marking as well the emergence of new leaders who would deliver God's people from their oppression (cf. *T. Mos.* 1:4-10; 9:6-7).[105]

In the symbolic order of space and time mapped in scriptures from Israel's beginnings to the present crisis, the flight to the wilderness signaled rejection of imperial rule and local policies and structures of collaboration; the expectation of God's deliverance; and a choice that only the covenant between God and Israel, and no decree of Antiochus, would shape identity and govern life in community. I mentioned above that Israel's traditions recording their history of enslavement and deportation provided a wellspring of hope and resources for resistance by testifying to God's actions on Israel's behalf, attributing agency and meaning-making to God, and promising future justice, liberation, restoration, and transformation. Like the heroes in 1 and 2 Maccabees, the apocalyptic writers studied in Part Three of this book find in the exodus and wilderness traditions a promise of deliverance and a pattern for faithful resistance to Antiochus's program of terror and de-creation.

---

105. Sievers, *The Hasmoneans and Their Supporters*, pp. 22-23, classifies this flight not as resistance but as evasion.

The Monstrosity of Imperial Rule

I have highlighted key responses to the terror tactics of Antiochus found in our sources. One important response was to reject the imperial spectacle and expose the inhumane character of Seleucid imperial rule. Israel's traditions concerning the creation of humankind associated the distinctive character of humanity created in the image (צלם) of God with the concept of rule (Gen 1:26).[106] Such rule incorporated notions of "wisdom and artful construction" and was fundamentally concerned with justice and the well-being of creation.[107] In Israel's sacred traditions, rule — the capacity and calling that distinguished human from animal — was thus understood as the exercise of temporal power in ways that mirrored and mediated the providential and creative care of God (cf. Dan 4:9). By contrast, the writer of Daniel revealed Antiochus as one who pretended to create but in fact destroyed, setting himself in the place of God (8:11, 25; 11:36; cf. 4:22) and deception in the place of wisdom (e.g., 8:25). In the seer's view, he provided no true security, protection, or benefaction. Through his policies of state terror he trampled on justice and became a predator toward the very people he was charged to protect.

I noted in chapter 1 the centrality of symbols in apocalyptic counter-discourse. A key strategy employed by the writers of the historical apocalypses in constructing discourses of resistance to Antiochus and his empire was the use of symbols to reveal the ways in which imperial rule contrasted with and violated the divine commission for humanity. The Animal Apocalypse portrays the predatory rule of the empires through animal symbolism (cf. Jer 51:34). During the period of Babylonian rule, the sheep that represent Israel are given over "to all the wild beasts, to devour them" (1 En. 89:68). The Hellenistic kings are similarly represented by eagles, vultures, kites, and ravens who blind and devour the flesh of the sheep (90:2-3). Enoch describes the fate of the people of Judea at the hands of their Hellenistic rulers this way: "And they left them neither flesh nor skin nor sinew, until only their bones remained; and their bones fell on the earth, and the sheep became few" (90:4). The Animal Apocalypse concludes with a contrasting eschatological vision of the just rule of a white bull, in whose presence these wild beasts and birds of heaven become afraid and make petition. They are finally transformed from predators into cattle, and are no longer violent (90:37-38).[108]

---

106. J. Richard Middleton, *The Liberating Image: The* Imago Dei *in Genesis 1* (Grand Rapids: Brazos, 2005), p. 55.

107. Middleton, *Liberating Image*, p. 89.

108. See Patrick A. Tiller, *A Commentary on the Animal Apocalypse of* I Enoch (Atlanta: Scholars Press, 1993), pp. 385, 388; George W. E. Nickelsburg, *1 Enoch 1: A Commentary on the Book of 1 Enoch, chapters 1–36; 81–108*, Hermeneia (Minneapolis: Fortress, 2001), pp. 406-7.

In similar fashion, the seer of Daniel symbolizes future just rule through the figure of "one like a human" (Dan 7:13). This figure evokes traditional conceptions of the image of God and communicates the fundamental character of rule in the time beyond empires as mediating divine providence and justice for God's people and for creation (contrast the king's idolatrous "image" or צלם in Dan 3). By contrast, the seer of Daniel envisions the empires not simply as predators but monsters, composite creatures mutated beyond the natural order (7:3-8).[109] The Hellenistic empires were most monstrous and terrifying of all. The seer describes the fourth beast, from which the horn of Antiochus rises, this way: "Now see a fourth beast, terrifying and hideous, with might untold and massive teeth of iron. Eating and crushing, it smashed with its feet whatever remained. It was mutated more than all the beasts before it (וְהִיא מְשַׁנְּיָה מִן־כָּל־חֵיוָתָא דִּי קָדָמַיהּ), and it had ten horns" (7:7). Through imagery of wild beasts and unnatural creatures, the seers communicated to their audiences that the empires that ruled over Judea had passed beyond the realm of the human, and humane, and beyond the limits of divinely ordained natural and social order, into the realm of the monstrous.[110]

109. I use "monster" here in the sense articulated by Noël Carroll, as "a being in violation of the natural order." *The Philosophy of Horror or Paradoxes of the Heart* (New York: Routledge, 1990), p. 40. Future investigation of early Jewish apocalypses through the lenses of horror and monster theory promises to illuminate the internal logic, grammar, and functions of apocalyptic symbolism. Two studies of Revelation have already made significant contributions in this direction: Tina Pippin, *Apocalyptic Bodies: The Biblical End of the World in Text and Image* (London: Routledge, 1999); Christopher A. Frilingos, *Spectacles of Empire: Monsters, Martyrs, and the Book of Revelation* (Philadelphia: University of Pennsylvania Press, 2004). In a similar vein, see Amy Kalmanofsky, *Terror All Around: Horror, Monsters, and Theology in the Book of Jeremiah* (London: Continuum, 2008).

110. The massacre of innocents in Jerusalem in 169 or 168 BCE led the epitomator to a similar characterization of Antiochus, often missed in translation: in his soul Antiochus had now become a wild beast (τεθηριωμένος τῇ ψυχῇ 2 Macc 5:11). Robert Doran, "The Second Book of Maccabees," *NIB*, vol. 4 (Nashville: Abingdon, 1996), pp. 179-299, 228, recognizes the contrast implicit in the metaphor: "Antiochus is not in control of himself, not properly human." Most translations understand ψυχή in this phrase as denoting affect, and so interpret the metaphor as pertaining to Antiochus's anger (cf. the discussion of Dan 11:30 in ch. 4). NAB translates "raging like a wild animal," while NRSV abandons the animal imagery altogether and simply translates, "raging inwardly." Schwartz translates, "his spirit maddened like a beast's" (2 *Maccabees*, p. 248). Goldstein's rendering of the verse comes closest to capturing the force of the animal imagery, although, like other translators, he understands the imagery primarily in affective terms: "With the fury of a wild beast he took the city, treating it as enemy territory captured in war" (*II Maccabees*, p. 245). While anger may be in view, "soul" (ψυχή) here denotes more than affect. The state of a king's ψυχή determines the character of his rule. Isocrates discusses the need for a king to "train his soul" (ψυχήν) in virtue (*Ad Nic.* 2.11). Note that acting like an "animal" is not always a bad thing in the moral world of 2 Maccabees, but even where it is positive it characterizes either the "raw" and "liminal" behavior of those who fled the city to avoid defilement (2 Macc

Divine Justice

In Daniel the succession of monsters is followed immediately by the appearance of the ancient one seated on a brilliant throne amidst a court of justice (7:9-10). I noted above that in treating the people of Jerusalem as newly conquered, Antiochus suspended all prior benefactions, all semblance of duty, and all obligation to protect. Judeans were no longer citizens or subjects, but enemies, criminals, and slaves. As such, he could slaughter and plunder them freely, and no earthly court would hold him accountable. It was precisely because Antiochus had suspended all law, positioning himself as sole sovereign but repudiating any commitment to justice, that the apocalyptic seers took such pains to assert a transcendent court of justice that would guarantee redress for victims of state violence and repression, judgment against the empire, and the establishment of a future just order among God's people.

Speaking the Unspeakable

These visions of judgment, redress, and restoration were ultimately a source of great hope and strength. But they did not erase the horror of Seleucid atrocities. While the experience of such horror defies expression, both healing and future direct action (whether resistant, restorative, or transformative) required remembrance.[111] As psychiatrist Judith Herman writes, "The ordinary response

---

5:27, 10:6) or conduct in battle much like that of Antiochus's army. When Judas and his men became "beast-like" (θηριώδει θυμῷ 10:35; θηριωδῶς 12:15), they refused mercy even to one who had fled and hidden (10:37), and "wrought unspeakable slaughters" upon a city (ἀμυθήτους ἐποιήσαντο σφαγὰς 12:16).

111. Discussing the function of Holocaust testimony, Lawrence L. Langer questions whether healing from such trauma is even possible. He writes, "Painful memories are not always disabling, and narratives about them — at least this is true of Holocaust testimony — rarely 'liberate' witnesses from a past they cannot and do not wish to escape. For them, forgetting would be the ultimate desecration, a 'cure' the ultimate illusion. As for renewal or rebirth, such monuments to hope cannot be built from the ruins of a memory crammed with images of flame and ash." "The Alarmed Vision: Social Suffering and Holocaust Atrocity," in *Social Suffering,* ed. Arthur Kleinman, Veena Das, and Margaret Lock (Berkeley: University of California Press, 1997), pp. 47-65, 54-55. I would distinguish, however, between healing, which may be partial and ongoing but efficacious nonetheless, and curing. It is perhaps trivializing even to observe that Antiochus's atrocities differed from those of the Holocaust in particulars as well as in scope. Yet there are commonalities, and in the face of those it is important to state that none of the writers studied in this volume wished to escape the horrors their people had seen. For them it was necessary to articulate them somehow, in iconic imagery and in narrative, to give witness and meaning and to demand a memorial. At the same time, all of the apocalyptic writings studied in this volume also offered visions of hope through a transformed future that empowered

to atrocities is to banish them from consciousness. Certain violations of the social compact are too terrible to utter aloud: this is the meaning of the word *unspeakable*."[112] At the same time, for individual and nation alike the only way forward through trauma is through remembrance and speech. Herman continues, "Remembering and telling the truth about terrible events are prerequisites both for the restoration of the social order and for the healing of individual victims."[113] Speaking the unspeakable is thus a necessary step in reconstituting the social self. We saw earlier that the epitomator crafted or preserved a memorial poem that began to bring the horror of massacre into view, refusing to surrender to the assault on life, order, and meaning (2 Macc 5:13). But the words chosen were not ordinary words. The epitomator changed registers from prose to poetry, reportage to lament, in a clipped but vivid style that prevented the memory of murder and disappearance from fading or dulling.[114]

Time, Memory, and Language

This tragedy is but one moment in the epitomator's story of terror, resistance, and restoration. The historical apocalypses similarly located Seleucid atrocities in Judea within a larger story. Herman has argued that trauma has the effect of stopping time, trapping its victims in a scene of terror that intrudes again and again into the present.[115] Past and future recede, such that victims of trauma may become disconnected from their history and unable to formulate hope. One of the reasons for this difficulty is that trauma records itself in the memory differently from other experiences, resisting narrative form. Herman writes that "traumatic memories lack verbal narrative and context; rather they are encoded in the form of vivid sensations and images."[116] To explain why this is so, Herman

---

the work of resistance. Having said this, I wish also to acknowledge the dilemma and difficulty of witnessing to atrocity: telling the story never can erase it. The personal cost — to those bearing witness and to those who consent to hear and see and feel their horror — is high. Many have argued that the cost of silence is higher. There is no clear or easy path in atrocity's wake.

112. Judith Herman, *Trauma and Recovery: The Aftermath of Violence — From Domestic Abuse to Political Terror* (New York: Basic Books, 1997), p. 1. Herman discusses the neurobiology of the "unspeakable" on pp. 239-40. Note that later in 2 Maccabees the epitomator labels Judas Maccabeus's slaughter of the people of Caspin "indescribable" or "unspeakable" (ἀμυθήτους, 2 Macc 12:16).

113. Herman, *Trauma and Recovery*, p. 1. See further pp. 175-95. See also Marcelo M. Suárez-Orozco, "Speaking of the Unspeakable: Toward a Psychosocial Understanding of Responses to Terror," *Ethos* 18, no. 3 (1990): 353-83.

114. Schwartz, *2 Maccabees*, pp. 258-59, recognizes the poetic quality of the verse.

115. Herman, *Trauma and Recovery*, p. 37.

116. Herman, *Trauma and Recovery*, p. 38.

draws on the theory of psychiatrist Bessel van der Kolk, who posits that during experiences of trauma and terror "the linguistic encoding of memory is inactivated, and the central nervous system reverts to the sensory and iconic forms of memory."[117] For psychiatrist Mardi Horowitz, because such trauma can challenge one's sense of identity and order in the world, the fragmented, iconic memory repeats — and continues to traumatize — until it is placed within a new ordering schema that allows the survivor to "understand."[118]

The historical apocalypses studied in this volume intervene into this traumatic rupture in time, reconnecting past, present, and future so that their audiences can reclaim their history and self and move forward again in hope. They answer powerful iconic images of terror and monstrous empires with even more powerful iconic images of the ordered and ordering presence, reality, and activity of God. Through the words of interpreting angels and seers they interpret the images, memories, and visions that defied linguistic codes, and assert their trustworthiness. They name confusion while opening the way for new understanding. They transform memory and relocate their individual and collective audiences within the story of God's provident care. Through the story and witness of the historical apocalypses, individual and community receive back language, time, and meaning, along with a new vision and possibility of hope.

Conclusion

From the first reprisals for Jason's failed revolt to the mission of Apollonius in 167 BCE, Antiochus's policies in Judea and Jerusalem aimed at reconquest not simply by force but also by state terror. According to 1 and 2 Maccabees, Antiochus's program of terror included slaughters, home invasion, abduction, and plunder of the temple, followed by a spectacular display of imperial order and power that culminated in massacre. Seleucid soldiers set fire to Jerusalem, destroying homes and razing its walls. They also fortified the Akra to serve as a local base for their military operations. Each of these measures aimed at social control and domination through the exercise of force and by creating a climate of fear, insecurity, and shame. They also aimed to dismantle and replace structures of order and meaning. From the standpoint of the apocalyptic writers, imperial spectacle offered a deceptive alternative to the life ordered by God.

First and 2 Maccabees and the historical apocalypses showcase a variety of

117. Herman, *Trauma and Recovery*, p. 39, summarizing Bessel van der Kolk, "The Trauma Spectrum: The Interaction of Biological and Social Events in the Genesis of the Trauma Response," *Journal of Traumatic Stress* 1 (1988): 273-90.
118. Herman, *Trauma and Recovery*, p. 39, citing Mardi Horowitz, *Stress Response Syndromes* (Northvale, NJ: Jason Aronson, 1986), pp. 93-94.

responses to this program of terror and conquest. The apocalyptic writers sought to expose the imperial spectacle as a deceptive and monstrous negation of life. They redirected attention from empire's chaos to the divine throne, heavenly worship, a future earthly temple, and books of truth, revealing God's plan for deliverance and judgment and a new just order to come. Wilderness became a symbolic seedbed for resistance, evoking traditions of liberation, theophany, and providence as well as covenant. These writers chose to speak the unspeakable, answering destruction and loss with lament and answering fear with a vision of hope. They developed new symbols and language to transform memory, resisting the fragmentation of self and time through a new visionary form that reconnected past, present, and future in a narrative governed by divine providence. In these ways apocalypse intervened in the logic of terror and so countered the empire's deadliest weapon.

Antiochus's policies of terror did not stop with the mission of Apollonius. In chapter 6 I turn to the edict of Antiochus and the religious persecution that followed. It is common to see in the edict and persecution a radical departure from earlier imperial policies, a shocking *novum* in the history of Hellenistic rule. The edict and persecution were unprecedented, to be sure, in the history of the world no less than in the history of the Hellenistic empires. Yet, as I argue in the chapter that follows, they were also a logical continuation of the Seleucid program of terror that followed Jason's revolt.

CHAPTER 6

The Edict of Antiochus: Persecution and the Unmaking of the Judean World

Late in the year 167 BCE, shortly after the mission of Apollonius, Antiochus IV issued an edict outlawing the practice of Jewish religion in Judea. Religious persecution followed, including killings and public tortures. Antiochus also instituted new religious practices, which his agents implemented by force. John Collins has noted that Antiochus's "attempt to change the religion of a people is extraordinary in antiquity, and lends itself to no ready explanation."[1] Given the lack of precedent in the Greco-Roman world, Elias Bickerman found the persecution "unintelligible in the pagan context."[2] This assessment led him to locate its genesis not within Seleucid circles, but among Judean elites, specifically among a putative group of Hellenizing reformers of Jewish religion led by the high priest Menelaus. Bickerman's hypothesis has been enormously influential, and also controversial. It has not won the day. Among the numerous objections that have been raised, I summarize here a few of the most important. As Erich Gruen has noted, Menelaus is nowhere associated with "Hellenistic reform."[3] Hellenizing was, rather, a charge leveled by the epitomator against Menelaus's opponent, Jason. While the epitomator is concerned with the allure and distraction of "Greek glories," including athletics (see ch. 3), the sources say nothing about religious reform.[4] Moreover, as I argued in chapter 3, Hellenism in it-

---

1. John J. Collins, "Cult and Culture: The Limits of Hellenization in Judea," in *Hellenism in the Land of Israel*, ed. John J. Collins and Gregory Sterling (Notre Dame: University of Notre Dame Press, 2001), pp. 38-61, 50.

2. Elias Bickerman, *The God of the Maccabees: Studies on the Meaning and Origin of the Maccabean Revolt*, trans. Horst R. Moehring (Leiden: Brill, 1979), p. xiii.

3. Erich S. Gruen, "Hellenism and Persecution: Antiochus IV and the Jews," in *Hellenistic History and Culture*, ed. Peter Green (Berkeley: University of California Press, 1993), pp. 238-64, 259.

4. Gruen, "Hellenism and Persecution," p. 260.

176

self was not the problem. Nor, as Collins has pointed out, can the new religious practices implemented by Antiochus and his agents be considered a reform of Judaism. They aimed rather at its suppression and replacement.[5] The measures taken in Judea and the processes by which they were formulated and implemented undoubtedly involved complex interactions between imperial and local officials. But we cannot ignore the fact that, as Collins has observed, "all our primary sources (Daniel, 1 and 2 Maccabees) ascribe primary responsibility to Antiochus Epiphanes."[6] Even though we lack clear precedent in the Hellenistic world for such a persecution, we would do well to understand it in relation to Antiochus's earlier policies in Judea and his broader political aims.

Similarly to Collins and Bickerman, Gruen calls the reversal in 167 BCE of earlier policies of religious toleration "baffling."[7] Yet Gruen nonetheless situates Antiochus's actions in Judea within a broader context. He argues that the king aimed through the persecution to salvage his reputation after the Day of Eleusis.[8] Gruen explains further, "Eradication of the creed and forcible conversion of the faithful would send a message throughout the ancestral kingdom of the Seleucids — the message that Antiochus had accomplished what no ruler before him had hoped to achieve: the abandonment of Jewish belief at Seleucid command."[9] In Gruen's analysis, the Judean religion became for Antiochus a kind of trophy, its eradication a feat. Judaism was admired far and wide for the ancient tradition it represented and "the tenacity with which its adherents clung to it"; its erasure thus posed a unique and public challenge.[10] The king imagined that his success would communicate his strength to the world.[11]

Gruen rightly recognizes that Antiochus's program of state terror aimed at solidifying and projecting his power well beyond the borders of Judea.[12] But questions remain. Whether a religious persecution would in fact bolster a king's reputation is unclear, especially in a context where such persecutions were unknown. The precise ramifications for Antiochus of the Day of Eleusis are also debatable (see ch. 4).[13]

5. Collins, "Cult and Culture," p. 51.

6. Collins, "Cult and Culture," p. 51. See also the assessment of Bruce William Jones, "Antiochus Epiphanes and the Persecution of the Jews," in *Scripture in Context: Essays on the Comparative Method,* ed. Carl M. Evans, William W. Hallo, and John B. White (Pittsburgh, PA: Pickwick, 1980), pp. 263-90, 272.

7. Gruen, "Hellenism and Persecution," p. 238.

8. Gruen, "Hellenism and Persecution," pp. 256-61.

9. Gruen, "Hellenism and Persecution," p. 263.

10. Gruen, "Hellenism and Persecution," p. 265.

11. Gruen, "Hellenism and Persecution," p. 264.

12. Gruen, "Hellenism and Persecution," p. 262.

13. See the response of M. Gwyn Morgan to Gruen's paper in *Hellenistic History and Culture,* ed. Peter Green (Berkeley: University of California Press, 1993), pp. 264-70.

The persecution surely aimed to magnify the glory of Antiochus and project his power onto the world stage. But it could only do so because it continued (and was designed to complete) his program of conquest and creation. Judean religion was not the prize. Reputation mattered, but was not the primary concern. The edict, persecution, and new religious practices were a means and a moment in the continual re-creation of empire. Though shocking and unprecedented, they nonetheless continued in the vein of Antiochus's earlier program of terror, completing the work of de-creation and implementing a new totalitarian order.

In this chapter I analyze the details of Antiochus's edict and persecution and the interpretation of these events found in our sources. I argue that Antiochus aimed through his edict and persecution at the unmaking and making of world and identity for the inhabitants of Judea in order to assert the empire as sole power, reality, and ground of being.[14] Antiochus himself would emerge as its creator and as true author (and authorizer) of identity.

As already noted, our most important sources for these events are Daniel and 1 and 2 Maccabees. Daniel's symbolic and allusive account provides neither dates nor names. Yet Daniel's iconic visions and even stories provide a frame and lenses for viewing Antiochus's actions. By beginning with Daniel we glimpse more clearly what was at stake for the apocalyptic writers who responded to Antiochus's program and for the audiences they encouraged in the work of resistance.

Daniel

The book of Daniel uses rich symbolism to give meaning to the horrors of persecution, placing Antiochus's actions within the larger frame of God's plan for God's people and actions on their behalf.[15] The words of Antiochus prove false and ineffective, by contrast with the books of truth (Dan 10:21), revelation (9:2), deliverance (12:1), and justice (7:10), and by contrast with the words of Daniel's visions (12:4). The destructive power of Antiochus is similarly revealed as derivative and finite, contrasting with the lifegiving and righteous power of God that

14. I adapt here the language of Elaine Scarry, who analyzes the structure of torture as the "making and unmaking of the world." *The Body in Pain: The Making and Unmaking of the World* (Oxford: Oxford University Press, 1985). Whether or not Antiochus used torture in the manner described in 2 Macc, the structure of torture as an act of power closely parallels the structure and aims of persecution. Thus Scarry's analysis offers helpful categories for understanding the methods and aims of Antiochus's persecution, and I will take up her work in my discussion of 2 Macc 6–7 at the end of this chapter.

15. Unless otherwise noted, translations of Daniel are my own.

governs heaven, earth, and time. Antiochus's assault on the holy ones will fail; holiness itself will be vindicated. The second half of the book of Daniel contains three major revelations concerning Antiochus, each composed (or completed) during the period of persecution in Judea. Two occur in symbolic dream visions and an angel's subsequent interpretation of the visions (7:7-8, 11, 19-26; 8:9-14, 23-25). The third (11:21-45) occurs in an angel's revelation to Daniel from the "book of truth" (10:21). These revelations are closely integrated with the stories in Daniel 1–6 (see discussion in the following chapter), so that revelations and stories illuminate each other. In the discussion that follows I focus on the three revelations in chapters 7, 8, and 11, with attention to the stories in Daniel where they illuminate the meaning of the revelations.

The visions and stories foreground motifs of power, speech, and time. The first vision portrays Antiochus as a horn with a boasting mouth (7:20) who denounces the Most High and wears down "the holy ones of the Most High" (7:25). I noted in the previous chapter that repeated traumas have a cumulative effect. The language of "wearing down" the holy ones suggests a sustained program of repression taking place over a period of time rather than a single decisive act. It also evokes the astonishing resilience of a people who were traumatized but not defeated by Antiochus's ongoing program of terror. The horn symbolizes military power, from which Antiochus derives the false confidence of the words he dares to speak against God. The speech of Antiochus recurs as a leading motif throughout the visions of Daniel (7:8, 11, 20, 25; 8:11, 23, 25; 11:32, 36), highlighting the important role of imperial discourse as well as resistant counterdiscourse in Antiochus's program of repression and Jewish responses to it. The interpreting angel further specifies some of the content of Antiochus's utterances: "he will imagine that he can change times and law" (7:25).

The referent of this expression will become clearer when we analyze the accounts concerning Antiochus's edict in 1 and 2 Maccabees. Within the book of Daniel, the phrase "change times" refers the reader back to the doxology in Daniel 2, pitting the pretensions of Antiochus against the confession of God's sovereignty, a sovereignty that extends to time itself. Daniel's doxology begins with the jussive, "may God's name be blessed מִן־עָלְמָא וְעַד־עָלְמָא" (2:20). While this latter expression might simply be translated "from age to age," or "forever and ever," the use of the prepositions מִן־ and עַד־ suggests the meaning "from the remotest past to the remotest future."[16] The words that follow spell out the ways in which God exercises wisdom and power in creation: God is "the one who changes the seasons and the times (וְהוּא מְהַשְׁנֵא עִדָּנַיָּא וְזִמְנַיָּא),

---

16. John J. Collins translates "from of old and forever." *Daniel: A Commentary on the Book of Daniel,* Hermeneia (Minneapolis: Fortress, 1993), pp. 150, 160.

causes kings to pass away (מְהַעְדֵּה), and causes kings to endure (וּמְהָקֵים)."[17] According to this prayer, God's wisdom, power, and being not only extend into the farthest reaches of time past and future, but they also manifest themselves in God's dominion over history and time itself. The emphatic pronoun הוּא makes plain the contrast between God and every other ruler. Kings exercise dominion on earth only within the temporal limits established by God. God alone changes times.[18]

This doxology connects closely with the action and dialogue of Daniel 2, in which the role of Nebuchadnezzar partly foreshadows the role later to be played by Antiochus. In this chapter Nebuchadnezzar demands of his advisors and diviners that they tell him his dream and its interpretation. Following the formal, scripted greeting "O king live forever!" (2:4; the vision that follows reveals the acclamation's irony), they assure him that no one can tell him the dream. Rather, if he reveals the dream, they will reveal its meaning. He responds, "I know for a fact that you are buying time" (2:8). The king's response evinces a view of time as commodity that can be bought or gained at will as well as an effort to control it. The following verse further links the king's anxiety concerning the dream and its interpretation — and his inability as king to command their revelation — with the theme of time. The king accuses the Chaldeans of conspiracy. "You have conspired (הִזְמִנְתּוּן) to make false and lying speeches before me until the time changes (עַד דִּי עִדָּנָא יִשְׁתַּנֵּא)" (2:9). The king recognizes that time itself sets a limit on his word and authority. A wordplay reveals that time is at the very root of his anxiety, for the verb with which he expresses this accusation, הִזְמִנְתּוּן ("you have conspired"), is a denominative verb derived from the noun זְמַן, "time." His reference to time's changing foreshadows the interpretation of his dream: with the passage of time God will bring change. Empire will succeed empire, until God effects the end of empire itself, shattering (2:44) the destructive powers (2:40) and filling the earth (2:35) with a new kingdom (2:44).[19]

17. In the Aramaic portions of Daniel the verbal root קוּם ("to set up, raise up, establish"), the noun קְיָם ("decree"), and the adjective קַיָּם ("enduring") are used together in ironic and sometimes comical counterpoint, especially but not only in the story of Darius's "immutable" decree in Dan 6 (e.g., 6:27). At the end of Dan 2 the same verb is used twice, once of God's action in establishing a kingdom that would never be destroyed, and once asserting that the kingdom would endure forever (2:44). The verbal root קוּם is then used seven times with reference to Nebuchadnezzar's setting up his statue in Dan 3. The juxtaposition and contrast underscore the folly of Nebuchadnezzar's statue, so close on the heels of his vision of the shattered statue in Dan 2.

18. "Change" is an important keyword in the book of Daniel. The etymological connection between the verbal root שְׁנָא "to change" (Aramaic) and the noun שָׁנָה "year" reminds the reader that the concept of change is fundamentally bound to the passage of time and is an important component of the understandings of time in early Jewish apocalyptic. In Daniel this connection between time and change is first made explicit in Dan 2.

19. Daniel's request to the king to give him time further develops the theme of time (Dan

The story and prayer in Daniel 2 would convey to readers and hearers that God is the one who knows and reveals the future; establishes and deposes kingdoms; and establishes and changes times. Yet, as noted above, in Daniel 7 we learn that in his overweening pride Antiochus IV Epiphanes set himself up to change times and the law (7:25). As I discuss further below, the times referred to have to do with the cultic calendar, that is, appointed times for worship and sacrifice, including the "taking away" of the daily offering or *tamid* (8:11-13; 11:31; 12:11) and the cessation (יַשְׁבִּית) of previous, ordained sacrifice and offering (9:27).

By changing the cultic calendar Antiochus aimed to assert and magnify his power in Judea. James VanderKam has argued that control of the cultic calendar was "essential for any group or person who desired to wield supreme religious authority in the community."[20] This religious authority was also a mark of political sovereignty.[21] Inherent in the effort to change the calendar, halt regular, existing religious practices, and replace them with new ones was an attempt to forcibly deny the sovereignty of the God the Jews worshiped and to co-opt their time-consciousness into an alternately constructed reality.[22]

2:16). While Nebuchadnezzar's ability to grant the request may betoken his authority, that authority will soon be relativized in light of God's power to change times and seasons (2:21). By contrast with Nebuchadnezzar's apparent inability even to recall his own dream, Dan 2 also calls attention to God's ability to reveal what will happen "in the future days" or "at the end of days" (2:28). The following verse again emphasizes the revelation of future time. Daniel tells the king his mind was stirred by a vision of "what will be after this" (2:29). The same phrase is repeated in 2:45, along with a final note of assurance that the vision is certain, trustworthy, and true.

20. James C. VanderKam, "2 Maccabees 6, 7A and Calendrical Change in Jerusalem," *JSJ* 12, no. 1 (1981): 52-74, 52.

21. VanderKam, "2 Maccabees 6, 7A and Calendrical Change," p. 52.

22. Events in twentieth-century Zaire and Cambodia provide instructive parallels. In Zaire, dictator Mobutu Sese Seko linked the celebration of Christmas with the ideology of European colonizers that he sought to negate and replace. In 1974 he therefore banned the celebration of Christmas, replaced Christian catechesis with training in *Mobutisme,* and replaced crucifixes with his own portrait. Philip Gourevitch, *We Wish to Inform You That Tomorrow We Will Be Killed with Our Families* (New York: Picador, 1999), p. 283; Michael Schatzberg, *The Dialectics of Oppression in Zaire* (Bloomington: Indiana University Press, 1991), p. 118. According to Schatzberg (p. 119), Mobutu was simultaneously characterized as a new messiah. A year later in Cambodia/Kampuchea, Pol Pot and the Khmer Rouge inaugurated their totalitarian regime with the declaration "This is Year Zero." Then followed genocide, deadly slave labor, prescribed diet and schedules (including a ten-day cycle of labor and rest), the banning of religion, and the erasure of local traditions (in the name of purging things "Western"), social structures, and even time-consciousness to create a radical new agrarian order. Howard Ball, *War Crimes and Justice: A Reference Handbook* (Santa Barbara, CA: ABC-CLIO, 2002), pp. 98-100. According to Ball (p. 100), Pol Pot "forced Muslims to eat pork and shot those who refused," a further parallel to the edict of Antiochus, on which see further below. In these examples control, repression, and reconfiguration of festal calendars and the reckoning of time combine with religious repression

As I discussed in chapter 3, in Seleucid Judea years were already reckoned according to the Seleucid Era — year zero was the year of the empire's beginning. The Seleucid administration reckoned not only years but also months and dates according to a Seleucid calendar that combined Babylonian and Macedonian systems for the months and counted thirty days in each month.[23] Yet in Jewish traditions the observance of sabbath, daily sacrifice, and the celebration of religious holidays, even the practice of praying at certain times, marked the cycle of days, weeks, months, seasons, and years as the structure of time ordained by God in creation and in the law. Judean religious life was thus organized in time around the very patterns ordained at creation, including the cycle of day and night, the seven-day cycle, lunar and solar cycles, and the cycle of seasons, according to a traditional calendar of appointed times. By following the cultic calendar and regular cultic practices Jews acknowledged divine sovereignty over creation and over time and participated in the created order. Antiochus's intervention into times and the law challenged divine sovereignty and sought to restructure the very order of the cosmos and human life within it. I discuss this reordering of time and human life in further detail below.

Like the first vision, the second vision uses imagery of the horn, focusing attention on its boastful opposition to the sanctuary and sacrificial cult:

> And it grew as high as the host of heaven, until it cast down to the earth some of the host and some of the stars, and it crushed them underfoot. Then it boasted of its greatness before the prince of heaven's host. It tore from his hands the daily sacrifice, so that the place of his sanctuary was overturned. Along with the daily sacrifice, a host was delivered into sin. Truth it threw down to the earth. It succeeded in everything it did. (8:10-12)

The horn pairs armed assault with performative speech, waging a battle against the army of heaven, the holy place, and worship of God that is also an assault against truth, the ground of knowledge and certainty. A holy one summarizes what Daniel has seen as "the vision of the daily sacrifice and the desolating sin, of handing over holiness and a host for trampling" (8:13). Daniel is told that at the conclusion of the period of desolation "holiness will be vindicated" (8:14).

The noun "holiness" (קֹדֶשׁ) in these verses is often rendered according to context as "holy place" or "sanctuary" (cf. Ex 26:33; 28:29, 35, 43; 29:30). Yet only

---

and the implementation of new cultural, religious, social, and political orders. The structure of time is fundamental to the ordering of human life in community. Modifying or controlling time's structure can be a key component of hegemony and domination.

23. On the Seleucid calendar, see Alan Edouard Samuel, *Greek and Roman Chronology: Calendars and Years in Classical Antiquity* (Munich: C. H. Beck, 1972), pp. 139-45. Samuel discusses distribution on pp. 144-45.

a few verses earlier the more specific noun מִקְדָּשׁ is used to designate "holy place" (Dan 8:11). While the sanctuary remains in view throughout the passage, the appearance of the abstract noun "truth" in 8:12 suggests that קֹדֶשׁ in 8:13-14 is also used as an abstract noun, evoking the broader meaning of "holiness." As an abstract noun it can describe an attribute of God (Ex 15:11; Amos 4:2; Ps 89:36; cf. 2 Macc 14:36) and God's name (Ps 33:21; 103:1; 105:3; etc.) or of things (Lev 5:15; 22:3; etc.), times (Ex 16:23; Neh 9:14), and people (Ex 22:30; Ezra 9:2) set apart by and for God and God's service. For the Chronicler it describes the modality by which the people consecrate themselves (2 Chron 31:18). If truth is the ground of certainty, holiness is the ground of identity and difference. It is the character of God's difference from humanity and the character of every time, place, person, and thing set apart as God's own. The words and actions of Antiochus, including his assault against the sanctuary and the holy ones, aimed to annul the divisions that separated holy from unholy, erasing identity and difference together.

Gabriel explains further to Daniel that at the height of his power this "king with brazen face, gifted in deception" (Dan 8:23; cf. 8:25 "deceit will grow in his hand") will "wreak unspeakable destruction" and "destroy the mighty and a people of holy ones" (8:24), killing many "in a time of rest" (8:25). The latter action may refer to Apollonius's sabbath massacre, or to other sabbath slaughters that will be examined in greater detail below. The repeated emphasis on outer appearance and deceptive speech as the prelude to destruction of the mighty and holy ones focuses attention on the lies that fuel the empire's deadly power games. This king will "strengthen his covenant with the many" (9:27), brokering power among the elite and manipulating the populace with false promises and empty benefactions predicated on the myth of imperial ultimacy (cf. 1 Macc 2:18; 2 Macc 7:24). While earlier imperial benefactions had supported the Jerusalem temple and its sacrificial cult, Gabriel reveals that Antiochus will terminate the regular sacrifices (prescribed in Ex 29:38-42) and introduce idolatrous practices in the holy place: "he will halt sacrifice and offering, on the wing of desolating abominations" (9:27).[24]

In the final revelation the angel gives further detail concerning the persecution: "He will pronounce doom against a holy covenant, taking action, and he will give renewed attention to ones who forsake a holy covenant. His forces will rise up and violate the sanctuary, the walled-fortress. They will take away the daily sacrifice and give [or 'set up'] the desolating abomination" (11:30-31).[25]

24. See Johan Lust, "Cult and Sacrifice in Daniel. The Tamid and the Abomination of Desolation," in *The Book of Daniel: Composition and Reception*, vol. 2, ed. John J. Collins and Peter W. Flint (Leiden: Brill, 2002), pp. 671-88.

25. The translation adopts the suggestion of Lust, "Cult and Sacrifice," p. 675: "giving" is closely paired with "taking away."

The precise referent or form of the desolating abomination remains obscure, yet it appears closely connected with new sacrificial practices.[26] According to 1 Maccabees 1:54, the abomination was erected on the altar of burnt offering. The epitomator states that "the altar was covered with abominable offerings that were forbidden by the laws" (2 Macc 6:5), while Josephus specifies that the sacrifices included swine and entailed the worship of "those whom [Antiochus] took to be gods" (A.J. 12.253). Johan Lust notes that repeatedly in Daniel the abomination replaces the halted daily offering, or *tamid,* suggesting that the abomination may simply have been a form of sacrifice or sacrificial altar.[27]

Helpful background for understanding the meaning of the term "abomination" (שִׁקּוּץ) in Daniel emerges from an examination of its uses in earlier biblical texts. In Deuteronomy and Ezekiel the word שִׁקּוּץ refers to the idols of Egypt, fashioned from wood, stone, gold, and silver (Deut 29:16; Ezek 20:7). They attract the eyes (עֵינָיו הַשְׁלִיכוּ Ezek 20:7-8; cf. 7:20), but to follow them is to abandon the covenant with the Lord (Deut 29:24-25). In the books of Kings the word שִׁקּוּץ names the Ammonite god Milcom (1 Kgs 11:5), the Moabite god Chemosh (1 Kgs 11:7; 2 Kgs 23:13), the Sidonian deity Ashtoreth (2 Kgs 23:13), and forms of divination and worship that were contrary to the covenant law code promoted by Josiah's reforms (23:24). In Zechariah the word is used to characterize the meat of the Philistines, referring to food that was forbidden for the Israelites to consume (Zech 9:7; cf. Isa 66:17).[28] Multiple passages in Jeremiah and Ezekiel refer to abominations in the temple (Jer 7:30; 32:34; Ezek 5:11), while the Chronicler describes repairs to the altar after the removal of "abominations" throughout Judea (2 Chron 15:8; cf. 1 Macc 4:43).

Whatever the object or practice now introduced, the phrase הַשִּׁקּוּץ מְשׁוֹמֵם highlights not only its forbidden and alien character, but also its ruinous effects (cf. 1 Kgs 9:8; 2 Chron 7:21; Ezek 6:4). The verbal root שׁמם calls to mind the

26. Bickerman, *God of the Maccabees*, pp. 69-71, suggested that a stone was erected on the holocaust altar and made into a "place and object of worship" (p. 71). The deity so represented would have been a syncretic blend of Israel's "god of heaven" and the Syrian "Baal-shamin" (p. 75). Jonathan Goldstein proposed that meteorites ("heaven's host" referred to in Dan 8:10-12) representing various gods were affixed to the altar as objects of worship. *I Maccabees: A New Translation with Introduction and Commentary*, Anchor Bible 41 (Garden City, NY: Doubleday, 1976), pp. 143-52.

27. Lust, "Cult and Sacrifice," p. 675. Lust has suggested further that the *polel* participle מְשׁוֹמֵם that follows the noun הַשִּׁקּוּץ focuses attention on the object's originator, namely Antiochus himself, calling him "desolator" or "the one who causes horror," just as the *qal* participle שֹׁמֵם names Antiochus as "destroyer" or "desolator" in Dan 9:27.

28. See Carol L. Meyers and Eric M. Meyers, *Zechariah 9–14*. Anchor Bible 25C (New York: Doubleday, 1993), pp. 114-15.

desolation decreed in the book of Leviticus as the consequence of forsaking the covenant (Lev 26:34-35, 43).[29] Yet this very echo also carries the hope that God will intervene to set things right. As I discuss in chapter 7, for the biblical writers the period of desolation allows the land to reclaim its lost sabbaths; after desolation follows restoration.[30]

Finally, where Daniel 9 spoke of the desolator's (i.e., Antiochus's) covenant with many (Dan 9:27), the final revelation names one holy covenant (11:28) against which Antiochus has issued his proclamation (11:30). Antiochus employs dishonest means to corrupt "those who betray the covenant" (11:32). Many found his threats and promises compelling. Among those who did not were the wise teachers "brought low by sword and flame, captivity and plunder" (11:33; cf. 11:35).[31] Gabriel's account of the persecution culminates by focusing attention once again on the words with which Antiochus assaults not only the holy people but also their God: "he will say unspeakable things against the God of gods" (11:36).

1 and 2 Maccabees

Antiochus's words of assault take concrete form in the edict and letters of Antiochus IV described in 1 and 2 Maccabees. Their accounts allow us to reconstruct events in fuller detail. According to 1 and 2 Maccabees, Antiochus's written words negated the written laws and embodied customs of the Judean people, revoking the privilege, granted by his own father, of living according to their ancestral laws. Royal command now opposed and replaced the word of former king and, as Antiochus would have it, former god, asserting the king's power to regulate the lives of his Judean subjects in minute detail and setting the power and authority of his own person in the place of God's.[32] The edict not only outlawed traditional practices but also ordained new ones, and prescribed for disobedience the penalty of death. The seeming power of the king's written word to adjudicate life and death provides an important point of reference for understanding the centrality of heavenly writing, including the "scroll

---

29. Of ninety-two occurrences of the verbal root in the Hebrew Bible, seven appear in Lev 26, making it the densest concentration of the root in a biblical text. Six appear in Ezek 36, which promises Israel's restoration (see the following note).

30. Lev 26:45; Isa 49:8, 19; 61:4; Ezek 36:3, 8-11, 34-36; 2 Chron 36:21-22.

31. In ch. 7 I give attention to the path of martyrdom foreseen and advocated by the writer(s) of Daniel's visions.

32. For an analysis of this and other Seleucid letters in 1 and 2 Macc using speech-act theory, see John Ma, "Seleukids and Speech-Acts: Performative Utterances, Legitimacy and Negotiation in the World of the Maccabees," *Scripta Classica Israelica* 19 (2000): 71-112.

of life" and scrolls or tablets that record deeds, judgments, and future events, not only in Daniel, but also in the early Enochic literature.[33]

Loss of Autonomia

The people of Judea may have been the only people in the Hellenistic world who believed, and publicly proclaimed, that their ancestral laws and customs were revealed and ordained by their God. They may also have been the only people whose body of written laws and teaching governed not only juridical and economic affairs but also worship and matters of daily conduct such as cooking, eating, and resting from labor. But they were not the only people in the Hellenistic world granted or denied the freedom to follow their own laws and customs.

From a political standpoint, revoking the right to follow ancestral laws amounted to revoking the last vestiges of Jerusalem's civic freedom or *autonomia*.[34] As I discuss further below, *autonomia* was typically expressed as the right to follow "one's own/ancestral laws" (νόμοις τοῖς ἰδίοις/πατρίοις χρῆσθαι, e.g., Polyb. 15.24.2-3; 18.46.5, 15). According to the epitomator, it was precisely "the ancestral laws" that the edict of Antiochus compelled Jews to forsake (ἀναγκάζειν τοὺς Ἰουδαίους μεταβαίνειν ἀπὸ τῶν πατρίων νόμων καὶ τοῖς τοῦ θεοῦ νόμοις μὴ πολιτεύεσθαι 2 Macc 6:1). The phrase "ancestral laws" recurs twice in declarations of resistance to the decree (7:2, 37).[35] After the death of Antiochus, according to 1 Maccabees, Antiochus's brother Demetrius offered

---

33. On writing and power in Daniel, see Donald C. Polaski, "*Mene, Mene Tekel, Parsin:* Writing and Resistance in Daniel 5 and 6," *JBL* 123, no. 4 (2004): 649-69. On heavenly writing in early Jewish apocalypses, see Leslie Baynes, "'My Life Is Written Before You': The Function of the Motif 'Heavenly Book' in Judeo-Christian Apocalypses, 200 B.C.E.–200 C.E." (Ph.D. diss., University of Notre Dame, 2005).

34. Mogens Herman Hansen cautions against using the English words "autonomy" and "autonomous" for the Greek words αὐτονομία and αὐτόνομος and suggests instead using the transliterated Greek words. "The 'Autonomous City-State.' Ancient Fact or Modern Fiction?" in *Studies in the Ancient Greek Polis*, ed. Mogens Herman Hansen and Kurt Raaflaub, Historia Einzelschriften 95 (Stuttgart: Franz Steiner Verlag, 1995), pp. 21-44, 22-23. I follow Hansen's suggestion here. In this chapter and elsewhere where I use the terms "autonomy" and "autonomous" I do not imply the Greek terms.

35. By contrast, 1 Macc generally refers to "the law" without further qualification, e.g., 1:49, 52, 56-57; 2:21, 26-27, 42, 48, 50, 58, 64, 67-68; 3:48, 56; 4:42, 47, 53; 10:14; 13:48; 14:14, 29. Verse 13:3 refers to "the laws" (pl.). This usage denies the authority of any other law, privileging the law of God alone and calling attention away from all other sources and guarantees. See, however, the reference in 3:29: "the laws/customs (νόμιμα) which were from the first days." This reference doesn't privilege *ancestral* customs per se but instead connects the laws with the origins and foundations of the people as a moment of creation, a beginning of and in time.

to restore to the people of Judea the right to live according to "their own laws" (τοῖς νόμοις αὐτῶν 10:37). He also offered to free them from tribute (10:29) and to surrender control of the Akra (10:32). Each of these freedoms was closely associated with *autonomia*. Combined, these references suggest that the edict of Antiochus amounted to, among other things, a revocation of Jerusalem's civic freedoms and the freedom of the region it governed.

A clearer understanding of *autonomia* in the Hellenistic world clarifies the meaning of Antiochus's edict as an act of imperial power.[36] Neither "civic freedom" nor *autonomia* was a fixed concept in the Hellenistic political lexicon.[37] Rather, Hellenistic cities enjoyed, negotiated,[38] and sometimes fought for[39] varying degrees of freedom and *autonomia*, the extent and limits of which were typically defined by the imperial powers that ruled or conquered them.[40] Bick-

36. Important treatments of *autonomia* include Elias Bickerman, "Autonomia. Sur un passage de Thucydide (I, 144, 2)," *RIDA*, 3rd series, 5 (1958): 313-44; Martin Ostwald, *Autonomia: Its Genesis and Early History* (Chico, CA: Scholars Press, 1982); Edmond Lévy, "Autonomia et éleuthéria au Vᵉ siècle," *RevPhil* 57:2 (1983): 249-70; A. B. Bosworth, "Autonomia: The Use and Abuse of Political Terminology," *SIFC*, 3rd series, 10 (1992): 122-52; Hansen, "The 'Autonomous City-State.'"

37. Sviatoslav Dmitriev, *City Government in Hellenistic and Roman Asia Minor* (Oxford: Oxford University Press, 2005), p. 291; Bosworth, "Autonomia," pp. 123, 151; Hansen, "The 'Autonomous City-State,'" p. 41.

38. According to Ostwald, the concept of *autonomia* emerges as a check on the power of Athens in relation to the allied Greek city-states; it receives clearest articulation in the charter of the second Athenian confederacy. Ostwald, *Autonomia*, pp. ix, 48-49.

39. See, e.g., Ostwald's treatment of the Mytilenean revolt (*Autonomia*, p. 43).

40. John Grainger has argued that, in the case of Seleucid Syria at least, most cities did not desire absolute independence, but preferred to accept limitations to their freedom in exchange for a king's protection and support. A notable exception is the Phoenician city Arados. *The Cities of Seleukid Syria* (Oxford: Oxford University Press, 1990), pp. 142-44, 148, 169-71. Grainger observes that even a formal grant of autonomy could serve as a "mask for continued royal control," while a city that lacked such a grant might still operate with a high degree of freedom (p. 171). But see the caveat of Erich S. Gruen, "The Polis in the Hellenistic World," in *Nomodeiktes: Greek Studies in Honor of Martin Ostwald*, ed. Ralph M. Rosen and Joseph Farrell (Ann Arbor: University of Michigan Press, 1993), pp. 339-54, 341-42. Citing the shock and elation of the Greeks in 196 BCE, when Titus Quinctius Flamininus announced the Roman grant of *autonomia* to their cities following the Second Macedonian War, Gruen argues that the grant of *autonomia* was no meaningless mask for imperial control but named a real and cherished freedom. The caveat is important, and Gruen's point is well made. The reality is nonetheless complex, for *autonomia* in this case was given meaning, and its limits prescribed, within a structure and map of international power relations shaped and delineated by Roman conquest and conditional withdrawal (cf. the conditions set for the Galatians by the Romans in 165 BCE, reported in Polyb. 31.1). Leo Raditsa describes the geopolitical map of this period in terms of a "split in the world which made it difficult to distinguish independence from aggression." "Bella Macedonica," in *Aufstieg und Niedergang der römischen Welt. Geschichte und Kultur Roms im Spiegel der neueren Forschung*, vol. 1, pt. 1, ed. Hildegard Temporini (Berlin: Walter de Gruyter, 1972), pp. 564-89, 582.

erman argues that the very concept of *autonomia* emerges in an imperial context in which civic freedom cannot be presumed, but is rather granted by an external power, such that the counterpart and background to *autonomia* is always a city's subjugation.[41] The freedom it names is imperfect because it is derived or contingent.[42]

In times of transition such as conquest a king (or the Roman Senate) might grant new freedoms, confirm old ones, or reestablish "lost" ones. Such was the case in 196 BCE, when Rome declared the freedom of eight cities following the Roman conquest of Macedon (Polyb. 18.46.5).[43] The Senate of Rome and the victorious general Titus Quinctius Flamininus declared the Greek cities "free, without garrison, without tribute, following their ancestral laws" (ἐλευθέρους ἀφρουρήτους ἀφορολογήτους νόμοις χρωμένους τοῖς πατρίοις 18.46.5; at 18.46.15 the same language is repeated, but ἰδίοις takes the place of πατρίοις; cf. also Appian, *Mac.*). Rome in this case did not want to undertake close management of affairs in Greece. Granting freedoms to the Greek cities was therefore advantageous for Rome. As Bickerman has noted, such grants of *autonomia* "could render the empire more elastic and, hence, more viable."[44]

Yet a city's freedoms were not always advantageous for the empire that ruled it, and the empire that granted *autonomia* could also take it away. In an earlier passage, Polybius uses a slightly expanded formula ("free from garrison, from tribute, from billeting of soldiers, and to follow their own laws," Polyb. 15.24.2-3) to report the Thasians' petition to Philip's general Metrodorus in 202-201 BCE. Philip grants the petition and the freedoms requested by the Thasians; in return, they accept him as ruler. But Polybius is skeptical of the value of such a grant. He writes, "Perhaps all kings, at the beginning of their rule, hold out the word 'freedom' and address those who share their goals as friends and allies; but when it comes to administering affairs, they no longer treat them as allies,

41. Bickerman, "Autonomia," pp. 327-28, 336-37, 340. Although the conjectured Persian setting has not won support, Bickerman's correlation between *autonomia* and empire remains an important insight. But see the recent treatment by Kurt Raaflaub, *The Discovery of Freedom in Ancient Greece* (Chicago: University of Chicago Press, 2005), pp. 152-53, who argues for a more positive and less restricted meaning in certain contexts.

42. Bickerman, "Autonomia," p. 337. See, however, the critique in Lévy, "Autonomia et éleuthéria," pp. 260-66. Lévy argues that *autonomia* denies the dependence Bickerman describes; he believes the term alludes to the possibility of freedom's absence in order to deny it (pp. 260-61). Yet, as Bosworth has argued, this very denial was frequently a tool of the conqueror, such that by the fourth century BCE the term *autonomia* was "discredited by association with the instrument of oppression" ("Autonomia," p. 149).

43. Specifically, the Corinthians, Phocians, Locrians, Euboeans, Achaeans of Phiotis, Magnesians, Thessalians, and Perrhaebians.

44. Bickerman, "Autonomia," p. 343: "Peut-être, l'*autonomia* aurait-il rendu l'empire plus élastique et, partant, mieux viable."

but instead behave in the manner of a despot" (Polyb. 15.24.4). As Martin Ostwald has observed, "from the view point of the major power [the grant of *autonomia*] is simply a declaration of [the major power's] willingness to refrain from exercising the power it has, a willingness which is in the control of the major power alone and depends on the historical circumstances in which it finds itself at any given time."[45] Barely concealed and sometimes plainly exposed within the granting of each freedom lay the possibility and threat of its loss.

Indeed, a conquered or reconquered city might lose some or all of its recognized freedoms as punishment for rebellion or for supporting the conqueror's enemies during the conflict.[46] Such measures communicated and effected a new configuration of power. As such they were intended to have not only punitive but also preventative force. By draining local resources, policing activity within the city and region, and undermining structures of self-governance, a monarch (or the Senate) could decrease the probability and effectiveness of future rebellions while also continuing to derive financial and strategic benefit from control of the city and its surrounding territory. Such measures would also serve as a warning to other cities and regions, discouraging open rebellion and encouraging submission.

In chapter 4, I discussed three marks of a city's freedom: (1) to be free from mandatory tribute (ἀφορολόγητος, cf. 1 Macc 11:28); (2) to be free from military occupation or garrison (ἀφρούρητος); and (3) to possess the right of self-governance according to native or self-determined laws and customs (αὐτό-νομος or νόμοις τοῖς ἰδίοις/πατρίοις χρῆσθαι, e.g., Polyb. 15.24.2-3). By contrast, mandatory tribute, a military garrison, and imposed laws and customs were all marks of subordination.[47] From the beginning of Antiochus's reign Judeans were already subject to tribute and garrison. Revoking the right to live according to their ancestral laws was continuous with the gradual erosion of freedoms in Judea and was intended as the last in a series of measures aiming at the region's total subordination. I discuss each mark of subordination in turn.

Though at times they chose to withhold it, Judeans had paid tribute to empires for centuries. At the beginning of Seleucid rule in Judea, Antiochus III's letter to Ptolemy brought some small relief, granting long-term tax exemptions to Jerusalem's community leaders and cultic functionaries and short-term tax relief to other residents. Yet only a few decades later, under the high-priesthoods of Jason and Menelaus, the city's financial burden had increased to

---

45. Ostwald, *Autonomia*, p. 9.

46. Raaflaub notes that "direct intervention in the constitutional sovereignty of a polis" first appears in the context of "suppressed rebellions." *Discovery of Freedom*, pp. 137-38, with supporting evidence in p. 326n114.

47. Cf. John Ma, *Antiochos III and the Cities of Western Asia Minor* (Oxford: Oxford University Press, 1999), p. 154, who calls the tribute a "formal marker of subjection."

crippling proportions. The new administrative appointments documented in 2 Maccabees 5:22-24 may have brought a new tax burden as well. Apollonius's title in 1 Maccabees, "Chief Tribute Collector" (ἄρχοντα φορολογίας, 1 Macc 1:29), suggests that he was sent in part to extract the tribute that Jerusalem's high priest had been unable to pay.

As discussed in chapter 2, the people of Jerusalem had also struggled with the presence of a foreign garrison since the Ptolemaic period. The expulsion of Ptolemy's soldiers that marked the transition to Seleucid rule in Judea had meant the influx of a new, Seleucid occupying force. Their ranks may have been small at first, but Apollonius brought with him overwhelming numbers of active soldiers — 22,000, according to the epitomator (2 Macc 5:24) — to garrison and police the city.

As we saw in chapter 4, tribute and garrison were intimately connected. That connection now intensified. On the basis of his study of a recently acquired Judean coin hoard containing sixteen specimens of a well-known bronze coin-type minted during the reign of Antiochus IV, Dan Barag has conjectured that during this period a Seleucid mint was established within the Akra, no doubt intended to facilitate the payment of tribute and taxes while also serving as a vehicle for Seleucid imperial propaganda.[48] Barag dates the Judean coins to the period between 167 BCE — the year of the edict — and 164 BCE.[49]

The coins Barag attributes to the Jerusalem mint carry on their obverse a portrait of Antiochus IV with a radiate head visually alluding to representations of the sun-god Helios and representing Antiochus's claim to be *theos epiphanes*, or "god manifest." On their reverse the coins portray a seated female figure holding in her right hand a statue of Nike, who in turn holds a victory wreath. The words ΑΝΤΙΟΧΟΣ ("Antiochus") and ΒΑΣΙΛΕΩΣ ("King"), written vertically, frame the image of the seated female figure. As one rotates the coin counterclockwise, the word "King" — written, of course, in the language of the empire — stands upon the back of her throne in large block letters that echo the throne's architectonic form.

Barag has suggested that the female figure personifies the city of Jerusalem.[50] Similar figures on related coin-types minted at Seleucia-on-Tigris and Susa likewise personify those cities.[51] For Georges Le Rider and Barag the similarities in representation across different regions indicate "royal control and probably the issue of directives sent from Antioch to these mints."[52] In light of

48. Dan Barag, "The Mint of Antiochus IV in Jerusalem: Numismatic Evidence on the Prelude to the Maccabean Revolt," *Israel Numismatic Journal* 14 (2002): 59-77.

49. Barag, "Mint of Antiochus IV in Jerusalem," p. 76.

50. Barag, "Mint of Antiochus IV in Jerusalem," p. 67.

51. Barag, "Mint of Antiochus IV in Jerusalem," p. 67.

52. Barag, "Mint of Antiochus IV in Jerusalem," p. 67; Georges Le Rider, *Suse sous les*

these directives and the political developments in Judea documented in previous chapters, it may be more accurate to identify the seated figure on the Judean coins not as Jerusalem but as "Antioch-in-Jerusalem" or even the Akra itself.[53] If Barag's identification is correct, the figure's holding victory in her hand would symbolically portray Antiochus's victory over the conquered people of Jerusalem and perhaps even victory over Egypt, as the Akra and the soldiers it housed delivered and secured for Antiochus the strategic region of Judea and the material and human resources it contained. The city or Akra would thus have become an emblem of Seleucid victory in war. The coins connected tribute to conquest, transforming the very image of the city into an icon of the empire it supported. Those who paid tribute would tender this image back to the empire, so that every payment was also a declaration of subjection and assimilation.

Imposed laws and customs removed the last vestige of formally recognized civic freedom, communicating total subjugation to the empire. Antiochus III had granted or confirmed the right to self-governance according to ancestral laws, and his *programma* confirmed local and ancestral norms concerning sacred space, the flesh of animals, and sacrifice. Now Antiochus IV revoked those privileges. Pitting his own manufactured customs and laws against those of the Mosaic law and Judean tradition,[54] he forced a choice between obedience to the king and obedience to God (1 Macc 2:19-22).

It is around this last point — the right to govern themselves (πολιτεύεσθαι) according to the ancestral laws (τῶν πατρίων νόμων) that were for Judeans also the laws of God (τοῖς τοῦ θεοῦ νόμοις 2 Macc 6:1) — that resistance took its clearest shape. To understand why we must take a closer look at the details of the royal edict and the persecution that followed.

Aims of the Edict and Persecution

First Maccabees refers to a kingdom-wide edict aiming to promote unity within the empire (1 Macc 1:41), while 2 Maccabees speaks of measures affecting only Judea and Samaria (2 Macc 6:2). We have good reason to doubt that an edict

---

Séleucides et les Parthes: Les trouvailles monétaires et l'histoire de la ville, Mémoires de la Mission archéologique en Iran 38 (Paris: P. Guethner, 1965), p. 291, cited in Barag, "Mint of Antiochus IV in Jerusalem," p. 67.

53. Cf. Barag, "Mint of Antiochus IV in Jerusalem," p. 75, who conjectures that the coins were meant to communicate the hellenization of Jerusalem.

54. Cf. the offer of Eumenes II, ca. 188 BCE, to "provide suitable laws" for his subjects the Toriaians if they could not agree on the laws they wanted for themselves. See Lloyd Jonnes and Marijana Ricl, "A New Royal Inscription from Phrygia Paroreios: Eumenes II Grants Tyriaion the Status of a Polis," *EA* 29 (1997): 1-29, l. 33.

was directed to all of the peoples (πάντα τὰ ἔθνη, 1 Macc 1:42) in the Seleucid empire.[55] Nonetheless, the report in 1 Maccabees may reflect an imperial declaration of motive designed to divert the attention and compassion of imperial agents and their collaborators away from the suffering Judean populace and toward the imagined need of the empire itself. Elaine Scarry notes that the fictional or false motive "has a fixed place in the formal logic of brutality," serving to endow "agency with agency, cause with cause," continuously misnaming and hiding the brutality's actual motivating causes and agents.[56]

At the same time, the purported motive also rings true. Vincent Gabrielsen's analysis of revolt and conquest, discussed in chapter 4, showed that the repression of revolt through the reenactment of conquest functioned to integrate the empire, providing kings with opportunities to consolidate power and assert a unifying system of order.[57]

Antiochus's motives surely included the stabilization of his entire dominion, but the means he had in view were the ongoing conquest and brutal subjugation of the people of Judea and its capital city. His agents had already killed and deported large portions of the population, plundered the temple, and undermined the foundations of security by leveling walls and houses and committing capricious acts of terror. He had disordered and reordered space and time, and the measures of his edict would continue in this vein. He now went further, aiming to dismantle and reorder the will of his surviving subjects, waging war on the embodied Judean self in all its social, religious, and historical particularity. The object of domination had become the body, mind, soul, and will of the Judean people.[58] He would accomplish this through a comprehensive program that included prohibitions, interventions into sacred and profane space, the compulsory institution of new ritual and dietary practices, the threat of punishment, and publicly advertised tortures and executions.

55. See the assessments of Peter Franz Mittag, *Antiochos IV. Epiphanes: Eine politische Biographie* (Berlin: Akademie Verlag, 2006), p. 260; Ma, "Seleukids and Speech-Acts," p. 90.

56. Scarry, *Body in Pain*, p. 58.

57. Vincent Gabrielsen, "Provincial Challenges to the Imperial Centre in Achaemenid and Seleucid Asia Minor," in *The Province Strikes Back: Imperial Dynamics in the Eastern Mediterranean*, ed. Björn Forsén and Giovanni Salmeri (Helsinki: Foundation of the Finnish Institute at Athens, 2008), pp. 15-44, 23, 25, 28.

58. Cf. Antonius C. G. M. Robben, *Political Violence and Trauma in Argentina* (Philadelphia: University of Pennsylvania Press, 2005), who speaks of the state's shift to the "battlefield of the mind" (p. 187) and the "conquest of people's psyches," aiming to get "inside their ideological convictions, political beliefs, emotions, and unconscious" (p. 189). He also writes that psychological torture was part of an "overall strategy in which the battlefield extended onto the human body and into the self and the mind." War was "fought on the uncharted terrain of the human soul" (p. 212). On forcing people to break taboos and violate religious and personal convictions as a means of destroying the self, see p. 217.

Prohibitions

I begin with the prohibitions. As noted above, according to 1 Maccabees, the supposedly universal edict required that all peoples abandon their particular customs (ἐγκαταλιπεῖν ἕκαστον τὰ νόμιμα αὐτοῦ 1 Macc 1:42). While we may reasonably doubt the edict's universality, the report reflects the perception that Antiochus sought to erase the particular identity of his Judean subjects. To this end Antiochus outlawed confession of Jewish identity. He also outlawed traditional sacrifices and drink offerings, sabbath observance, infant circumcision, possession of scrolls of the law, and consent to the law.

According to the epitomator, it was now forbidden to confess being "Judean," or "Jewish" (Ἰουδαῖον 2 Macc 6:6). I referred in chapter 3 to the "ethno-power games" of the Hellenistic kings, who could assert power by manipulating markers of ethnic, cultural, and religious identity.[59] In that chapter I also discussed the ways "Hellenism" could become a trope for the symbols of imperial power and domination that revoked the Jews' freedom to live according to their religious traditions, denied the sovereignty of their God, and threatened the lives of those Jews who would remain faithful to their ancestral religion. In this context, while their content was nonetheless fluid and contestable, political, ethnic, cultural, and religious identities did not stand apart from one another. For many, the term Judean could only also mean "worshiper of the Lord" or "Jew." By outlawing the very confession of Judaism — the freedom "simply" (ἁπλῶς) to speak one's being (εἶναι) out loud by publicly declaring "I am" a person belonging to this God, this place, and this people (6:6) — Antiochus not only forbade the expression of identity but also undermined the integrity of selfhood for people and for nation.

Antiochus regulated not only speech but also action. First Maccabees corroborates Daniel's report that Antiochus halted traditional worship by outlawing sacrifices and drink offerings in the temple (1 Macc 1:45). By halting daily sacrifices and other traditional modes of worship, Antiochus sought again to rupture the relationship between God and God's people, preventing them from expressing their obedience and from drawing near to God's presence in the manner prescribed for them by God and by their ancestors.

According to the epitomator it was also forbidden to keep the sabbath and the ancestral or traditional feasts (2 Macc 6:6). Proscribing sabbath observance and the keeping of festival days meant annulling the sacred calendar, denying God's power over time and over God's people. The book of Exodus commands that any who profane the sabbath be put to death; those who work on the sab-

---

59. The phrase is that of John Ma, "Kings," in *A Companion to the Hellenistic World*, ed. Andrew Erskine (Oxford: Blackwell, 2003), pp. 177-95, 188.

bath are to be cut off from the people (Ex 31:14). Compelling Jews to violate the sabbath was therefore a sentence of death, placing them outside the covenant community in which they had their life.

He similarly forbade circumcision. Within the scriptures and traditions of Jews a key mark of holiness, particularity, and covenant commitment was the circumcision of male infants on the eighth day of life. God charged Abraham with the circumcision of all the males in his household as a sign of covenant written in their flesh (Gen 17:10-14):

וְהָיְתָה בְרִיתִי בִּבְשַׂרְכֶם לִבְרִית עוֹלָם

So my covenant will be in your flesh as a covenant forever. (17:13)

By contrast, those not circumcised on the eighth day would remain outside the covenant. God instructs Abraham that a male who is uncircumcised will be cut off from the people, for to be uncircumcised is to break the covenant (17:14).

The command to circumcise male infants placed responsibility for their covenant belonging, and by extension belonging within the covenant people, in the hands of parents. The edict of Antiochus suggests that, in this period at least, that responsibility rested with their mothers, for the edict expressly forbade mothers to circumcise their sons (1 Macc 1:48). Women who circumcised (or had their children circumcised) were put to death (1:60), with babies hung from their necks. Their families and the individuals who performed the circumcision were also put to death (1:61). These circumcising mothers and their families are the first martyrs described in both 1 and 2 Maccabees.[60]

Second Maccabees tells the story of two women in particular who resisted the edict by circumcising their sons (2 Macc 6:10).[61] Tried and found guilty, the mothers were sentenced to death by public execution. According to the epitomator the babies' bodies were suspended from their mothers' breasts. The mothers and infants were then paraded through the city before being flung to their death from the wall (6:10). The wall, as noted in the previous chapter, is the sign and means of a city's protection.[62] Wall also marks inside from outside.

---

60. Jonathan A. Goldstein, *II Maccabees: A New Translation with Introduction and Commentary*, Anchor Bible 41A (New York: Doubleday, 1983), pp. 278-79; Daniel R. Schwartz, *2 Maccabees*, CEJL (Berlin: Walter de Gruyter, 2008), p. 270.

61. Not long after this report, Judas Maccabeus and the six thousand troops he had gathered would ask God to remember "the lawless (παρανόμου) destruction of innocent infants" (8:4; cf. 1 Macc 2:9; the translation is that of Schwartz, *2 Maccabees*, p. 320). This destruction may refer to the massacre memorialized at 2 Macc 5:13 or alternately, as Schwartz has suggested (p. 328), to the circumcised babies whose story is told at 6:10.

62. See also Robert Doran, "The Second Book of Maccabees," *NIB*, vol. 4 (Nashville: Abingdon, 1996), pp. 179-299, 233.

Although Jerusalem's walls had been demolished during the mission of Apollonius, the Akra remained fortified, and portions of the old wall undoubtedly remained in place. Hurling the bodies of circumcising mothers and their circumcised infants from the wall, whether from a battered remnant of the demolished wall or from the newly fortified wall of the Akra, effected a reversal of God's order for life in community. God had ordained that the uncircumcised male would remain outside the covenant and be "cut off from his people" (Gen 17:14 NRSV). Now the circumcised and circumcising, not the uncircumcised, were cut off from the people.

The edict of Antiochus opposed its own words to the words of scripture and divine teaching not only by forbidding the practices commanded by God in scripture, but also by forbidding scripture itself. Agents of the king confiscated, tore, and burned any scrolls of the law they found (1 Macc 1:56), and it became a capital offense to possess books of the covenant (1:57). I mentioned above the importance of speech and writing in the apocalyptic literature of resistance to Antiochus. Writing was an important medium of imperial hegemony. It was also a medium for resistance. It is not accidental that the apocalyptic writers committed to the creation of new scriptures in the face of Antiochus's programmatic banning and destruction of earlier authoritative writings. Resistance would also take shape in the continued reading and interpretation of Israel's earlier scriptures (see Part Three).

According to 1 Maccabees, the edict also made it a capital offense to *"consent"* to the law (1 Macc 1:57). Antiochus reached through and beyond the practices that gave form and testimony to belief, into the very minds, hearts, and wills of his subjects. They would approve what he approved, value what he valued, reject what he rejected. As I discussed in chapter 1, Antiochus exercised and effected domination not only through force and coercion, but also by assigning value and providing a framework for thought and belief.

Compulsory Practices

One way that he aimed to inculcate this framework was through new cultural and religious practices. These new practices were designed to negate and replace the embodied practices of covenant observance, reordering the behaviors of the Judean populace so that the structure of everyday life would provide visible and tangible testimony to Judean subjugation to the dominion of Antiochus. In particular, 1 Maccabees states that the edict mandated that inhabitants of Jerusalem and the cities of Judea follow "customs foreign to the land" (νομίμων ἀλλοτρίων τῆς γῆς, 1:44). Many Judeans complied by adopting "his worship" (τῇ λατρείᾳ αὐτοῦ), sacrificing to idols (τοῖς εἰδώλοις), profaning the sabbath (1:43), priests, and temple (1:46), and making themselves abominable (1:48). Second Maccabees provides further detail concerning the compulsory practices, specifying a monthly celebration of the king's birthday as well as participation in a festival honoring the god Dionysus.[63]

According to the epitomator, Jews were compelled to observe the king's birthday, a commemoration that included sacrifice and met with strong opposition on the part of the Jews: "On the monthly celebration of the king's birthday, the Jews were taken, under bitter constraint, to partake of the sacrifices" (2 Macc 6:7a NRSV).[64] VanderKam has argued that the reference to a newly mandated sacrifice in 1 Maccabees gives further detail concerning the king's birthday celebration (1 Macc 1:59 NRSV).[65] If correct, this identification places observance of the king's birthday on the twenty-fifth day of each month. In addition, 1 Maccabees states that this new monthly sacrifice was offered on "the altar that was on top of the altar of burnt offering" (1:59), the precise location of the desolating abomination (1:54). This detail suggests a basis for Judean resistance to the birthday celebration, for a new sacrifice connected with the desolating abomination would partake in its destructive power.

But this would not have been the only grounds for resistance to the king's birthday celebration. Such a celebration held power not only to destroy but also to create and reorder. Theories of ritual and symbol illuminate this creative and ordering power.

---

63. Schwartz (2 Maccabees, pp. 541-43) questions the historicity of these details. Jan Willem van Henten expresses similar reservation concerning the king's birthday celebration, suggesting that this was a practice known among the Ptolemies but not among the Seleucids. "Royal Ideology: 1 and 2 Maccabees and Egypt," in Jewish Perspectives on Hellenistic Rulers, ed. Tessa Rajak, Sarah Pearce, James Aitken, and Jennifer Dines (Berkeley: University of California Press, 2007), pp. 265-82, 273-77. Contrast, however, the treatment of Seleucid "ruler cult as social memory" in Ma, Antiochos III, pp. 219-26, which I discuss further below. Without further evidence it is impossible to establish the accuracy or inaccuracy of the epitomator's details. My own analysis suggests that the measures in question fit plausibly within Antiochus's program in Judea. Like the details concerning Antiochus's plundering of the temple, in the event these details are historically accurate, we do well to consider their significance. If Schwartz is correct, on the other hand, that the epitomator or his/her source has embellished the account of events by inventing these details or importing them from a Ptolemaic context, the argument of this chapter stands without them, as the details of Antiochus's program for which we have multiple attestation combined with evidence for Seleucid policy and practice elsewhere and at other times establish the pattern of de-creation and re-creation that I describe. The disputed details nonetheless play an important part in the subsequent interpretation of events in Jerusalem. Historically accurate or otherwise, this interpretation may nonetheless illuminate the logic of Antiochus's program.

64. Emil Schürer examined four inscriptions giving evidence for royal birthday cults in the Hellenistic world. "Zu II Mcc 6,7 (monatliche Geburtstagsfeier)," ZNW 2 (1901): 48-52.

65. VanderKam, "2 Maccabees 6, 7A and Calendrical Change," pp. 62-63. Against this view, see Schwartz, 2 Maccabees, pp. 541-42.

A mandated celebration of the king's birthday would merge the religious and political in a state-sponsored and -mandated ritual that repeatedly drew its participants into the very life of the king.[66] His birth would become a beginning made ever present, a past that would keep repeating, and a future that awaited them as surely as the moon waxed and waned.[67] Clifford Geertz has written of the "metaphysical theatre" of "state ceremonials" that are "designed to express a view of the ultimate nature of reality and, at the same time, to shape the existing conditions of life to be consonant with that reality; that is, theatre to present an ontology, and by presenting it, to make it happen — make it actual."[68] According to Craig Reynolds, state-sponsored and -mandated ceremonies "do not conceal the ordering function of the state. They enact it."[69] The birthday celebration enacted a novel ordering of life according to the life of the king. It also made of the Judean people participants in this new order.[70]

Indeed, rituals enact order in part by ordering the very people who partici-

---

66. Compare the explanation in Pope Leo I (Magnus)'s *Tractatus* concerning Christian celebration of Christ's birth (CCSL 138, 126:24-30): "When we worship the birth of our Lord and Savior, we are found to celebrate our own beginnings. Indeed Christ's engendering is the origin of the Christian people, and the birthday of the Head is the birthday of the body." Cited in Philippe Buc, *The Danger of Ritual: Between Early Medieval Texts and Social Scientific Theory* (Princeton: Princeton University Press, 2001), p. 254n19. Note that Buc's work provides an important critique of twentieth-century ritual theory and even the use of the term "ritual" as a sociological category. Moreover, Buc issues strong cautions concerning the use of anthropological categories to analyze rituals reconstructed from texts — texts are not raw data concerning what people actually did, and a writer's agency can vanish from sight in the attempt at reconstruction (p. 4). I am therefore conscious throughout my analysis that these new rites are being reported to us by the epitomator, and I have access only to the structures and meanings encoded within the epitomator's text.

67. Marsha Bol, "The Making of a Festival," in *Mexican Celebrations*, ed. Eliot Porter, Ellen Auerbach, Donna Pierce, and Marsha Bol (Albuquerque: University of New Mexico Press, 1990), pp. 109-15, 115, writes that festivals "mediate between the past and the future not only by giving its members a sense of tradition but also by providing continuity into the future."

68. Clifford Geertz, *Negara: The Theatre State in 19th Century Bali* (Princeton: Princeton University Press, 1980), p. 104.

69. Craig Reynolds, *Seditious Histories: Contesting Thai and Southeast Asian Pasts* (Seattle: University of Washington Press, 2006), p. 44.

70. Cf. William H. Beezley's analysis of the birthday celebrations of Mexican dictator Porfirio Diaz in "The Porfirian Smart Set Anticipates Thorstein Veblen in Guadalajara," in *Rituals of Rule, Rituals of Resistance: Public Celebrations and Popular Culture in Mexico*, ed. William H. Beezley, Cheryl English Martin, William E. French (Wilmington, DE: Scholarly Resources, 1994), pp. 173-90. In Beezley's analysis, government-sponsored rituals "used public performances of sacred and civic duties to instruct and inspire the people" (p. 174). They could provide "living tableaux of virtue" (p. 173) in which children would see the participation of their parents and lower classes the participation of the upper classes, such that observers would internalize the values and virtues being modeled by direct participants (p. 186).

pate. Summarizing the influential work of Erving Goffman, Randall Collins writes that "rituals are entraining; they exert pressures toward conformity and thus show one is a member of society."[71] They also "do honor to what is socially valued,"[72] and by the same token encode and assign value. According to Interaction Ritual Theory, ritual "creates cultural symbols" that become a shared focus of attention, creating greater solidarity and social cohesion around ritually invested persons, objects, values, and practices.[73] For Pierre Bourdieu such symbols have "a power of constituting the given . . . of making people see and believe, of confirming or transforming the vision of the world and thereby action on the world and thus the world itself."[74]

I have already discussed manifold ways in which the apocalyptic writers utilized the power of symbol to counter imperial domination. But to understand what the apocalyptic writers were doing, we must also understand the symbolic power exercised by the empire. In the king's birthday celebration, the king himself would be the central symbol. This constituting symbol of the king's person would continually, falsely assert the givenness of his empire from within the very space that formerly mapped and testified to the cosmic order created by Israel's God. The king's birthday celebration created and imposed not simply a symbol and order but also a ritual whose performance aimed to focus the attention of the Judean populace on the person of the king, unite them in loyalty to him, inculcate in them the values of the empire, and make them see, believe, and testify that his reality was given, knit into the fabric of the cosmos and located at its center.

He marked not only space, but also time. As I noted above, according to the epitomator, the birthday celebration was a monthly, recurring ritual. VanderKam argues that owing to its fixed date on the twenty-fifth day of the month the festival marked a departure not merely from the kinds of festivals Jews celebrated in the past, but also from the way in which festal time was reckoned.[75] The month was an interval of time whose passage was easily marked

71. Randall Collins, *Interaction Ritual Chains* (Princeton: Princeton University Press, 2004), p. 25, summarizing the work of Erving Goffman.

72. Collins, *Interaction Ritual Chains,* p. 25, summarizing Goffman.

73. Collins, *Interaction Ritual Chains,* pp. 32, 41, 48-49. On the use of ritual for the purposes of domination, see Randall Collins, *Conflict Sociology: Toward an Explanatory Science* (New York: Academic Press, 1975), p. 59.

74. Pierre Bourdieu, *Language and Symbolic Power,* ed. John B. Thompson, trans. Gino Raymond and Matthew Adamson (Cambridge, MA: Harvard University Press, 1991), p. 170.

75. VanderKam, "2 Maccabees 6, 7A and Calendrical Change," pp. 57-58. See also James C. VanderKam, *Calendars in the Dead Sea Scrolls: Measuring Time* (New York: Routledge, 1998), pp. 114-15. According to VanderKam, prior to the edict of Antiochus, Jerusalem's cultic festivals were reckoned according to a solar calendar. Concern for the importance of the solar calendar can be found in the early Enochic literature as well as in *Jub.* and at the Qumran community; both of

with reference to a heavenly body that was visible throughout the year, namely the moon. Yet, as I discussed above, the moon by itself was not the only means of reckoning time's passage or of fixing festival dates. Sun and seasons also marked the passage of time, a reality reflected in the Seleucid luni-solar calendar. In the words of Catherine Bell, the interweaving of lunar and solar calendrical systems yields "a rich set of associations between the seasons of nature and the rhythm of social life."[76] Natural cycles order life in community; at the same time "calendrical rites . . . impose cultural schemes on the order of nature."[77] They are thus "working interpretations of the natural and social worlds."[78] In this case interpretation aimed also to reconfigure the order of nature and human life.[79] The king's birthday festival imprinted the natural and social order with a recurring celebration of the king's entry into the world. Celebrating the king's entry into the world simultaneously celebrated his "entry" into the world of Judea. The new rites thus aimed to mark the end of conquest and the beginning of a new order in which the sovereignty of the king would no longer be contested, but would be fully integrated into the religious life and social memory of the conquered people.

John Ma's analysis of the Teian *Antiocheia* and *Laodikeia,* a ruler-cult festival honoring Antiochus III and Laodike, the parents of Antiochus IV, offers an

---

the latter apparently postdate the edict of Antiochus. According to the edict the cultic calendar would now be reckoned not according to the solar calendar favored in the Enochic literature and later by the author of *Jub.* and in the community at Qumran but rather according to a Seleucid luni-solar calendar. Philip R. Davies critiques VanderKam's argument and challenges his conclusions. "Calendrical Change and Qumran Origins: An Assessment of VanderKam's Theory," *CBQ* 45, no. 1 (1983): 80-89. At one point Davies asserts that, unlike the festivals themselves, "different calendrical calculations [were] merely incidental" (p. 87). Yet elsewhere Davies acknowledges the theological importance accorded to calendrical disputes in ancient Jewish literature (p. 88), although he locates "the origin of the calendrical discrepancy *as a theological issue*" (italics original) prior to the second century BCE (p. 89).

76. Catherine Bell, *Ritual: Perspectives and Dimensions* (Oxford: Oxford University Press, 1997), p. 102.

77. Bell, *Ritual*, p. 103.

78. Bell, *Ritual*, p. 103.

79. Bell gives two further examples of calendrical reform that aimed at social and political transformation and at countering religious practice and belief. At the dawn of the French Republic a new calendar signaled that "political history was started anew," marking a "total break between the old and new orders." The date September 22, 1792, provided a new "day one," while a ten-day week replaced the seven-day week around which Catholics structured their worship calendar. In Russia between 1929 and 1940 Stalin attempted (unsuccessfully) to implement five- and six-day weeks in order to prevent people from attending church. Bell, *Ritual*, p. 104, citing Eviatar Zerubavel, *Hidden Rhythms: Schedules and Calendars in Social Life* (Chicago: University of Chicago Press, 1981), p. 73. Zerubavel offers detailed analysis of the French Republican calendrical reform on pp. 82-96.

instructive parallel. The Teians established the festival following their conquest by Antiochus. Post-conquest, "ruler cult worked as 'instant memory': it created memory and hence meaning out of the confused present; the Teians . . . made sense of a potentially traumatic occurrence (armed takeover by the Seleukid empire, alarmingly resurgent under Antiochos III). . . . The [new] memories would . . . not be those of conquest, violence, submission by local communities which had no choice, but acceptable ones, consonant with civic pride, its sense of worth, its sense of participation in a process of exchange."[80] Celebration of the king's birthday in Jerusalem would have functioned in a similar fashion. According to the epitomator these rites were imposed from above rather than offered freely from below. Yet the inclusion of sacrifice in the monthly celebration of the king would gradually transform the imposed offering into an exchange of honor and benefaction. It would create new memories and a new orientation, a new social order to replace the one Antiochus had removed. Participation in the new sacrifices would secure royal protection and good will; it would also become a mark of civic belonging and pride and a new ground of identity.

According to the epitomator, Antiochus also compelled Judeans to participate in a festival honoring the god Dionysus: "And when a festival of Dionysus was celebrated, they were compelled to wear wreathes of ivy and to walk in the procession in honor of Dionysus" (2 Macc 6:7b). The meanings associated with the god Dionysus are complex.[81] The deity whom Karl Kerényi calls the "archetypal image of indestructible life"[82] has been characterized as a "destroyer of the household" and also "peacemaker."[83] These functions were not opposed to one another but were intimately connected. Through symbolic dissolution of the social bonds of family the rites of Dionysus also effected a city's salvation

80. Ma, *Antiochos III*, p. 225.

81. In Richard Seaford's analysis Dionysus embodies "irreducible cosmological ambiguity." *Reciprocity and Ritual: Homer and Tragedy in the Developing City-State* (Oxford: Oxford University Press, 1994), pp. 300-301, 367. See also Albert Henrichs, "'He Has a God in Him': Human and Divine in the Modern Perception of Dionysus," in *Masks of Dionysus*, ed. Thomas A. Carpenter and Christopher A. Faraone (Ithaca, NY: Cornell University Press, 1993), pp. 13-43, 18; and Albert Henrichs, "Between Country and City: Cultic Dimensions of Dionysus in Athens and Attica," in *Cabinet of the Muses: Essays on Classical and Comparative Literature in Honor of Thomas G. Rosenmeyer*, ed. Mark Griffith and Donald J. Mastronarde (Atlanta: Scholars Press, 1990), pp. 257-78, 258.

82. Karl Kerényi, *Dionysos: Archetypal Image of Indestructible Life* (Princeton: Princeton University Press, 1976).

83. "Destroyer of the household": Richard Seaford, "Dionysus as Destroyer of the Household: Homer, Tragedy, and the Polis," in *Masks of Dionysus*, ed. Thomas H. Carpenter and Christopher A. Faraone (Ithaca, NY: Cornell University Press, 1993), pp. 115-46. See also his *Dionysos* (New York: Routledge, 2006), pp. 95-98. "Peacemaker": Henrichs, "Between Country and City," p. 271.

and refounding.[84] In this way Antiochus could mark the transition from chaos to the restoration of order.

Jennifer Larson writes that, while Dionysus was "not a major civic or federal god, . . . his festivals [could] become essential to civic identity."[85] Worship of Dionysus entailed experiences of "surrender" and "liberation."[86] How did this experience translate into an expression of a city's salvation, and what might it have signaled for Jerusalem? The cult of Dionysus is perhaps best known, rightly or wrongly, for disorder and violence, made famous in the tragic myth of Euripides' *Bacchae.* Yet Richard Seaford has argued that in the move from myth to ritual, the ritual enactment of violence and disorder reduces them to "symbolic and predictable form. Potential disorder is contained in a traditional pattern."[87] The ritually enacted suspension of civic structure and order in the rites of Dionysus would ultimately confirm them.[88] In this way the cult of Dionysus could provide a city with a means to achieve unity and salvation.[89]

Xavier Riu highlights the connection between Dionysus's role in stabilizing the city and the flood myth, a connection honored in the Dionysian rites of the Athenian Anthesteria as well as other Dionysian festivals.[90] In his association with the great flood, Dionysus comes to symbolize the "cut" between past and present; the time before the reordering of the cosmos (effected by the Olympian sky-god Zeus); and the "disfounding" of the city.[91] Yet after the flood Dionysus guides humanity in the planting of the vine. From rites of disfounding proceed cultivation and civilization. The rites of Dionysus ritually guide the city to the moment of its (re)founding.[92]

In a manner similar to Seaford, Albert Henrichs emphasizes that, unlike myth, represented by the *Bacchae,* cult emphasizes "mutually beneficial reciprocity between the divine and human realms."[93] By contrast with the *Bacchae*'s frenzied maenadic rites, the Hellenistic cult of Dionysus "conveyed a vision of peace and rural tranquility."[94] Aristophanes' *Acharnians* provides a more apt model. Here the most famous symbols of Dionysian rites, wine and

84. Seaford, *Reciprocity and Ritual,* pp. 300-301.
85. Jennifer Lynn Larson, *Ancient Greek Cults: A Guide* (New York: Routledge, 2007), p. 126.
86. Larson, *Ancient Greek Cults,* p. 126.
87. Seaford, *Reciprocity and Ritual,* pp. 296-97.
88. Seaford, *Reciprocity and Ritual,* p. 301.
89. Seaford, *Reciprocity and Ritual,* p. 293.
90. Xavier Riu, *Dionysism and Comedy* (Oxford: Rowman & Littlefield, 1999), p. 75.
91. Riu, *Dionysism and Comedy,* p. 82.
92. Riu, *Dionysism and Comedy,* p. 82.
93. Henrichs, "Between Country and City," p. 258.
94. Henrichs, "Between Country and City," pp. 270-71.

the phallic thyrsus, symbolize not chaos or violence but an end of war and the dawn of peace. According to Henrichs, while Dionysus retained a dual and ambiguous nature, from the fourth century BCE onward his cultic associations were "benign, pastoral, and peaceful."[95]

Understanding the cult of Dionysus in this way suggests that Antiochus's mandate that Judeans participate in the Dionysian procession and sacrifices would have signified more than the imposition of foreign religion. By surrendering to the Dionysian rites Judeans would participate in the symbolic dissolution of existing social order followed by the city's "salvation" at the hands of Antiochus. Congruent with Antiochus's program of de-creation and re-creation, the Dionysian rites would signify the disfounding and refounding of the city, a cut between past and present that marked an end of violence and paved the way for a new order.

That new order would be symbolized in part through the renaming of the Jerusalem temple in honor of Olympian Zeus (2 Macc 6:2). Here a question arises: Was the rededication intended to identify Israel's God with Zeus, or to promote the cult of Zeus instead of Yhwh's?[96] I argue that even the suggested identification of Yhwh and Zeus entails a negation of all that Israel's traditions claimed for the Lord. Whatever forms worship took in the newly rededicated temple — whether they more closely resembled traditional practices of Judea, of Antiochus's native Syria, or of Zeus's homeland, Greece — the rededication was above all else an act of power celebrating Antiochus's conquest of Judea and promoting the power of the king.

Yhwh and Zeus shared certain roles and attributes in common, including kingship and dominion over the heavens. Yet while Israel's Lord ruled as sole deity, Olympian Zeus was celebrated not only as king over the heavens but as king over a pantheon of Greek gods. If the rededication of Yhwh's Jerusalem temple to Zeus Olympios meant identifying the Lord with Zeus, it could affirm the Lord's power only by assimilating Israel's God into the pantheon of Greek gods. While not denying the existence of Israel's God, this assimilation would deny the particularity of Israel's confession and election. Worse than meaningless, such an identification would lay claim to a tradition in order to negate it. The dissonance between the two far exceeded their commonalities. For example, the epithet "Olympios" named the deity's home as Mount Olympus. For Goldstein, this detail "identifies him as distinct from the Lord, who dwells on Mount Zion."[97] Calling Yhwh "Olympian Zeus," if such was the intent of the re-

95. Henrichs, "Between Country and City," p. 271.
96. Joann Scurlock has suggested that the rededication did not signal an equation of Yhwh with Zeus but rather a demotion, displacement, and subordination of Yhwh to the chief deity of the Greek pantheon. "167 BCE: Hellenism or Reform?" *JSJ* 31 (2000): 125-61, 132-33.
97. Goldstein, *II Maccabees,* p. 273.

dedication, could only contradict everything Judeans knew to be true about their history and life in covenant with God.

Whether through identification, disidentification, or a subtle combination of the two, rededicating the Jerusalem temple to Zeus Olympios was thus a negation of claims for the sole divinity of Yhwh and the history of this God with this people. It also entailed a positive set of claims about the deity now worshiped there. Based on his analysis of dedications to Olympian Zeus, Jon Mikalson has argued that this epithet evoked two aspects of the deity: "victory and the power of kingship."[98]

The kingship and power of the deity could symbolically reflect and ground the kingship and power of an earthly monarch, and for this reason the cult of Olympian Zeus was favored by kings.[99] In sixth-century Athens, the tyrant Peisistratus began constructing a monumental temple to Olympian Zeus, known as the Olympieion (Arist. *Pol.* 1313b).[100] His sons ruled as tyrants after his death, and the Olympieion remained an important project under their successive rule. With the end of tyranny and the inauguration of democratic reforms in 508/507 BCE, as Greg Anderson has written, "the vast Olympieion was consciously preserved in its unfinished state as a memorial to the folly of their 'tyranny.'"[101] It remained in this unfinished state until Antiochus IV himself undertook its completion.[102] Otto Mørkholm calls this building project the "most ambitious" of Antiochus's reign, contributing to his reputation as royal benefactor.[103] Yet royal benefaction went hand in hand with conquest, victory in war, and the domination of subject peoples. Mikalson observes that the temple of Olympian Zeus "was a monument of tyrants, kings, and emperors, and democratic Athenians wanted nothing to do with it."[104]

Antiochus was not the first Hellenistic king to promote the cult of Olympian Zeus as an expression of imperial power. According to Arrian, after conquering the city of Sardis in Asia Minor, Alexander the Great installed there a shrine to Zeus Olympios (*Anab.* 1.17.3-8). Sardis had been a regional capital in the Achaemenid Persian empire,[105] and it was the first such capital that Alexan-

---

98. Jon D. Mikalson, *Ancient Greek Religion*, 2nd ed. (Oxford: Wiley-Blackwell, 2010), p. 111.

99. Mikalson, *Ancient Greek Religion*, pp. 111-12.

100. For Aristotle, one aim of the building project was to keep the working poor both working and poor, so that they had neither the time nor the means to resist their oppression.

101. Greg Anderson, *The Athenian Experiment: Building an Imagined Political Community in Ancient Attica, 508-490 BCE* (Ann Arbor: University of Michigan Press, 2003), pp. 91-92.

102. It was not completed, however, until the time of Hadrian.

103. Otto Mørkholm, *Antiochus IV of Syria* (Copenhagen: Gyldendal, 1966), 58. Mørkholm cites Polyb. 26.1.11; Livy 41.20.8; Strabo 9.1.17; Vell. Pat. 1.10.1.

104. Mikalson, *Ancient Greek Religion*, p. 112.

105. For a rich treatment of acculturation, imperial ideology, and interaction in Persian

der conquered.[106] Conscious of history, ideology, and politics, and the connection of all of these with the cults of the gods, Alexander chose to install the shrine to Zeus Olympios on the city's acropolis, in the local palace. For Ma, this was an example of the "ethno-power games" played by Hellenistic kings and conquerors.[107] Linking power and particularity, they attributed power to the particular identity not of the ruled but of the ruler. As I discussed in chapter 3, for the Hellenistic kings that identity was "Greek" (or Macedonian); its symbolic expression therefore took consciously "Greek" forms. In the Judean coin-type minted during the reign of Antiochus, examined above, the pairing of Nike, or Victory, with the Greek words naming Antiochus "King" linked conquest with kingship and "Greek" with power. "Greek" forms imposed on or produced within other cultural institutions communicated the same link. As Ma writes, "the cultural manifestations of kingship, produced by the central institutions, were expressed in Greek. . . . These cultural phenomena represented Greek military superiority and right to rule."[108] Ma accordingly describes the shrine to Olympian Zeus at Sardis as "a symbolical manifestation of rule, but also the visible proclamation of [Alexander's] ethnic identity as Macedonian king come to this particular place, characterized by its traditions and history, associated with Lydian and Persian rule over Asia. . . . [The shrine could be read as] conspicuous because of its ethnic content, and expressing divinely sanctioned power."[109]

For Alexander the shrine to Olympian Zeus made a conspicuous claim about his place in history and about his power over the region and over the empire. Antiochus's rededication of the temple in Jerusalem to Olympian Zeus made a similar claim. By instituting in Jerusalem the cult of a Greek deity associated above all else with conquest and the power of kings, he announced his own victory in Jerusalem and asserted the power of his rule.[110] Continuing the erasure and denial of Judean identity and the unique God they worshiped, he replaced Judean particularity with a fictional identity that aimed solely to achieve and express the power of the king and the might of the empire. Compelling Judeans to participate in the cult of Zeus Olympios drew them into a

---

Sardis, see Elspeth R. M. Dusinberre, *Aspects of Empire in Achaemenid Sardis* (Cambridge: Cambridge University Press, 2003).

106. Ma, "Kings," p. 188.

107. Ma, "Kings," pp. 187-88.

108. Ma, "Kings," pp. 187-88.

109. Ma, "Kings," p. 189.

110. By contrast, the rededication of the temple at Gerizim to Zeus Xenios (2 Macc 6:2), a deity associated with hospitality, communicates power but not conquest. The Samaritans proved "hospitable" to Antiochus's policies, and had presumably not participated in Jason's revolt. Their city, therefore, did not need to be reconquered.

system of subjugation and patronage wherein resistance would be met with death, while worship, loyalty, and honor would be rewarded with benefaction, protection, and life.

The new cultic program had further ramifications for Judeans. First Maccabees uses the category of "profanation" or "defilement" to characterize various components of Antiochus's edict. One of the most extreme examples is the "desolating abomination" erected on the altar of whole-burnt offering; its stones were defiled (1 Macc 1:54; 4:43). Yet the writer of 1 Maccabees does not simply report that Antiochus profaned what was holy. He compelled the Judeans themselves to profane the sabbath and festival days (1:45); desecrate the sanctuary and its priests (1:46; see also 2 Macc 6:2); and defile themselves with impure or profane things (1 Macc 1:48).

Forcing Jews to violate sacred time and space and the boundaries between holy and unholy, pure and impure made them complicit in the work of de-creation. It was a violation of God's law intended simultaneously to negate God's sovereignty over creation and cut the ties of covenant that bound Judeans to their God. Defiling priests and sanctuary would render mediation between Judeans and their God ineffective, depriving them of the means to restore right relationship. By forcing Jews to defile themselves, Antiochus also decreated the individual and the community of belonging. By deconstructing their sense of rightness and belonging, he would place individuals on the outside of the world they had known, alien to their own law and people, until the law was forgotten and they had become another people entirely. According to 1 Maccabees, Antiochus forced Judeans to make themselves abominable "so that they might forget the law and change all their observances (δικαιώματα)" (1 Macc 1:49 NAB). δικαιώματα here denotes both the ordinances that structure life and the deeds or practices that situate the self within it. New laws and practices would take the place of the old, creating a new world and a new framework for identity and belief.

According to 1 Maccabees, the edict also compelled Judeans to build altars and shrines to idols and sacrifice pigs and other impure animals (1 Macc 1:47, 51). This prescription forced Judeans to violate the law of Moses on multiple counts. They would violate the Deuteronomic command to worship in the one place God had chosen, participating in the construction of alternative worship sites.[111] They would also violate the commandments against idolatry and laws concerning acceptable sacrifice. Antiochus appointed supervisors (ἐπισκόπους) throughout the region to oversee the new sacrifices (1:51). As with the other

111. Cf. Goldstein, *I Maccabees*, p. 222. Note that in the same verse the epitomator refers to the temple in Gerizim. The Samaritans viewed Gerizim as the place God had chosen for the temple, while for the Judeans it was Jerusalem.

practices proscribed and mandated by the edict, the penalty for noncompliance was death (1:50).

First Maccabees provides the further detail that "they" (either Judeans who have complied with the edict, the supervisors who oversaw the edict's implementation, or both) "burned incense" at the doors of houses and in the streets (1:55).[112] This practice removed the offering from its traditional place in cultic ritual to the public square. It went hand in hand with the stopping of the *tamid* and the imposition of new sacrificial practices. In the book of Exodus, Aaron is instructed to make a "regular incense offering" (קְטֹרֶת תָּמִיד) on the incense altar before the holy of holies (Ex 30:7-8). Kjeld Nielsen identifies this incense offering as part of the *tamid* sacrifice detailed in Exodus 29:38-42 (see also Num 28:2-8).[113] Not all incense was acceptable, however. "Strange" or "foreign" (זָרָה) incense was forbidden for use on the incense altar (Ex 30:9). Antiochus had abolished the daily sacrifices, introducing new sacrifices inside and outside the temple to replace those of the *tamid*. He apparently replaced the traditional incense offering with a new kind of incense offering, located not in the temple but in the streets. Streets are public spaces, signifying movement, direction, choice, and change. Antiochus's new religious practices literally permeated the air, suffusing the streets with the perfume of an alternative worship and an alternative order. This strange cloud also crossed thresholds, seeping into the protected and sacred spaces of family life and marking the homes of Judeans with the scent of empire. It also "covered over" a vital confession of God's sole sovereignty. Israel's religious traditions instructed the people of Judea to write on the doorways of their houses the confession of the sole being of God and the reminder to love God singly and wholeheartedly (Deut 6:4-6, 9). Regardless of the specific forms the observance of this command may have taken in second-century Judea,[114] for Jews familiar with the instructions of Deuteronomy 6 the incense burned at doorways would symbolically challenge the confession and commitment at the very heart of Judean religion.

Burning incense could be seen, smelled, and even tasted. Antiochus went a step further, mandating that Judeans eat impure food (1 Macc 1:62). Forcing Jews to eat impure food aimed to erase identity and difference, annul covenant, assert power, and reorder the Judean world.

Food was and is the source of sustenance, nourishment for the body. Yet nutritional value alone did not determine whether edible matter counted as

112. Goldstein has argued that the verb ἐθυμίων here means "they offered illicit sacrifices," rather than "they burned incense," on the grounds that the Greek word translates the Hebrew root קטר, "the verb used in the Bible for illicit sacrifice." *I Maccabees*, p. 225.

113. Kjeld Nielsen, *Incense in Ancient Israel* (Leiden: Brill, 1986), p. 70.

114. On this question, see Yehudah Cohn, *Tangled Up in Text: Tefillin and the Ancient World* (Providence: Brown University, 2008).

food for second-century Jews. The sacred traditions of Israel preserved detailed instructions concerning purity in the preparation of food as well as identifying which animals could be eaten — those that were pure — and which animals could not — those that were impure. Regardless of whether the meat of such animals might deliver to the human body necessary proteins, vitamins, minerals, or calories, if they were proscribed by Israel's sacred laws, they were not to be eaten as food.

For Luce Giard, food gives concrete form to "modes of relation between a person and the world" — we might add, between a people and the world. As such it is "one of the fundamental landmarks in space-time," a key to the mapping of the world and people's place within it.[115] As I noted in chapter 2, anthropologist Mary Douglas has made a compelling case that the laws concerning pure and impure animals, or those permitted and forbidden for eating, reflect an understanding and map of creation in which God has established categories, divisions, and boundaries. The holiness of the people Israel imitates the holiness of God, is constituted in being "set apart," and entails respect for the categories, divisions, and boundaries by which God has ordered all of creation, including the distinction between pure and impure animals. No practical logic governs the purity laws in their totality.[116] They are governed rather by the recognition that God has called God's people to order their lives according to God's will as manifested in creation, as revealed to God's prophet Moses, and as recorded and passed on in the Torah.

Many of the animals forbidden for consumption were wild, and were not dietary staples of Israel's neighbors. Thus abstaining from eating hare or tortoise

115. Luce Giard, "Doing-Cooking," in *The Practice of Everyday Life*, vol. 2: *Living and Cooking*, ed. Michel de Certeau, Luce Giard, and Pierre Mayol, trans. T. J. Tomasik (Minneapolis: University of Minnesota Press, 1998), p. 183. On the relation between food and national identity, see Bob Ashley, Joanne Hollows, Steve Jones, and Ben Taylor, *Food and Cultural Studies* (London: Routledge, 2004), pp. 75-89.

116. Cf. Giard, "Doing-Cooking," pp. 168, 185. Giard describes foodways of any given culture as "a system that is coherent and illogical, . . . arranged . . . according to a detailed code of values, rules and symbols" (p. 168). Contrast however Mary Douglas's insistence that the Levitical laws concerning food are, in fact, logical, although they are governed by plural logics. Mary Douglas, *Implicit Meanings: Essays in Anthropology* (London: Routledge, 1975), pp. 231-51. Giard's analysis resists strictly structuralist explanations, looking at acceptable and excluded foods in any culture as "an immense multientry combinatory set whose univocal inventory should be abandoned for a hundred reasons" ("Doing-Cooking," p. 185). "The food that is reserved, authorized, and preferred is the place of a silent piling up of an entire stratification of orders and counterorders that stem at the same time from an ethnohistory, a biology, a climatology, and a regional economy, from a cultural invention and a personal experience. Its choice depends on an addition of positive and negative factors, themselves dependent on objective determinations of time and space, on the creative diversity of human groups and individuals, on the indecipherable contingency of individual microhistories" (p. 185).

did not serve as a key marker of difference between the Jewish people and the Gentiles who lived among and around them. Pork, however, was a domestic animal commonly raised for food (by contrast with the camel, also forbidden to eat, which was raised primarily for use in travel and trade). Jewish abstention from pork was thus a highly visible marker of difference between Jews and certain Gentiles.[117] In his analysis of the signifying dimensions of food, Roland Barthes emphasizes the organization of difference: "Substances, techniques of preparation, habits, all become part of a system of differences in signification: and as soon as this happens, we have communication by way of food."[118] Part of what food communicates is identity and difference. The system of differences that structured its communication in ancient Judea was the system of purity and impurity preserved in the book of Leviticus. For the reasons cited above, the abstention from pork was perhaps the most well known of the Jewish dietary laws, and by the second century it had become an index of Jewish identity.[119] Antiochus's prescribed diet would erase this index of identity and with it the distinction between Jew and non-Jew. It would violate the boundaries of the Judean body and the boundary between pure and impure, compelling Jews to locate themselves within a world mapped not according to the will of the Creator God but according to the whim of the king. In the context of a persecution that sought to erase identity, undo creation, and annul the covenant, continuing to abstain from pork, even on pain of death, became a testimony, a marked choice for covenant, for holiness, for Yhwh, and for Jewishness.[120]

117. Discussing Zechariah's vision of the transformation of the "abominable" foodways of the Philistines, Carol and Eric Meyers observe that "food behaviors, which are part of daily life for all human beings, are thus the most representative of religious-ethnic practices that can be used to define one group as opposed to another" (*Zechariah 9–14*, p. 115). At the same time, Marvin Harris notes that in various periods Babylonians, Egyptians, and Phoenicians also abstained from pork. Thus, while an important index in context, abstention from pork would not have been an absolute marker of Jewish identity. *Good to Eat: Riddles of Food and Culture* (New York: Simon & Schuster, 1985), p. 83.

118. See Roland Barthes, "Toward a Psychosociology of Contemporary Food Consumption," in *Food and Culture: A Reader*, ed. Carole Counihan and Penny van Esterik, 2nd ed. (New York: Routledge, 2008), pp. 28-35, 30. Originally published as "Vers une psycho-sociologie de l'alimentation moderne," *Annales: Économies, Sociétés, Civilisations* 5 (1961): 977-86. Cf. Claude Lévi-Strauss, *The Origin of Table Manners* (New York: Harper & Row, 1978), p. 495.

119. It remained so in the first century CE. See Philo *Flacc.* p. 96. Philo reports that during the pogrom in Alexandria women believed to be Jews were brought onto a public stage and brought pork to eat. Those who ate it escaped further harm, while those who refused it were given over for further abuse. My thanks to Sean Burrus for calling my attention to this parallel. See also Tessa Rajak, "Dying for the Law: The Martyr's Portrait in Jewish-Greek Literature," in *The Jewish Dialogue with Greece and Rome: Studies in Cultural and Social Interaction* (Leiden: Brill, 2001), p. 129.

120. Douglas has argued that "whenever a people are aware of encroachment and danger, dietary rules controlling what goes into the body would serve as a vivid analogy of the corpus of

While the prescribed diet aimed to erase Judean identity, it also asserted Antiochus's power and providence. In the ancient Near Eastern world, the difficulties of producing or obtaining food, on the one hand, and the challenges of preserving surplus food for times of scarcity, on the other, strengthened the connection between food and power (cf. Gen 41–50). In his influential study of famine, social historian David Arnold describes the relationship between food and power as follows:

> Food was, and continues to be, power in a most basic, tangible, and inescapable form. To a degree which we in the well-fed world have perhaps ceased actively to acknowledge, food was not only essential for the maintenance of human life and bodily activity, but was also fundamental to the structures of dominance and dependency that arose out of this most vital of all commodities. Food (and the denial or absence of food that famine entailed) was (and remains even in a relatively secure and secularized society like our own) richly symbolic, a potent and recurrent motif in the semantics of kingship and statecraft, in the language and imagery of religion and culture.[121]

Multiple references to famine and its political consequences in 1 Maccabees reveal a world in which food could not be taken for granted (1 Macc 6:53-54; 9:24; 13:49). Jack Pastor describes the ways in which "cumulative and deleterious effects of the years of strife on the production and storage of food crops" affected loyalties during the Maccabean revolt.[122] In such a setting, provision of food was a mark of power and established a bond between the one who provided and the one who ate.[123]

Israel's traditions preserved the memory of miraculous feeding in the wilderness, encouraging and communicating a fundamental trust in the providence of God despite appearances and in the face of all improbability. That trust took further shape in the observance of ordinances that forbade gathering food on the sabbath, but promised that there would always be enough (Ex 16:23-30). Similar laws forbade working the land on the sabbath and in jubilee years (Lev 25:1-12; cf. 1 Macc 6:49). Moses promised to those who trusted in God's provision, "the land will yield its fruit, and you will eat your fill and live on it securely" (Lev 25:19 NRSV).

---

their cultural categories at risk." *Implicit Meanings*, pp. 249-50. She explains further, "The ordered system which is a meal represents all the ordered systems associated with it" (p. 250).

121. David Arnold, *Famine: Social Crisis and Historical Change* (New York: Basil Blackwell, 1988), pp. 3-4.

122. Jack Pastor, *Land and Economy in Ancient Palestine* (London: Routledge, 1997), pp. 58-61, esp. 61.

123. Carole M. Counihan, introduction to *Food and Gender: Identity and Power*, ed. Carole M. Counihan and Steven L. Kaplan (Amsterdam: Harwood Academic, 1998), p. 6.

The provision of food by the king, or his representative, mimicked the relationship of care and trust between God and Israel, replacing the bonds of covenant loyalty with bonds of submission to empire.[124] To accept the king's food was to accept the king's provision, to accept the substitution of king for God, and to offer in return for the king's generous bounty loyalty and allegiance. It was to take and assimilate into the body a regimen, a way of ordering life, that claimed the king as its source and as guarantor of survival. In such a system, the health of the subjugated body would translate into greater health and wealth for the empire itself.[125]

By compelling Judeans to consume pork on pain of death, the king did not merely seek to erase the outward signs of Jewish identity, and he did not merely shove his power down Judean throats. He continued his work of de-creation through the very erasure of distinctions, in the name of re-creating a unified Seleucid empire. By a change in diet he established a new order within the bodies and landscape of Judea.[126] I referred above to the ways in which the purity system provided a map of creation. Douglas explains further that categories of pure and impure foods participate in the mapping of "temple, altar, and sanctuary" as well as "the hard-won and hard-to-defend boundaries of the Promised Land."[127] By forcing Jews to eat pork Antiochus redrew the map, obliterating boundaries of purity, body, sanctuary, and nation and claiming the bodies, temple, and territory of Judea for himself.[128] Judea's de-creation paved the way for empire's re-creation. The map he drew on Judean bodies and landscape was simultaneously the map of his own empire, continually made new in the conquest of its subjects.

Resistance

If provision of food asserts power, so does its refusal. Those who refused to eat pork, whether publicly or privately, acted against Antiochus, severing and re-

124. S. N. Eisenstadt and L. Roniger emphasize the centrality of trust in patron-client relations in *Patrons, Clients, and Friends: Interpersonal Relations and the Structure of Trust in Society* (Cambridge: Cambridge University Press, 1984).

125. Arnold, *Famine*, p. 99: "Rulers recognized an identity of interest between themselves and the people, seeing in the prosperity and contentment of their subjects the surest foundation of their own wealth and power."

126. Characterizing the meaning of food in history, Giard offers the general dictum that "everything happens as if a specific alimentary diet expressed a world order, or rather, postulated in its very act the possible inscription of such an order on the world" ("Doing-Cooking," p. 180).

127. Douglas, *Implicit Meanings*, p. 269.

128. Giard characterizes the act of forcing another to eat certain foods as claiming possession of the body so compelled ("Doing-Cooking," p. 189).

fusing bonds of loyalty and submission and asserting the power of their traditions and their God.[129] First Maccabees says of those who resolved not to eat impure food that they "stood firm," "made themselves strong," or "exercised mastery" (ἐκραταιώθησαν 1 Macc 1:62).

Daniel 1 preserves a story of resistance through the refusal of food and drink. Daniel, Hananiah, Mishael, and Azariah are Judean captives in the court of the Babylonian king Nebuchadnezzar. Nebuchadnezzar plans to socialize and train the captives over a three-year period with the goal of preparing them for service in the royal court (Dan 1:5). As part of this program Nebuchadnezzar prescribes and provides for them a daily ration from "the king's menu" and from "the wine of his feasting" (1:5). For Daniel, eating from the king's menu and drinking from the wine of his feasting would be "defiling" or "polluting," and he determines not to comply (1:8). The story does not provide details as to what would have made the king's food and wine defiling for Daniel. One can well assume that they would not have been prepared according to Levitical purity laws. But the details that follow suggest that more is at stake. As Danna Nolan Fewell observes, "the food and wine are . . . symbols of political patronage."[130] The narrative raises the following questions: Who provides for the Judean captives? Who ensures their health and well-being? To whom will they render thanks for the sustenance of their bodies?

The diet Daniel requests in place of the royal menu is stark in its simplicity. Seeds or vegetables and water (1:12) would not have a high caloric content and would not be likely to make one "fat." Yet after ten days on this special diet Daniel and his friends "looked finer and fatter than all the boys who were eating the king's food" (1:15). Like the memory of manna in the wilderness, this detail emphasizes the miracle of divine provision. By refusing the diet the king had ordained for them and trusting that God would sustain and nourish their bodies, they asserted the provident power of God over against the power of the king. By the conclusion of this trial, God has given (נָתַן) them not only nourishment for their bodies but also "knowledge, mastery of all literature, and wisdom" (1:17).

The story moves from pollution to provision, suggesting that in this context one should not be understood apart from the other. Observing laws of purity meant fidelity to the order of life in covenant with God. The covenant also detailed God's responsibilities for the care of God's people, to sustain life, protect, deliver, and provide for them. Royal patronage pretended to offer the same provident care, full knowing that provision creates conditions of dependence

---

129. On refusing food as an act of power, see Counihan, introduction to *Food and Gender,* p. 6.

130. Danna Nolan Fewell, *Circle of Sovereignty: Plotting Politics in the Book of Daniel* (Nashville: Abingdon, 1991), p. 19.

and invites loyalty and allegiance. Eating the king's food and drinking the wine of his feasting would mean accepting his patronage and becoming dependent on the "care" he provided. The king would expect loyalty in return for rich food. By resisting pollution and refusing the king's food, Daniel, Hananiah, Mishael, and Azariah directed all loyalty to God, true provider of nourishment and wisdom.

In the time of the persecution the story in Daniel 1 served as an introduction to the entire book, urging the persecuted faithful to resist Antiochus's program and trust in divine providence. The epitomator preserves a similar tale of resistance in the months just prior to the persecution. I noted in chapter 5 that following the report of Apollonius's military parade and sabbath massacre the epitomator introduces the book's heroes, Judas Maccabeus and his group of ten, who retreated to the wilderness and there "continued to eat grass-like food, in order that they would not share in the defilement" (2 Macc 5:27). As in Daniel, so here, there is no explanation for the defilement. In the epitomator's account, this story precedes the report of the edict, which in 1 Maccabees contains the instruction that Judeans must eat pork and make themselves abominable. For this reason Joseph Sievers writes, "There was no reason before the decree of persecution to adopt a special diet in order to avoid defilement."[131] Nonetheless, by evoking Israel's wilderness traditions the story connects defilement with themes of trust, provision, and covenant fidelity, and ultimately denies Antiochus the power to order life in Judea. That power would belong only to God, to whom Judas and his band directed their allegiance.

The agents of Antiochus implemented the new religious program over a period of months, exercising tight surveillance over the inhabitants of Judea. Many Judeans complied with the edict, saving their lives and the lives of their children (1 Macc 1:52). But many resisted, even though their resistance met with violence (ἐν ἰσχύι 1:58) and earned a sentence of death (1:50, 57). They retained books of the covenant (1:57), circumcised their babies (1:60), observed sabbath (2 Macc 6:11), and refused to eat impure food (1 Macc 1:62). First Maccabees reports, "They preferred to die rather than to be defiled with unclean food or to profane the holy covenant; and they did die" (1:63 NAB).

In addition to the deaths of circumcising mothers and their families, both 1 and 2 Maccabees report the massacre of large groups who had retreated to caves or "hiding places in the wilderness" to observe the sabbath (2 Macc 6:11; 1 Macc 2:29-38). The epitomator reports death by burning, 1 Maccabees by armed assault; both place the massacres on the sabbath. In each case the victims welcomed death rather than violate the law ("let us all die in our innocence," 1 Macc

131. Joseph Sievers, *The Hasmoneans and Their Supporters: From Mattathias to the Death of John Hyrcanus I* (Atlanta: Scholars Press, 1990), p. 19.

2:37) and did nothing to defend themselves out of reverence for the sabbath: "the Jews neither replied to [the king's men and the men of the Akra] nor hurled a stone at them nor blocked the entrances to their hiding places" (1 Macc 2:36, Goldstein's translation); "they piously held back from defending themselves" (2 Macc 6:11). According to 1 Maccabees those who died in the desert numbered a thousand men, women, and children, along with their cattle.

The epitomator reports not only deaths but also tortures, giving elaborate accounts of the suffering and death of nine martyrs, the Judean elder Eleazar and a mother and seven sons, all of whom refused to eat pork at the king's command (2 Macc 6:18–7:42).[132] Their stories form the centerpiece and hinge of the book, as their innocent deaths restore right relationship between God and the Judean people and lead God to intervene to deliver their compatriots.[133] By portraying the efficacy of the martyrs' deaths the epitomator also reveals the delusions of Antiochus and the saving power of God (7:18, 34; 8:17-18, 24; 9:8).

Throughout this chapter I have explained the edict and persecution as a program of de-creation and re-creation that asserted the power of the empire and the king in the place of God. Tortures both public and private would contribute to Antiochus's program. Scarry's landmark study *The Body in Pain: The Making and Unmaking of the World* provides a framework for understanding torture as an act of power, de-creation, and re-creation.

In Scarry's analysis, torture consists of three elements: (1) inflicting pain; (2) objectifying pain's attributes; (3) and misreading pain as power by translating "those attributes into the insignia of the regime."[134] The attributes of pain that become emblems of the dominating power are (1) negation;[135] (2-3) "dissolution of boundaries" between the body's outside and inside, as pain comes from both places at once;[136] (4) a "conflation of private and public" that leaves no place secure;[137] (5) destruction of language;[138] (6) "obliteration of the con-

132. Jan Willem van Henten reviews the extensive literature on the source, form, and tradition history of the martyr accounts in 2 Macc 6–7. *The Maccabean Martyrs as Saviours of the Jewish People: A Study of 2 and 4 Maccabees* (Leiden: Brill, 1997), pp. 17-18n1.

133. See Van Henten, *Maccabean Martyrs*, pp. 28, 140-44. Following the martyrs' deaths Judas and his company of six thousand pray to God "to listen to [the martyrs'] blood crying out to him" (2 Macc 8:2-3). At the prayer's conclusion the epitomator reports that "the Lord's wrath had turned to mercy" (8:5), an answer not only to Judas's prayer but also to the prayer of the seventh martyred son, who gave his life asking only for God to show mercy to the people (7:37) and "through me and my brothers to bring to an end the wrath of the Almighty that has justly fallen on our nation" (7:38 NRSV).

134. Scarry, *Body in Pain*, p. 19.
135. Scarry, *Body in Pain*, p. 52.
136. Scarry, *Body in Pain*, pp. 52-53.
137. Scarry, *Body in Pain*, pp. 53-55.
138. Scarry, *Body in Pain*, p. 54, but see also 172.

tents of consciousness";[139] (7) totality;[140] and (8) the "ontological split" produced by the simultaneous perception and denial of pain's reality.[141]

I argued in chapter 1 that this very ontological split between mind and body, matter and spirit is a product of the domination system and serves its ends. Pain, like terror, helps the regime to achieve this split by annihilating "objects of complex thought and emotion" as well as "objects of the most elemental acts of perception . . . destroying one's ability simply to see."[142] Despite the pain inflicted on them, the mother and her sons each retained the ability to see (2 Macc 7:4, 16, 20, 28); they also insisted on the provident gaze of God (7:6, 35). Eleazar resisted the conflation of public and private, knowing that his actions would be an example for others (6:21-28, 31). All of them resisted the destruction of language by speaking what they knew to be true. The epitomator provides the further detail that the second brother and mother spoke "in their ancestral language" (τῇ πατρίῳ φωνῇ 7:8, 21, 27). In their trial this language connected them to place, history, people, and traditions that would be a source of certainty, hope, identity, and strength. Each of the martyrs insisted on maintaining the body's boundaries, refusing to ingest the pork that was offered and even forced into their mouths (6:19; 7:1-2). They refused to accord totality to pain or the suffering of the present moment, and instead set their sights on the totality of a world governed by God's law and created by God's design (7:23). They answered negation with bold declarations of will and confessions of faith (6:26, 30; 7:2, 6, 9, 11, 14, 16-17, 22-23, 28-38).

In similar fashion, against the totalizing claims and destructive aims of an empire that would convert human pain into signs of imperial power, the apocalypses offered new sight, restoring the ability to see to a people terrorized and tortured. They offered language, giving voice to suffering but also to hope, naming reality in the face of its denial. They resisted the ontological split by insisting on the integrity of mind and body and the necessary interrelationship between the visible and invisible realms. They denied the totality of pain and the totalizing claims of the empire by revealing the totality of God's dominion, creation, and human life in covenant with God.

Not everyone who resisted Antiochus embraced a martyr's death. First and 2 Maccabees both go on to tell the story of armed resistance, led first by Mattathias (1 Macc 2) and then by his son Judas Maccabeus (1 Macc 2:66; 2 Macc 8:5). This book will not add to the many, thorough accounts of the

---

139. Scarry, *Body in Pain,* p. 54.
140. Scarry, *Body in Pain,* pp. 54-56.
141. Scarry, *Body in Pain,* pp. 56-57, 48.
142. Scarry, *Body in Pain,* p. 54.

Maccabean revolt.[143] Yet I note that the Apocalypse of Weeks and Book of Dreams, the two Enochic historical apocalypses I study in Part Three, support armed resistance against the "structures of violence and deceit" and the armies of Antiochus. In chapters 9 and 10 I give sustained attention to the theological framework and interpretations of scriptural traditions that supported this response to the persecution.

Conclusion

The edict of Antiochus aimed to complete the work of Judea's reconquest and through it the re-creation of empire. As a political act, it revoked Judean *autonomia,* or civic freedom, announcing and effecting Judea's total subjection to the empire. But the edict aimed at more than subjugation. The edict launched a program of domination over Judean bodies, minds, souls, and wills. Antiochus intervened in the ordering of space, time, social structures, memory, and the human body, forbidding traditional religious practices and instituting a new order for religious and civic life. His edict aimed to replace Judean identity, history, and social memory with a new ground of being and belonging. It was a program of unmaking and making, de-creation and re-creation, with Antiochus the authorizer and maker of a new world, order, and identity for the inhabitants of Judea.

I noted in chapter 1 that the earliest extant examples of the literary form "historical apocalypse" — Daniel, the Apocalypse of Weeks, and the Book of Dreams — were all written during the reign of Antiochus IV Epiphanes. I argued in Part One that these apocalyptic writings must be understood as a literature of resistance.

To clarify what it was they were resisting, in Part Two I have reconstructed the conditions and objects of resistance in Seleucid Judea from the beginnings of Seleucid rule to the edict of Antiochus and the persecution he launched in 167 BCE.

In chapter 2 I highlighted the ideology of conquest that formed the basis of Hellenistic rule. Judea found itself at the heart of the Syrian wars between the Ptolemies and Seleucids, as they battled for control of the strategic region of Coele-Syria and Phoenicia. The late third and early second centuries BCE were a period of nearly ceaseless violence for the people of Judea. The transition to Seleucid rule in 200 BCE brought a temporary peace. Antiochus III confirmed for Judeans the right to live according to their ancestral laws and granted tax ex-

---

143. See especially Bezalel Bar-Kochva, *Judas Maccabaeus: The Jewish Struggle against the Seleucids* (Cambridge: Cambridge University Press, 1989).

emptions to Judea's leading citizens. Yet the Judean community experienced a high number of stressors and divisions even during the reign of Antiochus III, including military garrison, support for soldiers, personal and economic hardship in the aftermath of war, and significant gaps in the distribution of privilege between the ruling elite and lower classes. These tensions set the stage for resistance long before the reign of his son Antiochus IV.

In chapter 3, I examined conditions of domination and interaction between the Seleucid empire and its Judean subjects between the years 188 and 173 BCE. Analysis of the recently published Heliodorus stele revealed the logic of imperial benefaction as well as the beginnings of Seleucid encroachment into regional cultic administration. I also highlighted dynamics of reciprocity, calling attention to the agency of the Judean populace and its leaders in their interactions with the empire. These interactions included the negotiation of identity in the encounters between "Judaism" and "Hellenism" and in the face of imperial "ethno-power games."

In chapter 4, I drew attention to the broader context of the Sixth Syrian War between Antiochus IV Epiphanes and his Ptolemaic rivals during the years 170-168. In the midst of Antiochus's Egyptian campaigns, he received word of Jason's revolt in Jerusalem. I argued that Antiochus's reprisals against the revolt afforded him the opportunity to achieve the re-creation of empire through the reconquest of Judea.

Reconquest began with a program of terror, which I outlined in chapter 5. He would unmake the Judean world, destroying the foundations of security and hope, in order to substitute a world of his own making. That world took shape in the edict and persecution of 167 BCE. By these measures he sought to complete Judea's reconquest. These were the conditions and objects of resistance for the writers of Daniel, the Apocalypse of Weeks, and the Book of Dreams.

The destructive and reordering words of Antiochus opposed the creative and ordering words of God. The apocalyptic writers challenged and countered the king's program and reasserted the ground of identity and action through the creative reinterpretation of Israel's scriptural traditions and the writing of new texts that claimed the authority of tradition and divine revelation. Having established the historical context and with it the conditions and objects of resistance, in Part Three I examine these apocalyptic writings, readings, and visions of resistance.

PART THREE

APOCALYPTIC THEOLOGIES
OF RESISTANCE

Introduction to Part Three

Antiochus did not have the last word. Apocalypse answered the empire. The
writers of the apocalypses countered hegemonic cosmologies, imperial spectacle, and false claims to power by articulating and promulgating an alternative
vision of the world. They turned the symbols and values of the empire upside
down and asserted truth in the place of falsehood. They also countered domination and repression with a call to resistance.

Paul D. Hanson once characterized apocalyptic as an apolitical project in
which vision parted ways with reality.[1] For Hanson, visionary mythmaking had
abandoned "the prophetic task" of transforming the present order.[2] As he put
it, "When separated from the realism, the vision leads to a retreat into the world
of ecstasy and dreams and to an abdication of the social responsibility of translating the vision of the divine order into the realm of everyday earthly concerns."[3] The writers I study in Part Three did not retreat. They did not abandon
realism. Their visions portrayed reality in a new light in order to change not
only how their audiences saw, but also what they did.[4] They challenged readers
and hearers not to withdraw, but to engage. As we will see in our analysis of the

---

1. Paul D. Hanson, *The Dawn of Apocalyptic: The Historical and Sociological Roots of Jewish
Apocalyptic Eschatology*, rev. ed. (Minneapolis: Fortress, 1979), p. 26.

2. Hanson, *Dawn of Apocalyptic*, p. 29.

3. Hanson, *Dawn of Apocalyptic*, p. 30.

4. Cf. Marvin A. Sweeney, "The End of Eschatology in Daniel? Theological and Socio-
Political Ramifications of the Changing Contexts of Interpretation," *BibInt* 9, no. 2 (2001): 123-
40. I note, however, that I disagree with Sweeney concerning the kind of action the book supports. Sweeney states that the book supports the Maccabean revolt (p. 128). I argue against this
view in ch. 7.

Apocalypse of Weeks, some would aim precisely to transform social, political, and religious structures. For Hanson the command to Daniel to seal up the vision illustrates the split between the visionary and the real. I argue in the following chapter that the command does no such thing. He is right that "Daniel is not required to integrate" the realms of the cosmic and the mundane.[5] For these writers they are already integrated.[6] In fact, if Daniel has sealed the vision, and someone now reads it, it means the time of unsealing has arrived. The reader and the hearer must see what Daniel has seen. They must also live it.

One commonly noted feature of the literary genre apocalypse is that visions do not stand alone. They are framed by narrative. The historical reviews contained in many of the visions I study in Part Three also contain narrative. Their mythic qualities cannot be denied, but they are not therefore divorced from history. Instead, story and history bear within them the pattern of God's activity and a pattern for faithful human action. Thus, even as story provides a literary frame for vision, in the apocalyptic writings revelation provides a theological framework for action. Conjoining of story and vision matches the joining of practice and belief, providing a template for resistance to empire and to persecution.

In the remaining chapters I examine in detail three apocalyptic writings from Judea commonly dated to the reign of Antiochus IV: Daniel, the Apocalypse of Weeks, and the Book of Dreams. They are writings of resistance to Antiochus's program of terror, conquest, de-creation, and re-creation. As I have discussed in Parts One and Two, each text serves as resistant counterdiscourse. At the same time, each text calls its audience to take up resistance — effective action — against the empire and its ordering of the world.

These writers found a framework and models for resistance in Israel's scriptures. Even as Seleucid agents seized and burned scrolls of Torah, there were Jews who kept reading. Like Daniel, they searched the scriptures to perceive God's plan. They found themselves in Israel's stories and saw the future in the past.[7] Their revelations wove together vision and interpretation, so that each shaped the other. By a continual process of reading and writing, reception and production, they articulated Judean and Jewish identity, belief, and practice in the face of domination and persecution. Inventing tradition was an act

---

5. Hanson, *Dawn of Apocalyptic*, p. 19.

6. Mary Mills describes "the heavens and earth" in Daniel as "a single reality of cosmic dimensions." *Biblical Morality: Moral Perspectives in Old Testament Narratives* (Aldershot, UK: Ashgate, 2001), p. 192.

7. Reinhart Koselleck argues that "in order to even act . . . one must foresee the future," while "ideas about the future rest upon a structural repeatability derived from the past." *The Practice of Conceptual History: Timing History, Spacing Concepts,* trans. Todd Presner (Stanford: Stanford University Press, 2002), pp. 133, 137.

of resistance and an act of faith. By locating their own writings within an authoritative and sacred ancient tradition, the apocalyptic writers asserted divine sovereignty over imperial powers and divine authorization for the work of resistance. Yet these writers did not all draw on the *same* traditions. As I discuss in chapter 8, authoritative sacred writings from the Enochic tradition profoundly shaped the self-understanding, worldview, and program of resistance of the writers of the Apocalypse of Weeks and Book of Dreams.

Differences in worldview and self-understanding could give rise to different programs for resistance. While the programs of resistance envisioned and advocated by Daniel, the Apocalypse of Weeks, and the Book of Dreams share much in common, they also differ in significant ways, most notably in their stances toward martyrdom and armed resistance.

The writer(s) of Daniel, a book that dates to the early years of the persecution (ca. 165 BCE), advocated a stance of faithful waiting for God to act. They believed that angels would wage a decisive war on behalf of God's holy people; there would be no need to take up arms. Emphasizing nonviolent resistance and covenant obedience, they envisaged a role for the wise as teachers who would suffer martyrdom to preserve the covenant.

The views of another group are represented in the Apocalypse of Weeks and the Book of Dreams, portions of the composite work *1 Enoch* thought to have been composed between 170 and 165 BCE. This group expected that when God intervened, God would also arm the righteous remnant for victory against their oppressors. According to the Apocalypse of Weeks, in the time of judgment this righteous remnant would participate in executing God's vengeance against the wicked.

Each of these positions found precedent and warrant in the authoritative traditions of Israel. The resistant action they envision is based upon scriptural models and articulated in scriptural and theological terms. Moreover, for each writer the appropriate response to the persecution was grounded in specific theological convictions regarding the nature of the crisis and how God would effect deliverance for faithful Jews. Scriptural traditions provided an essential matrix in which these convictions were shaped. The broad spectrum of responses these writings represent, encompassing both nonviolent and violent forms of resistance, owes in part to the very diversity of views found within the scriptures they interpreted and the diversity of scriptures considered authoritative by the apocalyptic writers. Yet it should also be obvious that no tradition is self-interpreting. New revelations and insights influenced the ways in which these writers read the scriptures and interpreted them for the present situation. This dynamic and creative interplay between theology, hermeneutics, and ethics — or between the framework of belief, the practices of reading, and the shaping of resistant action — is a focus of Part Three.

I offer here a note concerning method. Robert Kraft has referred to the "tyranny of canonical assumptions," which leads even careful scholars to retroject into precanonical periods particular ways of thinking about the authoritative texts that would later be conceived as "biblical."[8] For Kraft these ways of thinking go hand in hand with a marginalization of "nonbiblical" writings (which Kraft prefers to call "parascriptural") and lead to an artificial and misleading bifurcation between "biblical" and "nonbiblical" or "extrabiblical" texts.

Kraft's point is well taken. At the same time, the second century BCE is a vital period in the formation of scriptures as scriptures, that is, written authoritative sacred texts, and in the development of scriptural hermeneutics.[9] Daniel's study of the scroll of Jeremiah and the angel's interpretation of the seventy-week prophecy in Daniel 9 provide a key example (cf. the vision of the flying scroll in Zech 5). Enoch's role as scribe and the prominent place of heavenly tablets in the Enochic literature further testify to the power of this scriptural principle, particularly within the scribal circles that generated these texts. These interpreters and writers sought through texts to arrive at and communicate knowledge of God's way, will, and plan for the future. Simply put, they viewed written texts as a source and record of revelation.

I have repeatedly stated that the writers of Daniel, the Apocalypse of Weeks, and the Book of Dreams were each heir to a set of scriptural traditions they viewed as authoritative, and each constructed his or her own discourse using, among other things, elements from those traditions.[10] Not all of these scriptural traditions claimed the same kind of authority.[11] For example, some prophetic texts claimed to record the "word of the Lord"; some wisdom texts claimed the authority of tradition or reason; some psalms presumably held authoritative status due to their use in the common prayer life of a community. And, as I discuss in chapter 8, the claims to revelation in the early Enochic literature stake out a unique authority that differs again from that claimed in the

8. See Robert Kraft's 2006 SBL presidential address, "Para-Mania: Beside, Before, and Beyond Bible Studies," *JBL* 126, no. 1 (2007): 5-27, 17, where he defines this phrase as "the temptation to impose on those ancients whom we study our modern ideas about what constituted 'scripture' and how it was viewed."

9. John C. Reeves, "Scriptural Authority in Early Judaism," in *Living Traditions of the Bible: Scripture in Jewish, Christian, and Muslim Practice*, ed. James E. Bowley (St. Louis: Chalice Press, 1999), pp. 63-84, 75-76.

10. Some of the traditions held to be authoritative by these writers would likely have been known in oral rather than written form.

11. Richard A. Horsley has demonstrated that the cultural repertory extended well beyond the written texts we now possess, but also concedes that "extant written texts constitute our only sources." *Scribes, Visionaries, and the Politics of Second Temple Judea* (Louisville: Westminster John Knox, 2007), p. 110.

Mosaic traditions. In addition, no one list of texts was held to be authoritative in this period, nor were the forms of authoritative texts yet fixed.[12] We do better to imagine a fluid deposit of tradition whose borders were still permeable and whose contents could become a site of contest as well as creativity.[13] While the writers I study do not all attribute to the same set of traditions equal levels of authority, all of them locate their own discourses within a matrix of authoritative received tradition.[14] They also make their own self-conscious claims to authority, such that Daniel, the Apocalypse of Weeks, and the Book of Dreams all present themselves as authoritative scripture, through which the will, way, and plan of God are made known.

I begin Part Three with a text familiar to most of my readers: chapter 7 examines the book of Daniel. Following Daniel I turn to the Enochic historical apocalypses, beginning with a consideration of Enochic authority in chapter 8, followed by a treatment of the Apocalypse of Weeks in chapter 9 and the Book of Dreams in chapter 10.

As I examine each text I focus on the program of resistant action the writer envisions for his or her audience and the means the writer uses to portray that action. These writers countered Antiochus's pretensions to be author and authorizer of world and identity by asserting the authority of revealed knowl-

12. James E. Bowley and John C. Reeves caution that "any particular text that one might use is one exemplar from one stage ('generation') in a long and complicated genealogy." "Rethinking the Concept of 'Bible': Some Theses and Proposals," *Henoch* 25 (2003): 3-18, 10. While we cannot claim that the text forms known to us are identical to those known to the writers studied here, the evidence from Qumran suggests that even as we acknowledge the diversity of ancient text forms we may also posit a high degree of continuity between earlier text forms and the ones known today. I prefer to work with the materials that are available to us rather than to let radical skepticism prevent us from exploring key dynamics in the creative use and invention of sacred tradition in this period.

13. See Horsley, *Scribes, Visionaries, and the Politics,* p. 164, for the view that in light of this fluidity, "we should not assume that the allegory [in the Animal Apocalypse] is drawing its details as well as its general sequence of events from 'biblical books.'" This is an important corrective to standard methodological assumptions in the study of this literature. At the same time, we must also recognize the increasing scriptural function of texts in this period and hold these insights in tension. Martha Himmelfarb argues that the writers of the early Enochic literature were self-consciously literary, situating their texts within a written tradition that included the texts later known as "biblical." *Ascent to Heaven in Jewish and Christian Apocalypses* (Oxford: Oxford University Press, 1993), pp. 98-103. See also Günter Reese, "Die Geschichte Israels in der Auffassung des frühen Judentums. Eine Untersuchung der Tiervision und der Zehnwochenapokalypse des äthiopischen Henochbuches, der Geschichtsdarstellung der Assumptio Mosis und der des 4. Esrabuches" (diss., Heidelberg University, 1967), pp. 21-47.

14. On the question of scriptures in the study of Enochic and other forms of Judaism in this period, see John C. Reeves, "Complicating the Notion of an 'Enochic Judaism,'" in *Enoch and Qumran Origins: New Light on a Forgotten Connection,* ed. Gabriele Boccaccini (Grand Rapids: Eerdmans, 2005), pp. 373-83, 376.

edge that testified to the creative and provident power of God. Each writer also understood right resistance in the light of God's being and actions, past, present, and future. I thus give attention to the theological framework for each program of resistance. Finally, I investigate the ways in which this theological framework and the interpretation of earlier scriptural traditions informed, undergirded, and shaped one another, just as they shaped and grounded each vision of resistance.[15]

15. I would like to acknowledge here that the idea for this portion of the study emerged from reading John J. Collins, *The Apocalyptic Vision of the Book of Daniel* (Missoula, MT: Scholars Press, 1977). Collins outlines a "Spectrum of Viewpoints" relating to resistance to Antiochus's persecution of the Jews (pp. 191-206). After considering the perspectives of Dan, 1 Macc, 2 Macc, *T. Mos*, and the Animal Apocalypse, Collins concludes that each document conceives of political resistance within a religious framework drawn from Israel's holy war traditions. Other treatments of the spectrum of responses to the persecution can be found in Édouard Will and Claude Orrieux, *Ioudaïsmos-hellènismos: essai sur le judaïsme judéen à l'époque hellénistique* (Nancy: Presses universitaires de Nancy, 1986); Joseph Sievers, *The Hasmoneans and Their Supporters: From Mattathias to the Death of John Hyrcanus I* (Atlanta: Scholars Press, 1990), pp. 21-26; André Lacocque, "The Socio-Spiritual Formative Milieu of the Daniel Apocalypse," in *The Book of Daniel in the Light of New Findings*, ed. A. S. van der Woude (Leuven: Leuven University Press, 1993), pp. 315-43, esp. 321-25; Stefan Beyerle, "The Book of Daniel and Its Social Setting," in *The Book of Daniel: Composition and Reception*, vol. 1, ed. John J. Collins and Peter Flint (Leiden: Brill, 2001), pp. 205-28; Stephen Breck Reid, *Enoch and Daniel: A Form Critical and Sociological Study of the Historical Apocalypses*, 2nd ed. (North Richland Hills, TX: BIBAL Press, 2004).

CHAPTER 7

Daniel

Studies on the book of Daniel as literature of resistance to empire have multiplied in recent years, owing in large part to shifts outside and within biblical studies. Indeed, since the appearance of Barbara Harlow's *Resistance Literature* in 1987, the categories of resistance and resistance literature have gradually entered the mainstream of literary criticism.[1] Six years after the publication of Harlow's seminal study, literary and cultural critic Edward Said's *Culture and Imperialism* called for "contrapuntal reading" that would examine not merely resistance but the interplay between resistance and imperialism.[2] Central to the intellectual project known as postcolonialism, empire and resistance have since become buzzwords throughout the humanities and social sciences. Even though the modern colonial moment properly begins in the sixteenth century CE, biblical studies are no exception. With the growth of postcolonial biblical criticism and the dawn of empire studies in biblical scholarship, scholars have increasingly brought the categories of empire and resistance to bear on biblical texts.[3]

No book of the Hebrew Bible so plainly engages and opposes the project of empire as Daniel.[4] Among the numerous recent studies that have analyzed the stories and visions of Daniel as a literature of resistance to empire, I give special

1. Barbara Harlow, *Resistance Literature* (New York: Routledge, 1987).

2. Edward Said, *Culture and Imperialism* (New York: Knopf, 1993), p. 66.

3. See, for example, the essays collected in Rasiah S. Sugirtharajah, ed., *The Postcolonial Biblical Reader* (Oxford: Blackwell, 2006). An assessment of the influence of postcolonial studies on biblical criticism can be found in Stephen D. Moore and Fernando Segovia, eds., *Postcolonial Biblical Criticism: Interdisciplinary Intersections* (London: T. & T. Clark, 2005).

4. Cf. the judgment of Danna Nolan Fewell: "The book of Daniel may be the Bible's foremost book of resistance against political domination." *The Children of Israel: Reading the Bible for the Sake of Our Children* (Nashville: Abingdon, 2003), p. 117.

attention here to the work of Daniel L. Smith-Christopher, David Valeta, Shane Kirkpatrick, Danna Nolan Fewell, and Jin Hee Han.[5]

In his *New Interpreter's Bible* commentary on Daniel, Smith-Christopher brought a theoretical edge — specifically the practical political theories of Frantz Fanon and Albert Memmi — to the study of Daniel as resistance literature.[6] Calling Daniel a "revolutionary book of resistance,"[7] Smith-Christopher emphasized the imperial context not only for the visions written during the reign of Antiochus IV, but also for the stories, many of which likely had origins in the Persian period.[8] "Most literary analysis of these stories," he wrote, "has tended to overlook their potent sociopolitical power as stories of resistance to cultural and spiritual assimilation of a minority to a dominant power."[9] In Smith-Christopher's analysis, storytelling was in itself an act of resistance, while dream visions opened up new possibilities and "a new approach to reality."[10]

Valeta names his debt to Smith-Christopher's work in the preface to his monograph *Lions and Ovens and Visions: A Satirical Reading of Daniel 1–6*.[11] Rather than postcolonial theory, however, Valeta uses the genre theory of linguist Mikhail Bakhtin to argue that the intentional mixing of genres of Daniel 1–6 creates a literary form comparable to Menippean satire.[12] Like classical Menip-

5. For treatment of smaller units, see: on Dan 1, Philip Chia, "On Naming the Subject: Postcolonial Reading of Daniel 1," in *The Postcolonial Biblical Reader*, ed. Rasiah S. Sugirtharajah (Oxford: Blackwell, 2006), pp. 171-84; on Dan 4, with a focus on globalization, Roland Boer, *Last Stop before Antarctica: The Bible and Postcolonialism in Australia*, 2nd ed. (Atlanta: SBL, 2008), pp. 37-55; on Dan 5 and 6, Donald C. Polaski, "*Mene, Mene, Tekel, Parsin:* Writing and Resistance in Daniel 5 and 6," *JBL* 123, no. 4 (2004): 649-69. For Chia the narrator "mirror[s] his/her resistance to colonial power through the character of God and the act of Daniel," particularly in Daniel's refusal of food and drink ("On Naming the Subject," p. 178). Polaski argues that subversive stories may nonetheless "secure the continued vitality of imperial power" (*"Mene, Mene, Tekel, Parsin,"* p. 668).

6. Daniel L. Smith-Christopher, "The Book of Daniel," *NIB*, vol. 7 (Nashville: Abingdon, 1996), pp. 19-152, 33 and passim. Smith-Christopher also draws on the teachings and example of Mahatma Gandhi. For a more extended treatment, see Daniel L. Smith-Christopher, "Gandhi on Daniel 6: Some Thoughts on a 'Cultural Exegesis' of the Bible," *BibInt* 1, no. 3 (1993): 321-38.

7. Smith-Christopher, "Book of Daniel," p. 32.

8. Smith-Christopher, "Book of Daniel," pp. 23-33.

9. Smith-Christopher, "Book of Daniel," p. 20.

10. On stories, see also Daniel L. Smith, *The Religion of the Landless: The Social Context of the Babylonian Exile* (Bloomington, IN: Meyer Stone, 1989), pp. 153-78. On visions: Smith-Christopher, "Book of Daniel," p. 107. See also Daniel L. Smith-Christopher, "Prayers and Dreams: Power and Diaspora Identities in the Social Setting of the Daniel Tales," in *The Book of Daniel: Composition and Reception*, vol. 1, ed. John J. Collins and Peter W. Flint (Leiden: Brill, 2001), pp. 266-90.

11. David Valeta, *Lions and Ovens and Visions: A Satirical Reading of Daniel 1–6* (Sheffield: Sheffield Phoenix, 2008).

12. On satire in Daniel as opposition to empire, see also Mary Mills, *Biblical Morality:*

Daniel

pea, Daniel's playful, multivoiced, and transgressive text combines elements of the fantastic and the comedic, the crude and the otherworldly, with a pointed and public concern for current issues. While earlier treatments of the tales in Daniel emphasized their comparatively favorable attitude toward foreign monarchs and, by extension, the empires they ruled,[13] Valeta's analysis exploits ambiguities and contradictions in the text to reveal its destabilizing power to oppose and undercut the imperial project.[14]

Kirkpatrick finds in the stories of Daniel 1–6 a competition between cultures and traditions. Social scientific models texture his reading of the tales as "literature of resistance to the perceived threat of Hellenistic cultural hegemony."[15] In Kirkpatrick's reading, the culture of the Babylonian and Persian courts within the story world is analogous to the Hellenistic tradition in the world of Daniel's audience. The wisdom of Daniel and his friends triumphs over that of the foreign courtiers, demonstrating the inferiority of the foreign tradition. In this way Daniel invites the reader to test and reevaluate "the Greek heritage."[16] Indeed, Daniel's rejection of the king's food is simultaneously the "refusal of an entire social system, specifically embodied in 'the literature and language of the Chaldeans' (Dan 1:4)."[17] The book models resistance to "the oppressor's tradition" and "sounds a call for its refusal and rejection."[18]

Kirkpatrick illumines many features of the stories in Daniel through his discussions of food, ritual, honor and shame, and patronage. Yet in his readings of the tales, and of the conflict between Judaism and Hellenism, Kirkpatrick overemphasizes the theme of refusal. As I argued in chapter 3, the relationship between Judaism and Hellenism is complex. Antiochus IV used markers of Greek culture to assert power, as had others before him. Antiochus IV also asserted power through the erasure of Judean identity and suppression of Jewish tradition. But even those who championed the covenant and resisted Antiochus's edict and persecution were not thereby refusing Greek culture or Hellenism per se.[19]

Moral Perspectives in Old Testament Narratives (Aldershot, UK: Ashgate, 2001), pp. 210-14; and Hector Avalos, "The Comedic Function of the Enumerations of Officials and Instruments in Daniel 3," *CBQ* 53, no. 4 (1991): 580-88.

13. E.g., Lawrence M. Wills, *The Jewish Novel in the Ancient World* (Ithaca, NY: Cornell University Press, 1995), p. 47.

14. See also David Valeta, "Court or Jester Tales? Resistance and Social Reality in Daniel 1–6," *PRSt* 32 (2005): 309-24.

15. Shane Kirkpatrick, *Competing for Honor: A Social-Scientific Reading of Daniel 1–6* (Leiden: Brill, 2005), p. 2.

16. Kirkpatrick, *Competing for Honor*, p. 63.

17. Kirkpatrick, *Competing for Honor*, p. 46.

18. Kirkpatrick, *Competing for Honor*, p. 38.

19. John J. Collins similarly notes that "Daniel does not view the issue as a conflict between

They were refusing imperial claims to ultimacy, by whatever means those claims were asserted.[20]

In Kirkpatrick's analysis of the tales in Daniel, the rejection of food stands for the rejection of an entire social system. But in fact, Daniel and his friends reject the food even as they begin to occupy and maneuver within a social system structured by the Babylonians. Rather than rejecting the Babylonian tradition, they master it.[21] They refuse one form of royal patronage, but accept others, evincing a "dual allegiance to both God and king."[22] In the words of John M. G. Barclay, they were both "using and refusing."[23]

Using James C. Scott's categories of public and hidden transcript (on which, see ch. 1), Fewell analyzes precisely this tension in her treatment of Daniel 1, titled "Resisting Daniel," in her book *The Children of Israel: Reading the Bible for the Sake of Our Children*.[24] Fewell is less enthusiastic about the power of the stories in Daniel as stories of resistance to assimilation.[25] She sees Daniel and his friends leading a double life, simultaneously resisting and conforming. They prosper not only through allegiance to God but also through service to the king.[26] Fewell's longer and earlier study, *Circle of Sovereignty*, traces this tension throughout the stories in Daniel.[27]

I concur with Fewell's assessment of the stories in Daniel 1–6. The stance they portray entails resistance but also accommodation. Daniel speaks language scripted by the empire ("O King, live forever!") and benefits from the patronage of the kings he serves. Yet I argued in chapter 1 that the book of

---

Judaism and Hellenism. His problem is with the conduct of a Hellenistic king, and consequently with gentile rule over Israel, but not with Hellenistic culture as such." "Daniel and His Social World," *Interpretation* 39 (1985): 131-43, 138.

20. See Walter Brueggemann, *The Word That Redescribes the World: The Bible and Discipleship* (Minneapolis: Augsburg Fortress, 2006), pp. 202, 205.

21. Contra Kirkpatrick, *Competing for Honor*, p. 51.

22. Danna Nolan Fewell, *Circle of Sovereignty: Plotting Politics in the Book of Daniel* (Nashville: Abingdon, 1991), p. 115.

23. John M. G. Barclay, "Using and Refusing: Jewish Identity Strategies under the Hegemony of Hellenism," in *Ethos und Identität: Einheit und Vielfalt des Judentums in hellenistisch-römischer Zeit*, ed. Matthias Conradt and Ulrike Steinert (Paderborn: Ferdinand Schöningh, 2002), pp. 13-25.

24. Fewell, *Children of Israel*, pp. 117-30.

25. Fewell identifies the stories themselves as part of a public transcript that covers over the horror of captivity and exile with "a folktale mentality," betraying memory even as it gives hope (*Children of Israel*, p. 130).

26. Fewell, *Children of Israel*, pp. 118-19, 123, 129.

27. Unfortunately, Fewell's treatment of the final six chapters of Daniel is brief (*Circle of Sovereignty*, pp. 119-25, shorter than any of the treatments of the individual chapters from Dan 1-6), and while it helpfully connects the visions with the stories it does not give sufficient attention to movement within the book.

Daniel does not serve as a hidden transcript, and I have repeatedly stated that the book opposes the project of empire. How do we reconcile these positions?

The structure of the book as a whole, including the enigmatic sequence of languages (1–2:3a in Hebrew; 2:3b–7:28 in Aramaic; 8–12 in Hebrew), provides a clue. I have argued elsewhere that the writer(s) who joined the stories to the visions made intentional use of two languages, Hebrew and Aramaic, to move their audience from a posture of partial accommodation and collaboration to one of total rejection of Seleucid hegemony and domination.[28]

From the time of Nebuchadnezzar's conquest of Judah in the early sixth century BCE, Judeans at home and abroad lived as subject people under a succession of foreign empires. Jeremiah's letter to the exiles provided a template for life under foreign domination: the exiles were to build lives — and houses — and they were to prayerfully seek the welfare of Babylon, for in its peace (or welfare, שָׁלוֹם) was also their own (Jer 29:7). Smith-Christopher characterizes the ethic Jeremiah prescribes as "limited co-operation and [nonviolent] social resistance" marked by "an engaged, strategic position towards authority and power that is cannily aware of the requirements for success and survival."[29] Judeans under Persian rule and in the early years of Hellenistic rule could embrace a similar ethic of "limited co-operation" (and resistance), as long as the law of the king also allowed Judeans to follow the law of their God. The tales in Daniel 3 and 6 portray the potential for conflict between the two laws, and communicate clearly that when there is a choice, faithful Judeans must choose only the law of God.

Through much of the history of foreign domination, such a choice did not appear necessary.[30] That situation changed when Antiochus issued his edict in 167 BCE.[31] For the writer(s) who composed Daniel 1–12, from this point forward resistance was the *only* faithful response to the empire. Writing between the time of the edict in 167 and the temple's rededication in 164 BCE, they incorporated familiar tales into a new composition, using the alternating languages of

28. Anathea E. Portier-Young, "Languages of Identity and Obligation: Daniel as Bilingual Book," *VT* 60 (2010): 98-115. Recognizing the book's complex composition history, in much of this chapter I refer not to a singular writer of Daniel but rather to "writers." This complex history does not remove intentionality from the joining of stories and visions in the composition and redaction of Dan 1–12 (MT).

29. Daniel L. Smith, "Jeremiah as Prophet of Nonviolent Resistance," *JSOT* 13, no. 43 (1989): 95-107, 102, 104.

30. Absent such a choice, the stories could teach one how to serve two masters simultaneously, providing a script for success under foreign domination. See W. L. Humphreys, "A Life-Style for the Diaspora: A Study of the Tales of Esther and Daniel," *JBL* 92 (1973): 211-23.

31. See also Collins, "Daniel and His Social World," p. 137.

Hebrew and Aramaic to underscore the change in situation and call an end to cooperation and accommodation.[32]

Sociolinguistic theory illuminates the way multilingual speakers and writers alternate between languages to create and signal a new context.[33] The writers of Daniel begin the book in Hebrew, evoking the history and traditions of Israel, the particularity of Judean identity, and the rights and obligations of covenant with the Lord. The shift to Aramaic in Daniel 2:3b highlights another social context and contract, a world of royal patronage that carries its own rights and obligations and makes competing claims on the identity and allegiance of Judeans. Yet with his edict and program of terror Antiochus IV would forfeit all claims to authority. With this situation in view, the vision of judgment in Daniel 7 heralds a decisive shift, using a language of empire to refute its claims and announce its end. The writers return to Hebrew in chapters 8–12, crafting from the language of Israel's Torah an apocalyptic language that frames identity solely within the covenant relationship between God and God's people. They invite those who have collaborated with the empire to perceive its true form and reject the false world it projected. They call the audience to find their place instead within the world of the visions, forsaking a stance of collaboration with the Seleucid empire in order to adopt a posture of resistance rooted in covenant and shaped by their new apocalyptic vision.

Han similarly focuses on the entire book of Daniel and its apocalyptic language. He argues that in place of the dominant construction of reality Daniel offered a new apocalyptic literacy that aimed to "radically revise the way of life, the way of perception, and the way of existence" for its audience.[34] Daniel's apocalyptic *paideia* (education) countered imperial hegemony, shaping its readers' imaginations by means of symbol, metaphor, and a new language of criticism and hope.[35]

Han's treatment of apocalyptic literacy in Daniel is highly suggestive, and dovetails with my own emphases on resistance to hegemony and the importance of teaching in Daniel. While Han speaks of a way of life, he focuses on perception and representation, asking how the writers of Daniel empowered their audience to see the world differently, a question I have considered in previous chapters.[36] In the present chapter I ask somewhat different questions: What did the writers of Daniel want their audience to do, and how did they

32. For Collins this dating "is established beyond reasonable doubt" ("Daniel and His Social World," p. 132).

33. Portier-Young, "Languages of Identity and Obligation," pp. 104-7.

34. Jin Hee Han, *Daniel's Spiel: Apocalyptic Literacy in the Book of Daniel* (Lanham, MD: University Press of America, 2008), pp. 1, 7, 9.

35. Han, *Daniel's Spiel*, pp. 8, 39-48, 95-110.

36. Han, *Daniel's Spiel*, pp. 97-98.

present this program for resistance? How was their vision of resistance shaped by their theology and interpretation of earlier scriptures? How did new revelation influence and shape each of these in turn? My approach is not opposed to Han's. Indeed, worldview, which I treat here under the rubric of theology, and literacy, especially the reading and interpretation of earlier scriptures, are central to my investigation of Daniel's program for resistance.

I argue in this chapter that the writers of Daniel outlined for their audiences a program of nonviolent resistance to the edict and persecution of Antiochus and the systems of hegemony and domination that supported his rule. New revelation provided an apocalyptic frame for covenant theology and offered hermeneutical keys for interpreting scripture in ways that anchored the writers' self-understanding and understanding of history, current events, and God's future action. Each of these in turn shaped a vision for resistance that included prayer, fasting, and penitence, teaching and preaching, and covenant fidelity even in the face of death. They presented their program for action through prediction and narrative modeling.

Toward the book's conclusion the revealing angel speaks of a group of *maśkîlîm*, or "wise teachers" (11:32-35; 12:3, 10). Repeated references to this group, their instrumental role in the book's final chapters, and meaningful repetition of the root *śkl* throughout the book (see further below) have suggested to many scholars that the writer(s) of Hebrew and Aramaic Daniel belong to this group of wise teachers.[37]

Can we say more about the *maśkîlîm?* Early attempts to identify this group with the *Hasidim* or Hasideans (οἱ Ἀσιδαῖοι) known from 1 Maccabees (2:42; 7:13; cf. 2 Macc 14:6) should be abandoned;[38] nor is it possible to identify the "teachers" of Daniel with another group known from our sources concerning the persecution. Yet if we cannot gain a picture of Daniel's "wise teachers" by identifying them with other known groups, it is nonetheless possible to construct a portrait from details within the text itself.[39] Philip R. Davies has highlighted the value of the symbols book, court (which in postexilic Yehud be-

---

37. Collins, "Daniel and His Social World"; Rainer Albertz, "The Social Setting of the Aramaic and Hebrew Book of Daniel," in *The Book of Daniel: Composition and Reception,* vol. 1, ed. John J. Collins and Peter W. Flint (Leiden: Brill, 2001), pp. 171-204; Stefan Beyerle, "Daniel and Its Social Setting," in *The Book of Daniel: Composition and Reception,* vol. 1, ed. John J. Collins and Peter W. Flint (Leiden: Brill, 2001), pp. 205-28.

38. See John Kampen, *The Hasideans and the Origin of Pharisaism: A Study in 1 and 2 Maccabees* (Atlanta: Scholars Press, 1988), pp. 22-31. See also Philip R. Davies, "Hasidim in the Maccabean Period," *JJS* 28 (1977): 127-40; John J. Collins, *The Apocalyptic Vision of the Book of Daniel,* Harvard Semitic Monographs 16 (Missoula, MT: Scholars Press, 1977), pp. 201-5.

39. Philip R. Davies, "The Scribal School of Daniel," in *The Book of Daniel: Composition and Reception,* vol. 1, ed. John J. Collins and Peter W. Flint (Leiden: Brill, 2001), pp. 247-65, 257.

comes "Temple and priests"), and secret for illuminating the social identity of Daniel's writers and the primary audience for which they wrote.[40] They are highly educated and literate, valuing activities of reading (including authoritative scriptures), interpretation, writing, and instruction.[41] They also value the temple and the traditional worship of God that transpired there.[42] Davies further speculates that they likely belong to the social class of scribally trained individuals that included "priests and other administrative officials."[43] Crucial in Davies' characterization is the recognition that the writers of Daniel were not among the disenfranchised or "powerless."[44] If they took a position on the margins, as Carol A. Newsom has argued, it was with respect to an imperial center.[45] In fact, however, they stood very close to the center, but they envisioned it differently, for in their view all things were governed by God, with justice.

Attention to the heavenly realm did not lead them to ignore earthly affairs,

40. Philip R. Davies, "Reading Daniel Sociologically," in *The Book of Daniel in the Light of New Findings*, ed. A. S. van der Woude (Leuven: Leuven University Press, 1993), pp. 345-61, 352.

41. See also Polaski, *"Mene, Mene, Tekel, Parsin"*; Michael A. Knibb, "'You Are Indeed Wiser Than Daniel': Reflections on the Character of the Book of Daniel," in *The Book of Daniel in the Light of New Findings*, ed. A. S. van der Woude (Leuven: Leuven University Press, 1993), pp. 399-411; P. Lampe, "Die Apokalyptiker — ihre Situation und ihr Handeln," in *Eschatologie und Friedenshandeln. Exegetische Beiträge zur Frage christlicher Friedensverantwortung*, ed. Ulrich Luz (Stuttgart: Katholisches Bibelwerk, 1981), pp. 59-114.

42. Moreover, Davies finds that in Daniel "the court is a positive symbol, the natural home and setting of the author's imagination" ("Reading Daniel Sociologically," p. 356). He adds, however, "The attitude to the Temple, like the attitude to foreign rule, is loaded with ambiguity" (p. 361).

43. Davies, "Reading Daniel Sociologically," p. 351. Paul L. Redditt argues that "the group responsible for the book of Daniel . . . was comprised of Jewish courtiers employed by the Seleucids." They flourished during the reign of Antiochus III, but suffered under Antiochus IV. "Daniel 11 and the Sociohistorical Setting of the Book of Daniel," *CBQ* 60 (1998): 463-74, 463. Redditt's view is similar to Victor Tcherikover's proposal concerning the Hasidim, who he believes were "elevated to a position of authority in every matter of law and justice, and thus became part of the ruling group in the Jewish theocracy" during the reign of Antiochus III. Victor Tcherikover, *Hellenistic Civilization and the Jews*, trans. S. Applebaum (Philadelphia: Jewish Publication Society, 1959; repr. with a pref. by John J. Collins, Peabody, MA: Hendrickson, 1999), p. 126. Yet Redditt's reconstruction differs sharply from Tcherikover's, since in the latter's view the Hasidim were "the chief scribes and authoritative interpreters of the regulations and commandments of the Torah" and also "the popular directors and leaders of the insurrection" (*Hellenistic Civilization*, p. 197), while Redditt understands the group responsible for Daniel to be "non-resistant" ("Daniel 11," p. 472).

44. See further Lester L. Grabbe, "The Social Setting of Early Jewish Apocalypticism," *JSP* 4 (1989): 27-47, 30-33; Beyerle, "Daniel and Its Social Setting," pp. 212-14.

45. Carol A. Newsom argues that ancient apocalyptic writers were "marginal" by choice, but exercised "various forms of social capital." Their position on the margins could be a source of power. *The Self as Symbolic Space: Constructing Identity and Community at Qumran* (Leiden: Brill, 2004), p. 48.

and revealed knowledge took shape alongside other forms of knowledge. The writers of Daniel evince a broad knowledge of international political affairs[46] as well as international and native traditions.[47] The wide array of sources used by the writers of Daniel and the values they placed on scriptural traditions, wisdom, and dream interpretation imply access to a broad cultural repertory, as Richard Horsley has noted:

> Literacy, the cultivation of a repertoire of high culture, and the production of literature were socially located and politically operative in circles of learned scribes. These intellectuals served as advisers and administrators in the imperial regimes of the ancient Near East, both in the central administration and in local institutions, such as the Jerusalem temple-state. . . . The *maskilim* were thus apparently dissident retainers who came into conflict with the aristocratic faction that controlled the temple-state. . . . These professional scribes were trained in a wide range of culture, including different kinds of wisdom. . . . [They] developed expressions of their own people's distinctive political-religious identity that conflicted with the culture and practices of the empire. . . . [They] could use their own indigenous forms of wisdom, such as cosmological knowledge and dream-interpretation (often in combination with prophetic traditions), to give expression to the political-economic interests of the subjugated Judeans that conflicted directly with the interests and power of the ruling empire. . . . The *maskilim* stood firm in the covenant against the dominant aristocratic faction that, in collusion with the imperial regime, abandoned it (Dan 11:28-35).[48]

Horsley notes that the *maśkîlîm* gave expression to the political and economic interests of the Judean people in the time of persecution. Yet it needs to be said

---

46. Collins, "Daniel and His Social World," p. 139.

47. On the use of Mesopotamian traditions, see Helge S. Kvanvig, *Roots of Apocalyptic: The Mesopotamian Background of the Enoch Figure and of the Son of Man* (Neukirchen: Neukirchener Verlag, 1988), pp. 345-613; Matthias Henze, *The Madness of King Nebuchadnezzar: The Ancient Near Eastern Origins and Early History of Interpretation of Daniel 4* (Leiden: Brill, 1999); Hector Avalos, "Daniel 9:24-25 and Mesopotamian Temple Rededications," *JBL* 117, no. 3 (1998): 507-11; Newsom, *Self as Symbolic Space*, p. 46. For critique of Kvanvig's proposal and attention to the Canaanite traditions informing Dan 7, see John J. Collins, "Stirring Up the Great Sea: The Religio-Historical Background of Daniel 7," in *The Book of Daniel in the Light of New Findings*, ed. A. S. van der Woude (Leuven: Leuven University Press, 1993), pp. 121-36. For a broader survey of proposals concerning the background of the visionary symbolism in Dan 7, see Jürg Eggler, *Influences and Traditions Underlying the Vision of Daniel 7:2-14: The Research History from the End of the 19th Century to the Present* (Göttingen: Vandenhoeck & Ruprecht, 2000).

48. Richard A. Horsley, *Scribes, Visionaries, and the Politics of Second Temple Judea* (Louisville: Westminster John Knox, 2007), pp. 173-74.

that they understood and expressed these in terms entirely theological: salvation and justice were from God.[49]

The *maśkîlîm* are not only the group among whom the book of Daniel originates, they also form part of the book's audience. The book would shape, exhort, and give comfort to those whose work of resistance to Antiochus's edict required vision, virtue, and strength. Yet the book is not a sectarian work aimed only at an "in-group."[50] The stories that once circulated independently were no doubt popular with other members of the literate scribal class, including those involved in the administration of Jerusalem's temple.[51] These successful Judean literati may well have identified with Daniel and his friends. The apocalyptic book of Daniel may have aimed to persuade such individuals not to comply with Antiochus's edict, but instead to fully embrace an alternative ethic and vision of reality.[52] The book also has another, likely nonliterate group in view. Stephen Breck Reid has noted the social implications of the *maśkîlîm*'s role in the instruction of "the many" (11:33; see further below).[53] By repeated references to "the many," the writers of Daniel project a lively engagement with and deep concern for the fate of others outside their group.[54] Even if "the many" do not read Daniel's scroll, they become a secondary audience

49. Susan F. Matthews writes, "Religious debates within Daniel are also economic and political debates. In the same way, . . . political matters are finally religious matters involving God's ultimate sovereignty." "When We Remembered Zion: The Significance of the Exile for Understanding Daniel," in *The Bible on Suffering: Social and Political Implications,* ed. Anthony J. Tambasco (Mahwah, NJ: Paulist, 2002), pp. 93-119, 94.

50. Cf. the judgment of Davies that the group's privilege "has no place for separatism, but belongs and operates within a wider community" ("Scribal School of Daniel," p. 253).

51. For a conflicting view, see Matthias Henze, "The Narrative Frame of Daniel: A Literary Assessment," *JSJ* 32, no. 1 (2001): 5-24. Henze argues that "the extravagant descriptions are wishful projections of the disenfranchised, reflecting the social misery of those who seek comfort in such fantasies. Hardly the product of the well-to-do Jews in exile, the legends originally circulated 'among the poorest of the Babylonian Jewry'" (p. 16).

52. *Pace* Davies, who states that "it is necessary to think of ancient literature as written for private, or even internal consumption, to reinforce the world-view of insiders and not to persuade outsiders" ("Reading Daniel Sociologically," p. 357).

53. Stephen Breck Reid, *Enoch and Daniel: A Form Critical and Sociological Study of the Historical Apocalypses,* 2nd ed. (North Richland Hills, TX: BIBAL, 1989), p. 114.

54. Beyerle suggests that, given the group's emphasis on secret, otherworldly knowledge, they may nonetheless have become "isolated and eventually disappeared" ("Daniel and Its Social Setting," p. 222). Yet the book emphasizes not simply secret knowledge, but its revelation and publication at the appropriate time (i.e., the time of the book's writing). Contra Beyerle, its otherworldly knowledge is also entirely *this-worldly.* For Beyerle, the way the book rearranges known symbols "within a visionary setting leaves them disconnected from the symbolic universe of everyday experience" (p. 225). I maintain that the book aims to transform perspectives on "this-world" by teaching the interrelationship between visible and invisible realities; the book's lively history of effects suggests that it enjoyed some measure of success.

for the book, for the *maśkîlîm* will "make them wise" by proclaiming and living its message and vision.

I indicated above that the writer(s) of Daniel present their program for resistance not only through prediction but also through narrative modeling. The examples of Daniel and his friends, who are also described as *maśkîlîm* (1:4), model for the book's audience resistance and faithful action.[55] David Satran has written of Daniel and similar legendary heroes that they "come to embody a 'classical religious style,' an index of belief and practice. The attitudes and activities ascribed to these figures awaken us to the values and concerns most central to the believing community. . . . These figures convert an ideal notion of virtue into something 'measurable, tangible, comprehensible.'"[56] The actions and beliefs of the heroes in the book of Daniel impress upon the moral imagination of its audience a vivid template for faithful praxis that is also a template for resistance.

As I noted above, scholarly consensus now holds that the tales of Daniel 1–6 (often called Daniel A) originally circulated independently of Daniel 7–12 (often called Daniel B), possibly originating in Diaspora but eventually finding an audience in Jerusalem.[57] Within the Hebrew and Aramaic book of Daniel, the tales take on new meaning.[58] Although the situations of the tales' heroes and of the *maśkîlîm* are not identical, they are partly analogous.[59] For Paul Ricoeur, it is because of this analogy that Daniel and his friends are an appropriate vehicle to "express the spirit of resistance to the present persecution."[60] Thus, the narrative presentations of Daniel, Shadrak, Meshak, and Abednego in exile serve as models or types for persecuted Judeans, and in particular for the *maśkîlîm*, or

55. See the remarks of Paul Ricoeur, foreword to André Lacocque, *The Book of Daniel*, trans. D. Pellauer, Eng. ed. rev. by author (Atlanta: John Knox, 1979), pp. xxi-xxiii: "The author proceeds to a fictional transference of his heroes into another time . . . [and so] constitutes the past as the model for his own time" (pp. xxi-xxii). The parenetic functions of the stories and visions unite in an "englobing performative function" of giving courage to the faithful (p. xxi).

56. David Satran, "Daniel: Seer, Philosopher, Holy Man," in *Ideal Figures in Ancient Judaism: Profiles and Paradigms*, ed. John J. Collins and George W. E. Nickelsburg (Chico, CA: Scholars Press, 1980), pp. 33-48, 33, drawing on the work of Clifford Geertz, Mary Douglas, and Victor Turner. Satran notes (p. 33n1), "The notion of virtue made '*messbar, greifbar, fassbar*' as an essential component of legendary narrative is formulated by A. Jolles, *Einfache Formen* (Tübingen: Niemayer, 1965), 23-61."

57. John J. Collins suggests a date in either the fourth or third century BCE. *Daniel: A Commentary on the Book of Daniel*, Hermeneia (Minneapolis: Augsburg, 1993), pp. 35-52.

58. H. L. Ginsberg, "The Composition of the Book of Daniel," *VT* 4 (1954): 246-75, 259.

59. Ricoeur, foreword to André Lacocque, *The Book of Daniel*, pp. xxii-xxiii.

60. Ricoeur, foreword to André Lacocque, *The Book of Daniel*, p. xxi. Compare Ida Fröhlich, *"Time and Times and Half a Time": Historical Consciousness in the Jewish Literature of the Persian and Hellenistic Eras* (Sheffield: Sheffield Academic, 1996), p. 12.

wise teachers, of the second century BCE.[61] They share a responsibility to impart knowledge of God and to remain faithful in the face of domination and death. The heroes in exile embody the ideals of the writers, and their actions constitute a pattern of behavior grounded in faith that the writers urge their audience to adopt.

At the same time, we cannot ignore important differences between the setting of the tales and the setting of persecution under Antiochus. As I noted above, the heroes of the tales in Daniel 1–6 have prospered under the rule of foreign kings, simultaneously serving king and God. By contrast, the future revealed in the visions and discourses of Daniel 7–12 leaves no room for service to the Seleucid king who has terrorized Judea. Does the nonviolent ethic of the tales in 1–6 yield therefore to a militant ethic in 7–12? No. As we will see, the book's call to resist Antiochus, his armies, and his empire did not entail armed resistance. Moreover, despite the change in setting, the heroes of the tales continued to model faithful resistance for those who suffered persecution. In their new context the stories in Daniel 1–6 encourage the victims of Antiochus's persecution to hold fast to their faith, and they provide them with models of right action.[62] The revelations given to Daniel in the book's second half provide them with the necessary framework to discern *which* actions are now called for.

The angelic figures who speak with Daniel provide further resources for resistance. In their role of revealing, interpreting, and imparting strength to the weak, not only do they model resistance for the *maśkîlîm*, they also make resistance possible. In the book of Daniel, the visible and invisible realms of earth and heaven form one reality, with each impacting the other. Consonant with this worldview, persons and events on earth not only mirror those in heaven, they interact with and participate in one another's being and reality. The wise teachers accordingly derive strength from their heavenly counterparts.[63] Daniel's commission from the revealing angel to proclaim the book's message becomes a commission for the readers as well. By their teaching and preaching they will counter imperial hegemony. By giving their bodies freely to sword and fire and by giving strength to others they will also deny Antiochus's power to dominate and coerce the people of Judea.

---

61. Smith-Christopher argues that the stories served as resistance literature well before their incorporation into the book of Daniel. "Gandhi on Daniel 6," pp. 333-38.

62. Philip R. Davies identifies "the association between the activity and the vindication of the 'wise' of chs. 11–12 and the wise heroes of chs. 1–6 [as] the key to the unity of the book." *Daniel,* Old Testament Guides (Sheffield: JSOT Press, 1985), p. 111.

63. On the heavenly counterpart in ancient Jewish literature, see Andrei A. Orlov, "Moses' Heavenly Counterpart in the *Book of Jubilees* and the *Exagoge* of Ezekiel the Tragedian," *Biblica* 88, no. 2 (2007): 151-73.

The People Who Know Their God Will Stand Strong and Act:
Strength, Knowledge, and Faithfulness

In the book's final revelatory discourse, the revealing angel describes for Daniel events to come in 167 BCE, including Antiochus's assault on the covenant (i.e., the edict), the halting of the *tamid,* and the desolating abomination (11:30-31). The angel then introduces in contrastive parallel two groups among the Judeans:

וּמַרְשִׁיעֵי בְרִית יַחֲנִיף בַּחֲלַקּוֹת וְעַם יֹדְעֵי אֱלֹהָיו יַחֲזִקוּ וְעָשׂוּ

Those who betray covenant he will corrupt with slick schemes,
But a people who know their God will stand strong, and they will act.
(11:32)

Whether seduced by the false promises of Antiochus or intimidated by the threat of death against themselves and their families, Judeans in the first group apparently comply with the edict and publicly trade their ancestral faith for the practices Antiochus now mandates. The verse's parallel structure suggests that their act of "covenant betrayal" will be matched by the second group's unwavering covenant commitment. Indeed, the phrase that names this second group, "the people who know their God" (עַם יֹדְעֵי אֱלֹהָיו), lends further support to this interpretation.

Knowledge itself is a key theme throughout the book of Daniel. Right knowledge is a precondition for right action, and its publication is therefore a key component of resistance (witness the book of Daniel itself). To "know God" is to know what God will do, to know that God is sovereign, to know God's commitment to God's people, and to know what God requires of them in turn. Knowledge of God strengthens the people and empowers them to remain steadfast in their covenant faith.

This observation brings us to the more technical sense of the phrase, which derives from ancient Near Eastern treaty formulations. Herbert Huffmon has examined the semantic range of the Hebrew verb *yādaʿ* in light of Hittite and Akkadian suzerainty treaties.[64] He cites this verse as an example of "*yādaʿ* in the sense of recognition of treaty or covenant stipulations as binding (resulting in appropriate behavior)."[65] The people's "knowing God" signals their intimate relationship with God.[66] They recognize God as sovereign and accept their mutual

64. Herbert B. Huffmon, "The Treaty Background of Hebrew *yādaʿ*," *BASOR* 181 (1966): 31-37.
65. Huffmon, "Treaty Background," p. 37.
66. E. W. Heaton, *The Book of Daniel* (London: SCM, 1956), p. 236.

covenant as binding. Confident of God's commitment to them, they in turn acknowledge and fulfill their own covenant obligations.[67] As Huffmon notes, the verse's contrastive parallelism strengthens the identification of knowledge of God and the action that results from it with covenant fidelity.[68] But the book of Daniel uses traditional covenant language in a new context. The book's visionary discourse adds to what was previously known about God and the relationship between God and God's people, revealing further dimensions to the covenant relationship and thereby giving new meaning to covenant faithfulness.

"The people who know their God" will resist the measures of Antiochus — they "will stand strong, and they will act" (יַחֲזִקוּ וְעָשׂוּ 11:32). But what will their resistance look like? I stated earlier that the book of Daniel presented to its second-century audiences a program of nonviolent resistance to Seleucid hegemony and domination. Yet others have found in these two verbs evidence that the book of Daniel promoted armed revolt against the Seleucid empire.[69] Taken by themselves, the verbs permit a range of interpretations encompassing both nonviolent and violent forms of resistance. Yet the book of Daniel equates the strength of the faithful not with arms, but with knowledge and understanding. Standing strong and acting means holding fast to the covenant, teaching, and thereby giving strength to others.

67. Cf. Delbert Hillers, *Covenant: The History of a Biblical Idea* (Baltimore: Johns Hopkins University Press, 1969), p. 122.

68. Some scholars depict a sharp contrast between the concerns of apocalyptic and halakhic literature. For example, Uriel Rappaport describes "two spiritual streams" in literature of Hellenistic-Roman Judaism: "One is the *Halakhic* with its concern for the actual performance of God's will, as known through his *Torah*. The second is the Apocalyptic, which, though sometimes very attentive to historical developments, was concerned with history only as a 'ladder to heaven.'" "Apocalyptic Vision and Preservation of Historical Memory," *JSJ* 23 (1992): 217-26, 225. This is a false dichotomy, however. Cf. the remarks of Christopher Rowland, "Apocalyptic Literature," in *It Is Written: Scripture Citing Scripture*, ed. D. A. Carson and H. G. M. Williamson (New York: Cambridge University Press, 1988), p. 175: "We are not dealing in the apocalypses with a phenomenon fundamentally opposed to the outlook of the torah. Those who find in the apocalypses a religious stream which is somehow opposed to the torah have to ignore the indebtedness which commentators like Knibb have noted [referring to Michael A. Knibb, "Apocalyptic and Wisdom in 4 Ezra," *JSJ* 13 (1982): 56-74]. To make the apocalypses a vehicle of salvation history among those circles opposed to the legal concerns of the scribes and proto-rabbis is to play down the importance of the apocalyptic tradition for rabbinic Judaism and to relegate the importance of the torah in the apocalypses."

69. John G. Gammie could write, "The use of the book to stir up support for the Maccabean Revolt is sufficiently well known and needs no further rehearsal here." "The Classification, Stages of Growth, and Changing Intentions in the Book of Daniel," *JBL* 95, no. 2 (1976): 191-204, 203. A verse that follows is also central to the debate. Since Porphyry, many have taken mention of "[a?] little help" in 11:34 as a reference to the Maccabees. This too has been construed in different ways (i.e., appreciative or belittling).

The verbs חזק and עשה both sometimes denote military action. Yet, in the case of עשה, in such instances the verb almost always has an object, and context makes the military meaning clear (e.g., Dan 11:7, on which see below).[70] It lacks an object here. While the semantic range of עשה is too broad and the verb's occurrence too frequent (2,640 times in the Hebrew Bible, 24 in Daniel) to draw firm conclusions from these occurrences, חזק is less common (292 times in the Hebrew Bible, 13 in Daniel; in the *hiphil* 117 times in the Hebrew Bible, 5 in Daniel, including this verse), and so merits a closer look. I will give special attention to other occurrences of חזק in Daniel. First I consider two instances where the verbs occur together, one in Daniel and one in Haggai.

In Daniel 11:7 the two verbs together describe the victorious assault of the king of the south against the fortress of the king of the north: וְעָשָׂה בָהֶם וְהֶחֱזִיק, "he will act against them and he will conquer/prevail." Here as in Daniel 11:32 חזק occurs in the *hiphil*, suggesting a tantalizing parallel.[71] Yet the meaning "prevail" or "conquer" for חזק in the *hiphil* and without an object (although בָּהֶם may in fact provide an object for both verbs) is unique to this verse. Moreover, by contrast with Daniel 11:32, in 11:7 the context and prepositional phrase בָּהֶם clarify the nature of the action as military assault. Both these elements are lacking in Daniel 11:32. Haggai 2:4 offers a closer parallel. The prophet exhorts Joshua, Zerubbabel, and all the people of the land to "be strong" or "take courage" (repeating the *qal* imperative חֲזַק three times) and "do," "act," or "work" (וַעֲשׂוּ). The work referred to is the rebuilding of the temple.[72] This is no military exploit but a demonstration of their commitment to perform the will of God and to ensure the right worship of Yhwh among those who dwell in the land.

Other uses of the verb חזק in Daniel further clarify the meaning of the phrase in Daniel 11:32. In Daniel 10, the revealing angel explains to Daniel that he (the angel) must soon return "to make war" (לְהִלָּחֵם) with the prince of Persia (10:20). After Persia, Greece comes (10:20). "Not a single one will stand strong (מִתְחַזֵּק) with me against them," he says, "except for Michael your prince" (10:21). The angel's reference to war in the preceding verse provides an explicitly military context for Michael's "standing strong" in 10:21. Yet the angel also reveals that the battle is theirs alone, and no one else will join them in the fight against the earthly princes — not Daniel, not another angel, nor anyone from among the Judean people (10:21).

Indeed, several times elsewhere in Daniel the verb חזק is predicated of the battling earthly powers, including Antiochus himself (11:1, 5, 6, 7), yet nowhere

---

70. By contrast, with the object שלום the verb can mean to "make" peace. Cf. Isa 27:5. The verb often refers simply to "doing" precepts of the law.

71. The verbs also appear together in Dan 11:6, but not in close conjunction.

72. Cf. Neh 6:9, where both verbs appear. Nehemiah prays to God to strengthen his hands for rebuilding the walls of Jerusalem.

in Daniel is it predicated of Judeans in a military context. Rather, the only other occurrences of חזק with reference to any Judean occur in exhortations to Daniel himself and references to Daniel's receiving strength from the angelic figure who touches him (10:18-19):

וַיֹּסֶף וַיִּגַּע־בִּי כְּמַרְאֵה אָדָם וַיְחַזְּקֵנִי
וַיֹּאמֶר אַל־תִּירָא אִישׁ־חֲמֻדוֹת שָׁלוֹם לָךְ
חֲזַק וַחֲזָק וּכְדַבְּרוֹ עִמִּי הִתְחַזַּקְתִּי
וָאֹמְרָה יְדַבֵּר אֲדֹנִי כִּי חִזַּקְתָּנִי

Then the one who looked human touched me again, and *he made me strong* [*piel*].
He said, "Do not fear, most precious man. Peace is with you.
Be strong [*qal*]. *Be strong* [*qal*]! And as he spoke with me *I stood strong* [*hitpael*],
And I said: "Let my lord speak, for *you have made me strong* [*piel*]!"

The verb's five occurrences in these two verses indicate that the writer here wished to place special emphasis on the motif of strength. I propose that the writer intended to establish a contrast between Daniel's strength and that of the battling earthly powers. As with Daniel himself, the prediction that the *maśkîlîm* will be strong refers not to their preparation for battle but to their firm resolve in the faith and their empowerment to proclaim the revelation they have received.

This contrast is borne out elsewhere in the book of Daniel. Apart from forms of חזק, the other word pertaining to strength which appears most often in Daniel (again, 13 times) is the noun כֹּחַ. Seven of its occurrences refer to the military and political strength of the leaders of the warring nations, particularly Antiochus IV.[73] The other five occurrences refer to the strength of Daniel and his friends (1:4; 10:8[x2], 16, 17). For the latter, in each case the context makes plain that the strength of these individuals has nothing to do with physical prowess and will not serve them on the battlefield. Rather, their "strength" consists in wisdom, understanding, and knowledge.

In Daniel 1:4 this strength enables them to stand (כֹּחַ בָּהֶם לַעֲמֹד) in the king's palace:

וּמַשְׂכִּילִים בְּכָל־חָכְמָה וְיֹדְעֵי דַעַת וּמְבִינֵי מַדָּע
וַאֲשֶׁר כֹּחַ בָּהֶם לַעֲמֹד בְּהֵיכַל הַמֶּלֶךְ

---

73. In the vision of the goat and the ram and its interpretation: 8:6, 7, 22, 24[x2]; and in the angel's final revelatory discourse, regarding the kings of the north and south: 11:6, 15, 25.

Though Nebuchadnezzar seeks to train them in Chaldean learning, Daniel utilizes his skills for the purpose of teaching, revealing, and interpreting the will of God. Later, when Daniel receives from God knowledge of Nebuchadnezzar's dream and its interpretation, Daniel identifies this wisdom with power or might. He attributes both to God:

$$\text{דִּי חָכְמְתָא וּגְבוּרְתָא דִּי לֵהּ־הִיא}$$

Wisdom and might are his alone! (2:20)

$$\text{חָכְמְתָא וּגְבוּרְתָא יְהַבְתְּ לִי}$$

You have given me wisdom and might. (2:23)

The Semitic root of the noun גְּבוּרָה, here translated "might," often, though not exclusively, connotes physical force or might in battle. In this case, however, the might God has shown is divine sovereignty over the universe and the power to reveal. Using the same word pair, Daniel thanks God for also granting him wisdom and might (2:23). In this story and throughout the book, Daniel's might is not that of a warrior, but rather that of a revealer. Daniel's power lies in his God-given capacities as teacher, proclaimer, and interpreter. Wisdom and knowledge, not weapons, are the strength of the faithful in the book of Daniel.

The writer's repeated references to the strength of Daniel prior to the book's final revelatory discourse (10:8-19) indicate that this interpretation holds for the second portion of the book as well. As noted above, forms of the verb חזק occur five times in these verses, while the noun כֹּחַ occurs four times.

According to Daniel, his vision of a man clothed in linen leaves him without strength: "I saw this great vision, but no strength was left in me: my very weight turned against me to pull and break me down. I could not keep my strength" (10:8). Some scholars have rightly connected this detail with the fact that Daniel has been in mourning for three weeks, abstaining from certain foods (10:3).[74] He has thus already been weakened by a relative lack of bodily sustenance. Moreover, the appearance of the angelic figure is itself psychically and physically devastating, and he cannot speak until "the one who seemed like a human" touches his lips (10:16).[75] Daniel then says to him, "during the vision I was wracked with pains, and I could not keep my strength. So how is it possible for my lord's servant to speak with my lord? For even now no strength rises in me, no breath remains in me" (10:16b-17). Sight without understanding is

74. E.g., Collins, *Daniel: A Commentary on the Book of Daniel*, p. 374.

75. Paul Redditt calls attention to the similar experiences of Ezekiel. *Daniel*, The New Century Bible Commentary (Sheffield: Sheffield Academic Press, 1999), p. 171.

devastating. Without understanding Daniel has no strength, and without strength he can neither stand, speak, nor receive and pass on the revelation.

Yet even before exhorting Daniel to "be strong," the man clothed in linen begins to reveal to Daniel what is required of him and empower him for the task. He touches him, shakes him up onto his hands and knees (10:10), calls him by name, and assures the seer of his favored status, instructing him:

הָבֵן בַּדְּבָרִים אֲשֶׁר אָנֹכִי דֹבֵר אֵלֶיךָ וַעֲמֹד עַל־עָמְדֶךָ

Grasp the meaning of the words I am saying to you. You must take your stand. (10:11)

The repetitive language in this final phrase, literally "stand upon your standing place," emphasizes the importance of Daniel's assuming an active posture. Yet the order of the commands is significant. Daniel's stance will be framed and supported by his understanding of the words he receives.

When Daniel takes his stand the angel tells him "do not fear" (10:12). Daniel's companions have just fled in terror (10:7), leaving him alone in the angel's presence. Elsewhere in the Hebrew scriptures this same injunction against fear accompanies similarly terrifying manifestations of divine presence (both theophanies and angelophany: Gen 15:1; 26:24; 46:3; Judg 6:23).[76] The words convey security and reassurance to one who trembles before a powerful mystery. But in the context of Antiochus's program of terror, the injunction to stand without fear takes on a further meaning, for the words of security and reassurance speak also to an audience who experience insecurity, anxiety, and terror as a result of Seleucid domination. Edgar W. Conrad has examined the assurance "do not fear" in contexts of warfare.[77] The audience of Daniel find themselves now in a similar setting, even though their role is not to fight. They need not fear this mystery of God. They also need not fear Antiochus and his armies or succumb to Seleucid tactics of terror (cf. Num 21:34; Deut 3:2; Josh 8:1; 10:8; 11:6; 2 Kgs 1:15; Ezek 2:6).

Finally, as I noted earlier, the angel tells Daniel חֲזַק וַחֲזָק, "Be strong. Be strong!" (10:19). The imperative of חזק, used here twice for emphasis, proleptically points to the same angel's use of the verb in his prediction that the *maśkîlîm* will "be strong" (11:32), examined above. Because the angel has spoken to him, Daniel reports that indeed he becomes strong: הִתְחַזַּקְתִּי (10:19). So

76. On its meanings in angelophanies in early Jewish literature, see Loren Stuckenbruck, *Angel Veneration and Christology: A Study in Early Judaism and the Christology of the Apocalypse of John* (Tübingen: Mohr, 1995), pp. 87-91.

77. Edgar W. Conrad, *Fear Not Warrior: A Study of 'al tîrā' Pericopes in the Hebrew Scriptures* (Chico, CA: Scholars Press, 1985).

strengthened, he is able to speak, and also to receive the revelation the angel brings: "Let my lord speak, for you have made me strong" (כִּי חִזַּקְתָּנִי 10:19). This exchange between the revealing/interpreting angel and Daniel further illuminates the meaning of the verb יְחַזִקוּ in 11:32. Here and throughout the book of Daniel, when predicated of God's faithful, language of strength refers not to physical prowess or warrior might, but rather to the power of knowledge and understanding derived from God as well as the capacity to receive and impart it.

An introductory verse informs us that in this vision Daniel does indeed receive understanding (בִּינָה) with which to understand the word, or matter, that has been revealed to him (10:1). We read further, וֶאֱמֶת הַדָּבָר וְצָבָא גָדוֹל, translated by the NRSV, "the word was true, and it concerned a great conflict" (10:1). That is, the angel's discourse sets forth the correct interpretation of the tumultuous events of history by affording the seer a panoramic view of cosmic proportions. "I have been sent," says the angel, "to help you understand (לַהֲבִינְךָ) what will happen to your people in the days to come" (10:14).

The true word Daniel receives reframes his vision so that he sees the terrible battles to come within the context of a greater cosmic battle, waged in heaven, in which God's own armies fight on behalf of God's persecuted people. Yet the heavenly host (צָבָא) who champion the faithful are invisible to all but the seer (10:7). Daniel's words must therefore represent the vision and reveal the invisible reality for those who live in the time of persecution, to give them right understanding, and to persuade and empower them to stand firm in the face of an apparently hopeless situation. When they learn that heaven's army fights on their behalf and that God has determined for them a favorable outcome, they will gain courage and strength in their own struggle to remain faithful.

Indeed, the language in 10:1 permits us to see another level of meaning. Not only is the word true (or "truth," אֱמֶת), but the word, the matter itself, is firmness or faithfulness, of God and God's people alike.[78] In his prayer (to which I return below), Daniel confessed that the people of Judea had failed to find wisdom in or make others wise through God's truth and faithfulness (לְהַשְׂכִּיל בַּאֲמִתֶּךָ 9:13). Now in the time of struggle the book's audience finds a watchword — "faithfulness" — encoded within the narrator's description of the angel's response to Daniel (10:1). They are to remain firm in their faith, believing in its truth and believing that God will be faithful to them. God's truth and faithfulness is their watchword; it is also the source of their wisdom and strength.

Isaiah's oracle to Ahaz during the Syro-Ephraimite crisis articulated a similar message in an earlier time: אִם לֹא תַאֲמִינוּ כִּי לֹא תֵאָמֵנוּ, "If you do not stand firm in faith, you shall not stand at all" (Isa 7:9 NRSV). Stated positively,

---

78. For this range of meanings, see BDB, p. 54.

Isaiah wishes Ahaz to know that the Lord will defend God's people. They need not and should not join the armed coalition against the overlord Assyria, but need only trust, hold fast, and wait.[79] Similarly, in providing the watchword אֱמֶת ("truth," "firmness," or "faithfulness") for the great battle ahead the book of Daniel conveys to its audience that their part in the struggle will not be armed resistance but covenant fidelity and trust in God.

Finally, a reading of the phrases וֶאֱמֶת הַדָּבָר וְצָבָא גָדוֹל in parallel yields a further level of meaning: the true words revealed to Daniel (i.e., the meaning and message of his visions) constitute the great earthly "army" of the faithful. While God's heavenly agents wage war on their behalf, the faithful are to take their stand and resist with the very words of the book, words of story and vision, truth and criticism, comfort and exhortation (cf. 10:21). With these words they arm themselves for victory against the deceptions of Antiochus.[80]

The book thus redefines "strength" for the faithful in stark contrast to that of the battling powers of Antiochus and his armies. While Antiochus is "portrayed as a symbol of violence and arrogance,"[81] "strength" for the persecuted Jews signifies above all the capacity to learn God's will and teach it to others. The very act of speaking the words of revelation and teaching their meaning gives strength in turn to those who hear them. So empowered, these too spread the word to remain true to the covenant. They are emboldened by the conviction that despite appearances, God is in control, God is faithful, and God will deliver.

The revealing and interpreting angel who speaks with Daniel empowers him. In so doing he also models for Daniel and the reader the interrelationship between imparting understanding and imparting the strength needed to stand firm in distress. The seer later adopts the role modeled by the angel and accepts the commission the angel has given him when he uses his strength to write his vision and its meaning for a future generation. As I discuss toward the conclusion of this chapter, Daniel in turn models this role for the *maśkîlîm* of the writer's time, who receive the commission anew.

<hr/>

79. Note that Assyria and Syria become typologically identified in the symbolic world of the writers of Daniel. The writers believe that prophecies regarding Yhwh's punishment/overthrow of Assyria will be fulfilled in their own time, with Syria, i.e., the Seleucid kingdom of Antiochus IV, as the antitype of Assyria. See Michael Fishbane, *Biblical Interpretation in Ancient Israel* (Oxford: Clarendon, 1985), p. 491; and Harold L. Ginsberg, "The Oldest Interpretation of the Suffering Servant," *VT* 3 (1953): 400-404.

80. Cf. Patricia M. McDonald, *God and Violence: Biblical Resources for Living in a Small World* (Scottdale, PA: Herald, 2004), pp. 245-77.

81. Fröhlich, *"Time and Times and Half a Time,"* p. 82.

Prayer and Penitence

Teaching, or making others wise, is the most prominent role assigned to the *maśkîlîm* in the time of persecution, and I return to it below. But it is not their only role. The book of Daniel also prescribes for the faithful a response of prayer and penitence. I called attention above to the angel's injunction, "Do not fear" (10:12). The basis for assurance is Daniel's own commitment to action: from the moment he set his heart to gain understanding and to humble himself before God, his words found a hearing (10:12). Indeed, the angel has come precisely "because of your words" (בִּדְבָרֶיךָ 10:12). But to what words does the angel refer? Daniel has not yet spoken in this chapter, save as narrator to the audience. The words that have prompted God to send the angel to him are the words of his prayer of confession, repentance, and petition in 9:4-19. Similarly, the angel's description of Daniel's setting his heart (נָתַתָּ אֶת־לִבְּךָ) to gain understanding and to humble himself before God (לְהִתְעַנּוֹת לִפְנֵי אֱלֹהֶיךָ 10:12) refers back to Daniel's actions in chapter 9 (9:2-3). Daniel models for the audience an appropriate response to the horrors that now surround them. They are to give their hearts to seek understanding and humble themselves before God. Later in the chapter I consider Daniel's act of reading (9:2), whereby he set his heart to gain understanding. Here I focus on Daniel's prayer and penitence, by which he set his heart to humble himself before God.

"Giving the heart" signals a commitment of mind and will. Daniel's action here is similar to the preparation for prayer described by Zophar in Job 11:13-15. Such preparation, according to Newsom, "disciplines and reorders the body."[82] Daniel's self-humbling took concrete form in the bodily postures and practices of penitence and prayer. He humbled his body through fasting, sackcloth, and ashes, testifying to human dependence on nourishment that comes from outside the body — and ultimately from God — and the finitude of mortal life that contrasts so sharply with God's eternal being (9:3). He also turned his face to God and prayed, making God the object of his attention and gaze and inviting God to look on his own weakness (9:3). Daniel's posture, like the praise Daniel offers in his prayer (9:4), recognizes the immensely greater power of God.[83] Yet the gulf between God and the humble penitent comprises more than a difference in power. It is also the difference between a righteous and faithful God and a sinful humanity. In his prayer Daniel confesses sin, praises God, and petitions God for mercy and deliverance (9:4-19).

---

82. Carol A. Newsom, *The Book of Job: A Contest of Moral Imaginations* (Oxford: Oxford University Press, 2003), pp. 109-10.

83. See further Newsom, *Book of Job*, p. 110: "The body of one at prayer thus structures an environment and implicitly assigns roles evocative of relationships of power that can be found in the social as well as religious sphere."

For Daniel's second-century audience, this discipline of penitence contradicts imperial claims to ultimacy. Fasting recognizes that God, not Antiochus, sustains life. Ashes remind the penitent that God created human beings from dust and destined them to die. By covering their body with ashes Daniel's audience could deny Antiochus IV's claims over their bodies, robbing his death threats of their coercive power. By affirming the relative weakness of humankind in relation to God they affirmed also the weakness of Antiochus, who was only human after all. By petitioning God, they would acknowledge God as sole patron and savior. Through penitence they reordered their own bodies and wills to give testimony to a cosmic order that differed sharply from the order proclaimed by the king.

According to Daniel's prayer, true order found expression in God's laws, delivered through the prophets (9:5-6, 11, 13). Daniel confesses that the Judeans have rebelled against God (9:5, 9) and stepped over God's law (9:11), incurring the "sworn oath written in the Torah of Moses" (9:11; cf. 9:13). By emphasizing covenant faithfulness (9:4) and voicing repentance for breaking God's commandments (9:5-15) the prayer would remind Daniel's audience that Judeans were bound by divine law, not the edict of Antiochus. Obedience to Torah spelled the difference between true life and death.

Yet the prayer in Daniel 9 is the only part of the book to mention "Torah" (9:10, 11[x2], 13). Moreover, Newsom has observed that while "the interpretation of prophetic scripture is central to the book," the writers of Daniel are not "preoccupied with specifically halakic discourse."[84] While Newsom is certainly correct, I propose that the prayer voices and inculcates a commitment to Torah that informs the entire book of Daniel. I have already noted the references to Israel's covenant with God in 11:22, 28, 30, and 32, as well as the covenantal background of the phrase "the people who know their God" in 11:32.[85] Even though, as I argued in chapter 2, we cannot assume that we know the exact contours of "Torah" and "ancestral law" for writers in our period,[86] Torah piety is nonethe-

84. Newsom, *Self as Symbolic Space*, p. 42; cf. 47.

85. Arie van der Kooij argues that the references to covenant in Dan 11 refer only to the temple cult, partly on the grounds that קדש in Dan 8 and 9 refers to the sanctuary. "The Concept of Covenant (Berît) in the Book of Daniel," in *The Book of Daniel in the Light of New Findings*, ed. A. S. van der Woude (Leuven: Leuven University Press, 1993), pp. 495-501, esp. 498. See my argument in ch. 6, however, that the meaning of קדש in chapter 8 (and in the phrase קדש ברית in 11:28, 30) should not be limited to the sanctuary, but should be taken to mean "holiness" in a broader sense.

86. Newsom observes that "[i]n second century Judaism terms such as 'torah,' 'Israel,' 'covenant,' 'righteousness' . . . became ideological signs. But as each group used those terms they did so with different 'accentuation'" (*Self as Symbolic Space*, pp. 10-11). Newsom treats "torah" at length (pp. 23-75). Her understanding of the role of language in articulating community and shaping identity is close to my understanding of how the prayer in Dan 9 creates and shapes

less central to the praxis of Daniel.[87] As I argued in the previous chapter, Daniel's desire to abstain from defiling foods suggests a strong commitment to Israel's purity laws (1:8).[88] In the new context of Antiochus's persecution that forced Jews to eat pork on pain of death, this story would exhort its audience to continue to observe the precepts of Torah despite the terror tactics of Antiochus. Conceptions of time, space, and holiness drawn from the book of Leviticus shape Daniel's theological framework, as apparently do traditions known from the book of Genesis.[89] As I discussed in the previous chapter, the writers of the visions and discourses in the latter half of the book are deeply concerned with Antiochus's assault on holiness and on the sanctuary, including the cessation of regular offering and the imposition of new, desolating offerings (e.g., 9:27). The edict of Antiochus that sought to annul the law of God constituted for the writers of Daniel "a writ of doom against a holy covenant" (11:30) and "unspeakable words against the God of gods" (11:36). As Rodney A. Werline notes, "The emphasis in Daniel on the covenant and its violation reveals that covenantal theology shapes the authors' worldview. . . . The authors interpret the events of the era through a covenantal lens and cast the opponents' religious and political actions as violations of the covenant."[90] Mention of Torah is clearly not the only mark of a Torah-shaped piety and praxis.

What the prayer names "Torah" is elsewhere in Daniel referred to as law. In the Aramaic portions of Daniel, God's law is referred to not as "Torah" but as דת (דָת אֱלָהֵהּ, "the law of his God," 6:6; Antiochus's changing times and "the

---

community among its audience (see below). She writes that "the Qumran community used language to constitute a world of meaning, a distinctive identity, a community of values, and a structure of selfhood" (p. 2).

87. Rex Mason, "The Treatment of Earlier Biblical Themes in the Book of Daniel," in *Perspectives on the Hebrew Bible: Essays in Honor of Walter J. Harrelson*, ed. James L. Crenshaw (Macon, GA: Mercer University Press, 1988), pp. 81-100, 94. On "law" in Daniel, see R. G. Kratz, "Reich Gottes und Gesetz im Danielbuch und im werdenden Judentum," in *The Book of Daniel in the Light of New Findings*, ed. A. S. van der Woude (Leuven: Leuven University Press, 1993), pp. 435-79; and Heinrich Hoffmann, *Das Gesetz in der frühjüdischen Apokalyptik* (Göttingen: Vandenhoeck & Ruprecht, 1999), pp. 71-121.

88. See also Collins, "Daniel and His Social World," p. 135.

89. On the importance of priestly traditions for Daniel, see Gabriele Boccaccini, *Roots of Rabbinic Judaism: An Intellectual History, from Ezekiel to Daniel* (Grand Rapids: Eerdmans, 2002), p. 186; and "The Covenantal Theology of the Apocalyptic Book of Daniel," in *Enoch and Qumran Origins: New Light on a Forgotten Connection*, ed. Gabriele Boccaccini (Grand Rapids: Eerdmans, 2005), pp. 39-44. On creation motifs, see Jacques B. Doukhan, "Allusions à la creation dans le livre de Daniel," in *The Book of Daniel in the Light of New Findings*, ed. A. S. van der Woude (Leuven: Leuven University Press, 1993), pp. 285-92.

90. Rodney A. Werline, "Prayer, Politics, and Social Vision in Daniel 9," in *Seeking the Favor of God*, vol. 2, *The Development of Penitential Prayer in Second Temple Judaism*, ed. Mark J. Boda, Daniel K. Falk, and Rodney A. Werline (Leiden: Brill, 2007), pp. 17-32, 29.

law," דָּת, 7:25), a loanword from the Persian noun *dâta*. I argued above that in these chapters the book's discourse responds directly to the context of empire. In imperial discourse, the terminology for the power exercised by earthly kings was not teaching, a primary connotation of "Torah," but "law," or דָּת (2:9; 6:8, 12, 15).[91] By using the same terminology to refer to God's ordering of human life, the writers of the Aramaic portions of Daniel were able to contrast the true sovereign power of God with the contingent and limited power of the earthly kings who ruled over Judea.[92] This rhetorical move does not displace Mosaic Torah, but locates it within a broader category and names it differently in order to assert its greater cosmic and political significance and to highlight competing claims to sovereignty over the lives of Judeans. The prayer, by contrast, foregrounds the particularity of Jewish faith by reference to the teaching of Moses, thereby constituting the book's audience as a people bound in covenant to God.

Differences between the prayer in Daniel 9 and its context raise a bigger question concerning the book's theology that is relevant for the discussion of resistance. The penitential prayer reflects, at its heart, a Deuteronomic theology of sin and punishment, cry and deliverance.[93] What does its inclusion signal here? Was it possible for the writers of Daniel simultaneously to teach that God had long ago appointed tribulations and the time of their end, and to commend a prayer that pleads with God to intercede and not delay? Did it make any sense to confess the sins of the nation, as though this were the cause of exile, or the cause of the persecution to come, when the book of Daniel never says, "this is because of your people's sins," but simply "this is what must be"? Put another way, is the Deuteronomistic theology of the prayer consistent with the apocalyptic theology — often called "deterministic" — found elsewhere in Daniel?[94]

91. Polaski notes that in Dan 6 royal power is equated with royal writing, i.e., the king's written law (*"Mene, Mene, Tekel, Parsin,"* p. 663).

92. See also Polaski, *"Mene, Mene, Tekel, Parsin,"* p. 661. By contrast, the term's use in Ezra 7:25 and elsewhere in Ezra places the "law" of God under the umbrella of the law of the king. According to Polaski, a similar move occurs by the conclusion of Dan 6 (p. 667). Fewell offers a similar reading: "When the worship of a god is established by the law, then the law out-powers the deity" (*Circle of Sovereignty,* pp. 117-18).

93. See Hans J. M. van Deventer, "The End of the End, Or, What Is the Deuteronomist (Still) Doing in Daniel?" in *Past, Present, Future: The Deuteronomistic History and the Prophets,* ed. Johannes C. de Moor and Harry F. van Rooy (Leiden: Brill, 2000), pp. 62-75. Van Deventer views the prayer as an addition to the book inserted just after Antiochus issued his edict and defiled the sanctuary. For van Deventer the prayer's Deuteronomistic theology answers the book's apocalypticism with a more viable response to the crisis drawn from Israel's traditions.

94. For a balanced view of the function of determinism in Daniel, see Bruce Jones, "Ideas of History in the Book of Daniel" (Ph.D. diss., Graduate Theological Union, 1972). On the blending of theological streams in Daniel, see Roger A. Hall, "Post-exilic Theological Streams and the Book of Daniel" (Ph.D. diss., Yale University, 1974).

Many scholars say no.[95] At stake is a view of history and of divine and human agency. How free are human beings to choose their course in the face of what has been decreed? Are human beings able to influence the course of events once God has planned them? In answer to the first question, Collins has noted that for the writer(s) of Daniel "neither determinism nor belief in supernatural powers detracts in any way from the seriousness of human action. While the course of events is predetermined, the fate of individuals is not."[96] The second question, meanwhile, misses the point of penitence and even of petition for our writers. I consider arguments concerning the status of the prayer, "original" or otherwise, before discussing its function in further detail.

In 1895 August von Gall called the prayer in Daniel 9 "a shoot on foreign soil."[97] In his judgment, it was not original to the book but an addition, much like the Prayer of Azariah and the Song of the Three Youths added to the Greek version of Daniel 3. Daniel's statement in 9:4, "And I prayed to the Lord my God and confessed and said," appeared to von Gall an unnecessary repetition in light of Daniel's statement in 9:3 ("I lifted my face to my Lord God, to seek prayer and mercy with fasting, sack-cloth, and ashes"). Von Gall found here an editorial seam, matched by Daniel's apparent narrative doubling of the prayer's conclusion in 9:20 and 21 (9:20 begins, וְעוֹד אֲנִי מְדַבֵּר וּמִתְפַּלֵּל; 9:21 similarly begins, וְעוֹד אֲנִי מְדַבֵּר בַּתְּפִלָּה).[98] For von Gall these seams merely signaled a greater difficulty: the theology of the prayer did not fit the theology of the book. Nowhere else in the book of Daniel is disaster — whether individual or collective — explicitly interpreted as punishment for sin. The righteous must endure tribulations, but they are never told that they have merited such suffering.[99]

Von Gall's assessment of the prayer would be followed by R. H. Charles and Aage Bentzen, among others.[100] Charles argued that the context demands not a prayer of repentance but rather a prayer of illumination.[101] In their Anchor Bible Commentary on Daniel, Louis Hartman and Alexander A. Di Lella put for-

95. See, for example, John J. Collins, *Daniel, with an Introduction to Apocalyptic Literature,* FOTL 20 (Grand Rapids: Eerdmans, 1984), p. 95. My discussion is indebted to Collins's thorough and judicious treatment of the question, though my conclusions differ from his.

96. Collins, "Daniel and His Social World," p. 141. Boccaccini argues that the book's "goal is to emphasize the centrality of perseverance for the individual and the personal liability of the individual independent of the destiny of the people of Israel as a whole" (*Roots of Rabbinic Judaism,* p. 200).

97. August Freiherrn von Gall, *Die Einheitlichkeit des Buches Daniel* (Giessen: Ricker, 1895), p. 126.

98. Von Gall, *Einheitlichkeit des Buches Daniel,* p. 123.

99. Von Gall, *Einheitlichkeit des Buches Daniel,* p. 125.

100. R. H. Charles, *A Critical and Exegetical Commentary on the Book of Daniel* (Oxford: Clarendon, 1929), pp. 226-35; Aage Bentzen, *Daniel* (Tübingen: Mohr, 1952), p. 75.

101. Charles, *Critical and Exegetical Commentary on the Book of Daniel,* p. 226.

ward similar arguments for viewing the prayer as a later insertion. They also noted that the prayer's smooth, classical Hebrew contrasts markedly with the "Aramaizing Hebrew" of the other portions of Daniel 8–12.[102]

The suggestion that the context requires a prayer for illumination finds a parallel in *4 Ezra* 12:7-9. There, Ezra has had a disturbing vision of an eagle with twelve wings and three heads. During the vision a lion speaks to Ezra and also to the eagle, pronouncing judgment that will spell hope for the earth (ch. 11). When Ezra wakes from his dream he is terrified, weary, and weak (*4 Ezra* 12:3-5), and prays to God for strength (12:6). In his prayer, he prays also for God to show him the interpretation and meaning of the vision, for this will bring him comfort (12:8). While the parallels with Daniel are striking, especially the correlation between strength and knowledge, these parallels arise because *4 Ezra* is dependent on the book of Daniel and reinterprets elements of the vision in Daniel 7. God answers Ezra's prayer by telling him, "the eagle you saw coming up from the sea is the fourth kingdom that appeared in a vision to your brother Daniel" (12:11).

By contrast, up to this point in Daniel 9, Daniel has not seen a vision, but has been reading scripture. Daniel "studied the scrolls to understand the number of years, according to the Lord's word to Jeremiah the prophet, that would fill up Jerusalem's sentence of desolation: it was seventy years" (Dan 9:2). In the next verse Daniel turns his face to God "to seek" (in) prayer and supplication with fasting, sackcloth, and ashes (9:3). By contrast with Daniel's reaction to the vision of the man clothed in linen, nowhere in the narrative frame does Daniel state that his reading of Jeremiah caused the kind of terror, confusion, or weakness Ezra reports, even though his earlier and later visions do occasion such responses (notably, not all at once; see 8:27; 10:8, 16-17; 12:8; cf. 7:15, 28). Although in places throughout the book Daniel does ask for understanding (7:16; 8:15; cf. 2:18; 12:8), in the narrative frame immediately surrounding the prayer he voices no such request. Rather, Daniel has already sought understanding precisely by reading the scriptures.[103] Though in his act of prayer Daniel "seeks" with prayer and supplication (תַּחֲנוּנִים), it is not stated that he thereby seeks illumination.[104] Rather, what he seeks appears to be God, to whom he directs his face. The noun תַּחֲנוּנִים and his fasting, sack-

---

102. Louis Hartman and Alexander A. Di Lella, *The Book of Daniel,* Anchor Bible 23 (New York: Doubleday, 1978), p. 246.

103. Aaron B. Hebbard finds here that "the claims of [the character Daniel] with regard to the Jeremiah text stand in contrast to what he admits in the previous two visions; that is, that here he understands the words of Jeremiah although he fails to understand completely the meaning of the angelic interpretations of the visions." *Reading Daniel as a Text in Theological Hermeneutics* (Eugene, OR: Pickwick, 2009), p. 186.

104. Noted also by Collins, *Daniel, with an Introduction to Apocalyptic Literature,* p. 90.

cloth, and ashes imply that he seeks also mercy (OG accordingly renders תַּחֲנוּנִים with ἔλεος).[105]

Gerald H. Wilson has pointed out that in Jeremiah 29 (one of two passages in Jeremiah to refer to the "seventy years"; see further below) precisely such prayer and "seeking" God precede the restoration that God promises will follow the seventy years of exile:[106] "Then when you call upon me and come and pray to me, I will hear you. When you search for me, you will find me; if you seek me with all your heart, I will let you find me, says the LORD, and I will restore your fortunes and gather you from all the nations and all the places where I have driven you, says the LORD, and I will bring you back to the place from which I sent you into exile" (Jer 29:12-14 NRSV). Jeremiah invites the reader to seek the Lord, promising that God will hear and effect restoration when the reader turns to God in prayer. Daniel's prayer does precisely this.[107] As John Collins has noted, "The traditional confession of sin and prayer for mercy is an appropriate reaction to the prophecy of Jeremiah" that Daniel has been reading.[108]

Although we can confidently reject the idea that the context demands a prayer for illumination, we cannot deny the difference in style between the prayer and its context noted by Hartman, Di Lella, and others. The prayer is a set piece. Yet identifying the prayer as a set piece with a style markedly different from that of its narrative context does not militate against its inclusion by the writers of the book of Daniel at the time when the twelve chapters of Hebrew and Aramaic Daniel were composed.[109]

Indeed, Bruce W. Jones has demonstrated that the writers integrated the prayer with the narrative in chapter 9 through the artistic use of repetition and wordplay.[110] Jones highlights the repetition of the *hiphil* infinitive לְהַשְׂכִּיל in 9:13 and 9:22 (with the second person singular suffix, לְהַשְׂכִּילְךָ), followed by the imperfect (with imperative force) וְתַשְׂכֵּל in 9:25. This repetition links the angel's revelation to Daniel with the faithfulness of God affirmed in Daniel's

---

105. See D. R. Ap-Thomas, "Some Aspects of the Root HNN in the Old Testament," *JSS* 2, no. 2 (1957): 128-48.

106. Gerald H. Wilson, "The Prayer of Daniel 9: Reflection on Jeremiah 29," *JSOT* 15, no. 48 (1990): 91-99.

107. See also Mark J. Boda, *Praying the Tradition: The Origin and Use of Tradition in Nehemiah 9* (Berlin: Walter de Gruyter, 1999), p. 32.

108. Collins, *Daniel, with an Introduction to Apocalyptic Literature*, pp. 90-91. See also Lev 26:41 and discussion of Dan 9:24-27 below.

109. By "composed" I refer to the creative process of "putting together" (the word's etymological sense) old and new material in one artfully conceived whole. James A. Montgomery suggests that "the second-century author may well have himself inserted such a prayer in his book for the encouragement of the faithful." *A Critical and Exegetical Commentary on the Book of Daniel*, ICC (New York: Charles Scribner's Sons, 1927), p. 362.

110. Bruce William Jones, "The Prayer in Daniel IX," *VT* 18 (1968): 488-93.

prayer. The angel empowers and calls on Daniel to understand and thereby remedy the collective failure to understand that Daniel has confessed (9:13). Jones also identifies a careful wordplay by which the angel answers Daniel's reference to the written "oath" (הַשְּׁבֻעָה) "poured out" (וַתִּתַּךְ) (9:11) by announcing "seventy weeks" (שָׁבֻעִים שִׁבְעִים 9:24) not written but engraved or determined, at the conclusion of which a decreed end is to be "poured out" (תִּתַּךְ) on the desolator (שֹׁמֵם, i.e., Antiochus 9:27). The angel thus points beyond the punishment of God's people by means of the seventy years of exile, focusing attention instead on the punishment of Antiochus at the conclusion of seventy weeks. The angel's discourse similarly takes up and transposes the prayer's reference to the desolated sanctuary (מִקְדָּשְׁךָ הַשָּׁמֵם 9:17) and the corresponding desolation of the people (שֹׁמְמֹתֵינוּ 9:18), bringing these into the frame of what God has decreed (נֶחֱרֶצֶת שֹׁמֵמוֹת 9:26); linking them with the desolating abominations (שִׁקּוּצִים מְשֹׁמֵם) of Antiochus IV; and declaring their end at the time appointed (9:27).[111]

In light of these links between the language of the prayer and the angel's discourse in Daniel 9:24-27, the "editorial seams" identified by von Gall appear not as clues to sloppy redaction but rather as a stylistic device aiming to highlight Daniel's act of prayer.[112] The differences in style between the prayer and its narrative context do not mark the text as a later insertion but instead suggest that the writers of Daniel 9 incorporated into the narrative either a traditional prayer or one composed from traditional language, specifically drawn from penitential liturgies.[113]

What does it mean to take seriously the prayer's liturgical character?[114] W. Sibley Towner accepts Jones's arguments that the prayer is original to Hebrew and Aramaic Daniel. But for Towner it signifies not through its (Deutero-

111. Jones, "The Prayer in Daniel IX," p. 491.

112. Collins states, "It is possible that such redundancy is simply a feature of the author's style and not necessarily indicative of redactional activity." He notes similar duplications in Dan 7 and 8 (*Daniel, with an Introduction to Apocalyptic Literature*, p. 91).

113. See, e.g., André Lacocque, "The Liturgical Prayer in Daniel 9," *HUCA* 47 (1976): 119-42; Davies, *Daniel*, pp. 61-62. John E. Goldingay suggests that the prayer "was composed by someone who knew this tradition well, probably both from study and from worship, and who instinctively but also consciously prayed in ways stimulated and hallowed by it." *Daniel*, WBC 30 (Dallas: Word, 1989), p. 234. See also Collins, *Daniel, with an Introduction to Apocalyptic Literature*, p. 91.

114. Daniel L. Smith-Christopher notes that "such prayers would not only be the documents of a literate elite, but would likely have been the public pronouncements around which large-scale identity would be constructed." *A Biblical Theology of Exile*, Overtures to Biblical Theology (Minneapolis: Fortress, 2002), p. 111. The shared, public setting of liturgical prayer would be an important site for the formation and transformation of "the many," so crucial to Daniel's vision for making many wise and righteous (e.g., 11:33; 12:3).

nomic) propositional content but as "an act of penitential devotion" appropriate to one "living between the times."[115] Collins follows Towner in asserting that it is *only* an act of piety. "The content of the prayer does not represent the theology of the angel or of the author of the book."[116] It is true that the prayer does not represent the angel's theology. By taking up keywords from Daniel's prayer the angel transposes and subsumes elements of the prayer into a new revelatory framework. But can Daniel's act of penitential prayer be so readily divorced from the prayer's content liturgical praxis or the theology that informs them, and is it accurate to say that the prayer in no way represents the theology of Daniel's writers? I argue instead that the writers of Daniel have consciously taken up and transposed "Deuteronomic" penitential theology and liturgical practice within an apocalyptic framework.

In support of this view I note that in Daniel 10 the angel approves Daniel's penitent attitude, stating that his words found a hearing from the moment he dedicated his heart to humbling himself before God (10:12). It is this attitude that the prayer evokes in the reader. It makes little sense to divorce Daniel's action of humbling himself before God, which the angel has specifically linked to Daniel's "words" (i.e., his prayer), from the penitential language that the prayer contains. Nor can this penitential language and Daniel's accompanying actions of fasting and putting on sackcloth and ashes be divorced from the Deuteronomic theology of sin-punishment-repentance-deliverance that undergirds them.

In chapter 6 I described the ways in which ritual entrains, ordering its participants. Liturgical prayer both expresses faith and forms the one who prays.[117] It shapes dispositions and attitudes, and thereby "opens up existence to a specific field of reality."[118] It enacts commitments.[119] It also forms community.[120]

---

115. W. Sibley Towner, "Retributional Theology in the Apocalyptic Setting," *USQR* 26 (1971): 203-14, 209, 213.

116. Collins, *Daniel: A Commentary on the Book of Daniel,* p. 360. By contrast, Boccaccini argues that "without the prayer of Dan 9, the book of Daniel as a whole would lack any internal logic" (*Roots of Rabbinic Judaism,* p. 184).

117. Donald E. Saliers, "Liturgy and Ethics: Some New Beginnings," *JRE* 7, no. 2 (1979): 173-89, 175.

118. Jean Ladrière, "The Performativity of Liturgical Language," in *Liturgical Experience of Faith,* ed. Herman A. P. Schmidt and David Noel Power (New York: Herder & Herder, 1973), pp. 50-62, 56. Cf. Werline, "Prayer, Politics, and Social Vision in Daniel 9," p. 20. I note that I became aware of Ladrière's work as well as that of Wade T. Wheelock (see below) through the work of Judith Marie Kubicki, *Liturgical Music as Ritual Symbol: A Case Study of Jacques Berthier's Taizé Music* (Leuven: Peeters, 1999).

119. Ladrière, "Performativity of Liturgical Language," p. 60. Cf. Saliers, "Liturgy and Ethics," p. 176: worship is "necessarily normative." Smith-Christopher (*Biblical Theology of Exile,* p. 120) describes the "integrative and transformative function" of postexilic penitential prayers.

120. Ladrière, "Performativity of Liturgical Language," pp. 58-59. Cf. Newsom, *Self as Sym-*

The prayer's mingling of singular and plural first person pronouns draws the book's audience into a shared praxis of worship with the character Daniel.[121]

Throughout the stories, visions, and discourses of Daniel a history is rehearsed, placing the relationship between Judeans and the empires that ruled them in a new apocalyptic perspective. The prayer rehearses a different history — that between the people of Judea and their God. In so doing, as Greg Carey puts it, the prayer "instills a theological set of values through which one may interpret both the past and the present."[122] The prayer opens both Daniel and the audience who reads and hears it to a field of reality that is differently articulated but not opposed to the field of the visions, nor finally separate from them. The field of reality to which the prayer opens its speakers and audience is the people's relationship with God. The vision in Daniel 7 showed God enthroned in majesty in heaven, enacting justice for the people of the holy ones. But within the book of Daniel, only the prayer draws the people to confess the majesty Daniel's vision has shown them, and only the prayer actively places this people in relationship with the God who will save them. The stories in Daniel 1–6 (esp. Daniel 4 and 5) taught the humbling of rulers, showing their proper status in relation to God. Only the prayer confesses and inculcates humility in God's people, and only the prayer constitutes them as people joined together in worship of God.

I argued in chapter 5 that Daniel's prayer denies Antiochus IV the power to control the people of Jerusalem through shaming.[123] Instead, the prayer gives meaning to shame only in relation to God's justice, faithfulness, and compassion, and this is part of the book's resistance to Antiochus.[124] It also makes a claim on Daniel's audience. Speaking of "a politics of penitence," Smith-Christopher highlights the relationship between penitential prayer, political power, and action: "To remind oneself constantly of the failure of power (in ancestors and kings) is to advocate an alternative mode of living."[125] He explains, "To call on God in the face of resisting dominance is a form of reidentification as a resistant people. The penitential prayers are a call to break with the past, to be an alternative people of

---

bolic Space, p. 1, regarding the Qumran community: "The community was constituted and maintained through speech-acts."

121. On the function of pronouns in liturgical language, see Wade T. Wheelock, "The Problem of Ritual Language: From Information to Situation," JAAR 50, no. 1 (1982): 49-71, 50-51.

122. Greg Carey, Ultimate Things: An Introduction to Jewish and Christian Apocalyptic Literature (St. Louis: Chalice, 2005), p. 46.

123. Smith-Christopher further highlights the way in which the prayer's reference to shame entails both ownership of the failures of the past and a commitment to an alternative way of life that embodies the values of the Mosaic Torah (Biblical Theology of Exile, pp. 120-23).

124. See also Werline, "Prayer, Politics, and Social Vision in Daniel 9," pp. 21, 23.

125. Smith-Christopher, Biblical Theology of Exile, p. 122.

God."[126] The prayer awakens the book's audience to the demands of covenant, to past failure, and to the possibility of renewal. Whether they pray individually or collectively, the act of praying constitutes them as community ("we have sinned") joined to one another in liturgical practices that counter the invented and imposed liturgies of Antiochus. It is precisely this false worship that has desolated the sanctuary. By characterizing the rupture they now experience as a result of sin, the prayer places all suffering and desolation within the governing framework of the relationship between God and God's people.

Even though the angel will give a different meaning to the desolations the book's audience experience, the prayer's theological assertions are neither incidental nor wholly negated.[127] They are rather actualized, subsumed, and, as Choon-Leong Seow puts it, recontextualized within a new revelatory frame.[128] The book makes room for two ways of telling the story. It affirms and inculcates an attitude, posture, and language of penitence. It takes up a language of liturgy that expresses and enacts a formative and indeed normative framework for the faith and lived experience of God's people in community. Praise and petition affirm that their deliverance can come only from God.

The angel's discourse, meanwhile, reveals that this framework alone is not enough, for it does not tell the whole story. The revelations provide a further framework, directing Daniel and the book's audience to perceive and understand further dimensions of the reality in which they find themselves and the future that will unfold. While the theology of the prayer and the theology of the revelations may seem incompatible, Pieter Venter describes this literary combination of two seemingly antithetical positions as "a typical *montage* technique where two ideas are put in synchronic relationship with each other to form a semantic frame for a new meaning that is 'beyond the sum of the independent meanings.'"[129] The penitential prayer and the apocalyptic revelation of future-history that follows each take on deeper meaning in light of the other.[130]

126. Smith-Christopher, *Biblical Theology of Exile*, p. 122.

127. *Pace* Jones, who argues that Gabriel's response replaces and corrects the prayer's Deuteronomistic view of history with a deterministic one ("The Prayer in Daniel IX").

128. Choon-Leong Seow, *Daniel*, Westminster Bible Companion (Louisville: Westminster John Knox, 2003), p. 144. Cf. Newsom, *Self as Symbolic Space*, p. 47. Werline notes that the dissonance between the Deuteronomic and apocalyptic theologies is finally unresolved: "The author's goal is not to be systematic, but to take back, to give meaning to, and to preserve key teachings and practices in a world that has suddenly discarded them" ("Prayer, Politics, and Social Vision in Daniel 9," p. 31).

129. Pieter Venter, "Daniel 9: A Penitential Prayer in Apocalyptic Garb," in *Seeking the Favor of God*, vol. 2, *The Development of Penitential Prayer in Second Temple Judaism*, ed. Mark J. Boda, Daniel K. Falk, and Rodney A. Werline (Leiden: Brill, 2007), pp. 33-49, 43.

130. For a sensitive treatment, see Donald Gowan, *Daniel*, Abingdon Old Testament Commentaries (Nashville: Abingdon, 2001), pp. 126-30.

The prayer in Daniel 9 follows upon the act of reading. Even though Daniel reads alone, his response as reader is to take up traditional words of prayer from Israel's liturgical and devotional traditions. New revelation follows. In this way, penitential traditions and practices of Jewish faith ground Daniel's practice of reading and prepare him for the revelation of new and necessary truth. At the same time, the revelation Daniel receives gives new meaning not only to what he has read but also to the practices of penitence and faith. Daniel's act of reading provides an example for future generations.[131] In the same way Daniel's act of praying, in and by which he has adopted the posture and attitude of the penitent and so humbled himself before the Lord, serves as an example for the persecuted Jews to follow.[132] Though not prevalent elsewhere in Daniel, the Deuteronomic theology which asserts that deliverance will follow upon repentance appears here in force to remind the audience that those who turn to God in repentance will be heard.

To Teach, to Fall, and to Make Righteous

The resistant action of the faithful in the time of persecution takes further shape in the angel's prediction in Daniel 11:33: "The wise among the people (מַשְׂכִּילֵי עָם) shall give understanding (יָבִינוּ) to many; for some days, however, they shall fall (וְנִכְשְׁלוּ) by sword and flame, and suffer captivity and plunder" (NRSV). I proposed above the translation "(wise) teachers" for the *hiphil* active participle *maśkîlîm*. Thus the phrase מַשְׂכִּילֵי עָם, translated by the NRSV as "the wise among the people," also conveys an active meaning: "ones who teach people," or "make people wise." Paul L. Redditt characterizes the *maśkîlîm* as those who instruct people "in their faith."[133]

Hans Kosmala's study of the semantic range of the participle *maśkîl* sheds further light on the nature of this instruction.[134] Overwhelmingly, says Kosmala, the passages in which the root *śkl* occur "are reflections on the knowledge of God, His miracles and deeds in creation and history, His supreme power over all mankind, His will and His pleasure that man should obey His word and the Torah He had given, and walk accordingly."[135] In his discussion of the passages in Daniel, he emphasizes in particular their understanding of God's actions, in-

---

131. Richard S. Briggs, *The Virtuous Reader: Old Testament Narrative and Interpretive Virtue* (Grand Rapids: Baker, 2010), p. 212.

132. Sharon Pace, *Daniel*, Smyth & Helwys Bible Commentary (Macon, GA: Smyth & Helwys, 2008), pp. 296-97.

133. Redditt, *Daniel*, p. 184.

134. Hans Kosmala, "Maśkîl," *JANESCU* 5 (1973): 235-41.

135. Kosmala, "Maśkîl," p. 235.

cluding those yet to come, and communicating that understanding to others.[136] He argues that the term carries the meaning of "teacher," signaling one who instructs others about God and what God expects from the faithful.[137]

A later verse in the angel's discourse confirms this meaning and adds further detail to Daniel's program of resistance:

וְהַמַּשְׂכִּלִים יַזְהִרוּ כְּזֹהַר הָרָקִיעַ
וּמַצְדִּיקֵי הָרַבִּים כַּכּוֹכָבִים לְעוֹלָם וָעֶד

The wise teachers will shine like the brilliance of heaven's vault,
Those who lead the many to righteousness, like the stars forever and ever.
(12:3)

Synonymous parallelism here portrays the glorious reward after death that awaits the *maśkîlîm*.[138] The verse's parallel structure also establishes a close link between their teaching function and their work of "leading the many to righteousness" (12:3). What this work entails becomes clearer in light of Gabriel's discourse in Daniel 9. There Gabriel explained to Daniel the purpose of the seventy weeks: "Seventy weeks have been decreed over your people and your holy city to complete the transgression (הַפֶּשַׁע), to end sins (חַטָּאוֹת), to atone for guilt (לְכַפֵּר עָוֹן), to bring eternal justice/righteousness (צֶדֶק), to seal vision and prophet, and to anoint the most holy place" (9:24). In Gabriel's revelation, the action of bringing eternal righteousness follows a threefold expression for the ending of an age of sin that culminates in atonement. The language of transgression, sins, and atoning for guilt evokes Israel's covenantal and priestly traditions, and suggests that the vision of a new age of righteousness and justice should also be understood in relation to Israel's covenant with God.[139] The persecution and activity of the *maśkîlîm* predicted in Daniel 11–12 occur in the final week of years foretold by Gabriel (9:27), at the cusp between the end of the era of sin and the dawn of the era of righteousness. In this context, their activity of "leading the many to righteousness" would appear to play a part in the "bringing of righteousness" that Ga-

136. Kosmala, *"Maśkîl,"* p. 239.

137. Kosmala finds the use of the term here very similar to that found later at Qumran (*"Maśkîl,"* pp. 240-41).

138. On the classification of this verse as poetry or prose, see Stanislav Segert, "Poetic Structures in the Hebrew Sections of the Book of Daniel," in *Solving Riddles and Untying Knots: Biblical, Epigraphic, and Semitic Studies in Honor of Jonas C. Greenfield,* ed. Ziony Zevit, Seymour Gitin, and Michael Sokoloff (Winona Lake, IN: Eisenbrauns, 1995), pp. 261-75, 269-71.

139. Cf. Devorah Dimant, "The Seventy Weeks Chronology (Dan 9,24-27) in the Light of New Qumranic Texts," in *The Book of Daniel in the Light of New Findings,* ed. A. S. van der Woude (Leuven: Leuven University Press, 1993), pp. 57-76, 60-61. But note that Dimant finds here an allusion to a future messianic priest.

briel has foretold. In this way the *maśkîlîm* participate in fulfilling the prophecy of Daniel 9:24. They may also play a role in effecting atonement, as I argue below.

I indicated above that righteousness should be understood here in relation to covenant obedience. In my discussion of the prayer in Daniel 9 I also argued that Gabriel's discourse recasts Deuteronomistic traditions and theology within an apocalyptic framework. These insights clarify the relationship between the teaching of the *maśkîlîm* and their activity of leading many to righteousness. By instructing the persecuted in (and by) the practice of Torah, the proper interpretation of scriptures, and the apocalyptic vision revealed to Daniel, the *maśkîlîm* impart knowledge of God's faithfulness, God's sovereignty, and God's will for the Judean people. With this knowledge they also impart the strength to hold fast to the covenant. By these actions they lead the many to righteousness, even at the cost of death.

The very suffering and death of the *maśkîlîm* are seen by the writers of Daniel as efficacious:[140]

וּמִן־הַמַּשְׂכִּילִים יִכָּשְׁלוּ

לִצְרוֹף בָּהֶם וּלְבָרֵר וְלַלְבֵּן

עַד־עֵת קֵץ כִּי־עוֹד לַמּוֹעֵד

> Then some of the teachers will be brought low
> To refine in them, to purify, and to cleanse
> Until an end time — it remains for an appointed season. (11:35)

The "end time" here appears to correspond to the end of sin and transgression, and hence the moment of atonement, earlier foretold by Gabriel (9:24). Although the words used here for refining (צרף), purifying (ברר), and cleansing (לבן) are relatively uncommon and do not occur in the Pentateuch, each none-theless has cultic associations elsewhere in Israel's scriptures.[141] The prophet Malachi proclaims concerning the priests that God "will sit as a refiner (מְצָרֵף) and purifier of silver, and he will purify the descendants of Levi and refine them like gold and silver, until they present offerings to the LORD in righteousness" (Mal 3:3 NRSV). In Isaiah 52:11 the root ברר appears in the command to those who carry the vessels of the Lord to make themselves pure. And in Psalm 51:9 the verbal root לבן (אַלְבִּין) is closely associated with the removal of sin (cf. Isa 1:18) and occurs in parallel with purification (וְאֶטְהָר) achieved through cultic

---

140. Contra Albertz who interprets יִכָּשְׁלוּ to mean "they will stumble," based on a common meaning of the *niphal* to refer to "the failure of an action and/or the bad end of the wicked" ("Social Setting of Daniel," p. 193). The occurrence of the *niphal* in 11:33, where the context is clearly death by "sword and flame," clarifies the verb's meaning here.

141. For ברר, see Vinzenz Hamp, "ברר brr," *TDOT* 2:308-12, esp. 310-11.

rites (cf. Lev 14:4-57). These associations with priestly rites for the removal of sin and purification and with the purity required of those who handle the temple vessels and make sacrifices before God suggest a connection between the atonement foretold by Gabriel and the suffering and deaths of the *maśkîlîm*, for it is through sacrifice that priests would traditionally make atonement for the sins of the people (Lev 4:20, 26, 31, 35; 9:7; etc.). Yet the temple had been defiled by Antiochus's desolating abomination, and the daily offering had ceased. Other forms of sacrifice to Yhwh, including those intended to atone for sins, would also have ceased. These had been replaced by forms of sacrifice the writers of Daniel considered abominable. According to Gabriel's revelation, atonement would still take place. But in the absence of regular cultic sacrifice, atonement would be achieved by other means.[142]

A question arises, nonetheless, as to who receives the action of "refining, purifying, and cleansing" achieved through the suffering and death of the *maśkîlîm*. For Collins, "The purification bespeaks an interest in individual salvation as distinct from (though not opposed to) the deliverance of the nation. The death of the martyrs is not vicarious. They are the ones who are purified."[143] Yet the verse's grammar does not require such a reading, and the web of associations I have identified between the actions of the *maśkîlîm* and the atonement for sin suggests otherwise. It would appear that the humble self-sacrifice of the *maśkîlîm* (cf. Daniel's own self-humbling, and Lev 23:28-29) will play some part in atonement for the sins of the many, just as they play a part in bringing in righteousness by making the many righteous.

The repetition of the same three verbs (refining, צרף; purifying, ברר; and cleansing, לבן) in Daniel 12:10 further strengthens the connection between the deaths of the *maśkîlîm* and the fate and activity of the many, although their precise relationship is not entirely clear. There the angel states that

יִתְבָּרֲרוּ וְיִתְלַבְּנוּ וְיִצָּרְפוּ רַבִּים וְהִרְשִׁיעוּ רְשָׁעִים
וְלֹא יָבִינוּ כָּל־רְשָׁעִים וְהַמַּשְׂכִּלִים יָבִינוּ

> Many will purify themselves, they will cleanse themselves, and they will be refined, but the wicked will be declared guilty. None of the wicked will understand, but the wise teachers will understand. (12:10)

As Collins has noted, the shift in subject here from the wise to "many" (or a collapse of the two) may be a "sign of a different hand."[144] Whether or not this is so, do the reflexive verbs יִתְבָּרֲרוּ וְיִתְלַבְּנוּ — many will purify and cleanse

---

142. Davies, "Reading Daniel Sociologically," p. 360.
143. Collins, *Daniel: A Commentary on the Book of Daniel,* p. 386.
144. Collins, *Daniel: A Commentary on the Book of Daniel,* p. 400.

themselves — militate against an interpretation of the deaths of the *maśkîlîm* as effecting atonement for others, including the many? Not necessarily. As I noted above, the call to rejoice in Isaiah 52:11 includes the command to those who would handle the sacred vessels (i.e., those who would serve as cultic intermediaries between God and the people and make offerings on the people's behalf) to "purify yourselves" (הַבָּרוּ, *niphal*). While this verse does not portray the same group involved in making atoning sacrifices, yet it nonetheless reminds us that purification may not only be an effect of atonement. Intermediaries who will offer sacrifice must also make themselves pure *before* handling the sacred vessels and *before* offering sacrifice (i.e., before making atonement). Thus purification is also a preparation for making atonement.

A close reading of Isaiah 52–53, which I consider in greater detail below, may have suggested such a need to the writers of Daniel. In Isaiah 52, only two verses after the command to those who carry the vessels of the Lord to "purify yourselves" (52:11), the Servant Song begins. Crucial to the self-understanding of the *maśkîlîm* (see below), the song contains a vision of vicarious suffering and atonement: "On him was the punishment that made us whole" (53:5 NRSV); his life is given "as an offering for sin" (53:10). As I discuss below, the *maśkîlîm* of Daniel applied to themselves a corporate understanding of Isaiah's Suffering Servant, and it may be that the writer of Daniel 12:10 envisioned the circle of *maśkîlîm* expanding to include "many" as a result of successful teaching. In this vision of the future these "many" may in turn have effected atonement for others in Judea, beyond the circle of the wise teachers. It is possible that they would purify themselves in preparation for their atoning self-sacrifice.

Finally, the verbal roots ברר and צרף have connotations not only of purification but also of testing, a theme prevalent in the narratives of Daniel 1, 3, and 6 (cf. Isa 48:10; Ps 26:2; 66:10).[145] The heroes in Daniel 3 and 6 also share with the *maśkîlîm* of the angel's revelation a willingness to surrender their bodies to death rather than forsake the practices of their faith or worship another god, thereby denying earthly kings the power to coerce apostasy from Jewish faith. These links direct us to examine the ways in which the heroes in these stories served as models for the *maśkîlîm* in their final trials.

Daniel 1, 3, and 6: Stories of Faithfulness

Daniel 1 introduces the theme of testing through abstention from defiling foods. While the narrative does not identify the precise purity issues at stake,[146]

---

145. Mason, "Treatment of Earlier Biblical Themes," p. 92.
146. See discussions in Collins, *Daniel: A Commentary on the Book of Daniel*, pp. 141-43;

I noted in the previous chapter that abstaining from the king's food and the wine of his feasting asserts and maintains distinctively Jewish identity in an environment that threatens to extinguish it.[147] In addition, like fasting, abstention is a way for Judeans under foreign domination to order life according to the will of God and acknowledge God alone as true patron, provider, and source of life.[148] Rather than ingratiate themselves to their foreign ruler, in this instance they rely on their God to nourish and sustain them. They specifically ask their overseer to put them to the test (נַסׁ־נָא, 1:12; cf. 1:14). Because of their steadfastness and willingness to be tested, God grants Daniel, Shadrak, Meshak, and Abednego the gift of exceptional wisdom and understanding (1:17). The knowledge they receive will later empower them to stand up to foreign kings, proclaiming God's word and proclaiming their faithfulness to the worship of Yhwh alone.

In Daniel 3, Shadrak, Meshak, and Abednego defy the king's command to bow down and worship the golden statue the king has erected, full knowing that on refusing they will be cast into a blazing furnace.[149] The king demands, "Who is the god who will deliver you from my hand?" (3:15).

Nebuchadnezzar's words echo the arrogant taunt of the Rabshakeh of Sennacherib, king of Assyria.[150] After cataloging the nations defeated by Sennacherib's armies, he asks, "Who among all the gods of these countries have saved their countries out of my hand, that the LORD should save Jerusalem out of my hand?" (Isa 36:20 NRSV). Readers would recall that God heard these words and, through the prophet Isaiah, counseled the people not to fear, for the Lord would deliver them (37:6). The armies of Assyria would turn back from Jerusalem, and the enemy would be destroyed. When the Rabshakeh scoffs at this assurance, Hezekiah turns to prayer, praising God as sovereign of heaven

---

Fewell, *Circle of Sovereignty,* pp. 18-19; W. Sibley Towner, *Daniel* (Atlanta: John Knox, 1984), pp. 24-26; Collins, "Daniel and His Social World," p. 135.

147. See Gowan, *Daniel,* pp. 47-48; Mary Mills, "Household and Table: Diasporic Boundaries in Daniel and Esther," *CBQ* 68, no. 3 (2006): 408-20; Kirkpatrick, *Competing for Honor,* pp. 40-66.

148. See Fewell, *Circle of Sovereignty,* pp. 18-19.

149. In OG the story was joined with the Prayer of Azariah and the Song of the Three Youths. On the dating of the prayer and its theology of atonement, possibly through martyrdom, see Klaus Koch, *Die Reiche der Welt und der kommende Menschensohn: Studien zum Danielbuch,* ed. Martin Rösel (Neukirchen-Vluyn: Neukirchener Verlag, 1995), pp. 66-82. The prayer seems to have been composed in a Semitic language between 167 and 164 BCE, but most scholars locate its authorship outside the circle responsible for Hebrew and Aramaic Daniel. The theology of the prayer is similar to that of the prayer in Dan 9, discussed above. See discussion in Collins, *Daniel: A Commentary on the Book of Daniel,* pp. 198-203.

150. Also observed by Charles, *Critical and Exegetical Commentary on the Book of Daniel,* p. 68; Collins, *Daniel: A Commentary on the Book of Daniel,* p. 187.

and earth (37:16) and petitioning, "save us from his hand" (37:20). To this request God responds once more, declaring to the blasphemer and to the faithful that all that has transpired, even the successes of the enemy, God determined long ago. Now in his arrogance the foreign king has overstepped his ordained role, and God will thwart him, acting to defend the people of Judah (37:35). He sends an angel to smite the enemy. One hundred and eighty-five thousand Assyrians die in the siege of Jerusalem, yet the people of Judah wield no weapon (37:36).

By means of this echo, the writer underscores the analogy between earlier events and the current crisis, emboldening the audience to remain faithful and submit to the test. God determined the course of events long ago. Long ago God raised up an army and retained the power to destroy it. God established a ruler and retained the power to depose him. The same is true now. This is the very message Daniel delivered to Nebuchadnezzar in chapter 2, where the sequence of four kingdoms yields finally to God's intervention to establish God's own rule and the rule of the chosen people upon the earth.[151] Vision and story alike assure the audience that whatever the appearance, God remains in control of events and will deliver when God chooses. The promise of resurrection for the faithful in 12:1-4 further assures them that even if they are given to a violent death in this life, God will ultimately reward their fidelity with deliverance from evil. God delivers the three young men from the hand of Nebuchadnezzar, and he will deliver the *maśkîlîm* of a later age. The faithful who have died will rise to eternal life and shine like the stars, sharing in the company of God's angels.

Yet the story of Shadrak, Meshak, and Abednego retreats one step and urges the faithful to give their lives regardless of any reward they might expect (Dan 3:17-18).[152] Like the three young men, they are to seek no guarantee, ask nothing of God, but give their lives for their faith simply because it is right. This message is not contrary to the promise of vindication — the story concludes with the heroes' miraculous deliverance. It rather instills in the persecuted the conviction that acting for their own sake, for God's, and for one another's all aim toward the one end of covenant fidelity. Self-sacrifice does not negate this goal but allows them to attain it.

As God sent an angel to deliver the besieged Jerusalemites in the time of Isaiah, so God sends an angel into the furnace to deliver the three young men. Awed by their rescue, Nebuchadnezzar blesses God. His description of the actions of the three young men offers a portrait of faithful resistance: "Blessed be the God of Shadrak, Meshak, and Abednego, who sent his angel to rescue his

---

151. The narratives in Dan 4 and 5 deliver the same message. On Dan 5, see Fröhlich, *"Time and Times and Half a Time,"* p. 41.

152. See Collins, *Daniel: A Commentary on the Book of Daniel,* pp. 188, 194.

servants who put their trust in him. They flouted the king's word and gave over their bodies, because they would not serve and they would not worship any god but their God" (3:28). The three young men model resistance for the *maśkîlîm*. They trust in God, defy the king's edict, refuse to worship any God but Yhwh, proclaim their faith out loud and in public, and surrender their bodies to death, not to apostasy.

In chapter 6, Daniel, too, exhibits his willingness to die rather than compromise his service to God. The king's courtiers determine to engineer Daniel's downfall but see no way to bring him down, save by criminalizing his very obedience to "the law of his God" and thus the actions by which he demonstrates his fidelity (6:5). They therefore convince the king to outlaw supplication made to anyone but the king during a period of thirty days (6:7, 9). Like the edict of Antiochus, their manipulations prohibit and legislate religious practice for the purposes of power. Daniel resists. He not only continues to pray to God three times daily but does so with windows open, refusing to hide the practice of his faith (6:10). He thus models for the audience of the book not only the importance of prayer in time of religious oppression, but also the courage to worship God openly and in defiance of the king's law, whatever the cost.[153]

When Daniel is brought before King Darius, the king expresses his wish to deliver Daniel (6:14). While the audience hears a contrast to Nebuchadnezzar's arrogant boast in 3:15, the final message will be the same. Even Darius must concede in the end that only God, and not he, can deliver (6:16). In the present context, the king's failure reminds the people suffering at the hands of Antiochus and his agents that their promises to those who would abandon the covenant are only meaningless deceptions. Antiochus has no power to deliver, for in the ultimate trial he has no power at all.

Daniel's refusal to obey Darius's decree and his insistence on constant prayer before God model one form of resistance for the persecuted. Yet the pacific words he delivers to the king in the wake of his ordeal also exclude a form of resistance. To Darius's query concerning his well-being (6:20), Daniel responds with the traditional court greeting, "O king, live forever!" (6:21).[154] He then attributes his salvation to his innocence before God, adding further (וְאַף) that he has done no injury to the king (6:22). In the verse that follows, the narrator confirms that Daniel suffered no harm because he trusted in God

---

153. See Smith-Christopher, "Gandhi on Daniel 6"; Mason, "Treatment of Earlier Biblical Themes," pp. 85-86.

154. On this expression, see P. A. H. de Boer, "Vive le roi!" *VT* 5, no. 3 (1955): 225-31. According to de Boer, in its biblical usage, this expression functions like an oath of allegiance that acknowledges the king's relative power over life and death but does so within the context of a greater divine authority. The king must ever answer to God, who is the source of the king's longevity.

(6:23).[155] Implicit in Daniel's innocence, and consequent to his trust in God, is his refusal to harm the very individual who has outlawed the practice of his faith and even decreed his death.[156] The *maśkîlîm* will not seek to harm or injure Antiochus or his agents. Their resistance is nonviolent.

As noted above, the original composition of this story and of those in Daniel 1 and 3 very likely did not take place during the Antiochian persecution. Yet in their present context they demonstrate specific modes of nonviolent resistance for the faithful in this crisis.[157] These modes of resistance are grounded in trust in God and require of the faithful a willingness to yield their bodies to death rather than compromise their faith. Later in the chapter I examine how the writer of Daniel developed these themes further by identifying the *maśkîlîm* with the Suffering Servant of Isaiah 52–53.

Waiting for the End

I have argued so far that the book of Daniel urges Judeans persecuted by Antiochus IV to adopt specific forms of nonviolent resistance, namely setting their heart to gain understanding, including studying the scriptures (see further below); humbling themselves, including fasting, prayer, and penitence; teaching God's message to the people; defying the decrees of Antiochus and persevering in the practices of their faith even at the cost of their lives; giving an example to others; and giving strength to others. The effect of their actions will be to make others wise and lead others to righteousness. Through their suffering and death they may also participate in atonement. Giving themselves willingly to the test, they are called to trust in God to the very end.[158]

Indeed, toward the conclusion of Daniel's final vision, the angel tells him,

155. Cf. Redditt, "Daniel 11," p. 469.

156. Trust in God can lead the faithful to refrain from violent action because they view the final overturning of the oppressor as the work of God alone. Cf. Redditt, "Daniel 11," p. 474. On the use of wordplay in the narrator's declaration of Daniel's innocence and its theological significance, see Bill T. Arnold, "Wordplay and Narrative Techniques in Daniel 5 and 6," *JBL* 112, no. 3 (1993): 479-85, 485.

157. Edwin Good takes the stories of 1–6 as "a comedy of subversion from the inside," which reading, he argues, "seriously undermines the notion that they were composed in order to stiffen Jewish resistance to persecution." "Apocalyptic as Comedy: The Book of Daniel," *Semeia* 32, no. 1 (1984): 41-70, 55-56. Yet this observation speaks to the stories as separate from the visions, and not to their present function within the book as a whole.

158. Heaton (*Book of Daniel*, p. 82) summarizes the ethic of the stories as follows: "The qualities which are most strongly stressed are those demanded by the crisis of persecution — unswerving loyalty to the Law (1.8; 3.18; 6.5), the duty of prayer and thanksgiving (2.18, 23; 6.9f.), and the courageous exercise of a complete trust in God (3.18, 28; 6.23)."

"Blessed is the one who waits (הַמְחַכֶּה) and reaches" the appointed number of days (12:12).[159] The book's final verse then dismisses Daniel, instructing him to go his way and rest, assuring him that at the end of days he will rise (or "stand," תַעֲמֹד) for his reward (12:13). I discuss below how Daniel's dismissal effectively creates a space for the book's audience to enter into the world of the visions and assume their own stance within the struggle. This intended audience lives in Daniel's future. His voice from the past and the written words he has recorded for them provide a framework for understanding the crisis that besets them and for knowing what action they must take. While Daniel must rest until the end, their task will be to persevere against Antiochus and to resist with all the resources Daniel's book has given them. Like Daniel in the lion's den and the three young men in the furnace, they wait for God to show forth God's power and justice.

In Daniel 2:34, the seer informs King Nebuchadnezzar that the statue of his dream will be destroyed by a stone hewn "by no hands" (דִּי־לָא בִידַיִן). Gabriel will later use a very similar phrase ("without a hand," בְּאֶפֶס יָד) to reveal to Daniel the means for shattering the horn of Antiochus (8:25). Both verses would indicate to the second-century audience that God, not human hands or power, would initiate and complete the action that would bring to an end the oppressive rule of Antiochus. The shattered pieces of the statue in Daniel 2 will be swept away by the wind (רוּחָא), like chaff from the threshing floor (2:35). The image is one of God's judgment (cf. Jer 51:33; Hos 13:3), executed by divine spirit, and not by human hands (contrast the Apocalypse of Weeks; see ch. 9). The people of God wait for this judgment and for God to establish them in the new kingdom God will give them (2:35, 44; 7:14, 18, 22, 27).[160]

This theme of waiting grounded in the expectation of God's justice found earlier expression in Isaiah and in the Psalms. Gordon Zerbe finds in Daniel 12:12 a possible allusion to "the Isaianic tradition of taking the stance of trust and waiting in view of God's exclusive prerogative for security and defense," anchored here by means of a verbal echo of Isaiah 30:18.[161] In this verse, Isaiah as-

159. John J. Collins translates "blessed are they who stand firm . . ." and finds in this verse a summary of "the message of the preceding visions." "Apocalyptic Eschatology as the Transcendence of Death," *CBQ* 36, no. 1 (1974): 21-43, 42.

160. See Choon-Leong Seow, "From Mountain to Mountain: The Reign of God in Daniel 2," in *A God So Near: Essays on Old Testament Theology in Honor of Patrick D. Miller,* ed. Brent A. Strawn and Nancy R. Bowen (Winona Lake, IN: Eisenbrauns, 2003), pp. 355-74.

161. Gordon Zerbe, "'Pacifism' and 'Passive Resistance' in Apocalyptic Writings: A Critical Evaluation," in *The Pseudepigrapha and Early Biblical Interpretation,* ed. J. H. Charlesworth and C. A. Evans (Sheffield: JSOT Press, 1993), pp. 65-95, 73-74. Does Daniel reject armed resistance? Zerbe is cautious: "It is clear that Daniel should be identified as a piece of resistance literature. But while it is probable that Daniel promotes passive resistance, it is merely possible that Daniel additionally rejects military action categorically and thus represents a pacifistic perspective" (p. 75).

serts God's justice. He then calls for the people to repent so that the Lord may respond to them with mercy (Isa 30:19). Isaiah promises: "Therefore the LORD waits to be gracious to you; therefore he will rise up to show mercy to you. For the LORD is a God of justice; blessed are all those who wait for him" (30:18 NRSV).[162] As noted above, these last words are echoed in the benediction of Daniel 12:12.

While Daniel 12:12 is commonly viewed as providing a revised timetable for the book in light of unfolding events,[163] its echo of Isaiah 30:18 may nonetheless shed light on traditions that shaped the theological outlook of the writers of Daniel and the ethic they envisioned during the persecution. Further thematic parallels between Isaiah 30 and the message of Daniel suggest that this may be the case. These include a common emphasis on written prophecy for future days (Isa 30:8), the idea of God as teacher (30:20) (comparable to that of God as the source of wisdom and knowledge in Daniel), the image of winnowing as a metaphor for God's judgment on the nations (30:28), and an emphasis on Torah observance (30:21) and rejection of apostasy (30:22). Moreover, in these verses Isaiah counsels the people of Jerusalem that their strength (גְּבוּרָה; see the discussion of this term above) lies not in horses (i.e., in the apparatus of war) but in repentance and rest (30:15; on rest, cf. Dan 12:13). Should they choose to rely on the steeds of war to deliver them in safe flight from their persecutors, they will only discover that the enemy rides more swiftly than they (30:16). Rather than flee, they must remain. They will find salvation in quiet and in trust (30:15). God will effect judgment on the nations and deliverance for the chosen people (30:27-33). By recalling the words of the prophet Isaiah, the writers/editors of Daniel would recapitulate at the book's conclusion the message of faithful waiting for God's decisive action already emphasized throughout the work.

But in Isaiah and in Daniel the stance of waiting on God is not passive.[164]

---

162. Elsewhere Isaiah asserts, "I will wait (וְחִכִּיתִי) for the Lord . . . and I will wait/hope in (וְקִוֵּיתִי)" the Lord (8:17).

163. See Collins, Daniel: A Commentary on the Book of Daniel, pp. 400-401. Against this view, see Boccaccini, Roots of Rabbinic Judaism, p. 200.

164. The book of Daniel's emphasis on divine initiative and action has led many to call the book's stance passive or quietistic. Yet designating Daniel as "quietistic" misapplies the term. Strictu sensu, quietism refers to the seventeenth-century mystical doctrines of Miguel de Molinos, while broadly speaking "Quietism is any form of mystical piety that stresses interior passivity to the neglect of exterior practice." Bernard McGinn, The Essential Writings of Christian Mysticism (New York: Random House, 2006), p. 502. De Molinos advocated mystical annihilation of the self through meditation, and consequent absorption into the divine. The strict quietist retreats from the world and strives to achieve a passive rather than active state, though some later adaptations of quietism take a more active approach to the contemplative life. See further McGinn, Essential Writings of Christian Mysticism, pp. 144-48, 501-8. The book of Daniel

Daniel

In a much later passage, the writer of Isaiah offers a prayer of penitence, asking God to "rend the heavens and come down" to work miracles for the people and to vindicate the sanctuary (Isa 63:15–64:12). In this context the prophet asserts, "No eye has seen any God besides you, who works for those who wait for him" (64:4 NRSV). Again, the prophet emphasizes the importance of waiting for God's salvation. But the verse that follows clarifies that waiting for God also involves *doing*. In referring to God's saving actions, the prophet proclaims: "You meet those who gladly do right, who remember you in your ways" (64:5 NRSV). For Daniel waiting is also active. In waiting the faithful are called to stay the course, to remain firm in Torah observance and the praxis of resistance outlined for them elsewhere in the book until God intervenes to set things right once for all.[165] Even the expectation of resurrection to new life presupposes a commitment to right action in the old life.[166] By making many righteous and so thwarting the edict of Antiochus, they prepare a people for God's judgment. It is with this active stance that they wait for the divine judge to mete out reward and punishment to the righteous and the wicked.[167]

Reading and Writing Scripture: Creative Reinterpretation and New Revelation

I stated in the introduction to Part Three that even as Antiochus's soldiers gathered and burned scrolls of Israel's scriptures, there were Judeans who kept reading and writing. As will by now be obvious, the writers of Daniel were among them. Reading and writing alike were part of their program of resistance to the empire. The book's visionary ethic is informed by Israel's sacred scriptural tra-

---

neither sets forth mystical doctrine, nor, as this chapter shows, exemplifies or advocates a passive retreat from the world. The book's interest in reward and punishment after death is also contrary to quietistic teaching.

165. Heaton summarizes the message of the book as follows: "The true Israelite was called upon, not to fight back, but to endure with unflinching loyalty. The power was of God and not of himself" (*Book of Daniel*, p. 19).

166. Collins discusses this function of the promise of resurrection for shaping the praxis of the faithful. Eschatological hope and present experience are interdependent. Regarding future expectation in Daniel, Wisdom of Solomon, and 1 Enoch, he summarizes, "The objective is that people should live justly . . ." ("Apocalyptic Eschatology," pp. 76-77).

167. The psalmic tradition of waiting for the Lord may also lie behind the exhortation and blessing in Dan 12:12. See especially Pss 25, 27, 37, 40, etc.; see also Pss 37, 34, 69, on waiting and trust instead of wrath in response to abuse, and Ps 46 (be still, do not trust in weapons, but Yhwh's exclusive prerogative for deliverance and vengeance). See also Gordon M. Zerbe, *Non-Retaliation in Early Jewish and New Testament Texts: Ethical Themes in Social Contexts* (Sheffield: JSOT Press, 1993), p. 30n37.

265

ditions at every turn, even as new revelations reinterpret scriptures, history, and present reality in a radically new light.[168] At various points in this chapter I have considered the way particular echoes of scripture function in the book of Daniel, giving special attention to themes of trust and waiting for God's salvation. Here I examine in greater detail the writers' creative interpretations of Jeremiah's seventy-year prophecy (Jeremiah 25 and 29) and Isaiah's Servant Song (Isa 52:13–53:12). These interpretations shaped their vision of history and self-understanding and played a key role in framing their program of resistance to Antiochus.

Judith Newman has documented the "scripturalization" of prayer in Second Temple Judaism.[169] The phenomenon Newman describes — "the reuse of biblical texts or interpretive traditions to shape the composition of new literature"[170] — relies on a development within early Judaism whereby written word becomes authoritative scripture. Yet authoritative word was not thereby fixed. It was authoritative because it spoke to the communities that read it, and it could speak to them because it spoke fresh in each new age. The writers of early Jewish apocalypses typically used scripture differently from the prayers Newman analyzes. Yet fundamental to their project was the interpretation and writing of scripture as scripture — written authoritative text.[171] Interpreting and writing scripture were not separate endeavors, but knit together.

I have already mentioned Daniel's references to the Torah of Moses (9:13), "the scrolls" (9:2), and "the word of the Lord to Jeremiah the prophet" (9:2). Elsewhere, however, the writers of Daniel refrain from directly naming the scriptures they read, and instead use and interpret scripture in ways that are "allusive and indirect."[172] This richly evocative style is hardly unique to Daniel — it is rather a hallmark of apocalyptic discourse, matched by a similar use of symbols and language.[173] The use of symbol within the visions and the multivalent, even cryptic language of the angelic revelations draw readers into an imaginative world where they must actively participate in seeking and constructing meaning even as they receive interpretation from and with the leg-

168. For Davies the frequent allusions to scripture in Daniel indicate the writer's profound familiarity with its texts, such that "whole phrases and ideas come as readily to mind as the writer's own words" (*Daniel*, p. 71). In Heaton's view these scriptural texts provide a "framework or pattern of belief in terms of which new experience and new situations could be judged" (*Book of Daniel*, p. 81).

169. Judith H. Newman, *Praying by the Book: The Scripturalization of Prayer in Second Temple Judaism* (Atlanta: Scholars Press, 1999).

170. Newman, *Praying by the Book*, pp. 12-13.

171. Rowland, "Apocalyptic Literature," pp. 170-89, 170-71, 183.

172. Rowland, "Apocalyptic Literature," p. 170.

173. John J. Collins, *The Apocalyptic Imagination: An Introduction to Jewish Apocalyptic Literature*, 2nd ed. (Grand Rapids: Eerdmans, 1998), pp. 17-19.

endary seer and sage, Daniel. In the same way, echoes of scripture in Daniel draw the reader into a complex interface with multiple texts,[174] inviting them to search the scriptures and find understanding even as they receive a new frame for their interpretation.[175] While earlier scriptures are hardly the sole authority or source for the writers of Daniel,[176] they are nonetheless an essential matrix and shaping influence, a resource for resistance, and a site of engagement that awakens the book's audience to their history and identity in order to show them the path they are called to follow in the present moment and in the future.

Studying the Scrolls: Seventy Weeks of Years

In the story world of Daniel, after the last Babylonian king has died, "Darius the Mede received the kingdom" (6:1). Repeated references to the "law of Media and Persia" (6:9, 13, 16) associate Darius's rule with the Persian empire, while the reference to Daniel's prospering "during the rule of Darius the Mede and during the rule of Cyrus the Persian" would help readers remember that it was during the reign of the Persian king Cyrus, who conquered Babylon in 539 BCE, that Judeans were permitted to return from exile in Babylonia to their native land. For many Judeans, this return marked exile's end.

As I noted above, the prophet Jeremiah had long before delivered an oracle to the people of Judah concerning the exile. Because they had not listened to the prophets of Yhwh (Jer 25:4), but served and worshiped other gods (25:6-7), the Lord would bring Nebuchadnezzar to devastate the land (25:9-11). The people of Judah would "serve the king of Babylon seventy years" (25:11 NRSV), at the end of which God would punish him by bringing another nation against Babylonia (25:12). Babylon came as Jeremiah foretold, and devastated the land of Judah. Between the years 597 and 587, many Judeans went into captivity in Babylon. Jeremiah would later write to the exiles concerning their time there. Although I quoted a portion of this passage above, it bears repeating here:

> For thus says the LORD: Only when Babylon's seventy years are completed will I visit you, and I will fulfill to you my promise and bring you back to this place. For surely I know the plans I have for you, says the LORD, plans for your welfare and not for harm, to give you a future with hope. Then when you call upon me and come and pray to me, I will hear you. When you search for me,

174. Heaton, *Book of Daniel*, p. 81.

175. Rowland accordingly prescribes for modern interpreters a "subtle approach, allowing full weight to the often allusive character of reference to Scripture and the complexity of the relationship" ("Apocalyptic Literature," p. 170).

176. Collins, *Apocalyptic Vision*, p. 81.

you will find me; if you seek me with all your heart, I will let you find me, says the LORD, and I will restore your fortunes and gather you from all the nations and all the places where I have driven you, says the LORD, and I will bring you back to the place from which I sent you into exile. (Jer 29:10-14 NRSV)

According to the oracle in this letter, at the end of seventy years God would fulfill the promise to bring them back to their native land. God invited them to call upon and seek God; at that time God would restore their fortunes. If one reads Jeremiah 25 and 29 together, one expects that the restoration would occur in the same year as the fall of Babylon, for both are promised at the end of seventy years.[177]

In the story world of Daniel, that year is the first year of King Darius's rule. At the beginning of chapter 9, Daniel gives the date twice so we do not miss its significance (9:1-2). We would therefore expect, and apparently Daniel would expect, that since Babylon has fallen, the hour of restoration and the end of exile is at hand. But Daniel has seen two visions in which empire succeeds empire, with Greek kings still to follow after the kings of Media and Persia (8:20-21). His own people will continue to suffer (7:25, 8:24), and will not receive their kingdom (7:27) until the fourth beast has been judged (7:26) and a king of Greece is shattered without the touch of a hand (8:25). What does this mean? How can he reconcile Jeremiah's words with the visions he has seen? And what is to happen now, in year one of Darius's rule? As I noted above, "to understand the number of years, according to the Lord's word to Jeremiah the prophet, that would fill up Jerusalem's sentence of desolation — it was seventy years" — Daniel studies "in the scrolls" (9:2).

Jeremiah's prophecy occupied other biblical writers as well. Writing in Yehud after the return, Zechariah and the Chronicler both refer to the seventy years, although only the Chronicler mentions Jeremiah by name. While these books would not have been known to Daniel, they may well have been known to the writers of Daniel.[178] The revelation Daniel receives concerning the seventy years draws on earlier traditions but also breaks with them in dramatic fashion.[179]

177. I do not go into calculations here. The duration of an exile that begins in 597 or 587 BCE and ends in 539 BCE is shorter than seventy years. The number seventy is symbolic and possibly conventional. See, e.g., Avalos, "Daniel 9:24-25 and Mesopotamian Temple Rededications," p. 507.

178. Collins, *Daniel: A Commentary on the Book of Daniel*, p. 349.

179. Collins, *Daniel: A Commentary on the Book of Daniel*, p. 349. Mason, however, sees the writer of Daniel combining Jeremiah's prophecy regarding the exile and "the Chronicler's theological interpretation of its purpose and significance" (i.e., that exile was a purifying process in accordance with the law and prophets) and applying these to his or her own time. Biblical predictions regarding deliverance from exile in Ezekiel and Isaiah similarly inform the writer's understanding of imminent deliverance from the persecution ("Treatment of Earlier Biblical Themes," p. 93).

In "the second year of Darius" (Zech 1:7) the prophet Zechariah hears an angel ask, "O LORD of hosts, how long will you be without mercy for Jerusalem and the cities of Judah that have felt your anger these seventy years?" (Zech 1:12 NAB).[180] The angel receives an answer, and announces it to Zechariah (1:13-17): the time of mercy is now (1:16). The temple will be rebuilt in Jerusalem, the glory of the Lord will dwell within the holy city (2:9), and God will punish the nations whose horns have "tossed Judah, Israel, and Jerusalem" (2:2-4, 11-13). Zechariah proclaims an end to the seventy years of Judah's domination and desolation.

The Chronicler similarly declared the end of the seventy years. Moreover, by reading Jeremiah in concert with the book of Leviticus, the Chronicler could interpret the period of captivity not simply as punishment but as a sabbath for the land.[181] Toward the conclusion of the book of Leviticus, the Lord proclaims through Moses both blessings for those who would follow God's laws and observe the commandments (26:3) and curses for those who do not obey but reject God's law and break the covenant (26:14-15). The curses include exile and devastation/desolation:[182]

> So devastated (וַהֲשִׁמֹּתִי) will I leave the land that your very enemies who come to live there will stand aghast (וְשָׁמְמוּ) at the sight of it. You yourselves I will scatter among the nations at the point of my drawn sword, leaving your countryside desolate (שְׁמָמָה) and your cities deserted. Then shall the land retrieve its lost sabbaths during all the time it lies waste (הָשַׁמָּה), while you are in the land of your enemies; then shall the land have rest and make up for its sabbaths during all the time that it lies desolate (הָשַׁמָּה), enjoying the rest that you would not let it have on the sabbaths when you lived there. (Lev 26:32-35 NRSV)

Elsewhere in Leviticus sabbath is prescribed as a way for people and land to participate in the holiness of God, ordering time, space, and human life according to the patterns of creation and God's will. The work week culminated in a day of rest that mirrored God's rest following the work of creation. In the same way, six years of working the land would be followed by a year of rest, or sabbath year (25:2-7). But the people had not always kept the sabbaths. The book of Leviticus envisioned future exile as a time of rest that would return to the land the sabbaths its inhabitants had failed to observe. In this way Leviticus brings even the calamities of history into the plan of God and rhythm of creation. The Chronicler followed suit, interpreting the Babylonian exile as sabbath: "All this

---

180. Zechariah 7:5 also refers to the seventy years.

181. Fishbane, *Biblical Interpretation*, p. 481.

182. I have indicated each place where the root שׁמם occurs, for in Daniel this root provides an important link between the angel's interpretation of the seventy years and the actions of Antiochus, "the desolator" (שֹׁמֵם, 9:27).

was to fulfill the word of the LORD spoken by Jeremiah: 'Until the land has retrieved its lost sabbaths, during all the time it lies waste it shall have rest while seventy years are fulfilled'" (2 Chron 36:21 NAB).

Leviticus 26 ends with the promise of return from captivity, for God will not reject the people wholesale but will remember the covenant (Lev 26:44-45). For the Chronicler, this promise, and the prophecy of Jeremiah, had been fulfilled. The seventy years ended during the reign of the Persian king Cyrus the Great, whose decree permitted the Judeans in captivity to return to Yehud and rebuild the temple of Yhwh (2 Chron 36:22-23). The land had recovered its sabbaths, the exile had ended, and the people had been saved; they were no longer being punished for sins of the past.

The writers of Daniel live long after these events were to have taken place. But the revelation they entrust to their readers makes a sobering claim: in the second century, even though the people had returned to the land and the temple had been rebuilt, yet the exile had not ended, salvation had not been achieved, and Israel was still suffering.[183] Jeremiah's seventy years were in fact seventy weeks of years, or 490 years (Dan 9:24-27). But the hour of salvation and the end of "exile," captivity, and suffering were at hand.[184] Michael Knibb summarizes the position of Daniel 9:24-27 this way: "The exile was now, and only now, to have its proper end, and in the author's view everything that had happened between the carrying away into captivity of the Jewish people and the time of Antiochus was of little importance. Rather, this period is seen as a unity whose characteristic is sin. We are in a situation where the exile is understood as a state that is to be ended only by the intervention of God and the inauguration of the eschatological era."[185] In view of centuries of foreign domination that culminated in Antiochus's edict and program of terror, the writers of Daniel could assert that the people who lived now in Judea lived in captivity. They were slaves to another Babylon, another idolatrous empire that had confused itself with God. Their holy city was again devastated, and even within Judea they were cut off from land and temple. But captivity did not render them helpless or passive. By recognizing their present situation as continuing exile they could better understand the present danger of apostasy and the threat it posed to their identity as people of God, and know how to respond.

183. Newsom notes that this new interpretation of Jeremiah's prophecy "is articulated in an allusive or even coded form (Dan 9:24-27), suggesting that truth has yet further reserves of mystery" (*Self as Symbolic Space*, p. 50). Klaus Koch finds behind this revelation a view of history that divided world-time into seven epochs. "Die mysteriösen Zahlen der judäischen Könige und die apokalyptischen Jahrwochen," *VT* 28, no. 1 (1978): 433-41.

184. Mason, "Treatment of Earlier Biblical Themes," p. 96.

185. Michael Knibb, "The Exile in the Literature of the Intertestamental Period," *HeyJ* 17, no. 3 (1976): 253-72, 255.

We saw above that the Chronicler interpreted Jeremiah's prophecy in concert with Leviticus. As Michael Fishbane has shown, so did the writers of Daniel.[186] Daniel found in Leviticus not only a connection between exile and sabbath, but also the multiplication of seven times seven that would yield a type of jubilee. In Leviticus, the punishment for disobedience did not begin with exile and desolation. First would come disease and conquest (Lev 26:16-17). If these did not elicit obedience, God would discipline "sevenfold" (שֶׁבַע, 26:18). If the people continued to disobey, God would "continue to" or "again" (יָסַפְתִּי) strike "sevenfold" (26:21). After continued disobedience, God would strike sevenfold again (26:24) and again (26:28), finally bringing about the promised exile and desolation. Here in Leviticus the multiplier seven refers not to years, but to severity. Yet the association between this final, sevenfold punishment and sabbaths for the land may have suggested to the writers of Daniel a further connection with the jubilee year described in Leviticus 25. There Moses announces to the people the sacred order of years in the land they will inhabit, and prescribes the way that extended cycles of time will structure their life in community. After seven sabbatical cycles, or seven weeks of years (seven times seven years), on the Day of Atonement, the Israelites will sanctify the jubilee year. The jubilee would be a holy year of release, redemption from servitude, and forgiveness of debt, when land would be returned (25:8-55). Israel's jubilee traditions thus ordered not only time but space: land belongs to God, and the people hold it in tenure; it is holy and is to be used for purposes ordained by God for the welfare of God's people.[187] The jubilee also signaled the ordering of the people's social and economic life according to principles of justice.[188] By declaring that the period decreed for desolation would be seventy weeks of years, the writers of Daniel not only made sense of the long history of foreign domination, they also countered Antiochus's interventions into the ordering of time, space, and human life for the people of Judea.

Gabriel's timetable emphasized the sabbatical and thus the created structure of historical time. He announced a grand-jubilee,[189] which brought even the horrifying events of 167 BCE into a familiar pattern of liberation that was linked to Israel's history of captivity and salvation. Ordering time, space, and

186. Fishbane, *Biblical Interpretation*, pp. 487-89.

187. Jeffrey A. Fager, *Land Tenure and the Biblical Jubilee: Uncovering Hebrew Ethics through the Sociology of Knowledge* (Sheffield: Sheffield Academic Press, 1993), pp. 116-18; John Sietze Bergsma, *The Jubilee from Leviticus to Qumran: A History of Interpretation* (Leiden: Brill, 2007), 63-65.

188. Fager, *Land Tenure and the Biblical Jubilee*, pp. 78, 108-11, 115-18.

189. See Bergsma, *Jubilee from Leviticus to Qumran*, p. 225. Bergsma (*Jubilee from Leviticus to Qumran*, pp. 225-27) counters the objections of Goldingay (*Daniel*, p. 267) that the writers do not explicitly refer to jubilees.

human life according to the jubilee also asserted an ordering of power. God, not Antiochus, is the "owner" of people and land and the one who has established the order of creation and life in it. God has similarly ordained a time of foreign rule. For the audience of Daniel that time would soon come to an end, and Antiochus would be left with no power at all.

In the book of Leviticus, the jubilee was closely associated with the Day of Atonement. The two remain connected in Daniel.[190] As we saw above, Gabriel proclaims that the seventy weeks have been decreed in part "to atone for sins" and "to bring in everlasting righteousness" (Dan 9:24). As I noted earlier, his words look forward to the actions of the *maśkîlîm* who "lead many to righteousness" and whose deaths may participate in the work of atonement. John Bergsma argues that the jubilee gave the Day of Atonement "socio-economic expression" in the life of the people.[191] Reconciliation between God and the people corresponded to a regular return to just order in the land. This link between atonement and the jubilary commitment to justice and the ordering of life in community according to the holiness and will of God suggests that the writers of Daniel believed the teaching, suffering, and martyrdom of the *maśkîlîm* would contribute to the transformation and restoration of a just and holy order of life in Judea.

Suffering Servants

This understanding of the role of the *maśkîlîm* was shaped by their identification with the Suffering Servant of Isaiah 52:13–53:12. In 1953, both William Brownlee and H. L. Ginsberg published articles demonstrating that the book of Daniel's portrait of the *maśkîlîm* depends on Isaiah 52:13–53:12 and identifies the wise teachers of the writers' time with the Suffering Servant.[192] This view has received broad acceptance among scholars.[193] The table on page 273 illustrates the primary verbal links and points for comparison.

190. Fishbane concludes that "the inherent contradiction between the fact that Jeremiah's oracle had a clearly determined end, and the fact that the termination of the cycle of sabbaticals of wrath in Lev. 26 was conditional upon human confession and divine grace, was resolved in the process: Daniel's confession led to a revelation of the timetable of divine historical activity, consoling the repentant one by declaring that the culmination of doom and the onset of restoration were equally nigh" (*Biblical Interpretation*, p. 489).

191. Bergsma, *Jubilee from Leviticus to Qumran*, pp. 91-92, 227.

192. W. H. Brownlee, "The Servant of the Lord in the Qumran Scrolls I," *BASOR* 132 (1953): 8-15; and Ginsberg, "The Oldest Interpretation of the Suffering Servant," pp. 400-404.

193. E.g., George W. E. Nickelsburg, *Resurrection, Immortality, and Eternal Life in Intertestamental Judaism and Early Christianity*, exp. ed. (Cambridge: Harvard University Press, 2006), pp. 38-41, 91-108; Mason, "Treatment of Earlier Biblical Themes," pp. 94-96; Collins, *Daniel: A Commentary on the Book of Daniel*, pp. 385, 393; Hartman and Di Lella, *Book of Daniel*, p. 300.

Isaiah 52:13–53:12	Daniel
יַשְׂכִּיל 52:13, meaning "he will prosper"; translated in LXX "he will understand" (συνήσει).	Forms of the verb שׂכל *(hiphil)* occur at 1:4, 17; 7:8 (Aramaic); 9:13, 22, 25; 11:33, 35; 12:3, 10, always with reference to wisdom, understanding, or teaching. The last four occurrences refer to the "wise teachers."
The song foregrounds the servant's relationship to "(the) many" (רַבִּים 52:14, 15; 53:11, 12; see further below).	Repeated references to "(the) many" in Daniel 11 and 12 clarify the mission of the *maśkîlîm* (11:33; 12:3; cf. 11:34, 12:10; see further below).
"By his knowledge (בְּדַעְתּוֹ) my righteous servant will make the many righteous" (יַצְדִּיק צַדִּיק עַבְדִּי לָרַבִּים 53:11).	The *maśkîlîm* "make the many righteous" (מַצְדִּיקֵי הָרַבִּים 12:3).
"Many nations (גּוֹיִם רַבִּים) . . . will contemplate (הִתְבּוֹנָנוּ)" what is revealed through the servant (52:15).	The *maśkîlîm* "will give the many understanding" (וּמַשְׂכִּילֵי עָם יָבִינוּ לָרַבִּים 11:33).
Reconciling/atoning function: In parallel with the statement that the servant "will make the many righteous," the prophet declares that the servant "will bear their guilt" (עֲוֹנֹתָם הוּא יִסְבֹּל 53:11). He will also "take away the sin of many, and intercede for the sinners" (וְהוּא חֵטְא־רַבִּים נָשָׂא וְלַפֹּשְׁעִים יַפְגִּיעַ 53:12). He bears the people's suffering (53:4) and guilt (53:6), making himself a sacrifice (53:10) that effects reconciliation: "on him was the punishment that made us whole" (53:5).	Possible atoning function: "Making many righteous" in Daniel 11:33 echoes Gabriel's reference to bringing righteousness at the conclusion of seventy weeks, at the time of the end of transgression (הַפֶּשַׁע) and sin (חַטָּאת *Qere*) and atonement for guilt (עָוֹן 9:24). References to purification and cleansing in 11:35 and 12:10 strengthen this connection. Daniel's self-humbling (וּלְהִתְעַנּוֹת 10:12) recalls the command to the Israelites to humble themselves (וְעִנִּיתֶם) on the Day of Atonement, which would take place on the seventh day of the tenth month (Lev 23:27), and may model preparation for atonement for the *maśkîlîm*.

Both Ginsberg and Brownlee have also noted connections between the servant's exaltation and reward after death and the glorious future promised to the *maśkîlîm*.[194] Isaiah proclaims, "See, my servant will prosper (יַשְׂכִּיל), he will be raised and lifted up, and he will be very high" (52:13). After describing his death ("cut off from the land of the living," 53:8; "with the wicked his grave," 53:9), the prophet explains that if the servant "gives his life as an offering for sin, he shall see his descendants in a long life" (53:10 NAB). The *maśkîlîm* would also be raised up from dusty earth (cf. Isa 53:2, "dry ground," NRSV), not simply to long life but to eternal life (Dan 12:2). While the angel's promise that they will shine like the stars in the firmament (12:3) — the highest place imaginable — is cast as a simile, George W. E. Nickelsburg notes that in view of the connection between Daniel and the servant poem the promise may reflect an interpretation of Isaiah 52:13 that envisions "literal exaltation to heaven."[195]

Brownlee suggests a further connection between the servant poem and Daniel 8:24-25. Gabriel reveals that a king (*sc.* Antiochus IV) "will destroy (וְהִשְׁחִית) the mighty (עֲצוּמִים) and a people of holy ones" (8:24); he will "destroy many in a time of rest" (יַשְׁחִית רַבִּים 8:25). Brownlee sees here a connection to Isaiah 53:12, where "the mighty" and "the many" also appear in parallel. Among them the Servant will receive his portion and reward (cf. Dan 12:2).[196]

Having identified the multiple connections between the portraits of the *maśkîlîm* and "the many" in Daniel and Isaiah's servant poem, it remains to specify how these identifications shaped Daniel's vision of resistance to Antiochus IV. The writers of Daniel found in Isaiah's Servant a model for non-violent (לֹא־חָמָס עָשָׂה 53:9) transformational revelatory praxis. Like the Servant's witness, the teaching of the *maśkîlîm* would have far-reaching political implications. For the writers of Daniel the poem underscored the instrumentality of knowledge and gave meaning to innocent suffering and death, promising that through self-sacrifice the will of the Lord would prosper (cf. Isa 53:10).

We saw above that the *maśkîlîm* would lead many to righteousness in part by their verbal and written instruction. By interpreting Isaiah's declaration, "my servant יַשְׂכִּיל" (52:13), as referring to instruction, the writers of Daniel replaced the expectation of earthly reward ("he will prosper") with visionary and missionary praxis. Daniel and his friends had received rich rewards from the foreign kings they served, prospering greatly (Dan 2:49; 3:30; 5:29; 6:4, 28). Antiochus also doled out rewards of spoil to those who served and endorsed him, but at a price (11:24, 39). According to the writers of Daniel, for Judeans

194. See also Bentzen, *Daniel*, p. 52; Fishbane, *Biblical Interpretation*, p. 493.

195. Nickelsburg, *Resurrection, Immortality, and Eternal Life*, p. 41.

196. A typographic error identifies the verse as 43:12 (Brownlee, "Servant of the Lord," p. 13). Brownlee also discerns a link between Antiochus's destructive activity (וְהִשְׁחִית) and the Servant's "disfigurement" (מִשְׁחַת 52:14).

that price was too high. They therefore transmuted "prosperity" into wisdom. Even when they have received their true reward after death the *maśkîlîm* "will shine" (יַזְהִרוּ 12:3), giving light by which others might see (the verb can also mean "teach"; cf. Ex 18:20).[197]

In emphasizing knowledge, sight, and revelation the writers of Daniel in fact followed Isaiah's servant poem closely. The poem emphasizes the disjunction between misperception and true reality: judgments based solely on appearances fail to grasp God's purpose and therefore assign value incorrectly (Isa 53:2). "The many" were appalled/desolated by the Servant's appearance (52:14);[198] the speakers of the poem rightly reckoned him afflicted by God but failed to perceive the reason God had done so (53:4-5, 10); they despised him and "held him of no account" (53:3 NRSV). Although the Servant is "silent" in the face of persecution — he does not protest his own condemnation and death (53:7) — he also reveals realities previously unseen and unheard (52:15; cf. 53:1), with profound political consequences. His revelation impacts many nations and causes kings to shut their mouths (52:15). In and through his suffering the Servant also receives revelation: "out of/from the affliction of his person he will see" (53:11).[199] His knowledge is instrumental (בְּדַעְתּוֹ 53:11; cf. 53:3: וִידוּעַ חֹלִי "knowing sickness"), whether for his own fulfillment or for making the many righteous (53:11).[200]

The revelations of the book of Daniel would likewise correct failures of perception. To those who judged solely on appearances they would reveal a deeper, invisible reality. In its light the values of the empire would be turned upside down. Before the truth of Daniel's revelations Antiochus the deceiver (Dan 8:25) would have nothing meaningful to say. As in Isaiah, so in Daniel, the revelation of God's power (cf. Isa 53:1) and will to save could transform knowledge of human weakness into a source of strength (cf. 53:3, 11).

In Isaiah's servant poem, the suffering of the righteous servant brings about wholeness, welfare, peace, and healing for others (53:5), making reparation for their sins. Is this also true for the *maśkîlîm?* Nowhere do the writers of Daniel make this atoning function explicit.[201] For this reason, despite the many connec-

---

197. Cf. Nickelsburg, *Resurrection, Immortality, and Eternal Life,* p. 41n85.

198. The servant's appearance "beyond human form" may have taken on additional meaning for the writers of Daniel, who speculated that the wise teachers would "shine like the stars," i.e., the angels (cf. Dan 10:5-6), and who in some way associated the holy ones with the one "like a human being" (7:13-14, 18, 27).

199. OG, 1Q Isᵃ, and 1Q Isᵇ have the direct object "light."

200. The interpretation depends on whether one reads the term בְּדַעְתּוֹ with the preceding verb or the one that follows it.

201. Martin Hengel with Daniel P. Bailey, "The Effective History of Isaiah 53 in the Pre-Christian Period," in *The Suffering Servant: Isaiah 53 in Jewish and Christian Sources,* ed. Bernd Janowski and Peter Stuhlmacher (Grand Rapids: Eerdmans, 2004), pp. 75-146, 92.

tions to Isaiah's servant poem, Davies finds it "improbable" that the *maśkîlîm* make the many righteous by means of their suffering and death. They do so rather by their teaching.[202] Yet the book's revelatory discourse is thick with allusions and echoes that suggest a more complicated picture. The writers of Daniel do not proclaim that the suffering and death of the *maśkîlîm* will atone, but through a dense web of allusions they suggest it is possible. Perhaps the writers were themselves uncertain, or unwilling to make explicit a teaching that had not fully been revealed to them. Contrary to the assertion of Davies, however, suffering and death in the face of persecution were nonetheless part of the efficacious teaching of the *maśkîlîm*. They would suffer because they refused to comply with the edict of Antiochus, and refused to abandon the practices and confession of their ancestral faith. They would die because their witness was public, and their refusal plainly known. They were willing to die because they believed in God's faithfulness. Their suffering and death thus testified to their confession and choice, giving an example to many that was also a proof of faith.

Commissioning the Reader

While the teaching of the *maśkîlîm* is conveyed in part through their suffering and death, it is also conveyed through the book of Daniel itself. Thus, once circulated, the book itself performs this teaching function on behalf of its writer(s). In this way, as Davies puts it, "Daniel is not *about* understanding and 'making righteous'; it performs that function itself."[203] Reader response criticism informs Davies' analysis of the way the book draws the audience in, equips them for the task of resistance, and finally commissions them to act. Beginning with stories in the third person, the writer first lets the reader observe Daniel and his friends from a distance, admiring them and learning from their example. In the first visions, the audience is drawn in closer to identify with Daniel, hearing the book's message for them as well as for Daniel. In the latter visions, as Daniel recedes and finally disappears (the visions are for a later time, he is to "go his way"), the audience remains alone with the text that has been written down and preserved especially for them. The angel's words now speak to them alone, and they are fully absorbed in Daniel's project.[204] This narrative technique accomplishes the goal of the book, which is to impart wisdom and make many righteous, and ensures that this work will continue.[205]

202. Davies, *Daniel*, pp. 110-11. See also Collins, *Daniel: A Commentary on the Book of Daniel*, p. 386 (quoted above).

203. Davies, *Daniel*, p. 118.

204. Davies, *Daniel*, p. 125.

205. Davies, *Daniel*, p. 126.

Redditt adopts this reading from Davies, noting that Daniel's failure to comprehend the visions in 7–12 sets up the transition whereby Daniel himself fades and leaves the audience to receive revelation and commission directly from the angel. The goal of the book, he argues, is to ensure that they understand where Daniel does not. "At that point, the readers, the community of the wise, are equipped to assume Daniel's role and lead the Jewish community in the last days."[206] This reading helps to explain what Edwin Good has seen as a "narrative flaw in Daniel's reception of the truth about the second century during the sixth." He describes the revelation of the last chapters as "purely verbal event, told to but not participated in by the receptor."[207] Yet by this point in the work, the receptor is now no longer Daniel alone but also the future audience or reader. While Daniel is told to seal the book and go to his rest, the reader receives the commission to trust, teach, and make righteous.

Conclusion

The book of Daniel is resistance literature. Antiochus IV asserted power in Judea by his edict, his army, and his program of terror and de-creation. The writers of Daniel resisted with language and symbol, limiting and even negating the power of Antiochus by writing, proclaiming, and teaching an alternative vision of reality. Weaving together story, vision, liturgical prayer, and revelatory discourse, they crafted a composite work of powerfully resistant counterdiscourse to Seleucid hegemony. They also presented their readers with a program of active nonviolent resistance.

The writers of Daniel belonged to a group of "wise teachers," or *maśkîlîm*, who formed a primary audience for the book. While the *maśkîlîm* apparently belonged to Jerusalem's scribal elite, they had a mission to "the many" (i.e., the people of Judea, who formed a secondary audience for the book); the writers aimed at their conversion to wisdom and righteousness. They may also have aimed to persuade other members of Jerusalem's scribal elite to forsake collaboration with the Seleucid regime.

Resistance to Antiochus IV's edict and persecution would entail covenant faithfulness in the face of death. Faithfulness would require strength. For the writers of Daniel, strength came from knowledge; both came from God. Just as an angel gave Daniel understanding and strength to stand, so would the book give understanding and strength to its readers to stand firm against the edict of Antiochus, persist in the practices of Torah, and teach and strengthen others in turn.

206. Redditt, "Daniel 11," p. 474.
207. Good, "Apocalyptic as Comedy," p. 62.

Daniel and his friends modeled resistance and faithful praxis for the book's audience. They were to give their hearts to practices of penitence and prayer, humbling themselves before God, just as Daniel had done. Liturgical prayer constituted the book's audience as a community sharing common commitments, language, and attitudes as well as a common history and future as God's people. New revelation gave new meaning to history and future alike.

An angel's prediction revealed that in the time of persecution not only would the wise teachers of the people make many wise, they would lead many to righteousness. They would also fall by sword, flame, and captivity. The writers may have believed that by their sacrificial deaths they would participate in effecting atonement for their people. They viewed the suffering and death of the *maśkîlîm* as efficacious, leading to purification and also offering to others a visible proof of faith.

In an earlier age, Daniel, Shadrak, Meshak, and Abednego surrendered their own bodies to death rather than forsake the practices of their faith or worship another god. Their stories provided the readers of Daniel with models of fidelity rooted in trust and outspoken, nonviolent resistance to royal coercive power.

The visions of Daniel revealed God's timetable and plan for deliverance. Divine, not human, initiative would bring about the end of empire. The book of Daniel urged its readers to wait on God's deliverance even as they persisted in nonviolent resistance to the edict and persecution of Antiochus IV.

Reading, interpreting, and writing scripture played a key role in the book of Daniel's program of nonviolent resistance. Interpretations of Jeremiah's seventy-year prophecy and the servant poem of Isaiah 52:13–53:12 shaped their vision of history and future as well as their self-understanding. New revelation reinterpreted Jeremiah's prophecy to refer to seventy weeks of years, placing even the actions of Antiochus IV within a sabbatical framework that revealed God's plan for history. Connections to sabbath and jubilee countered Antiochus's program of de-creation by reasserting God's ordering of time, space, and human life as well as an order of power. The conjoining of motifs of jubilee and atonement suggests that the present work of the *maśkîlîm* would contribute to establishing a just and holy order of life in Judea at the end of the era of domination. The writers of Daniel identified the *maśkîlîm* with the Servant in Isaiah 52:13–53:12, and found in the Servant a model for nonviolent transformational revelatory praxis. The poem gave meaning to their suffering and underscored the efficacy of knowledge and revelation.

At the book's conclusion, Daniel himself recedes and the reader must take up the work of resistance the writers have envisioned. The book offers hope, critique, vision, and strength, commissioning its readers to teach, pray, and make righteous, to study and to speak, to humble themselves and surrender to death, and always to remain faithful to the covenant, trusting in God's salvation.

The writers of Daniel were not the only seers to envision and proclaim a program of resistance to the edict and persecution through apocalyptic writings. Others wrote in the name of Enoch and Moses. In chapter 8 I introduce the Enochic texts.

CHAPTER 8

Enochic Authority

The writers of Daniel located their revolutionary counterdiscourse within a centuries-old tradition associated with a legendary figure from their people's past who had lived in exile and spoken truth to kings. Other seers located their discourse within a tradition that claimed an even longer history, reaching past the time of empires, election, and the great flood to a time before the fall of angels and the corruption of human knowledge. They wrote in the name of the righteous scribe Enoch.[1] They resisted imperial and local structures of violence and deceit, and they resisted Antiochus's persecution. These were the writers of the Enochic Apocalypse of Weeks and Book of Dreams.[2]

While the Enochic writers shared with the writers of Daniel a common fund of scriptures, other scriptures vitally shaped their self-understanding and

---

1. On the roles and titles of Enoch in the early Enoch literature, see Andrei A. Orlov, *The Enoch-Metatron Tradition* (Tübingen: Mohr Siebeck, 2005), pp. 40-85.

2. Scholars have perceived a literary relationship between the two apocalypses. While most posit dependence of the Book of Dreams on the Apocalypse of Weeks, it has not been possible to establish with certainty which text precedes the other. See George W. E. Nickelsburg, *1 Enoch 1: A Commentary on the Book of 1 Enoch, Chapters 1–36; 81–108*, Hermeneia (Minneapolis: Fortress, 2001), p. 360. Stephen Breck Reid maintains that the writer of the Book of Dreams had before him the Book of the Watchers, the Astronomical Book, and the Apocalypse of Weeks. "The Sociological Setting of the Historical Apocalypses of 1 Enoch and the Book of Daniel" (Ph.D. diss., Emory University, 1981), p. 79. For a different reconstruction, see Andreas Bedenbender, *Der Gott der Welt tritt auf den Sinai: Entstehung, Entwicklung und Funktionsweise der frühjüdischen Apokalyptik* (Berlin: Institut Kirche und Judentum, 2000), pp. 120-22. Bedenbender argues for the priority of the Animal Apocalypse over the Apocalypse of Weeks, both in terms of tradition history and date of composition. He adduces the former's interest in the salvation of all Israel versus the latter's more narrow focus on the chosen elect and the views of the temple found in each. He detects behind the Apocalypse of Weeks a disappointment in the outcome of the Maccabean uprising. 4Q212 provides a *terminus ante quem* for the Apocalypse of Weeks in the middle of the first century BCE (*Gott der Welt*, pp. 120-22).

vision of resistance, especially the Enochic Book of Watchers (*1 En.* 1–36).[3] This early portion of *1 Enoch,* tentatively dated to the third century BCE,[4] draws on a variety of sources while also reshaping and expanding the narrative known from Genesis 6–8 regarding the descent of heavenly beings, the corruption of humankind, and God's judgment by means of the flood.[5] Its accounts of sin, the role of the righteous, and the nature of God's justice shape the worldview of these two writers and their responses to the crisis faced by Judeans between the years 175 and 164 BCE. The writers of the Apocalypse of Weeks and Book of Dreams appear to have held the Book of the Watchers on a

3. See Nickelsburg, *1 Enoch 1,* pp. 359-60, 422-23. Nickelsburg notes, for example, that the beginning of the Apocalypse of Weeks imitates that of the Book of the Watchers, while the language used to describe the righteous, sinners, and salvation mirrors that found in *1 Enoch* 1–5 and 10:16–11:2, which passages, like the Apocalypse of Weeks, also describe the end time (p. 422). Situating the authority of the traditions in *1 En.* 1–36 in relation to the authority of other scriptures for the writer of the Animal Apocalypse, Nickelsburg writes: "From a historical-critical point of view, 1 Enoch 6–11 is an elaboration on a biblical text, and surely the author of the Vision saw it as the definitive way to read Genesis 6–8. At the same time, it is likely that the author accepted chs. 6–11 and the rest of the received Enochic tradition as parts of a larger sacred tradition that also included the Law and some of the Prophets" (p. 359).

4. For a brief survey of divergent proposals, see James H. Charlesworth, "A Rare Consensus among Enoch Specialists: The Date of the Earliest Enoch Books," *Henoch* 24 (2002): 225-34, 233. Some debate remains concerning the date of *1 En.* 1–5, which appear to serve as an introduction for the Book of the Watchers. For a mid-third-century date, see Nickelsburg, *1 Enoch 1,* p. 7. For a later date ("some decades before 167 BCE"), see Andreas Bedenbender, "The Place of the Torah in the Early Enoch Literature," in *The Early Enoch Literature,* ed. Gabriele Boccaccini and John J. Collins (Leiden: Brill, 2007), pp. 65-79, 78; and *Gott der Welt,* pp. 215-17.

5. On the exegetical relationship between the Book of the Watchers and Gen 6–8, see Philip S. Alexander, "The Enochic Literature and the Bible: Intertextuality and Its Implications," in *The Bible as Book: The Hebrew Bible and the Judaean Desert Discoveries,* ed. Edward D. Herbert and Emanuel Tov (London: The British Library, 2002), pp. 57-68, esp. 65; James C. VanderKam, "The Interpretation of Genesis in *1 Enoch,*" in *The Bible at Qumran: Text, Shape, and Interpretation,* ed. Peter W. Flint (Grand Rapids: Eerdmans, 2001), pp. 129-48; Philip S. Alexander, "From Son of Adam to Second God: Transformations of the Biblical Enoch," in *Biblical Figures Outside the Bible,* ed. Michael Stone and Theodore Bergren (Harrisburg, PA: Trinity Press International, 1998), pp. 87-122; J. H. le Roux, "The Use of Scripture in *1 Enoch* 6–11," *Neot* 17 (1983): 28-38; Devorah Dimant, "The Angels Who Sinned" (Ph.D. diss. [in Hebrew], Jerusalem: Hebrew University, 1971). See also Devorah Dimant, "1 Enoch 6–11: A Fragment of a Parabiblical Work," *JJS* 53 (2002): 223-37. Dimant argues here that the composer of the Book of the Watchers extracted *1 En.* 6–11 from a Hebrew parabiblical source that was similar to the *Genesis Apocryphon* in its technique of exegetically reworking and expanding a "biblical" text. For the Book of the Watcher's use of scriptural material outside of Genesis, see Lars Hartman, *Asking for a Meaning: A Study of 1 Enoch 1–5* (Lund: CWK Gleerup, 1979); Michael A. Knibb, "The Use of Scripture in *1 Enoch* 17–19," in *Jerusalem, Alexandria, Rome: Studies in Ancient Cultural Interaction in Honour of A. Hilhorst,* ed. Florentino García Martínez and Gerard P. Luttikhuizen (Leiden: Brill, 2003), pp. 165-78.

par with other scriptures and possibly accorded it even higher authoritative status.[6]

This observation requires us to reconsider long-cherished views of Judaism in the second century BCE. A familiar scholarly narrative of Second Temple Judaism posits one type of normative Judaism, influentially characterized by E. P. Sanders as "Common Judaism."[7] Common Judaism refers to a religious framework shared by all who would have identified themselves as Jews in Palestine in the Second Temple period. For Sanders, this framework could be summarized under the rubric of "covenantal nomism"[8] in which the law or Torah, more or less loosely identified with the Pentateuch, provided the basis for a common Jewish understanding of covenant.[9] Priests associated with the Jerusalem tem-

---

6. Helge S. Kvanvig stresses the importance of the Book of the Watchers as a shaping influence on the Apocalypse of Weeks, forming "the basis for the protology in the two first weeks and for the eschatology in the three last. The story is also the key to understand what is going on in the author's own time, in the seventh week. The story frames the whole history of Israel as it is recorded from the third to the sixth weeks. Although we can recognise the events in this history from the books that became the Hebrew Bible, the basic perspective on history is Enochic." "Cosmic Laws and Cosmic Imbalance: Wisdom, Myth and Apocalyptic in Early Enochic Writings," in *The Early Enoch Literature*, ed. Gabriele Boccaccini and John J. Collins (Leiden: Brill, 2007), pp. 139-58, 149-50.

7. E. P. Sanders, *Judaism: Practice and Belief, 63 BCE–66 CE* (Philadelphia: Trinity Press International, 1992), pp. 45-314.

8. E. P. Sanders summarizes "covenantal nomism" as follows: "(1) God has chosen Israel and (2) given the law. The law implies both (3) God's promise to maintain the election and (4) the requirement to obey. (5) God rewards obedience and punishes transgression. (6) The law provides for means of atonement, and atonement results in (7) maintenance or re-establishment of the covenantal relationship. (8) All those who are maintained in the covenant by obedience, atonement and God's mercy belong to the group which will be saved." *Paul and Palestinian Judaism: A Comparison of Patterns of Religion* (Philadelphia: Fortress, 1977), p. 422. With regard to *1 En.*, which Sanders notes does not contain all these elements, he suggests that enough of them are present to warrant thinking the others are presupposed: "Thus one can note the requirement of obedience and infer that something must have been given to be obeyed, even though the giving of the law is not rehearsed" (p. 423). For a "polythetic" revision of the idea of Common Judaism, see James Davila, *The Provenance of the Pseudepigrapha: Jewish, Christian, or Other?* (Leiden: Brill, 2005), pp. 19-21. Davila identifies "widely shared traits" while creating greater space for recognizing differences among forms of Judaism in this period. Davila suggests that "Enochic Judaism, while accepting the same historical narrative and probably many of the same scriptures [as Zadokite Judaism], focused on the elements associated with Enoch rather than Moses. . . . It seemed to have accepted the concept of a covenant (perhaps associated with Enoch or Abraham rather than Moses) and a Levitical priesthood, but the relationship of the latter to the Zadokite priesthood remains unclear" (p. 20).

9. For a nuanced understanding of the relationship between the Torah of Moses and the books we know as the Pentateuch, see Hindy Najman, *Seconding Sinai: The Development of Mosaic Discourse in Second Temple Judaism* (Leiden: Brill, 2003). In her discussion of Ezra/Nehemiah, for example, Najman writes, "Even if there was a collection of writings known as the

ple cult served as authoritative experts in the interpretation of Torah, as did other teachers with scribal expertise. This interpreted Torah served as the basis for Jewish practice and belief in the Second Temple period.

J. T. Milik's discovery at Qumran of fragments of four of the five booklets belonging to the corpus known to us as *1 Enoch* (including portions of the Apocalypse of Weeks and Book of Dreams) prepared the ground for a major shift in how scholars think about Second Temple Judaism.[10] The finds at Qumran substantiated the antiquity of texts previously known only through later translations, and enabled scholars to establish dates for the early Enochic literature in a period when many of the texts that later came to be viewed as biblical were still being written and edited. The revised dating of the earliest (by most reckonings, ca. third century BCE) Enochic booklets — the Astronomical Book (*1 En.* 72–82) and the Book of the Watchers (*1 En.* 1–36) — called for a fresh look at Judaism in this and subsequent periods. Yet the full significance of this discovery has only begun to be realized.[11] While Sanders's investigation into Second Temple Judaism included a treatment of the Enochic literature,[12]

Torah of Moses, and even if the term 'Torah of Moses' was often used to refer to this collection, it does not follow that the primary function of the term was to *name* this collection of writings. Instead, it may well be that the primary function of this term was to confer authority" (p. 116). The Pentateuch would have been the "preeminent" example, but not the only one. "Torah of Moses" would thus not designate a literary corpus, but rather serve as a category and a claim to authority.

10. J. T. Milik, ed., with the collaboration of Matthew Black, *The Books of Enoch: Aramaic Fragments of Qumrân Cave 4* (Oxford: Clarendon, 1976), p. vi. He discovered the first of these fragments in 1952.

11. Our understanding of the origins of Jewish apocalypticism provides one illustration of this point. Referring to the influential reconstructions of the origins of Jewish apocalypticism by Otto Plöger (*Theokratie und Eschatologie* [Neukirchen: Neukirchener Verlag, 1959]) and Paul D. Hanson (*The Dawn of Apocalyptic* [Philadelphia: Fortress, 1975]), Kvanvig observes that "neither for Plöger nor for Hanson did the Scriptures of Enoch have any relevance for the origin of apocalyptic" ("Cosmic Laws and Cosmic Imbalance," p. 140). Milik's publication of the Aramaic fragments from Qumran, with its arguments for revised dating, did not appear until 1976, helping to explain the veritable absence of Enochic literature from their studies. Similarly, while Sanders's *Paul and Palestinian Judaism* was published in the following year, a telling footnote indicates that he was still awaiting publication of these fragments at the time of writing (*Paul and Palestinian Judaism*, p. 346n1). Following Milik's publication of these fragments (and the publication of W. Lambert, "Enmeduranki and Related Matters," *JCS* 21 [1967]: 126-38), James C. VanderKam was among those who recognized the importance of the Enochic traditions for understanding the origins of apocalyptic literature and thought. He published the early fruits of his research in *Enoch and the Growth of an Apocalyptic Tradition*, CBQMS 16 (Washington, DC: Catholic Biblical Association of America, 1984). Helge Kvanvig's erudite study *Roots of Apocalyptic: The Mesopotamian Background of the Enoch Figure and of the Son of Man* (Neukirchen: Neukirchener Verlag, 1988) independently followed similar lines of thought.

12. Sanders, *Paul and Palestinian Judaism*, pp. 346-62. Sanders concluded that "within the framework of apocalyptic, we find much the same pattern of religion as we found in the rab-

increased scholarly attention to the Enochic traditions in recent decades requires us to ask whether the earlier picture was too monochrome.[13] Helge Kvanvig states the problem this way:

> In the discussion about groups and ideologies in the second temple period the scope is often limited to Palestine, and the religious and cultural worldview formed within what is constructed as Judaism. In this narrow perspective the Enoch literature with its emphasis on primeval time as the time when the basic conditions of reality were laid and the basic revelations about them were given, seems as something exotic compared to what is regarded as main stream Judaism.[14]

Gabriele Boccaccini has similarly noted that prior to the Qumran discoveries, "1 Enoch was still struggling against the impediments of its 'noncanonical' status and its dubious reputation as a bizarre and marginal pseudepigraphon."[15]

We are fortunate in the past decade to have witnessed a major increase in scholarly attention to the Enochic literature, bringing it to a more central position in the study of Second Temple Judaism. Boccaccini has identified "the rediscovery of Enochic Judaism" as "one of the major achievements of contemporary scholarship."[16] To the groundbreaking scholarship published in the

---

bis. . . . We still find that salvation depends on election and that what is necessary to *maintain* the elect state — to be righteous — is to maintain loyalty and obedience to God and his covenant" (p. 362).

13. For example, Gabriele Boccaccini criticizes the circularity of Sanders's treatment of the Parables of Enoch. "Finding a Place for the Parables of Enoch within Second Temple Jewish Literature," in *Enoch and the Messiah Son of Man: Revisiting the Book of Parables*, ed. Gabriele Boccaccini (Grand Rapids: Eerdmans, 2007), pp. 263-89, 269-70. In this essay, Boccaccini identifies five paradigms within Second Temple Judaism that coexisted and interacted: Wisdom, Apocalyptic, Messianic, Covenantal, and Enochic. Contra Sanders, he notes that no single paradigm is shared by all Second Temple Jewish texts. Of the five, Boccaccini argues that only the covenantal paradigm is missing from the Parables ("Finding a Place," pp. 268-69). For a critique of Boccaccini's concept of paradigm and choices, see Matthias Henze, "The Parables of Enoch in Second Temple Literature: A Response to Gabriele Boccaccini," in *Enoch and the Messiah Son of Man: Revisiting the Book of Parables*, ed. Gabriele Boccaccini (Grand Rapids: Eerdmans, 2007), pp. 290-98. Other possibilities suggested by Henze include cosmological/astronomical and prophetic paradigms (pp. 292-93).

14. Helge S. Kvanvig, "*Jubilees* — Between Enoch and Moses: A Narrative Reading," *JSJ* 35 (2004): 243-61, 260.

15. Gabriele Boccaccini, "Introduction: From the Enoch Literature to Enochic Judaism," in *Enoch and Qumran Origins: New Light on a Forgotten Connection*, ed. Gabriele Boccaccini (Grand Rapids: Eerdmans, 2005), pp. 1-14, 1.

16. Gabriele Boccaccini, "Qumran and the Enoch Groups: Revisiting the Enochic-Essene Hypothesis," in *The Bible and the Dead Sea Scrolls*, vol. 1: *Scripture and the Scrolls*, ed. James H. Charlesworth (Waco, TX: Baylor University Press, 2006), pp. 37-66, 60.

decades following Milik's publication of the Aramaic fragments[17] have now been added the efforts of scores of scholars participating in the Enoch Seminar, which first met in 2001.[18] The work of these scholars has advanced our understanding of the Enochic literature and given rise to lively debates about the place of the Enochic traditions within Second Temple Judaism.

Distinctive Features of the Early Enochic Literature

Central to these debates is the recognition that certain key features of the early Enochic booklets contrast markedly with other texts that would later become known as biblical from this and earlier periods.[19] Most prominent among these are (1) astronomical concerns; (2) alternative cosmology, including a mythic account of the origins of evil; (3) alternative epistemology; and (4) the elevated role of Enoch.

17. For bibliography of scholarship on *1 En.* in previous decades, see Lorenzo DiTommaso, *A Bibliography of Pseudepigrapha Research 1850-1999* (Sheffield: Sheffield Academic Press, 2001), pp. 355-430; Florentino García Martínez and Eibert J. C. Tigchelaar, "*1 Enoch* and the Figure of Enoch: A Bibliography of Studies 1970-1988," *RevQ* 14 (1989-1990): 149-74; Matthew Black, "A Bibliography on 1 Enoch in the Eighties," *JSP* 5 (1989): 3-16. The works of James C. VanderKam, Helge S. Kvanvig, George W. E. Nickelsburg, and Patrick Tiller have been especially influential.

18. D. D. Swanson writes, "The study of the Enochic literature is rapidly becoming a growth industry, and the Enoch Seminar is a cottage industry in itself." Review of Gabriele Boccaccini, ed., *Enoch and Qumran Origins: New Light on a Forgotten Connection, JSOT* 30 (2006): 161-62, 161. Information about the Enoch Seminar can be found at www.enochseminar .org. Topics of the biennial Seminar have included: "The Origins of Enochic Judaism" (2001); "Enoch and Qumran Origins" (2003); "Enoch and the Messiah Son of Man: Revisiting the Book of Parables" (2005); "Enoch and the Mosaic Torah: The Evidence of Jubilees" (2007); "Enoch, Adam, and Melchizedek: Mediatorial Figures in *2 Enoch* and Second Temple Judaism" (2009). The work of the Seminar has been published in the following volumes: Gabriele Boccaccini, ed., *The Origins of Enochic Judaism* (Turin: Zamorani, 2003); Gabriele Boccaccini, ed., *Enoch and Qumran Origins: New Light on a Forgotten Connection* (Grand Rapids: Eerdmans, 2005); Gabriele Boccaccini, ed., *Enoch and the Messiah Son of Man: Revisiting the Book of Parables* (Grand Rapids: Eerdmans, 2007); Gabriele Boccaccini and John J. Collins, eds., *The Early Enoch Literature* (Leiden: Brill, 2007); P. Bertalotto and T. Hanneken, eds., "Short Papers on Jubilees Presented at the Fourth Enoch Seminar," *Henoch* 30, no. 1 (2008); Gabriele Boccaccini and Giovanni Ibba, *Enoch and the Mosaic Torah: The Evidence of Jubilees* (Grand Rapids: Eerdmans, 2009). Others will no doubt follow in course. In addition to the essays, the volumes contain valuable bibliography to help scholars navigate the ever-growing corpus of secondary literature.

19. Michael E. Stone observes that these distinctive features might be explained in one of three ways: "new, indigenous developments of Judaism"; the result of influence from foreign traditions; or material that had been present within native traditions but not known to us previously due to transmission history. "The Book of Enoch and Judaism in the Third Century B.C.E.," *CBQ* 40 (1978): 479-92, 483. While Stone finds the third explanation most compelling, perhaps a combination of the three is closer to the mark (pp. 490-91).

Astronomical Concerns

The astronomical, indeed scientific, concerns of the earliest Enochic literature we possess (the Astronomical Book in particular) added an entirely new set of concerns to our picture of Second Temple Judaism, especially by comparison with evidence from more familiar biblical texts.[20] As do other elements of the Enochic traditions, this astronomical speculation shows a strong influence from Babylonian traditions.[21] Yet these traditions are not taken over wholesale. They are adapted within a framework shaped by native traditions and theology. John Collins highlights the development of these scientific concerns within a mythological framework and idiom,[22] while Mark Adam Elliott calls attention to their "serious reflection upon the cosmic implications of the covenant."[23] Klaus Koch shows that the creative adaptations of Mesopotamian material in the Astronomical Book aimed to preserve "the freedom of God and humankind," by contrast with the deterministic foundations of Babylonian astrology and divination.[24] The astronomical concerns of the Astronomical Book and the Book of the Watchers thus represent creative blending and adapting of traditional theological elements with Mesopotamian motifs and forms of knowledge in a new historical and cultural moment.

20. Stone, "The Book of Enoch and Judaism," pp. 487-92; George W. E. Nickelsburg, "'Enoch' as Scientist, Sage, and Prophet: Content, Function, and Authorship in 1 Enoch," *SBLSP* 38 (1999): 203-30. Nickelsburg observes: "For the authors of these texts, natural science and divine science constitute a unity." He connects this knowledge with the book's aim "to exhort its audience to right conduct" (pp. 219, 223). See also Phillip Alexander, "Enoch and the Beginning of Jewish Interest in Natural Science," in *The Wisdom Texts from Qumran and the Development of Sapiential Thought*, ed. Charlotte Hempel, Armin Lange, and Hermann Lichtenberger (Leuven: Peeters, 2002), pp. 223-43.

21. For a study of Babylonian influence on the Astronomical Book, see Matthias Albani, *Astronomie und Schöpfungsglaube* (Neukirchen: Neukirchener Verlag, 1994), pp. 163-272. See also Klaus Koch, "Die Anfänge der Apokalyptik in Israel und die Rolle des astronomischen Henochbuches," *Vor der Wende der Zeiten* (Neukirchen: Neukirchener Verlag, 1996), pp. 3-44. Carol A. Newsom has described the openness to sources of knowledge located at the boundaries, in this case the astronomical traditions of Babylonian learning, as a characteristic feature of apocalyptic as "outsider" discourse. *The Self as Symbolic Space: Constructing Identity and Community at Qumran* (Leiden: Brill, 2004), pp. 48-49.

22. John J. Collins, "Theology and Identity in the Early Enoch Literature," *Henoch* 24 (2002): 57-62, 59.

23. Mark Adam Elliott, "Covenant and Cosmology in the Book of the Watchers and the Astronomical Book," *Henoch* 24 (2002): 23-38, 31.

24. Klaus Koch, "The Astral Laws as the Basis of Time, Universal History, and the Eschatological Turn in the Astronomical Book and the Animal Apocalypse of 1 Enoch," in *The Early Enoch Literature*, ed. Gabriele Boccaccini and John J. Collins (Leiden: Brill, 2007), pp. 119-37, 126.

Alternative Cosmology

While there is certainly some overlap between the biblical and Enochic cosmologies, in the Enochic literature cosmology becomes a crucial shaping factor in human life.[25] A key focus of Enochic cosmology is the origin of evil, which affects not only human life but the very workings of the cosmos.[26] While the origin of evil as such is not a major focus of most biblical texts, the problem of evil often is. They offer not one explanation but several.[27] Among these, sin holds a prominent place, and is understood primarily in terms of human violation of the covenant with God. The Eden myth underscores the centrality of human freedom in the choice between sin and obedience to God. External forces did not cause humans to sin. Kept in check by God's providential governance, chaos is part of the created order (e.g., Job 40:15-21; 41) and does not threaten its stability or integrity.[28]

The Enochic literature introduces an alternative theodicy.[29] The Astronom-

---

25. On the cosmology of the early Enochic literature, see Koch, "Astral Laws"; Kvanvig, "Cosmic Laws and Cosmic Imbalance"; Koch, "Die Anfänge der Apokalyptik"; David R. Jackson, *Enochic Judaism: Three Defining Paradigm Exemplars* (London: T. & T. Clark, 2004), pp. 139-50; Kelley Coblentz Bautch, *A Study of the Geography of 1 Enoch 17–19: "No One Has Seen What I Have Seen"* (Leiden: Brill, 2003), pp. 258-64; Klaus Koch, "Die Gesetze des gestirnten Himmels als Manifestationen der Herrschaft Gottes über Raum und Zeit," in Klaus Koch, *Die aramäische Rezeption der hebräischen Bibel: Studien zur Targumik und Apokalyptik*, ed. Martin Rösel (Neukirchen-Vluyn: Neukirchener Verlag, 2003), pp. 21-42; Norman Cohn, *Cosmos, Chaos, and the World to Come: The Ancient Roots of Apocalyptic Faith* (New Haven: Yale University Press, 2001), pp. 176-87; Carol A. Newsom, "The Development of 1 Enoch 6–19: Cosmology and Judgment," *CBQ* 42 (1980): 310-29.

26. See Paolo Sacchi, *Jewish Apocalyptic and Its History,* trans. William J. Short (Sheffield: Sheffield Academic Press, 1990). Sacchi emphasizes the soteriological implications of the Book of the Watchers' view of evil: "Evil appears as a disorder which cannot be traced back either to God or to the human person. . . . If evil comes from the sphere above the human, salvation too . . . can only come from the same sphere" (p. 57). See also Gabriele Boccaccini, *Roots of Rabbinic Judaism: An Intellectual History, From Ezekiel to Daniel* (Grand Rapids: Eerdmans, 2002), pp. 90-99.

27. See James L. Crenshaw, *Defending God: Biblical Responses to the Problem of Evil* (Oxford: Oxford University Press, 2005).

28. Boccaccini characterizes what he terms the Zadokite worldview in which God's governance over creation maintained order at all times, keeping cosmic forces of chaos in check and either punishing or forgiving human sin (*Roots of Rabbinic Judaism*, pp. 73-82).

29. Andreas Bedenbender argues that, as representative texts of Mosaic and Enochic Judaism respectively, Genesis and the Book of the Watchers each acknowledge the view of the origin of evil found in the "competing tradition" by casually incorporating its elements as *minor* strands in an account that places true emphasis elsewhere. "Traces of Enochic Judaism within the Hebrew Bible," *Henoch* 24 (2002): 39-48, 45-46. I would argue that the presence of these minor strands reveals that the traditions are not mutually exclusive, and are not intended to be so. We appear to be dealing with a question of emphasis, not mutually exclusive truth claims.

ical Book portrays a sympathy between "deviation" in the celestial and human realms (*1 En.* 80:1-8). In "the days of the sinners" (*1 En.* 80:2) the "heads of the stars" would deviate from their assigned courses (80:6; see also 18:15: "The stars . . . did not come out in their appointed times"; cf. 21:4–6), and in so doing disrupt the seasons (80:2-5) and lead human beings into religious error (80:7).[30] In this theodicy, human beings are susceptible to influence from the world of angels and spirits, both good and evil. This influence limits and challenges but does not negate human freedom.[31] Nor does it remove human responsibility.[32]

While the Book of the Watchers shows familiarity with the primeval history known from Genesis 1–11, this early Enochic text testifies to a very different mythic framework for understanding the origins of evil and the means for overcoming it.[33] In the early Enochic literature, as Paolo Sacchi notes, "Eschatology and protology are two sides of the same coin," such that "the things that happened in the beginning are the cause of the life we live now, and at the same time they are the things to be put right at the end of time."[34] The Apocalypse of Weeks develops this framework further in a "historical-eschatological theodicy" that emphasizes the final triumph of justice. The theodicy of the Book of Dreams has a similar historical-eschatological orientation, while offering a more universal vision of salvation, restoration, and right relationship.[35]

30. Translations of *1 En.* in this chapter are those of George W. E. Nickelsburg and James C. VanderKam, *1 Enoch: A New Translation* (Minneapolis: Fortress, 2004).

31. Koch, "Astral Laws," p. 126.

32. Gabriele Boccaccini, "Enochians, Urban Essenes, Qumranites: Three Social Groups, One Intellectual Movement," *The Early Enoch Literature*, ed. Gabriele Boccaccini and John J. Collins (Leiden: Brill, 2007), pp. 301-27, 311-12; Nickelsburg, *1 Enoch 1*, p. 46.

33. For Boccaccini, this is the central idea at the heart of Enochic Judaism: "The catalyst of Enochic Judaism was a unique concept of the origin of evil that made the 'fallen angels' (the 'sons of God' also recorded in Gen 6:1-4) as ultimately responsible for the spread of evil and impurity on earth" (*Roots of Rabbinic Judaism*, p. 90). He elaborates that it is not the presence of the myth of the fallen angels that is distinctive, as it can be found also in Gen 6:1-4, but rather the fact that it was developed in the Book of the Watchers into "the central paradigm for the origin of sin and evil" and linked with the figure of Enoch (p. 96).

34. Paolo Sacchi, "The Theology of Early Enochism and Apocalyptic: The Problem of the Relation between Form and Content of the Apocalypses; the Worldview of the Apocalypses," *Henoch* 24 (2002): 77-85, 80. But note Newsom's observation regarding chs. 12–16: "Eschatology appears to be only one aspect (and certainly not the major one) in the resolution of the problem" of evil. Of even greater importance to the writer is the fact that God exercises control in the present (both the present within the story and that in which the audience lives), limiting evil's effects even before the eschaton ("Development of *1 Enoch* 6–19," p. 316).

35. Kvanvig, "Cosmic Laws and Cosmic Imbalance," p. 152. George W. E. Nickelsburg comments that this universalism, present in "several strata" of *1 En.*, should "caution us against an uncritical application of the term 'sectarian' to these documents." "*1 Enoch* and Qumran Origins," *SBLSP* 25 (1986): 341-60, 357.

The interest in cosmology also has a feature that Eibert Tigchelaar identifies as "dimensional."[36] I would argue that, for the Book of the Watchers especially, the interest in providing a visionary map of the extent of the cosmos ties in with its interest in mapping the places of judgment and reward and the seat of God's power: in each case, visionary mapping puts the powers "in their place." In the Book of the Watchers, Enoch witnesses the judgment against the fallen watchers for forsaking their place and transgressing divinely ordained boundaries (*1 En.* 12:4; 15:3, 7). They are consequently bound, restricting all future movement. They are also removed from the places they sought to inhabit and confined instead to a deserted place (*1 En.* 10:4), beyond the mountain throne of God (18:8-10) at "the edge of the great earth" where "the heavens come to an end" (18:10). The stars that have transgressed are confined to a no-space, at "the end of heaven and earth" (18:14), with no firmament above them and no solid ground below them (18:12; 21:1). The place of reward, by contrast, is located by the house of God, the eternal king (25:5). These places of reward and punishment are each located by reference to God's royal throne and dwelling, such that the fundamental point of orientation is the seat of divine royal power and judgment.

Places of punishment and reward are a major part of Enoch's visionary journey, but, as Carol Newsom has argued, there is a broader interest in mapping the "royal dominion," charting the extent of the cosmos (*1 En.* 33:1–36:4); identifying its center (26:1); locating its treasuries (17:3; 18:1), armory (17:2), and natural resources (18:6-8; 24:2-5; 28:1–32:4); and revealing its hidden workings (18:1-5; 23:1-4; 33:1–36:4).[37] This cosmic cartography exceeds the limits of imperial space, as celestial guides lead the visionary to the ends of the earth and throughout the divine dominion. The cosmic vision subordinates all other modalities of organizing space, including the efforts of the empires.

Those efforts took concrete form in maps and descriptions of the known world. When Alexander and his generals conquered the Levant (and elsewhere), they brought with them cartographers. Alexander "not only conquered

36. Eibert Tigchelaar, *Prophets of Old and the Day of the End: Zechariah, the Book of Watchers, and Apocalyptic* (Leiden: Brill, 1996), p. 262. See also Pieter M. Venter, "Spatiality in Enoch's Journeys (1 Enoch 12–36)," in *Wisdom and Apocalypticism in the Dead Sea Scrolls and in the Biblical Tradition*, ed. Florentino García Martínez (Leuven: Leuven University Press, 2003), pp. 211-30. On the Enochic construction of space as a strategy of resistance, see further Pieter Venter, "Spatiality in the Second Parable of Enoch," in *Enoch and the Messiah Son of Man: Revisiting the Book of Parables*, ed. Gabriele Boccaccini (Grand Rapids: Eerdmans, 2007), pp. 403-12.

37. Newsom, "Development of *1 Enoch* 6–19," p. 325. While Newsom does not here develop in great detail the anti-imperial implications of her thesis, she argues that the cosmology of the Book of the Watchers amounts to a cosmic expression of divine power, conveying its message of hope through royal imagery and motifs (pp. 325-27).

the eastern regions, he also explored them. For that purpose he had at his disposal a group of specialists called 'bematists', whose duty it was to measure and calculate distances covered by the main body of the army as well as by special detachments. In addition to this they also recorded their observations on the native population, flora, fauna and other matters of interest in the territory through which they passed."[38] Mapping was a key to successful conquest. Mapping the extent of the known world was also a way to communicate Alexander's universal dominion. For the warring generals and dynasts that succeeded him, maps served expansionist ambitions and also served as tools for building and maintaining the machinery of domination. Maps would have served not only for warfare, but for "political propaganda, boundary making, [and] the preservation of law and order."[39] Maps could assert ownership of land and property, and would have been used to identify sources of revenue for the empire and to chart and safeguard paths of tribute. They were crucial for establishing and maintaining the economic and political interdependence of colonies and the empires that ruled them.

As Simon Ryan has noted, maps "create and manipulate reality as much as they record it."[40] The Enochic visionaries countered imperial cartography and its ideology of dominance with the alternative geography revealed in Enoch's heavenly journey. Enoch's own freedom of movement across geographical boundaries signals divinely granted freedom from imperial control, while the confinement of the watchers and stars presages a time when the imperial powers themselves will forfeit the freedoms they have stolen.[41] By narrating this heavenly journey the Enochic visionaries witnessed to the much broader, cosmic, and truly universal dominion of God that gave the lie to Hellenistic imperial claims to absolute power. "Mapping" the cosmos in this way was thus a key strategy in countering imperial ideology and asserting in its place a cosmic theology of divine sovereignty.

38. Klaus Geus, "Space and Geography," in *A Companion to the Hellenistic World*, ed. Andrew Erskine (Oxford: Blackwell, 2003), pp. 232-45, 237. See also Peter Whitfield, *New Found Lands: Maps in the History of Exploration* (London: Routledge, 1998), p. 8. Cf. Alexander's interest in flora and fauna to the description of plants in *1 En.* 28:1–32:4 and animals in 33:1-2.

39. John Bryan Harley, *The New Nature of Maps: Essays in the History of Cartography* (Baltimore: Johns Hopkins University Press, 2001), p. 55.

40. Simon Ryan, "Inscribing the Emptiness: Cartography, Exploration and the Construction of Australia," in *De-Scribing Empire: Post-colonialism and Textuality*, ed. Chris Tiffin and Alan Lawson (London: Routledge, 1994), pp. 115-130, 116.

41. Cf. Steve Pile, "Introduction: Opposition, Political Identities and Spaces of Resistance," in *Geographies of Resistance*, ed. Steve Pile and Michael Keith (London: Routledge, 1997), pp. 1-32, 16, 29. For further treatment of the ways domination and resistance play out in space and its representation, see Joanne P. Sharp, Paul Routledge, Chris Philo, and Ronan Paddison, eds., *Entanglements of Power: Geographies of Domination/Resistance* (London: Routledge, 2000).

Alternative Epistemology

Christopher Rowland identifies epistemology as the key to apocalyptic literature.[42] The early Enochic literature is no exception. Rowland argues that in the Second Temple period, believers increasingly sought knowledge of God's will and ways from the growing body of scriptural texts. But interpretation of sacred scriptures constituted, in Rowland's terminology, an "indirect mode of discernment" made less reliable by the need for new interpretation in new eras (such as the need to reinterpret Jeremiah's seventy years in Dan 9) and by the availability at any given time of multiple conflicting or competing interpretations.[43]

Rowland's suggestion is similar to that of James L. Crenshaw in his study of prophetic conflict.[44] For example, Jeremiah 28 narrates the competing predictions and recommended courses of action of Jeremiah and Hananiah. While both of them claimed to speak for Yhwh, they could not both be right. History vindicated Jeremiah, yet his contemporaries had no way to confirm or deny the validity of his claims until after the predicted events had transpired. This example highlights the fact that all claims to religious authority will compete, and none can be directly verified. For Crenshaw this burden of verification was an impetus behind the embrace and development of both apocalyptic and wisdom epistemologies. Wisdom schools proposed observation of the created world as a path to certainty about God's will. Yet the Enochic concept of astral deviation demonstrates that even this "direct" mode of access was subject to competing interpretations.[45] As previously noted, deviation in the natural realm corresponding to deviation in the supernatural realm could mislead even the most careful observer.

This example highlights a distinctive feature of apocalyptic epistemology, with its focus on the supernatural world. Sacchi proposes that this knowledge of the "spirit world" complements two other sources: "knowledge of the world," which we would associate with wisdom epistemology, and "knowledge of tradition," including the interpretation of authoritative texts. Knowledge of the su-

---

42. Christopher Rowland, *The Open Heaven: A Study of Apocalyptic in Judaism and Early Christianity* (New York: Crossroad, 1982), p. 11. See also J. Louis Martyn, "Epistemology at the Turn of the Ages: 2 Corinthians 5.16," in *Christian History and Interpretation: Studies Presented to John Knox*, ed. William R. Farmer, C. F. D. Moule, and Richard R. Niebuhr (Cambridge: Cambridge University Press, 1967), pp. 269-87. Critical discussion of Rowland's position, with a contrasting emphasis on eschatology, can be found in M. C. de Boer, "Paul and Apocalyptic Eschatology," in *The Encyclopedia of Apocalypticism*, ed. John J. Collins, vol. 1, *The Origins of Apocalypticism in Judaism and Christianity* (New York: Continuum, 2000), pp. 345-83, 351-54.

43. Rowland, *The Open Heaven*, p. 10.

44. James L. Crenshaw, *Prophetic Conflict: Its Effect upon Israelite Religion* (Berlin: Walter de Gruyter, 1971), pp. 106-9.

45. See Jackson, *Enochic Judaism*, pp. 139-202.

pernatural world "continually reveals truths that do not deny those of this world, but transcend them and constitute the underlying reason for them. The world, history and tradition itself make sense only if seen against the backdrop of the spirit world, revealed by those who are raised up to it."[46] Sacchi helps us to see that the question of certainty may not be the major epistemological issue driving the Enochic claims to revelation. Rather, there is a concern with reinterpreting knowledge available through other sources — scriptures, oral traditions, other cultures, observation of the created world — in light of this transcendent revelation not otherwise available to humankind. The transcendent revelation provides the framework through which all other forms of knowledge are viewed and in relation to which they are evaluated and given new meaning.

Knowledge as such is a key interest of the Enochic traditions. The Book of the Watchers in particular takes great pains to identify the source and validity of different forms of knowledge and to relate these to the exercise of power, both good and bad (1 En. 5:8-9; 7:1; 8:1-4; 9:5-11; 10:3, 8; 13:2; 14:3, 22). Through analogy with the fallen watchers, the Book of the Watchers exposes as false and destructive the transgressive knowledge on which empire is founded (16:3). At the same time, just as the Book of the Watchers' visionary map of the cosmos asserts the universal dominion of God and the attendant contingency of earthly powers, so its discourse about knowledge relativizes all other epistemological claims — including those of surrounding cultures and of the empires — in relation to the deposit of Enochic revelation.

The Enochic literature grounds its epistemology in Enoch's direct access to the supernatural realm. Thus the elevated role of the figure of Enoch is a key to the alternative epistemology of the Enochic literature.

Elevated Role of Enoch

Enoch son of Jared can only be called a minor character in the primeval history of Genesis.[47] His birth is announced with little fanfare at Genesis 5:18. We learn his age (sixty-five) at the time when he begets his son Methuselah (Gen 5:21). He is then said to have walked with God (הָאֱלֹהִים, understood in the Book of the Watchers as "divine beings," i.e., angels) and to have fathered sons and daughters during the remaining three hundred years of his life (5:22). His days are reckoned as three hundred and sixty-five years (5:23). The final enigmatic comment on his life follows:

46. Sacchi, "Theology of Early Enochism," pp. 82-83.
47. On the biblical figure of Enoch, see VanderKam, *Enoch and the Growth of an Apocalyptic Tradition*, pp. 23-51. VanderKam establishes here that the writer of the Enoch material in Genesis drew on Mesopotamian traditions about Enmeduranki.

וַיִּתְהַלֵּךְ חֲנוֹךְ אֶת־הָאֱלֹהִים וְאֵינֶנּוּ כִּי־לָקַח אֹתוֹ אֱלֹהִים

"Enoch walked with God; then he was no more, because God took him."
(5:24 NRSV)

Enoch appears again in the Chronicler's genealogy (1 Chron 1:3), and in Sirach 44:16 and 49:14.

The central importance of Enoch within the Enochic literature stands in stark contrast to his slender profile in these verses. It is not the place here to trace the development of the figure of Enoch that stands behind and within the early Enochic literature.[48] At present it is necessary only to note (1) the link between Enoch's unique role and status and the epistemological claims of the Enochic literature; (2) the link that is forged between Enoch, the etiology and paradigm of sin elaborated in the myth of the descent of the watchers (cf. Gen 6:1-4), and the subsequent judgment that includes the flood (cf. Gen 6:5–8:22); and, as I argue in chapters 9 and 10, (3) the importance of the *example* of Enoch for the writers and their intended audience.[49] I will note additional details concerning the elevated status of Enoch as I consider the debate regarding the relationship between Enochic and Mosaic claims to authority.

---

48. For an excellent treatment of this development, see Orlov, *The Enoch-Metatron Tradition*, pp. 23-85.

49. Mark Adam Elliott highlights the *"implicit but essential relationship between the figure and the righteous community"* (italics original). He asserts that *"paradigmatic* figures functioned to define the community in terms of its behavior and circumstances." *The Survivors of Israel: A Reconsideration of the Theology of Pre-Christian Judaism* (Grand Rapids: Eerdmans, 2000), p. 469. While I am not sure I would characterize their function as "defining," I argue in this book that they model appropriate and even necessary behavior. Martha Himmelfarb similarly observes, "The narrative identification with the pseudepigraphic hero, then, is more than a device to lend authority to the apocalypse; it is an integral part of its message." *Ascent to Heaven in Jewish and Christian Apocalypses* (Oxford: Oxford University Press, 1993), p. 104. But for Himmelfarb it is an interior identification only. She sees the heavenly ascent in early apocalyptic literature as conveying "human possibility" and "the status of the righteous in the universe," operating within the mind of the reader but effecting nothing outside the imagination (meaning they had no magical or ritual significance, p. 114). John J. Collins expresses a similar view: "The apocalyptic vision does not, of course, have a publicly discernible effect on the historical crisis, but it provides a resolution in the imagination by evoking a sense of awe and instilling a conviction." "The Apocalyptic Technique: Setting and Function in the Book of Watchers," *CBQ* 44 (1982): 91-111, 111. This understanding focuses on the aim of consolation but gives little attention to exhortation, or to the way in which an alternative vision of the cosmos, heavenly court, or history creates a new framework for action (e.g., by redefining the boundaries of what is possible and real). The possibility of reimagining reality, as through the alternative geography revealed to Enoch in the Book of the Watchers, can have sociopolitical implications reaching far beyond the mind of the reader.

Enochic Authority in the Hellenistic Imperial Context

I have identified four distinctive and interrelated features of the Enochic literature by comparison with other Jewish scriptures known from this and earlier
periods, namely astronomical concerns, alternative cosmology, alternative epistemology, and the elevated role and status of the figure of Enoch. We will see
that each shapes the vision of resistance in the Apocalypse of Weeks and Book
of Dreams. These distinctive concerns and the vitality of the traditions in which
they find expression have led scholars to speak of an "Enochic Judaism." If we
posit an Enochic Judaism, the question remains, what is its relationship to what
Sanders has called Common Judaism?[50] What is its relation to other "Judaisms"
we might identify in the third and second centuries BCE? And what has this to
do with resistance to empire in the reign of Antiochus IV Epiphanes? While
scholars have increasingly seen an internal polemic within Judaism, I shift the
focus to the imperial context. I argue that Enochic authority challenges not
Moses, but the empire and its collaborators.

In an influential but controversial reconstruction, Boccaccini views
Enochic Judaism as a priestly reform or protest movement that began in reaction to developments within what he calls "Zadokite Judaism."[51] Zadokite Judaism represents for Boccaccini the dominant form of Judaism among the
priestly establishment in Jerusalem prior to the persecution under Antiochus IV Epiphanes. While the label Zadokite is intended to evoke its priestly
orientation, the most important body of teaching Boccaccini associates with
this form of Judaism is the Mosaic Torah preserved in the Pentateuch. Within
this Zadokite tradition the figure of Moses serves as a major mediator figure
and primary source of religious authority. In Boccaccini's reconstruction, the
alternative cosmology and epistemological claims of the Enochic literature represent direct challenges to the worldview and authority of the religious establishment in Jerusalem. The exalted figure of Enoch could be said to vie with
Moses, putative author of the books of the Pentateuch, each serving as guarantor of a competing worldview and competing claims to authority.[52]

To the extent that Moses and "his" Torah authorized the priestly establishment of the Jerusalem temple, the Enochic traditions may have arisen and
gained currency among individuals or groups of highly educated Jews who

50. I use the term "Enochic Judaism" provisionally, as it appears to have heuristic value.
But as I state below, I do not believe we have sufficient evidence to posit a *sectarian* or *separatist*
Enochic group in the third and early second centuries BCE.

51. See esp. Boccaccini, *Roots of Rabbinic Judaism*, pp. 43-111. For Boccaccini, Daniel presents a "Third Way" between the two (pp. 151-201).

52. In the forceful phrasing of Bedenbender, "the wisdom of Enoch *eo ipso* meant a challenge to the revelation received by Moses" ("Traces of Enochic Judaism," p. 40).

wished to claim a different kind of religious authority. This much seems obvious, for the epistemological claims of the Enochic traditions do indeed seek to establish the Enochic revelations as authoritative in a way that the biblical Mosaic traditions do not claim. Moreover, their content is quite different from the Mosaic Torah known to us through the Pentateuch. But many questions remain. Do we imagine an intra-group dialogue, perhaps even a complementary relationship, among individuals within the same priestly and scribal circles, some claiming Mosaic authority, others claiming Enochic authority, but all located within one shared religious system?[53] Or do we imagine an inter-group conflict, in which the writers and tradents of the Enochic traditions actively seek to challenge the religious claims of those whose authority is centered around the Jerusalem temple?[54] If the latter, with respect to what do they seek to challenge those who claim the authority of Moses and his Torah?[55] Do they reject the authority of Torah? Or do they seek rather to supplement, recontextualize, and reinterpret it?[56] To what ends?

I briefly survey below the evidence that some scholars interpret to suggest that the early Enochic traditions represent a set of counterclaims to Mosaic authority and even possible rejection of Torah as such.[57] This evidence includes the following: (1) the absence of direct citation of Pentateuchal material; (2) the absence of explicit parallels to the Pentateuchal commandments; (3) a single reference to "covenant"; (4) the apparent dissociation between Sinai and the giving of the law; (5) the fact that Moses does not figure in the As-

53. Benjamin Wright III argues for a priestly-scribal location for the Enochic writers and tradents in "1 Enoch and Ben Sira: Wisdom and Apocalypticism in Relationship," in *The Early Enoch Literature,* ed. Gabriele Boccaccini and John J. Collins (Leiden: Brill, 2007), pp. 159-76. Elsewhere he suggests that the Book of the Watchers contains a "mild" internal critique of the Jerusalem priesthood. See Benjamin Wright III, "Ben Sira and the Book of the Watchers on the Legitimate Priesthood," in *Intertextual Studies in Ben Sira and Tobit: Studies in Honor of Alexander A. Di Lella,* ed. Jeremy Corley and Vincent Skemp (Washington, DC: Catholic Biblical Association of America, 2005), pp. 241-54, 247.

54. Tigchelaar suggests rather that the critique focuses on priests who have *left* the Jerusalem temple and taken up residence in Samaria (*Prophets of Old,* pp. 198-203).

55. We also need to ask to what extent we can delineate the precise contours of Torah in this period, Mosaic or otherwise. Richard A. Horsley notes that "the continuing composition of alternative texts of Torah, such as *Jubilees* and the *Temple Scroll,* suggests strongly that the Pentateuchal books had no monopoly on authority among texts of Mosaic torah." *Scribes, Visionaries, and the Politics of Second Temple Judea* (Louisville: Westminster John Knox, 2007), p. 118.

56. Hindy Najman discusses the aim of certain Second Temple writings "not to replace, but rather to *accompany* traditions already regarded as authoritative, and thus to provide those traditions with their proper interpretive context" (*Seconding Sinai,* p. 44).

57. See also the careful summary of the state of the question in Coblentz Bautch, *Study of the Geography,* pp. 289-99.

tronomical Book, the Book of the Watchers, or the Apocalypse of Weeks, while the Book of Dreams does not identify Moses as lawgiver or covenant mediator; and (6) the elevated role and status of Enoch. As I consider each point, I discuss other ways the evidence has been construed and stake out the position adopted in the present study. While it will not be possible to provide definitive answers to all, or even most, of the questions posed above, I hope to offer a fresh perspective by looking beyond the inner-Jewish discursive setting to the multicultural imperial context in which the Enochic literature takes shape. I argue that the ultimate rival to Enochic claims to authority is not Moses but the empire.

1. *The absence of direct citation of Pentateuchal material.* Pentateuchal material is present in *1 Enoch* in the form of allusions and even quotations, but quotations are never identified as such and the Mosaic traditions are never named as scripture or cited as an authoritative source.[58] The fact that *1 Enoch* makes heavy use of Mosaic and other scriptural traditions without using quotation formulas or direct attributions suggests that *1 Enoch* seeks to locate itself within the living scriptural tradition of Israel and even appropriate the authority of earlier scriptures. At the same time, *1 Enoch* does not overtly ground its authority in that of other scriptures or other mediator figures. Rather, the Enochic booklets claim an independent and direct authority grounded in the figure of Enoch and the revelations he has received and handed on.[59]

2. *The absence of explicit parallels to the Pentateuchal commandments.* George Nickelsburg has observed that there are no explicit parallels to the Pentateuchal commandments in *1 Enoch*.[60] Though *1 Enoch* is certainly interested in human conduct, it does not spell out guidelines for a righteous and holy life.[61] From this evidence, Sacchi concludes: "The ancient Enochians had no law comparable to that of the Zadokites."[62] But his conclusion stretches the evidence. *First Enoch* returns again and again to the theme of divine judgment, distinguishing not only between rebellious and faithful heavenly beings but also between righteous and wicked humans. Nickelsburg has argued that, lacking explicit criteria for judgment in the Enochic corpus, we should assume im-

---

58. Bedenbender, "The Place of the Torah," p. 65.

59. Kenneth E. Pomykala, "A Scripture Profile of the Book of the Watchers," in *The Quest for Context and Meaning: Studies in Biblical Intertextuality in Honor of James A. Sanders,* ed. Craig A. Evans and Shemaryahu Talmon (Leiden: Brill, 1997), pp. 263-84, 281-83.

60. Nickelsburg, *1 Enoch 1,* 51; George W. E. Nickelsburg, "Enochic Wisdom: An Alternative to the Mosaic Torah?" in *Hesed ve-Emet: Studies in Honor of Ernest S. Frerichs,* ed. Jodi Magness and Seymour Gitin (Atlanta: Scholars Press, 1998), pp. 123-32, 126. Coblentz Bautch summarizes the slender evidence for halakhic concerns in *1 En.* in *Study of the Geography,* pp. 290-94.

61. Cf. Sanders, *Paul and Palestinian Judaism,* p. 348.

62. Sacchi, "Theology of Early Enochism," p. 80.

plicit criteria.[63] Might those implicit criteria include Mosaic Torah, as well as the preaching of Israel's prophets that grew up alongside it? Lars Hartman has argued in great depth for the dependence of *1 Enoch* 1–5 on the covenant traditions preserved in the Pentateuch, especially those found in Deuteronomy, as well as Israel's prophetic traditions.[64] In light of this dependence, we might read *1 Enoch*'s silence regarding Pentateuchal commandments not as rejection but as tacit acceptance.

At the same time, it is clear that the criteria for judgment in *1 Enoch* cannot be limited to Mosaic Torah or the witness of Israel's prophets. The revealed wisdom handed down within the Enochic literature itself forms part of the criteria for judgment.[65] The universal and cosmic scope of Enoch's revelations, including but not limited to its astronomical concerns, contrasts with the particular focus of Pentateuchal legislation and the covenant between the Lord and Israel. Kenneth Pomykala illustrates this shift in scope by examining the role of "heaven" and "earth" in Deuteronomy and in the Book of the Watchers. Whereas in Deuteronomy heaven and earth are invoked as witnesses to the covenant and law, in the Book of the Watchers they are the "standard of obedience." Pomykala suggests that for this early Enochic text "the moral order is lodged not in the Sinai law, but in the natural order."[66]

It must also be noted that the lack of halakhic parallels results from differences in literary form and focus. James VanderKam reminds us that "certain kinds of literature are more likely to handle certain topics . . . and to ignore others. . . . This does not entail that their authors objected to other teachings, only that they did not consider them in the surviving contexts."[67] Similarly, though a strong proponent of the view that the earliest Enochic traditions rep-

---

63. George W. E. Nickelsburg, "Enochic Wisdom and Its Relationship to the Mosaic Torah," in *The Early Enoch Literature*, ed. Gabriele Boccaccini and John J. Collins (Leiden: Brill, 2007), pp. 81-94, 84. Cf. Sanders, *Paul and Palestinian Judaism*, p. 423: "One can note the requirement of obedience and infer that something must have been given to be obeyed, even though the giving of the law is not rehearsed."

64. Hartman, *Asking for a Meaning*, passim.

65. Nickelsburg, "Enochic Wisdom and Its Relationship," p. 84.

66. Pomykala, "Scripture Profile," p. 266. See also Elliott, "Covenant and Cosmology," pp. 32-36.

67. James C. VanderKam, "Mapping Second Temple Judaism," in *The Early Enoch Literature*, ed. Gabriele Boccaccini and John J. Collins (Leiden: Brill, 2007), pp. 1-20, 19. Cf. the remarks of Lester Grabbe: "Care should be taken about drawing conclusions from omissions, especially in short texts. An author will not necessarily put all his concerns in every text he writes or edits." He also cautions that what is most important to an author may be assumed rather than talked about. "The Parables of Enoch in Second Temple Jewish Society," in *Enoch and the Messiah Son of Man: Revisiting the Book of Parables*, ed. Gabriele Boccaccini (Grand Rapids: Eerdmans, 2007), pp. 386-402, 387.

resent a challenge to Mosaic authority, Andreas Bedenbender notes that the "absence of strict parallels to Mosaic laws is easily to be explained by reference to the nature and scope of the text. In Genesis 1–11 there are very few commandments as well."[68] Nickelsburg suggests that the literary forms of commandment or halakhic commentary simply did not suit the writer's primary goal of exhortation.[69]

Finally, some have suggested that the absence of such parallels reflects a desire on the part of the writer(s) to avoid anachronism: Enoch lives before the time of the giving of the law to Israel. Therefore it would not make sense for his corpus to refer to the commandments revealed to Israel at that later time. Yet, as Collins has observed, the writer of *Jubilees* made Mosaic law a central concern despite the work's focus on the patriarchal period.[70] Perhaps more to the point, the primeval setting common to Genesis 1–11 and the Book of the Watchers provides a universal and cosmic framework that does not prescind the particular history of Israel, but precedes and also transcends it.[71] Pomykala argues precisely this point in his analysis of the "Scripture Profile of the Book of the Watchers."[72] He calls attention to the pluralistic context of Hellenism into which the book spoke. In such a setting, claims to authority explicitly grounded in the traditions of Israel's election may have been rhetorically ineffective.[73] This is not to deny the centrality of election motifs within the Enochic corpus. It is to assert, rather, that the writer of the Book of the Watchers preferred to locate the authority of its truth-claims in primeval, cosmic, and universal terms. I will explore the implications of this observation in greater detail below.

3. *A single reference to "covenant."* Closely related to the absence of halakhic parallels is the near absence of references to "covenant" in *1 Enoch*.[74] Covenant is mentioned explicitly only in *1 Enoch* 93:6. Scholars interpret this absence in different ways. On the one hand, as Nickelsburg notes, "to judge from what the

---

68. Bedenbender, "The Place of the Torah," p. 68. He suggests that the writers of the Book of the Watchers did not object to the "main body of the Mosaic commandments," but rather to the symbolic universe constructed by the redacted Pentateuch (p. 71).

69. Nickelsburg, "Enochic Wisdom and Its Relationship," p. 92.

70. Collins, "Theology and Identity," p. 58.

71. VanderKam, "Interpretation of Genesis in *1 Enoch*," pp. 142-43. I note here that while in this essay VanderKam emphasizes the relative unimportance of the Sinai covenant in the Book of the Watchers and in the Animal Apocalypse, in a later essay he highlights the importance of the Sinai covenant via the crucial metaphor of "seeing" in the Animal Apocalypse. See James C. VanderKam, "Open and Closed Eyes in the Animal Apocalypse (*1 Enoch* 85–90)," in *The Idea of Biblical Interpretation: Essays in Honor of James L. Kugel*, ed. Hindy Najman and Judith Newman (Leiden: Brill, 2004), pp. 279-92.

72. Pomykala, "Scripture Profile," p. 279.

73. Pomykala, "Scripture Profile," p. 279.

74. Nickelsburg, "Enochic Wisdom and Its Relationship," p. 83.

authors of 1 Enoch have written and not written, the Sinaitic covenant and Torah were not of central importance for them."[75] Yet arguments from silence are tricky, to say the least. Elliott cautions that absence of covenantal language does not imply rejection of the covenant framework as a "life-structuring given." Rather, the presence of covenantal patterns of thought can be detected throughout the Book of the Watchers and the Astronomical Book, particularly in their emphasis on reward and punishment.[76] The Deuteronomistic foundation of the concepts of blessing and curse, reward and punishment in these books suggests to Elliott that the writers and tradents of the Enochic literature wanted to maintain the authority of Moses and his teachings while at the same time asserting a greater authority for Enoch and his teachings.[77] Just as they appropriated the astronomical science of Babylonian tradition within a covenantal framework, so too they reworked traditional covenant categories within a cosmic framework.[78]

4. *The apparent dissociation between Sinai and the giving of the law.* The Astronomical Book does not mention Sinai explicitly. Yet, in its description of the "four quarters" of the earth, it alludes to Sinai as the site of divine descent to earth and/or earthly dwelling place of God (*1 En.* 77:1). In this verse God's theophanic descent from the heavenly to the earthly realm serves as the point of reference and orientation for the southern quarter of the earth. The introduction to the Book of the Watchers explicitly names Sinai as a site of theophany, portraying the Holy One as a warrior who marches with his army (*1 En.* 1:4) for judgment (1:9) but also to make peace and grant blessing (1:8): "The Great Holy One will come forth from his dwelling, and the eternal God will tread from thence upon Mount Sinai" (1:4). The association of Sinai with theophany for the purpose of battle appears to draw on an ancient tradition found also in Judges 5:4-5 and Psalm 68:9, where the march of the Lord, "this one of Sinai" (זה סיני), causes mountains to quake, disturbing even the mightiest fixtures of the earth. Elsewhere in the Book of the Watchers, Kelley Coblentz Bautch finds allusions to Sinai at *1 Enoch* 18:8; 24:3; and 25:3.[79] Together these passages suggest that Sinai serves in the book's geography as the location of God's throne, to which God would descend to dispense blessing and judgment (*1 En.* 25:3-4). Thus, while Sinai is important in the Astronomical Book and the Book of the Watchers, it is not explicitly linked to the giving of law to Israel. Rather, it is the

---

75. Nickelsburg, "Enochic Wisdom: An Alternative to the Mosaic Torah?" p. 124.

76. Elliott, "Covenant and Cosmology," p. 38. Elliott extends Lars Hartman's insights concerning *1 En.* 1–5 further into the corpus of early Enochic literature in *Survivors of Israel*, pp. 245-307.

77. Elliott, "Covenant and Cosmology," p. 38.

78. Elliott, "Covenant and Cosmology," pp. 37-38.

79. Coblentz Bautch, *Study of the Geography,* pp. 120-25, 295.

place where the Holy One descends. This does not exclude God's descent for the giving of the law. It may well include this descent under a more general rubric.[80] That is to say, within the Enochic framework, the descent for the giving of the law may be one instance of a type of descent in which God "makes peace" and grants blessing for the righteous and chosen (*1 En.* 1:8). Yet God also descends to lead his divine army into battle, executing judgment upon the wicked (*1 En.* 1:4, 9). This dimension of divine descent holds far greater prominence in the early Enochic literature than the tradition of the giving of the law at Sinai, which is nowhere explicitly mentioned. Repeated references to the throne of God underscore that in the Book of the Watchers Sinai serves above all as a geographical marker of divine earthly sovereignty, signaling God's active engagement in and providential care for the affairs of humankind.[81]

What is the evidence from the Apocalypse of Weeks and Book of Dreams? The Apocalypse of Weeks refers to "visions of the holy and righteous," a covenant or law, and a tabernacle, but not Sinai itself (*1 En.* 93:6). Given the schematic and allusive style of this apocalypse, one should refrain from drawing strong conclusions from this omission. It names no other places, nor does it refer directly to divine descent of any kind. In the Book of Dreams, Sinai appears as "the summit of a high rock" (*1 En.* 89:29-33). It holds its traditional place in Israel's history as the site of terrifying theophany in the wilderness following the deliverance from oppression. The Animal Apocalypse narrates "that sheep's" (i.e., Moses') encounters with the Lord of the sheep on the summit in an episode filled with references to the open and closed eyes of the flock. In chapter 10 I explore in greater detail links between this imagery of open and closed eyes and the themes of revelation, awareness, and obedience. Here I simply note that while the Animal Apocalypse does not mention the giving of the law to Moses at Sinai, it nonetheless links Sinai with revelation and obedience and contains clear allusions to the narrative of the giving of the law known from Exodus. The fact that the Enochic narrator introduces the motif of "open eyes" in the verse preceding the Sinai event suggests that the writer views the revelation at Sinai as continuous with earlier revelation and even contained within it, but not the sole or even primary instance of divine revelation. The Enochic visions, including the Book of Dreams itself, provide a broader deposit of revelation that does not deny but encompasses the revelation to Moses at Sinai.[82]

5. *Moses does not figure in the Astronomical Book, the Book of the Watchers, or the Apocalypse of Weeks, and the Book of Dreams does not identify Moses as*

80. Hartman, *Asking for a Meaning,* pp. 42-48, discusses the topos of Sinai theophany, and identifies other texts (from *L.A.B.,* Targums, *Exod. Rab.,* etc.) that link Sinai with eschatological judgment and universal accountability.

81. And again, this providential care need not exclude the giving of the law itself.

82. Cf. Newsom, *Self as Symbolic Space,* p. 49.

lawgiver or covenant mediator. The absence of Moses from the Astronomical Book and the Book of the Watchers does not seem remarkable. The only humans named in the Book of the Watchers live in the age before the flood: Enoch himself (passim), Jared (*1 En.* 6:5), Lamech (10:1, 3), and Noah (10:2), and the brothers Abel and Cain (22:7). Neither book contains a review of history, and, with the exception of Noah, no human figure from Enoch's future plays any role in either text. Moses' role in the historical apocalypses is more significant. While the Apocalypse of Weeks mentions "covenant" (*1 En.* 93:6), it does not refer to Moses himself. By contrast, the terse apocalypse refers to four other human figures: Enoch (93:3), Noah (93:4), Abraham (93:5), and Elijah (93:8). By contrast, Moses plays an important role in the Animal Apocalypse, and he is one of only a few "sheep" to be transformed into "human" form (89:36).[83] In the symbolic world of the Animal Apocalypse, this metamorphosis signals his elevation to angelic status, and is hardly consistent with a polemic against Mosaic authority as such. At the same time, Moses is not explicitly identified in this text as lawgiver or covenant mediator.[84] In chapter 10 I examine the role of Moses in the Animal Apocalypse in greater detail. I argue there that he serves as a major exemplar for the community of the righteous. He is commissioned to testify, modeling righteous prophetic activity as well as armed resistance to apostasy. He interacts directly with the Lord of the sheep and with the earthly powers that oppress them. Yet he is not portrayed as covenant mediator. As Nickelsburg has noted, the Animal Apocalypse "transfers the role of mediator, recipient of revelation, and lawgiver from Moses to Enoch."[85]

This type of transfer may occur already in the Book of the Watchers. For example, the book incorporates elements of the priestly benediction, passed on from the Lord to Moses, and from Moses to Aaron and the priests (Num 6:22-27), into the oracle of blessing spoken by Enoch. Just as the Book of the Watchers (esp. *1 En.* 1–5) adapts features of the Deuteronomistic covenant framework to construct its vision of judgment, blessing, curse, and witness, it also borrows the very words attributed to Moses, reshaping them and placing them in the mouth of Enoch. In so doing the Book of the Watchers relativizes

---

83. Cf. the transformation of Noah in *1 En.* 89:1, 9. Noah's transformation may be a later interpolation, as it is not attested in the Aramaic fragments from Qumran. Patrick A. Tiller, *A Commentary on the Animal Apocalypse of 1 Enoch* (Atlanta: Scholars Press, 1993), pp. 259, 267.

84. The extant portions of the *Exagoge* of Ezekiel also refrain from explicitly associating Moses with the law or covenant. Yet this does not imply a diminishment of Moses. Rather, the text elevates Moses, seating him on the throne of God. In the *Exagoge,* as John J. Collins has noted, "The authority of Moses, at least in the fragments we have, is related not to the law but to his ascent to the divine throne." *Between Athens and Jerusalem: Jewish Identity in the Hellenistic Diaspora,* 2nd ed. (Grand Rapids: Eerdmans, 2000), p. 229.

85. Nickelsburg, "Enochic Wisdom and Its Relationship," p. 89.

Moses' role as covenant mediator and authorizer of Israel's cultic practice and polity. Enoch's temporal priority means that Moses' words echo Enoch's, not the other way around. The Moses of the Pentateuch will follow in Enoch's footsteps. In this way *1 Enoch* does not silence Mosaic discourse, but subsumes and even reinforces it, drawing it within the compass of Enochic revelation.

6. *The elevated role and status of Enoch.* In the early Enochic literature, the elevated stature of Enoch clearly dwarfs the relatively modest figure of Moses, who, as noted above, appears only in the Book of Dreams.[86] Three aspects of Enoch's characterization, namely his temporal priority, his righteousness, and his translation to heaven, have suggested to other scholars that the Enochic traditions claim not simply an alternative but also a superior form of authority. I propose that these three features do not constitute a polemic against Moses and the traditions in his name, but rather strengthen the claims of the Enochic traditions against those of the Hellenistic empires. I consider each of them in turn.

a. *Enoch lived in the generation before the flood and never died.* It is argued that Enoch's greater antiquity accords temporal priority to his revelations by comparison with the revelation given to Moses.[87] While this is true, it is also the case that antediluvian wisdom was prized in Mesopotamian traditions that became familiar to Jews exiled in Babylon and to those who had returned from there to Judea, Samaria, and Galilee.[88] The many correspondences between the figure of Enoch and Enmeduranki, a major pre-flood Babylonian wisdom hero, suggest that if an epistemological polemic exists here, it is firstly against Babylonian, not Mosaic, traditions.[89] That is, the claims for Enochic revelation assimilate but also compete with those of nonnative traditions that were influential in the broader religious and cultural milieu.

As a recipient of knowledge before the flood, Enoch provides a unique continuity between the antediluvian and postdiluvian periods. He receives revelation about the cosmos *before* the age of cosmic disorder (80:1-8). At the same time, his foreknowledge of the flood matches his foreknowledge of future disorder, or sin, and judgment. He can testify to the unfolding of God's providential plan over a span of time that encompasses most of human history. Because

86. Of course, in the Enochic literature the figure of Enoch dwarfs *all* other human figures, not only Moses.

87. Boccaccini, *Beyond the Essene Hypothesis: The Parting of the Ways between Qumran and Enochic Judaism* (Grand Rapids: Eerdmans, 1998), p. 74.

88. Karel van der Toorn, "Why Wisdom Became a Secret: On Wisdom as a Written Genre," in *Wisdom Literature in Mesopotamia and Israel,* ed. Richard Clifford (Atlanta: SBL, 2007), pp. 21-29.

89. On "Mesopotamian Antediluvian Traditions," see Kvanvig, *Roots of Apocalyptic,* pp. 160-213.

he has not died, Enoch remains available as an ongoing source of knowledge and perduring guarantor of truth.[90]

b. *Enoch was righteous* (1 *En.* 1:2; 12:4; 15:1; cf. 84:1; cf. *Jub.* 10:17). The emphasis on Enoch's righteousness contrasts with the biblical portrait of Moses, a murderer and fugitive at the time of his call (Ex 2:12-15). Moreover, in response to God's summons, Moses asserts his ineloquence, making it clear that he is not called because of skill or merit (Ex 4:10). To the extent that Enoch's righteousness authorized his revelation, his superior moral standing lent a higher authority to his writings. Yet the contrast and even the claim for higher authority do not require us to infer a polemic against Moses, who is nowhere criticized in the early Enochic literature, or against the traditions that bear his name.

The emphasis on Enoch's righteousness results first of all from an exegetical detail. As noted above, Genesis 5:22 and 5:24 refer to Enoch's walking with God, often understood not only as a description of intimate relationship but also of Enoch's moral rectitude. The close proximity of this detail with the notice that God "took him" suggested to interpreters a causal link between Enoch's righteousness and his ascension (cf. Heb 11:3-5). In the Book of the Watchers, Enoch's righteousness is directly linked with his visionary experience: "Enoch, a righteous man whose eyes were opened by God, who had the vision of the Holy One and of heaven, which he showed me" (1 *En.* 1:2). Hartman suggests that Enoch's righteousness added efficacy to his words of blessing: "Such an access to divine secrets cannot be accorded to anyone without qualifications, and so Enoch is explicitly called 'righteous', and probably this righteousness, in the eyes of our author as in those of other Jews, made Enoch capable of a unique closeness to the Holy One in heaven. When a man of such qualities stands behind a blessing of this kind, the truth and trustworthiness of the oracle are ascertained in two ways . . . : on the one hand, he is trustworthy as a stalwart witness to the divine secrets which God has revealed to him; on the other, the 'blessing' of such a powerful personality is so loaded that it, so to speak, shapes the future."[91] Enoch's righteousness is linked not only with his visionary activity and his spoken words of blessing, but also with his scribal activity (1 *En.* 12:4; 15:1). The link between Enoch's righteousness and his

---

90. Bedenbender argues that the present text of Genesis contains subtle polemical details inserted by Zadokite redactors to counter Enochic claims to authority. These included the reckoning of his age as 365 years and the statement "he was no more" (וְאֵינֶנּוּ), which Bedenbender argues conveyed the message "he is gone, and he has nothing left. *Finis*" ("Traces of Enochic Judaism," p. 43). See also Philip R. Davies, "And Enoch Was Not, For Genesis Took Him," in *Biblical Traditions in Transmission: Essays in Honour of Michael A. Knibb*, ed. Charlotte Hempel and Judith Lieu (Leiden: Brill, 2006), pp. 97-107.

91. Hartman, *Asking for a Meaning*, p. 126.

unique scribal role serves to establish the validity and authority of his written witness, including the writings that bear his name.[92]

c. *Enoch was translated to heaven and from that location had unique and enduring access to heavenly knowledge.*[93] Moses, by contrast, received his revelation in an earthly setting during a finite period of time. Moses came down from the mountain, while Enoch remains in heaven. This final point of difference returns us once again to the cosmic and universal scope of the Enochic revelations. Above, I suggested ways in which the unique claims made for the Enochic revelations countered imperial constructions of reality. Enoch's privileged view of heavenly realities and his guided tour of the ends of the earth challenged imperial claims to authority in ways that Mosaic revelation could not do. The scope of Mosaic revelation was too "earth-bound," local, and particular to fully undercut the ideology that supported imperial ambitions of world domination. As political philosophers Michael Hardt and Antonio Negri assert, the "local" is insufficient to combat a global empire. Empire "can be effectively contested only on its own level of generality."[94] By this understanding, it is only when the local is joined to the universal that it can succeed against the empire.[95] Enoch's priority, righteousness, and access to heavenly mysteries all underscore the universal and cosmic scope of a knowledge that will challenge the authority not of Moses, but of the empire.

In the final analysis, I concur with Nickelsburg, who cautions that *"the non-Mosaic character of most of 1 Enoch does not add up to an* anti-*Mosaic bias or polemic."*[96] While we cannot assert that all Jews agreed on the importance and interpretation of Mosaic Torah in this period,[97] silence about the Torah need not

92. Annette Yoshiko Reed, "Heavenly Ascent, Angelic Descent, and the Transmission of Knowledge in 1 Enoch 6–16," in *Heavenly Realms and Earthly Realities in Late Antique Religions,* ed. Annette Yoshiko Reed and Ra'anan Boustan (Cambridge: Cambridge University Press, 2004), pp. 47-66, 48. On Enoch's role as scribe in the early Enoch literature, including the title "scribe of righteousness," see Orlov, *The Enoch-Metatron Tradition,* pp. 50-59.

93. Orlov, *The Enoch-Metatron Tradition,* p. 258. Orlov argues for "ongoing polemic and competition" between the Enochic and Mosaic traditions. With respect to the heavenly setting of Enoch's revelations, he writes: "The advantage here is clearly in the hands of the Enochic hero."

94. Michael Hardt and Antonio Negri, *Empire* (Cambridge, MA: Harvard University Press, 2000), p. 206.

95. Hardt and Negri, *Empire,* p. 362.

96. Nickelsburg, "Enochic Wisdom and Its Relationship," p. 88 (emphasis original). See also Pierluigi Piovanelli, "'Sitting by the Waters of Dan,' or the 'Tricky Business' of Tracing the Social Profile of the Communities That Produced the Earliest Enochic Texts," in *The Early Enoch Literature,* ed. Gabriele Boccaccini and John J. Collins (Leiden: Brill, 2007), pp. 257-81, 272. For Piovanelli, the parallels between 1 *En.* 1:3c-9 and Deuteronomy 33 invite the reader "to see in Enoch a forerunner of Moses and in Moses a continuator of Enoch" (p. 274).

97. Citing 1 Macc 1:11-15, David Noel Freedman and David Miano, "People of the New Cov-

imply opposition.[98] There is no evidence that the early Enochic literature rejects the Pentateuchal laws as such. Indeed, the booklets contain no polemic whatsoever against specific Mosaic teachings.[99] Nor is the figure of Moses vilified. Where he does appear, he is exalted. He serves as a model of prophetic witness, resistance to apostasy, and engagement with temporal powers, to be imitated in the reader's own day. But he is not presented as the mediator of revelation or of the covenant. Instead, the role of mediator is transferred to Enoch.

When we locate within the multicultural imperial setting the distinctive features of the early Enochic literature, namely its scientific concerns, alternative cosmology, alternative epistemology, and the elevated role and status of Enoch, we begin to see something besides internal Jewish polemics at work. Rather than pitting Enoch against a rival Moses, or, more accurately, tradents of Enochic traditions against the wielders of Mosaic authority, I suggest that we focus our attention on what work the figure of Enoch does in this setting that Moses does not. The unique status and experience of Enoch as living antediluvian hero, righteous scribe, and cosmic visionary allow his writings to look and speak outward into the broader, pluralistic context and there engage the discourses of the empire. The figure of Enoch and the traditions handed on in his name authorize a new understanding of the world that answers a new set of circumstances.[100] In fashioning this new vision the Enochic writers adapt elements of the Pentateuchal, prophetic, and wisdom traditions, even as they fuse them with elements drawn from Babylonian, Persian, and Greek traditions and reposition them all within the framework of Enochic revelation.[101]

---

enant," in *The Concept of the Covenant in the Second Temple Period*, ed. Stanley E. Porter and Jacqueline C. R. de Roo (Leiden: Brill, 2003), pp. 7-26, 20, rightly observe: "We know that not all of the Jewish people felt that adherence to the Law was necessary."

98. Hindy Najman cautions against relying on an argument from silence to claim opposition to Mosaic torah. Review of G. Boccaccini, *Beyond the Essene Hypothesis*, *AJSR* 26 (2002): 352-54.

99. Bedenbender believes that the writers of the Book of the Watchers were not opposed to the "main body of the Mosaic commandments," but rather "the symbolic universe the Zadokites had created by reshaping the Torah," by which I take him to mean a priestly redaction of the Pentateuch, including the material found in large portions of Leviticus and Genesis 1. "The Place of the Torah," p. 71. He arrives at this view by following Boccaccini's reconstruction of Enochic opposition to the Zadokite view of an ordered universe.

100. Nickelsburg, "Enochic Wisdom and Its Relationship," p. 92. Nickelsburg here suggests that the cultural shifts and uncertainties of the Hellenistic period generated a "daily cognitive dissonance" that required new answers to old questions about evil and sin, order and disorder, along with assurances of an ordered future in which the righteous would still have their reward. The distinctive emphases on cosmology and theodicy and the attendant non-Mosaic character of the early Enochic literature are best understood in light of the historical and cultural context in which this literature took shape.

101. Elliott cautions against leaning so heavily on the Babylonian roots of Enochic cosmol-

A similar view is expressed by Pieter van der Horst, who locates the burgeoning Enochic traditions within the intensified "meeting of cultures" of the Hellenistic period. For van der Horst, the Enochic traditions are active players in a competition between cultures, each claiming greater antiquity.[102] In my view, while van der Horst is absolutely right to call attention to the pluralistic matrix in which these traditions take shape, we do not see in the early Enochic literature evidence of a competition between cultures as such. But we do see a set of claims about knowledge. The writers and tradents of the Enochic corpus recognized the relationship between knowledge and power.[103] They understood that the empires that exerted temporal rule on the earth relied on their own claims to knowledge — including scientific knowledge, mapping, and knowledge about the future — to project a worldview that supported and perpetuated their correlative claims to power. They understood that to combat imperial power they would need to undermine and surpass these claims to knowledge.[104]

While Mesopotamia was no longer the locus of colonial rule, yet it was as a result of their encounter with Mesopotamian imperial power that the Israelite and Judean people had their closest encounter with Mesopotamian ways of studying, interpreting, and narrating the universe. The Hellenistic world in which Judea was subject to repeated conquest and successive rule by the Ptolemaic and Seleucid empires was a mixed cultural heritage. Babylonian, Greek, and native traditions mingled freely in the province of Coele-Syria and Phoenicia. The tradents of the Enochic corpus did not reject wholesale the forms of knowledge they encountered in this colonial meeting of cultures. But they

---

ogy that the "Hebrew" matrix is ignored. For Elliott the Enochic tradents adhere to a "conservative Judaism steeped in monotheism and Torah" ("Covenant and Cosmology," p. 27), adapting Babylonian astronomy within a covenant framework (p. 28). Overall, he suggests that "*adaptation*' was the operating method of the Enochic writers just as it was the operating method of a number of the authors of the Hebrew Scriptures." Mark Adam Elliott, "Origins and Functions of the Watchers Theodicy," *Henoch* 24 (2002): 63-75, 74. For more detailed exposition, see Elliott, *Survivors of Israel*. Compare also the insight of Lester Grabbe, "The Social Setting of Early Jewish Apocalypticism," *JSP* 4 (1989): 27-47, 35-36: "The expression of apocalyptic and related movements usually makes use of a wide range of resources in the cultural environment" (p. 35), including elements from "native" and "imported" culture. "Even when the message focuses on a 'return to old paths', it often masks what is really a mixture of old and new" (p. 36).

102. Pieter W. van der Horst, "Antediluvian Knowledge: Jewish Speculations about Wisdom from before the Flood in Their Ancient Context," in *Jüdische Schriften in ihrem antikjüdischen und urchristlichen Kontext*, ed. Hermann Lichtenberger and Gerbern S. Oegema (Gütersloh: Gütersloher Verlagshaus, 2002), pp. 163-81, 181.

103. Cf. Kvanvig's analysis of the "structure of knowledge" and the "structure of power" in the Book of the Watchers (*Roots of Apocalyptic*, pp. 97-98, 296; cf. 333).

104. Hardt and Negri assert that "the real revolutionary practice refers to the level of *production*. Truth will not make us free, but taking control of the production of truth will" (*Empire*, p. 156).

sought to bring each form of knowledge within the purview of knowledge revealed to Enoch by the one God. In so doing they could position all claims to knowledge, including those that underwrote the power claims of the empires, in relation to authoritative revelation from the highest ruler, God.

Finally, as I discussed in chapter 2, to whatever extent Mosaic Torah served as a basis for the "ancestral laws" referred to in the Seleucid charter, by 200 BCE the empire had already commandeered Moses for its own cause, simply through the publicly inscribed act of authorizing the continued use of ancestral traditions as the basis for local and regional governance. This did not negate the value of Mosaic traditions as a resource for resistance. Yet if Moses was to this extent a "company man" prior to the period of the persecution, with his authority bearing a royal stamp of approval, the grander epistemological claims of the Enochic literature had the potential to extricate Moses and his teachings from their subordinate position under the imperial thumb.[105] Effective resistance at this level would require an epistemology grounded in alternative and higher claims to authority. In this struggle, the Enochic claims to authority do not invalidate the authority of Moses or of Israel's other sacred traditions. Rather, they assimilate these within a broader framework that transcends the limits of the particular, local, and terrestrial, reaching beyond to assert a universal authority against the ideology of empire.

Who Were They?

Boccaccini's reconstruction of Enochic and Zadokite Judaism has enormous heuristic value, compelling scholars to take a closer look at the distinctive features and worldview of the Enochic literature. Yet it will be clear from the preceding analysis that I do not see evidence in the early Enochic literature for a polemic between competing religious groups. Nor is it clear to me that we can construct an Enochic religious or social group as such behind the various writings now collected in *1 Enoch*, as some have tried to do.[106] Annette Yoshiko

---

105. The *Exagoge* of Ezekiel may accomplish something similar through other means and within a different cultural setting. Orlov's analysis of the *Exagoge* highlights Ezekiel's transfer of Enochic attributes to Moses, including the heavenly journey and astronomical concerns (*The Enoch-Metatron Tradition,* pp. 260-76). For Orlov this text reflects another stage in the polemic between Enochic and Mosaic traditions, with the elevation of one figure meaning the diminishment of the other. To my mind, the enthronement of Moses suggests political concerns, raising questions about the relationship between Mosaic Torah and governance, both temporal and cosmic (*Exagoge* 67-90).

106. Grabbe notes that "an apocalypse or related form may not represent the thinking of a tightly knit community but rather reflect attitudes found much more broadly in society" ("So-

Reed questions whether these Enochic traditions should be seen as reflecting a single movement: "To what degree does the unity within 1 Enoch reflect the production of its parts within a single socioreligious sphere, and to what degree is the appearance of unity created retrospectively by the act of collection?"[107] On the basis of this uncertainty, Reed cautions against positing a unitary "Enochic Judaism" as distinctive from a unitary Mosaic or Zadokite Judaism.[108] She proposes a more fluid understanding of Judaism in this period, with an awareness of the ways different traditions, Enochic and otherwise, would influence one another across the lines of various groups and intellectual movements. VanderKam calls attention to "the many examples of cross-fertilization attested in the sources," in light of which no divisions should be drawn too neatly.[109] Even those scholars who have argued most strenuously for the polemic between Mosaic/Zadokite and Enochic Judaism call attention to what is shared between the writers and tradents of the Enochic literature and other Jews from this period. Bedenbender issues this caution: "The literary feud between both groups should not be overestimated. . . . Seen from a little distance, both factions of Palestinian Judaism did not look so much unlike each other."[110] Boccaccini similarly suggests that while the different movements he

---

cial Setting," p. 36). Patrick Tiller has also cautioned against the search for social groups behind texts: "Books like Daniel, Enoch, Sirach or other books of the period should no longer be mined for theological evidence of groups that were either the same or different. Rather they are evidence that their writers and compilers belonged to a class of professional sages and teachers, trained in the traditions of aristocratic and/or apocalyptic wisdom (whether native or foreign), whose politically charged teachings had an impact on their own and subsequent generations." "The Sociological Settings of the Components of 1 Enoch," in *The Early Enoch Literature*, ed. Gabriele Boccaccini and John J. Collins (Leiden: Brill, 2007), pp. 237-55, 255.

107. Annette Yoshiko Reed, "Interrogating 'Enochic Judaism': 1 Enoch as Evidence for Intellectual History, Social Realities, and Literary Tradition," in *Enoch and Qumran Origins: New Light on a Forgotten Connection*, ed. Gabriele Boccaccini (Grand Rapids: Eerdmans, 2005), pp. 336-44, 341.

108. Cf. the hesitations expressed by Jeff S. Anderson, "From 'Communities of Texts' to Religious Communities: Problems and Pitfalls," in *Enoch and Qumran Origins: New Light on Forgotten Connections*, ed. Gabriele Boccaccini (Grand Rapids: Eerdmans, 2005), pp. 351-55, 353. Despite his hesitation about identifying groups behind the texts, Anderson does endorse the idea of "religious communities" that edited and passed on the Enochic traditions (p. 355).

109. VanderKam, "Mapping Second Temple Judaism," p. 20. Florentino García Martínez urges scholars to respect the "messiness" of the evidence we have. "Conclusion: Mapping the Threads," in *The Early Enoch Literature*, ed. Gabriele Boccaccini and John J. Collins (Leiden: Brill, 2007), pp. 329-35, 333.

110. Bedenbender, "Traces of Enochic Judaism," pp. 45-46. Contrast Sacchi's position in the same volume, laid out in "Theology of Early Enochism," pp. 77-85. In view of the differences he identifies between them, Sacchi suggests, "It appears that the only thing that early Enochism and Zadokitism have in common is that they both worship the same God" (p. 80). This surely overstates the differences between the two.

identifies within Judaism in this period each had "their own distinct identity," they shared "a common sense of membership to the same religious community."[111] If this is so, then it makes little sense to speak of "Enochic Judaism" as something morphologically distinct from "Zadokite" or "Mosaic" Judaism.

If we refrain from reconstructing a landscape filled with opposed groups, exclusive communities, or rival camps, we nonetheless find evidence in the early Enochic literature for the creativity and diversity within Judaism in this period. Moreover, we find in this literature a living and organic tradition that values traditional modes of revelation while making unique claims for the authority of Enochic revelation in the midst of a new cultural pluralism and in response to imperial claims to ultimate power and, by the time of the Apocalypse of Weeks and the Book of Dreams, unprecedented religious crisis.

Moreover, if we cannot with certainty locate the writers and tradents of the early Enochic literature within a discrete social or religious group, we can — as with the writers of Daniel — venture a few remarks as to their social profile.[112] In fact, their social profile is in many respects the same. Earlier views of apocalypticism located the writers of apocalypses among society's powerless and deprived, portraying them as belonging to small groups who were alienated from structures of power and met in secret to transmit their visionary teachings. This view has now been discredited as reductionist and sociologically imprecise.[113] Like the writers of Daniel, the writers and tradents of the early Enochic literature were hardly powerless. They were literate and they were writers of texts. These facts alone place them among their society's elite. But we can say more: They knew and alluded to a variety of scriptural texts. They knew and utilized motifs from Greek mythology. They assimilated and adapted forms of Babylonian learning. They used all these traditions in complex and sophisticated ways. From these data we can conclude that they were intellectuals steeped in the multicultural environment and in the religious traditions of Israel. They were interested in history, politics, and the future. They engaged in critique and exhortation. Far from an alienated group, they were engaged in regional affairs and deeply concerned with the global and local exercise of power. We can place them among the class of scribes and sages. This suggests a connection to the Jerusalem Temple establishment and to the regional government and its imperial superstructure, as these are the major em-

---

111. Boccaccini, *Roots of Rabbinic Judaism*, p. 36.

112. Attempts to illuminate their social profile, setting, and location, can be found in Tiller, "The Sociological Settings"; Wright, "1 Enoch and Ben Sira"; Reid, "Sociological Setting," pp. 233-34; and Randal Argall, *1 Enoch and Sirach: A Comparative Literary and Conceptual Analysis of the Themes of Revelation, Creation and Judgment* (Atlanta: Scholars Press, 1995), pp. 7-8.

113. For a summary and critique of this view, see Stephen L. Cook, *Prophecy and Apocalypticism: The Postexilic Social Setting* (Minneapolis: Fortress, 1995), pp. 1-84.

ployers of scribes known to us in this period. Yet the exact nature of that connection is unclear.

Whether they critiqued structures of power from the inside or from the outside, it is unlikely that they sought to hide their views. As I argued in chapter 1, attribution of authorship to Enoch was not a cloaking device, but served rather to ground their radical epistemological claims and locate their discourse within a particular authoritative tradition. The extant texts do not contain instructions for keeping their revelations secret. Enoch instructs Methuselah to "keep the book written by your father so that you may give (it) to the generations of the world" (*1 En.* 82:1). The writers and tradents of the early Enochic literature appear bold in their engagement with powers and in their prophetic witness, as the following chapters show. They were activists, and sought by their witness to condemn the wicked and rouse other Jews to awareness and action. The writer of the Book of Dreams was critical of those whose eyes were closed, but also envisioned a time when "the eyes of all" would be opened (*1 En.* 90:35). The popularity of the early Enoch literature at Qumran and the high regard in which the writers of later Enochic writings, *Jubilees,* and the letter of Jude held the early Enochic literature testify to the influence of their teaching and writings.[114]

Languages

Finally, a word is in order concerning languages. At some time after their original dates of composition the Apocalypse of Weeks and Book of Dreams were incorporated into the composite work now known as *1 Enoch.*[115] This book, which was preserved as canonical scripture in the Ethiopic church, survives *in toto* only through a late (between the fourth and sixth centuries CE) translation into Ge'ez, or Classical Ethiopic.[116]

From the time of its rediscovery in the West in the nineteenth century,[117]

---

114. See Annette Yoshiko Reed, *Fallen Angels and the History of Judaism and Christianity: The Reception of Enochic Literature* (Cambridge: Cambridge University Press, 2005).

115. Nickelsburg, *1 Enoch 1,* pp. 21-26, has argued that they were crafted to fit an Enochic testament.

116. Edward Ullendorff, *Ethiopia and the Bible* (London: Oxford University Press, 1968).

117. The Scottish explorer James Bruce brought to Europe three copies of *Enoch* in 1773. One he deposited in the Bibliothèque Nationale in Paris, one in the Bodleian Library at Oxford, and one he retained for his private library. The book received no scholarly attention until the work of Richard Laurence, who published a translation of the Bodleian manuscript in 1821. Laurence in this first edition of his translation posited a Semitic original for the document. Richard Laurence, *The Book of Enoch, an apocryphal production, supposed to have been lost for ages; but discovered at the close of the last century in Abyssinia; now first translated from an Ethiopic Ms. in the Bodleian Library* (Oxford: J. H. Parker, 1821).

scholars suspected a Semitic *Vorlage* for the work. Aramaic fragments from Qumran, first published by J. T. Milik in 1975, have since led to a broad consensus that the book was originally composed in Aramaic. Some scholars have also argued that, similarly to the book of Daniel, *1 Enoch* was composed partly in Aramaic and partly in Hebrew. This thesis cannot be proved or disproved on the basis of the current evidence.[118]

Comparison of the Ethiopic version with the Aramaic fragments and with extant portions of an early Greek translation have led to the further conclusion that the Ethiopic translation was based upon a Greek *Vorlage,* which was in turn translated from a Semitic *Vorlage.*[119] Edward Ullendorff and Michael Knibb have presented arguments for an Aramaic *Vorlage* for portions of the Ethiopic text as well, and it is possible that the Ethiopic text was corrected in places against an Aramaic original.[120] The Ethiopic translation of *1 Enoch* occurred as part of the translation of the Old and New Testaments.[121]

In light of this complex textual situation, in analyzing the Apocalypse of Weeks and Book of Dreams one works at times from a fragmentary text in the original language, at times from a primary translation, and most often from a secondary translation made half a millennium later than the original composition. Such a situation naturally poses some difficulties for literary analysis, and calls for a cautious and sensitive approach to the text.[122] Knibb issues the fur-

---

118. Cf. Nickelsburg, *1 Enoch 1,* p. 9: "The discovery of the Qumran Aramaic Enoch MSS. makes it virtually certain that Aramaic was the language in which chaps. 1–36, the Book of Giants, and chaps. 72–107 were composed, although the authors may have drawn on some Hebrew sources."

119. Nickelsburg, *1 Enoch 1,* p. 15.

120. Edward Ullendorff, "An Aramaic 'Vorlage' of the Ethiopic Text of Enoch?" *Atti del Convegno Internazionale di Studi Etiopici,* Problemi attuali di scienza e di cultura 48 (Rome: Accademia Nazionale dei Lincei, 1960), pp. 259-67. See also Michael A. Knibb, *The Ethiopic Book of Enoch, A New Edition in the Light of the Aramaic Dead Sea Fragments,* vol. 1 (Oxford: Clarendon, 1978), pp. 37-46.

121. For a full treatment of this process, see Michael A. Knibb, *Translating the Bible: The Ethiopic Version of the Old Testament* (Oxford: Oxford University Press, 1999); and Ullendorff, *Ethiopia and the Bible.*

122. Nickelsburg's procedures for establishing text and translation provide a useful starting point (*1 Enoch 1,* pp. 18-20). See further Michael A. Knibb, "Interpreting the Book of Enoch: Reflections on a Recently Published Commentary," *JSJ* 33, no. 4 (2002): 437-50, 442-43, who cautions that we cannot simply treat the versions as translations of one another, but must view each as a witness to a distinct textual tradition. Where "more than one textual witness is extant," Knibb favors translating the witnesses in parallel rather than attempting to provide one translation that aims to approximate a posited original. Erik Larson, however, argues for the close relationship between the Greek and Aramaic texts, indicating that "the Greek manuscripts actually belong to the same stream of textual transmission as the Qumran Aramaic fragments," and most discrepancies between the two owe to scribal error. "The Relation between the Greek and

ther caveat that the text forms we have cannot be placed in direct relationship to one another. That is, we cannot assume that the Ethiopic translation translates the Greek version available to us, or that the Greek fragments we possess translate the version known from our extant Aramaic fragments.[123] Where they are extant, I consider the readings of the Aramaic and Greek texts alongside the Ethiopic, giving preference in most cases first to the Aramaic (where a coherent reading survives or can be reconstructed with some confidence), second to the Greek, and third to the Ethiopic.[124]

Aramaic Texts of Enoch," in *The Dead Sea Scrolls Fifty Years after Their Discovery, Proceedings of the Jerusalem Congress, July 20-25, 1997* (Jerusalem: Israel Exploration Society, 2000), pp. 434-44, 439. Larson also discusses translation technique (pp. 440-44). On relevant recent textual discoveries and the benefits of improved technologies in reconstructing the text(s) of *1 En.*, see Michael Langlois, "Les Manuscrits Araméens D'Hénoch: Nouvelle Documentation et Nouvelle Approche," in *Qoumran et judaïsme du tournant de notre ère: Actes de la Table ronde, Collège de France, 16 novembre 2004*, ed. André Lemaire and Simon C. Mimouni (Leuven: Peeters, 2006), pp. 111-21.

123. Michael Knibb, "The Book of Enoch or Books of Enoch?" in *The Early Enoch Literature*, ed. Gabriele Boccaccini and John J. Collins (Leiden: Brill, 2007), pp. 21-40, 29.

124. Knibb cautions further, "Restorations, however plausible, remain hypothetical, and important as the Aramaic is, we remain dependent on the Greek translation, insofar as it survives, and the Ethiopic version for our knowledge of the bulk of the text of the book" ("The Book of Enoch or Books," p. 33).

CHAPTER 9

The Apocalypse of Weeks:
Witness and Transformation

The "righteous" will witness. They will uproot foundations of violence and the structure of deceit. They will wield a sword. Enoch's apocalyptic vision and discourse of resistance in some ways differs sharply from Daniel's. By contrast with Daniel's twelve chapters, the Apocalypse of Weeks (*1 En.* 93:1-10 + 91:11-17) contains the report of a single vision in seventeen verses.[1] Yet this one, brief vision is no less concerned with the fate of the world. And while it has not yet become fashionable to write about the Apocalypse of Weeks as resistance literature, its program for resistance is no less radical.[2]

---

1. The Aramaic fragment 4QEn^g 1 iv 13-26 (= 4Q212) preserves 93:9-10 followed immediately by 91:11-17, while the Ethiopic text locates the last seven verses earlier in the Epistle of Enoch. Josef T. Milik, ed., with the collaboration of Matthew Black, *The Books of Enoch: Aramaic Fragments of Qumrân Cave 4* (Oxford: Clarendon, 1976), pp. 245-72, 48. For differing explanations for the state of the Ethiopic, see James C. VanderKam, "Studies in the Apocalypse of Weeks (1 Enoch 93:1-10; 91:11-17)," *CBQ* 46 (1984): 511-23, 518; and Matthew Black, "The Apocalypse of Weeks in the Light of 4Q En^g," *VT* 28, no. 4 (1978): 469. See also George W. E. Nickelsburg, *1 Enoch 1: A Commentary on the Book of 1 Enoch, Chapters 1–36; 81–108,* Hermeneia (Minneapolis: Fortress, 2001), pp. 414-15. For challenges to Milik's reconstruction, see Eibert J. C. Tigchelaar, "Evaluating the Discussions Concerning the Original Order of Chapters 91–93 and Codicological Data Pertaining to 4Q212 and Chester Beatty XII Enoch," in *Enoch and Qumran Origins: New Light on a Forgotten Connection,* ed. Gabriele Boccaccini (Grand Rapids: Eerdmans, 2005), pp. 220-23; and Daniel C. Olson, "Recovering the Original Sequence of 1 Enoch 91–93," *JSP* 11 (1993): 69-94. See further Loren Stuckenbruck, *1 Enoch 91–108,* CEJL (Berlin: Walter de Gruyter, 2007), pp. 49-53.

2. This is not to say that scholars have not identified in it a program of resistance. See Richard A. Horsley, *Scribes, Visionaries, and the Politics of Second Temple Judea* (Louisville: Westminster John Knox, 2007), p. 167. On the Apocalypse of Weeks and apocalyptic literature as resistance to Hellenism, see Andreas Bedenbender, *Der Gott der Welt tritt auf den Sinai: Entstehung, Entwicklung und Funktionsweise der frühjüdischen Apokalyptik* (Berlin: Institut Kirche und Judentum, 2000), pp. 111-42.

Perhaps the earliest extant example of the genre historical apocalypse, the Apocalypse of Weeks records a revelation to Enoch concerning the entire history — and future — of the world.[3] Three media of transmission — visual, aural, and written — establish the authority of his revelation and locate its source in heaven. Enoch has seen "the vision of heaven," heard words from the watchers and holy ones, and read the heavenly tablets (93:2). He offers this comprehensive revelation ("I have learned everything . . . I read everything," 93:2) as a testament to his children.[4] While references to the vision of heaven, angelic mediators, and heavenly tablets emphasize the heavenly source of saving knowledge — it is certain, uncorrupted by the false knowledge of the fallen watchers — Enoch's mediation makes this knowledge accessible to the apocalypse's earthly, human audience. With it, they will begin to transform the world around them.

Enoch's vision (it is also called a "parable" or "discourse") divides history into ten weeks followed by weeks without number. While Enoch himself lives in the first week (93:3), the writer and audience live at the conclusion of the seventh week (93:9-10; 91:11). Using the device of *vaticinia ex eventu* (reporting known events from the past in the form of a prophecy concerning the future), weeks one through six contain the writer's interpretation of past events (93:3-8) and week seven an interpretation and program for resistance in the present (93:9-10; 91:11).[5] Weeks eight through ten and the unnumbered weeks that follow convey a vision of the future, including judgment to come, righteousness on earth, and a new heaven (91:11-17). While Enoch's vision asserts continuity between past, present, and future, it opens toward a transformed future. With this radical future-orientation, the apocalypse assures the reader of God's providence and plan for creation while also revealing to the righteous what they must do.

The Apocalypse of Weeks shares many of these features with Daniel. Both works use apocalyptic vision to interpret history, imagine a future judgment and just order on earth, and commission their audience for the work of resistance. In both works the future actions of the faithful are revealed by angelic

3. On the genre, see John J. Collins, *The Apocalyptic Imagination: An Introduction to Jewish Apocalyptic Literature,* 2nd ed. (Grand Rapids: Eerdmans, 1998), pp. 62-65; and John J. Collins, "Introduction: Towards the Morphology of a Genre," *Semeia* 14 (1979): 1-20.

4. On the characteristics of the genre "testament," see Anitra Bingham Kolenkow, "The Literary Genre 'Testament,'" in *Early Judaism and Its Modern Interpreters,* ed. Robert A. Kraft and George W. E. Nickelsburg (Philadelphia: Fortress, 1986), pp. 259-67. Unless otherwise noted, translations of *1 Enoch* are from George W. E. Nickelsburg and James C. VanderKam, *1 Enoch: A New Translation* (Minneapolis: Fortress, 2004). I replace their "sons" with "children."

5. Cf. Ithamar Gruenwald, "A Case Study of Scripture and Culture: Apocalypticism as Cultural Identity in Past and Present," in *Ancient and Modern Perspectives on the Bible and Culture: Essays in Honor of Hans Dieter Betz,* ed. Adela Yarbro Collins (Atlanta: Scholars Press, 1996), pp. 252-80, 270-71.

figures from a heavenly book or tablets. Both works equip their audiences with knowledge necessary for their prophetic task. And both works counter Antiochus's intervention into the ordering of time and space by asserting a divinely ordained sabbatical and jubilary structure for time and human life. Despite similarities, there are key differences as well. Daniel's visions assure the faithful that they will not have to fight, for heavenly battles will determine the course of events on earth. In the Apocalypse of Weeks, as in Daniel, earthly and heavenly realms mirror and interact with one another. Yet, as John Gammie has noted, "the notion of heavenly battles" is "virtually absent" in *1 Enoch*.[6] The emphasis lies instead on judgment. The "righteous" will wield a sword of judgment on earth (91:11-12). God equips them, but the task of transforming the present world order is theirs to carry out.[7] Moreover, only when a new order has been established on earth does God execute judgment on the fallen watchers of heaven (91:15). After this final judgment earth's transformation is matched by the appearance of a new heaven (91:16).[8]

I indicated above that the writer and audience live at the conclusion of the seventh week. When do we date the work? The Apocalypse of Weeks' literary dependence on earlier portions of *1 Enoch* (especially the Book of Watchers) and the probable dependence of *Jubilees* on the Apocalypse of Weeks narrow the range of dates to the period between the late third and early second centuries BCE, or the period leading up to and including Seleucid rule in Judea.[9] We find further clues within the text of the apocalypse. On the one hand, the vision's symbolic and allusive style employs broad strokes and few details. The apocalypse names no one but Enoch (93:1, 2, 3) and offers no dates save the numbering and division of weeks, a period of time whose limit is never defined. Nonetheless, a clearer picture emerges as we compare the description of the seventh week — the writer's present — with what we know about the period of Seleucid rule in Judea (see Part Two).

6. John G. Gammie, "Spatial and Ethical Dualism in Jewish Wisdom and Apocalyptic Literature," *JBL* 93, no. 3 (1974): 356-85, 368.

7. This is in contrast to the Book of the Watchers, on whose opening verses those of the Apocalypse of Weeks are modeled. Although the Book of the Watchers is likewise introduced as "concerning the elect" (*1 En.* 1:2), the verses that follow speak immediately of God's theophany and direct intervention for judgment and transformation (1:3-9). To the righteous, God will give peace and prosperity (1:8), but they are not expected to participate in the judgment of the wicked (1:9). Moreover, in the Book of the Watchers the gift of wisdom to the elect *follows* the transformation of the world (5:8).

8. For Stephen Breck Reid, the "new political regime" described in 91:12-13 "is a prefiguring of the new creation" of 91:15-17. "The Sociological Setting of the Historical Apocalypses of 1 Enoch and the Book of Daniel" (Ph.D. diss., Emory University, 1981), p. 101.

9. See Nickelsburg, *1 Enoch 1*, pp. 440-41. *Jub.* 4:18 seems to refer to the Apocalypse of Weeks.

The description of the seventh week begins with the prediction that "there will arise a perverse generation . . . and all its deeds will be perverse" (93:9). The description of a "perverse [or apostate] generation" and its deeds suggests practices of idolatry associated with foreign peoples. As George W. E. Nickelsburg has observed, the wording "perverse generation" (Ethiopic *tewled 'elut*) is identical to the Ethiopic translation of the phrase עִקֵּשׁ דּוֹר in Deuteronomy 32:5, suggesting that the original text also preserved an echo of Deuteronomy 32:5.[10] There the phrase refers to Israelites who have worshiped foreign gods: "They provoked [the LORD] with strange gods and angered him with abominable idols. They offered sacrifice to demons, to 'no-gods,' to gods whom they had not known before, to newcomers just arrived, of whom their fathers had never stood in awe" (Deut 32:16-17 NAB; cf. Dan 11:38).[11] By borrowing the unique phrase "perverse generation" to describe the writer's own time, the writer invites the reader to identify deeds of the present generation with those described in Deuteronomy 32:15-21, specifically the worship of foreign gods. In both Deuteronomy 32 and the Apocalypse of Weeks that worship is closely associated with foreign domination.

The fact that the perverse generation is said in the Apocalypse of Weeks to "arise" implies a sudden and unexpected beginning at a specific moment in time. James VanderKam accordingly suggests that this "apostate generation" refers to "the rise of a strong hellenizing party in Jewish society at the beginning of Antiochus IV's reign."[12] Loren Stuckenbruck similarly sees here a reference to those who embraced the "Hellenising reforms in Jerusalem" initiated by Jason.[13] Yet I determined in chapter 3 that while Jason's initiatives invited "Greek glories" to compete with, displace, and reshape traditional values, we have no evidence that Jason's gymnasium, ephebate, and citizen rolls in any way compromised the forms of Judean religion. Hellenizing reforms did not directly translate into religious apostasy.

But imperial and local activity soon did. The Heliodorus stele, also examined in chapter 3, reveals that beginning in the reign of Seleucus IV, the Seleucid regime increasingly intervened in the oversight of temple cults in the Palestinian region for the purposes of tighter fiscal control, promoting an ideology of inter-

---

10. Nickelsburg, *1 Enoch 1*, p. 447. This phrase does not occur elsewhere in the Hebrew Bible, but compare the similar phrase דּוֹר תַּהְפֻּכֹת (Deut 32:20) from the same passage, translated "perverse generation" by NRSV.

11. The song concludes by praising the God who "avenges the blood of his servants and purges his people's land" (Deut 32:43 NAB). The Apocalypse of Weeks takes up many of the themes of Moses' song.

12. James C. VanderKam, *Enoch and the Growth of an Apocalyptic Tradition*, CBQMS 16 (Washington, DC: Catholic Biblical Association of America, 1984), p. 147.

13. Stuckenbruck, *1 Enoch 91–108*, p. 62.

dependence that served imperial interests. Antiochus IV's appointment of Menelaus as Jerusalem's high priest in Jason's place made a further step in this direction and spelled the end of the Zadokite high-priesthood. According to the epitomator, Menelaus assisted Antiochus in entering and robbing the Jerusalem temple, violating traditional understandings of purity and sacred space and symbolically challenging God's role as sovereign creator while also interrupting temple worship. Menelaus's complicity in Antiochus's theft could only be construed as a form of idolatry, giving loyalty to king before God. Menelaus and Lysimachus themselves stole and sold wrought gold objects from the temple, perhaps sacred vessels, for their own personal and political gain. The early years of Antiochus's rule thus witnessed increasing imperial intervention into the conduct of Jerusalem's temple cult alongside the increasing corruption of Jerusalem's temple leadership. The temple was a locus of governance, a privileged site of mediation between God and people, and a center of religious teaching. Corrupt leadership could exploit and defraud the local and regional populace, fail to mediate between heaven and earth, and lead a generation astray.

Full-scale idolatry would soon be imposed from above, in the form of Antiochus's edict and the practices it mandated. While a number of scholars date the Apocalypse of Weeks during the persecution itself, others hesitate on the grounds that neither Antiochus's edict nor the temple's desecration receives direct mention in the description of the seventh week.[14] They instead assign a date earlier in Antiochus's reign, between the years 175 and 167 BCE.[15] But the

14. During the persecution: Klaus Koch, "History as a Battlefield of Two Antagonistic Powers in the Apocalypse of Weeks and in the Rule of the Community," in *Enoch and Qumran Origins: New Light on a Forgotten Connection,* ed. Gabriele Boccaccini (Grand Rapids: Eerdmans, 2005), pp. 185-99, 187, and Klaus Koch, "Sabbat, Sabbatjahr und Weltenjahr: Die apokalyptische Konstruktion der Zeit," *Ars Semiotica* 29 (1977): 69-86; Andreas Bedenbender, "Reflection on Ideology and Date of the Apocalypse of Weeks," in *Enoch and Qumran Origins: New Light on a Forgotten Connection,* ed. Gabriele Boccaccini (Grand Rapids: Eerdmans, 2005), pp. 200-203; Ferdinand Dexinger, *Henochs Zehnwochenapokalypse und offene Probleme der Apokalyptikforschung* (Leiden: Brill, 1977), p. 139. No mention of persecution and desecration: VanderKam, *Enoch and the Growth of an Apocalyptic Tradition,* p. 148; Stuckenbruck, *1 Enoch 91–108,* p. 61; Florentino García Martínez, *Qumran and Apocalyptic: Studies on the Aramaic Texts from Qumran* (Leiden: Brill, 1992), p. 92.

15. For the later date, see VanderKam, "Studies in the Apocalypse of Weeks," p. 521; and VanderKam, *Enoch and the Growth of an Apocalyptic Tradition,* pp. 143-49. Matthew Black, in consultation with James C. VanderKam, *The Book of Enoch or 1 Enoch: A New English Edition* (Leiden: Brill, 1985), p. 288, also supports this dating. François Martin, finding no allusion to the Maccabees or to the persecution in the Apocalypse of Weeks, dates the work to "un peu avant 170." *Le Livre d'Hénoch traduit sur le texte éthiopien* (Paris: Letouzey et Ané, 1906), p. xcv. Stuckenbruck suggests "ca. 175-170 BCE" (*1 Enoch 91–108,* p. 62). Note that Stuckenbruck is confident of the priority of the Apocalypse of Weeks over the Animal Apocalypse (p. 62). By contrast, Andreas Bedenbender dates the Apocalypse of Weeks "after 167 BCE." "The Place of the Torah in

apocalypse may not be as silent concerning the edict and persecution as has been perceived. The next verses provide further clues: "And at its conclusion, the chosen will be chosen . . . and they will uproot the foundations of violence, and the structure of deceit in it, to execute judgment" (93:10; 91:11). Together "the foundations of violence and the structure of deceit" likely refer broadly to the physical structures that house unjust rule, social systems of domination, and the hegemony that supports them. The architectonic metaphors of "foundations" and "structure" provide a first clue.[16] Elsewhere in the Apocalypse of Weeks the activity of building has as its object physical houses of worship that are also closely associated with the governing structures of society. The verb "to build" occurs twice in the apocalypse, first in reference to Solomon's temple, which mediated divine sovereignty within the temple state (93:7), and second in reference to the eschatological temple, which will accompany right government marked by God's sole rule and universal obedience to divinely revealed law (91:13-14). The closely connected architecture of worship and rule (they are also syntactically linked: "the temple of the kingdom," 91:13; cf. 93:7) provides a metonym for social structures of governance, whether just or unjust.

In the seventh week, these structures are characterized by violence and deceit. Deceit likely includes false revelation, false cosmology, imperial manipulations, spectacle, and enticements, and the authorizing claims that underwrite them, as well as opposition to God's law, as I argue below.[17] Each forms part of the hegemony that supports domination. We have seen the central role of violence in the ideology and practice of the Hellenistic kings, including Antiochus IV, whose troops now occupied Jerusalem. The writers of Daniel recognized that deceit and violence are foundations of imperial power (recall that deceit was a key motif in Daniel's characterization of Antiochus; see ch. 6), and challenged both by locating power in true knowledge. The Book of the Watchers wove together its critiques of the violence of the Hellenistic kings and generals and false, misleading, and dangerous knowledge, at the level of both imperial cosmology and cultic leadership (see ch. 1). A similar perspective likely informs the writer of the Apocalypse of Weeks, who was deeply influenced by the Book of the Watchers (see ch. 8).

---

the Early Enoch Literature," in *The Early Enoch Literature,* ed. Gabriele Boccaccini and John J. Collins (Leiden: Brill, 2007), pp. 65-79, 67. This dating is a key component of his argument for the *Mosaierung* of the second-century BCE Enochic literature. See also Bedenbender, *Gott der Welt,* p. 120.

16. For the architectonic use of the Aramaic noun אֻשׁ here, cf. Ezra 4:12, where it is used to refer to the rebuilding of Jerusalem and its walls ("they are repairing the foundations"), and 5:16, where it refers to the foundations for the temple (Sheshbazzar "laid the foundations of the house of God in Jerusalem").

17. On deceit, see also Black, *Book of Enoch,* p. 292.

It is frequently noted that, despite references to Solomon's temple and the eschatological temple, the Apocalypse of Weeks makes no mention of the second temple. More probably the second temple *is* mentioned, in the reference to "the foundations of violence and the structure of deceit" (91:11). That is, in light of increasing imperial involvement in the administration of the temple cult and increasing corruption of Jerusalem's priests, culminating in the temple's rededication and new role as the regional center of an imperially mandated cultus, the Apocalypse of Weeks likely considers the second temple to be part of the physical apparatus of unjust rule and a structural foundation for imperial hegemony and the propagation of false knowledge and claims to authority. The foundations of violence likely also included the newly fortified Akra. The physical structures of temple and Akra were key components in Antiochus's program of conquest, terror, de-creation, and re-creation. Without them Antiochus's edict could never have been enforced.

Seen in this light, the Apocalypse of Weeks' reference to the "foundations of violence and the structure of deceit" may well include the edict and persecution and the entire apparatus of imperial and local rule by which they were enacted. Its dimensions were physical, social, religious, and epistemological. The edict's sudden imposition of new religious practices in 167 BCE provides the most logical referent for the "perverse/apostate generation" (93:9). Like the reference in Daniel to a group who "betray the covenant" (Dan 11:32), it refers to those who complied with Antiochus's edict, abandoning the traditional practices of Jewish faith and adopting new practices in their place.[18]

Enoch states that in the eighth week "a sword will be given to all the righteous" (*1 En.* 91:12). Some have seen in this image a reference to the Maccabean revolt.[19] Yet, as Stuckenbruck, VanderKam, and others have noted, the eighth week remains in the writer's future, not the present.[20] The writer may belong to a group that is planning armed resistance to the measures of Antiochus in the immediate future. But the moment has not yet arrived. I therefore propose a date for the Apocalypse of Weeks in 167 BCE, just prior to the beginning of the Maccabean revolt.

The book's audience is the "righteous" community of the writer's own time. We cannot identify the "righteous" of the Apocalypse of Weeks with a particular known social group (see also ch. 8).[21] Nonetheless, as John J. Collins

---

18. Reid identifies the apostate generation with the foreign rulers and their Jewish allies. In the current climate, he argues, the Enochic writer has come to see government service as tantamount to political and religious treason ("Sociological Setting," p. 136n39).

19. E.g., Dexinger, *Henochs Zehnwochenapokalypse*, pp. 137-40.

20. Stuckenbruck, *1 Enoch 91–108*, pp. 61-62; VanderKam, *Enoch and the Growth of an Apocalyptic Tradition*, pp. 148-49.

21. Patrick Tiller cautions that language of "community" or "group" often implies "an or-

notes, they appear to be "self-consciously different from other Jews of their time."[22] Yet this difference is cast in terms not sociological, but theological.[23] We may therefore speak of this group of "righteous" as a community in the theological sense.

Another group also features prominently in the Apocalypse of Weeks — the "wicked." The apocalypse portrays righteousness, on the one hand, and violence, deceit, and sin, on the other, as opposing forces in the history of the world.[24] This ethical dualism complements and grounds the spatial (earth and heaven) and temporal (past and future, or old and new order) dualisms that structure the apocalyptic worldview the text projects.[25] Moreover, the ongoing opposition between righteousness and its negative counterparts and the final resolution of that conflict are key structuring motifs of the apoca-

---

ganized social structure," but nothing in 1 En. provides incontrovertible evidence for the existence of such a social group or details as to its structure. "The Sociological Context of the Dream Visions of Daniel and 1 Enoch," in *Enoch and Qumran Origins: New Light on a Forgotten Connection*, ed. Gabriele Boccaccini (Grand Rapids: Eerdmans, 2005), pp. 23-26, 26. As John J. Collins notes (in addressing the question of a relationship between the writers of the Apocalypse of Weeks and the Essene movement), "We simply do not know how the 'chosen righteous' of the Apocalypse of Weeks were organized, but we have no warrant for assuming that they lived a common life in the manner attributed to the Essenes." "'Enochic Judaism' and the Sect of the Dead Sea Scrolls," in *The Early Enoch Literature*, ed. Gabriele Boccaccini and John J. Collins (Leiden: Brill, 2007), pp. 283-99, 294-95.

22. John J. Collins, "Response: The Apocalyptic Worldview of Daniel," in *Enoch and Qumran Origins: New Light on a Forgotten Connection*, ed. Gabriele Boccaccini (Grand Rapids: Eerdmans, 2005), pp. 59-66, 63. As George W. E. Nickelsburg observes, the Apocalypse of Weeks "claims for certain people a special identity tied to revealed wisdom"; "the claim of special knowledge and sometimes chosenness . . . implies that certain other people are *not* the chosen and do *not* have this special knowledge." "Response: Context, Text, and Social Setting of the Apocalypse of Weeks," in *Enoch and Qumran Origins: New Light on a Forgotten Connection*, ed. Gabriele Boccaccini (Grand Rapids: Eerdmans, 2005), pp. 234-41, 237.

23. Matthias Henze, "Enoch's Dream Visions and the Visions of Daniel Reconsidered," in *Enoch and Qumran Origins: New Light on a Forgotten Connection*, ed. Gabriele Boccaccini (Grand Rapids: Eerdmans, 2005), pp. 17-22, 21.

24. See Koch, "History as a Battlefield." Koch sees *qushṭa*, not divine or human agency, as the driving force in history (p. 191).

25. Gammie argues that the ethical dualism is conceptually prior to the other forms of dualism, and that apocalyptic dualism differs from that found in wisdom literature only by its deferral of consequences for righteous and wicked behavior to an eschatological plane (thus they are distinguished by the "temporal dualism" that is characteristic of apocalyptic but not wisdom literature; "Spatial and Ethical Dualism," pp. 378, 384). He finds the "traditional vocabulary of sapiential ethical dualism" throughout 1 En. (p. 378). Note that Koch, however, locates the origin of the Apocalypse of Weeks' ethical dualism in Iranian traditions ("History as a Battlefield"). Reid writes that the ethical dualism of the Apocalypse of Weeks "reinforces, and even legitimates, the group's own role in the course of history," adding further that it "legitimates the status of the group as the instrument of the sacred" ("Sociological Setting," pp. 102-3).

lypse itself.[26] Although the first week is a time of righteousness (93:3), deceit and violence emerge in the second (93:4).[27] Sin increases in the remainder of the second week (93:4), but in the week that follows, Abraham is chosen as the plant of righteous judgment; the plant of righteousness will go forth from him for eternity (93:5). The fourth week brings "visions of the holy and righteous" alongside the giving of a law or covenant (93:6), while the sixth week is a time of universal apostasy (93:8).[28] Thus far Enoch has not referred to righteousness and wickedness within the same week. These opposing forces seem rather to vie continually with one another so that first one has ascendancy and then the other.[29] It is only in the pivotal seventh week — the writer's own time — that the two forces appear together. A perverse generation arises (93:9) but so too do the witnesses of righteousness (93:10). These forces now stand opposed, so that the righteous, in part by their testimony, uproot the foundations of violence and structure of deceit that support the wicked deeds of the perverse generation (91:11). The opposition continues to play out in the eschatological eighth week, the time of earthly judgment. The phrase "all the righteous" contrasts directly with "all the wicked" (91:12). Again in 91:14, "righteous law" and the "path of eternal righteousness" contrast with "all the deeds of wickedness," which now have vanished from the earth. The opposition of powers in heaven matches that on earth. The "watchers of the eternal heaven" who face condemnation in the tenth week (91:15) contrast with the "powers of the heavens" who will shine forever (91:16). In 91:17, the word pair "piety and righteousness" contrasts finally with "sin," which will never be mentioned again.

In all, the keywords "righteousness" (or "justice") and "righteous" occur twelve times in the Apocalypse of Weeks, appearing in nine out of seventeen verses. The forces and works opposed to righteousness are variously characterized as deceit and violence (93:4; 91:11), sin (91:17), iniquity (93:4), blindness and straying from wisdom (93:8), perverse deeds (93:9), and "deeds of wickedness" (91:14). Those who commit such deeds are characterized as "sinners" (93:4), "a perverse generation" (93:9), and "the wicked" (91:12).

The recurrence of such language highlights the Apocalypse of Weeks' ethi-

---

26. Cf. Nickelsburg, *1 Enoch 1*, pp. 441, 454-56; Matthias Henze, "The Apocalypse of Weeks and the Architecture of the End Time," in *Enoch and Qumran Origins: New Light on a Forgotten Connection*, ed. Gabriele Boccaccini (Grand Rapids: Eerdmans, 2005), pp. 207-9.

27. On the pairing of *shiqra* and *ḥamsa* in other contemporary literature, see Koch, "History as a Battlefield," p. 192.

28. There is some debate over the interpretation of *sher'ata* in 93:6 and its relation to the Mosaic covenant/torah. See Bedenbender, "Reflection on Ideology and Date of the Apocalypse of Weeks," pp. 200-203.

29. See Koch, "History as a Battlefield," esp. p. 191.

cal concerns, encompassing dimensions social, political, and religious, each intimately bound up with the other, and each dependent on sight, knowledge, and wisdom. On the one hand, terms such as violence and deceit have obvious reference to "social" sins and unjust socioeconomic and political structures.[30] We will see below that the writer characterizes the future actions of the righteous in a way that, by contrast, emphasizes economic and social justice. On the other hand, as already indicated, the references to blindness and straying and the language referring to "a perverse generation" and perverse deeds refer also to religious apostasy. The celebratory descriptions of the temple of Solomon and the new temple to be built in the end time place a contrasting emphasis on right worship (93:7; 91:13). Thus for the Apocalypse of Weeks righteousness encompasses both social justice and religious piety, which combine to form, in Klaus Koch's words, "the order of life."[31] Its negative counterpart includes religious apostasy as well as the whole domination system. The social, political, and religious crimes perceived by the writer are organically and structurally linked in the image of "the foundations of violence and the structure of deceit," just as a just social order and religious piety grow from one plant of righteousness and truth.

The apocalypse begins with the birth of Enoch in the first week. In weeks two through six, the writer alludes to the following figures and events known also from Israel's scriptures: in week two, Noah, the flood, and the Noachic covenant; in week three, the election of Abraham and his offspring; in week four, the Sinai theophany, the giving of the law, and the building of the wilderness tabernacle; in week five, the building of Solomon's temple; and in week six, the apostasy of the period of the divided kingdom, the ascension of Elijah, the burning of the temple, and the dispersion of God's chosen people.

The Apocalypse of Weeks' schematic overview of past, present, and future asserts a unity within history.[32] Typologies between the eras of deceit and violence (weeks two and seven) and between the "first end" (the flood) and the latter end (eschatological judgment) invite readers to find an analogue to their own situation in events of the past and to expect God to act now as God had then.[33]

---

30. In explaining the meaning of the verb from this root, H. Haag writes that its "socio-ethical aspect . . . stands in the foreground from the very outset." "חמס," *TDOT* 4:479-87, 479. He adds, "The primary context of *chāmās* is society" (p. 483). At the same time, "all *chāmās* is ultimately directed against Yahweh" (p. 480).

31. Koch, "History as a Battlefield," p. 197.

32. For the Apocalypse of Weeks' complex understanding of history (entailing linearity, parallelism, and alternation), see Henze, "The Apocalypse of Weeks and the Architecture of the End Time."

33. While God is not named as an actor in the Apocalypse of Weeks, God's agency is implied throughout.

But they are not to wait passively. God's action (including the election of the righteous) calls forth human action, including participation in the judgment to come.[34] In the words of Stephen Breck Reid, the Apocalypse of Weeks is "activistic," expecting humans "to be the chief agent[s] of change."[35] To this end the writer outlines for the audience their own role as obedient witnesses to truth and agents of divine justice on earth in weeks seven and eight (93:10; 91:11-12), while also inviting them to perceive continuity between their present and future role and that of the "righteous" in the past. For example, Abrahamic and exodus traditions inform the vision of the righteous economy of the new kingdom in the eighth week. The reference to Elijah in week six foreshadows the prophetic role of the righteous as well as their active, even armed opposition to promoters of false teaching and idolatry (cf. 1 Kgs 18:40; 19:1; Mal 3:24; see also ch. 10). Typologies between the Solomonic and eschatological temples and between the Mosaic and future eternal law shape its vision of worship and faithful praxis. Like the visions of Daniel, this schematic vision of history both consoles and exhorts: Enoch's predictions affirm God's will and power to save the innocent and renew the earth, while also outlining the instrumental role of the "righteous" in God's transformative plan.

To gain a clearer picture of the program for resistance and transformation in the Apocalypse of Weeks, I begin with the description of the "righteous" in its introduction (93:2). Their parallel identifications as "children of righteousness," chosen ones, and "plant of truth" emphasize radical dependence, election, and obligation to obey and bear good fruit. As I have already noted, elsewhere in the apocalypse, language of righteousness and truth finds its negative counterpart in language of iniquity, wickedness, violence, and deceit. By characterizing the "righteous" over against the "wicked," the apocalypse highlights the active stance the "righteous" will take in the seventh and eighth weeks.

The writer's program of resistance takes clearest shape in the predictions concerning week seven. The "righteous" will witness, in both a prophetic and legal sense (93:10; 91:11). Equipped with special revelation and wisdom, they will root out structures of violence and deceit, domination and hegemony, in order

---

34. *Pace* Koch, "History as a Battlefield," pp. 191, 194, who deemphasizes human and divine agency in the Apocalypse of Weeks. I would argue that the passive verbs "will be saved," "will be chosen," and "will be given," do not aim to deemphasize agency, which is understood in each case, but highlight the change in status conferred on the subject by the event in question. George E. Mendenhall writes of a "constant 'feedback'" loop between "religious conviction and sociopolitical reality" in the biblical worldview. "The link between the two was, first of all, the experiences identified as divine action, and, second, the whole complex of religious obligation (in other words, the covenant)." *The Tenth Generation: The Origins of the Biblical Tradition* (Baltimore: Johns Hopkins University Press, 1973), p. 72.

35. Reid, "Sociological Setting," pp. 104, 136n44.

to establish an alternative, just order. Further details concerning the Apocalypse of Weeks' vision of resistance and transformation emerge from the writer's predictions concerning the role of the "righteous" in the eschatological future, from the time of judgment beginning in the eighth week to the beginning of God's eternal and righteous kingdom on earth (91:12-14).

The Righteous

"Concerning the children of righteousness, and concerning the chosen of eternity [or, 'of the world'], and concerning the plant of truth, these things I say to you and I make known to you, my children" (93:2). Enoch's first words in the Apocalypse of Weeks identify "the righteous community" as the subject of his prophecy and testament.[36] The rhetorical device of direct address ("I say to you and I make known to you, my children," 93:2) invites the intended audience to identify with the implied audience, Enoch's children,[37] and also with those variously described throughout the apocalypse as "chosen," "righteous," "plant of truth" (93:2), "plant of righteousness" (93:5), and "plant of righteous judgment" (93:5). The variations among these latter three descriptions of the faithful community as plant point to their major interrelated tasks. The reference to truth highlights their role as witnesses. Righteousness foregrounds their active commitment to justice and their faithfulness toward Yhwh. Righteous judgment looks forward to their eschatological role in enacting the Lord's judgment on earth.

As Enoch's children, the "righteous" receive his testament and inherit the wisdom and vision revealed to him in heaven. The address to Enoch's children thus establishes the writer's own community as heirs to the revelations and traditions associated with Enoch, the wisdom and knowledge they convey, and the authority associated with his name.[38] The phrase "children of righteousness" reinforces this identification while also identifying the community's defining characteristic as righteousness or justice, entailing righteous deeds, "order of life," and participation in the outworking of divine justice (93:2).[39]

Their characterization as "children" emphasizes two further points. The

---

36. Nickelsburg, *1 Enoch 1*, p. 441.

37. Nickelsburg, *1 Enoch 1*, p. 442.

38. See also Stuckenbruck, *1 Enoch 91–108*, p. 73.

39. Koch objects to the translation "righteousness" for *qushṭa*, but does not propose an alternative translation. He outlines an understanding of *qushṭa* as "the order of life, as well as the source of righteous and true *behavior*" ("History as a Battlefield," p. 191). It fuses an Iranian concept with the understanding of צדק found in the traditions of Israel ("History as a Battlefield," p. 197).

first is their radical dependence on God's provident care.[40] Parents give children food, clothing, shelter, protection, care, and love. Parents also educate their children — teaching them skills, practical wisdom, and to distinguish right from wrong. This latter point highlights the mutual responsibility of parent and child, comparable to the covenant relationship between Yhwh and Israel. The designation "children of righteousness" thus evokes not only God's protective care but also their filial obligations to the Lord. The Lord protests in Malachi, "A son honors his father, and a servant fears his master; If then I am a father, where is the honor due to me?" (Mal 1:6 NAB). In Hosea, God similarly laments Ephraim's failure to give piety and loyalty due the divine parent. God threatens Ephraim's infidelity with the sword (Hos 11:6; cf. Ex 20:12; Deut 5:16; 21:18-21). The same duty of child to divine parent and penalty for disobedience (*1 En.* 91:12) are implied in the Apocalypse of Weeks' identification of the faithful as "children of righteousness."

Enoch next refers to them as "the chosen ones of eternity" *(ḥeruyāna 'ālam)*. Reconstructing the Aramaic text בחירי עלמא, Josef T. Milik translates this phrase, "the elect of the world."[41] Indeed, both the Ethiopic *'ālam* and the Aramaic עלמא can mean either "eternity" or "the world."[42] This multivalent language conveys two notions. One, the elect are chosen from and for the sake of the world.[43] Two, their special status and commission endure for all time.[44] The passive participle "chosen" implies divine agency.[45] Their election highlights God's initiative and their eternal dependence on God's free choice (cf. Deut 7:6-9).[46]

The elect are chosen from a world that has given itself over to sin. They are called to stand apart from the prevailing ethos of violence and deceit, and to witness to the way of righteousness in their lives and teaching. But as I indi-

---

40. The dependence of the elect on God is a major theme in *1 En.* 37–71 as well. In the writer's view, according to R. H. Charles, "all righteous living is the outcome of dependence on God." *The Book of Enoch; or 1 Enoch, translated from the editor's Ethiopic Text and edited with the introduction, notes and indexes of the first edition wholly recast, enlarged and rewritten together with a reprint from the editor's text of the Greek fragments* (Oxford: Clarendon, 1912), p. cvi.

41. Nickelsburg reconstructs, בחירי עולמין (*1 Enoch 1*, p. 442).

42. Wolf Leslau, *Comparative Dictionary of Geʿez (Classical Ethiopic): Geʿez-English, English-Geʿez, with an Index of the Semitic Roots* (Wiesbaden: Harrassowitz, 1987), p. 61; Marcus Jastrow, *Dictionary of the Targumim, Talmud Babli, Yerushalmi, and Midrashic Literature* (New York: Judaica, 1996), p. 1084.

43. See Carroll Stuhlmueller, "God in the Witness of Israel's Election," in *God in Contemporary Thought*, ed. Sebastian Matczak (New York: Learned Publications, 1977), pp. 349-78, 362.

44. Stuckenbruck (*1 Enoch 91–108*, pp. 73-74) prefers to emphasize the temporal sense, with its message of enduring election.

45. According to G. Quell, of the 164 occurrences of the verb בחר, "to choose," in the Hebrew scriptures, God is the agent of the active verb 92 times and in all 13 occurrences of the adjective בחיר. "Ἐκλέγομαι," *TDNT* 4:144-92, 146.

46. Stuhlmueller stresses "divine initiative" ("God in the Witness," p. 353).

cated above, they are chosen not only from the world, but also for the world's sake.[47] The two sides of this one coin are also seen in God's promises to Abraham (Gen 12:3; 22:18; cf. 18:18), in the prophetic vision of Israel as light to the nations, and in the Isaianic Servant Songs.[48] According to these traditions, the nations will find blessing and/or salvation through the elect people Israel. Thus the calling of the elect is a pivotal moment in the history of salvation of the world. They play a key role in God's plan for renewing creation and bringing all people together in right worship and conduct (1 En. 93:10; 91:11-17).

Election could have political dimensions as well. Carroll Stuhlmueller notes that the two components of election theology, namely separation from the many and special commission, are united in Israel's royal traditions.[49] In these traditions a chosen king is commissioned with the roles of judge, leader in wartime, overseer of building projects (including the temple), and shepherd/pastor of his people. In all these roles he acts as proxy for God. Saul, David, Absalom, and Solomon were each identified as chosen by God. The later Davidic governor Zerubbabel, viewed by contemporaries in postexilic Yehud as a messianic figure, was also called God's "chosen."[50] Yet, for the writer of the Apocalypse of Weeks, the king currently reigning over God's people — Antiochus IV — is not chosen by God, nor is the high priest the king has appointed. Rather, the "righteous" have been chosen precisely to resist the apostate ruling powers of their day. Stuhlmueller has noted that "when royalty within Israel degenerated to its condition outside Israel and lost its particularly Israelite character, then the quality of the king's being Yahweh's 'chosen' or 'elect' one is returned to all people — partially in Deuteronomy; completely in Deutero-Isaiah (Isa 55:3)."[51] A similar development takes place in the Apocalypse of Weeks: in the absence of an elect king, the righteous elect will not only resist the dominating power, they will also assume many of the prerogatives and duties named above.

The Apocalypse of Weeks' theology of election appears to draw on Deutero-Isaiah in this and other respects. The apocalypse will later identify the elect with the offspring of Abraham (1 En. 93:5). Deutero-Isaiah explicitly linked the choosing of Abraham's offspring with service to the Lord ("But you, Israel, my servant, Jacob, whom I have chosen, the offspring of Abraham, my friend . . . you are my servant. I have chosen you," Isa 41:8-9 NRSV). For Stuhlmueller, in this Isaianic passage "'Servant' brings out clearly one of the essential components of 'election,'

47. On the relationship between particularism and universality as it relates to election, see Joel S. Kaminsky, *Yet I Loved Jacob: Reclaiming the Biblical Concept of Election* (Nashville: Abingdon, 2007).
48. Cf. Stuhlmueller, "God in the Witness," p. 351.
49. Stuhlmueller, "God in the Witness," p. 353.
50. Stuhlmueller, "God in the Witness," p. 358.
51. Stuhlmueller, "God in the Witness," p. 359.

i.e., a special commission for a particular work."[52] Isaiah 43:10 offers further detail: "You are my witnesses — the oracle of Yahweh — my servant, whom I have chosen, that you may know and trust in me, and understand that I am God."[53] *First Enoch* 91:10 apparently draws on Isaiah 43 and Deutero-Isaiah more broadly in linking the key concepts of election, witness, knowledge, and service.[54]

Enoch next characterizes the community of the faithful as "plant of truth" (*1 En.* 93:2; *takla retʿ*).[55] The plant metaphor recurs throughout the Apocalypse of Weeks (93:4, 5, 8, 10; 91:11). In the third week God would choose a "plant of righteous judgment" (Abraham), from whom would go forth "the plant of righteousness forever and ever" (93:5).[56] As "chosen root" (93:8) the holy people are called to be righteous and yield the fruit of God's justice.[57] Their designations "plant of truth" and "plant of righteous judgment" foreshadow the active role of the "righteous" in witnessing against deceit, uprooting foundations of violence, and executing God's judgment.[58]

Metaphor was a powerful symbolic tool for envisioning resistance. It evoked a rich set of associations, some of which were drawn from scriptural traditions. The plant language in the Apocalypse of Weeks closely echoes *1 Enoch* 10:16, where the "plant of righteousness and truth" replaces wicked deeds with "deeds of righteousness." In other scriptures, a plant watered by

---

52. Stuhlmueller, "God in the Witness," p. 365.

53. Following translation in Stuhlmueller, "God in the Witness," p. 367.

54. Black, *Book of Enoch*, p. 291, writes of the role of the chosen in 91:10 that "according to En^g l iv 12 its role is to be that attributed to the 'servant of the Lord' in Second Isaiah, viz., to be 'true witnesses' (i.e. of the Lord); cf. Isa 43:10, 12 and 1QS 8.6 (עֵדֵי אמת)." See also Matthew Black, *The Scrolls and Christian Origins: Studies in the Jewish Background of the New Testament* (New York: Charles Scribner's Sons, 1961), pp. 128f.

55. This is the reading of gmtT^9. q gives *takla ṣedq*. β gives *takla ṣedq waretʿ*, an apparent conflation. Nickelsburg, *1 Enoch 1*, p. 435. Nickelsburg does not support Milik's reconstruction of the Aramaic, in which Milik departs from the threefold parallelism. I follow Nickelsburg's judgment that the threefold parallelism is an important stylistic element in this verse.

56. Koch notes that here Abraham is not a full-grown plant himself, but a sprout, more "the *germ* of the transformation of the field of *qushṭa* into the whole of a human society than a final representation of it" ("History as a Battlefield," pp. 192-93).

57. Cf. Prov 12:3, 12. Mark Adam Elliott argues that the plant motif is best understood in the light of "soteriological dualism." *The Survivors of Israel: A Re-Consideration of the Theology of Pre-Christian Judaism* (Grand Rapids: Eerdmans, 2000), p. 330. But see Loren Stuckenbruck, "The Plant Metaphor in Its Inner-Enochic and Early Jewish Context," in *Enoch and Qumran Origins: New Light on a Forgotten Connection*, ed. Gabriele Boccaccini (Grand Rapids: Eerdmans, 2005), pp. 210-12, who argues that in the Apocalypse of Weeks the plant motif "is not made to carry the restricted sense of a 'community of chosen ones'" as it would in "sectarian" literature (p. 211).

58. Stuckenbruck observes, "The plant here most likely refers to the *human* community of those who will survive the judgement into the future eschatological age of blessing, peace, and unhindered productivity" (*1 Enoch 91–108*, p. 77).

right teaching will bear fruit of righteousness and flourish forever in the land. Psalm 1 declares that the one who follows the Lord's teaching "is like a tree planted beside streams of water, which yields its fruit in season, whose foliage never fades, and whatever it produces thrives" (Ps 1:3 JPS). Similarly, Moses likens the words of his instruction to rain or dew, "like a downpour upon the grass, like a shower upon the crops" (Deut 32:2 NAB).

From the nurturing word of God sprouts a plant of truth in Psalm 85. Here the psalmist prays for God to give life to the people (Ps 85:7), restoring the faithful (85:9) and granting prosperity to those who worship God (85:10) so that the land will yield its fruit once more (85:13). The psalmist listens eagerly for God's saving word (85:9). God's activity will manifest itself in the union of virtues, namely loyalty and truth, righteousness/justice and peace; divine virtues will give life to human virtues. The language of union signifies the mutual loyalty between God and people, the single heart of the people who will cherish the truth of God's law, the practices of righteousness by which they embody God's justice, and the peace God has proclaimed for them to enjoy. The psalmist describes this union in erotic ("faithfulness and truth will meet; righteousness [צֶדֶק] and peace will kiss," 85:11) and agricultural language ("Truth will spring [תִּצְמָח] from the earth; justice [צֶדֶק] will look down from heaven," 85:12). The metaphors anticipate the bearing of fruit in righteousness for all the earth.

Isaiah 45:8 preserves a comparable image. Here the prophet foretells the restoration the Lord will enact through Cyrus after the Babylonian exile: "Let justice (צֶדֶק) descend, O heavens, like dew from above, like gentle rain let the skies drop it down. Let the earth open and salvation bud forth; let justice also spring up!" (NAB). In this case, God's justice is the rain that waters the earth, bringing forth the fruit of salvation. Brought to life by God's righteousness, human righteousness (וּצְדָקָה) springs up (תַצְמִיחַ) from the earth.

By using the imagery of the plant of truth and righteousness, the Apocalypse of Weeks develops themes it shares with these and other scriptural texts. The plant of righteousness is nourished by God's word and the word of God's emissaries, which includes for our writer the words of Enoch and his followers. The plant nourished on the word of truth bears fruit in the practices of justice and righteous deeds (1 En. 91:17).

The Seventh Week: Witness, Uproot, Enact Justice

A different plant metaphor — uprooting violence and deceit — appears in the description of the seventh week.[59] Enoch's vision of the conclusion of the sev-

---

59. In the second week deceit and violence were said to "sprout" (1 En. 93:4).

enth week offers the clearest picture of the Apocalypse of Weeks' program of resistance:

י[תבחרון ב[חירי]ן לשהדי קשט מן נ[צבת] קשט על[מ]א

די שבעה פ[עמי]ן חכמה ומדע תתיה[ב להון]

ולהון עקרין אשי חמסא ועבד שקרא בה למעבד [דין][60]

The chosen will be chosen as witnesses of righteousness from the eternal plant of righteousness, to whom will be given sevenfold wisdom and knowledge. And they will uproot the foundations of violence, and the structure of deceit in it, in order to effect justice.[61] (93:10; 91:11)

In this description resistance takes three interrelated forms: witnessing, uprooting, and effecting justice.

Prior to Milik's publication in 1976 of the Aramaic fragments of *1 Enoch*, the idea of witnessing did not figure in scholarly treatments of the role of the righteous in the Apocalypse of Weeks.[62] This is because the Ethiopic translation lacks the phrase "chosen as witnesses of righteousness," reading instead "the chosen/elect just" or "the elect of justice."[63] Yet witnessing is central to the apocalypse's program for resistance. Witness counteracts deceit by giving public testimony to truth.

The "righteous" are equipped for witness by the gift of knowledge and wisdom. The passive verb תתיהב ("will be given," 93:10; cf. "will be chosen" earlier in the same verse), repeated twice in 91:12 (ויתיהבון; תתיהב), implies God as the unnamed agent who makes possible the work of the righteous.[64] God orchestrates earthly events from behind the scenes, revealing God's will to the chosen and empowering them to act on God's behalf.

60. I follow Milik's edition with reconstructed text.

61. I have replaced Nickelsburg's "to execute judgment" with "to effect justice." See further below.

62. But see now Matthew Black, *Book of Enoch; Scrolls and Christian Origins;* and "The 'Two Witnesses' of Rev. 11:3f. in Jewish and Christian Apocalyptic Tradition," in *Donum Gentilicum: New Testament Studies in Honor of David Daube,* ed. E. Bammel, C. K. Barrett, and W. D. Davies (Oxford: Clarendon, 1978), pp. 227-37; and James C. VanderKam, "1 Enoch, Enochic Motifs, and Enoch in Early Christian Literature," in *The Jewish Apocalyptic Heritage in Early Christianity,* ed. James C. VanderKam and William Adler (Minneapolis: Fortress, 1996), pp. 33-101.

63. See Milik, *Books of Enoch,* p. 267. As Milik has noted, "the Ethiopic version thus lost the important theological idea of the testimony of the just at the end of time" (p. 267).

64. These forms are technically reflexive, but are passive in meaning. See further Alger F. Johns, *A Short Grammar of Biblical Aramaic,* rev. ed. (Berrien Springs, MI: Andrews University Press, 1972), p. 38: "It is important to note that these 'reflexive' conjugations may often have a true *passive* meaning, as well as their expected reflexive meaning."

The content of the sevenfold (i.e., perfect) wisdom and knowledge given to the witnesses likely includes the Apocalypse of Weeks itself and earlier Enochic revelations.[65] Their prophetic testimony will prepare the way for God's judgment (cf. Jer 29:23) by issuing a call for covenant faithfulness and by spreading the salvific teachings of the Enochic tradition.[66] As Koch has observed, they appear to have a mission to their fellow Judeans.[67] Throughout the Enochic corpus, revealed knowledge of the cosmic order, history, and future reflects the will of God and provides the framework for conceiving right action. This wisdom and knowledge would enable the "righteous" to lead others to a new awareness of what God requires and empower them to take a stand against the measures of Antiochus and the deceit and false teaching that had now, in their view, led a generation into sin, idolatry, and violence.[68]

Equipped with perfect knowledge, the chosen witnesses will uproot the foundations of violence and structure of deceit (cf. Jer 1:9-10; Sir 49:7).[69] In the Apocalypse of Weeks violence and deceit characterize both the present day and the period before the flood, establishing a typology between the pervasive sinfulness of the prediluvian period and that of the present. Because the apocalypse adapts this typology from the Book of the Watchers, a consideration of themes of violence and deceit in the Book of the Watchers illuminates their meaning in the Apocalypse of Weeks, clarifying the objects of resistance.

In the Book of the Watchers, evil enters the world when the sexual union of

65. Charles, *Book of Enoch; or 1 Enoch*, p. 229. Randal A. Argall has noted that "in the Enochic corpus, the expression 'to give/be given wisdom' . . . is a technical term for the reception of revelation." *1 Enoch and Sirach: A Comparative Literary and Conceptual Analysis of the Themes of Revelation, Creation and Judgment* (Atlanta: Scholars Press, 1995), p. 42.

66. On knowledge as salvific in this verse, see Reid, "Sociological Setting," p. 87; and Nickelsburg, *1 Enoch 1*, p. 448. For "witness to" specific doctrinal content in biblical usage, cf. Josh 22:34, where the Transjordanian altar is to serve as witness "that the Lord is God." K. Luke separates the legal from the religious senses of witness. "The Biblical Idea of Marturia," in *Service and Salvation: Nagpur Theological Conference on Evangelization*, ed. Joseph Pathrapankal (Bangor: Theological Publications in India, 1973), pp. 113-24, 116. But the religious sense seems to derive from the metaphor of legal action transposed to a divine plane, while action on the divine plane gives meaning to that on the human plane (see, e.g., Isa 44:7-8). Note that *Tg. Isa.* consistently uses סהד for עֵד here and elsewhere. Johannes C. de Moor, ed., *A Bilingual Concordance to the Targum of the Prophets*, vol. 10 (Leiden: Brill, 2002), p. 348.

67. Koch, "History as a Battlefield," p. 193.

68. Cf. Nickelsburg, *1 Enoch 1*, p. 448.

69. Koch interprets the Aramaic in a passive sense ("History as a Battlefield," p. 194). In its place the Ethiopic text has a passive construction, *yetgazzamu 'ašrāwa 'amaḍā*, "the roots of iniquity shall be cut off." By using the noun *'ašrāwa* (roots) in this verse, the translator emphasizes the verbal contrast between the chosen root (*šerew*) of 93:9 and the sinful roots of 91:11. Black, however, proposes that the phrase "race of the chosen root" is a corruption for "captains of the host," and thus *šerew ḥeruy* for *sarwē/sarāwita ḥayl* (*Book of Enoch*, p. 291).

watchers and the daughters of humankind (*1 En.* 6:1–7:1) leads to the revelation of forbidden mysteries (7:1) and the birth of a race of giants who consume human livelihood and devour human beings (7:3-5). In a second account of sin's origins, the revelation of forbidden mysteries to humankind again spells destruction (8:1; 9:1, 9).[70] The blood of humans poured out on the earth witnesses to the pervasive wickedness of a people corrupted by illicit unions and forbidden revelation (9:1).[71] An Aramaic fragment preserves here the word [ו]חמסה, "[and] violence," paired closely with wickedness: "all the earth was filled with wickedness and violence" (9:1; cf. Gen 6:11).[72] The writer of the Apocalypse of Weeks uses the same word to characterize the violence of the second and seventh weeks (*1 En.* 93:4; 91:11).[73] While the word "deceit" (שקר, *1 En.* 93:4; 91:11) does not appear in the Book of the Watchers' account of the watchers' crimes, this keyword similarly develops the epistemological critique already present in the earlier text.

For the late-third-century writer and audience of the Book of the Watchers, the primeval narrative of the revelation of forbidden knowledge and the violent crimes that accompanied it served as a type for their own situation, allowing them to critique the violence, power, and knowledge claims of the Hellenistic kings and generals who fought over Judea while also critiquing religious leadership within Judea (see chs. 1, 8, and above). The writer of the Apocalypse of Weeks further adapts the narrative of the antediluvian period and the judgment on the watchers, giants, and wicked humans. For this writer too, past events constitute types for the present and future, providing a symbolic vocabulary for critique and for a vision of resistance.

Usage of the terms violence and deceit in the Hebrew scriptures sheds further light on their meaning in the Apocalypse of Weeks. In the Hebrew scriptures, the term violence (חָמָס) refers to assault on the human person, including physical attacks on the body and unjust acquisition of wealth by the

---

70. On the relationship between the two accounts, see Carol A. Newsom, "The Development of 1 Enoch 6–19: Cosmology and Judgment," *CBQ* 42 (1980): 310-29.

71. Milik has reconstructed here the Aramaic [חשע]ר. In *1 En.* 9:1 G⁸ has reference only to αἷμα "bloodshed"; G⁸¹ follows the reference to much bloodshed with the parallel description of πᾶσαν ἀσέβειαν καὶ ἀνομίαν; in G⁸² the last two elements are reversed, yielding πᾶσαν ἀνομίαν καὶ ἀσέβειαν. In 9:9, G⁸ reads, "the whole earth was filled with blood(shed) and injustice" (ὅλη ἡ γῆ ἐπληρώθη αἵματος και ἀδικίας); G⁸ omits "blood." G⁸ refers to "lawless deeds" (ἀνομημάτων) in 9:10; G⁸ to "injustices" or "oppressions" (ἀδικημάτων). On the blood of the slain as witness, cf. also *1 En.* 22:6-7, where the spirit of Abel continually brings suit against Cain.

72. Milik, *Books of Enoch*, pp. 157-60.

73. See Milik, *Books of Enoch*, pp. 264-68, 360-61. Milik notes that in 93:4 the phrase is slightly different in the Ethiopic, which states that in the seventh week "will arise great wickedness, and deceit will have sprung up" (p. 265). For the use of the Ethiopic "injustice" rather than "violence" here, see Milik, *Books of Enoch*, p. 267.

rich and powerful.[74] The term thus encompasses a range of social sins having to do mainly with domination and oppression.[75] H. Haag defines חָמָס as "cold-blooded and unscrupulous infringement of the personal rights of others, motivated by greed and hate and often making use of physical violence and brutality."[76]

In Hebrew scriptures the word "deceit" (שֶׁקֶר) frequently refers to public speech opposed to God's law, including false witness and false prophecy. Jeremiah condemns the deceit of scribes who have altered the law of the Lord (Jer 8:8) and false-dealing priests (6:13; 8:10; cf. 5:31; 7:4). Isaiah similarly condemns rulers who have "taken shelter in deceit" (Isa 28:15). In Isaiah (44:20) and Jeremiah (10:14; 16:19; 51:7) the term refers also to false gods.[77] It can also refer to breaking faith, including covenant obligation.[78] In Psalm 119 deceit (שֶׁקֶר) characterizes those who stray from the law: "You spurn all who go astray from your statutes; for their cunning is in vain" (Ps 119:118 NRSV). The faithful one thus declares, "Truly I direct my steps by all your precepts; I hate every false way" (119:128 NRSV; cf. 119:29, 104), and again, "I hate and abhor falsehood, but I love your law" (119:163 NRSV). These statements foreground the opposition between Torah, the teaching of God's law and its precepts, and deceit, which represents false teaching and the deceptive practices of those who have abandoned the way of God's law. The psalmist further specifies that by their deceit those who forsake the law persecute the faithful (119:78, 86). For readers steeped in Israel's traditions, the term deceit in the Apocalypse of Weeks would thus evoke themes of opposition to and perversion of the law of God, even persecution, as well as false prophecy, false witness, corrupt leadership, breaking covenant faith, and idolatry.[79]

Violence and deceit are explicitly linked several times in the Hebrew Bible. In Deuteronomy 19 the phrases "witness of violence" (עֵד־חָמָס Deut 19:16) and "witness of deceit" (i.e., false witness, עֵד־שֶׁקֶר 19:18) are used interchangeably to convey the notion that accusing an innocent person of breaking the law is an act of violence (19:18).[80] Such a pairing might take on new meaning in the after-

74. Haag, "חָמָס," *TDOT* 4:483.
75. Haag, "חָמָס," *TDOT* 4:480.
76. Haag, "חָמָס," *TDOT* 4:482.
77. Cf. E. Carpenter and M. Grisanti, "שׁקר," *NIDOTTE* 4:247-49.
78. Carpenter and Grisanti, "שׁקר," *NIDOTTE* 4:248.

79. Though the word שׁקר does not occur in Daniel, we saw in ch. 6 that the theme of deceit is important for that writer as well. In Daniel the actions of Antiochus are several times characterized by intrigue, lies, and deceit (Dan 8:23, 25; 11:21, 23, 27, 32). It is through such deceit that he gains power (11:21), opposes the holy ones (8:25), and seduces the people of God to the path of apostasy (11:32).

80. In Ps 27:12, the psalmist pleads with the Lord regarding such deceitful witnesses: "Do not give me up to the will of my adversaries, for false witnesses have risen against me, and they

math of Antiochus's edict, when Judeans were being tried and sentenced to death for following God's law. The prophet Micah joins the two terms in a different context, condemning an unjust economy: "Your wealthy are full of violence; your inhabitants speak lies, with tongues of deceit in their mouths" (Mic 6:12 NRSV). As we have seen, systems of domination, named here violence, are inextricably linked to deceit. The writer of the Apocalypse of Weeks envisioned a program of resistance that would root them out together.

I noted above that the writer employs the architectural metaphor of "foundations" to refer to the physical structures and social infrastructures that support the domination system.[81] Within this system, deceit is a tool of hegemony, an instrument for unjust gain, a means of perverting justice and divine law to the advantage of those in power, and a vehicle for false religious teachings that support the ruling ideology, including the edict of Antiochus. In its reference to uprooting foundations and structure the Apocalypse of Weeks combines the architectural metaphor with an organic one, echoing a similar mixing of metaphors in Jeremiah's prophetic commission: "See, I have appointed you this day over the nations and over the kingdoms, to pull up and pull down; to destroy and overthrow; to build and to plant" (Jer 1:10). The organic image of pulling vegetation up by its roots calls to mind natural cycles of growth and death, firmly locating even oppressive ruling powers within the created order of life. The architectural imagery calls attention to structures of power that give the appearance of fixity and permanence but in fact have their origin in time, through human effort. As surely as they are built up from the ground, they can be torn down by the prophetic word. Jeremiah's prophetic precedent and the central position of wisdom and knowledge in the description of the activity of the chosen in the seventh week suggest that in the Apocalypse of Weeks the act

---

are breathing out violence" (NRSV). In Ps 7:14-16, the psalmist predicts that schemers will reap the reward of their violent plots: "See how they conceive evil, and are pregnant with mischief, and bring forth lies. They make a pit, digging it out, and fall into the hole that they have made. Their mischief returns upon their own heads, and on their own heads their violence descends" (NRSV). The pairing of violent deeds, i.e., bloodshed, and deceit can also be found in Prov 6:16-19, which offers a catalog of sins detestable to the Lord: "There are six things that the LORD hates, seven that are an abomination to him: haughty eyes, a lying tongue, and hands that shed innocent blood, a heart that devises wicked plans, feet that hurry to run to evil, a lying witness who testifies falsely, and one who sows discord in a family" (NRSV).

81. Note that in Dan 4, Nebuchadnezzar's kingdom was portrayed as a tree. When the king failed to acknowledge God's sovereignty, the tree was cut down, but its roots were left. Daniel explains that this "means that your kingdom shall be preserved for you," to be reestablished when Nebuchadnezzar learns that God is the true sovereign. In the current crisis, however, as perceived by both the writer of Daniel and the writer of the Apocalypse of Weeks, the time is coming when the present kingdom will be replaced. Thus its structures must finally be uprooted.

of uprooting takes place first of all through the act of witnessing. True witness will eradicate violence and deceit.[82]

They will do so in order to effect or enact justice ([דין] למעבד 1 En. 91:11).[83] The term for justice, here דין,[84] encompasses both retributive and supportive justice.[85] In terms of earthly justice, it can refer to right administration (cf. Zech 3:7), advocacy for the poor and needy, and vindication of the oppressed.[86] As God's justice, it refers both to the punishment of sinners (among Israel, the nations, and all the earth) and to protection and succor for the faithful.[87] The term's use in this verse suggests a role for the chosen as defenders of the dominated people of Judea and accusers of the perverse generation, giving their witness a legal and juridical component (1 En. 91:11).[88] The reference to executing righteous judgment by means of a sword in the eighth week (91:12) develops this meaning further, suggesting that the "righteous" will serve as witnesses (and later executioners; God will serve as judge) in the trial for the capital crimes of the wicked.[89] According to Israel's ancestral laws, such capital crimes could include murder (Ex 21:12; Lev 24:17; Deut 19:12-13; etc.), idolatry (Ex 22:20; Deut 13:6-16; etc.), false prophecy (Deut 13:5-6; 18:20; cf. Zech 13:3), and blasphemy (Lev 24:15-16).[90] It would not be difficult to imagine the Apocalypse

82. A proverb declares, "the witness of truth (עֵד אֱמֶת) saves lives" (Prov 14:25); cf. Isa 19:20. For witness as advocate/intercessor, cf. Mal 2:12 and Job 16:19.

83. Cf. 1Qap Gen^ar XX, 14: עבד לי דין מנה, "obtain/do/effect justice for me from him."

84. Assuming that Milik's reconstruction is correct. Nickelsburg adopts Milik's reading as the basis for his translation here (Nickelsburg, 1 Enoch 1, p. 436).

85. See Vinzenz Hamp, "דין," TDOT 3:190-91.

86. Hamp, "דין," TDOT 3:190-91.

87. Hamp, "דין," TDOT 3:190.

88. In the prophetic literature, "witness" frequently serves as preface to God's judgment, e.g., in Mal 3:5; Mic 1:2; and Jer 29:20-23. In these passages God assumes the roles of both witness and judge. Cf. Luke, "Biblical Idea of Marturia," p. 118. Note, however, that God's judging occurs because human judging has failed. Action against the state must come from outside or above the human system of governance. Cf. Mendenhall, Tenth Generation, p. 92.

89. Numbers 35:30 and Deut 17:6 require multiple witnesses to convict of a capital crime (cf. Deut 19:15). For the calling or designating of witnesses in the matter of Israel's covenant fidelity, see Deut 30:19; 31:19, 26; Josh 24:22, 27. See also Herbert B. Huffmon, "The Covenant Lawsuit in the Prophets," JBL 78 (1959): 273-95. According to Huffmon, witnesses in the covenant lawsuit can "serve as an indication or guarantee that an unfulfilled obligation exists, which justifies Yahweh in actually invoking the curses of the covenant" (p. 293). On witnesses as accusers and enforcers in ancient Near Eastern treaty contexts, see Timo Veijola, "The Witness in the Clouds: Ps 89:38," JBL 37 (1988): 413-17; Theodore E. Mullen, "The Divine Witness and the Davidic Royal Grant: Ps 89:37-38," JBL 102, no. 2 (1983): 207-18; George E. Mendenhall, Law and Covenant in Israel and the Ancient Near East (Pittsburgh: Biblical Colloquium, 1955), p. 35.

90. Deuteronomy 19:12-13 outlines the conditions for execution of a murderer by the victim's blood avenger. The elders of the city of refuge are to "hand over" the murderer to the avenger for execution (cf. wording in 1 En. 91:12). Moses instructs, "Do not look on [the mur-

of Weeks' audience linking each of these crimes with the actions of Antiochus and those who propagated, enforced, or complied with his edict. Those who gave witness would be those willing to speak truthfully about the horrors wrought in Jerusalem and Judea during Antiochus's reign.

The deferral of the execution of sinners until the eighth week (*1 En.* 91:12), however, implies that, while the foundations of domination and the works of deceit are rooted out in the seventh week, perpetrators may yet have an opportunity for repentance and reconciliation before they are finally called to account for their deeds.[91] The witnessing of the elect would thus have a corrective function, summoning Judeans who had strayed to return to faithfulness and honor God's law once more.[92] In a comprehensive study of legal terminology and concepts in the Hebrew Bible, Pietro Bovati examines the relational and communal dimension of righteousness (צְדָקָה), a concept that no doubt informs the Apocalypse of Weeks' understanding of "righteousness" despite the difference in terminology.[93] Bovati asserts that righteousness has to do not simply with the relationship between subjects in general, but that between just and unjust subjects within a community. He writes, "the most difficult, but at the same time the most decisive relationship is the one that the just establishes with the unjust (or those considered so): the just is called upon in fact not only to deal correctly with the other, but to *re-establish justice,* so as to promote a right relationship between all the members of the society."[94] The book of Nehemiah identifies this same prophetic role of calling for repentance and reestablishing right relationship with that of witnessing against the people on God's behalf.[95] In Nehemiah 9, Ezra confesses to God the sins of Israel's ancestors: "They slew your prophets, who bore witness against them in order to bring them back to you" (Neh 9:26

---

derer] with pity, but purge from Israel the stain of shedding innocent blood, that you may prosper" (NAB). Jeremiah was nearly handed over to the people to be put to death for false prophecy (26:24; 38:16). Other capital crimes included failure to observe the Sabbath (Ex 31:14-15), "grave sins against parents" (Ex 21:15, 17; Lev 20:9; and Deut 21:18-21), and sexual crimes (Lev 20 and 21; Deut 22:22). See Roland de Vaux, *Ancient Israel, Its Life and Institutions,* trans. John McHugh (New York: McGraw-Hill, 1961), p. 158.

91. Contra Black, *Book of Enoch,* p. 294, who sees the execution of judgment occurring in stages, with judgment against Israel's enemies, both internal and external, described in the seventh week, followed by a judgment against all humanity in the eighth week.

92. Cf. Pietro Bovati, *Re-establishing Justice: Legal Terms, Concepts and Procedures in the Hebrew Bible,* trans. Michael J. Smith (Sheffield: JSOT Press, 1994), p. 19.

93. Cf. Koch, "History as a Battlefield," p. 197.

94. Bovati, *Re-establishing Justice,* p. 19. Italics original.

95. In Amos 3:13 the prophet delivers to his audience the command from the Lord to bear witness against Jacob. This witnessing appears to coincide with the prophetic role referred to in Amos 3:7-9. Luke writes that "in the Old Testament the prophet is first and foremost a witness to his contemporaries, inasmuch as his preaching will make them realize that there is a spokesman of God in their midst" ("Biblical Idea of Marturia," p. 119).

NAB). As punishment, God handed them over to their enemies, but when the people repented God delivered them. The cycle repeats itself, and Ezra continues, "You bore witness against them, in order to bring them back to your law" (9:29 NAB), "bearing witness against them through your spirit, by means of your prophets" (9:30 NAB). When they again failed to heed the prophetic witness, God again handed them over to the power of their enemies (9:30 NAB).

In the Apocalypse of Weeks, those "wicked" who fail to heed the prophetic testimony of the "righteous" will be handed over not to a foreign enemy, but to the "righteous" themselves. This is in conformity with Deuteronomy 17:7, which prescribes that the witnesses who testify against the perpetrator of a capital crime must also partake in the execution: "At the execution the witnesses are to be the first to raise their hands against him; afterward all the people are to join in. Thus shall you purge the evil from your midst" (Deut 17:7 NAB).[96]

While witnessing thus plays a key role in correcting sinners and bringing the "wicked" to justice, the phrase "to enact justice" ([דין] למעבד) likely also refers to its supportive dimensions, suggesting a program of transformative resistance that counteracts the deeds of apostasy and work of deceit and establishes in their place a new just order in the seventh week.[97] Following Milik's reconstructed text, the root עבד occurs a total of six times in verses 1 Enoch 93:9-10 and 91:11-17.[98] I list these occurrences in the table below:

93:9	וכול עבד[והי בט]עותא	"and all its deeds shall be (done) in apostasy"
91:11	עבד שקרא	"the work/structure of falsehood"
	למעבד [דין]	"to effect justice"
91:12	למעבד דין קשוט	"to execute righteous judgment"
91:14	וכול עב[די ר]שעיא יעברו[ן]	"and all the workers/doers of wickedness shall pass away"
91:17	טבא וקש טא יעבדון	"they shall do/work good and righteousness"

96. Cf. Deut 13:7-12. See Mendenhall, *Tenth Generation*, pp. 90-91. See also 1QS 8:6: They are to be "true witnesses to judgment, and the chosen of grace to atone for the land, and to render to the wicked their desert." See discussion in Black, *Scrolls and Christian Origins*, pp. 128-29.

97. On supportive justice, cf. Hamp, "דין," *TDOT* 3:188. The occurrence of this radical transformation of the social order in the seventh week (and through the agency of sevenfold wisdom) evokes traditions of the biblical jubilee. VanderKam likewise links the periodization in the Apocalypse of Weeks with the jubilee, "a concept unusually rich in the symbolism of liberty and release" (*Enoch and the Growth of an Apocalyptic Tradition*, p. 156).

98. Black reconstructs the verb יתעבד in 91:15, with reference to the judgment on the watchers, where Milik has יתנקם (*Book of Enoch*, p. 294).

In these repeated uses of the root עבד, "to do or make," we see an alternating sequence of wrong and right action. The work of the righteous soon counters the deeds of the apostate generation and the work or structure of deceit, so that justice and righteousness eradicate and take the place of falsehood. The total passing of the workers of wickedness in 91:14 finds its contrasting parallel in the general announcement of 91:17 that the remaining inhabitants of the earth will "do piety and righteousness."[99] For the Apocalypse of Weeks, righteous human action is the fruit of a transformed world order even as it brings that transformation about.

A Sword to Execute Righteous Judgment

In the eighth week, a time of righteousness, "a sword will be given to all the righteous, to execute righteous judgment on all the wicked, and they will be delivered into their hands" (91:12).[100] Here, as above, it is God who will give, providing a sword to the "righteous" and handing over the "wicked" into their power. The task of the "righteous" is to enact God's justice against the "wicked."[101] The execution of the guilty is, in this apocalypse, the final step in eradicating evil and reestablishing justice on earth (cf. *1 Enoch* 16).

While the phrase למעבד דין קשוט clarifies that the sword is for executing judgment against the "wicked" (91:12), the sword is a weapon of war, and in other scriptural traditions the sword is frequently an instrument of divine justice within a military context (e.g., Ps 76).[102] Similarly, the phrase "to be given into the hands of" another, or "to give x into the hands of y," occurs frequently both in scenes of judgment and of warfare (with the two often combined; see

99. Milik believes the implicit subject of the verb here to be human beings. The Ethiopic uses an impersonal construction that does not reflect the verb "to do" (*Books of Enoch*, p. 269). Nickelsburg prefers the verb used in the Aramaic (*1 Enoch 1*, 437).

100. "All the righteous" seems to designate a larger group than that which was active in the seventh week. Cf. Nickelsburg, *1 Enoch 1*, p. 448.

101. Cf. Ezra 7:26: "All who will not obey the law of your God and the law of the king, let judgment be strictly executed (דִּינָה לֶהֱוֵא מִתְעֲבֵד) on them, whether for death or for banishment or for confiscation of their goods or for imprisonment" (NRSV).

102. On the relation between legal and military connotations of judgment by the sword, see Susan Niditch, "The Ban as God's Justice," in *War in the Hebrew Bible: A Study in the Ethics of Violence* (Oxford: Oxford University Press, 1993), 56-77. Otto Kaiser distinguishes the "sword of justice" (e.g., 1 Kgs 3:24; Isa 66:16) from the sword as "military weapon," but notes that, "as a glance at Isa. 34.5f. shows, together with the consideration that war can be an instrument of divine punishment (Ex. 22:23[24]; Lev. 26:25, 33; Isa. 1:20; 3:25; Am. 7:11, 17; 9:10; etc.), the distinction is often vague, especially in the theological language of the prophets." "חֶרֶב," *TDOT* 5:155-65, 157. This would seem to be the case here. See below.

below). Which did the writer envision?[103] Does the verse describe a court scene in which the "wicked" are handed over to the "righteous" for execution, a battle in which the "righteous," armed by God, defeat their enemies, or both?[104]

The image of the sword together with the stereotyped language of "giving into the hands" can be found in three types of texts preserved in the Hebrew Bible. The first type has to do with warfare, especially as typified in the conquest narratives of Joshua.[105] This type holds potential significance for our writer inasmuch as the promise of possessions later in the eighth week may echo the promises to Abraham and his descendants that find their fulfillment in the traditions of exodus, conquest, and entry into the land. Yet given the overarching theme of judgment in the present verse, these traditions do not provide the main theological and conceptual framework for the writer's image of the sword in the eighth week.

The second type of text in which one finds both the language of handing over and the imagery of the sword is legal, dealing with capital punishment.[106] While the sword is not the primary means of execution of the death penalty in Israel's extant legal traditions, in the book of Deuteronomy it is the prescribed means of judgment against idolaters among God's people in the land and those

103. I noted above that the Apocalypse of Weeks departs from the model of the Book of the Watchers by assigning the work of execution to the "righteous," rather than to the angels. Do the "righteous" here imitate the angels?

104. VanderKam writes, "the sword of the eighth week (the events of which are otherwise purely eschatological) can be explained plausibly as a reference to the sort of eschatological war that is depicted in other Jewish sources" (*Enoch and the Growth of an Apocalyptic Tradition*, p. 149).

105. In such contexts, those given over may be either Israelites or their enemies. When Israel is the one being handed over, the phrase most often refers to punishment by God at enemy hands, but sometimes appears in expressions of fear (e.g., Deut 1:27) and corresponding promises that the Israelites will *not* be handed over (e.g., Isa 36:15; 37:10). With victory in war come land and spoils. Thus, in narratives of conquest and war, after enemies are given over into Israel's hands, the Israelites occasionally acquire possessions and wealth, providing a parallel to the sequence in 1 En. 91:12-13. When such victory is granted by God (usually implied in the "giving over" formula), then the land and spoils may be seen as fulfilling God's promises to prosper the faithful people. The following examples are by no means exhaustive. Regarding enemies handed over to the Israelites: Ex 23:31; Num 21:2, 34; Deut 2:24, 30; 3:2-3; Josh 2:24; 6:2; 8:1, 7, 18 (8:18 also refers to "the sword that is in your hands"); 10:8, 19, 30, 32; 11:8; 21:44; 24:8, 11, where the language refers to the conquest of Canaan and its peoples. In Deut 7:24 the formula refers to this conquest within the context of the covenant blessings for obedience, which also include the promise of possessions. The latter theme is elaborated further in Deut 8:12-20, which reminds the Israelites that they obtained their wealth by God's hand. Joshua 21:44 notes that after all the enemies had been given into their hands, the Lord gave the Israelites rest, and every promise came to pass, including the possession of their lands and much wealth (22:8). Deuteronomy 20:13 and 21:10 use the phrase in rules for warfare.

106. On the use of the sword in executing legal judgments, see Kaiser, "חֶרֶב," *TDOT* 5:161-64; Bovati, *Re-establishing Justice*, p. 381.

who have led them astray: "If, in any of the cities which the LORD, your God, gives you to dwell in, you hear it said that certain scoundrels have sprung up among you and have led astray the inhabitants of their city to serve other gods whom you have not known, you must inquire carefully into the matter and investigate it thoroughly. If you find that it is true and an established fact that this abomination has been committed in your midst, you shall put the inhabitants of that city to the sword, dooming the city and all life that is in it, even its cattle, to the sword" (Deut 13:12-15 NAB). Moses here charges the entire people with the duty to carry out the sentence against idolaters from the land. Elsewhere in Deuteronomy, elders have responsibility for capital cases, acting according to God's instructions and thus serving as agents of God's justice. The community are again bound to carry out the sentence handed down to them by the elders (21:18-21).[107] In other scriptures, when a chosen king ruled over God's people, he held judicial power (cf. 1 Sam 8:5) by virtue of his divine commission and was therefore responsible for administering justice (cf. 2 Sam 8:15).[108] But in the Apocalypse of Weeks, the governing classes themselves — king, high priest, and no doubt some among the elders — are among those who stand accused before God, so that the "righteous" receive the commission to execute judgment on them directly from God and God's prophetic agents within the Enochic circle.

In this respect, the program of action envisioned for the faithful by the writer of the Apocalypse of Weeks shares elements with a third type of text that combines juridical and military elements. When a nation's leaders (i.e., those responsible for the enacting of justice) are themselves corrupt or faithless, Yhwh frequently acts against them and in their stead as plaintiff, witness, and judge.[109] In such cases, Yhwh calls upon members of the human community to execute the sentence. Yhwh may use one nation or group to execute divine judgment upon another, often, but not exclusively, by means of military incursion.[110]

---

107. With reference to stoning, de Vaux notes, "The collective character of communal justice was thus expressed to the end" (*Ancient Israel*, p. 159). Mendenhall writes regarding the death of slaves that "the community itself is charged with exercising the executive authority of Yahweh to punish the murderer, and thus at the same time giving (posthumous) redress to the murdered slave" (*Tenth Generation*, pp. 90-91).

108. See de Vaux, *Ancient Israel*, pp. 150-52.

109. Compare de Vaux's description of cases presented before the elders of a community, in which an elder might serve as both witness and judge (*Ancient Israel*, p. 157).

110. In Lev 26:25 it is part of the covenant curse/vengeance upon Israel for disobedience. The model of Israel being given over to its enemies on account of its sins is articulated in Ezra 9:7 (NRSV): "From the days of our ancestors to this day we have been deep in guilt, and for our iniquities we, our kings, and our priests, have been handed over to the kings of the lands, to the sword, to captivity, to plundering, and to utter shame, as is now the case" (cf. also Neh 9:27-30). Other examples abound, including Isa (47:6, re Babylon), Jer (20:4, 5; 21:7, with explicit mention of the sword; 21:10; 22:25; 27:6; 29:21; ch. 32; ch. 34), and Ezek (chs. 7, 16, 23, 30, 31, 39).

Finally, it is often difficult to draw strict boundaries between these different types of texts that use the language of "giving into the hands" and sword.[111] In the present instance, the writer draws on the latter two types, envisioning a scene of judgment that partakes of elements from each. Thus, the nature and setting of the judgment scene remain open to interpretation, perhaps intentionally. The writer may have imagined that the witnessing of the "righteous" in the seventh week would leave few "wicked" remaining in the eighth, and that these might be handed over for execution following the appropriate legal proceedings (by analogy with the judgment on the watchers in the Book of the Watchers; cf. 1 En. 91:15), whether these proceedings would take place before a divine or human judge. Yet the writer may also envision the "righteous" participating in a divinely sanctioned, armed revolt that would execute and establish justice on earth, as discussed above.[112] The "righteous" wait on God's future action to equip them for their work of judgment. It is possible that they also wait to see how earthly events unfold in the remainder of the seventh week before determining their course of action in the eighth.

Beyond Resistance: Righteous Economy, Temple, and the Kingdom of the Great One

When they have completed the work of judgment, the "righteous" "will acquire possessions in righteousness, and the temple of the kingdom of the Great One will be built in the greatness of its glory for all the generations of eternity" (91:13). By contrast with the violence and deceit of the seventh week, the writer here envisions a new economy of justice and right social relations.[113] The

111. For example, in the conquest narratives of Joshua, the peoples of the land are given over into the hand of Joshua and the Israelites he leads because of God's promise to them. In Judg, however, the same peoples are said to be handed over, and often Israel handed over to them, as judgment for sins committed.

112. Nickelsburg speaks here of "the militant activity of the righteous as they execute divine judgment on their enemies by means of violent death" (1 Enoch 1, pp. 448-49; cf. 464).

113. Cf. Nickelsburg, 1 Enoch 1, p. 449. For a biblical example of the unrighteous acquisition of property that may have been in the mind of the writer of the Apocalypse of Weeks (given the probable reference to Elijah in week six), compare 1 Kgs 21, the story of Ahab's seizure of Naboth's vineyard, made possible by the deceptions and violence orchestrated by Jezebel. The prophet Elijah brings to Ahab the accusation and condemnation from the Lord: "The LORD says: after murdering, do you also take possession?" (1 Kgs 21:19 NAB). Abraham, by contrast, models the righteous acquisition of possessions, which is tied to the promise of possessions for his descendants in Gen 15 and 17. Nickelsburg has noted that the Aramaic word for "possessions" used in 1 En. 91:13 (נכסין) is the same word used in 1Qap Gen^ar XX-XXII to describe the wealth and possessions of Abraham and members of his family (1 Enoch 1, p. 449). The wealth of

paired references to acquiring possessions in righteousness and building the new temple envision a total restructuring of society, now called "the kingdom of the Great One" (91:13). Parallels between the Apocalypse of Weeks and biblical exodus traditions suggest that possessions and temple are likely connected in another way — the possessions may provide materials and funding for the construction of the new temple. Acquiring possessions would likely be understood as a reward for righteousness and the fulfillment of God's promise to Abraham in Genesis 15, as I argue below. But it would also serve the purpose of promoting worship of God and establishing a locus of divine rule on earth.

"Possessions" indicate first of all the basic building blocks of the Judean economy. Stuckenbruck emphasizes that "the term for 'possessions' in the Aramaic (נכסין) does not, in this context, so much denote lavish, material wealth associated with precious metals and jewellery as it refers to domestic, agricultural, and agrarian goods."[114] Acquiring these basic goods in righteousness means human thriving within a just economy. Israel's legal and prophetic traditions would have given the audience ample guidance for establishing and maintaining such an economy.[115]

The reference to possessions may also be taken as a promise of reward to the "righteous" for their fidelity, in line with the covenant promises known from Deuteronomy (e.g., Deuteronomy 28 and 30), reversing their earlier experience of domination.[116] This promise also appears to echo God's promise to Abraham regarding the Israelites' enslavement to and departure from Egypt. Three factors strengthen the likelihood that the promise of possessions for the oppressed descendants of Abraham, made to Abraham in Genesis 15 and first realized in the exodus narrative, forms part of the background for the prediction in this verse: (1) the importance of the figure of Abraham and the promise regarding his seed for the writer of the Apocalypse of Weeks

---

the patriarchs is a major theme of the Genesis narratives (Gen 12:5, 16, 20; 13:1-6; 17:23, 27; 20:14; 24:1; 24:10, 22, 35, 53; 25:5-6) and signifies God's blessing (24:35; 26:12-13; 33:11). For themes of social and economic justice and injustice in the Epistle of Enoch as a whole (*1 En.* 92–105), see George W. E. Nickelsburg, "Riches, the Rich, and God's Judgment in 1 Enoch 92–105 and the Gospel according to Luke," *NTS* 25 (1979): 324-44.

114. Stuckenbruck, *1 Enoch 91–108*, p. 136.

115. Stuckenbruck notes by contrast the economic injustice portrayed in Jer 22:13: "Woe to the one who builds his house without righteousness, and his upper rooms without justice" (*1 Enoch 91–108*, p. 137n269).

116. See Black, *Book of Enoch*, p. 293. E. P. Sanders views the "themes of revelation and the promise of restoration and reversal" as *"generative"* for Dan 7–12, the Animal Apocalypse, and *1 En.* 91–104. "The Genre of Palestinian Jewish Apocalypses," in *Apocalypticism in the Mediterranean World and the Near East: Proceedings of the International Colloquium on Apocalypticism, Uppsala, August 12-17, 1979*, ed. David Hellholm (Tübingen: JCB Mohr [Paul Siebeck], 1983), pp. 447-60.

(*1 En.* 93:5);[117] (2) the prominent place of the wilderness period in the writer's historical review (93:6); and (3) thematic parallels between the exodus narrative and that of the new order to be established beginning in the eighth week in the Apocalypse of Weeks. A closer look at relevant texts in Genesis and Exodus brings these parallels into view.

In Genesis, God promises to Abraham that, following judgment on the dominating power, the chosen people will acquire possessions: "But I will bring judgment on the nation they serve, and in the end they shall come out with great possessions" (Gen 15:14 NRSV). The Israelites' suffering and deprivation in Egypt enriched the ruling class that enslaved them, in particular through their conscripted labor in Pharaoh's building program (Ex 1:11-14). In that context architecture gave tangible form to the crimes an unjust ruler perpetrated against God and God's people. The foundations of violence were sunk by Hebrew slaves compelled to obey a violent master. Justice for these slaves was both restorative and retributive, including liberation, compensation, and "great acts of judgment" (7:4 NAB) on the ruler who denied them the freedom of self-governance and right worship of their God as taught to them by Moses (5:2; 8:28; 9:7; 10:10-28; etc.). God identifies the Israelites as God's firstborn son, and demands their liberation "that he may worship me" (4:23 NRSV). God resolves further to bring God's people to a prosperous and spacious land as their possession (6:8), replacing their suffering and want with comfort and abundance (3:8, 17). The promises of justice, liberation, and wealth all find their first fulfillment in the exodus narrative. God tells Moses God will ensure that when the Israelites leave Egypt they will not go "empty-handed" (3:21-22). The Israelites ask their Egyptian neighbors for silver, gold, and clothing (12:35), and the Lord ensures that they receive "whatever they asked for" (12:36). During their wilderness journey the Israelites give their possessions for building and furnishing the sanctuary (35:20-29).

The writer of the Apocalypse of Weeks has established a typology between this early, formative period in Israel's history and the eschatological period, just as the writer has foregrounded the continuity between Abraham as chosen plant in week three and the witnesses chosen from this same plant in week seven. So, for example, just as the giving of the law follows the liberation from bondage in Egypt and is narrated in *1 Enoch* 93:6 (the fourth week), so too an eternal law is to be revealed in the ninth week following the final passing of wickedness from the earth (91:14). In Genesis the promises to Abraham were

---

117. Against this view see Reid, "Sociological Setting," pp. 135-36n36, who holds that the reference to Abraham in week three "indicates nothing." He explains that "Abraham was such a popular figure in intertestamental literature and often depicted as the father of Judaism that such a depiction in 1 Enoch is not a major contribution to the interpretation of the passage."

linked to God's command to "walk in my presence and be blameless" (Gen 17:1 NAB). In Exodus the promise of wealth for his descendants became linked to their worshiping Yhwh according to the instructions of Moses. Similarly, in the Apocalypse of Weeks righteousness is the condition of ownership and stewardship in the new era. Finally, as in Exodus, so in *1 Enoch* 91:13, acquiring possessions in righteousness immediately precedes the building of the new sanctuary, highlighting once again the connection between religious practice and social order, or between the architecture of rule and worship and the economy of justice.[118] It also reveals the linking of blessing and righteousness, gift and responsibility.

A verbal allusion to Zech 6:13 in the prediction concerning the new temple develops this connection further. The account of the eighth week continues, "and the temple of the kingdom of the Great One will be built in the greatness of its glory" (*1 En.* 91:13). The Aramaic, partially reconstructed by Milik, reads as follows: ויתבנא היכל [מ]ל[כ]ות רבא ברבות זוה (91:13). Milik notes that the writer here borrows the language of Zechariah 6:13:

וְהוּא יִבְנֶה אֶת־הֵיכַל יְהוָה וְהוּא־יִשָּׂא הוֹד

And he will build the temple of the Lord, and he will bear (or lift) glory.

In Zechariah, the subject is Zerubbabel, the Davidic heir who governs the province of Yehud after the return from exile. He is called a "shoot" or "branch" (צֶמַח) who will spring up (יִצְמָח) and, as ruler, oversee and complete the rebuilding of God's temple.[119] He will adopt the royal insignia and sit upon his appointed throne (6:13). This messianic prophecy develops themes from Isaiah 11, which had promised a shoot from the stump and root of Jesse (Isa 11:1), there referring to the anticipated ruler Hezekiah, descended from the house of David. His reign would be characterized by wisdom, understanding, knowledge, fear of the Lord, and justice. While the prophet Zechariah drew upon Isaianic imagery to characterize an era of renewal marked by the rebuilding of the temple and the reestablishment of a Davidic ruler on the throne, the Apocalypse of Weeks reshapes Zechariah's prophetic language, carrying with it powerful themes of wisdom, piety, and justice drawn from Isaiah 11, into a new vision of the age to come.

118. Nickelsburg suggests that the combination of the two motifs of possessions and the rebuilding of the temple "is probably a reflex of Isa 60:5-11 and Hag 2:6-9, which speak of the flow of wealth to Jerusalem and of the glory and splendor of the eschatological city" (*1 Enoch 1*, p. 449).

119. On royal use of צמח, see Joyce G. Baldwin, "ṣemaḥ as a Technical Term in the Prophets," *VT* 14, no. 1 (1964): 93-97.

While the temple remains at the center of Enoch's vision, the Apocalypse of Weeks does not envision a Davidic messiah. Instead, the king is God. The lack of reference to a royal messianic figure, Davidic or otherwise, thus points un-equivocally to divine sovereignty. Though the writer of the apocalypse foresees an earthly kingdom, it is no longer home to sin. No longer is a ruler needed to mediate God's justice to the people, for all people are now just (1 En. 91:17). Nor is an earthly ruler responsible for rebuilding the temple. The passive language may imply once again that God is agent (but cf. 93:6-7), likely aided by the work of the righteous human community whose will is now in perfect synchrony with God's.

Moreover, although the Apocalypse of Weeks retains the organic imagery of a plant, explored in detail above, that plant is not a Davidic shoot but the plant of righteousness and righteous judgment descended from Abraham.[120] The plant's origin with Abraham and not the family of David broadens the scope of election and responsibility and adumbrates the writer's emphasis on universal righteousness in the ninth week when "righteous law will be revealed to all the children of the whole earth," and "all humankind" will practice righteousness (91:14). Between weeks three through seven repetition of the word "chosen" indicated an ever narrower group of elect. As sin grew and threatened to choke the earth, it fell to the lot of a small group of the "righteous" to break its hold and tear its roots from the ground through the proclamation of God's truthful word. With this work accomplished, in the eighth week *all* the "righteous" would participate in God's work of justice against the "wicked." Now with this too done, in the ninth week all who remain upon the earth will receive the revelation of God's law and walk according to God's ways. Thus in the Apocalypse of Weeks particularity yields to universality. Indeed, in accordance with the promise to Abraham known from Genesis, all nations find blessing through his seed (Gen 22:18; cf. Gen 18:18; Sir 44:21), for it is through the work of those chosen from his plant that the way is prepared for the universal kingdom of righteousness.

The righteous economy and temple building of the eighth week are not properly acts of resistance. The "wicked" have all been judged, and although "deeds of wickedness" do not vanish until the ninth week, there is no indication of opposition at the conclusion of the eighth. Instead, the vision of a just economy, new temple, and divine kingdom makes it possible for the audience to imagine an alternative to the reality they presently inhabit. In the phrase "ac-quiring possessions in righteousness," the accent falls squarely on the final word, emphasizing an order of social, political, and economic life qualitatively different from the foundations of violence and structure of deceit. By focusing

120. Milik, *Books of Enoch*, p. 268.

attention on the glory of the future temple, the writer of the Apocalypse of Weeks could locate future divine rule outside the current temple and Akra and draw attention away from the distracting and deceptive glamour of these and other structures of power, while insisting on the central place of worship in the order of human life. By naming this order "the kingdom of the Great One," the apocalypse undercuts all other claims to power and rule and identifies God as the definitive measure of value. This vision of the future provided orientation for resistance to Antiochus's edict and persecution.

Conclusion

During the persecution, the apocalyptic vision of weeks told a people their story, revealed to them their identity, and showed them a future they believed worth fighting for. In a time of unprecedented confusion it equipped them with knowledge and wisdom for witness. Earlier Enochic traditions asserted the fundamental connection between violence and false knowledge. Developing the typology between the age before the flood and the age of Hellenistic imperial rule, the Apocalypse of Weeks commissioned its audience to uproot the foundations of violence and the structure of deceit of their own day, and directed every act of resistance toward righteousness, justice, truth, and the order of life revealed by God. The apocalypse also envisioned a future time when the "righteous" would be given a sword to execute judgment on the "wicked" in order to enact and establish justice. After judgment the "righteous" would acquire possessions in righteousness and participate in the building of the new temple. Those who had struggled to find a center in a desolated city would find a point of orientation in this vision of a future just economy, future temple, and the kingdom of the Great One. This vision was shaped by Israel's sacred traditions concerning the promise to Abraham and the exodus from Egypt as well as prophetic promises of future king and temple. Yet Enoch's vision claimed an even higher authority — the vision of heaven, the words of the watchers and holy ones, and the heavenly tablets. The edict of Antiochus had no comparable authority. The witness of the "righteous" children of Enoch would reveal it to be false, and deny it the power to order life in Judea. The true order of life was righteousness and the law of God.

CHAPTER 10

The Book of Dreams: See and Cry Out

The Enochic Book of Dreams (1 *En.* 83–90) counters imperial hegemony by calling the people of Judea to open their eyes and ears. They must see and hear God's law, given to Moses and preached by the prophets, and the order of creation, written in the course of the stars. They must see past and future, a flood vision, Israel's story with God and empires, the end of domination, and God's joy in the peace of all peoples.

When they see, the people of Judea will understand and obey God's will. They will not stray from the path they must follow. They will also cry out. With open eyes they will know that some stars had fallen and some shepherds (i.e., angels given authority over Judeans from the time of Jerusalem's first conquest by the Babylonians through the time of its reconquest by Antiochus IV) had defied the justice of God. Although Antiochus IV is not named or imaged, the Book of Dreams calls its readers to resist his edict and persecution with prayer and prophetic preaching and to fight against his armies.

The Book of Dreams contains two visions. In the first vision Enoch sees the destruction of the earth in the great flood. He responds with lament and intercessory prayer. The second vision portrays Israel as sheep and God as the "Lord of the sheep." Although shepherds are assigned to watch over them, wild animals attack the sheep. Enoch sees God put their enemies to flight, split the earth for them, and give them a sword. He also sees God judge the stars, the shepherds, and the blinded sheep. All the sheep who remain on earth become good. God removes their old "house" and builds for them a new one.

Antiochus IV imposed on Judea a program of de-creation and re-creation, assigning to himself the roles of creator and provider and commanding his subjects to obey his edict and forsake their tradition, identity, and God. The Book of Dreams resisted by giving new life to past traditions in a story that spanned past, present, and future; by modeling prayer; by asserting the identity of the

346

faithful as sheep who belonged to one owner throughout their history; and by calling for obedience to God alone. The book undercuts Antiochus's authority by denying him a role in the story. In the second vision angelic shepherds, not kings, had authority over Judeans in the age of Seleucid domination. This apocalypse asserted God's role as sovereign creator and just judge. God — not Antiochus — ordered and cared for the universe. And for this reason, as dire as the persecution was, the situation was not hopeless. Israel's traditions, especially flood and exodus narratives, established God's pattern of intervention and care.[1] The Book of Dreams revealed to its audience that God would act again to judge, save, and create anew.

Israel's traditions — including the very scriptures Antiochus IV burned and proscribed — provided a key for unlocking the meaning of the present crisis and the pattern of things to come. They held a pattern not only for God's action, but also for human action. Action followed understanding. The writer emphasized worship and fidelity to divinely revealed teaching. Against the measures of Antiochus, Enoch sees a group of lambs engaged in prophetic activity, calling for repentance and obedience to divine law. Through prayer this group also interceded with God on behalf of God's flock. Enoch himself models these same roles in the first dream vision.

By contrast with the heroes of Daniel's final vision (see ch. 7), Enoch sees the lambs accept the leadership of Judas Maccabeus and take up arms against Antiochus IV and those who enforced his program of terror, de-creation, and re-creation. The writer of the Book of Dreams believed that God and the heavenly scribe would fight with them to end foreign rule in Judea. Even the sword they carried would be given by God. After victory, God would judge. Then earth and creatures would be transformed. In contrast to the Apocalypse of Weeks, the faithful would not help to execute judgment, though they would, as in the Apocalypse of Weeks, participate in the new order to come.

I pause briefly to address the date and integrity of the Book of Dreams. I follow a majority of scholars in accepting its unity and in assigning a date for its composition between the years 165 and 160 BCE (i.e., during the Maccabean revolt).[2] Within the book, the second vision, or Animal Apocalypse (*1 En.* 85:1–

---

1. Carol A. Newsom argues that God's preservation of the righteous is a guiding theme of the work: "The specific intention of the piece I take as a proof that though God permits the existence of powers inimical to his elect, yet he will never allow them to perish utterly but will secure their ultimate victory." "Enoch 83–90: The Historical Résumé as Biblical Exegesis" (unpublished Ph.D. seminar paper, Harvard University, 1975), p. 33.

2. The following scholars all assume or argue for the integrity of the work and propose dates within this range: Stephen Breck Reid, "The Sociological Setting of the Historical Apocalypses of 1 Enoch and the Book of Daniel" (Ph.D. diss., Emory University, 1981), p. 105; James C. VanderKam, *Enoch and the Growth of an Apocalyptic Tradition* (Washington, DC: Catholic Bib-

90:38), is distinguished both by its length and by its sustained use of animal symbolism/allegory. Some scholars have accordingly treated the Animal Apocalypse in isolation from the remainder of the Book of Dreams.[3] Yet the thematic unity of the whole militates against discussing either vision in isolation from the other or from their shared narrative framework.[4] The writer has woven together multiple pieces of tradition to form one coherent message.

---

lical Association of America, 1984), pp. 161-63; David Bryan, *Cosmos, Chaos and the Kosher Mentality* (Sheffield: Sheffield Academic, 1995), pp. 37-38; Robert G. Hall, *Revealed Histories: Techniques for Ancient Jewish and Christian Historiography* (Sheffield: Sheffield Academic Press, 1991), pp. 62-68; J. T. Milik, ed., with the collaboration of Matthew Black, *The Books of Enoch: Aramaic Fragments of Qumrân Cave 4* (Oxford: Clarendon, 1976), p. 44; Matthew Black, in consultation with James C. VanderKam, *The Book of Enoch or 1 Enoch: A New English Edition* (Leiden: Brill, 1985), pp. 19-20; R. H. Charles, *The Book of Enoch; or 1 Enoch, translated from the editor's Ethiopic Text and edited with the introduction, notes and indexes of the first edition wholly recast, enlarged and rewritten together with a reprint from the editor's text of the Greek fragments* (Oxford: Clarendon, 1912), p. 179. George W. E. Nickelsburg dates the Animal Apocalypse to this period but allows only that the date of the composition of the Animal Apocalypse provides a terminus post quem for the composition of the first vision and so the Book of Dreams as a whole. *1 Enoch 1: A Commentary on the Book of 1 Enoch, Chapters 1–36; 81–108*, Hermeneia (Minneapolis: Fortress, 2001), p. 347. Patrick Tiller writes, "There is some indication that the unity of the two dream-visions is the result of editorial activity and not of common authorship." *A Commentary on the Animal Apocalypse of 1 Enoch* (Atlanta: Scholars Press, 1993), p. 98. He concludes, "Since there are no indications of common authorship and there are definite traces of redactional activity to unite the two dream-visions, it seems certain that the *An. Apoc.* was originally an independent work. It is impossible to say whether the first dream-vision was also once independent since its narrative framework is precisely that of the present text (first person narrative)" (pp. 99-100). When I speak of unity I do not exclude the possibility that the two visions were composed at different times and then joined together within a common narrative framework, with possibly more than one layer of redactional activity.

    3. E.g., Tiller, *Commentary;* Bryan, *Cosmos;* Paul Porter, *Metaphors and Monsters: A Literary Critical Study of Daniel 7 and 8* (Lund: Gleerup, 1983), pp. 43-60; Ida Fröhlich, *"Time and Times and Half a Time": Historical Consciousness in the Jewish Literature of the Persian and Hellenistic Eras* (Sheffield: Sheffield Academic, 1996), pp. 82-90; Daniel Assefa, *L'Apocalypse des animaux (1 Hen 85–90): une propagande militaire?* (Leiden: Brill, 2007). Nickelsburg suggests that the first vision came later, "shaped from traditional material . . . for the purpose of providing a companion piece to what is now the second dream vision" (*1 Enoch 1*, p. 347). Black, by contrast, thinks the first dream vision may have been an earlier source given prominent place by the composer of the Book of Dreams (*Book of Enoch*, p. 20). A similar view is advanced by Philip Tite, who believes that the first vision originated prior to the Animal Apocalypse but was not paired with the Animal Apocalypse until after the revolt had succeeded. "Textual and Redactional Aspects of the Book of Dreams (1 Enoch 83–90)," *BTB* 31 (2001): 106-20. Yet elements of the redacted text (for example, Enoch's reaction in 90:41-42) that indicate for Tite a later date of composition make equal sense in the period of persecution and revolt. See further below.

    4. Charles writes that the Book of Dreams is the "most complete and self-consistent of all the sections" of Enoch (*Book of Enoch; or 1 Enoch*, p. 179). Black echoes Charles's characterization of the Book of Dreams as the most "self-consistent" portion of *1 Enoch* (*Book of Enoch,*

A recent study challenges the consensus view concerning the date and militant outlook of the Animal Apocalypse. In his book *L'Apocalypse des animaux (1 Hen 85–90): une propagande militaire?* Daniel Assefa argues that the bulk of the Animal Apocalypse originated prior to the persecution, perhaps during the Syrian wars between the Ptolemies and Seleucids.[5] He answers the question in his title negatively — the apocalypse did not originally serve as military propaganda; its original version was nonviolent.[6] He offers several reasons for suggesting the earlier date: (1) The text of the Animal Apocalypse portrays the Hellenistic period as the most difficult for God's people but makes no clear reference to Antiochus.[7] (2) The apocalypse does not oppose itself to political power, but to blindness.[8] (3) The universal focus of the final vision of transformation (e.g., 90:30) transcends any particular crisis.[9] (4) The Animal Apocalypse is too long, imaginative, and complex to have been composed in a time of great crisis, but would have required a longer period for its composition.[10] (5) In the apocalyptic review of history, the vision's heroes are not militant figures and thus do not model militant activity.[11] (6) The Animal Apocalypse is critical of the second temple, whereas defense of the temple was a key motivator in the movement of armed resistance to Antiochus.[12] (7) Verses portraying the Maccabean revolt (90:13-15, 19, 31, 38) interrupt the logic of the narrative.[13] Assefa argues that in the proposed earlier setting the apocalypse critiqued the wars of the Diadochoi and the blindness of Judeans who were forsaking re-

---

p. 19). VanderKam writes that "as the AA dominates the BD and there is no indication in the text which would suggest that the apocalypse was written by someone other than the writer of the entire BD, establishing a date for the AA should reveal the date for the complete booklet" (*Enoch and the Growth of an Apocalyptic Tradition*, p. 161). Reid argues from thematic coherence for the literary unity of the whole, noting that the first dream vision report introduces the second, and arguing that the two portions cannot be understood apart from one another ("Sociological Setting," p. 105). Bryan reviews recent arguments for treating the book as a unity, analyzing thematic parallels and shared concerns. He suggests that "the case for the unity of the two dreams is not to be dismissed lightly" (*Cosmos*, pp. 37-38). Nickelsburg treats elements of the narrative frame as redaction (e.g., 90:39-42), but finds that the Book of Dreams "as a whole has a certain unity" (*1 Enoch 1*, p. 408). Newsom finds that the first vision "serves as the hermeneutical key for the proper interpretation of the subsequent beast vision" ("Enoch 83–90," p. 8).

5. Assefa, *L'Apocalypse des animaux*, pp. 214-15.
6. Assefa, *L'Apocalypse des animaux*, p. 214.
7. Assefa, *L'Apocalypse des animaux*, pp. 208-9.
8. Assefa, *L'Apocalypse des animaux*, p. 223.
9. Assefa, *L'Apocalypse des animaux*, p. 321.
10. Assefa, *L'Apocalypse des animaux*, p. 208.
11. Assefa, *L'Apocalypse des animaux*, p. 254.
12. Assefa, *L'Apocalypse des animaux*, pp. 217-19.
13. Assefa, *L'Apocalypse des animaux*, pp. 123-24.

vealed tradition. But it did not advocate armed revolt. Passages in the Animal Apocalypse referring to the sword of the faithful and armed resistance under the leadership of Judas Maccabeus were inserted by a redactor in the period of the Maccabean revolt.

Assefa's literary analysis of the Animal Apocalypse is astute, and his treatment of the book's theological vision advances our understanding considerably. At the same time, while his theory that an earlier version of the Animal Apocalypse was modified in the time of persecution cannot be disproved, I do not find the evidence sufficient to persuade.

1. It is true that no prominent figure in the Animal Apocalypse can be identified as Antiochus, but an argument from silence, or lack of prominence, cannot carry the weight of Assefa's theory. Of events known to us, the persecution remains the best fit for the circumstances portrayed in these verses. The apocalypse envisions the end of Hellenistic rule (90:5), but identifies its conclusion as a period when blindness (including religious apostasy) and attacks against the sheep intensify. The apocalypse envisions imminent divine intervention and judgment precisely because the sheep are being attacked and devoured (e.g., 90:11). Failure to mention or image Antiochus (or any other earthly king in the postexilic period) apart from the general imagery of the Hellenistic imperial armies (or the peoples they represent) as beasts and birds (90: 2, 8, 11, 13, 16, 18-19) is an act of discursive resistance that negates his and other imperial claims to authority and refuses him a starring role in Israel's story. He is but one among a host of predators and scavengers, all of whom will flee before the Lord of the sheep.

2. Concerning the second point, I have called attention throughout this study to the ways in which hegemony supports domination. Blindness is not in itself political power. But blindness supports the project of the empire. The transparently political book of Daniel redefines power as wisdom — this in itself is an act of resistance. In the Book of Dreams themes of sight and blindness keep the main focus on perception, reception, understanding, and obedience to God, constantly relativizing, even minimizing, the power of temporal rulers. This too is an act of resistance, and is not inconsistent with other forms of opposition to the empire, be they nonviolent or violent.

3. The universality of the book's final vision does indeed transcend any particular crisis. That is its power. I have asserted that against the totalizing claims of the empire the apocalyptic writers offered a different totalizing narrative. But the universal encompasses and responds to the particular. Throughout the Animal Apocalypse particular events participate in a cyclic, transhistorical pattern that reveals their meaning and discloses God's future action. Antiochus and his armies had devastated the city and profaned the temple. The Animal Apocalypse promised that God would answer the destructive horror of

Antiochus's program of terror and de-creation by building a new house far greater than the last one. The vision of all peoples living peacefully together in the house answers the Judeans' experience of warfare and occupation.

4. The argument that the book's literary complexity would have required a longer period of composition cannot be supported. Any academic who has coveted her neighbor's c.v. knows that some people think more powerfully and write more quickly — or with greater discipline — than others. A crisis might shut down literary operations. Or, a crisis that threatened everything that mattered could kick a determined writer into high gear. The writer of the Book of Dreams would not have been the only creative visionary who galvanized resistance to Antiochus's persecution with a complex and imaginative series of visions. I do not deny that the book incorporates earlier traditions. But the work's complexity necessitates neither an earlier nor a less stressful date.

5. I agree with Assefa that the Animal Apocalypse is not a work of military propaganda. Yet there is nothing in the proposed original version that suggests opposition to military activity or to militant defense of the faith on the part of God's sheep. To call the proposed original form of the Animal Apocalypse nonviolent ignores references in that text to Moses' militancy and the military activity of Israel's judges and kings. Both Moses and Elijah model for the book's audience militant defense of right worship. The description of the actions of the lambs echoes their stories, suggesting that the Animal Apocalypse's understanding of prophetic witness included armed defense of the faith.

6. From Part Two of this study it should be clear that the temple held a central position in Israel's symbolic and political landscape, and for this reason Antiochus's program of de-creation and re-creation gave special attention to the temple, its leadership, resources and furnishings, and worship life. For these same reasons the temple became a focal point of resistance to the program of Antiochus. Yet his edict did not only violate the temple, and did not only target Judeans who supported its legitimacy. Despite the prominence of the temple in the story of resistance in 2 Maccabees, there is no reason to exclude from the Maccabean resistance movement a group of Jews who opposed the administration of the current Jerusalem temple cult.

7. Finally, while scholars have long puzzled over the apparent doublet in *1 Enoch* 90:13-19,[14] the view that verses 90:13-15 and 19 interrupt the logic of the text depends on how one reconstructs the text's logic. These verses may well constitute a revision to the narrative. But the revision may have occurred close in time to the original composition, as Patrick Tiller has argued.[15] The writer of added verses may have been the writer of the original work or someone very

---

14. See Tiller, *Commentary,* pp. 63-78.
15. Tiller, *Commentary,* p. 76.

close in ideology and theology.[16] In the end, we are still left with an apocalypse from the period of the persecution whose vision of resistance includes armed revolt.

Interpreting the Present through the Past

In the Book of Dreams, Enoch relates two visions to his son Methuselah. He narrates both in past tense. He has seen the future of the world and of God's chosen people not as something that will happen, but as something that already has happened. The device underscores that the outline of God's plan for the future has already been made known in events of the past.[17] The use of symbolic and allegorical imagery contributes further to the portrayal of past as paradigm.[18] In the first dream report, Enoch tells Methuselah that he saw the coming flood and describes his own prayerful response of lament, praise, and petition. In the second vision report, or Animal Apocalypse, he relates all of human history in three eras, divided by God's judging activity in the flood and the final judgment. Like the Apocalypse of Weeks, the Book of Dreams establishes a typology between these two events. Enoch's response to the first vision accordingly provides a model for the audience who receive a vision of their own future in the Animal Apocalypse. I argue that Enoch's response to the vision models a key component in the writer's program for resistance to Antiochus's edict and persecution. The description of the activity of the lambs/rams in the second vision (90:6-19) further develops the Book of Dreams' program of resistance. In this description, allusive language evokes the actions of past prophetic leaders who, like Enoch, model resistance for the lambs.

In narrating his dream visions, Enoch simultaneously interprets history and other scriptures. In the Animal Apocalypse, this interpretation is embedded in the vision itself. A large part of this symbolic narrative retells Israel's Primary History (85–89),[19] while its account of events since the exile interprets key

---

16. Tiller, *Commentary*, p. 78.

17. Carol A. Newsom argues that the writer of the Book of Dreams sought in the past a pattern for the future. "The Past as Revelation: History in Apocalyptic Literature," *Quarterly Review* 4, no. 3 (1984): 40-53, 43.

18. John J. Collins, *The Apocalyptic Imagination: An Introduction to Jewish Apocalyptic Literature*, 2nd ed. (Grand Rapids: Eerdmans, 1998), p. 70.

19. See table in Nickelsburg, *1 Enoch 1*, p. 358. He comments there, "The outline of Enoch's account of human history and most of its details have been drawn from the narrative biblical books: Genesis–2 Kings, and perhaps Ezra–Nehemiah." Nickelsburg calls attention to the work of Günter Reese, "Die Geschichte Israels in der Auffassung des frühen Judentums. Eine Untersuchung der Tiervision und der Zehnwochenapokalypse des äthiopischen Henochbuches,

prophetic texts.[20] The writer's portrayal of the persecution, the resistance of the righteous, and God's intervention for salvation and judgment must be understood in the light of these interpretations of earlier authoritative traditions. The interpretations are shaped in turn by new revelations.

The First Dream Vision: Supplication

In his first dream, Enoch sees a "terrible vision" (83:2) of heaven thrown down on the earth and earth swallowed in the abyss (83:3-4).[21] Enoch cries out, "The earth has been destroyed!" (83:5). His grandfather Mahalalel tells him, "Mighty is the vision of your dream (in) the secrets of all the sin of the earth. It must sink into the abyss, and it will be utterly destroyed" (83:7). These words, which echo Enoch's own, suggest that the earth itself must sink and be destroyed. But they are ambiguous, and may instead mean that the earth must sink not for its own destruction, but for the destruction of the sin that has defiled it. Allusions in the vision to the fall of the watchers and subsequent flood as narrated in the Book of the Watchers (*1 En.* 1–36) lend further weight to this interpretation. In that book, a similar pronouncement yields to a vision of the earth not destroyed, but cleansed from sin.

Allusions to the Book of the Watchers in the Book of Dreams' first dream vision include references to the fall of the watchers and the subsequent judgment on them for their crimes. In the Book of Dreams Enoch sees heaven "thrown down and taken away, and it fell down upon the earth" (*1 En.* 83:3). This falling of heaven reflects the initial descent of the watchers (*1 En.* 6; cf. 86:1-3), while the image of heaven thrown down evokes their condemnation by God. Just as heaven is "taken away" in this first dream vision, so in the earlier book the watchers are bound and taken away to await their judgment (*1 En.* 10:4, 12). The two accounts likewise share the motif of the abyss (10:6, 13; 83:4, 7).[22] A verbal echo of the Book of the Watchers further strengthens the tie between the two accounts, and helps clarify the ambiguity regarding the earth's fate. Enoch and Mahalalel's declarations echo the words of the angel Sariel, who tells Noah, "The earth will be completely destroyed" (10:2).[23] But the Book of the Watchers

---

der Geschichtsdarstellung der Assumptio Mosis und der des 4. Esrabuches" (diss., Heidelberg University, 1967), pp. 21-47, who shows "that the author is dependent on the biblical texts rather than traditions behind them" (*1 Enoch 1*, p. 358n6).

20. See discussion in Newsom, "Enoch 83–90," pp. 25-27; Nickelsburg, *1 Enoch 1*, p. 359.

21. Unless otherwise noted, translations of *1 Enoch* are from George W. E. Nickelsburg and James C. VanderKam, *1 Enoch: A New Translation* (Minneapolis: Fortress, 2004).

22. In the Book of the Watchers the abyss is not water but fire.

23. Black's translation (*Book of Enoch*, p. 30). Arthur Heath Jones translates, "the whole

continues with an account of the flood God will send to destroy not earth, but sin. God says to Michael, "I will destroy all iniquity from the face of the earth, and every evil work shall come to an end" (10:16). The righteous will escape destruction (10:17), and the earth itself will endure (10:18-19). Mahalalel's instructions to Enoch similarly mitigate the present vision of total destruction, and Enoch prays that not earth but sinners will be destroyed (84:6). This shift underscores the efficacy of intercessory prayer for salvation of the righteous and renewal of the earth.

Even as the language of the first dream vision echoes and alludes to the account of the fall of the watchers and the flood in the Book of the Watchers, the writer also typologically links this event and its interpretation to events narrated in the second dream vision.[24] Renarrated in the Animal Apocalypse, the flood emerges as a type of the final judgment.[25] I noted above that in the Animal Apocalypse these two events mark the end of the first and second eras respectively. These eras share a cyclic structure of sin, oppression, cry and deliverance, patterned on that found in the Deuteronomistic History.[26] This cycle repeats throughout the narrative, most notably in events surrounding the exodus. The typology between flood, exodus, and final judgment links paradigmatic events from Israel's history to the present crisis.

Use of language from exodus traditions to describe the flood in Enoch's first dream vision anticipates the renarration of that event in the second vision. In this way, portrayals of type and antitype (flood, exodus, and final judgment) shape one another. In the first dream vision, the earth is swallowed into the abyss, hills sink down, trees are thrown down, and these also sink into the abyss (83:4). Paired with water and flood imagery, repeated language of sinking, throwing down, and swallowing recalls the destruction of the Egyptians in the Reed Sea as recounted in Moses' and Miriam's songs in Exodus 15.[27] God "hurled" and "cast" Pharaoh's armies into the sea (Ex 15:1, 4, 21), so that they "went down" into the depths (15:5) and "sank like lead" in the waters (15:10), until the earth (i.e., Sheol) "swallowed" them.

Israel's sacred traditions identified Egypt as the first empire to dominate God's people. According to the exodus story, God heard the enslaved people when they cried out, and appointed prophets and performed miracles to deliver

---

earth will be destroyed." *Enoch and the Fall of the Watchers* (Ph.D. diss., Vanderbilt University, 1989), p. 387. Nickelsburg translates, "the whole earth will perish" (*1 Enoch 1*, p. 215).

24. Of the first vision Collins writes, "This brief vision is a paradigm of judgment, a reminder that the whole world could be destroyed. It implies the contingency of the world, its dependence on its Maker. It need not refer to any particular crisis" (*Apocalyptic Imagination*, p. 68).

25. See Nickelsburg, *1 Enoch 1*, 379; Tiller, *Commentary*, pp. 286-87, 365.

26. Cf. Newsom, "Enoch 83–90," pp. 12-16, 32.

27. Black, *Book of Enoch*, p. 254.

them. Egypt, like the watchers and their offspring, became for our writer a type of future oppressors. The cry of the Hebrew slaves would sound again in the cries of the lambs. Moses and Aaron would be models for future prophets, including members of the writer's own community, while the crossing of the Reed Sea would prefigure God's future deliverance of the lambs and judgment against Antiochus and his armies.

The image of trees cut from their roots, thrown away, and sinking to the abyss (*1 En.* 83:4) recalls another text concerning Egypt's fate in a later age, the allegory of Ezekiel 31.[28] There trees represent nations or earthly powers. God commissions the prophet to teach Egypt's king (Ezek 31:2) to discern his own future by looking to the past, recalling that Assyria was once such a great tree (31:3-9) but was cut down (31:12). No other tree would reach such heights again,

> For they are all consigned to death, to the lowest part of the Netherworld, together with human beings who descend into the Pit. Thus said the Lord GOD: on the day it went down to Sheol, I closed the deep over it and covered it; I held back its streams, and the great waters were checked. I made Lebanon mourn deeply for it, and all the trees of the field languished on its account. I made nations quake at the crash of its fall, when I cast it down to Sheol with those who descend into the Pit; and all the trees of Eden, the choicest and best of Lebanon, all that were well watered, were consoled in the lowest part of the netherworld. They also descended with it into Sheol, to those slain by the sword, together with its supporters, they who had lived under its shadow among the nations. (31:14-17 NJPS)

As Assyria was a great tree, so is Egypt, and they will share the same fate, "brought down with the trees of Eden to the lowest part of the netherworld" (31:18 NJPS). Enoch's first vision adopts several elements of Ezekiel's symbolism and imagery.[29] The two passages share the motifs of cutting down trees, casting

---

28. Scholars have long recognized the Book of Dreams' use of Ezek 34 in developing the symbolism of shepherd and sheep and the identification of the nations with ravenous beasts in the Animal Apocalypse. Newsom suggests the further parallel to Ezek 31 in light of the tree imagery in the first dream vision of the Book of Dreams ("Enoch 83–90," p. 9).

29. God's judgment against that other great oppressor, Babylon, also shapes Enoch's vision. The fall of heaven recalls not only the fall of the watchers, but also Isaiah's taunt over Babylon, the "morning star" and "son of the dawn" who has fallen from heaven (Isa 14:12) and at last ceases from his raging. The Lord broke the rod (14:5) of this oppressor who persecuted the peoples of the earth. The image of the ruler's "rod" or "staff" evokes the image of ruler as shepherd, and so the allusion to this passage here looks ahead to the judgment in the Animal Apocalypse of those shepherds (angelic rulers or angels of specific nations) who likewise oppressed and persecuted God's people beyond the commission they received from God. Sheol awaits the fallen ruler (Isa 14:9, 11, 16, 20; cf. *1 En.* 83:4).

or throwing them down, and their descent into Sheol or the abyss. This commonality suggests that in the Book of Dreams, too, the trees may represent world powers, less appropriate for the time of the flood (though in that context they may represent the watchers and/or their giant offspring), but wholly appropriate to the period of the persecution. By adapting elements of Ezekiel's oracle, the writer emphasizes God's sovereignty over world powers and assures the audience that like the watchers, like Pharaoh and his armies, and like the tree of Assyria, Antiochus and his supporters will fall.

Just as typology linked events and world powers, it also linked the actions of the righteous in Enoch's time to the actions of the righteous in the writer's present. The vision-report of the first vision and the introductory frame of the second vision encourage the audience to identify themselves not only as antitypes of the righteous Noah and the remnant saved from the flood, but also heirs and antitypes of Enoch, whose intercession helped to save them.

In the book of the Watchers God promised that a righteous plant or seed would be planted and established from Noah forever (1 En. 10:3), a "plant of righteousness" (10:16) that will escape the flood (10:17). After that, all will become righteous to "serve and bless" and "worship" God (10:21). Like the Apocalypse of Weeks, the Book of Dreams borrows the Book of the Watchers' plant imagery and its vision of the future. In the Book of Dreams, Enoch petitions the Lord to spare a remnant of his posterity on earth (1 En. 84:5) and establish them "as a seed-bearing plant forever" (84:6). As in the Apocalypse of Weeks, the audience are to identify with this plant, Enoch's righteous descendants and heirs saved by Enoch's merits. The plant thus prefigures those who will see the end of the persecution and the beginning of a new age in which all will serve, bless, and worship God (90:28-36). They too will be righteous, mindful of their calling to serve, bless, and worship the Lord, and will model their actions on those of their ancestor Enoch.[30]

Careful repetition of the vocative "my son" (or "my child," waldeya) throughout the report of the first dream vision and in the introductory framework of the second vision invites the audience to make this identification. The book opens with the address, "And now, my son, Methuselah, I will show you everything; the visions that I saw I will recount before you" (83:1).[31] Immedi-

---

30. In the Book of Dreams, Enoch himself "anticipates" or models the fulfillment of these promises of 10:22 in his prayer of 84:2-6. He blesses the Lord three times in three consecutive verses (83:11–84:2) and calls himself the Lord's "servant" at the conclusion of his prayer (84:6).

31. Adopting the translation offered by Nickelsburg in his commentary (1 Enoch 1, p. 348). This translation takes better account of the Ethiopic as it is written ("everything" or "all," kwello, is singular, while "visions" is plural; see p. 349), eliminates the difficulty of identifying "all the visions" with "two visions" in the verse that follows (83:2), and parallels the similar statement in 83:10, "I will show you everything."

ately, the audience identifies with Enoch's son Methuselah as recipient of the dream reports. In the preface to his prayer Enoch again addresses Methuselah as "my son" and repeats much of his earlier promise: "I will show you everything, my son, Methuselah" (83:10).[32] Enoch repeats this promise at the introduction to the second dream vision (85:1). The promise's three occurrences introduce and unite the three major segments of the book: the first dream, the intercessory prayer, and the second dream. The first also introduces the whole.

Through this repeated direct address, the writer reminds the readers that the work is intended for them, children of Enoch. The Ethiopic *weled* can mean not only "son" or "child," but also "disciple."[33] This broader sense of the word includes as Enoch's children those who have kept the Enochic writings and sought to live by and propagate their teachings. Enoch also states, "my prayer I wrote down for the generations of eternity" (*1 En.* 83:10). The readers who identify with the righteous remnant of Enoch's posterity thus receive the prayer with the understanding that it is especially for them, both for their salvation and for them to take up and pass on.[34] They are called to emulate his prayerful response to the vision, receiving anew the mandate given Enoch by his own ancestor and with it a model for the action they must take. It is in this sense that the prayer is "for them," for it shows them by what grace they themselves have survived upon the earth and how they are to intercede for the faithful in their own day.

In the introduction to the Book of Dreams, Enoch summarizes his response to the visions: "I made supplication about them to the Lord" (83:2).[35] The motif of supplication recurs throughout the first vision report (83:2, 8, 10; 84:5). This prospective verse alerts the reader to its importance.

After reporting the content of the first vision, Enoch says that Mahalalel asked him why he "cries out" and "laments" (83:6). We will see that language of crying out and lamenting recurs also at key points in the Animal Apocalypse. Crying out will signify both prayer (crying out to God) and prophetic activity (crying out to/over/against one's fellows),[36] while lament, like crying out, can

---

32. I depart slightly from Nickelsburg's translation to better reflect the verbatim repetition. Cf. Black, *Book of Enoch*, p. 71.

33. See Wolf Leslau, *Comparative Dictionary of Ge'ez (Classical Ethopic): Ge'ez-English, English-Ge'ez, with an Index of the Semitic Roots* (Wiesbaden: Harrassowitz, 1987), p. 613. Its semantic range is comparable to that of Hebrew בֵּן, which can indicate membership in a group/guild, as in בֶּן־נָבִיא (Amos 7:14).

34. According to Nickelsburg, "In stating that he wrote it down 'for the generations of eternity,' Enoch gives his prayer a status parallel to his other writings (see 82:2-3). Thus the author implies that the prayer for survival from the flood will be significant for those who live in the latter days and wish to survive the final judgment (cf. 84:4)" (*1 Enoch 1*, pp. 350-51).

35. Black's translation (*Book of Enoch*, p. 71).

36. Cf. Jer 20:8 (verbal root זעק).

be a call for heavenly aid. Here Enoch's outcry and lament signal his immediate distress but also anticipate his formal act of supplication to follow.

Enoch moves immediately from lament to this formal act of prayer. After Mahalalel interprets the vision, he commands Enoch, "Arise, and make supplication to the Lord of glory, since you are faithful, that a remnant may remain upon the earth, and that he may not obliterate the whole earth" (83:8).[37] The proper response to the vision is prayer. Here Mahalalel outlines Enoch's intercessory role. He will pray to God on behalf of the earth, to preserve a remnant for the future. God will hear Enoch because he is faithful. Enoch obeys: "I arose and prayed and made supplication and request" (83:10); "I lifted up my hands in righteousness and blessed" God (84:1).[38] In his prayer Enoch foregrounds his intercessory role: "I make supplication and request" (84:5).

While the primary emphasis in the report of Enoch's response to the first vision falls on this action of prayer/intercession, before he petitions he meditates on the created order. Enoch goes outside and looks upon God's creation (83:11). There Enoch sees the rising sun, the setting moon, stars, the earth, "and everything. . . ." The description begins with a realistic report of what Enoch and any other person would have seen at this hour. Yet the sweeping reference to "everything" God made "from the beginning" recalls both Enoch's otherworldly journeys narrated in the Book of the Watchers and in the Astronomical Book of 1 Enoch, in which Enoch is shown all of God's creation and given understanding of its mysteries, and the description of the regularity of heavenly bodies and the created order on earth in 1 Enoch 2:1–5:3. In the book of Dreams the narrative conjoins two kinds of sight: common sight, or what anyone can perceive about reality, nature, and God by observing the world, and special sight, given only to the privileged visionary and the heirs to his traditions. Sight in the Book of Dreams thus signifies the understanding that comes from attending to these twin sources of knowledge about God and the world. It also signifies obedience to God's will that results from that understanding.

Seeing creation leads Enoch to "bless the Lord of judgment" and ascribe majesty to God (83:11; 84:2; cf. 90:39). This linking of judgment to creation takes up the common Enochic motif of nature's obedience to God's will.[39] The regu-

---

37. Cf. 2 Kgs 5:11, where Na'aman expects the prophet to "stand and call on the name of the Lord," to intercede for him. Rising and standing as a posture for prayer appears to have roots in both royal/legal/courtroom practice (on the analogy of God as divine judge to whom one may make one's plea or case) and in liturgy. The two surely have influenced one another. In Job 30:20, 28 the human legal sphere merges with petition to God. For liturgical practice, see Neh 9:5, 1 Chron 23:30, 2 Chron 20:9, Ps 135:2-3.

38. Cf. Lam 2:19. An example of instructions for prayer similar to those given Enoch by Mahalalel is found in Tob 6:17.

39. This motif appears in the first chapters of the Book of the Watchers, which introduce

larity of the sun's movement in its course discloses God's cosmic sovereignty. By the same principles with which God has ordered the cosmos, God has also laid out the consequences for obedience and disobedience. The steady example of the sun in its course thus quietly hints at the punishment in store for the wicked, while also promising salvation for the righteous. In this way recognition of God as creator implies recognition of God as ruler and judge and leads Enoch to glorify God. Enoch's prayer returns to the theme of God's sovereign power (84:2-3).

Enoch now tells Methuselah, "I spoke with the breath of my mouth and with a tongue of flesh, which God has made for humankind, that they might speak with it" (84:1).[40] This description of the human faculty of speech echoes *1 Enoch* 14:2, where it introduces Enoch's role in reprimanding the watchers: "In this vision I saw in my dream what *I now speak with a tongue of flesh and with the breath of my mouth, which the Great One has given to humankind, to speak with them* and to understand with the heart. As he destined and created humankind to understand the words of knowledge, so he created and destined me to reprimand the watchers" (14:2-3; italics added for emphasis).[41] Whoever possesses the gifts of speech and understanding must also reprimand sinners — even those who are powerful — and hold them accountable for their crimes. A closer look at the context of the earlier passage illuminates the function of the echo of 14:2 in 84:1.

In the Book of the Watchers Enoch mediates between the heavenly angels and the fallen watchers. The angels of God commission Enoch to deliver the sentence of judgment on the watchers and their children. The angels instruct him that "concerning their children, in whom they rejoice, the slaughter of their beloved ones they will see, and over the destruction of their children they will lament and make petition forever, and they will have no mercy or peace" (12:6).[42] Enoch is also to tell Asael, "You will have no relief or petition, because of the unrighteous deeds that you revealed" (13:2).

Yet when Enoch speaks to the fallen watchers, they disregard his message and formulate their petition (13:3-6), asking Enoch to intercede for them before God (13:4). Enoch writes out their petition and recites it before God, but it is

---

the entire corpus of *1 En.* There, as here, recognizing God's sovereign role as judge (*1 En.* 1:9) is closely linked to contemplation of the regular rising and setting of the heavenly luminaries (2:1) and the order of all that is upon the earth (2:2–5:3).

40. I substitute "humankind" for Nickelsburg's "sons of the flesh of man."

41. Again, I substitute "humankind" for Nickelsburg's "sons of men," and "humans" for "men." I have left "sons" in place where the reference is to the watchers themselves, as the narrative turns on the fact that they were male (emphasized in the Animal Apocalypse's description of their genitalia) and desired to have intercourse with human women.

42. Here and below I have substituted the translation "children" for Nickelsburg's "sons."

swiftly rejected (13:6-7).[43] God sends Enoch to reprimand the fallen watchers once again (13:8). He tells them, "I wrote up your petition, and in the vision it was shown to me thus, that you will not obtain your petition for all the days of eternity; but judgment has been consummated in the decree against you . . . you will see the destruction of your children, your beloved ones . . . you will not obtain your petition concerning them, nor concerning yourselves. You will be petitioning and making supplication . . . but you will not be speaking any word from the writing that I have written" (14:4-7). Because of their transgressions these watchers cannot even hope for the intercession of the righteous Enoch to save them.[44] The very words of prayer are now denied to them, for they are not worthy to speak them.

As I noted above, in the Book of Dreams the introduction to Enoch's intercessory prayer for the faithful remnant (84:1) repeats the statement from *1 Enoch* 14:2 with only slight variation. The major difference is the absence of reprimand.[45] While the Book of the Watchers foregrounds Enoch's role in chastising the watchers and revealing the fate decreed for them, the Book of Dreams foregrounds his role in praying for the preservation of the faithful remnant. The allusion in 84:1 to 14:1-2 highlights the contrast between them. The watchers' fruitless supplication and denied petition in the Book of the Watchers contrasts with Enoch's righteous prayer in the Book of Dreams. While he could not intercede for the watchers and their children, he could intercede for his own children. The petition of the watchers was rejected because of their sinfulness. Enoch's would be heard and granted because of his righteousness and that of his children. In this way, the writer emphasizes the righteousness of the Enochic community over against the sinfulness of the watchers and the present-day oppressors these prefigure, and shows the different rewards for each. The writer also models for the audience the intercessory role they are to take in the present crisis, as they prepare for a final judgment comparable to the first.

Finally, Enoch's prayer in *1 Enoch* 84 closely parallels that of the archangels in *1 Enoch* 9. In his commentary on the latter text, Nickelsburg observes that "In 1 Enoch 84 a version of the present prayer is placed in the mouth of Enoch and is revised (including the addition of a petition) to fit the seer's situation."[46]

---

43. Compare Jer 7:16; 11:14.

44. Nickelsburg observes that for the watchers, "No amount of prayer and petition in the future will change things" (*1 Enoch 1*, p. 253).

45. Within the story world of *1 En.*, this first vision and Enoch's intercession for humankind would have occurred before he was asked to intercede for the fallen watchers and before he was commissioned to deliver their sentence of doom.

46. Nickelsburg, *1 Enoch 1*, p. 206. He provides a chart mapping out the parallel portions of the two prayers on p. 352.

Using very similar language, both prayers treat the plight of humankind on the eve of the flood, but each emphasizes a different dimension of the crisis.

In *1 Enoch* 9 the angels report that the souls of humankind are bringing suit before heaven on account of the violence and bloodshed that filled the earth after the fall of the watchers and the birth of the giants. The angels accordingly petition for justice (9:3), taking it upon themselves to bring this suit before the heavenly throne (9:4-11). In so doing they act as intercessors.[47] In this role they contrast with the fallen watchers, whom God chastised for seeking humans to petition on their behalf rather than petitioning on behalf of humans (15:2). The angels call God to task, seeking clearance to begin their work of enacting God's judgment. Their prayer comprises three parts: praise of God's power and knowledge (9:4-5), rehearsal of the crimes of the watchers and the plight of humans (9:6-10), and a concluding complaint (9:11). Because the angels wish to know what punishment awaits the watchers and their children, the bulk of the prayer focuses on their crimes (9:6-9). They charge God, "You see these things and you permit them" (9:11). Now they are eager for judgment. If God knows, God must also act, and God must make known to them what lies in store. They receive in response instructions for the preservation of Noah and his family and the punishment of the watchers and their children.

How does the Book of Dreams adapt the prayer? The prayers differ in speaker, goal, emphasis, and tone. Most obvious is the difference in speaker. Though he will later be translated into heaven, Enoch is no angel. He does not at this stage in the tradition possess the supernatural powers of the archangels, whose work in the Book of the Watchers is to execute divine judgment on earth. The angels pray for their instructions so that they may perform this work. Enoch, on the other hand, has already received his instructions (from Mahalalel). His role is more modest, but no less important. In the portion of the prayer most similar to *1 Enoch* 9, Enoch also introduces a motif not present in the earlier prayer, namely his concern for the salvation of the earth. The speakers' different goals shape the structure and emphasis of the prayers. The prayers differ also in tone. Enoch does not chastise. His tone remains reverent throughout, so that, by contrast with the angels' complaint, Enoch concludes his prayer with the humble entreaty, "Hide not your face from the prayer of your servant, O Lord" (84:6). Divine wrath already threatens humanity (84:4). Rather than calling God to the task of justice, Enoch appeals for mercy.

His praise lays the foundation for his petition. God is all-powerful and can therefore destroy the earth, but since "nothing is too difficult" for God (84:3), God can also save it. The wisdom that attends God's throne (84:3) ensures God's just judgments, and so divine wrath is surely justified, but that same wis-

---

47. See Nickelsburg, *1 Enoch 1*, pp. 208-10.

dom may also prompt God to guarantee the salvation of a righteous few, and the salvation of the earth on their behalf.[48] Finally, Enoch develops the theme of God's eternal nature. The angels had addressed the Lord as "God of the ages" whose "throne of your glory (exists) for every generation for the generations that are from eternity," and blessed God's name "for all the ages" (9:4). Enoch multiplies eternities further still. God's power, reign, and majesty "abide forever and forever and ever"; "all the heavens are [God's] throne forever"; "and all the earth is your footstool forever and forever and ever" (84:2; cf. Isa 66:1). Enoch asks God not to destroy the earth, lest "there be eternal destruction" (1 En. 84:5). The earth, God's footstool, must endure as part of the eternal cosmic order.

In adapting the angels' prayer in 1 Enoch 9 for Enoch's act of intercession, the Book of Dreams outlines a role for Enoch and also for his children that is similar to that of the angels but more limited in scope. Both serve as intercessors. While the angels seek justice against the criminals, Enoch seeks mercy for the victims of their violence. In a new situation, the Book of Dreams calls Enoch's successors to imitate Enoch, petitioning God to show mercy on the righteous. His doxology provides the theological foundations for their petition and their hope. Yet their role would also differ from Enoch's. By adapting an earlier prayer, the writer demonstrates for the audience how they might creatively reshape traditions of the past to address God in the present hour of need.

Enoch's differing responses to the first and second visions, reported in the Book of Dreams' narrative frame, hint at the different work required of Enoch's posterity. After the second vision, Enoch reports: "And I awoke and blessed the Lord of righteousness and gave him glory.[49] And after that I wept bitterly, and my tears did not cease until I could no longer endure it, but they were running down because of what I had seen; for everything will come to pass and be fulfilled, and every deed of humanity was shown to me in its order. That night I remembered the first dream. I wept because of it, and I was disturbed because I had seen the vision" (90:39-42).[50] Even when assured of the glorious kingdom of the end time, Enoch cries and laments because he has seen suffering and destruction in the history of God's people. Yet Enoch does not offer a prayer of supplication after the second vision. Why? Enoch's role was to intercede for the generation of the flood, to ensure that a righteous remnant would remain on

---

48. Cf. Gen 18:25.

49. Cf. Josh 7:19; Ps 29:1-2; 96:7-8; Isa 42:12. These examples reveal that giving glory to God affirms God's sovereign might, highlighting roles as judge, cosmic ruler, and warrior.

50. There is some debate as to whether these verses are "original" to the Book of Dreams, yet, as Nickelsburg notes, they summarize the vision, show Enoch's reaction, and tie together the first and second visions, giving a "certain unity" to the Book of Dreams as a whole (1 Enoch 1, p. 408).

the earth, and to pass on his visions and prayer for future generations. As at the conclusion of Daniel, so in the Book of Dreams responsibility for the future resides now with the audience. Just as Enoch saved the earth and a remnant upon it by his merits, so this remnant must intercede to save the faithful from persecution and establish a new order on earth. The sudden shift from joy (90:38) to sorrow returns the reader to the present moment.[51] They must take up Enoch's lament and petition to help ensure the joyful outcome.

The Second Dream Vision: The Animal Apocalypse

The second dream vision, or Animal Apocalypse, reveals that lament, prayer, and petition are only part of the Book of Dreams' program of resistance. The book also calls its audience to prophetic witness and armed revolt. In his second vision Enoch sees the persecution of Judeans during the reign of Antiochus IV. Among them Enoch sees a group of lambs: "And behold, lambs were born of those white sheep, and they began to open their eyes and to see and to cry out to the sheep" (90:6). The lambs are a new group, continuous with the white sheep who in the Animal Apocalypse symbolize the elect of Israel, but also distinguished from them by their sight and actions.[52] The writer of the Book of Dreams identifies with this group and views their actions as part of God's plan for restoring right worship and delivering God's people. The latter have been blind, their eyes pecked out by those who rule them (90:2).[53] They falter now, increasingly heedless of God's word. This new group opens their eyes, sees, and cries out to their companions. These actions point to the lambs' capacity for right perception, their obedience to God's revealed will, and their prophetic role in calling others to faithfulness.

They Began to Open Their Eyes and to See

I discussed above the dual meaning of sight in the Book of Dreams.[54] At one level, sight refers to knowledge and understanding derived both from attention

51. Cf. Nickelsburg, *1 Enoch 1*, p. 408.
52. Tiller describes them as "an unsuccessful, militant, pro-independence, religious reform group in Judea" (*Commentary*, p. 102). Their history includes evangelism, "forcible opposition from others within Israel," "unsuccessful armed revolt," and "later adherence to the Maccabees" (p. 350).
53. Cf. Num 33:55: "But if you do not drive out the inhabitants of the land before you, those whom you allow to remain will become as barbs in your eyes" (see also Josh 23:13).
54. On the meaning of sight and blindness in the Animal Apocalypse, see Beate Ego,

to the workings of the created order and from revealed knowledge, including the Enochic revelations.[55] It is the sight of the sage and the visionary, passed on as a gift to those who receive their teachings and read their writings.[56] At another level, sight means observing the laws of God.[57] To look is to look to God and the path God has revealed; to see is to see what God has done for the people and what they owe God in turn.[58]

The two levels of signification complement one another. Right understanding leads to right action, while observing the law opens the door to deeper insight. We may compare the words of two psalms, one which requests of the Lord, "Open my eyes, that I may look upon the wonders of your law" (Ps 119:18), and another which declares, "The commandment of the Lord is clear, enlightening the eyes" (19:8).[59]

"Vergangenheit im Horizont eschatologischer Hoffnung: Die Tiervision (1 Hen 85–90) als Beispiel apokalyptischer Geschichtskonzeption," in *Die antike Historiographie und die Anfänge der christlichen Geschichtsschreibung*, ed. Eve-Marie Becker (Berlin: Walter de Gruyter, 2005), pp. 171-95, 178-80; James C. VanderKam, "Open and Closed Eyes in the Animal Apocalypse (1 Enoch 85–90)," in *The Idea of Biblical Interpretation. Essays in Honor of James L. Kugel*, ed. Hindy Najman and Judith Newman (Leiden: Brill, 2004), pp. 279-92; Nickelsburg, *1 Enoch 1*, pp. 379-81; Tiller, *Commentary*, pp. 292-93; Reese, "Geschichte," pp. 34-36; Newsom, "Enoch 83–90," pp. 30-31.

55. Contra Tiller, *Commentary*, p. 292. While Tiller finds "no warrant" for the view that "sight also represents an esoteric wisdom such as that possessed by Enoch," *1 En.* 1:2 and the Animal Apocalypse use language of seeing to describe Enoch's visionary experience.

56. James L. Crenshaw discusses this Sumerian riddle: "Whoever enters it has closed eyes; whoever departs from it has eyes that are wide open. What is it?" The answer is the tablet house or school. *Education in Ancient Israel: Across the Deadening Silence* (New York: Doubleday, 1998), pp. 116-20, 155.

57. For VanderKam, sight in the Animal Apocalypse signifies "proper relationship" between Israel and God ("Open and Closed Eyes," p. 280). References to seeing in the Sinai pericope in Exodus and the explanation of the name "Israel" in Gen 32:28 provide the main sources for the imagery of sight in the Animal Apocalypse (p. 287). He explains, "The author uses the expression beginning at or near Sinai in order to express the special event, the covenant, that took place there. . . . Israel truly enfleshes the meaning of its revealed name — the one who sees God — when it obeys God, when it accepts his covenantal will disclosed at Sinai and obeys it" (p. 292).

58. Cf. Deut 3:21; 4:9, 34; 6:22; 7:19; 10:21; 11:9; 29:1; 29:3. For Tiller the parallel between the moment when the sheep first begin to open their eyes (89:28) and Exod 15:25b-26 determines the meaning of sight in the Book of Dreams as "possession of God's law and obedience to it" (*Commentary*, p. 292). Ego connects awareness and obedience: "Dabei ist 'Sehend-Werden' wohl als Ausdruck für Gotteserkenntnis, die auch die praktische Seite der Gebotserfüllung einschließt, aufzufassen" ("Vergangenheit," p. 180).

59. The image of opening eyes occurs also in the book of Gen and in 2 Kgs. In the story of Adam and Eve in the garden of Eden, sight was equated with wisdom and knowledge (Gen 3:5, 7). The serpent promised the first humans, "Your eyes will be opened, and you will be like gods, knowing good and evil" (3:5; cf. 3:7). For John Skinner opening eyes here "denotes a sudden ac-

The connotation of obedience to the will of God is best understood by comparison with the other occurrences of the image of open eyes and its opposite, eyes that are blind, earlier in the Animal Apocalypse. The image of open eyes first appears in *1 Enoch* 89:28. The wording there is identical to that in 90:6 with only a variation in word order. Following the exodus from Egypt, the sheep "began to open their eyes and see" *(wa'aḥazu yekšetu 'a'yentihomu wayer'ayu).*

Yet before long the eyes of the sheep begin to go blind *('aḥazu yeṣṣallalu 'a'yentihomu* 89:32). They can no longer see the path that was shown them *('ar'ayomu),* and so begin to stray.⁶⁰ The path is that of the Lord of the sheep, who shepherds them (89:28); it represents the will of God revealed by Moses.⁶¹ The episode of the golden calf that follows illustrates the consequences of blindness. When Moses descends from the mountain, he finds "most of [the sheep] blinded and straying" (89:33).⁶² Blindness leads to idolatry. In a similar vein, in the Apocalypse of Weeks blindness symbolized the apostasy of the period of the divided kingdom (93:8). So too in the Animal Apocalypse, at that time the sheep abandoned the temple and "went astray in everything, and their eyes were blinded" (89:54).

Those with sight must lead the blind to safety. Moses successfully returns the straying flock to their folds (89:35). The judges were sometimes able to do the same and could even help the blinded sheep to see again. Enoch describes the period of the judges in this way: "And sometimes their eyes were opened, and sometimes they were blinded, until another sheep arose and led them and brought them all back, and their eyes were opened." For our writer, Judas Maccabeus will occupy a similar role (90:10).

---

quisition of new powers of perception through supernatural influence." *A Critical and Exegetical Commentary on Genesis* (New York: Charles Scribner's Sons, 1910), p. 75. Hagar's eyes were also opened. After an angel appears to her and reveals her child's future, Hagar names God "El-Ro'i," God of Vision, or God of Seeing (Gen 16:13). The same God later opens Hagar's eyes so that she sees a well of water, the source of salvation and life for her and her son (21:19). In 2 Kgs 6:14-17, a king has sent out his army to seize the resisting prophet Elisha. Seeing the city surrounded by the king's forces, Elisha's servant conveys his alarm to the prophet. He in turn prays to God to "open his eyes that he may see" (2 Kgs 6:17 NRSV). God opens the eyes of the servant (6:17), who now sees another army, the army of God, so that the mountain is "full of horses and chariots of fire" (6:17). In this case, God-given sight means the ability to see the host of heaven preparing to do battle on behalf of God's chosen servants. The Animal Apocalypse similarly opens its readers' eyes to see the forces of heaven that will aid the resisting lambs in their fight against the armies of Antiochus (*1 En.* 90:14-15, 18-19).

60. Blindness or failing sight and sin, including apostasy, are linked in various ways in the Pentateuch. See Lev 20:4; Deut 16:19; 28:65; 29:4.

61. Cf. Ps 119:4-5, 15.

62. Cf. Isa 53:6: "We had all gone astray like sheep, each following his own way." The image of straying sheep occurs also in Deut 22:1; Jer 50:17; cf. also Matt 18:12; 1 Pet 2:25.

The Book of Dreams conjoins the meaning of sight as obedience with that of sight as perception and reception, so that each is contingent on the other. As in the first vision, so in the second, sight symbolizes a knowledge of and attention to God's will that leads to obedience, knowledge of God's creation, and the ability to see things as they are and know what lies in store.

David Suter has also suggested that in the early Enochic literature sight signifies the visionary experience of God's holiness and glory.[63] In the Animal Apocalypse this experience is mediated through references to the theophany at Sinai (89:30-31), the throne/judgment vision (90:20-27), and the vision of the new house (90:29-36). Enoch's report of the Sinai theophany is thoroughly visual, with particular emphasis on the visual perception of the terrifying majesty and power of the Lord of the sheep: "And after that, I saw the Lord of the sheep who stood before them, and his appearance was majestic and fearful and mighty, and all those sheep saw him and were afraid before him" (89:30). The sheep who witnessed the Lord's glory at Sinai nonetheless strayed from their path: they refused or could not sustain the vision of glory ("We cannot stand before our Lord or look at him," 89:31) and became blind (89:32). The Enochic revelation holds a key to opening the eyes of the sheep through its vision of the future. The same Lord who appeared to the sheep on the Sinai summit would intervene for their salvation, would sit enthroned in judgment on their behalf, and would build a house for them. At the conclusion of the Animal Apocalypse Enoch reports, "And the eyes of all were opened, and they saw good things; and there was none among them that did not see" (90:35). Visual perception of God's holiness and glory in the Animal Apocalypse evokes confidence in the sovereign power and plan of God, even in the face of destructive and oppressive temporal powers.

As heirs to the Enochic traditions, the lambs who opened their eyes in 90:6 possess such sight. Use of sight-language to describe Enoch's visionary experience throughout the Animal Apocalypse highlights the necessity of sight-as-perception for the reception and understanding of the Enochic revelations, just as it is the necessary condition for right action in the time of crisis. A verbal echo of 1 Enoch 1:2 reinforces this point. The image of the opening of the lambs' eyes in 90:6 echoes the description of Enoch that introduces the Enochic corpus: "Enoch, a righteous man whose eyes were opened by God, who had the vision of the Holy One and of heaven, which he showed me. From the words of the watchers and holy ones I heard everything; and as I heard everything from them, I also understood what I saw" (1:2).[64]

63. David Suter, "Temples and the Temple in the Early Enoch Tradition: Memory, Vision, and Expectation," in *The Early Enoch Literature,* ed. Gabriele Boccaccini and John J. Collins (Leiden: Brill, 2007), pp. 195-218, 217.

64. This passage in turn echoes the words of the seer Balaam in Num 24. Balaam's third oracle provided a model for the writers of the Book of the Watchers and the Apocalypse of Weeks

As in the introduction to the Apocalypse of Weeks (93:2), so here the act of seeing is paired with hearing and understanding.[65] The verse also links Enoch's open eyes with his righteousness. The catchword "righteous" establishes a kinship of identity between Enoch and the righteous chosen, the intended recipients of Enoch's revelations who are destined for victory and salvation. They are so identified in the superscription in the preceding verse: "The words of the blessing with which Enoch blessed the righteous chosen who will be present on the day of tribulation, to remove all the enemies; and the righteous will be saved" (1:1).

The echo of the earlier description of Enoch in the Animal Apocalypse's description of the lambs thus accomplishes two things. It identifies the lambs both as recipients of Enoch's revelations and as the righteous chosen of 1:1, for whom Enoch's words are intended. It further emphasizes the importance of their knowledge and understanding of the Enochic revelations for the work that they perform in the end time, for their own salvation and that of their fellow Jews.

The use of sight language throughout the Animal Apocalypse to denote Enoch's visionary experience reinforces the symbolism of sight as perception and reception. Forms of the verb *re'ya* "to see" (cognate with Hebrew ראה) occur eighty-three times in the Animal Apocalypse.[66] Enoch is the subject in all but seventeen instances. Enoch refers eleven times to his "vision" *(rā'y;* with suffix *rā'eya),* and refers to his eyes on three occasions (86:1; 87:2; 89:2). The use of sight language to characterize the lambs thus emphasizes not only their obedience to God's law, but also their status as heirs to the Enochic visionary tradition. This language also points to apprehension of those visions, including

---

(Nickelsburg, *1 Enoch 1*, pp. 137-38). Was it also in the mind of the writer of the Book of Dreams? In Num 22, the Lord opened the eyes of the seer Balaam (Num 22:31), so that he saw the angel of the Lord and so came to know the will of God (22:34). As a result of his vision, Balaam could only speak true words God would place in his mouth (22:35). When his eyes were opened, Balaam thus received deeper understanding of God's will (cf. 24:1, where Balaam "sees" that his actions please the Lord), and both a mandate and the capacity to deliver true prophetic speech. Moreover, with eyes opened Balaam is able to "see" the armed angel of the Lord (22:31), and to "see" and "regard" Israel (23:9; 24:2). He calls himself "the man whose eye is true [or 'open'] . . . one who hears the words of God, who sees the vision of the Almighty, who falls down, but with eyes uncovered" (24:3-4 NRSV). In 24:15-16 Balaam repeats this proclamation, adding between the descriptions of his hearing and sight the detail that he is the one who "obtains knowledge from the Most High" (24:16 NJPS), specifically a vision of Israel's victory and the destruction of its enemies in the distant future: "What I see for them is not yet, What I behold will not be soon" (24:17-19; cf. *1 En.* 1:3). Later messianic use of this passage is well known.

65. While the three verbs see, hear, and understand each refer to a different mode of perception, together they denote the total and perfect reception of revelation (as in Deut 29:4). Because of this close relationship, one can conjure the other (metonymy), or each singly can represent the whole to which they belong (synecdoche).

66. Most occurrences (sixty) are first person perfects from the G-stem. Four are causative, meaning "to show."

those contained in the Book of Dreams itself, as a precondition for right action in the hour of crisis.[67]

... And to Cry Out to the Sheep

Moved now to action, the lambs strive to open the eyes of their fellow Judeans. To make others see, they must also make them hear. In "crying out to" *(wayeṣreḥu ḥaba)* the sheep (90:6), the lambs take on the role of teachers and prophets, passing on their salvific teaching and exhorting their fellow Judeans to covenant fidelity.

In this prophetic and teaching role, the lambs follow an example already set within the Book of Dreams by the figures of Moses and the prophets of the divided kingdom, including Elijah. The catchword "cry out" *(ṣarḥa)* links the activity of the lambs with that of Elijah and his contemporaries. The catchword "testify" *(yāsmeʿ/yāsmeʿu)* further links the activity of these prophets with that of Moses (and Aaron), tracing a fundamental continuity of action from the archetypal prophet and teacher Moses through to the prophets of the divided kingdom and on to the community of the righteous in the era of persecution. We will see that not only does the righteous community of the writer's time inherit the prophetic commissions of Moses and Elijah, but they also follow their examples in merging the prophetic role with that of militant defenders of the faith.

In the Book of Dreams, language of "crying out" describes not only the lambs' activity, but also the prophetic activity of Elijah, who "cried out *(waṣarḥa)* over the sheep" who had strayed and abandoned God's temple (89:52).[68] Elijah called the Israelites to resist assimilation and return to right worship of the Lord (1 Kgs 18:20-39). The lambs did the same for Judeans.

67. Nickelsburg comments that "the Enochic authors explicitly tie their soteriology to the possession of right knowledge. Actions are, of course, important, but they are possible only if one is rightly informed. The gaining of that information is pivotal for this sapiential-apocalyptic tradition" (*1 Enoch 1*, p. 50). He calls the opening of eyes in 90:6 a "divinely prompted religious awakening from the apostate blindness that has characterized Israel since the time of Manasseh" (p. 361). The group described as lambs believe "that they have received revelation about the correct law for the conduct of the cult. Their claims of revelation are tied to visionary experience but are also rooted in the learned exposition of sacred tradition that included the Pentateuch, the Prophets, and the Enochic material" (p. 362).

68. For use of verbs צעק/זעק "to cry out" to describe prophetic speech toward humans, see Jonah 3:7 and possibly Jer 20:8. The verb used to describe Elijah's prophetic speech to the Israelites in 1 Kgs 18 is simply אמר, "to speak." By the more intensive verb "cry out" the writer (or translator) connects prophecy with other types of "cries" in the Book of Dreams designated by this verb (Ethiopic ṣarḥa), including prayers of lament and intercession, battle summons, and cries for help.

Elijah occupies a central position in the Animal Apocalypse's description of prophetic activity in the divided kingdom (*1 En.* 89:51-53).[69] When the sheep began to stray the Lord "summoned some from among the sheep and sent them to the sheep, and the sheep began to kill them" (89:51). Elijah alone escaped: "It sprang away and cried out over the sheep." The Israelites wanted to kill him also, but he, like Enoch, was taken up by God (89:52). The Lord then sent many others "to testify *(yāsmeʿu)* and lament *(wayaʿawyewu)* over them" (89:53). The passage portrays God's sending of prophets in two waves; in the interval between them Elijah holds the field alone. Yet they all share the commission to return the straying sheep to right worship. To this end, Elijah cries out over the sheep. The prophets who follow him continue his work of testimony. They also take up the work of lament. While they address their testimony to the wayward Israelites, they address their lament to God, crying out for divine help in the face of a seemingly impossible task.

In 1 Kings 18, Elijah cries out to the people not only to effect their return to the Lord, but also to rally them to forceful resistance against those who introduced and propagated false religion. Once he wins their affirmation that "the Lord alone is God" (1 Kgs 18:39 NJPS), he commands them, "Seize the prophets of Baal, let not a single one of them get away" (18:40 NJPS). They comply, and Elijah executes the captives (18:40). Awareness of the episode is implicit in the Book of Dreams' statement that the sheep "wished to kill" Elijah after his earlier escape and subsequent crying out, for in Kings it is clear that Jezebel intends to kill Elijah in retaliation for the murder of her prophets (19:2).[70] The purge of the Baal prophets thus lurks just below the surface of the Book of Dreams' retelling of 1 Kings 18–19. We will see below that in the Book of Dreams too the prophetic call to religious reform soon merges with the call to arms.

The sighted lambs of *1 Enoch* 90:6 suffer just like the prophets of 89:51. The ravens (*viz.*, the Seleucids) seized one of the lambs, then devoured the sheep (*1 En.* 90:8). The one lamb who was seized (often identified with Onias III) contrasts with Elijah, the one sheep who escapes and is not killed. The next verse reports that the remaining lambs sprouted horns (i.e., took up arms, 90:9), now merging into one the role of prophet and militant defender of the faith.

The verbal and thematic links between the description of the lambs in *1 Enoch* 90 and of Elijah and the prophets of the Lord in 89:51-53 serve another purpose for our writer. By highlighting the earlier persecution of the faithful

---

69. Nickelsburg has observed a ring structure in these verses (*1 Enoch 1*, p. 384).

70. His life was endangered prior to the purge of the Baal prophets, but this first threat on Elijah's life is resolved in the Book of Dreams with the first notice that Elijah "escaped safely and was not killed." The threat recurs after he cries out over the sheep, and thus after the episode at Carmel.

messengers of God (cf. 1 Kgs 18:13; 19:2), the writer of the Book of Dreams draws attention to the common circumstances of the community of the righteous in the time of Antiochus's edict and persecution and of the prophets of the Lord in Elijah's time.[71] The community of the righteous could see themselves, like the former prophets, as sent by God to restore right worship among God's people. They could find in prophetic figures from the past a model for the present. Elijah's central position in the passage and his elevation to a special status alongside Enoch (1 En. 89:52) point further to his exemplary status for our writer. His solitary stand among would-be murderers and his ultimate escape from death provide the audience with models of courage and of God's intervention to deliver the faithful ("The Lord of the sheep saved it from the hands of the sheep," 89:52).

The other major prophetic exemplar for our writer is Moses,[72] who receives in 89:17-18 a commission to testify.[73] This commission parallels and prefigures the one later given to the prophets who followed Elijah and continued his work.[74] Moses (and Aaron) will testify (yāsmeʿ 89:17; waʾasmeʿu 89:18) against the Egyptians "not to touch the sheep" (89:17). In the period of crisis, Moses, like Elijah, provides a model for the prophetic activity of the righteous, who must testify now to the faltering Judeans.

Like Elijah, Moses also provides the righteous with a model for armed resistance to apostasy when the prophetic word fails. We saw that in retelling the events at Sinai, the writer adverts to the episode of the golden calf ("The flock began to go blind," 89:32), a type of future apostasy. The Book of Dreams foregrounds the story of Moses' rally of the Levites to slaughter the idolaters (89:35; Ex 32:25-29).[75] In Exodus, Moses instructs the Levites who respond to his call:

71. Tiller, Commentary, 352; Nickelsburg, 1 Enoch 1, 361. For Newsom these prophets "prefigure" the group described in 90:6 ("Enoch 83–90," p. 21).

72. Samuel also appears in the Book of Dreams, but his actions are limited to observing Saul's disobedience and appointing/anointing his successor (89:44-46). There is no clear sense in which the lambs/rams of ch. 90 emulate the activities of Samuel in this book, and thus he cannot be seen as an exemplar.

73. The Ethiopic verbal root samʿa overlaps substantially in meaning with the Hebrew root שמע, but its G-stem can also signify bearing witness or testifying. The causative stem found in 89:18 also has this meaning (cf. Ex 23:1, and Prov 21:28). Aramaic and Greek are not extant for the three verses in which this verb occurs with this sense in the Book of Dreams, so we cannot be sure of the Vorlage.

74. The verb "to testify" recurs also in the account of the heavenly scribe's intercession for the sheep: "He testified (wayesammeʿ) in his presence against all the shepherds" (89:76). In this case testimony is testimony to God, urging God to act and setting the stage for the final judgment. Testimony to/against humans necessarily serves a different purpose.

75. Newsom notes the emphasis, finding here "an allusion to the attacks of pious Jews upon their apostate fellows in the early days of the uprising against Antiochus" ("Enoch 83–90," pp. 17-18).

"Thus says the Lord, the God of Israel, put your sword on your hip, every one of you! Now go up and down the camp, from gate to gate, and slay your own kinsmen, your friends, and neighbors" (32:27). Exodus thus presents the arming of the faithful and slaughter of idolaters as a divine mandate, a motif we also saw in the Apocalypse of Weeks. By contrast with the Apocalypse of Weeks, however, both in Exodus 32 (32:34) and in the Book of Dreams this activity is separate from God's judging activity. In the Book of Dreams the slaughter reestablishes right worship: "And that sheep took other sheep with it and went against those sheep that had strayed and began to slaughter them, and the sheep were afraid of it. And that sheep returned all the straying flock to their folds" (1 *En.* 89:35). To the extent that the episode of the golden calf was a type of apostasy, the actions of Moses and the Levites provided a paradigm for future responses to apostasy. The Book of Dreams' narration emphasizes the outcome: taking up arms against idolaters results in a return to right worship.

Against the edict of Antiochus, the lambs take on a prophetic role similar to that of Elijah, crying out and urging the sheep to resist false religion and return to right worship. Like the prophets who followed Elijah, and like Moses who preceded them, they testify to the will of God and exhort the people to return to covenant obedience. Moses also models the merging of prophetic and militant roles to achieve religious reform.

The lambs' prophetic cry and testimony fall on deaf ears: "But [the sheep] did not listen to them nor attend to their words, but they were extremely deaf, and their eyes were extremely and excessively blinded" (1 *En.* 90:6-7).[76] In these verses, a framing device places the actions of speaking and (not) hearing (B/B′) within the context of seeing and not seeing (A/A′). In this way the writer emphasizes right perception as a precondition for right action/obedience to God's will. The chiasm may be diagrammed as follows:

> A   They began to open their eyes and see
> B   and cry out to those sheep
> B′   but they did not listen to them
>   nor attend to their words
>   but they were extremely deaf
> A′ And their eyes were extremely and excessively blinded.

Within this chiastic structure, triple emphasis falls on hearing/attending to the words of God's messengers, which in this case the sheep have failed to do. The

---

76. Several variant readings exist for 90:7: "they afflicted them" instead of "they did not listen to them"; "and they prevailed" instead of "excessively." While these variants suggest a persecution of the lambs by the sheep, it is unclear which reading is original. See notes in Nickelsburg, 1 *Enoch 1*, p. 389, and Tiller, *Commentary,* pp. 351-52.

opening verses of the second dream vision share a similar emphasis, where the same framing device occurs in slightly different form. There Enoch tells Methuselah (85:1-2):

> A   I saw a second dream,
>   And I will show all of it to you, my son,
>   B   And Enoch lifted up and said to his son Methuselah
>   To you I speak, my son,
>   B' Hear my words
>   And incline your ear
> A'   To the dream vision of your father.

In these verses to show is to speak. To hear and attend to Enoch's words is to receive the revelation given to the seer in a vision and accept its authority. In so doing, the audience will distinguish themselves from the blind sheep who failed to hear the cry.

In this way the writer tells the audience, *it is not too late.* Not long ago the message of the faithful was ignored, their testimony failed, and the people continued to be swept up in a growing tide of idolatry and assimilation. But, as we will see below, the tide quickly turns and battle begins. By urging the audience to hear and attend, the writer calls them to dwell not on the failure of the past, but on the work yet to be done.[77] In the context of war, the cry of the lambs will take new direction and meaning as a plea for heavenly aid.

Horns Came Out on Those Lambs

Amidst a people blind and deaf, victimized by their Seleucid overlords, the chosen lambs grow horns (i.e., they take up arms, 90:8-9).[78] These verses signal a clear departure from the nonviolent program of resistance advocated by the writer of Daniel and move a step beyond the scene of execution envisioned in the Apocalypse of Weeks. While each of these writers envisions a role for the faithful in spreading salvific teachings and revelations, each differs in his or her understanding of the battle that would ensue and the role of the faithful in it. For the writer of Daniel, the battle would be waged in heaven; the faithful would not need to take up arms. In the Apocalypse of Weeks, the righteous would be given a sword only at the hour of judgment, when the wicked were handed over to them to execute God's sentence. By contrast, the lambs of the

---

77. Tiller, *Commentary,* p. 115.

78. Citing 1 Sam 2:1, Assefa argues that horns need not connote force (*L'Apocalypse des animaux,* p. 317). Yet military connotations are present even in Hannah's song.

Book of Dreams neither wait for the final judgment nor go gently to slaughter. They sprout horns, maturing into rams, and do battle on earth.

One sheep sprouts a great horn (90:9). The sheep represents Judas Maccabeus.[79] In the Book of Dreams Judas is not only military leader of the resistance movement, but also champion of orthodoxy. He "looked upon" the sheep, and their eyes opened (90:10a).[80] In this respect Judas follows the leadership pattern established in the Animal Apocalypse during the period of the judges.[81] Judas, like the judges, emerges as a charismatic military and religious leader in a time of apostasy and oppression. His effectiveness in "opening the eyes" of the sheep and so bringing about a return to right belief and practice corresponds to reports in 1 Maccabees of his commitment to the law and his actions against apostate Jews.[82] In the Book of Dreams Judas also "cried out" to the sheep *(waṣarḥu lomu)*, and "the rams saw it [Judas], and they all rallied to him" (90:10b).[83] The "cry" that in earlier verses signaled prophetic activity here becomes a summons to battle.[84] The rams' sight enables them to recognize Judas's leadership and marshal under his command.

By contrast with Judas (and later the rams), the sheep remain silent while birds attack and devour them (90:11). They have not taken up arms and do not resist their attackers. They also fail to address God in prayer or neighbor in exhortation.[85] As I have argued in preceding chapters, resistance includes lament. While the sheep remain silent, the rams take on the role of intercessors. Crying out to God in the hour of need, they will stand in the breach on behalf of land, people, and law.

79. Cf. Judas's "great horn" to 1 Macc 2:66: "Judas Maccabeus has been a mighty warrior from his youth; he shall command the army for you and fight the battle against the peoples" (NRSV).

80. Cf. Isa 35:5; 42:6-7.

81. Cf. also the role of Moses following the episode of the golden calf (89:34-35). The writer of the Book of Dreams does not style Judas after the kings of the united monarchy, who are also described as rams. His activity is much closer to that of Moses, the judges, and the prophets of the divided kingdom. This writer considered the period of the united monarchy to be relatively free from apostasy, while these other periods were not, and thus afforded a better analogy to the present situation.

82. Cf. 1 Macc 2:20-22, 42-44, 46, 48, 64.

83. For Judas's cry as battle summons and exhortation, cf. 2 Macc 8:1, 15:8-11. For the rally to Judas, cf. 1 Macc 2:67-68.

84. The verbs זעק/צעק frequently indicate a call to arms: צעק in Judg 7:23, 24; 10:17; 12:1; 1 Sam 13:4; 2 Kgs 3:21; זעק in Josh 8:16; Judg 4:10, 13; 6:34, 35; 12:2; 18:22; 1 Sam 14:20.

85. As in 85:7 and 89:20, silence signals the ceasing or absence of lament and outcry. See also Tiller, *Commentary*, p. 357.

They Lamented and Cried Out

When the rams (the sighted lambs who sprouted horns) witnessed the birds of prey "tearing the sheep in pieces and flying upon them and devouring them," "they lamented and cried out" (*ya'awayyewu wayeṣarreḥu* 90:11). Repetition of the verb "to cry out" with different connotations throughout the narrative connects different forms of speech, including prophecy, prayers of lament and intercession, battle summons, and, as we will see below, the cry for help in battle. The righteous are bound ever to speak out. From the midst of battles, the rams now pray and make supplication, actions modeled earlier in the Book of Dreams by Enoch.[86]

Their lament and cry echo Enoch's following his first vision, as well as those of the slaves in Egypt, reported in 89:15-20. The typology of flood-exodus-eschaton here provides a model for lament and prayer along with the promise of God's saving response. The writer highlights this typology within the second dream vision by using the same word pair ("to lament" and "to cry out") to describe the actions of Enoch, the slaves, and the rams.

When he witnesses the sufferings of God's people during the period of the divided kingdom, Enoch cries out and calls to God (*'eṣrāḥ wa'eṣawwe'o*). Enoch continues to grieve (*waḥazanku*) as he witnesses the destruction of the temple (89:67) and laments again as he sees the events of the exile (*'aḥazku 'ebki wa'a'awyu* "I began to cry and lament" 89:69). Just before the birth of the sighted lambs, Enoch vocalizes his lament once more (*ṣarāḥku wa'awyawku* 90:3). As a response to the second vision, however, Enoch's laments are ineffectual. I argued above that Enoch's success as intercessor was limited to the salvation of the righteous remnant after the flood, for which he petitioned following the first vision. It would fall to those descended from the remnant to pray again in the hour of persecution, as Enoch taught them, to seek deliverance for the faithful and punishment for their oppressors.

The slaves in Egypt also lamented and cried out. Responding to conditions of oppression and the drowning of their babies at the hands of the Egyptians, the sheep "began to cry out (*yeṣreḥu*) because of their young and to make complaint (*wayesakkeyu*) to their Lord" (89:15). While Moses escaped to the wilderness, the sheep continued to lament and cry out (*ya'awayyewu wayeṣarreḥu*), and petitioned/prayed to their Lord/owner (*wayese'elewwo la'egzi'omu* 89:16).[87]

---

86. The writer reintroduces the motif of intercession in the description of the recording angel who intercedes and petitions on behalf of the sheep (*wayāstabaqqwe'o ba'enti'ahomu wayese''elo* 89:76). Enoch uses the same two verbs in the intercessory prayer that follows his vision of the flood: "I make supplication and ask that you will fulfill for me my prayer" (*'astabaqwe' wa'ese''el kama tāqem lita se'lateya* 84:5).

87. The same verb *sa'ala*, and its cognate accusative occur in Enoch's prayer: *wa'ese'el kama tāqem lita se'lateya*, "I ask that you fulfill for me my prayer" (84:5).

Following Moses' and Aaron's commission to testify to the Egyptians, the latter dealt more harshly still with the Hebrew slaves, so that the sheep cried out yet again (ṣarḥu 89:19). Just as God heard these cries and acted to deliver the slaves from oppression, so God would hear the cries of the faithful rams in the battle preceding the end time and act for their deliverance. The prophets' initial failure does not preclude God's ultimate victory, nor does it signal an end to the work they must do.

As in the Book of Dreams, so in earlier traditions the exodus events provided a paradigm of the cry to God for help and God's saving response (cf. its use in Josh 24:7; 1 Sam 12:8; 1 Kgs 8:51-53; Neh 9:9; cf. Isa 19:20). That cry first goes out in Exodus 2:23, a verse that is echoed in *1 Enoch* 89:16. The cry and response also holds a central place in the Deuteronomistic cycle of apostasy-punishment-repentance-deliverance (cf. Judg 2:18, 1 Sam 12:8-11).[88] This cycle is a major structuring element in the Animal Apocalypse, with the cry of God's people marking the turning point of each new era.[89]

Solomon's prayer in 1 Kings 8 provided a template for cry in crisis, showing "what Israel should do in the hour of judgment."[90] According to Judith Newman, it served "as a programmatic statement . . . that God should respond in a certain way and help the Israelites in certain situations," offering to those who could not worship in the Jerusalem temple "the reassurance that their own prayers would be answered by God."[91] In Solomon's prayer the exodus gives assurance of God's response to prayer (1 Kgs 8:51, 53). Looking also to the future, Solomon prays, "If your people go out to battle against their enemy, by whatever way you shall send them, and they pray to the LORD toward the city that you have chosen and the house that I have built for your name, then hear in heaven their prayer and their plea, and maintain their cause" (8:44-45 NRSV; see also 2 Chron 6:34-35). He entreats God to hear God's people "whenever they call on you" (1 Kgs 8:52). The Chronicler models Jehoshaphat's later prayer on Solomon's, while placing additional emphasis on the future efficacy of the cry: "If disaster comes upon us, the sword, judgment, or pestilence, or famine, we

---

88. Hans Walter Wolff, "The Kerygma of the Deuteronomic Historical Work," trans. Frederick C. Prussner, in *The Vitality of Old Testament Traditions*, ed. Walter Brueggemann and Hans Walter Wolff, 2nd ed. (Atlanta: John Knox, 1975), pp. 83-100, 87.

89. On the use of this cycle in the Animal Apocalypse, see Nickelsburg, *1 Enoch 1*, p. 359. The Book of Dreams' audience shared with the exilic audience of the Deuteronomistic Historian lack of national sovereignty or legitimate king and lack of ("properly") functioning temple cult. They also viewed themselves as Israel's remnant.

90. Wolff, "Kerygma," pp. 91-92.

91. Judith H. Newman, *Praying by the Book: The Scripturalization of Prayer in Second Temple Judaism* (Atlanta: Scholars Press, 1999), p. 52. Newman also notes the references to this prayer in 1 Macc 7:37-38 and 2 Macc 2:8 (p. 52n61).

will . . . cry to you in our distress, and you will hear and save" (2 Chron 20:9 NRSV).[92] The prayers of Solomon and Jehoshaphat articulate a theology of prayer and response central to our writer's program of resistance. Prayer is efficacious. God's response to the cry in Egypt established for God's people a sure pattern: whatever their sufferings, if they turn to God and cry out, trusting in God's salvation, God will hear and deliver, even in time of war.

In the events surrounding both the flood and the exodus, God heard the cry and intervened to save God's people and punish their oppressors.[93] Our writer wished to show that God would again deliver when the people cried out in prayer. To make this point, the writer uses similar language to describe God's saving actions in response to each of the three cries.[94] This thematic repetition reinforces the typology of flood-exodus-eschaton. The reports of the flood and the exodus in the Book of Dreams share imagery of darkness/blindness (1 En. 89:4, 21), rising/swelling waters (89:26), the opening of fissures (89:3) and splitting of the waters (89:24), covering or engulfing (89:3, 5, 8, 26), and the perishing and sinking of the oppressors (89:6, 27). When God intervenes to help the rams during the final battle, we again see themes of darkness (90:15), splitting (now the earth, 90:18), sinking of the enemies (now into the earth, 90:18), and covering (90:18). In this way the writer portrays God's future saving action as consistent with God's actions in the past.

War Traditions

Now the ram Judas also cries out *(waṣarḥa)* "that its help might come" (90:13).[95] Judas's cry effects a turning point in the war and in the narrative. The angelic scribe "helped it and showed it everything; his help came down to that

92. Note that the Chronicler's version of Solomon's prayer closely follows that in Kings, though it omits the references to the exodus. Isaiah also counted on God's response to the cry for help: "He will be gracious to you when you cry out; as soon as he hears he will answer you" (Isa 30:19 NAB). This verse follows on the injunction to wait for the Lord, a passage that played an important role in shaping the stance of active waiting advocated by the writer of Daniel. Trito-Isaiah likewise promises that God will save the righteous in distress: "Then you shall call, and the Lord will answer, you shall cry for help, and he will say, 'Here I am'" (58:9 NAB). The prayer in Neh 9 likewise emphasizes the importance of the cry, in its description of the period of the judges (Neh 9:27).

93. The cry is not present in Genesis's flood account, but is an important element in the Book of the Watchers (see 1 En. 7:6; 8:4; 9:3), culminating in the angels' declaration to God, "And now behold, the souls of those who have come to an end cry out and petition as far as the gates of heaven, and their moaning has gone up" (9:10).

94. Nickelsburg, 1 Enoch 1, pp. 379, 401; and Tiller, Commentary, pp. 286-87, 365.

95. On the cry to God for help in battle, cf. 1 Chron 5:20; 2 Chron 13:14, 18.

ram" (90:14). God intervenes and turns the tide of the battle in favor of the Judeans. Finally, the sheep are given a sword and pursue the enemy to kill them (90:19). The host of beasts and birds flee before them. As noted above, God's intervention in this final battle follows a pattern of God's intervention for salvation and judgment in the era of the flood and the exodus.[96]

The theophanies that follow Judas's cry draw on divine warrior traditions that exhibit a synergistic understanding of warfare, in which neither God nor God's people fight alone, but both enter the fray together (cf. Deut 20:4).[97] In the Hebrew scriptures Joshua 10 provides the first major illustration of the Lord fighting with and for Israel. Parallels between this episode and the battle scene(s) in *1 Enoch* 90:9-19 suggest that the writer of the Book of Dreams may have had this episode in mind while composing his or her account of the final battle(s).

In Joshua, five Amorite kings mustered to attack the Gibeonites, who had made peace with Joshua, and Joshua and his warriors went to aid the people of Gibeon (Josh 10:5-7). The Lord told Joshua, "Do not fear them, for I have handed them over to you; not one of them shall stand before you" (10:8 NRSV). When Joshua marched on the enemy, "The Lord threw them into a panic before Israel" (10:10 NRSV). Joshua defeated and pursued the Amorites. As they fled, the Lord hurled hailstones at them from the sky: "There were more who died because of the hailstones than the Israelites killed with the sword" (10:11 NRSV).

After this first intervention and victory, Joshua prayed to God, calling on the sun and moon to stand still while Israel takes vengeance on the Amorites (10:12-13). The sun halted in its course (10:13), "for the LORD fought for Israel" (10:14 NRSV). The narrator reports, "There has been no day like it before or since, when the LORD heeded a human voice" (10:14 NRSV). As the enemy fled, Joshua instructed his army to pursue them (10:19).

After describing Joshua's subsequent victories, the narrator reports, "Joshua took all these kings and their land at one time, because the LORD God of Israel fought for Israel" (10:42 NRSV). Joshua would later remind the Israel-

---

96. Cf. Tiller, *Commentary*, p. 4; Newsom, "Enoch 83–90," p. 14.

97. On *1 Enoch*'s use of the divine warrior motif, see Randal Argall, 1 Enoch *and Sirach: A Comparative Literary and Conceptual Analysis of the Themes of Revelation, Creation and Judgment* (Atlanta: Scholars Press, 1995), pp. 167-84; Nickelsburg, *1 Enoch 1*, pp. 43-44. Newsom observes, "The authors of apocalyptic did draw heavily on the divine warrior material but felt relatively little compulsion to present it in a form determined by the inner logic of that tradition" ("Enoch 83–90," p. 37). On synergy, see Patrick Miller, *The Divine Warrior in Early Israel* (Cambridge, MA: Harvard University Press, 1973). This synergism also informs 2 Macc and pervades the *War Scroll*. By contrast, in 1 Macc God is the "help" of the Maccabees and equips and strengthens them (especially Judas) for victory, but neither God nor God's angels enter the battle. See also Judg 4:14; 5:4-5, 20; 6:12; 7:22.

ites how God fought with them: "For the LORD has driven out before you great and strong nations; and as for you, no one has been able to withstand you to this day. One of you puts to flight a thousand, since it is the LORD your God who fights for you, as he promised you" (23:9-10 NRSV). This synergy in battle testified to the Lord's provident care for the covenant people, accomplishing God's promises and bringing them victory in seemingly impossible circumstances.

In its present form the battle account in *1 Enoch* 90 shares characteristics with Joshua 10. The assemblage of eagles, kites, vultures, ravens, and wild beasts[98] in *1 Enoch* 90:16 corresponds in number to the five kings assembled against Joshua. In both narratives God intervenes twice in the course of battle, and the enemy flees twice. Both also share the motif of the Israelites pursuing the enemy in their final flight after God's decisive intervention.[99] In Joshua 10, they pursue them knowing that the Lord has delivered the enemy into their hands; in *1 Enoch* 90:19 they do so equipped with a sword given to them by the Lord. Finally, both Joshua and Judas make a unique request within the narrative, which God immediately honors. Joshua asks God to stay the sun in its course; the narrator tells us that never before or since did God so honor the request of a mortal. Judas cries out to God "that his help might come," a phrase that has no exact parallel in other extant scriptures. The writer of the Book of Dreams thus places a similar emphasis on the uniqueness of Judas's request, which is both consistent with earlier cries to God in the book, but set apart from them in its specificity. Judas's help comes immediately. The heavenly scribe and the Lord both enter the fray, ensuring victory for the righteous.

Judas shares with Joshua the role of military leader who emphasizes obedience to the Mosaic covenant. In his opening the eyes of the sheep, Judas is portrayed in the manner of the judges in the Animal Apocalypse, but also like Joshua, their immediate predecessor. Indeed, it was Joshua who read the teachings of Moses before the Israelites, reminding them of the covenant blessings and curses (Josh 8:30-35), shortly before the campaign against the Amorites. He would later exhort the Israelites to follow the Torah of Moses (23:6) and to serve the Lord rather than the gods of the Amorites who lived in the land (24:15), mindful of the covenant and all the wonders the Lord had performed on their behalf (24:2-13). The Book of Dreams imagined that like Joshua, Judas would bring Judeans to covenant fidelity, that they might reject the religion now practiced by people who lived in their midst, follow the law of Moses, and worship

98. Or "wild sheep" or "wild asses." See Tiller, *Commentary*, p. 363.

99. Tiller notes the structural similarity (victory accomplished by God followed by pursuit of the enemy) but does not note that both have a doubling of this sequence (*Commentary*, p. 365).

the Lord in the pleasant land. By highlighting similarities between the battles led by Judas and Joshua, the writer underscores the necessity of covenant fidelity in the Judean struggle against the program of Antiochus.

The period of Joshua's leadership in the Book of Dreams is described in idyllic terms: "And I saw the sheep until they were entering a good place and a pleasant and glorious land. And I saw those sheep until they were satisfied, and that house was in their midst in the pleasant land" (*1 En.* 89:40). This idyllic description prefigures the ideal age that would follow the final defeat of Israel's enemies. The repetition of the phrase "pleasant land" in 90:20, the construction of the new house in 90:29, and the use of idyllic imagery throughout 90:29-38 all emphasize this point. Yet the writer also portrays this ideal future in terms that far outstrip the glories of the past.

Conclusion

In a persecution that opposed the words of God and the scriptures and practices of the Jewish faith, the Book of Dreams found models for resistance in Israel's sacred traditions and in the examples of revered figures of the past. The writer outlines a program of resistance in two ways: (1) Through Enoch's example in the first vision report and in the prayer that follows; and (2) in the second vision's description of the lambs' resistance. In this description, echoes of language used earlier to describe the actions of Moses, Elijah, and Joshua direct the reader to emulate their examples.

As I discussed in chapter 1, it is common to imagine resistance as armed revolt, and this book's program of resistance certainly included this. But resistance includes all effective action that aims to limit, oppose, reject, or transform hegemonic institutions and cosmologies as well as systems, strategies, and acts of domination. The Book of Dreams envisioned resistance to imperial hegemony through the transmission of revelatory traditions and through prophetic preaching that called and empowered God's people to open their eyes. Lament and intercessory prayer opposed the destructive power of Antiochus and the temptation to comply with his edict. Praise affirmed an alternative cosmology and God's power to save. By continuing to practice their ancestral religion and championing the covenant the faithful also rejected and limited Antiochus's power to dominate and reconfigure the lives of Judeans and the land they inhabited.

In chapter 1 I also noted that resistance influences outcomes. According to the Book of Dreams, the action of the righteous could influence the fate of the world. In the first vision report, the writer invites the reader to identify with the righteous remnant saved from the flood, children of Noah and of Enoch. It is for them that the Enochic revelations and writings are intended, so that they may be saved in the final trial and save others by their merits and actions. A carefully constructed typology between the flood and the eschaton (before which the writer and righteous community now stand) shows the reader that the fate of the world is not yet determined but hangs upon their righteousness and their actions in the hour of crisis.

Both the Deuteronomistic cycle of sin, oppression, cry, and deliverance and the typology between flood and eschaton shaped the structure of the Book of Dreams. Our writer's interpretation of events of the exodus further developed the theology of cry and response. The writer extended the typology between flood and eschaton (comparable to that found in the Apocalypse of Weeks) to a cyclic typology of flood-exodus-eschaton. Both the flood and the exodus provided surety for God's salvation of the righteous and punishment of their oppressors, which would play out in the Book of Dreams in both the final battle and the final judgment. Hints of the exodus in the first vision looked ahead to the importance of the cry of God's people in the time of terror and persecution.

The report of Enoch's response to the first vision similarly emphasizes prayer. Enoch models intercession, a key form of resistance for our writer. In developing this role, the writer adapts two portions of the Book of the Watchers, one in which Enoch interceded for the fallen watchers, and one in which the angels interceded for humanity. In the Book of Dreams Enoch intercedes for the righteous and records his prayer for them so that they too may take up this work.

Enoch's response to the vision also points to the saving power of the Enochic revelations and wisdom. They counter hegemony, allowing readers to pierce the veil of imperial deception and perceive the world as it is. Sight and perception lead to understanding and right action. The writer's theological vision links God's creation, human obedience, divine sovereignty, and the coming judgment, so that a meditation on the created order hints at the future in store for the righteous and the wicked, promising reward for the faithful and an end to the reign of Antiochus.

In the narration of Enoch's second dream vision, commonly known as the Animal Apocalypse, the righteous are described as a group of lambs. Like Enoch, they possess sight, a sign that they are obedient to the covenant and heirs to the Enochic visionary tradition. Their first task is to cry out as prophets. Like Elijah and the prophets of old, they are to preach repentance, calling Israel to return and to resist the tide of Antiochus's edict and armies. They are to share the salvific knowledge they have inherited.

Moses provides this group with a model for calling the faithful to arms against apostasy. The lambs grow horns and accept the leadership of Judas Maccabeus, who has risen up like one of the judges to lead them in battle and bring the people back to right worship. As the battle ensues, the lambs/rams lament and cry, now to God. They echo the lament and cry of both Enoch and the exodus people, reflecting again the typology between flood-exodus-eschaton. By using this language to describe the actions of the rams, the writer emphasizes the intercessory role of the righteous, which they continue to perform even as they partake in the battle.

Finally, the battle accounts reveal a synergistic understanding of war, in which the faithful fight with the help of the Lord and the heavenly scribe. The account in the book of Joshua of Joshua's battle against the Amorites provided a kind of template for the final battle, in which Judas appears as a second Joshua. By this parallel, the writer shows that what is at stake in the battle is nothing less than covenant fidelity. Judas's cry for help elicits God's direct intervention and marks a turning point in the war, highlighting again the efficacy and necessity of prayer.

Conclusion

In an age of foreign domination, war, and terror, early Jewish apocalypses prompted their readers to look through and beyond visible, familiar phenomena to apprehend God's providential ordering of space, time, and created life. While exposing the violence and deceit of empire and its collaborators, they revealed powerful angelic, semi-divine, and divine actors at work in and beyond human experience and history. Shared memory, interpretation of past and present, and a new vision of the cosmos shaped hope for a transformed future. The apocalypses asserted a threatened identity and covenant and empowered their readers for resistance.

Hellenistic rule in Judea set the stage for resistance and for the emergence of the literary genre apocalypse. Alexander the Great conquered Judea, along with much of the known world, in 332 BCE. After his death his successors and their empires battled for the territories he had conquered. Between 274 and 168 BCE, the Ptolemies and Seleucids fought six "Syrian wars" for control of Judea and the wider province of Coele-Syria and Phoenicia. During these struggles, the Book of the Watchers, the earliest known "heavenly journey" apocalypse, challenged imperial hegemony and offered in its place an alternative epistemology and cosmology. By recasting myths and motifs from native, Greek, and Babylonian traditions, the Book of the Watchers critiqued Hellenistic rulers, their armies, and their ideology of conquest as well as the Jewish cultic leaders who allied themselves with the imperial administration. The righteous scribe Enoch mediated knowledge not only of the cosmos and the ancient past but also of God's plan and will for the future. For apocalyptic writers of a later generation, these Enochic traditions became an authoritative source of revelation and resource for resistance.

The leaders and populace of Judea negotiated identity, commitments, and survival throughout the decades of Hellenistic conquest and rule. During the

Fifth Syrian War, Judean leaders transferred allegiance and aid to Antiochus III. By 200 BCE Judea had a new, Seleucid king. Antiochus III confirmed the freedom of Judeans to follow their ancestral laws. The freedom was partial. Judeans paid tribute and taxes to the Seleucid government, and Jerusalem's citadel became a garrison for Seleucid troops. As agents of the empire exercised ever tighter control over local and regional administration, Judeans rebelled. Antiochus IV Epiphanes answered revolt with reconquest, aiming to crush Judean resistance through force and terror. In 167 BCE he banned Judean ancestral laws and the confession and practice of Jewish faith. His armies punished disobedience with death.

The historical apocalypses Daniel, the Apocalypse of Weeks, and the Book of Dreams oriented a terrorized people through these traumas to a vision of a future ordered by divine justice. Prophetic visions of past, present, and future asserted the transience and finitude of temporal powers. These earliest extant historical apocalypses articulated a resistant counterdiscourse to the discourse and project of empire. They also envisioned, advocated, and empowered resistant action.

Part One (ch. 1) provided a theoretical framework for studying these earliest Jewish apocalypses as literature of resistance, giving attention to social relations and context, including systems, structures, and strategies of domination and hegemony. Domination can refer both to social and ideological structures that create and maintain conditions of subordination and to such directly political and coercive forms of social control as torture, execution, enslavement, plunder, policing, and military occupation. Hegemony refers to nonviolent forms of control exercised through cultural institutions, systems of patronage, and the structured practices of everyday life. Hegemony maps the universe and people's place within it, asserting as normative and universal particular and contingent constructions of reality. It orders, divides, and assigns value. As it becomes internalized, this hegemonic cosmology invisibly constrains thought, behavior, and imagination.

Although the terms domination and hegemony are proper to modern, not ancient, discourse, they nonetheless provide descriptive categories for analyzing the conditions and objects of resistance for the earliest Jewish apocalypses and their audiences. They resisted not only foreign domination but also systems and structures of regional and local collaboration with the empires. The discourse of the earliest extant apocalypses and the actions they advocated aimed to limit, oppose, reject, and transform these complex, shifting, and plural systems, strategies, and acts of domination as well as hegemonic institutions, cosmologies, and claims for the location and legitimation of power and knowledge. Apocalyptic language, symbol, and vision gave readers tools and frameworks for thinking beyond hegemonic constructions of reality. Theologies affirming God's power and providence as Creator and restorer of life and guarantor of justice counteracted the coercive rule of Antiochus IV and its totalitarian claims over the bodies of his Judean subjects.

Earlier studies of resistance to the Hellenistic empires located the earliest Jewish historical apocalypses within a broader matrix of resistance literature in the Hellenistic Near East, suggesting that their writers drew on literary *topoi* known from other Near Eastern and Greco-Roman traditions. Samuel Eddy identified further commonalities between resistance to Hellenistic rule in Judea and elsewhere in the ancient Near East, including theologies of kingship and the role of local cults.

In recent years, studies of resistance in the ancient world have taken a theoretical turn. James C. Scott's categories of public and hidden transcript have opened the way for more nuanced analyses of systems of domination and forms of resistance previously neglected or misunderstood. Despite the popularity and usefulness of these categories, the writers of Daniel, the Apocalypse of Weeks, and the Book of Dreams were up to something very different from the off-stage resistance Scott identifies in his analyses of hidden transcripts. The dichotomy between hidden and public can accompany a set of false dualisms: invisible and visible, spirit and matter, mind and body, thought and action, belief and praxis. Generated by the domination system, such dualisms serve the purposes of empire. The apocalyptic writers studied in this book reject those dualisms and insist that the interconnectedness of the invisible and visible realms requires also the joining of thought and action, belief and praxis. Their faith in unseen realities — including divine kingship, angelic mediation, and future resurrection — leads not to a denial of the visible world and its constraints on thought and action but rather to a denial of their ultimacy and, as a result, to a different and direct confrontation and engagement with realities both seen and unseen.

The apocalyptic writers studied in this volume all use the device of pseudonymity, attributing their revelations to either Daniel or Enoch. Within the apocalypses, Daniel and Enoch mediate and authorize revelation and model faithful reception and response. Pseudonymity confers authority and signals participation in an existing discourse, locating authority within a tradition of revelatory discourse that testifies to an alternative source of power and vision of reality. The narrative of revelation reveals the contingency of self and empire. What is commonly called apocalyptic determinism thereby deconstructs illusions of autonomy while simultaneously (despite popular misperceptions) insisting on human freedom. Apocalyptic revelations of divine providence, will, and action summon readers to answer with corresponding awareness, commitment, and praxis.

Part Two (chs. 2–6) examined the conditions of Hellenistic rule in Judea, with special attention to the period of Seleucid domination. Modern historiographic accounts have commonly portrayed the first three decades of Seleucid rule in nearly idyllic terms, with their happy rhythm suddenly and inexplicably interrupted by the decree and persecution of Antiochus IV in 167 BCE. Closer scrutiny reveals multiple stressors and divisions in Judea from the beginning of Seleucid rule. The fifth Syrian war itself brought hardship to Judea, including injury, captivity, and loss of life, the burden of provisions for Antiochus's troops and elephants, and damage to land and structures, likely including the temple in Jerusalem. After the war, in addition to the economic strain of tribute and taxes, military occupation brought loss of land, displacement, and more slavery. The transition to Seleucid rule was marked by rapid political change, internal division, and unequal distribution of resources and privileges.

In this period, temple, priests, and sacred laws each mediated between the Jews and their God. They also occupied complex positions in the relationship between Judeans and the empire that governed them. As loci of governance, interaction, memory, and identity, temple cult and other living traditions — oral, embodied, and written — formed the heart of early Jewish theologies of resistance.

Events and circumstances in the wider Mediterranean world shaped those in Judea, as I explored in chapter 3. Indemnities to Rome and ambitions for expansion prompted Seleucid kings to identify provincial temples as sources of revenue. Though often dismissed by historians as a minor episode, the account of Heliodorus's attempted incursion into and robbery of the Jerusalem temple in 2 Maccabees 3:4–4:1 takes on new significance in light of the recently published Heliodorus stele. The stele displayed a dossier of correspondence dating to 178 BCE from Seleucus IV to Heliodorus and other regional officials concerning the oversight of temples in Coele-Syria and Phoenicia. Its rhetoric of royal piety and benefaction promoted tighter financial control through an ideology of interdependence. Read together, the ancient sources reveal the increasing encroachment of imperial administration into cultic life, a development that exacerbated tensions and divisions in the Judean community. They also reveal interaction, reciprocity, and negotiation between Judean leadership and imperial officials.

Cultural interaction and negotiation took place alongside and within the political. Historians have long employed the trope of Judaism versus Hellenism to explain Judean resistance to Seleucid rule. The trope oversimplifies even as it names a real tension. Antiochus IV came to power in 175 BCE. Shortly thereafter, the Oniad Jason purchased from the king the high-priestly office and the privilege of introducing in Jerusalem a gymnasium, ephebate, and Antiochene citizenship. These innovations linked Judean political power with Hellenistic cultural forms that reshaped Judean bodies and civic identity. But when the Hasmoneans revolted against Seleucid domination eight years later, or when Jason himself rebelled in 169 or 168 BCE, they were not fighting against Hellenism, nor did Hellenism kill the first Jewish martyrs. Judaism and Hellenism — both of them always already hybrid and porous — were not opposing forces. I noted above that some Hellenistic traditions provided models and sources for Jewish resistance to Seleucid rule. Yet by 167 BCE, when "Hellenism" became associated with a power that aimed to erase particular Jewish identity, resisters emphasized alternate sources of power and identity for the people of Judea. These included religious traditions and praxis and cultural forms seen as particular to, or indexical of, Judaism. They also included revelation, angels, and God.

If Hellenism was not the primary object of resistance, neither was Judaism's eradication the primary goal of Antiochus IV's assault on Judea. It was a means of reconquest by which he sought to re-create his empire. Between the years 170 and 168 BCE, Antiochus IV fought the Ptolemaic empire for control of Coele-Syria and Phoenicia in the Sixth Syrian war. I argued in chapter 4 that during this period or at the war's conclusion Jason's revolt gave Antiochus the opportunity to secure and consolidate his power in this prized but contested region, magnifying himself as creator, source, and sovereign.

In chapter 5 I brought trauma theory and studies of modern state terror to bear in analyzing events in Judea between the years 169 and 167 BCE (prior to the edict and persecution) and the responses to them in the historical apocalypses. Antiochus's reprisals in Judea included assault and abduction, home invasion, and plunder of the temple. Military parade turned massacre as Seleucid soldiers set fire to the capital city and leveled its houses. The contrast between Jerusalem's broken walls and the newly fortified Akra gave stark testimony to Seleucid power. Antiochus's program of terror created a climate of insecurity and shame. The writers of the apocalypses intervened in the logic and program of terror, revealing divine order and transcendent meaning in the midst of suffering. They voiced lament and visions of hope. They resisted fragmentation with symbol and language, reconnecting past, present, and future in a continuous narrative of God's providential care.

Chapter 6 examined the edict and persecution by which Antiochus aimed to complete the conquest of Judea. Revoking Judean civic freedom, he banned ancestral religion, mandating in its place new religious practices and civic rituals that reordered space, time, and human life. Drawing on the work of Elaine Scarry, I argued that Antiochus used negation, dissolution of boundaries, insecurity, destruction of language, annihilation of thought and vision, totality, and the creation of an "ontological split" to project the power of the Seleucid empire. Judean resistance took many forms, including revolt, martyrdom, teaching, and writing. The writers of the apocalypses resisted the unmaking of world and identity by offering new sight, naming terror and hope, insisting on the integrity of reality, and denying the ultimacy of the pain Antiochus inflicted and the power he claimed. In its place they asserted the totality of heavenly rule, divine creation, sacred knowledge, and life in covenant with God.

A close examination of these apocalypses in Part Three (chs. 7–10) underscored the relationship between vision, interpretation, and praxis. Daniel called its readers to outspoken, nonviolent resistance to the edict of Antiochus, the lies of empire, and the terror of Seleucid rule. Against empire they were to wield knowledge. The teachers who formed the book's primary audience would lead their people to wisdom and righteousness through liturgical prayer, fasting, penitence, and public preaching that gave witness to the book's apocalyptic vision of past, present, and future. Narrative joined with prediction to provide models of hope, trust, and faithful action, including a willingness to give over their bodies to death in time of persecution. New revelation provided interpretive keys for reading Torah and prophets, uncovering a pattern for life in covenant and assurance of salvation. Angelic interpretation of Jeremiah 25 and 29 emphasized the providential ordering of historical time, place, and community. The wise teachers of Daniel identified their own mission with that of the Servant in Isaiah 52:13–53:12. For both, the revelation of divine power in human weakness had profound political consequences.

According to legend, the captive Daniel entered exile with the leaders of Judah. He interpreted visions and delivered God's word of judgment to the kings of Babylon. He also saw a future in which empire succeeded empire, leading at last to the age of Seleucid domination. In this future God brought about empire's end, replacing Antiochus's reign of terror with the eternal just rule of one like a human being.

Sacred stories told of another seer, Enoch, who journeyed to heaven in an age long before Daniel, before empires ruled God's elect, and before the fateful descent of watchers (angels) corrupted the created order and human knowledge. Enoch's cosmic visions revealed hidden dimensions of heaven and earth, space and time, wickedness and righteousness, and the life of God and creatures. As early as the Book of the Watchers, Enoch's visions provided ancient epistemological foundations for critique of Hellenistic imperial violence and claims to knowledge and power. The Apocalypse of Weeks and Book of Dreams grounded not only critique but also calls to resistance in the authority of Enochic discourse.

By comparison with other early Jewish texts, the early Enochic booklets exhibit a number of distinctive features, including astronomical concerns, alternative cosmology, alternative epistemology, and the elevated role of Enoch. As scholars have increasingly attended to these distinctive features and to the vitality of Enochic traditions in early Judaism, questions have arisen concerning the relation between "Enochic" and "Mosaic" Judaism, or between the authority of Enochic traditions and that of Mosaic Torah. Chapter 8 argued that Enochic authority did not primarily compete with Mosaic authority, although it subsumed it. It challenged the hegemonic claims of empire and its collaborators. Its map of the divine realm countered imperial cosmology. Claims for Enoch's temporal priority, righteousness, and access to heavenly mysteries allowed Enochic writers to transcend the limits of the particular, local, and terrestrial to assert a universal authority against the ideology of empire.

From this standpoint, the Apocalypse of Weeks, examined in chapter 9, called the righteous to witness, to uproot foundations of violence and the structure of deceit, and wield a sword in the time of judgment. I dated this brief apocalypse during the reign of Antiochus IV Epiphanes, in the year 167 BCE, following the edict but prior to the beginning of the Maccabean revolt. The vision structures the human story according to the sabbatical rhythms of created time and a typological correspondence between past and future, while simultaneously tracing an opposition between truth and righteousness, or the "order of life," on the one hand, and falsehood and wickedness on the other. God's election and gift of knowledge and wisdom would empower the righteous for effective testimony that would transform the current order, eradicating the "foundations of violence and structure of deceit" that included the physical, social, religious, and epistemological dimensions of domination and hegemony in Seleucid Judea. The chosen righteous would then execute capital punishment against the wicked. The anticipated rule of "the Great One" provided the fundamental point of orientation and measure of value in the midst of Seleucid claims to order Judean life. The just economy of the future kingdom would have its foundation in the worship of God.

Chapter 10 concluded the study of apocalyptic theologies of resistance in early Judaism with an analysis of the Enochic Book of Dreams, a composition dating between the years 165 and 160 BCE. In Enoch's first-person account of two dreams and his responses to them, narrative typology yokes together visions of past, present, and future, calling readers to resist Antiochus's edict and persecution with prayer, preaching, and warfare. Linking creation, obedience, divine sovereignty, and judgment, the book emphasized doxology, right worship, and the appeal to God for mercy and aid.

Enoch's first vision heralded earth's destruction by flood. He responded with lament, praise, and petition that changed the fate of the world. His second vision, commonly called the Animal Apocalypse, told the story of humankind from their creation to the descent of the stars, through the flood, to the election of Israel, through their history of slavery and liberation, wilderness revelation, settlement, monarchy, and division, blindness, exile, and foreign domination. It also told of their resistance, God's intervention to help them in a day of battle, and an eternal age of justice marked by judgment against their oppressors, the conversion of the nations, and the joy of God. This vision represents humankind as animals, with God's chosen people portrayed as sheep, governed sometimes by shepherds but ever belonging to their Lord.

The Book of Dreams presented its vision for resistance in Enoch's account of his response to his dreams and the actions of the lambs/rams with open eyes. The description of their activity also echoed that of earlier figures in the vision, including Moses, Elijah, and Joshua, calling readers to emulate these leaders from the past in their prophetic summons to obedience, militant action, and petition to God. Alone among the extant historical apocalypses dating to the era of Seleucid domination, the Book of Dreams plainly advocated resistance through armed revolt. But if it differed from Daniel and the Apocalypse of Weeks in this respect, it shared with them an insistence on the power of knowledge, the importance of obedience and right worship, and a vision of resistance through preaching that would counter imperial hegemony by enabling others to see.

The image of open eyes vividly captures the insistence in each apocalypse on the interrelation of knowledge and obedience, vision and praxis, that formed the heart of apocalyptic theologies of resistance to empire in early Judaism. Apocalyptic faith maintained that what could be seen on the surface told only part of the story. It looked as if Antiochus would destroy God's people, the covenant, holiness itself. It looked as if empire wielded power over life and death. A people with open eyes could look through and beyond appearances to perceive the order of all creation and the enduring rule of God. They could name the violence and deception of imperial domination and hegemony, but also see in history a pattern for deliverance to come. They could see their own path and not stray from it, remaining faithful to God's law. And they could behold a future for humankind, Jerusalem and Judea, earth and heaven, marked by justice, righteousness, and joy.

Epilogue

Among the many questions that lie beyond the scope of this book, I propose five topics for future study, which I hope some of my readers will take up:

1. The subversive use of nonnative traditions;
2. The relationship between the genres apocalypse and testament;
3. The function of narratives of resistance in ancient Jewish historiographic literature;
4. Methodological reflection on the relation between ancient and modern state terror; and
5. Implications of this study for modern (and postmodern) theology.

1. The subversive use of nonnative traditions

I noted in chapters 1 and 8 that the Enochic writers employed not only native traditions but also Babylonian, Iranian, and Greek traditions, which they deftly reworked into a revelatory monotheistic framework. The writers of Daniel did the same. Their appropriation of nonnative traditions clearly reflects the multicultural situation of Jews in the postexilic period. At the same time, it also represents a conscious strategy of resistance to empire. Though not every instance of borrowing is subversive, we would do well to give greater attention to how such adaptations function in the early apocalyptic literature. By appropriating elements from traditions of the various empires that had ruled their people over the centuries, the apocalyptic writers could engage and subvert imperial claims to knowledge and power. By locating bodies of knowledge and forms of revelation such as the Babylonian astronomical lore and the interpretation of dreams and visions within the sphere of wisdom revealed by God to God's faithful, our writers could undercut the very foundations of imperial claims to authority. Similarly, understandings of dualism drawn from Persian religious discourse could be merged with native traditions of ethical dualism to portray forces of oppression as opposed to the order of life but ultimately subject to divine judgment. Systematic attention to appropriation and subversion of nonnative traditions as a conscious strategy of resistance in early apocalyptic literature awaits future study and would complement the attention given in the present study to how writers of early Jewish apocalypses deployed and reshaped native traditions in the work of resistance to imperial domination and persecution.

2. The relationship between the genres apocalypse and testament

In this book I have examined some of the earliest Jewish apocalypses, with sustained attention to three historical apocalypses written in Judea during the reign of Antiochus IV Epiphanes. Jacob Licht and Adela Yarbro Collins have argued that an early edition of another apocalyptic text, the *Testament of Moses*, was also written in response to the persecution of Jews by Antiochus, and many scholars have since accepted their arguments.[1] Although I included a chapter on the *Testament of Moses* in my dissertation, I did not include it in this book, for two reasons.[2] First, while arguments for a first edition of the *Testament of Moses* during the persecution by Antiochus are strong, the date of the work remains in dispute. I did not wish to base the conclusions of this study on a work that could not be securely dated to the period of Hellenistic rule in Judea. Second, I have focused in this book on the genre apocalypse as resistance literature. While the *Testament of Moses* also functions as resistance literature and has many apocalyptic elements, most scholars agree that it is not properly an apocalypse because it lacks an angelic mediator.[3] It is rather a testament, purporting to contain Moses' last words to his successor, Joshua, before Moses departs earthly life.

Like apocalypse, "testament" is a well-attested genre in the literature of late Second Temple Judaism.[4] Yet the boundary between the two is not always clear.

1. Jacob Licht, "Taxo, or the Apocalyptic Doctrine of Vengeance," *JJS* 12 (1961): 95-104; Adela Yarbro Collins, "Composition and Redaction of the Testament of Moses 10," *HTR* 69 (1976): 179-86. See also George W. E. Nickelsburg, *Resurrection, Immortality, and Eternal Life in Intertestamental Judaism*, exp. ed. (Cambridge, MA: Harvard University Press, 2006), pp. 61-64. Against this view, see most recently Kenneth Atkinson, "Taxo's Martyrdom and the Role of the *Nuntius* in the *Testament of Moses*: Implications for Understanding the Role of Other Intermediary Figures," *JBL* 125, no. 3 (2006): 453-76, 457-67.

2. Anathea E. Portier-Young, "Theologies of Resistance in Daniel, the Apocalypse of Weeks, the Book of Dreams, and the Testament of Moses" (Ph.D. diss., Duke University, 2004).

3. See John J. Collins, "The Jewish Apocalypses," *Semeia* 14 (1979): 21-59, 45-46; and John J. Collins, "The Testament (Assumption) of Moses," in *Outside the Old Testament*, ed. Marinus de Jonge (Cambridge: Cambridge University Press, 1985), pp. 146-47.

4. See Anitra Bingham Kolenkow, "The Literary Genre 'Testament,'" in *Early Judaism and*

Many apocalypses exhibit elements of the testamentary genre (e.g., portions of *1 En., Jub.,* and *2 Bar.*), while the testament, in Michael Stone's words, "was considered particularly apt for the passing on of eschatological or cosmic secrets," content commonly associated with apocalypses.[5]

Earlier studies sometimes contrasted the two genres by emphasizing the ethical dimensions of the testamentary genre and deemphasizing those of apocalyptic literature.[6] This distinction no longer holds.[7] Among other things, the present study has foregrounded ethical concerns in some of the earliest apocalypses. A future study might begin from the assumption that both genres show a high degree of interest in ethics, and examine similarities and differences in how and in what contexts each kind of text seeks to shape the ethic of its audience.

To this end, if they are not to be distinguished by the content of their teaching, the example of the *Testament of Moses* focuses attention on differences in the location and construction of authority. In other respects, the *Testament of Moses* resembles the apocalypses studied in this volume. Like those apocalypses, it counters the horrors of imperial violence with a prophetic vision that unites past, present, and future. It presents a program for effective, resistant action and draws readers' attention to a powerful heavenly figure who will act to bring about the kingdom of God on earth. A great human figure from the past, in this case Moses, mediates the vision to his successor and to the writer's audience. But unlike the apocalypses studied in this volume, Moses' revelation does not originate with an angelic revealer. The vision's authority derives from Moses' knowledge of God's word and purpose (*T. Mos.* 1:11-12), which in turn seems connected to the fact that God designed *(excogitavit et invenit)* Moses, who had been "prepared from the beginning of the world,"

Its Modern Interpreters, ed. Robert A. Kraft and George W. E. Nickelsburg (Philadelphia: Fortress, 1986), pp. 259-67, 259; and John J. Collins, "The Testamentary Literature in Recent Scholarship," in *Early Judaism and Its Modern Interpreters,* ed. Robert A. Kraft and George W. E. Nickelsburg (Philadelphia: Fortress, 1986), pp. 268-78, 278.

5. Michael E. Stone, "Apocalyptic Literature," in *Early Judaism and Its Modern Interpreters,* ed. Robert A. Kraft and George W. E. Nickelsburg (Philadelphia: Fortress, 1986), pp. 383-442, 418.

6. See the literature reviewed in Kolenkow, "The Literary Genre 'Testament,'" pp. 262-64. Kolenkow focuses on authority, suggesting that the subject matter dictates the kind of authority needed: "Apocalyptic teaching needs heavenly authority (vision or trip to heaven); ethical teaching needs the authority of experience; and both assume reward and punishment" (p. 264).

7. On the ethical concerns of apocalyptic literature, consider David Aune, "The Apocalypse of John and the Problem of Genre," *Semeia* 36 (1986): 65-96, 87, 90-91; and Adela Yarbro Collins, "Introduction: Early Christian Apocalypticism," *Semeia* 36 (1986): 1-11, 6-7. Against this view, see Frederick David Mazzaferri, *The Genre of the Book of Revelation from a Source Critical Perspective* (Berlin: Walter de Gruyter, 1989), pp. 169-70.

to be covenant mediator (*arbiter testamenti,* 1:14). While its exalted claims for Moses' status "from the beginning" cannot be considered paradigmatic for the testamentary genre, the emphasis on Moses' mediation and the absence of an angelic mediator draw our attention to the different ways apocalypse and testament each construct authority.

Discussions of authority in apocalyptic literature have often focused on the presumed need to validate a prophetic vision of the future in order to render a book's vision more persuasive and therefore more effective in consoling and exhorting its audience. David Aune offers more nuance in suggesting the aim rather of encouraging the audience "to modify their cognitive and behavioral stance in conformity with transcendent perspectives."[8] Apocalyptic claims for knowledge counter other knowledge claims, including the claims of empire. To accept one set of knowledge claims is thus to reject others, and thereby orient oneself within the world. In the face of hegemony, knowledge itself has salvific power, and frames proper action.

Discussions of authority in testamentary literature have given greater attention to the exemplary character of the speaker. This exemplary function is often overlooked in the study of authority in apocalyptic literature, but was an important focus of Part Three of the present study. Chains of transmission in the historical apocalypses from revealer to mediator to recipient establish a parallel within the text to the chain of transmission from writer to text to audience. We saw that persons in the chain of transmission within the text may also model right action for the audience. This is both similar to and different from the construction and function of authority in testamentary literature.

Moreover, while discussions of authority in testamentary literature tend to highlight moral authority derived from life experience, in the *Testament of Moses* we find that Moses is far more than a moral exemplar, although he is that.[9] He mediates covenant (*T. Mos.* 1:14) and intercedes for the people (11:10-11, 14). He also mediates knowledge of the future. If we date a first edition of the *Testament of Moses* to the period of Seleucid hegemony in Judea, then we might ask what it would have meant for a writer to locate visionary authority in the person of Moses and to dramatize the passage of mediatorial offices to Joshua, his "successor for the people and for the tabernacle of the testimony" (1:7), during a persecution that proscribed the Torah and interrupted Jerusalem's cultic worship.[10] The

8. Aune, "The Apocalypse of John and the Problem of Genre," p. 87.

9. E.g., Kolenkow, "The Literary Genre 'Testament,'" p. 264. In *T. Mos.* 3:11 Moses predicts that in the time of distress Israel's tribes will reckon his authority in part by reference to his sufferings: *Nonne hoc est quod testabatur nobis tum Moyses in profetis, qui multa passus est in Aegypto et in Mari Rubro et in heremo annis XL?*

10. The translation is that of Johannes Tromp, *The Assumption of Moses: A Critical Edition with Commentary* (Leiden: Brill, 1993), p. 7.

location of authority and forms of mediation portrayed in the text and effected by the text also raise questions concerning the social location of the writer and his or her relationship to and assessment of other authoritative and mediatory persons, groups, institutions, and social forms in the time of crisis.

For Andrew Welburn issues of authority in the linking of new apocalyptic revelation with older traditions are a key to the emergence of the testamentary genre: "It is not hard to see that the authority of a patriarchal figure provides a crucial link between the cosmic-apocalyptic revelations of these works and the historical tradition of Judaism. The emergence of the distinctive 'testamentary' documents with a series of recognizable features seems therefore to indicate a particular stage in the attempt, in certain Jewish circles, to reconcile with biblical authority apocalyptic and related forms of esoteric knowledge."[11] Whether or not this explains the emergence of the genre, in the *Testament of Moses,* Moses' introductory words to Joshua thematize the relationship between "new" revelation and other authoritative traditions. Moses tells Joshua that the text of the testament itself authenticates the trustworthiness *(scribturam hanc ad recognoscendam tutationem)* of *other* books he gives to Joshua (1:16). Johannes Tromp interprets these as books of the law.[12] The visionary testament now authorizes the law itself, even as it gives instructions (and, for the audience, assurances) concerning its preservation (1:17).

In light of such issues, study of the location, construction, and function of authority in the genres testament and apocalypse would lead to a better understanding of the relationship between the genres more generally. The construction of authority in each shapes the identity and ethic of their audiences. Does the presence or absence of an angelic revealer substantially alter how this occurs, and, if so, in what ways? Attention to specific texts would reveal how the construction of authority in each relates to the knowledge and identity claims of competing sources of authority, including but not limited to empire, and how it relates to other, recognized sources of authority, such as "the law," other scriptures and traditions, and other forms of mediation. Different loci of authority may correspond to different epistemological claims and differences in worldview. Alternately, they may reflect differences in emphasis, subject, or originary context. The *Testament of Moses* would provide an apt starting point for such a study, leading to a more nuanced understanding of the relationship between the genres apocalypse and testament.

11. Andrew J. Welburn, *From a Virgin Womb: The Apocalypse of Adam and the Virgin Birth* (Leiden: Brill, 2008), p. 31.

12. Tromp, *Assumption of Moses,* p. 147.

3. The function of narratives of resistance in ancient Jewish historiographic literature

Throughout this book I have examined the early Jewish apocalypses as resistance literature, with attention to the ways in which visions within a narrative framework both functioned as resistant discourse and presented programs for resistance to their audiences. To understand the context and circumstances in which they arose and to locate them within a spectrum of responses to those circumstances, in Part Two of this study I relied heavily on 1 and 2 Maccabees as historical sources for the period of Seleucid rule in Judea. But what may seem too obvious to require comment is that, while 1 and 2 Maccabees contain narratives of resistance, they are *not* resistance literature. How, then, do narratives of resistance function in these ancient historiographic writings?

Both 1 and 2 Maccabees represent the interests and interpretations of writers in a later period. Their accounts are necessarily shaped by the commitments and structures of institutions that sponsor and facilitate their historiography. These institutions might include both state and cult (ultimately unified under the leadership of one high priest/king) as well as the professional class of scribes and scholars to which these history writers belonged. Both 1 and 2 Maccabees have been interpreted as propaganda, whether for the Hasmoneans, the Judean state, or the temple.[13] To understand how narratives of resistance function within these writings we must give attention to the commitments and structures that shape the histories.

Michel de Certeau observes that historiographic writings hide precisely these relationships, purporting instead to "speak the 'real'" of the past they represent.[14] In so doing they serve a positive function: they bridge the divisions between past and present in order to erase divisions within the present, offering their audiences common points of reference, common symbols, common values, and most importantly, common story.[15] This common story — in this case a (national) story of struggle and triumph, a *story of resistance* — creates for the readers a sense of unity and shared national, ethnic, and religious identity.[16]

---

13. The status of 1 Macc as propaganda legitimating the claims of the Hasmonean dynasty is, according to Joseph Sievers, "one of the few points on which there is hardly any disagreement among scholars." *The Hasmoneans and Their Supporters: From Mattathias to the Death of John Hyrcanus I* (Atlanta: Scholars Press, 1990), p. 2. See also Jonathan Goldstein, *I Maccabees,* Anchor Bible 41 (Garden City, NY: Doubleday, 1976), pp. 6-7, 77. On 2 Macc as temple propaganda, see Robert Doran, *Temple Propaganda: The Purpose and Character of 2 Maccabees,* CBQMS 12 (Washington, DC: Catholic Biblical Association of America, 1981).

14. Michel de Certeau, "History: Science and Fiction," in *The Certeau Reader,* ed. Graham Ward (Oxford: Blackwell, 2000), pp. 37-52, 39-40.

15. Certeau, "History," p. 41.

16. For Certeau histories are pedagogical, normative, and "militantly nationalist" ("History," p. 43).

Such an identity is not primordially or biologically given, but constructed through story, symbol, and practice.[17]

Moreover, history looks forward, and is fundamentally ethical in its orientation, with a power to "transform, reorient, and regulate the space of social relations."[18] Historiography is performative: "In making believers, it produces an active body of practitioners."[19] While Certeau focuses on the political, ethical, and social spheres, we must also add the religious; for ancient history writers these spheres were not to be separated.[20] Stories of resistance in 1 and 2 Maccabees contribute to the portrayal of a divinely legitimated dynastic state, on the one hand, and a divinely protected city on the other, with aims of instilling in readers a unified identity and praxis stemming from shared story and belief.[21]

Stories of resistance in 1 and 2 Maccabees thus help to produce and shape a shared national, ethnic, or religious identity (or a combination of these) and unified practices in the face of divisions between past and present and divisions within the present.[22] Detailed analysis of these divisions as well as textually projected identities and practices would further our understanding of the function of stories of resistance in ancient Jewish historiographic literature.

4. Methodological reflection on the relation between ancient and modern state terror

In chapter 5 I applied insights from studies of modern state terror, including what R. J. Rummel calls "democide," or murder by government, to my analysis of events in second-century Judea. To my knowledge, scholars only began to study state terror in recent years, and began with the modern regimes that were staring them in the face. It is more difficult to imagine horrors more than two thousand years distant. I have hoped that comparisons between ancient and modern state terror might bring into sharper focus the magnitude of such atrocities, their effects, and what it meant to respond to them one way or another. At the same time, such comparisons are methodologically imprecise. I hope that future studies will investigate the extent to which state terror is and is

---

17. Anthony D. Smith, *National Identity* (London: Penguin, 1991), pp. 19, 29.

18. Certeau, "History," p. 43.

19. Certeau, "History," p. 43.

20. Cf. Sievers, *The Hasmoneans and Their Supporters*, p. 10.

21. Consider the emphasis on shared worship practices in 2 Macc 1:18; 2:16, and its relation to the hope for ingathering (2:18).

22. Cf. Jane M. Jacobs's analysis of how narratives of Aboriginal resistance to colonial violence are deployed within a broader project of Australian national reconciliation and unification in "Resisting Reconciliation: The Secret Geographies of (Post)colonial Australia," in *Geographies of Resistance*, ed. Steve Pile and Michael Keith (London: Routledge, 1997), pp. 203-18.

not a transhistorical phenomenon and also identify the historical particulars that distinguish its ancient and modern forms, helping us to achieve greater methodological precision.

5. Implications of this study for modern (and postmodern) theology

I have written this book primarily for specialists and students in the fields of ancient Judaism and biblical studies. At the same time, I hope this study will make a contribution to discussions outside my disciplinary subfield. Even though the book of Daniel belongs to the canons of Jewish and Christian scripture, and *1 Enoch* is considered authoritative scripture by many Christians in Africa and beyond, modern theology sits uneasily with these and other ancient apocalyptic texts and with "apocalyptic" ways of imagining and representing time, cosmos, and created life.[23] For some a conflation of apocalypticism with gnosticism leads to the false assumption that the apocalypses oppose the invisible realm to the visible realm, or spirit to matter. Apocalyptic literature is then presumed to be anti-incarnational, representing a flight from particular, embodied, human existence and a denial of reality.[24] Others find it impossible to reconcile apocalyptic faith with scientific reasoning, and have followed Rudolf Bultmann's program of demythologizing seemingly irrational elements of an apocalyptic worldview and reinterpreting them in existential terms.

Lieven Boeve has noted that even as modern theologians reject apocalyptic symbols and "sentiment" as "too mythological, too dangerous, too literal, too speculative, too escapist," popular culture embraces them.[25] Visions of the end sell briskly at the box office, where they provide temporary relief for collective anxieties in a confusing cybernetic world that claims everything and nothing for human existence.[26] The reality is that apocalyptic "sentiment" appeals not only to restless consumers in the industrial Two-Thirds World; globally, apocalyptic hope is thriving. To give one example, Christians in southern Sudan identify with Shadrak, Meshak, and Abednego, "falling in the fire."[27] They sing,

23. As Johann Baptist Metz observes, "In systematic theology proper, apocalypticism has for the most part been proscribed in the name of a more congenial, existentially or evolutionistically colored eschatology." *A Passion for God: The Mystical Political Dimension of Christianity,* ed. and trans. J. Matthew Ashley (Mahwah, NJ: Paulist Press, 1998), p. 191.
24. Cf. the assessment of Christopher McMahon, "Imaginative Faith: Apocalyptic, Science Fiction Theory, and Theology," *Dialog: A Journal of Theology* 47, no. 3 (2008): 271-77, 271.
25. Lieven Boeve, "God Interrupts History: Apocalypticism as an Indispensable Theological Conceptual Strategy," *Louvain Studies* 26 (2001): 195-216, 196.
26. Boeve, "God Interrupts History," p. 196.
27. Marc Nikkel, *Why Haven't You Left: Letters from the Sudan,* ed. Grant Lemarquand (New York: Church Publishing, 2006), p. 45; see also pp. 56-57. According to Lemarquand, "Daniel 3 has been one of the most important biblical stories for Sudanese Christians" (*Why*

Let us give thanks to the Lord in the day of devastation . . .
When we unite our hearts and beseech the Lord, and have hope,
   then the bad spirit has no power.
God has not forgotten us.
Evil is departing and holiness is advancing;
This is the transformation which throws the earth into convulsions.[28]

Southern Sudan's twenty-year civil war wreaked horrors on its people. And in the midst of these horrors, conversions to Christianity — a thoroughly apocalyptic Christianity — increased as never before. I gave attention in this study to the effects of terror and trauma in second-century Judea, as well as to the creative ways Judeans responded to them. The study of terror and trauma is haunting, and I do not hope to return to it any time soon. At the same time, what I found in my research convinced me that we live today in a world more deeply traumatized and terrorized than many of us dare to imagine. Rummel estimates that worldwide in the twentieth century governments killed 262,000,000 of their own people.[29] I have argued that apocalyptic literature emerged as a literature of resistance to violent rule, and apocalyptic hope took shape as a response to terror and trauma. A recent and necessary trend in theology, as in many disciplines, is attention to globalization. A truly global theology must confront global trauma and terror. A pressing question is what kind of resource the ancient apocalypses are and are not for such theology.

For Ithamar Gruenwald, apocalypticism is too dangerous. He finds in it an expression of anxiety that can "breed monstrous manifestations of violence."[30] This violence arises from "dualistic estrangement of the 'other,' the animalization of the enemy, and the radicalization of social and political issues."[31] In the light of such violent "othering," Gruenwald calls for an end to apocalypticism.[32] Jonathan Z. Smith responds to Gruenwald that "apocalypticism seems no more inherently violent than other religious modes — or, for that matter, other spheres of human culture."[33] Is "dualistic estrangement of the 'other'" a

---

Haven't You Left, p. 45n18). I thank Susan Eastman for sharing this book with me and calling my attention to the apocalyptic tenor of Christian hope in Sudan.

28. Nikkel, *Why Haven't You Left*, p. 106.

29. Rudolph J. Rummel, "20th Century Democide," n.p. [cited 12 Feb 2010]. Online: http://www.hawaii.edu/powerkills/20TH.HTM.

30. Ithamar Gruenwald, "A Case Study of Scripture and Culture: Apocalypticism as Cultural Identity in Past and Present," in *Ancient and Modern Perspectives on the Bible and Culture: Essays in Honor of Hans Dieter Betz,* ed. Adela Yarbro Collins (Atlanta: Scholars Press, 1998), pp. 252-80, 279.

31. Gruenwald, "A Case Study of Scripture and Culture," p. 254.

32. Gruenwald, "A Case Study of Scripture and Culture," p. 280.

33. Jonathan Z. Smith, "Cross-Cultural Reflections on Apocalypticism," in *Ancient and*

necessary or constitutive component of classical apocalypticism and its modern analogues?

Contrasting with Gruenwald's call for an end to apocalypticism, political theologian Johann Baptist Metz insists on the possibility and even necessity of a nonviolent apocalyptic theology that entails hope for one's enemy.[34] Metz finds in apocalypticism not flight from the world but its temporalization, and deep engagement with human suffering.[35] Out of and within this temporal awareness emerge radical hope, longing for justice, and trust in God; these in turn "provide a foundation for the seriousness of a liberating praxis and emphasize the urgent and critical character of human responsibility."[36]

David Tracy similarly emphasizes the political, public, and historical character of apocalyptic discourse (Tracy's primary focus here is on New Testament texts), its attention to the real, and its capacity to respond to human suffering. He submits as a corrective for Christian systematic theology "Apocalyptic's challenge and reminder of the explosive intensification and negations needed within all other genres."[37] It stands also

> as a challenge to all the privileged to remember the privileged status of the oppressed, the poor, the suffering in the scriptures; as a challenge to all the living not to forget the true hope disclosed in these texts of a future from God for all the dead; as a challenge to all wisdom and all principles of order to remember the pathos of active suffering untransformable by all thought ordering cosmos and ethos; as a challenge to each to remember all. . . .[38]

Tracy has more recently come to focus on questions of divine incomprehensibility and comprehensibility, hiddenness and revelation. Faced with the impossibility of "direct communication with God," Tracy emphasizes the fragment, "something that sparks into the realm of the infinite yet disallows a totalizing

---

Modern Perspectives on the Bible and Culture: Essays in Honor of Hans Dieter Betz, ed. Adela Yarbro Collins (Atlanta: Scholars Press, 1998), pp. 281-85, 284.

34. J. Matthew Ashley, "Johann Baptist Metz," in *The Blackwell Companion to Political Theology,* ed. Peter Scott and William T. Cavanaugh (Oxford: Blackwell, 2004), pp. 241-55, 252.

35. Metz, *A Passion for God,* p. 83. In his translations and critical studies, J. Matthew Ashley has made Metz's apocalyptic political theology more widely available to an English-speaking audience. In addition to editing, translating, and introducing a collection of Metz's essays in *A Passion for God,* Ashley has also edited and translated Metz's *Faith in History and Society: Toward a Practical Fundamental Theology* (New York: Crossroad, 2007) and has published his own study of Metz's theology, *Interruptions: Mysticism, Politics and Theology in the Work of Johann Baptist Metz* (Notre Dame: University of Notre Dame Press, 1998).

36. Boeve, "God Interrupts History," p. 212.

37. David Tracy, *The Analogical Imagination: Christian Theology and the Culture of Pluralism* (New York: Crossroad, 1981), p. 265.

38. Tracy, *Analogical Imagination,* pp. 265-66.

approach, and at the same time opens up material realities."[39] For Tracy, "apocalyptic" is a necessary but (and necessary because) "fragmentary form" opening into injustice and terror, balanced by another fragmentary form, the apophatic mystical tradition. Like Tracy, J. Matthew Ashley balances apocalyptic *kataphasis* with mystical *apophasis,* saying with unsaying, and claims for knowledge with confessions of *ignorantia.*[40] In chapter 1 I argued that apocalypses offered in place of the totalizing discourses of empire an equally totalizing discourse of their own. Yet Tracy's emphasis on fragments and Ashley's retrieval of *ignorantia* remind the reader that what is glimpsed and revealed by the seer is only partial. Even when the seer claims to have seen and heard "everything" (1 *En.* 1:2; 93:2), the apocalypse never makes full disclosure. What each apocalypse says about its own revelation, about knowledge itself, and the limits of human knowing, has ramifications for a global theology that confronts domination, suffering, and death with discourse and vision — apocalyptic or otherwise — of justice, healing, hope, and life.

39. "An Interview with David Tracy," by Lois Malcolm, *The Christian Century* (Feb. 13-20, 2002): 24-30.

40. J. Matthew Ashley, "Apocalypticism in Political and Liberation Theology: Toward an Historical *Docta Ignorantia,*" *Horizons* 27, no. 1 (2000): 22-43, 38-39.

Bibliography

Aeschines. *Against Timarchos.* Translated with introduction and commentary by Nick Fisher. Clarendon Ancient History. Oxford: Oxford University Press, 2001.

Aeschylus. *Prometheus Bound.* Translated by James Scully with introduction and notes by C. John Herington. Oxford: Oxford University Press, 1975.

Aeschylus. *Prometheus Bound.* Edited and translated with introduction and commentary by A. J. Podlecki. Oxford: Aris & Phillips, 2005.

Affortunati, Monica, and Barbara Scardigli. "Aspects of Plutarch's Life of Publicola." In *Plutarch and the Historical Tradition,* edited by Philip Stadter, pp. 109-31. London: Routledge, 1992.

Agamben, Giorgio. *Homo Sacer: Sovereign Power and Bare Life.* Translated by Daniel Heller-Roazen. Stanford, CA: Stanford University Press, 1998. Translation of *Homo Sacer: Il potere sovrano e la nuda vita.* Torino: Einaudi, 1995.

Ahmad, Aijaz. "The Politics of Literary Postcoloniality," *Race and Class* 36, no. 3 (1995): 1-20.

Albani, Matthias. *Astronomie und Schöpfungsglaube.* Neukirchen: Neukirchener Verlag, 1994.

Albertz, Rainer. *A History of Israelite Religion in the Old Testament Period,* vol. 2: *From the Exile to the Maccabees.* Translated by John Bowden. Louisville: Westminster John Knox, 1994.

———. "The Social Setting of the Aramaic and Hebrew Book of Daniel." In *The Book of Daniel: Composition and Reception,* vol. 1, edited by John J. Collins and Peter W. Flint, pp. 171-204. Leiden: Brill, 2001.

Alexander, Philip S. "Enoch and the Beginning of Jewish Interest in Natural Science." In *The Wisdom Texts from Qumran and the Development of Sapiential Thought,* edited by Charlotte Hempel, Armin Lange, and Hermann Lichtenberger, pp. 223-43. Leuven: Peeters, 2002.

———. "The Enochic Literature and the Bible: Intertextuality and Its Implications." In *The Bible as Book: The Hebrew Bible and the Judaean Desert Discoveries,* edited by Edward D. Herbert and Emanuel Tov, pp. 57-58. London: The British Library, 2002.

———. "From Son of Adam to Second God: Transformations of the Biblical Enoch." In

Biblical Figures Outside the Bible, edited by Michael E. Stone and Theodore A. Bergren, pp. 87-122. Harrisburg, PA: Trinity Press International, 1998.

Anderson, Benedict. *Imagined Communities: Reflections on the Origin and Spread of Nationalism.* London: Verso, 1983.

Anderson, Greg. *The Athenian Experiment: Building an Imagined Political Community in Ancient Attica, 508-490 BCE.* Ann Arbor: University of Michigan Press, 2003.

Anderson, Jeff S. "From 'Communities of Texts' to Religious Communities: Problems and Pitfalls." In *Enoch and Qumran Origins: New Light on a Forgotten Connection,* edited by Gabriele Boccaccini, pp. 351-55. Grand Rapids: Eerdmans, 2005.

Aperghis, G. G. *The Seleukid Royal Economy: The Finances and Financial Administration of the Seleukid Empire.* Cambridge: Cambridge University Press, 2004.

Appian. *The Foreign Wars.* Translated by Horace White. New York: Macmillan, 1899.

Ap-Thomas, D. R. "Some Aspects of the Root HNN in the Old Testament," *Journal of Semitic Studies* 2, no. 2 (1957): 128-48.

Argall, Randal. 1 Enoch *and Sirach: A Comparative Literary and Conceptual Analysis of the Themes of Revelation, Creation and Judgment.* Atlanta: Scholars Press, 1995.

Arnold, Bill T. "Wordplay and Narrative Techniques in Daniel 5 and 6," *Journal of Biblical Literature* 112, no. 3 (1993): 479-85.

Arnold, David. *Famine: Social Crisis and Historical Change.* New York: Basil Blackwell, 1988.

Ashley, Bob, Joanne Hollows, Steve Jones, and Ben Taylor. *Food and Cultural Studies.* London: Routledge, 2004.

Ashley, J. Matthew. "Apocalypticism in Political and Liberation Theology: Toward an Historical *Docta Ignorantia,*" *Horizons* 27, no. 1 (2000): 22-43.

———. *Interruptions: Mysticism, Politics and Theology in the Work of Johann Baptist Metz.* Notre Dame: University of Notre Dame Press, 1998.

———. "Johann Baptist Metz." In *The Blackwell Companion to Political Theology,* edited by Peter Scott and William T. Cavanaugh, pp. 241-55. Oxford: Blackwell, 2004.

Assefa, Daniel. *L'Apocalypse des animaux (1 Hen 85–90): Une propagande militaire? Approches narrative, historico-critique, perspectives théologiques.* Leiden: Brill, 2007.

Atkinson, Kenneth. "Taxo's Martyrdom and the Role of the *Nuntius* in the *Testament of Moses:* Implications for Understanding the Role of Other Intermediary Figures," *Journal of Biblical Literature* 125, no. 3 (2006): 453-76.

Aubet, María Eugenia. *The Phoenicians and the West: Politics, Colonies, and Trade.* Translated by Mary Turton. Cambridge: Cambridge University Press, 2001.

Aune, David. "The Apocalypse of John and the Problem of Genre," *Semeia* 36 (1986): 65-96.

Austin, M. M. "Hellenistic Kings, War and the Economy," *Classical Quarterly* 36 (1986): 450-66.

———. "The Seleukids and Asia." In *A Companion to the Hellenistic World,* edited by Andrew Erskine, pp. 121-33. Oxford: Blackwell, 2003.

Avalos, Hector. "The Comedic Function of the Enumerations of Officials and Instruments in Daniel 3," *Catholic Biblical Quarterly* 53, no. 4 (1991): 580-88.

———. "Daniel 9:24-25 and Mesopotamian Temple Rededications," *Journal of Biblical Literature* 117, no. 3 (1998): 507-511.

Bagnall, Roger S., and Peter Derow. *Greek Historical Documents: The Hellenistic Period.* Chico, CA: Scholars Press, 1981.

Bibliography

———. *The Hellenistic Period: Sources in Translation*. Oxford: Blackwell, 2004.

Bahrani, Zainab. "Assault and Abduction: The Fate of the Royal Image in the Ancient Near East," *Art History* 18, no. 3 (1995): 363-82.

———. *The Graven Image: Representation in Babylonia and Assyria*. Philadelphia: University of Pennsylvania Press, 2003.

Baldwin, Joyce G. "Ṣemaḥ as Technical Term in the Prophets," *Vetus Testamentum* 14, no. 1 (1964): 93-97.

Ball, Howard. *War Crimes and Justice: A Reference Handbook*. Santa Barbara, CA: ABC-CLIO, 2002.

Barag, Dan. "The Mint of Antiochus IV in Jerusalem: Numismatic Evidence on the Prelude to the Maccabean Revolt," *Israel Numismatic Journal* 14 (2002): 59-77.

Barbalet, J. M. "Power and Resistance," *British Journal of Sociology* 4 (1985): 531-48.

Barclay, John M. G. *Jews in the Mediterranean Diaspora: From Alexander to Trajan (323 BCE–117 BCE)*. Berkeley: University of California Press, 1996.

———. "Using and Refusing: Jewish Identity Strategies under the Hegemony of Hellenism." In *Ethos und Identität: Einheit und Vielfalt des Judentums in hellenistisch-römischer Zeit*, edited by Matthias Konradt and Ulrike Steiner, pp. 13-25. Paderborn: Ferdinand Schöningh, 2002.

Bar-Kochva, Bezalel. *Judas Maccabaeus: The Jewish Struggle against the Seleucids*. Cambridge: Cambridge University Press, 1989. Repr. 2002.

———. *The Seleucid Army: Organization and Tactics*. Cambridge: Cambridge University Press, 1976.

Barr, James. *The Semantics of Biblical Language*. London: Oxford University Press, 1961.

Barth, Fredrik. Introduction to *Ethnic Groups and Boundaries: The Social Organization of Cultural Difference*. Edited by Fredrik Barth. Long Grove, IL: Waveland Press, 1998.

Barthes, Roland. "Toward a Psychosociology of Contemporary Food Consumption." In *Food and Culture: A Reader*, 2nd ed., edited by Carole Counihan and Penny van Esterik, pp. 28-35. New York: Routledge, 2008. Translation of "Vers une psycho-sociologie de l'alimentation moderne," *Annales: Économies, Sociétés, Civilisations* 5 (1961): 977-86.

Bartlett, John R. *1 Maccabees*. Sheffield: Sheffield Academic Press, 1998.

Bartsch, Shadi. *Actors in the Audience: Theatricality and Doublespeak from Nero to Hadrian*. Cambridge, MA: Harvard University Press, 1998.

Baumgarten, Albert. *The Flourishing of Jewish Sects in the Maccabean Era: An Interpretation*. Leiden: Brill, 1997.

Baynes, Leslie. "'My Life Is Written Before You': The Function of the Motif 'Heavenly Book' in Judeo-Christian Apocalypses, 200 B.C.E.–200 C.E." Ph.D. diss., University of Notre Dame, 2005.

Beacham, Richard C. *Spectacle Entertainments of Early Imperial Rome*. New Haven: Yale University Press, 1999.

Beard, Mary. *The Roman Triumph*. Cambridge, MA: Harvard University Press, 2007.

Bechtel, Lyn M. "Shame as a Sanction of Social Control in Biblical Israel: Judicial, Political, and Social Shaming," *Journal for the Study of the Old Testament* 16, no. 49 (1991): 47-76.

Bechtel Huber, Lyn. "The Biblical Experience of Shame/Shaming: The Social Experience of Shame/Shaming in Biblical Israel in Relation to Its Use as Religious Metaphor." Ph.D. diss., Drew University, 1983.

Bedenbender, Andreas. *Der Gott der Welt tritt auf den Sinai: Entstehung, Entwicklung und Funktionsweise der frühjüdischen Apokalyptik.* Berlin: Institut Kirche und Judentum, 2000.

———. "The Place of the Torah in the Early Enoch Literature." In *The Early Enoch Literature,* edited by Gabriele Boccaccini and John J. Collins, pp. 65-79. Leiden: Brill, 2007.

———. "Reflection on Ideology and Date of the Apocalypse of Weeks." In *Enoch and Qumran Origins: New Light on a Forgotten Connection,* edited by Gabriele Boccaccini, pp. 200-203. Grand Rapids: Eerdmans, 2005.

———. "Traces of Enochic Judaism within the Hebrew Bible," *Henoch* 24 (2002): 39-48.

Beezley, William H. "The Porfirian Smart Set Anticipates Thorstein Veblen in Guadalajara." In *Rituals of Rule, Rituals of Resistance: Public Celebrations and Popular Culture in Mexico,* edited by William H. Beezley, Cheryl English Martin, William E. French, pp. 173-90. Wilmington, DE: Scholarly Resources, 1994.

Bell, Andrew. *Spectacular Power in the Greek and Roman City.* Oxford: Oxford University Press, 2004.

Bell, Catherine M. *Ritual: Perspectives and Dimensions.* Oxford: Oxford University Press, 1997.

———. *Ritual Theory, Ritual Practice.* Oxford: Oxford University Press, 1992.

Bentzen, Aage. *Daniel.* Tübingen: Mohr, 1952.

Bergsma, John Sietze. *The Jubilee from Leviticus to Qumran: A History of Interpretation.* Leiden: Brill, 2007.

Berquist, Jon. *Controlling Corporeality: The Body and the Household in Ancient Israel.* New Brunswick, NJ: Rutgers University Press, 2002.

———. *Judaism in Persia's Shadow: A Social and Historical Approach.* Minneapolis: Fortress, 1995.

———. "Postcolonialism and Imperial Motives for Canonization," *Semeia* 75 (1996): 15-35.

———. "Resistance and Accommodation in the Persian Empire." In *In the Shadow of Empire: Reclaiming the Bible as a History of Faithful Resistance,* edited by Richard A. Horsley, pp. 41-58. Louisville: Westminster John Knox, 2008.

Bertalotto, P., and T. Hanneken, eds. "Short Papers on Jubilees Presented at the Fourth Enoch Seminar," *Henoch* 30, no. 1 (2008).

Bevan, Edwyn R. *The House of Seleucus,* vol. 2. London: E. Arnold, 1902.

Beyerle, Stefan. "The Book of Daniel and Its Social Setting." In *The Book of Daniel: Composition and Reception,* vol. 1, edited by John J. Collins and Peter W. Flint, pp. 205-8. Leiden: Brill, 2001.

Bhabha, Homi K. *The Location of Culture.* London: Routledge, 1994.

Bhayro, Siam. "Daniel's 'Watchers' in Enochic Exegesis of Genesis 6:1-4." In *Jewish Ways of Reading the Bible,* edited by George Brooke, pp. 58-66. Oxford: Oxford University Press, 2000.

Bickerman, Elias. "Autonomia. Sur un passage de Thucydide (I, 144, 2)," *Revue Internationale des Droits de l'Antiquité* 3rd series, 5 (1958): 313-44.

———. "La charte séleucide de Jérusalem," *Revue des études juives* 100 (1935): 4-35.

———. *The God of the Maccabees: Studies on the Meaning and Origin of the Maccabean Revolt.* Translated by Horst Moehring. Leiden: Brill, 1979. Translation of *Der Gott der Makkabäer: Untersuchungen über Sinn und Ursprung der makkabäischen Erhebung.* Berlin: Schocken, 1937.

———. "Une proclamation séleucide relative au temple de Jérusalem," *Syria* 25 (1946-1948): 67-85.

Bilde, Per, Troels Engberg-Pedersen, Lise Hannestad, and Jan Zahle, eds. *Religion and Religious Practice in the Seleucid Kingdom.* Aarhus: Aarhus University Press, 1990.

Billows, Richard. "Cities." In *A Companion to the Hellenistic World,* edited by Andrew Erskine, pp. 196-215. Oxford: Blackwell, 2003.

Black, Matthew. "The Apocalypse of Weeks in the Light of 4Q En^g," *Vetus Testamentum* 28, no. 4 (1978): 464-69.

———. "A Bibliography on 1 Enoch in the Eighties," *Journal for the Study of the Pseudepigrapha* 5 (1989): 3-16.

———. *The Scrolls and Christian Origins: Studies in the Jewish Background of the New Testament.* New York: Charles Scribner's Sons, 1961.

———. "The 'Two Witnesses' of Rev. 11:3f. in Jewish and Christian Apocalyptic Tradition." In *Donum Gentilicum: New Testament Studies in Honor of David Daube,* edited by E. Bammel, C. K. Barrett, and W. D. Davies, pp. 227-37. Oxford: Clarendon, 1978.

Black, Matthew, in consultation with James C. Vanderkam. *The Book of Enoch or 1 Enoch, a New English Edition with Commentary and Textual Notes.* Studia in Veteris Testamenti Pseudepigraphica 7. Leiden: Brill, 1985.

Boccaccini, Gabriele. *Beyond the Essene Hypothesis: The Parting of the Ways between Qumran and Enochic Judaism.* Grand Rapids: Eerdmans, 1998.

———. "The Covenantal Theology of the Apocalyptic Book of Daniel." In *Enoch and Qumran Origins: New Light from a Forgotten Connection,* edited by Gabriele Boccaccini, pp. 39-44. Grand Rapids: Eerdmans, 2005.

———, ed. *Enoch and Qumran Origins: New Light from a Forgotten Connection.* Grand Rapids: Eerdmans, 2005.

———, ed. *Enoch and the Messiah Son of Man: Revisiting the Book of Parables.* Grand Rapids: Eerdmans, 2007.

———. "Enochians, Urban Essenes, Qumranites: Three Social Groups, One Intellectual Movement." In *The Early Enoch Literature,* edited by Gabriele Boccaccini and John J. Collins, pp. 301-27. Leiden: Brill, 2007.

———. "Finding a Place for the Parables of Enoch within Second Temple Jewish Literature." In *Enoch and the Messiah Son of Man: Revisiting the Book of Parables,* edited by Gabriele Boccaccini, pp. 263-89. Grand Rapids: Eerdmans, 2007.

———. "Introduction: From the Enoch Literature to Enochic Judaism." In *Enoch and Qumran Origins: New Light on a Forgotten Connection,* edited by Gabriele Boccaccini, pp. 1-14. Grand Rapids: Eerdmans, 2005.

———, ed. *The Origins of Enochic Judaism.* Turin: Zamorani, 2003.

———. "Qumran and the Enoch Groups: Revisiting the Enochic-Essene Hypothesis." In *The Bible and the Dead Sea Scrolls,* vol. 1: *Scripture and the Scrolls,* edited by James H. Charlesworth, pp. 37-66. Waco, TX: Baylor University Press, 2006.

———. *Roots of Rabbinic Judaism: An Intellectual History, From Ezekiel to Daniel.* Grand Rapids: Eerdmans, 2002.

Boccaccini, Gabriele, and John J. Collins, eds. *The Early Enoch Literature.* Leiden: Brill, 2007.

Boccaccini, Gabriele, and Giovanni Ibba, eds. *Enoch and the Mosaic Torah: The Evidence of Jubilees.* Grand Rapids: Eerdmans, 2009.

Boda, Mark J. *Praying the Tradition: The Origin and Use of Tradition in Nehemiah 9*. Berlin: Walter de Gruyter, 1999.

Boer, Roland. *Last Stop Before Antarctica: The Bible and Postcolonialism in Australia*, 2nd ed. Atlanta: Society of Biblical Literature, 2008.

Boeve, Lieven. "God Interrupts History: Apocalypticism as an Indispensable Theological Conceptual Strategy," *Louvain Studies* 26 (2001): 195-216.

Bol, Marsha. "The Making of a Festival." In *Mexican Celebrations*, edited by Eliot Porter, Ellen Auerbach, Donna Pierce, and Marsha Bol, pp. 109-15. Albuquerque: University of New Mexico Press, 1990.

Bonasso, Miguel. *Recuerdo de la Muerte*. Mexico City: Editiones Era, 1984.

Bonfante, Larissa. *Etruscan Dress*. Baltimore: Johns Hopkins University Press, 2003.

———. "Nudity as Costume in Classical Art," *American Journal of Archaeology* 93 (1989): 543-70.

Bonnet, Corinne. *Melqart: Cultes et mythes de l'Héraclès tyrien en Méditerranée*. Leuven: Peeters, 1988.

Bosworth, "Autonomia: The Use and Abuse of Political Terminology," *Studi Italiani di Filologia Classica*, 3rd series, 10 (1992): 122-52.

Botterweck, G. J., and H. Ringgren, eds. *Theological Dictionary of the Old Testament*. Translated by J. T. Willis, G. W. Bromiley, and D. E. Green. 15 vols. Grand Rapids: Eerdmans, 1974-.

Bourdieu, Pierre. *Language and Symbolic Power*. Edited by John B. Thompson. Translated by Gino Raymond and Matthew Adamson. Cambridge, MA: Harvard University Press, 1991.

———. *Outline of a Theory of Practice*. Translated by Richard Nice. Cambridge: Cambridge University Press, 1977. Translation of *Esquisse d'une théorie de la pratique, précédé de trois études d'ethnologie kabyle*. Geneva: Librairie Droz, 1972.

Bovati, Pietro. *Re-establishing Justice: Legal Terms, Concepts and Procedures in the Hebrew Bible*. Translated by Michael J. Smith. Journal for the Study of the Old Testament Supplement 105. Sheffield: JSOT Press, 1994.

Bowersock, G. W. "The Mechanics of Subversion in the Roman Provinces." In *Opposition et résistances à l'empire d'Auguste à Trajan*, edited by Kurt Raaflaub, Adalberto Giovannini, and Denis van Berchem, pp. 291-317. Entretiens sur l'Antiquité classique 33. Geneva: Fondation Hardt, 1987.

Bowley, James E., and John C. Reeves. "Rethinking the Concept of 'Bible': Some Theses and Proposals," *Henoch* 25 (2003): 3-18.

Boyarin, Daniel. *Dying for God: Martyrdom and the Making of Christianity and Judaism*. Stanford: Stanford University Press, 1999.

Braund, David. "After Alexander: The Emergence of the Hellenistic World, 323-281." In *A Companion to the Hellenistic World*, edited by Andrew Erskine, pp. 19-34. Oxford: Blackwell, 2003.

Bremmer, Jan M. "Remember the Titans!" In *The Fall of the Angels*, edited by Christoph Auffarth and Loren Stuckenbruck, pp. 35-61. Leiden: Brill, 2004.

Briant, Pierre. "The Seleucid Kingdom and the Achaemenid Empire." In *Religion and Religious Practice in the Seleucid Kingdom*, edited by Per Bilde, Troels Engberg-Pedersen, Lise Hannestad, and Jan Zahle, pp. 40-65. Aarhus: Aarhus University Press, 1990.

Briggs, Richard S. *The Virtuous Reader: Old Testament Narrative and Interpretive Virtue*. Grand Rapids: Baker, 2010.

Bringmann, Klaus. *Hellenistische Reform und Religionsverfolgung in Judäa: Eine Untersuchung zur jüdisch-hellenistischen Geschichte (175-163 v. Chr.).* Göttingen: Vandenhoeck & Ruprecht, 1983.

―――. *A History of the Roman Republic.* Cambridge: Polity, 2007.

Brinton, Crane. *The Anatomy of Revolution,* revised and enlarged ed. New York: Vintage, 1965.

Brownlee, William H. "The Servant of the Lord in the Qumran Scrolls I," *Bulletin of the American Schools of Oriental Research* 132 (1953): 8-15.

Brueggemann, Walter. "Faith in the Empire." In *In the Shadow of Empire: Reclaiming the Bible as a History of Faithful Resistance,* edited by Richard A. Horsley, pp. 25-40. Louisville: Westminster John Knox, 2008.

―――. *The Word That Redescribes the World: The Bible and Discipleship.* Minneapolis: Augsburg Fortress, 2006.

Bryan, David. *Cosmos, Chaos and the Kosher Mentality.* Sheffield: Sheffield Academic Press, 1995.

Buc, Philippe. *The Dangers of Ritual: Between Early Medieval Texts and Social Scientific Theory.* Princeton: Princeton University Press, 2001.

Burkert, W. *The Orientalizing Revolution: Near Eastern Influence on Greek Culture in the Early Archaic Age.* Translated by M. E. Pinder and W. Burkert. Cambridge, MA: Harvard University Press, 1992.

Carey, Greg. "The Book of Revelation as Counter-Imperial Script." In *In the Shadow of Empire: Reclaiming the Bible as a History of Faithful Resistance,* edited by Richard A. Horsley, pp. 157-82. Louisville: Westminster John Knox, 2008.

―――. *Elusive Apocalypse: Reading Authority in the Revelation to John.* Macon, GA: Mercer University Press, 1999.

―――. *Ultimate Things: An Introduction to Jewish and Christian Apocalyptic Literature.* St. Louis: Chalice, 2005.

Carroll, Noël. *The Philosophy of Horror or Paradoxes of the Heart.* New York: Routledge, 1990.

Carson, D. A., and H. G. M. Williamson, eds. *It Is Written: Scripture Citing Scripture.* New York: Cambridge University Press, 1988.

Castelli, Elizabeth A. *Martyrdom and Memory: Early Christian Culture Making.* New York: Columbia University Press, 2007.

Castriota, David. *Myth, Ethos, and Actuality: Official Art in Fifth Century Athens.* Madison: University of Wisconsin Press, 1992.

Chaniotis, Angelos. "Foreign Soldiers — Native Girls? Constructing and Crossing Boundaries in Hellenistic Cities with Foreign Garrisons." In *Army and Power in the Ancient World,* edited by Angelos Chaniotis and Peter Ducrey, pp. 99-114. Stuttgart: Franz Steiner Verlag, 2002.

―――. *War in the Hellenistic World: A Social and Cultural History.* Oxford: Blackwell, 2005.

Charles, Michael. "Elephants at Raphia: Reinterpreting Polybius 5.84-5," *Classical Quarterly* 57 (2007): 306-311.

Charles, R. H. *The Book of Enoch; or 1 Enoch, translated from the editor's Ethiopic Text and edited with the introduction, notes and indexes of the first edition wholly recast, enlarged and rewritten together with a reprint from the editor's text of the Greek fragments.* Oxford: Clarendon, 1912.

——. *A Critical and Exegetical Commentary on the Book of Daniel.* Oxford: Clarendon, 1929.

Charlesworth, James H. "A Rare Consensus among Enoch Specialists: The Date of the Earliest Enoch Books," *Henoch* 24 (2002): 225-34.

Charlesworth, James H., and Craig A. Evans, eds. *The Pseudepigrapha and Early Biblical Interpretation.* Sheffield: JSOT Press, 1993.

Chia, Philip. "On Naming the Subject: Postcolonial Reading of Daniel 1." In *The Postcolonial Biblical Reader,* edited by Rasiah S. Sugirtharajah, pp. 171-84. Oxford: Blackwell, 2006.

Ciszek, D. "Elephas maximus." No pages. Cited 2 April 2008. Online: http://animaldiversity .ummz.umich.edu/site/accounts/information/Elephas_maximus.html

Coblentz Bautch, Kelley. *A Study of the Geography of 1 Enoch 17–19: "No One Has Seen What I Have Seen."* Leiden: Brill, 2003.

Cohen, Andrew C. *Death Rituals, Ideology, and the Development of Early Mesopotamian Kingship: Toward a New Understanding of Iraq's Royal Cemetery at Ur.* Leiden: Brill, 2005.

Cohen, Getzel M. "The 'Antiochenes in Jerusalem'. Again." In *Pursuing the Text: Studies in Honor of Ben Zion Wacholder on the Occasion of His Seventieth Birthday,* edited by John C. Reeves and John Kampen, pp. 243-59. Sheffield: Sheffield Academic Press, 1994.

——. *The Hellenistic Settlements in Europe, the Islands, and Asia Minor.* Berkeley: University of California Press, 1995.

——. *The Hellenistic Settlements in Syria, the Red Sea Basin, and North Africa.* Berkeley: University of California Press, 2006.

——. *The Seleucid Colonies: Studies in Founding, Administration and Organization.* Wiesbaden: Frank Steiner Verlag GMBH, 1978.

Cohen, Shaye. *The Beginnings of Jewishness: Boundaries, Varieties, Uncertainties.* Berkeley: University of California Press, 1999.

Cohn, Norman. *Cosmos, Chaos, and the World to Come: The Ancient Roots of Apocalyptic Faith.* New Haven: Yale University Press, 2001.

Cohn, Yehudah. *Tangled Up in Text: Tefillin and the Ancient World.* Brown Judaic Studies 351. Providence: Brown University, 2008.

Collins, Adela Yarbro. "Composition and Redaction of the Testament of Moses 10," *Harvard Theological Review* 69 (1976): 179-86.

——. "Introduction: Early Christian Apocalypticism," *Semeia* 36 (1986): 1-11.

Collins, John J. "Apocalyptic Eschatology as the Transcendence of Death," *Catholic Biblical Quarterly* 36, no. 1 (1974): 21-43.

——. *The Apocalyptic Imagination: An Introduction to Jewish Apocalyptic Literature,* 2nd ed. Grand Rapids: Eerdmans, 1998.

——. "The Apocalyptic Technique: Setting and Function in the Book of the Watchers," *Catholic Biblical Quarterly* 44 (1982): 91-111.

——. *The Apocalyptic Vision of the Book of Daniel.* Harvard Semitic Monographs 16. Missoula, MT: Scholars Press, 1977.

——. *Between Athens and Jerusalem: Jewish Identity in the Hellenistic Diaspora,* 2nd ed. Grand Rapids: Eerdmans, 2000.

——. "Cult and Culture: The Limits of Hellenization in Judea." In *Hellenism in the Land of Israel,* edited by John J. Collins and Gregory E. Sterling, pp. 38-61. Notre Dame: University of Notre Dame Press, 2001.

————. *Daniel: A Commentary on the Book of Daniel.* Hermeneia. Minneapolis: Fortress, 1993.

————. *Daniel, First Maccabees, Second Maccabees, with an Excursus on the Apocalyptic Genre.* Old Testament Message 15. Wilmington, DE: Michael Glazier, 1981.

————. *Daniel, with an Introduction to Apocalyptic Literature.* Forms of the Old Testament Literature 20. Grand Rapids: Eerdmans, 1984.

————. "Daniel and His Social World," *Interpretation* 39 (1985): 131-43.

————. "'Enochic Judaism' and the Sect of the Dead Sea Scrolls." In *The Early Enoch Literature,* edited by Gabriele Boccaccini and John J. Collins, pp. 283-99. Leiden: Brill, 2007.

————. "Introduction: Towards the Morphology of a Genre," *Semeia* 14 (1979): 1-20.

————. "The Jewish Apocalypses," *Semeia* 14 (1979): 21-59.

————. *Jewish Cult and Hellenistic Culture: Essays on the Jewish Encounter with Hellenism and Roman Rule.* Leiden: Brill, 2005.

————. "Response: The Apocalyptic Worldview of Daniel." In *Enoch and Qumran Origins: New Light on a Forgotten Connection,* edited by Gabriele Boccaccini, pp. 59-66. Grand Rapids: Eerdmans, 2005.

————. "Sibylline Oracles." In *Old Testament Pseudepigrapha,* vol. 1: *Apocalyptic Literature and Testaments,* edited by James H. Charlesworth, pp. 317-472. New York: Doubleday, 1983.

————. "Stirring Up the Great Sea: The Religio-Historical Background of Daniel 7." In *The Book of Daniel in the Light of New Findings,* edited by A. S. Van der Woude, pp. 121-36. Leuven: Leuven University Press, 1993.

————. "Temporality and Politics in Jewish Apocalyptic Literature." In *Apocalyptic in History and Tradition,* edited by Christopher Rowland and John Barton, pp. 26-43. London: Sheffield Academic Press, 2002.

————. "The Testamentary Literature in Recent Scholarship." In *Early Judaism and Its Modern Interpreters,* edited by Robert A. Kraft and George W. E. Nickelsburg, pp. 268-78. Philadelphia: Fortress, 1986.

————. "Theology and Identity in the Early Enoch Literature," *Henoch* 24 (2002): 57-62.

Collins, John J., and Peter Flint, eds. *The Book of Daniel: Composition and Reception.* Leiden: Brill, 2001.

Collins, John J., and George W. E. Nickelsburg, eds. *Ideal Figures in Ancient Judaism: Profiles and Paradigms.* Chico, CA: Scholars Press, 1980.

Collins, John J., and Gregory E. Sterling, eds. *Hellenism in the Land of Israel.* Notre Dame: University of Notre Dame Press, 2001.

Collins, Randall. *Conflict Sociology: Toward an Explanatory Science.* New York: Academic Press, 1975.

————. *Interaction Ritual Chains.* Princeton: Princeton University Press, 2004.

Conrad, Edgar W. *Fear Not Warrior: A Study of 'al tîrā' Pericopes in the Hebrew Scriptures.* Chico, CA: Scholars Press, 1985.

Cook, Stephen L. *Prophecy and Apocalypticism: The Postexilic Social Setting.* Minneapolis: Fortress, 1995.

Cotton, Hannah, and Michael Wörrle. "Seleukos IV to Heliodoros: A New Dossier of

Royal Correspondence from Israel," *Zeitschrift für Papyrologie und Epigraphik* 159 (2007): 191-205.

Counihan, Carole M. Introduction to *Food and Gender: Identity and Power.* Edited by Carole M. Counihan and Steven L. Kaplan. Amsterdam: Harwood Academic, 1998.

Crawford, Michael Hewsom. *Roman Republican Coinage.* Cambridge: Cambridge University Press, 1974.

Crenshaw, James L. *Defending God: Biblical Responses to the Problem of Evil.* Oxford: Oxford University Press, 2005.

———. *Education in Ancient Israel: Across the Deadening Silence.* New York: Doubleday, 1998.

———. *Prophetic Conflict: Its Effect upon Israelite Religion.* Berlin: Walter de Gruyter, 1971.

Crowther, Nigel B. *Athletika: Studies on the Olympic Games and Greek Athletics.* Nikephoros 11. Hildesheim: Weidmann, 2004.

———. "Euexia, Eutaxia, Philoponia. The Contests of the Greek *gymnasion*," *Zeitschrift für Papyrologie und Epigraphik* 85 (1983): 301-4.

———. "More on 'dromos' as a Technical Term in Greek Sport," *Nikephoros* 6 (1993): 33-37.

Daspit, Toby, and John A. Weaver. "Rap (in) the Academy." In *Imagining in the Academy: Higher Education and Popular Culture,* edited by Susan Edgerton, pp. 89-104. New York: RoutledgeFalmer, 2005.

Davies, Philip R. "And Enoch Was Not, for Genesis Took Him." In *Biblical Traditions in Transmission: Essays in Honour of Michael A. Knibb,* edited by Charlotte Hempel and Judith Lieu, pp. 97-107. Leiden: Brill, 2006.

———. "Calendrical Change and Qumran Origins: An Assessment of VanderKam's Theory," *Catholic Biblical Quarterly* 45, no. 1 (1983): 80-89.

———. *Daniel.* Old Testament Guides. Sheffield: JSOT Press, 1985.

———. "Daniel in the Lions' Den." In *Images of Empire,* edited by Loveday Alexander, pp. 160-78. Sheffield: Sheffield Academic Press, 1991.

———. "Hasidim in the Maccabean Period," *Journal of Jewish Studies* 28 (1977): 127-40.

———. "Reading Daniel Sociologically." In *The Book of Daniel in the Light of New Findings,* edited by A. S. Van der Woude, pp. 345-61. Leuven: Leuven University Press, 1993.

———. "The Scribal School of Daniel." In *The Book of Daniel: Composition and Reception,* vol. 1, edited by John J. Collins and Peter W. Flint, pp. 247-65. Leiden: Brill, 2001.

Davila, James. *The Provenance of the Pseudepigrapha: Jewish, Christian, or Other?* Leiden: Brill, 2005.

De Boer, M. C. "Paul and Apocalyptic Eschatology." In *The Origins of Apocalypticism in Judaism and Christianity,* edited by John J. Collins, pp. 345-83. Vol. 1 of *The Encyclopedia of Apocalypticism.* New York: Continuum, 2000.

De Boer, P. A. H. "'Vive le roi!'" *Vetus Testamentum* 5, no. 3 (1955): 225-31.

Debord, Guy. *Comments on the Society of the Spectacle,* 2nd ed. Translated by Malcolm Imrie. London: Verso, 1998.

De Certeau, Michel. "History: Science and Fiction." In *The Certeau Reader,* edited by Graham Ward, pp. 37-52. Oxford: Blackwell, 2000.

De Souza, Philip. "Greek Warfare and Fortification." In *The Oxford Handbook of Engineering and Technology in the Classical World,* edited by John Peter Oleson, pp. 673-90. Oxford: Oxford University Press, 2008.

Deventer, Hans van. "The End of the End, Or, What Is the Deuteronomist (Still) Doing in

Daniel?" In *Past, Present, Future: The Deuteronomistic History and the Prophets,* edited by Johannes C. de Moor and Harry F. van Rooy, pp. 62-75. Leiden: Brill, 2000.

Dexinger, Ferdinand. *Henochs Zehnwochenapokalypse und offene Probleme der Apokalyptikforschung.* Leiden: Brill, 1977.

Dimant, Devorah. "1 Enoch 6–11: A Fragment of a Parabiblical Work," *Journal of Jewish Studies* 53 (2002): 223-37.

———. "The Angels Who Sinned." Ph.D. diss. [in Hebrew]. Hebrew University of Jerusalem, 1971.

———. "The Seventy Weeks Chronology (Dan 9,24-27) in the Light of New Qumranic Texts." In *The Book of Daniel in the Light of New Findings,* edited by A. S. Van der Woude, pp. 57-76. Leuven: Leuven University Press, 1993.

DiTommaso, Lorenzo. *A Bibliography of Pseudepigrapha Research 1850-1999.* Sheffield: Sheffield Academic Press, 2001.

Dmitriev, Sviatoslav. *City Government in Hellenistic and Roman Asia Minor.* Oxford: Oxford University Press, 2005.

Doran, Robert. "The First Book of Maccabees." In *The New Interpreter's Bible,* vol. 4, pp. 1-178. Nashville: Abingdon, 1996.

———. "The High Cost of a Good Education." In *Hellenism in the Land of Israel,* edited by John J. Collins and Gregory E. Sterling, pp. 94-115. Notre Dame: University of Notre Dame Press, 2001.

———. "Independence or Co-Existence: The Responses of 1 and 2 Maccabees to Seleucid Hegemony," *Society of Biblical Literature Seminar Papers* 38 (1999): 94-103.

———. "Jason's Gymnasion." In *Of Scribes and Scrolls: Studies on the Hebrew Bible, Intertestamental Judaism, and Christian Origins Presented to John Strugnell on the Occasion of His Sixtieth Birthday,* edited by Harold W. Attridge, John J. Collins, and Thomas H. Tobin, pp. 99-109. Lanham, MD: University Press of America, 1990.

———. "Jewish Education in the Seleucid Period." In *Second Temple Studies III: Studies in Politics, Class and Material Culture,* edited by Philip R. Davies and John M. Halligan, pp. 116-32. London: Sheffield Academic Press, 2002.

———. "The Second Book of Maccabees." In *The New Interpreter's Bible,* vol. 4, pp. 179-299. Nashville: Abingdon, 1996.

———. *Temple Propaganda: The Purpose and Character of 2 Maccabees.* Catholic Biblical Quarterly Monograph Series 12. Washington, DC: Catholic Biblical Association of America, 1981.

Douglas, Mary. *Implicit Meanings: Essays in Anthropology.* London: Routledge, 1975.

———. *Purity and Danger: An Analysis of Concepts of Pollution and Taboo.* London: Routledge, 2002.

Doukhan, Jacques B. "Allusions à la creation dans le livre de Daniel." In *The Book of Daniel in the Light of New Findings,* edited by A. S. Van der Woude, pp. 285-92. Leuven: Leuven University Press, 1993.

Dowden, Ken. *The Uses of Greek Mythology.* London: Routledge, 2005.

Droge, Arthur J., and James D. Tabor. *A Noble Death: Suicide and Martyrdom Among Christians and Jews in Antiquity.* San Francisco: HarperSanFrancisco, 1992.

Duncan-Jones, R. P. "The Choenix, the Artaba, and the Modius," *Zeitschrift für Papyrologie und Epigraphik* 21 (1976): 43-52.

Dusinberre, Elspeth R. M. *Aspects of Empire in Achaemenid Sardis.* Cambridge: Cambridge University Press, 2003.

Duvall, Raymond D., and Michael Stohl. "Governance by Terror." In *The Politics of Terrorism*, 3rd ed., edited by Michael Stohl, pp. 231-71. New York: M. Dekker, 1988.

Eckstein, Arthur M. *Moral Vision in the Histories of Polybius.* Berkeley: University of California Press, 1995.

Eddy, Samuel K. *The King Is Dead: Studies in the Near Eastern Resistance to Hellenism, 334-31 B.C.* Lincoln: University of Nebraska Press, 1961.

Edgar, C. C., ed. *Zenon Papyri, Catalogue général des antiquités égyptiennes du Musée du Caire.* 5 vols. Cairo: Imprimerie de l'Institut français d'archéologie orientale, 1925-1940.

Edmondson, Jonathan C. "The Cultural Politics of Public Spectacle in Rome and the Greek East, 167-166 BCE." In *The Art of Ancient Spectacle,* edited by Bettina Bergmann and Christine Kondoleon, pp. 77-95. Studies in the History of Art 56. New Haven: Yale University Press, 1999.

Eggler, Jürg. *Influences and Traditions Underlying the Vision of Daniel 7:2-14: The Research History from the End of the 19th Century to the Present.* Göttingen: Vandenhoeck & Ruprecht, 2000.

Ego, Beate. "God's Justice: The 'Measure for Measure' Principle in 2 Maccabees." In *The Books of the Maccabees: History, Theology, Ideology. Papers of the Second International Conference on the Deuterocanonical Books. Pápa, Hungary, 9-11 June, 2005,* edited by Géza G. Xeravits and József Zsengellér, pp. 141-54. Leiden: Brill, 2007.

————. "Vergangenheit im Horizont eschatologischer Hoffnung: Die Tiervision (1 Hen 85–90) als Beispiel apokalyptischer Geschichtskonzeption." In *Die antike Historiographie und die Anfänge der christlichen Geschichtsschreibung,* edited by Eve-Marie Becker, pp. 175-95. Berlin: Walter de Gruyter, 2005.

Eisenstadt, Shmuel N., and Luis Roniger. *Patrons, Clients and Friends: Interpersonal Relations and the Structure of Trust in Society.* Cambridge: Cambridge University Press, 1984.

Elliott, Mark Adam. "Covenant and Cosmology in the Book of the Watchers and the Astronomical Book," *Henoch* 24 (2002): 23-38.

————. "Origins and Functions of the Watchers Theodicy," *Henoch* 24 (2002): 63-75.

————. *The Survivors of Israel: A Reconsideration of the Theology of Pre-Christian Judaism.* Grand Rapids: Eerdmans, 2000.

Elliott, Neil. "The Anti-Imperial Message of the Cross." In *Paul and Empire: Religion and Power in Roman Imperial Society,* edited by Richard A. Horsley, pp. 167-83. Harrisburg, PA: Trinity Press International, 1997.

————. *The Arrogance of Nations: Reading Romans in the Shadow of Empire.* Minneapolis: Fortress Press, 2008.

————. "Strategies of Resistance and Hidden Transcripts in the Pauline Communities." In *Hidden Transcripts and the Arts of Resistance: Applying the Work of James C. Scott to Jesus and Paul,* edited by Richard A. Horsley, pp. 97-122. Atlanta: Society of Biblical Literature, 2004.

Fager, Jeffrey A. *Land Tenure and the Biblical Jubilee: Uncovering Hebrew Ethics through the Sociology of Knowledge.* Sheffield: Sheffield Academic Press, 1993.

Feldman, Allen. *Formations of Violence: The Narrative of the Body and Political Terror in Northern Ireland.* Chicago: University of Chicago Press, 1991.

Femia, Joseph. *Gramsci's Political Thought: Hegemony, Consciousness, and the Revolutionary Process.* Oxford: Oxford University Press, 1981.

Fewell, Danna Nolan. *The Children of Israel: Reading the Bible for the Sake of Our Children.* Nashville: Abingdon, 2003.

————. *Circle of Sovereignty: Plotting Politics in the Book of Daniel.* Nashville: Abingdon, 1991.

Finkelstein, Israel. "The Territorial Extent and Demography of Yehud/Judea in the Persian and Early Hellenistic Periods," *Revue biblique* 117, no. 1 (2010): 39-54.

Fischer, T. "Zur Seleukideninschrift von Hafzibah," *Zeitschrift für Papyrologie und Epigraphik* 33 (1979): 131-38.

Fishbane, Michael. *Biblical Interpretation in Ancient Israel.* Oxford: Clarendon, 1985.

Flaig, Egon. *Ritualisierte Politik: Zeichen, Gesten, und Herrschaft im Alten Rom.* Göttingen: Vandenhoeck & Ruprecht, 2003.

Fleischer, Robert. "Hellenistic Royal Iconography on Coins." In *Aspects of Hellenistic Kingship,* edited by Per Bilde, Troels Engberg-Pedersen, Lise Hannestad, and Jan Zahle, pp. 28-40. Aarhus: Aarhus University Press, 1996.

Flusser, David. "The Four Empires in the Fourth Sibyl and in the Book of Daniel," *Israel Oriental Studies* 2 (1978): 148-75.

Foucault, Michel. *Discipline and Punish: The Birth of the Prison,* 2nd ed. Translated by Alan Sheridan. New York: Vintage, 1995.

————. "What Is an Author?" Translated by Josué Harari. In *Textual Strategies: Perspectives in Post-Structuralist Criticism,* edited by Josué Harari, pp. 141-60. Ithaca, NY: Cornell University Press, 1979.

Foxhall, Lin. *Olive Cultivation in Ancient Greece: Seeking the Ancient Economy.* Oxford: Oxford University Press, 2007.

Fraenkel, Eduard. "The Giants in the Poem of Naevius," *The Journal of Roman Studies* 44 (1954): 14-17.

Frank, Arthur W. "For a Sociology of the Body: An Analytical Review." In *The Body: Social Process and Cultural Theory,* edited by Mike Featherstone, Mike Hepworth, and Bryan S. Turner, pp. 36-102. London: Sage, 1991.

Freedman, David Noel, ed. *Anchor Bible Dictionary.* 6 vols. New York: Doubleday, 1992.

Freedman, David Noel, and David Miano. "People of the New Covenant." In *The Concept of the Covenant in the Second Temple Period,* edited by Stanley E. Porter and Jacqueline C. R. de Roo, pp. 7-26. Leiden: Brill, 2003.

Friedman, Jonathan. "Notes on Culture and Identity in Imperial Worlds." In *Religion and Religious Practice in the Seleucid Kingdom,* edited by Per Bilde, Troels Engberg-Pedersen, Lise Hannestad, and Jan Zahle, pp. 14-39. Aarhus: Aarhus University Press, 1990.

Frilingos, Christopher A. *Spectacles of Empire: Monsters, Martyrs, and the Book of Revelation.* Philadelphia: University of Pennsylvania Press, 2004.

Fröhlich, Ida. *'Time and Times and Half a Time': Historical Consciousness in the Jewish Literature of the Persian and Hellenistic Eras.* Sheffield: Sheffield Academic Press, 1996.

Fuchs, Harald. *Der geistige Widerstand gegen Rom in der antiken Welt.* Berlin: Walter de Gruyter, 1938.

Furtwangler, Albert. *The Authority of Publius: A Reading of the Federalist Papers.* Ithaca, NY: Cornell University Press, 1984.

Futrell, Alison. *Blood in the Arena: The Spectacle of Roman Power.* Austin: University of Texas Press, 1997.

————. *The Roman Games: A Sourcebook.* Oxford: Blackwell, 2006.

Gabrielsen, Vincent. "Piracy and the Slave Trade." In *A Companion to the Hellenistic World*, edited by Andrew Erskine, pp. 389-404. Oxford: Blackwell, 2003.

——. "Provincial Challenges to the Imperial Centre in Achaemenid and Seleucid Asia Minor." In *The Province Strikes Back: Imperial Dynamics in the Eastern Mediterranean*, edited by Björn Forsén and Giovanni Salmeri, pp. 15-44. Helsinki: Foundation of the Finnish Institute at Athens, 2008.

Gall, August Freiherrn von. *Die Einheitlichkeit des Buches Daniel*. Giessen: Ricker, 1895.

Gammie, John G. "The Classification, Stages of Growth, and Changing Intentions in the Book of Daniel," *Journal of Biblical Literature* 95, no. 2 (1976): 191-204.

——. "Spatial and Ethical Dualism in Jewish Wisdom and Apocalyptic Literature," *Journal of Biblical Literature* 93, no. 3 (1974): 356-85.

Gampel, Yolanda. "Reflections on the Prevalence of the Uncanny in Social Violence." In *Cultures Under Siege: Collective Violence and Trauma*, edited by Antonius C. G. M. Robben and Marcelo M. Suárez-Orozco, pp. 48-69. Cambridge: Cambridge University Press, 2000.

García Martínez, Florentino. "Conclusion: Mapping the Threads." In *The Early Enoch Literature*, edited by Gabriele Boccaccini and John J. Collins, pp. 329-35. Leiden: Brill, 2007.

——. *Qumran and Apocalyptic: Studies on the Aramaic Texts from Qumran*. Leiden: Brill, 1992.

García Martínez, Florentino, and Eibert J. C. Tigchelaar. "1 Enoch and the Figure of Enoch: A Bibliography of Studies 1970-1988," *Revue de Qumran* 14 (1989-1990): 149-74.

——. *The Dead Sea Scrolls Study Edition*. 2 vols. Leiden: Brill, 2000.

Gardner, Gregg. "Jewish Leadership and Hellenistic Civic Benefaction in the Second Century B.C.E.," *Journal of Biblical Literature* 126 (2007): 327-43.

Gauthier, Philippe, and Miltiades B. Hatzopoulos. *La loi gymnasiarchique de Beroia*. Athens: Centre de recherché de l'antiquité grecque et romaine, 1993.

Geertz, Clifford. *Negara: The Theatre State in Nineteenth-Century Bali*. Princeton: Princeton University Press, 1980.

Gera, Dov. *Judaea and Mediterranean Politics, 219-161 B.C.E.* Leiden: Brill, 1998.

Geus, Klaus. "Space and Geography." In *A Companion to the Hellenistic World*, edited by Andrew Erskine, pp. 232-45. Oxford: Blackwell, 2003.

Giard, Luce. "Doing-Cooking." In *The Practice of Everyday Life*, vol. 2: *Living & Cooking*, edited by Michel de Certeau, Luce Giard, and Pierre Mayol, pp. 149-248. Translated by Timothy J. Tomasik. Minneapolis: University of Minnesota Press, 1998.

Gilmore, David D., ed. *Honor and Shame and the Unity of the Mediterranean*. Washington, DC: American Anthropological Association, 1987.

Ginsberg, Harold L. "The Composition of the Book of Daniel," *Vetus Testamentum* 4, no. 3 (1954): 246-75.

——. "The Oldest Interpretation of the Suffering Servant," *Vetus Testamentum* 3, no. 4 (1953): 400-404.

Goldingay, John E. *Daniel*. Word Biblical Commentary 30. Dallas: Word Books, 1989.

Goldstein, Jonathan. *I Maccabees: A New Translation with Introduction and Commentary*. The Anchor Bible 41. Garden City, NY: Doubleday, 1976.

——. *II Maccabees: A New Translation with Introduction and Commentary*. The Anchor Bible 41A. New York: Doubleday, 1984.

Goldstone, Jack A., and John F. Haldon. "Ancient States, Empires, and Exploitation: Problems and Perspectives." In *The Dynamics of Ancient Empires: State Power from Assyria to Byzantium,* edited by Ian Morris and Walter Scheidel, pp. 3-29. Oxford: Oxford University Press, 2009.

Good, Edwin M. "Apocalyptic as Comedy: The Book of Daniel," *Semeia* 32, no. 1 (1984): 41-70.

Goodblatt, David. "From Judeans to Israel: Names of Jewish States in Antiquity," *Journal for the Study of Judaism in the Persian, Hellenistic, and Roman Periods* 29, no. 1 (1998): 1-36.

Gorman, Michael. *Cruciformity: Paul's Narrative Spirituality of the Cross.* Grand Rapids: Eerdmans, 2001.

Gottwald, Norman K. "Early Israel as an Anti-Imperial Community." In *In the Shadow of Empire: Reclaiming the Bible as a History of Faithful Resistance,* edited by Richard A. Horsley, pp. 9-24. Louisville: Westminster John Knox, 2008.

Gourevitch, Philip. *We Wish to Inform You That Tomorrow We Will Be Killed with Our Families: Stories from Rwanda.* New York: Picador, 1999.

Gowan, Donald. *Daniel.* Abingdon Old Testament Commentaries. Nashville: Abingdon, 2001.

Grabbe, Lester. "The Hellenistic City of Jerusalem." In *Jews in the Hellenistic and Roman Cities,* edited by John R. Bartlett, pp. 6-21. London: Routledge, 2002.

———. "The Jews and Hellenization: Hengel and His Critics." In *Second Temple Studies III: Studies in Politics, Class, and Material Culture,* edited by Philip R. Davies and John M. Halligan, pp. 52-66. Journal for the Study of the Old Testament Supplement Series, 340. London: Sheffield Academic Press, 2002.

———. "The Parables of Enoch in Second Temple Jewish Society." In *Enoch and the Messiah Son of Man: Revisiting the Book of Parables,* edited by Gabriele Boccaccini, pp. 386-402. Grand Rapids: Eerdmans, 2007.

———. "The Social Setting of Early Jewish Apocalypticism," *Journal for the Study of the Pseudepigrapha* 4 (1989): 27-47.

Grainger, John D. *The Cities of Seleukid Syria.* Oxford: Oxford University Press, 1990.

———. *Hellenistic Phoenicia.* Oxford: Clarendon, 1991.

———. *The Roman War of Antiochus the Great.* Leiden: Brill, 2002.

Gramsci, Antonio. *Selections from the Prison Notebooks.* Edited and translated by Quintin Hoare and Geoffrey Nowell Smith. London: Lawrence & Wishart, 1971.

Green, Peter. *Alexander to Actium: The Historic Evolution of the Hellenistic Age.* Berkeley: University of California Press, 1990.

Gruen, Erich S. "Hellenism and Persecution: Antiochus IV and the Jews." In *Hellenistic History and Culture,* edited by Peter Green, pp. 238-74. Berkeley: University of California Press, 1993.

———. *The Hellenistic World and the Coming of Rome.* Berkeley: University of California Press, 1984.

———. *Heritage and Hellenism: The Reinvention of Jewish Tradition.* Berkeley: University of California Press, 1998.

———. "The Polis in the Hellenistic World." In *Nomodeiktes: Greek Studies in Honor of Martin Ostwald,* edited by Ralph M. Rosen and Joseph Farrel, pp. 339-54. Ann Arbor: University of Michigan Press, 1993.

———. "Seleucid Royal Ideology," *Society of Biblical Literature Seminar Papers* 38 (1999): 24-53.

Gruenwald, Ithamar. "A Case Study of Scripture and Culture: Apocalypticism as Cultural Identity in Past and Present." In *Ancient and Modern Perspectives on the Bible and Culture: Essays in Honor of Hans Dieter Betz,* edited by Adela Yarbro Collins, pp. 252-80. Atlanta: Scholars Press, 1998.

Habicht, Christian. "The Seleucids and Their Rivals." In *The Cambridge Ancient History,* vol. 8: *Rome and the Mediterranean to 133 BCE.* Edited by A. E. Astin, F. W. Walbank, M. W. Fredriksen, and R. M. Ogilvie, pp. 324-87. Cambridge: Cambridge University Press, 2000.

Hadley, R. A. "Royal Propaganda of Seleucus I and Lysimachus," *Journal of Hellenic Studies* 94 (1974): 50-65.

———. "Seleucus, Dionysus, or Alexander?" *Numismatic Chronicle* 14 (1974): 9-13.

Hall, Catherine. "Histories, Empires and the Post-colonial Moment." In *The Post-Colonial Question: Common Skies, Divided Horizons,* edited by Iain Chambers and Lidia Curti, pp. 65-77. London: Routledge, 1996.

Hall, Edith. *Inventing the Barbarian: Greek Self-Definition through Tragedy.* Oxford: Oxford University Press, 1991.

Hall, Jonathan. *Hellenicity: Between Ethnicity and Culture.* Chicago: University of Chicago Press, 1999.

Hall, Robert. *Revealed Histories: Techniques for Ancient Jewish and Christian Historiography,* JSPSS 6. Sheffield: Sheffield Academic Press, 1991.

Hall, Roger Alan. "Post-exilic Theological Streams and the Book of Daniel." Ph.D. diss., Yale University, 1974.

Han, Jin Hee. *Daniel's Spiel: Apocalyptic Literacy in the Book of Daniel.* Lanham, MD: University Press of America, 2008.

Hanhart, Robert, ed. *Septuaginta: Vetus Testamentum Graecum,* vol. IX.2: *Maccabaeorum Liber II.* Göttingen: Vandenhoeck & Ruprecht, 1976.

Hansen, Mogens Herman. "The 'Autonomous City-State': Ancient Fact or Modern Fiction?" In *Studies in the Ancient Greek Polis,* edited by Mogens Herman Hansen and Kurt Raaflaub, pp. 21-44. Historia Einzelschriften 95. Stuttgart: Franz Steiner Verlag, 1995.

Hanson, Karen. "Dressing Down, Dressing Up: The Philosophical Fear of Fashion." In *Aesthetics in Feminist Perspective,* edited by Hilde S. Hein and Carolyn Korsmeyer, pp. 229-42. Bloomington: Indiana University Press, 1993.

Hanson, Paul D. *The Dawn of Apocalyptic: The Historical and Sociological Roots of Jewish Apocalyptic Eschatology.* Philadelphia: Fortress, 1975. Repr., 1979.

Harari, Josué V. "Critical Factions/Critical Fictions." In *Textual Strategies: Perspectives in Post-Structuralist Criticism,* edited by Josué Harari, pp. 17-72. Ithaca, NY: Cornell University Press, 1979.

Hardt, Michael, and Antonio Negri. *Empire.* Cambridge, MA: Harvard University Press, 2000.

Harley, John Bryan. *The New Nature of Maps: Essays in the History of Cartography.* Baltimore: Johns Hopkins University Press, 2001.

Harlow, Barbara. *Resistance Literature.* New York: Routledge, 1987.

Harrington, Daniel. *The Maccabean Revolt: Anatomy of a Biblical Revolution.* Wilmington, DE: Michael Glazier, 1988.

Harris, Marvin. *Good to Eat: Riddles of Food and Culture.* New York: Simon & Schuster, 1985.

Hartman, Lars. *Asking for a Meaning: A Study of 1 Enoch 1–5*. Lund: CWK Gleerup, 1979.

Hartman, Louis F., and Alexander A. Di Lella. *The Book of Daniel*. Anchor Bible 23. New York: Doubleday, 1978.

Hatzopoulos, Miltiades B. "Quaestiones Macedonicae: lois, decrets, et epistates dans les cités Macedoniennes," *Tekmeria* 8 (2003): 27-60.

Hayes, John, and Sara Mandell. *The Jewish People in Classical Antiquity: From Alexander to Bar Kochba*. Louisville: Westminster John Knox, 1998.

Haynes, Douglas, and Gyan Prakash. "Introduction: The Entanglement of Power and Resistance." In *Contesting Power: Resistance and Everyday Social Relations in South Asia*, edited by Douglas Haynes and Gyan Prakash, pp. 1-22. Berkeley: University of California Press, 1991.

Heaton, Eric W. *The Book of Daniel*. London: SCM Press, 1956.

Hebbard, Aaron B. *Reading Daniel as a Text in Theological Hermeneutics*. Eugene, OR: Pickwick, 2009.

Heinen, Heinz. "The Syrian-Egyptian Wars and the New Kingdoms of Asia-Minor." In *The Cambridge Ancient History*, vol. 7, part 1: *The Hellenistic World*, edited by A. E. Astin, F. W. Walbank, M. W. Fredriksen, and R. M. Ogilvie, pp. 412-45. Cambridge: Cambridge University Press, 1984.

Hellholm, David, ed. *Apocalypticism in the Mediterranean World and the Near East: Proceedings of the International Colloquium on Apocalypticism, Uppsala, August 12-17, 1979*. Tübingen: JCB Mohr, 1983.

Hengel, Martin. *Judaism and Hellenism: Studies in Their Encounter in Palestine during the Early Hellenistic Period*. 2 vols. Philadelphia: Fortress, 1974.

Hengel, Martin, and Daniel P. Bailey. "The Effective History of Isaiah 53 in the Pre-Christian Period." In *The Suffering Servant: Isaiah 53 in Jewish and Christian Sources*, edited by Bernd Janowski and Peter Stuhlmacher, pp. 75-146. Grand Rapids: Eerdmans, 2004.

Henrichs, Albert. "Between Country and City: Cultic Dimensions of Dionysus in Athens and Attica." In *Cabinet of the Muses: Essays on Classical and Comparative Literature in Honor of Thomas G. Rosenmeyer*, edited by Mark Griffith and D. J. Mastronarde, pp. 257-78. Atlanta: Scholars Press, 1990.

———. "'He Has a God in Him': Human and Divine in the Modern Perception of Dionysus." In *Masks of Dionysus*, edited by Thomas A. Carpenter and Christopher A. Faraone, pp. 13-43. Ithaca, NY: Cornell University Press, 1993.

Henten, Jan Willem van. *The Maccabean Martyrs as Saviours of the Jewish People: A Study of 2 and 4 Maccabees*. Leiden: Brill, 1997.

———. "Royal Ideology: 1 and 2 Maccabees and Egypt." In *Jewish Perspectives on Hellenistic Rulers*, edited by Tessa Rajak, Sarah Pearce, James Aitken, and Jennifer Dines, pp. 265-82. Berkeley: University of California Press, 2007.

Henze, Matthias. "The Apocalypse of Weeks and the Architecture of the End Time." In *Enoch and Qumran Origins: New Light on a Forgotten Connection*, edited by Gabriele Boccaccini, pp. 207-9. Grand Rapids: Eerdmans, 2005.

———. "Enoch's Dream Visions and the Visions of Daniel Reconsidered." In *Enoch and Qumran Origins: New Light on a Forgotten Connection*, edited by Gabriele Boccaccini, pp. 17-22. Grand Rapids: Eerdmans, 2005.

———. *The Madness of King Nebuchadnezzar: The Ancient Near Eastern Origins and Early History of Interpretation of Daniel 4*. Leiden: Brill, 1999.

————. "The Narrative Frame of Daniel: A Literary Assessment," *Journal for the Study of Judaism in the Persian, Hellenistic, and Roman Periods* 32, no. 1 (2001): 5-24.

————. "The Parables of Enoch in Second Temple Literature: A Response to Gabriele Boccaccini." In *Enoch and the Messiah Son of Man: Revisiting the Book of Parables,* edited by Gabriele Boccaccini, pp. 290-98. Grand Rapids: Eerdmans, 2007.

Herman, Judith. *Trauma and Recovery: The Aftermath of Violence — From Domestic Abuse to Political Terror.* New York: Basic Books, 1997.

Hillers, Delbert. *Covenant: The History of a Biblical Idea.* Baltimore: Johns Hopkins University Press, 1969.

Himmelfarb, Martha. *Ascent to Heaven in Jewish and Christian Apocalypses.* Oxford: Oxford University Press, 1993.

————. "Judaism and Hellenism in 2 Maccabees," *Poetics Today* 19, no. 1 (1998): 19-40.

Hindess, Barry. "Power, Interests and the Outcome of Struggles," *Sociology* 16, no. 4 (1982): 498-511.

Hobsbawm, Eric. "Introduction: Inventing Traditions." In *The Invention of Tradition,* edited by Eric Hobsbawm and Terence Ranger, pp. 1-14. Cambridge: Cambridge University Press, 1983.

Hoffmann, Heinrich. *Das Gesetz in der frühjüdischen Apokalyptik.* Göttingen: Vandenhoeck & Ruprecht, 1999.

Hoglund, Kenneth. "The Material Culture of the Seleucid Period in Palestine: Social and Economic Observations." In *Second Temple Studies III: Studies in Politics, Class and Material Culture,* edited by Philip R. Davies and John M. Halligan, pp. 67-73. London: Sheffield Academic Press, 2002.

Holleran, Claire. "The Development of Public Entertainment Venues in Rome and Italy." In *'Bread and Circuses': Euergetism and Municipal Patronage in Roman Italy,* edited by Kathryn Lomas and Tim Cornell, pp. 46-60. London: Routledge, 2003.

Horowitz, Mardi. *Stress Response Syndromes.* Northvale, NJ: Jason Aronson, 1986.

Horsley, Richard A., ed. *Hidden Transcripts and the Arts of Resistance: Applying the Work of James C. Scott to Jesus and Paul.* Atlanta: Society of Biblical Literature, 2004.

————, ed. *In the Shadow of Empire: Reclaiming the Bible as a History of Faithful Resistance.* Louisville: Westminster John Knox, 2008.

————. *Jesus and Empire: The Kingdom of God and the New World Disorder.* Minneapolis: Fortress, 2003.

————, ed. *Oral Performance, Popular Tradition, and Hidden Transcript in Q.* Atlanta: Society of Biblical Literature, 2006.

————, ed. *Paul and Empire: Religion and Power in Roman Imperial Society.* Harrisburg, PA: Trinity Press International, 1997.

————. *Scribes, Visionaries, and the Politics of Second Temple Judea.* Louisville: Westminster John Knox, 2007.

Horst, Pieter W. van der. "Antediluvian Knowledge: Jewish Speculations about Wisdom from before the Flood in Their Ancient Context." In *Jüdische Schriften in ihrem antikjüdischen und urchristlichen Kontext,* edited by Hermann Lichtenberger and Gerbern S. Oegema, pp. 163-81. Gütersloh: Gütersloher Verlagshaus, 2002.

Houghton, Arthur. *Coins of the Seleucid Empire from the Collection of Arthur Houghton.* New York: The American Numismatic Society, 1983.

Houghton, Arthur, and Catherine Lorber. *Seleucid Coins: A Comprehensive Catalog, Part I:*

Seleucus through Antiochus III, vol. 1. New York: The American Numismatic Society, 2002.

Howgego, C. J. "Why Did Ancient States Strike Coins?" *Numismatic Chronicle* 150 (1990): 1-25.

Huffmon, Herbert B. "The Covenant Lawsuit in the Prophets," *Journal of Biblical Literature* 78 (1959): 273-95.

————. "The Treaty Background of Hebrew *yāda'*," *Bulletin of the American Schools of Oriental Research* 181 (1966): 31-37.

Humphreys, W. L. "A Life-Style for the Diaspora: A Study of the Tales of Esther and Daniel," *Journal of Biblical Literature* 92 (1973): 211-23.

Hutchinson, John, and Anthony Smith. Introduction to *Ethnicity.* Edited by John Hutchinson and Anthony Smith. Oxford Readers. Oxford: Oxford University Press, 1996.

Isaacman, Allen, and Barbara Isaacman. "Resistance and Collaboration in Southern and Central Africa, c. 1850-1920," *International Journal of African Historical Studies* 10 (1977): 31-62.

Isaacman, Allen, Michael Stephen, Yussuf Adam, Maria João Homen, Eugenio Macamo, and Augustinho Pililão. "'Cotton Is the Mother of Poverty': Peasant Resistance to Forced Cotton Production in Mozambique, 1938-1961," *International Journal of African Historical Studies* 13 (1980): 581-615.

Jackson, David R. *Enochic Judaism: Three Defining Paradigm Exemplars.* London: T. & T. Clark, 2004.

Jacobs, Jane M. "Resisting Reconciliation: The Secret Geographies of (Post)colonial Australia." In *Geographies of Resistance,* edited by Steve Pile and Michael Keith, pp. 203-18. London: Routledge, 1997.

Jastrow, Marcus. *Dictionary of the Targumim, Talmud Babli, Yerushalmi, and Midrashic Literature.* New York: Judaica, 1996.

Johns, Alger F. *A Short Grammar of Biblical Aramaic,* rev. ed. Berrien Springs, MI: Andrews University Press, 1972.

Jones, Arthur Heath. "Enoch and the Fall of the Watchers: 1 Enoch 1–36." Ph.D. diss., Vanderbilt University, 1989.

Jones, Bruce William. "Antiochus Epiphanes and the Persecution of the Jews." In *Scripture in Context: Essays on the Comparative Method,* edited by Carl D. Evans, William H. Hallo, and John B. White, pp. 263-90. Pittsburgh: Pickwick, 1980.

————. "Ideas of History in the Book of Daniel." Ph.D. diss., Graduate Theological Union, 1972.

————. "The Prayer in Daniel IX," *Vetus Testamentum* 18, no. 4 (1968): 488-93.

Jonnes, Lloyd, and Marijana Ricl. "A New Royal Inscription from Phrygia Paroreios: Eumenes II Grants Tyriaion the Status of a Polis," *Epigraphica Anatolica* 29 (1997): 1-29.

Kalmanofsky, Amy. *Terror All Around: Horror, Monsters, and Theology in the Book of Jeremiah.* London: Continuum, 2008.

Kaminsky, Joel S. *Yet I Loved Jacob: Reclaiming the Biblical Concept of Election.* Nashville: Abingdon, 2007.

Kampen, John. *The Hasideans and the Origin of Pharisaism: A Study in 1 and 2 Maccabees.* Atlanta: Scholars Press, 1988.

Kasher, Aryeh. *Jews and Hellenistic Cities in Eretz-Israel. Relations of the Jews in Eretz-Israel with the Hellenistic Cities during the Second Temple Period (332 BCE–70 CE)*. Tübingen: J. C. B. Mohr (Paul Siebeck), 1990.

Kasinec, Wendy F., and Michael A. Polushin. Introduction to *Expanding Empires: Cultural Interaction and Exchange in World Societies from Ancient to Early Modern Times*, edited by Wendy F. Kasinec and Michael A. Polushin. Wilmington, DE: Scholarly Resource Books, 2002.

Keefe, Alice. "Rapes of Women/Wars of Men," *Semeia* 61 (1993): 70-98.

Kennell, Nigel M. *The Gymnasium of Virtue: Education and Culture in Ancient Sparta*. Chapel Hill: University of North Carolina Press, 1995.

———. "New Light on 2 Maccabees 4:7-15," *Journal of Jewish Studies* 56, no. 1 (2005): 10-24.

Kerényi, Karl. *Dionysos: Archetypal Image of Indestructible Life*. Princeton: Princeton University Press, 1976.

Kirkpatrick, Shane. *Competing for Honor: A Social-Scientific Reading of Daniel 1–6*. Leiden: Brill, 2005.

Kittel, G., and G. Friedrich, eds. *Theological Dictionary of the New Testament*. Translated by G. W. Bromiley. 10 vols. Grand Rapids: Eerdmans, 1964-1976.

Klawans, Jonathan. *Purity, Sacrifice, and the Temple: Symbolism and Supersessionism in the Study of Ancient Judaism*. Oxford: Oxford University Press, 2006.

Knibb, Michael A. "Apocalyptic and Wisdom in 4 Ezra," *Journal for the Study of Judaism in the Persian, Hellenistic, and Roman Periods* 13 (1982): 56-74.

———. "The Book of Enoch or Books of Enoch?" In *The Early Enoch Literature*, edited by Gabriele Boccaccini and John J. Collins, pp. 21-40. Leiden: Brill, 2007.

———. *The Ethiopic Book of Enoch: A New Edition in the Light of the Aramaic Dead Sea Fragments*, 2 vols. Oxford: Clarendon, 1977-1978.

———. "The Exile in the Literature of the Intertestamental Period," *Heythrop Journal* 17, no. 3 (1976): 253-72.

———. "Interpreting the Book of Enoch: Reflections on a Recently Published Commentary," *Journal for the Study of Judaism in the Persian, Hellenistic, and Roman Periods* 33, no. 4 (2002): 437-50.

———. *Translating the Bible: The Ethiopic Version of the Old Testament*. Oxford: Oxford University Press, 1999.

———. "The Use of Scripture in 1 Enoch 17–19." In *Jerusalem, Alexandria, Rome: Studies in Ancient Cultural Interaction in Honour of A. Hilhorst*, edited by Florentino García Martínez and Gerard P. Luttikhuizen, pp. 165-78. Leiden: Brill, 2003.

———. "'You Are Indeed Wiser Than Daniel': Reflections on the Character of the Book of Daniel." In *The Book of Daniel in the Light of New Findings*, edited by A. S. Van der Woude, pp. 399-411. Leuven: Leuven University Press, 1993.

Koch, Klaus. "Die Anfänge der Apokalyptik in Israel und die Rolle des astronomischen Henochbuches." In *Vor der Wende der Zeiten*. Neukirchen: Neukirchener Verlag, 1996.

———. "The Astral Laws as the Basis of Time, Universal History, and the Eschatological Turn in the Astronomical Book and the Animal Apocalypse of 1 Enoch." In *The Early Enoch Literature*, edited by Gabriele Boccaccini and John J. Collins, pp. 119-37. Leiden: Brill, 2007.

———. "Daniel und Henoch — Apokalyptik im Antiken Judentum." In *Apokalyptik und kein Ende?* edited by Bernd U. Schipper and Georg Plasger, pp. 31-50. Göttingen: Vandenhoeck & Ruprecht, 2007.

———. "Die Gesetze des gestirnten Himmels als Manifestationen der Herrschaft Gottes über Raum und Zeit." In *Die aramäische Rezeption der hebräischen Bibel: Studien zur Targumik und Apokalyptik,* by Klaus Koch. Edited by Martin Rösel, pp. 21-42. Neukirchen-Vluyn: Neukirchener Verlag, 2003.

―――. "History as a Battlefield of Two Antagonistic Powers in the Apocalypse of Weeks and in the Rule of the Community." In *Enoch and Qumran Origins: New Light on a Forgotten Connection,* edited by Gabriele Boccaccini, pp. 185-99. Grand Rapids: Eerdmans, 2005.

―――. "Die mysteriösen Zahlen der judäischen Könige und die apokalyptischen Jahrwochen," *Vetus Testamentum* 28, no. 4 (1978): 433-41.

―――. *The Rediscovery of Apocalyptic: A Polemical Work on a Neglected Area of Biblical Studies and Its Damaging Effects on Theology and Philosophy.* London: SCM Press, 1972.

―――. *Die Reiche der Welt und der kommende Menschensohn: Studien zum Danielbuch.* Edited by Martin Rösel. Neukirchen: Neukirchener Verlag, 1995.

―――. "Sabbat, Sabbatjahr, und Weltenjahr: Die apokalyptische Konstruktion der Zeit," *Ars Semiotica* 29 (1977): 69-86.

Kolenkow, Anitra Bingham. "The Literary Genre 'Testament.'" In *Early Judaism and Its Modern Interpreters,* edited by Robert A. Kraft and George W. E. Nickelsburg, pp. 259-67. Philadelphia: Fortress, 1986.

Kolk, Bessel van der. "The Trauma Spectrum: The Interaction of Biological and Social Events in the Genesis of the Trauma Response," *Journal of Traumatic Stress* 1 (1988): 273-90.

Kooij, Arie van der. "The Concept of Covenant (Berît) in the Book of Daniel." In *The Book of Daniel in the Light of New Findings,* edited by A. S. Van der Woude, pp. 495-501. Leuven: Leuven University Press, 1993.

Koselleck, Reinhart. *The Practice of Conceptual History: Timing History, Spacing Concepts.* Translated by Todd Presner. Stanford: Stanford University Press, 2002.

Kosmala, Hans. "*Maśkîl,*" *Journal of the Ancient Near Eastern Society of Columbia University* 5 (1973): 235-41.

Kraft, Robert A. "Para-Mania: Beside, Before, and Beyond Bible Studies," *Journal of Biblical Literature* 126, no. 1 (2007): 5-27.

Kraft, Robert A., and George W. E. Nickelsburg. *Early Judaism and Its Modern Interpreters.* Philadelphia: Fortress, 1986.

Kratz, G. "Reich Gottes und Gesetz im Danielbuch und im werdenden Judentum." In *The Book of Daniel in the Light of New Findings,* edited by A. S. Van der Woude, pp. 435-79. Leuven: Leuven University Press, 1993.

Krause, Deborah. *1 Timothy.* London: T. & T. Clark, 2004.

Kristeva, Julia. *Powers of Horror: An Essay on Abjection.* Translated by Leon S. Roudiez. New York: Columbia University Press, 1982.

Kubicki, Judith Marie. *Liturgical Music as Ritual Symbol: A Case Study of Jacques Berthier's Taizé Music.* Leuven: Peters, 1999.

Kvanvig, Helge S. "Cosmic Laws and Cosmic Imbalance: Wisdom, Myth and Apocalyptic in Early Enochic Writings." In *The Early Enoch Literature,* edited by Gabriele Boccaccini and John J. Collins, pp. 139-58. Leiden: Brill, 2007.

―――. "*Jubilees* — Between Enoch and Moses. A Narrative Reading," *Journal for the Study of Judaism in the Persian, Hellenistic, and Roman Periods* 35 (2004): 243-61.

————. *Roots of Apocalyptic: The Mesopotamian Background of the Enoch Figure and of the Son of Man*. Neukirchen: Neukirchener Verlag, 1988.

Kyle, Donald G. *Sport and Spectacle in the Ancient World*. Oxford: Blackwell, 2007.

Lacocque, André. *The Book of Daniel*. Translated by David Pellauer. Atlanta: John Knox Press, 1979.

————. "The Liturgical Prayer in Daniel 9," *Hebrew Union College Annual* 47 (1976): 119-42.

————. "The Socio-Spiritual Formative Milieu of the Daniel Apocalypse." In *The Book of Daniel in the Light of New Findings*, edited by A. S. van der Woude, pp. 315-43. Leuven: Leuven University Press, 1993.

Ladrière, Jean. "The Performativity of Liturgical Language." In *Liturgical Experience of Faith*, edited by Herman A. P. Schmidt and David Noel Power, pp. 50-62. New York: Herder & Herder, 1973.

Lambert, W. "Enmeduranki and Related Matters," *Journal of Cuneiform Studies* 21 (1967): 126-38.

Lampe, P. "Die Apokalyptiker — ihre Situation und ihr Handeln." In *Eschatologie und Friedenshandeln. Exegetische Beiträge zur Frage christlicher Friedensverantwortung*, edited by Ulrich Luz, pp. 59-114. Stuttgart: Katholisches Bibelwerk, 1981.

Langer, Lawrence L. "The Alarmed Vision: Social Suffering and Holocaust Atrocity." In *Social Suffering*, edited by Arthur Kleinman, Veena Das, and Margaret Lock, pp. 47-65. Berkeley: University of California Press, 1997.

Langlois, Michael. "Les Manuscrits Araméens d'Hénoch: Nouvelle Documentation et Nouvelle Approche." In *Qoumran et judaïsme du tournant de notre ère: actes de la table ronde, Collège de France, 16 novembre 2004*, edited by A. Lemaire and S. C. Mimouni, pp. 111-21. Leuven: Peeters, 2006.

Larson, Erik. "The Relation between the Greek and Aramaic Texts of Enoch." In *The Dead Sea Scrolls Fifty Years after Their Discovery, Proceedings of the Jerusalem Congress, July 20-25, 1997*, pp. 434-44. Jerusalem: Israel Exploration Society, 2000.

Larson, Jennifer Lynn. *Ancient Greek Cults: A Guide*. London: Routledge, 2007.

Laurence, Richard. *The Book of Enoch, an apocryphal production, supposed to have been lost for ages; but discovered at the close of the last century in Abyssinia; now first translated from an Ethiopic Ms. in the Bodleian Library*. Oxford: J. H. Parker, 1821.

Le Rider, Georges. "Un essai de réforme monétaire sous Antiochos IV en 173/2? Remarques sur l'idée d'une pénurie d'argent dans les Etats hellénistiques au IIe siècle." In *Recherches récentes sur le monde hellénistique: Actes du colloque international organisé à l'occasion du 60e anniversaire de Pierre Ducrey (Lausanne, 20-21 novembre 1998)*, edited by Regula Frei-Stolba and Kristine Gex, pp. 269-79. Berlin: Peter Lang, 2001.

————. "Les ressources financières de Séleucos IV (187-175) et le paiement de l'indemnité aux Romains." In *Essays in Honour of Robert Carson and Kenneth Jenkins*, edited by Martin Price, Andrew Burnett, and Roger Bland, pp. 49-67. London: Spink, 1993.

————. *Suse sous les Séleucides et les Parthes: Les trouvailles monétaires et l'histoire de la ville*. Mémoires de la Mission archéologique en Iran 38. Paris: P. Geuthner, 1965.

Le Roux, J. H. "The Use of Scripture in 1 Enoch 6–11," *Neotestamentica* 17 (1983): 28-38.

Leslau, Wolf. *Comparative Dictionary of Ge'ez (Classical Ethiopic): Ge'ez-English, English-Ge'ez, with an Index of the Semitic Roots*. Wiesbaden: Harrassowitz, 1987.

Levenson, Jon. *Creation and the Persistence of Evil*. San Francisco: Harper & Row, 1985. Repr. Princeton: Princeton University Press, 1994.

Levine, Lee I. *Jerusalem: Portrait of the City in the Second Temple Period (538 B.C.E.–70 C.E.)*. Philadelphia: Jewish Publication Society, 2002.

———. *Judaism and Hellenism in Antiquity: Conflict or Confluence?* Seattle: University of Washington Press, 1998.

Lévi-Strauss, Claude. *The Origin of Table Manners*. New York: Harper & Row, 1978.

Lévy, Edmond. "Autonomia et éleuthéria au Ve siècle," *Revue de philologie* 57, no. 2 (1983): 249-70.

Licht, Jacob. "Taxo, or the Apocalyptic Doctrine of Vengeance," *Journal of Jewish Studies* 12 (1961): 95-104.

Lieu, Judith. "Not Hellenes but Philistines? The Maccabees and Josephus Defining the 'Other,'" *Journal of Jewish Studies* 53, no. 2 (2002): 246-63.

Lipschits, Oded. "Persian Period Finds from Jerusalem: Facts and Interpretations," *The Journal of Hebrew Scriptures* 9, no. 20 (2009): 1-30.

Liverani, Mario. *Myth and Politics in Ancient Near Eastern Historiography*. Edited by Zainab Bahrani and Marc Van De Mieroop. Ithaca, NY: Cornell University Press, 2004.

Loader, William. *Enoch, Levi, and Jubilees on Sexuality: Attitudes toward Sexuality in the Early Enoch Literature, the Aramaic Levi Document, and the Book of Jubilees*. Grand Rapids: Eerdmans, 2007.

Luke, K. "The Biblical Idea of Marturia." In *Service and Salvation: Nagpur Theological Conference on Evangelization*, edited by Joseph Pathrapankal, pp. 113-24. Bangor: Theological Publications in India, 1973.

Lust, Johan. "Cult and Sacrifice in Daniel: The Tamid and the Abomination of Desolation." In *The Book of Daniel: Composition and Reception*, vol. 2, edited by John J. Collins and Peter W. Flint, pp. 671-88. Leiden: Brill, 2002.

Ma, John. *Antiochos III and the Cities of Western Asia Minor*. Oxford: Oxford University Press, 1999.

———. "Kings." In *A Companion to the Hellenistic World*, edited by Andrew Erskine, pp. 177-95. Oxford: Blackwell, 2003.

———. "'Oversexed, Overpaid, and Over Here': A Response to Angelos Chaniotis." In *Army and Power in the Ancient World*, edited by Angelos Chaniotis and Peter Ducrey, pp. 115-95. Stuttgart: Franz Steiner Verlag, 2002.

———. "Seleukids and Speech-Acts: Performative Utterances, Legitimacy and Negotiation in the World of the Maccabees," *Scripta Classica Israelica* 19 (2000): 71-112.

MacMullen, Ramsay. *Enemies of the Roman Order: Treason, Unrest, and Alienation in the Empire*. Cambridge, MA: Harvard University Press, 1966.

Martin, François. *Le Livre d'Hénoch traduit sur le texte éthiopien*. Paris: Letouzey et Ané, 1906.

Martyn, J. Louis. "Epistemology at the Turn of the Ages: 2 Corinthians 5.16." In *Christian History and Interpretation: Studies Presented to John Knox*, edited by William R. Farmer, C. F. D. Moule, and Richard R. Niebuhr, pp. 269-87. Cambridge: Cambridge University Press, 1967.

Mason, Rex A. "The Treatment of Earlier Biblical Themes in the Book of Daniel." In *Perspectives on the Hebrew Bible: Essays in Honor of Walter J. Harrelson*, edited by James L. Crenshaw, pp. 81-100. Macon, GA: Mercer University Press, 1988.

Mason, Steve. "Jews, Judeans, Judaizing, Judaism: Problems of Categorization in Ancient

History," *Journal for the Study of Judaism in the Persian, Hellenistic, and Roman Periods* 38 (2007): 457-512.

Massa-Pairault, Françoise-Hélène. *La gigantomachie de Pergame ou l'image du monde.* Athens: École française d'Athènes, 2007.

Matthews, Susan F. "When We Remembered Zion: The Significance of the Exile for Understanding Daniel." In *The Bible on Suffering: Social and Political Implications,* edited by Anthony J. Tambasco, pp. 93-119. Mahwah, NJ: Paulist, 2002.

Matthews, Victor H. "Honor and Shame in Gender-Related Legal Situations in the Hebrew Bible." In *Gender and Law in the Hebrew Bible and the Ancient Near East,* edited by Victor H. Matthews and Tikva Frymer-Kensky, pp. 97-112. London: T. & T. Clark, 2004.

Mazzaferri, Frederick David. *The Genre of the Book of Revelation from a Source Critical Perspective.* Berlin: Walter de Gruyter, 1989.

McDonald, Patricia M. *God and Violence: Biblical Resources for Living in a Small World.* Scottdale, PA: Herald, 2004.

McGing, Brian. "Population and Proselytism: How Many Jews Were There in the Ancient World?" In *Jews in the Hellenistic and Roman Cities,* edited by John R. Bartlett, pp. 88-106. London: Routledge, 2002.

———. "Subjection and Resistance: To the Death of Mithridates." In *A Companion to the Hellenistic World,* edited by Andrew Erskine, pp. 71-89. Oxford: Blackwell, 2003.

McGinn, Bernard. *The Essential Writings of Christian Mysticism.* New York: Random House, 2006.

McGrail, Seán. "Sea Transport, Part 1: Ships and Navigation." In *The Oxford Handbook of Engineering and Technology in the Classical World,* edited by John Peter Oleson, pp. 606-37. Oxford: Oxford University Press, 2008.

McMahon, Christopher. "Imaginative Faith: Apocalyptic, Science Fiction Theory, and Theology," *Dialog: A Journal of Theology* 47, no. 3 (2008): 271-77.

Mendels, Doron. "The Five Empires: A Note on a Propagandistic *Topos,*" *American Journal of Philology* 102 (1981): 330-37.

———. "A Note on the Tradition of Antiochus IV's Death," *Israel Exploration Journal* 31 (1981): 53-56.

———. *The Rise and Fall of Jewish Nationalism.* New York: Doubleday, 1992.

Mendenhall, George E. *Law and Covenant in Israel and the Ancient Near East.* Pittsburgh: Biblical Colloquium, 1955.

———. *The Tenth Generation: The Origins of the Biblical Tradition.* Baltimore: The Johns Hopkins University Press, 1973.

Merbach, Mitchell B. *The Thief, the Cross, and the Wheel: Pain and the Spectacle of Punishment in Medieval and Renaissance Europe.* Chicago: University of Chicago Press, 1999.

Metz, Johann Baptist. *Faith in History and Society: Toward a Practical Fundamental Theology.* Translated by J. Matthew Ashley. New York: Crossroad, 2007.

———. *A Passion for God: The Mystical Political Dimension of Christianity.* Edited and translated by J. Matthew Ashley. Mahwah, NJ: Paulist Press, 1998.

Meyers, Carol L. *The Tabernacle Menorah: A Synthetic Study of a Symbol from the Biblical Cult.* Missoula, MT: Scholars Press, 1976.

Meyers, Carol L., and Eric M. Meyers. *Zechariah 9–14.* The Anchor Bible 25C. New York: Doubleday, 1993.

Middleton, J. Richard. *The Liberating Image: The* Imago Dei *in Genesis 1.* Grand Rapids: Brazos Press, 2005.

Mikalson, Jon. D. *Ancient Greek Religion,* 2nd ed. Oxford: Wiley-Blackwell, 2010.

Milgrom, Jacob. *Leviticus: A Book of Ritual and Ethics: A Continental Commentary.* Minneapolis: Fortress, 2004.

Milik, J. T., ed., with the collaboration of Matthew Black. *The Books of Enoch: Aramaic Fragments of Qumrân Cave 4.* Oxford: Clarendon, 1976.

Millar, Fergus. "The Background to the Maccabean Revolution: Reflections on Martin Hengel's 'Judaism and Hellenism,'" *Journal of Jewish Studies* 29, no. 1 (1978): 1-21.

―――. "The Problem of Hellenistic Syria." In *Hellenism in the East: The Interaction of Greek and Non-Greek Civilizations from Syria to Central Asia after Alexander,* edited by Amélie Kuhrt and Susan Sherwin-White, pp. 110-33. Berkeley: University of California Press, 1987.

Miller, Daniel. "The Limits of Dominance." In *Domination and Resistance,* edited by Daniel Miller, Michael Rowlands, and Christopher Tilley, pp. 63-79. London: Unwin Hyman, 1989.

Miller, Daniel, Michael Rowlands, and Christopher Tilley. Introduction to *Domination and Resistance,* edited by Daniel Miller, Michael Rowlands, and Christopher Tilley. London: Unwin Hyman, 1989.

Miller, Patrick. *The Divine Warrior in Early Israel.* Cambridge, MA: Harvard University Press, 1973.

Mills, Mary. *Biblical Morality: Moral Perspectives in Old Testament Narratives.* Aldershot, UK: Ashgate, 2001.

―――. "Household and Table: Diasporic Boundaries in Daniel and Esther," *Catholic Biblical Quarterly* 68, no. 3 (2006): 408-20.

Mirzoeff, Nicholas. *The Visual Culture Reader.* London: Routledge, 1998.

Mitchell, Timothy. "Everyday Metaphors of Power," *Theory and Society* 19 (1990): 545-77.

Mittag, Peter Franz. *Antiochos IV. Epiphanes: Eine politische Biographie.* Berlin: Akademie Verlag, 2006.

Montgomery, James A. *A Critical and Exegetical Commentary on the Book of Daniel.* International Critical Commentary. New York: Charles Scribner's Sons, 1927.

Moor, Johannes C. de, ed. *A Bilingual Concordance to the Targum of the Prophets,* vol. 10. Leiden: Brill, 2002.

Moore, Barrington, Jr. *Injustice: The Social Bases of Obedience and Revolt.* White Plains, NY: M. E. Sharpe, 1978.

Moore, Stephen D. *God's Gym: Divine Male Bodies of the Bible.* London: Routledge, 1996.

Moore, Stephen D., and Fernando Segovia, eds. *Postcolonial Biblical Criticism: Interdisciplinary Intersections.* London: T. & T. Clark, 2005.

Morgan, M. Gwyn. "The Perils of Schematism: Polybius, Antiochus Epiphanes, and the 'Day of Eleusis,'" *Historia: Zeitschrift für Alte Geschichte* 39, no. 1 (1990): 37-76.

―――. "Response to Erich S. Gruen." In *Hellenistic History and Culture,* edited by Peter Green, pp. 264-70. Berkeley: University of California Press, 1993.

Mørkholm, Otto. *Antiochus IV of Syria.* Copenhagen: Gyldendal, 1966.

Mullen, Theodore E. "The Divine Witness and the Davidic Royal Grant: Ps 89:37-38," *Journal of Biblical Literature* 102, no. 2 (1983): 207-18.

Najman, Hindy. Review of G. Boccaccini, *Beyond the Essene Hypothesis. Association for Jewish Studies Review* 26 (2002): 352-54.

———. *Seconding Sinai: The Development of Mosaic Discourse in Second Temple Judaism.* Leiden: Brill, 2003.

Neer, Richard T. "Framing the Gift: The Siphnian Treasury at Delphi and the Politics of Public Art." In *The Cultures within Ancient Greek Culture: Contact, Conflict, Collaboration,* edited by Carol Dougherty and Leslie Kurke, pp. 129-52. Cambridge: Cambridge University Press, 2003.

Newby, Zahra. *Greek Athletics in the Roman World: Victory and Virtue.* Oxford: Oxford University Press, 2005.

Newel, Edward T. *The Coinage of the Eastern Seleucid Mints: From Seleucus I to Antiochus III.* Numismatic Studies I. New York: The American Numismatic Society, 1938.

Newman, Judith H. *Praying by the Book: The Scripturalization of Prayer in Second Temple Judaism.* Atlanta: Scholars Press, 1999.

Newsom, Carol A. *The Book of Job: A Contest of Moral Imaginations.* Oxford: Oxford University Press, 2003.

———. "The Development of 1 Enoch 6–19: Cosmology and Judgment," *Catholic Biblical Quarterly* 42 (1980): 310-29.

———. "Enoch 83–90: The Historical Résumé as Biblical Exegesis." Unpublished Seminar Paper, Harvard University, 1975.

———. "The Past as Revelation: History in Apocalyptic Literature," *Quarterly Review* 4, no. 3 (1984): 40-53.

———. *The Self as Symbolic Space: Constructing Identity and Community at Qumran.* Leiden: Brill, 2004.

Nickelsburg, George W. E. *1 Enoch 1: A Commentary on the Book of 1 Enoch, Chapters 1–36; 81–108.* Hermeneia. Minneapolis: Fortress, 2001.

———. "1 Enoch and Qumran Origins," *Society of Biblical Literature Seminar Papers* 25 (1986): 341-60.

———. "Apocalyptic and Myth in 1 Enoch 6–11," *Journal of Biblical Literature* 96, no. 3 (1977): 383-405.

———. "'Enoch' as Scientist, Sage, and Prophet: Content, Function, and Authorship in 1 Enoch," *Society of Biblical Literature Seminar Papers* 38 (1999): 203-30.

———. "Enochic Wisdom: An Alternative to the Mosaic Torah?" In *Hesed ve-emet: Studies in Honor of Ernest S. Frerichs,* edited by Jodi Magness and Seymour Gitin, pp. 123-32. Atlanta: Scholars Press, 1998.

———. "Enochic Wisdom and Its Relationship to the Mosaic Torah." In *The Early Enoch Literature,* edited by Gabriele Boccaccini and John J. Collins, pp. 81-94. Leiden: Brill, 2007.

———. "Response: Context, Text, and Social Setting of the Apocalypse of Weeks." In *Enoch and Qumran Origins: New Light on a Forgotten Connection,* edited by Gabriele Boccaccini, pp. 234-41. Grand Rapids: Eerdmans, 2005.

———. *Resurrection, Immortality, and Eternal Life in Intertestamental Judaism.* Harvard Theological Studies 56. Exp. ed. Cambridge, MA: Harvard University Press, 2006.

———. "Riches, the Rich, and God's Judgment in 1 Enoch 92–105 and the Gospel According to Luke," *New Testament Studies* 25 (1979): 324-44.

Nickelsburg, George W. E., and James C. VanderKam. *1 Enoch: A New Translation.* Minneapolis: Fortress, 2004.

Niditch, Susan. "War, Women, and Defilement in Numbers 31," *Semeia* 61 (1993): 39-58.

———. *War in the Hebrew Bible: A Study in the Ethics of Violence.* Oxford: Oxford University Press, 1993.

Nielsen, Kjeld. *Incense in Ancient Israel.* Leiden: Brill, 1986.

Nikkel, Marc. *Why Haven't You Left: Letters from Sudan.* Edited by Grant Lemarquand. New York: Church Publishing, 2006.

Norsa, M., G. Vitelli, V. Bartoletti, et al., eds. *Papiri greci e latini.* 15 vols. Florence: Pubblicazioni della Società Italiana per la ricerca dei papiri greci e latini in Egitto, 1912-1979.

Olson, Daniel C. "Recovering the Original Sequence of *1 Enoch* 91–93," *Journal for the Study of Pseudepigrapha* 11 (1993): 69-94.

Orlov, Andrei A. *The Enoch-Metatron Tradition.* Tübingen: Mohr Siebeck, 2005.

———. "Moses' Heavenly Counterpart in the *Book of Jubilees* and the *Exagoge* of Ezekiel the Tragedian," *Biblica* 88, no. 2 (2007): 151-73.

Osborne, Brian S. "Landscapes, Memory, Monuments, and Commemoration: Putting Identity in Its Place," *Canadian Ethnic Studies Journal* 33, no. 3 (2001): 39-77.

Ostwald, Martin. *Autonomia: Its Genesis and Early History.* Chico, CA: Scholars Press, 1982.

Otto, Walter. "Zur Geschichte der Zeit des 6. Ptolemäers," *Abhandlungen der Bayerischen Akademie der Wissenschaften* 11 (1934).

Pace, Sharon. *Daniel.* Smyth & Helwys Bible Commentary. Macon, GA: Smyth & Helwys, 2008.

Paltiel, Eliezer. "The Treaty of Apamea and the Later Seleucids," *Antichthon* 13 (1979): 30-41.

Pappas, Nickolas. "Fashion Seen as Something Imitative and Foreign," *British Journal of Aesthetics* 48, no. 1 (2008): 1-19.

Pastor, Jack. *Land and Economy in Ancient Palestine.* London: Routledge, 1997.

Patterson, Orlando. *Slavery and Social Death: A Comparative Study.* Cambridge, MA: Harvard University Press, 1982.

Pattison, Stephen. *Shame: Theory, Therapy, Theology.* Cambridge: Cambridge University Press, 2000.

Peristiany, J. G., ed. *Honour and Shame: The Values of Mediterranean Society.* Chicago: University of Chicago Press, 1966.

Perkins, Judith. *The Suffering Self: Pain and Narrative Representation in the Early Christian Era.* London: Routledge, 2003.

Pestman, P. W., ed. *Greek and Demotic Texts from the Zenon Archive.* Leiden: Brill, 1980.

Pile, Steve. "Introduction: Opposition, Political Identities and Spaces of Resistance." In *Geographies of Resistance,* edited by Steve Pile and Michael Keith, pp. 1-32. London: Routledge, 1997.

Piovanelli, Pierluigi. "'Sitting by the Waters of Dan,' or the 'Tricky Business' of Tracing the Social Profile of the Communities That Produced the Earliest Enochic Texts." In *The Early Enoch Literature,* edited by Gabriele Boccaccini and John J. Collins, pp. 257-81. Leiden: Brill, 2007.

Pippin, Tina. *Apocalyptic Bodies: The Biblical End of the World in Text and Image.* London: Routledge, 1999.

Plöger, Otto. *Theocracy and Eschatology.* Translated by S. Rudman. Oxford: Blackwell, 1968. Translation of *Theokratie und Eschatologie.* Neukirchen: Neukirchener Verlag, 1959.

Polaski, Donald. "*Mene, Mene, Tekel, Parsin:* Writing and Resistance in Daniel 5 and 6," *Journal of Biblical Literature* 123, no. 4 (2004): 649-69.

Pole, J. R., ed. *The Federalist*. Indianapolis: Hackett, 2005.

Pollard, Nigel. *Soldiers, Cities, and Civilians in Roman Syria*. Ann Arbor: University of Michigan Press, 2000.

Pomykala, Kenneth E. "A Scripture Profile of the Book of the Watchers." In *The Quest for Context and Meaning: Studies in Biblical Intertextuality in Honor of James A. Sanders*, edited by Craig A. Evans and Shemaryahu Talmon, pp. 263-84. Leiden: Brill, 1997.

Porter, Paul. *Metaphors and Monsters: A Literary Critical Study of Daniel 7 and 8*. Lund: Gleerup, 1983.

Portier-Young, Anathea. "Languages of Identity and Obligation: Daniel as Bilingual Book," *Vetus Testamentum* 60, no. 1 (2010): 98-115.

———. "Theologies of Resistance in Daniel, the Apocalypse of Weeks, the Book of Dreams, and the Testament of Moses." Ph.D. diss., Duke University, 2004.

Raaflaub, Kurt. *The Discovery of Freedom in Ancient Greece*. Chicago: University of Chicago Press, 2005.

Raaflaub, Kurt, Adalberto Giovannini, and Denis van Berchem, eds. *Opposition et resistances à l'Empire d'Auguste à Trajan*. Entretiens sur l'Antiquité classique 33. Geneva: Fondation Hardt, 1987.

Raditsa, Leo. "Bella Macedonica." In *Aufstieg und Niedergang der römischen Welt: Geschichte und Kultur Roms im Spiegel der neueren Forschung*, Tl. I, Bd. 1, edited by Hildegard Temporini, pp. 564-89. Berlin: Walter de Gruyter, 1972.

Rajak, Tessa. "Dying for the Law: The Martyr's Portrait in Jewish-Greek Literature." In *The Jewish Dialogue with Greece and Rome: Studies in Cultural and Social Interaction*, pp. 99-133. Leiden: Brill, 2001. Repr. from *Portraits: Biographical Representation in the Greek and Latin Literature of the Roman Empire*, edited by M. J. Edwards and Simon Swain, pp. 39-68. Oxford: Oxford University Press, 1997.

———. "Hasmonean Kingship and the Invention of Tradition." In *Aspects of Hellenistic Kingship*, edited by Per Bilde, Troels Engberg-Pedersen, Lise Hannestad, and Jan Zahle, pp. 99-116. Aarhus: Aarhus University Press, 1996.

Rappaport, Uriel. "Apocalyptic Vision and Preservation of Historical Memory," *Journal for the Study of Judaism in the Persian, Hellenistic, and Roman Periods* 23 (1992): 217-26.

Redditt, Paul L. *Daniel*. The New Century Bible Commentary. Sheffield: Sheffield Academic Press, 1999.

———. "Daniel 11 and the Sociohistorical Setting of the Book of Daniel," *Catholic Biblical Quarterly* 60 (1998): 463-74.

Reed, Annette Yoshiko. *Fallen Angels and the History of Judaism and Christianity: The Reception of Enochic Literature*. Cambridge: Cambridge University Press, 2005.

———. "Heavenly Ascent, Angelic Descent, and the Transmission of Knowledge in 1 Enoch 6–16." In *Heavenly Realms and Earthly Realities in Late Antique Religions*, edited by Annette Yoshiko Reed and Ra'anan Boustan, pp. 47-66. Cambridge: Cambridge University Press, 2004.

———. "Interrogating 'Enochic Judaism': 1 Enoch as Evidence for Intellectual History, Social Realities, and Literary Tradition." In *Enoch and Qumran Origins*, edited by Gabriele Boccaccini, pp. 336-44. Grand Rapids: Eerdmans, 2005.

Reed, David. "Rethinking John's Social Setting: Hidden Transcript, Anti-Language, and the Negotiation of the Empire," *Biblical Theology Bulletin* 36 (2006): 93-106.

Reese, Günter. *Die Geschichte Israels in der Auffassung des frühen Judentums: Eine Untersuchung der Tiervision und der Zehnwochenapokalypse des äthiopischen Henochbuches, der Geschichtsdarstellung der Assumptio Mosis und der des 4 Esrabuches.* Berlin: Philo, 1999. Reprint of diss., Heidelberg University, 1967.

Reeves, John C. "Complicating the Notion of an 'Enochic Judaism.'" In *Enoch and Qumran Origins*, edited by Gabriele Boccaccini, pp. 373-83. Grand Rapids: Eerdmans, 2005.

————. "Scriptural Authority in Early Judaism." In *Living Traditions of the Bible: Scripture in Jewish, Christian, and Muslim Practice*, edited by James E. Bowley, pp. 63-84. St. Louis: Chalice Press, 1999.

Reid, Stephen Breck. *Enoch and Daniel: A Form Critical and Sociological Study of the Historical Apocalypses*, 2nd ed. North Richland Hills, TX: BIBAL, 2004.

————. "The Sociological Setting of the Historical Apocalypses of 1 Enoch and the Book of Daniel." Ph.D. diss., Emory University, 1981.

Reiner, Erica. *Astral Magic in Babylonia.* Transactions of the American Philosophical Society, vol. 85, pt. 4. Philadelphia: American Philosophical Society, 1995.

Reynolds, Craig J. *Seditious Histories: Contesting Thai and Southeast Asian Pasts.* Seattle: University of Washington Press, 2006.

Ricoeur, Paul. Foreword to *The Book of Daniel*, by André Lacocque. Translated by D. Pellauer. English rev. ed. Atlanta: John Knox, 1979.

Rieger, Joerg. *Christ and Empire: From Paul to Postcolonial Times.* Minneapolis: Fortress, 2007.

————. "Christian Theology and Empires." In *Empire: The Christian Tradition: New Readings of Classical Theologians*, edited by Kwok Pui-lan, Don H. Compier, and Joerg Rieger, pp. 1-13. Minneapolis: Fortress, 2007.

Riu, Xavier. *Dionysism and Comedy.* Oxford: Rowman & Littlefield, 1999.

Robben, Antonius C. G. M. "The Assault on Basic Trust: Disappearance, Protest, and Reburial in Argentina." In *Cultures Under Siege: Collective Violence and Trauma*, edited by Antonius C. G. M. Robben and Marcelo M. Suárez-Orozco, pp. 70-101. Cambridge: Cambridge University Press, 2000.

————. "The Fear of Indifference: Combatants' Anxieties about the Political Identity of Civilians during Argentina's Dirty War." In *Societies of Fear: The Legacies of Civil War, Violence, and Terror in Latin America*, edited by Kees Koonings and Dirk Kruijt, pp. 125-40. New York: Zed Books, 1999.

————. *Political Violence and Trauma in Argentina.* Philadelphia: University of Pennsylvania Press, 2005.

————. "State Terror in the Netherworld: Disappearance and Reburial in Argentina." In *Death, Mourning, and Burial: A Cross-Cultural Reader*, edited by Antonius C. G. M. Robben, pp. 134-48. Oxford: Blackwell, 2004.

Robert, Louis. Review of Franz Georg Maier, *Griechische Mauerbauinschriften. Gnomon* 42 (1970): 579-603.

Rochberg, Francesca. *The Heavenly Writing: Divination, Horoscopy, and Astronomy in Mesopotamian Culture.* Cambridge: Cambridge University Press, 2004.

Rowland, Christopher. "Apocalyptic Literature." In *It Is Written: Scripture Citing Scripture*, edited by D. A. Carson and H. G. M. Williamson, pp. 170-89. New York: Cambridge University Press, 1988.

————. *The Open Heaven: A Study of Apocalyptic in Judaism and Early Christianity.* New York: Crossroad, 1982.

Rudolf-Wicker, Hans. "From Complex Culture to Cultural Complexity." In *Debating Cul-*

tural Hybridity: Multi-Cultural Identities and the Politics of Anti-Racism, edited by Pnina Werbner and Tariq Modood, pp. 29-45. London: Zed Books, 1997.

Rummel, Rudolph J. "20th Century Democide." No pages. Cited 12 Feb. 2010. Online: http://www.hawaii.edu/powerkills/20TH.HTM.

———. *China's Bloody Century: Genocide and Mass Murder Since 1900.* Rutgers, NJ: Transaction Publishers, 1991.

———. *Death by Government.* New Brunswick, NJ: Transaction Publishers, 1997.

———. *Democide: Nazi Genocide and Mass Murder.* Rutgers, NJ: Transaction Publishers, 1992.

———. *Lethal Politics: Soviet Genocides and Mass Murders 1917-1987.* Rutgers, NJ: Transaction Publishers, 1990.

Ryan, Simon. "Inscribing the Emptiness: Cartography, Exploration and the Construction of Australia." In *De-Scribing Empire: Post-colonialism and Textuality,* edited by Chris Tiffin and Alan Lawson, pp. 115-30. London: Routledge, 1994.

Saatsoglou-Paliadeli, Chryssoula. "Aspects of Ancient Macedonian Costume," *The Journal of Hellenic Studies* 113 (1993): 122-47.

Sacchi, Paolo. *The History of the Second Temple Period.* Sheffield: Sheffield Academic Press, 2000.

———. *Jewish Apocalyptic and Its History.* Translated by William J. Short. Sheffield: Sheffield Academic Press, 1990.

———. "The Theology of Early Enochism and Apocalyptic: The Problem of the Relation between Form and Content of the Apocalypses; the Worldview of the Apocalypses," *Henoch* 24 (2002): 77-85.

Said, Edward. *Culture and Imperialism.* New York: Knopf, 1993.

Saliers, Donald E. "Liturgy and Ethics: Some New Beginnings," *Journal of Religious Ethics* 7, no. 2 (1979): 173-89.

Salimovich, Sofia, Elizabeth Lira, and Eugenia Weinstein. "Victims of Fear: The Social Psychology of Repression." In *Fear at the Edge: State Terror and Resistance in Latin America,* edited by Juan E. Corradi, Patricia Weiss Fagen, and Manuel Antonio Garretón, pp. 72-89. Berkeley: University of California Press, 1992.

Salmeri, Giovanni. "Empire and Collective Mentality: The Transformation of *eutaxia* from the Fifth Century BC to the Second Century AD." In *The Province Strikes Back: Imperial Dynamics in the Eastern Mediterranean,* edited by Björn Forsén and Giovanni Salmeri, pp. 137-55. Helsinki: The Finnish Institute of Athens, 2008.

Samuel, Alan E. *Greek and Roman Chronology: Calendars and Years in Classical Antiquity.* Munich: C. H. Beck, 1972.

Sánchez, David. *From Patmos to the Barrio: Subverting Imperial Myths.* Minneapolis: Fortress, 2008.

Sanders, E. P. "The Genre of Palestinian Jewish Apocalypses." In *Apocalypticism in the Mediterranean World and the Near East: Proceedings of the International Colloquium on Apocalypticism, Uppsala, August 12-17, 1979,* edited by David Hellholm, pp. 447-60. Tübingen: JCB Mohr (Paul Siebeck), 1983.

———. *Judaism: Practice and Belief, 63 BCE–66 CE.* Philadelphia: Trinity Press International, 1992.

———. *Paul and Palestinian Judaism: A Comparison of Patterns of Religion.* Philadelphia: Fortress, 1977.

Sansone, David. *Greek Athletics and the Genesis of Sport*. Berkeley: University of California Press, 1992.

Sasson, Jack M. "Circumcision in the Ancient Near East," *Journal of Biblical Literature* 85 (1966): 473-76.

Satran, David. "Daniel: Seer, Philosopher, Holy Man." In *Ideal Figures in Ancient Judaism: Profiles and Paradigms*, edited by John J. Collins and George W. E. Nickelsburg, pp. 33-48. Society of Biblical Literature Septuagint and Cognate Studies 12. Chico, CA: Scholars Press, 1980.

Scala, Rudolf von. *Die Studien des Polybios*. Stuttgart: Kohlhammer, 1890.

Scanlon, Thomas F. *Eros and Greek Athletics*. Oxford: Oxford University Press, 2002.

Scarry, Elaine. *The Body in Pain: The Making and Unmaking of the World*. Oxford: Oxford University Press, 1985.

Schäfer, Peter. *The History of the Jews in the Greco-Roman World,* rev. ed. London: Routledge, 2003.

Schatzberg, Michael. *The Dialectics of Oppression in Zaire*. Bloomington: Indiana University Press, 1991.

Schiffman, Lawrence H. *From Text to Tradition: A History of Second Temple and Rabbinic Judaism*. Hoboken, NJ: Ktav, 1991.

Schmitt, Carl. *Political Theology: Four Chapters on the Concept of Sovereignty*. Chicago: University of Chicago Press, 2005.

Schniedewind, William. *How the Bible Became a Book*. Cambridge: Cambridge University Press, 2004.

Schürer, Emil. "Zu II Mcc 6,7 (monatliche Geburtstagsfeier)," *Zeitschrift für die neutestamentliche Wissenschaft und die Kunde der älteren Kirche* 2 (1901): 48-52.

Schüssler Fiorenza, Elisabeth. *The Power of the Word: Scripture and the Rhetoric of Empire*. Philadelphia: Fortress, 2007.

Schwartz, Daniel R. *2 Maccabees*. CEJL. Berlin: Walter de Gruyter, 2008.

——. "Antiochus IV Epiphanes in Jerusalem." In *Historical Perspectives from the Hasmoneans to bar Kokhba in Light of the Dead Sea Scrolls: Proceedings of the Fourth International Symposium of the Orion Center for the Study of the Dead Sea Scrolls and Associated Literature, 27-31 January, 1999*, edited by David Goodblatt, Avital Pinnick, and Daniel R. Schwartz, pp. 45-56. Leiden: Brill, 2001.

——. "Why Did Antiochus Have to Fall (II Maccabees 9:7)?" In *Heavenly Tablets: Interpretation, Identity and Tradition in Ancient Judaism*, edited by Lynn LiDonnici and Andrea Lieber, pp. 257-64. Leiden: Brill, 2007.

Schwartz, Seth. *Imperialism and Jewish Society, 200 B.C.E. to 640 C.E.* Princeton: Princeton University Press, 2001.

Scott, James C. *Domination and the Arts of Resistance: Hidden Transcripts*. New Haven: Yale University Press, 1990.

——. *Weapons of the Weak: Everyday Forms of Peasant Resistance*. New Haven: Yale University Press, 1985.

Scurlock, Joann. "167 BCE: Hellenism or Reform?" *Journal for the Study of Judaism in the Persian, Hellenistic, and Roman Periods* 31 (2000): 125-61.

Seaford, Richard. *Dionysos*. New York: Routledge, 2006.

——. "Dionysus as Destroyer of the Household: Homer, Tragedy, and the Polis." In *Masks of Dionysus*, edited by Thomas H. Carpenter and Christopher A. Faraone, pp. 115-46. Ithaca, NY: Cornell University Press, 1993.

————. *Reciprocity and Ritual: Homer and Tragedy in the Developing City-State.* Oxford: Oxford University Press, 1994.

Segert, Stanislav. "Poetic Structures in the Hebrew Sections of the Book of Daniel." In *Solving Riddles and Untying Knots: Biblical, Epigraphic and Semitic Studies in Honor of Jonas C. Greenfield,* edited by Ziony Zevit, Seymour Gitin, and Michael Sokoloff, pp. 261-75. Winona Lake, IN: Eisenbrauns, 1995.

Seow, Choon-Leong. *Daniel.* Westminster Bible Companion. Louisville: Westminster John Knox, 2003.

————. "From Mountain to Mountain: The Reign of God in Daniel 2." In *A God So Near: Essays on Old Testament Theology in Honor of Patrick D. Miller,* edited by Brent A. Strawn and Nancy R. Bowen, pp. 335-74. Winona Lake, IN: Eisenbrauns, 2003.

Sharp, Joanne P., Paul Routledge, Chris Philo, and Ronan Paddison, eds. *Entanglements of Power: Geographies of Domination/Resistance.* London: Routledge, 2000.

Sherwin-White, Susan M. "Seleucid Babylonia: A Case Study for the Installation and Development of Greek Rule." In *Hellenism in the East: The Interaction of Greek and Non-Greek Civilizations from Syria to Central Asia after Alexander,* edited by Amélie Kuhrt and Susan Sherwin-White, pp. 1-31. Berkeley: University of California Press, 1987.

Sherwin-White, Susan M., and Amélie Kuhrt. *From Samarkhand to Sardis: A New Approach to the Seleucid Empire.* Berkeley: University of California Press, 1993.

Sievers, Joseph. *The Hasmoneans and Their Supporters: From Mattathias to the Death of John Hyrcanus I.* Atlanta: Scholars Press, 1990.

————. "Jerusalem, the Akra, and Josephus." In *Josephus and the History of the Greco-Roman Period: Essays in Honor of Morton Smith,* edited by Fausto Parente and Joseph Sievers, pp. 195-209. Leiden: Brill, 1994.

Skinner, John. *A Critical and Exegetical Commentary on Genesis.* New York: Charles Scribner's Sons, 1910.

Sluka, Jeffrey A. "Introduction: State Terror and Anthropology." In *Death Squad: The Anthropology of State Terror,* edited by Jeffrey A. Sluka, pp. 1-45. Philadelphia: University of Pennsylvania Press, 2000.

Smith, Anthony D. "Chosen Peoples: Why Ethnic Groups Survive," *Ethnic and Racial Studies* 15, no. 3 (1992): 440-49.

————. *National Identity.* London: Penguin, 1991.

Smith, Daniel L. "Jeremiah as Prophet of Nonviolent Resistance," *Journal for the Study of the Old Testament* 13, no. 43 (1989): 95-107.

————. *The Religion of the Landless: The Social Context of the Babylonian Exile.* Bloomington, IN: Meyer Stone, 1989.

Smith, Jonathan Z. "Cross-Cultural Reflections on Apocalypticism." In *Ancient and Modern Perspectives on the Bible and Culture: Essays in Honor of Hans Dieter Betz,* pp. 281-85, edited by Adela Yarbro Collins. Atlanta: Scholars Press, 1998.

Smith, Mark S. *The Early History of God: Yahweh and the Other Deities in Ancient Israel,* 2nd ed. Grand Rapids: Eerdmans, 2002.

Smith-Christopher, Daniel L. *A Biblical Theology of Exile,* Overtures to Biblical Theology. Minneapolis: Fortress, 2002.

————. "The Book of Daniel." In *The New Interpreter's Bible,* vol. 7, pp. 19-152. Nashville: Abingdon, 1996.

————. "Gandhi on Daniel 6: Some Thoughts on a 'Cultural Exegesis' of the Bible," *Biblical Interpretation* 1, no. 3 (1993): 321-28.

432

―――. "Prayers and Dreams: Power and Diaspora Identities in the Social Setting of the Daniel Tales." In *The Book of Daniel: Composition and Reception,* vol. 1, edited by John J. Collins and Peter Flint, pp. 266-90. Leiden: Brill, 2001.

Spatafora, Andrea. "Hellénisme et Judaïsme: Rencontre ou Confrontation: Étude de 1 M 1,11-15, 2 M 4,7-20 et Sg 1,16–2,24," *Science et Esprit* 56, no. 1 (2004): 81-102.

Spek, Robartus van der. "Darius III, Alexander the Great, and Babylonian Scholarship." In *A Persian Perspective: Essays in Memory of Heleen Sancisi-Weerdenburg,* edited by Wouder Henkelman and Amélie Kuhrt, pp. 289-346. Leiden: Nederlands Instituut voor het nabije Oosten, 2003.

Spiegelberg, W., ed. *Die Demotischen Urkunden des Zenon-Archivs.* Dem. Stud. 8, Nos. 1–25. Leipzig: Hinrichs, 1929.

Stephens, Susan A. *Seeing Double: Intercultural Poetics in Ptolemaic Alexandria.* Berkeley: University of California Press, 2003.

Stevens, Marty E. *Temples, Tithes, and Taxes: The Temples and the Economic Life of Ancient Israel.* Peabody, MA: Hendrickson, 2006.

Stiebert, Johanna. *The Construction of Shame in the Hebrew Bible: The Prophetic Contribution.* London: Sheffield Academic Press, 2002.

Stone, Michael E. "Apocalyptic Literature." In *Early Judaism and Its Modern Interpreters,* edited by Robert A. Kraft and George W. E. Nickelsburg, pp. 383-442. Philadelphia: Fortress, 1986.

―――. "The Book of Enoch and Judaism in the Third Century B.C.E.," *Catholic Biblical Quarterly* 40 (1978): 479-92.

Stubbs, Monya A. "Subjection, Reflection, Resistance: An African American Reading of the Three-Dimensional Process of Empowerment in Romans 13 and the Free Market Economy." In *Navigating Romans through Cultures: Challenging Readings by Charting a New Course,* edited by Yeo Khiok-khng (K.K.), pp. 171-97. London: Continuum, 2004.

Stuckenbruck, Loren. *1 Enoch 91–108.* CEJL. Berlin: Walter de Gruyter, 2007.

―――. *Angel Veneration and Christology: A Study in Early Judaism and the Christology of the Apocalypse of John.* Tübingen: Mohr, 1995.

―――. "The Plant Metaphor in Its Inner-Enochic and Early Jewish Context." In *Enoch and Qumran Origins: New Light on a Forgotten Connection,* edited by Gabriele Boccaccini, pp. 210-12. Grand Rapids: Eerdmans, 2005.

Stuhlmueller, Carroll. "God in the Witness of Israel's Election." In *God in Contemporary Thought,* edited by Sebastian Matczak, pp. 349-78. New York: Learned Publications, 1977.

Suárez-Orozco, Marcelo M. "Speaking of the Unspeakable: Toward a Psychosocial Understanding of Responses to Terror," *Ethos* 18, no. 3 (1990): 353-83.

Sugirtharajah, Rasiah S., ed. *The Postcolonial Biblical Reader.* Oxford: Blackwell, 2006.

Sukumar, Raman. *The Living Elephants: Evolutionary Ecology, Behavior, and Conservation.* Oxford: Oxford University Press, 2003.

Suter, David. "Fallen Angel, Fallen Priest: The Problem of Family Purity in 1 Enoch," *Hebrew Union College Annual* 50 (1979): 115-35.

―――. "Revisiting Fallen Angel, Fallen Priest," *Henoch* 24 (2002): 137-42.

―――. "Temples and the Temple in the Early Enoch Tradition: Memory, Vision, and Expectation." In *The Early Enoch Literature,* edited by Gabriele Boccaccini and John J. Collins, pp. 195-218. Leiden: Brill, 2007.

Swain, Joseph Ward. "The Theory of the Four Monarchies: Opposition History under the Roman Empire," *Classical Philology* 35, no. 1 (1940): 1-21.

Swanson, D. D. Review of Gabriele Boccaccini, ed., *Enoch and Qumran Origins: New Light on a Forgotten Connection*. *Journal for the Study of the Old Testament* 30 (2006): 161-62.

Sweeney, Marvin A. "The End of Eschatology in Daniel? Theological and Socio-Political Ramifications of the Changing Contexts of Interpretation," *Biblical Interpretation* 9, no. 2 (2001): 123-40.

Sweet, Waldo E. *Sport and Recreation in Ancient Greece: A Sourcebook with Translations.* Oxford: Oxford University Press, 1987.

Taussig, Michael. "Culture of Terror — Space of Death: Roger Casement's Putumayo Report and the Explanation of Torture," *Comparative Studies in Society and History* 26 (1984): 467-97.

Taylor, James Ellis. "Seleucid Rule in Palestine." Ph.D. diss., Duke University, 1979.

Tcherikover, Victor. *Hellenistic Civilization and the Jews.* Translated by S. Applebaum. Philadelphia: Jewish Publication Society, 1959. Repr. with pref. by John J. Collins. Peabody, MA: Hendrickson, 1999.

Terdiman, Richard. *Discourse/Counter-Discourse: The Theory and Practice of Symbolic Resistance in Nineteenth Century France.* Ithaca, NY: Cornell University Press, 1985.

"Tetradrachm of Seleucus I [Iran, excavated at Pasargadae] (1974.105.9)." No pages. Cited 23 April 2008. Online: http://www.metmuseum.org/toah/ho/04/wam/ho_1974.105.9 .htm

Thiel, John. *Senses of Tradition: Continuity and Development in Catholic Faith.* Oxford: Oxford University Press, 2000.

Thorne, J. A. "Warfare and Agriculture: The Economic Impact of Devastation in Classical Greece," *Greek, Roman, and Byzantine Studies* 42 (2001): 225-53.

Tigchelaar, Eibert J. C. "Evaluating the Discussions Concerning the Original Order of Chapters 91–93 and Codicological Data Pertaining to 4Q212 and Chester Beatty XII Enoch." In *Enoch and Qumran Origins: New Light on a Forgotten Connection*, edited by Gabriele Boccaccini, pp. 220-23. Grand Rapids: Eerdmans, 2005.

———. *Prophets of Old and the Day of the End: Zechariah, the Book of Watchers, and Apocalyptic.* Leiden: Brill, 1996.

Tiller, Patrick A. *A Commentary on the Animal Apocalypse of* 1 Enoch. Atlanta: Scholars Press, 1993.

———. "The Sociological Settings of the Components of 1 Enoch." In *The Early Enoch Literature*, edited by Gabriele Boccaccini and John J. Collins, pp. 237-55. Leiden: Brill, 2007.

Tite, Philip. "Textual and Redactional Aspects of the Book of Dreams (1 Enoch 83–90)," *Biblical Theology Bulletin* 31 (2001): 106-120.

Toorn, Karel van der. "Why Wisdom Became a Secret: On Wisdom as a Written Genre." In *Wisdom Literature in Mesopotamia and Israel*, edited by Richard Clifford, pp. 21-29. Atlanta: Society of Biblical Literature, 2007.

Torres-Rivas, Edelberto. "Epilogue: Notes of Terror, Violence, Fear and Democracy." In *Societies of Fear: The Legacies of Civil War, Violence, and Terror in Latin America*, edited by Kees Koonings and Dirk Kruijt, pp. 285-300. New York: Zed Books, 1999.

Towner, W. Sibley. *Daniel.* Atlanta: John Knox Press, 1984.

———. "Retributional Theology in the Apocalyptic Setting," *Union Seminary Quarterly Review* 26, no. 3 (1971): 203-14.

Tracy, David. *The Analogical Imagination: Christian Theology and the Culture of Pluralism.* New York: Crossroad, 1981.

———. "An Interview with David Tracy." By Lois Malcolm. *The Christian Century* (Feb. 13-20, 2002): 24-30.

Trelstad, Marit, ed. *Cross Examinations: Readings on the Meaning of the Cross Today.* Minneapolis: Fortress, 2006.

Tromp, Johannes. *The Assumption of Moses: A Critical Edition with Commentary.* Leiden: Brill, 1993.

Ullendorff, E. "An Aramaic *'Vorlage'* of the Ethiopic Text of Enoch?" In *Atti del Convegno Internazionale di Studi Etiopici.* Problemi attuali di scienza e di cultura 48, pp. 259-67. Rome: Accademia Nazionale dei Lincei, 1960.

———. *Ethiopia and the Bible.* London: Oxford University Press, 1968.

Valeta, David. "Court or Jester Tales? Resistance and Social Reality in Daniel 1–6," *Perspectives in Religious Studies* 32 (2005): 309-24.

———. *Lions and Ovens and Visions: A Satirical Reading of Daniel 1–6.* Sheffield: Sheffield Phoenix, 2008.

———. "Polyglossia and Parody: Language in Daniel 1–6." In *Bakhtin and Genre Theory in Biblical Studies,* edited by Roland Boer, pp. 91-108. Atlanta: Society of Biblical Literature, 2007.

VanderKam, James C. "1 Enoch, Enochic Motifs, and Enoch in Early Christian Literature." In *The Jewish Apocalyptic Heritage in Early Christianity,* edited by James C. VanderKam and William Adler, pp. 33-101. Minneapolis: Fortress, 1996.

———. "2 Maccabees 6, 7A and Calendrical Change in Jerusalem," *Journal for the Study of Judaism in the Persian, Hellenistic, and Roman Periods* 12, no. 1 (1981): 52-74.

———. *Calendars in the Dead Sea Scrolls: Measuring Time.* New York: Routledge, 1998.

———. *Enoch and the Growth of an Apocalyptic Tradition.* Catholic Biblical Quarterly Monograph Series 16. Washington, DC: Catholic Biblical Association of America, 1984.

———. *From Joshua to Caiaphas: High Priests after the Exile.* Minneapolis: Fortress, 2004.

———. *From Revelation to Canon: Studies in the Hebrew Bible and Second Temple Literature.* Leiden: Brill, 2000.

———. "The Interpretation of Genesis in *1 Enoch.*" In *The Bible at Qumran: Text, Shape, and Interpretation,* edited by Peter W. Flint, pp. 129-48. Grand Rapids: Eerdmans, 2001.

———. "Mapping Second Temple Judaism." In *The Early Enoch Literature,* edited by Gabriele Boccaccini and John J. Collins, pp. 1-20. Leiden: Brill, 2007.

———. "Open and Closed Eyes in the Animal Apocalypse (*1 Enoch* 85–90)." In *The Idea of Biblical Interpretation: Essays in Honor of James L. Kugel,* edited by Hindy Najman and Judith Newman, pp. 279-92. Leiden: Brill, 2004.

———. "Studies in the Apocalypse of Weeks (*1 Enoch* 93:1-10; 91:11-17)," *Catholic Biblical Quarterly* 46 (1984): 511-23.

VanGemeren, W. A., ed. *New International Dictionary of Old Testament Theology and Exegesis.* 5 vols. Grand Rapids: Zondervan, 1997.

Vaux, Roland de. *Ancient Israel: Its Life and Institutions.* Translated by John McHugh. New York: McGraw-Hill, 1961.

Veijola, Timo. "The Witness in the Clouds: Ps 89:38," *Journal of Biblical Literature* 37 (1988): 413-17.

Venter, Pieter. "Daniel 9: A Penitential Prayer in Apocalyptic Garb." In *The Development of Penitential Prayer in Second Temple Judaism,* edited by Mark J. Boda, Daniel K. Falk, and Rodney A. Werline, pp. 33-49. Vol. 2 of *Seeking the Favor of God.* Leiden: Brill, 2007.

———. "Spatiality in Enoch's Journeys (1 Enoch 12–36)." In *Wisdom and Apocalypticism in the Dead Sea Scrolls and in the Biblical Tradition,* edited by Florentino García Martínez, pp. 211-30. Leuven: Leuven University Press, 2003.

———. "Spatiality in the Second Parable of Enoch." In *Enoch and the Messiah Son of Man: Revisiting the Book of Parables,* edited by Gabriele Boccaccini, pp. 403-12. Grand Rapids: Eerdmans, 2007.

Versnel, H. S. *Triumphus: An Inquiry into the Origin, Development and Meaning of the Roman Triumph.* Leiden: Brill, 1970.

Vian, Francis. *La guerre des géants: le mythe avant l'époque hellénistique.* Paris: Librairie C. Klincksieck, 1952.

Vidal-Naquet, Pierre. "The Black Hunter and the Origin of the Athenian *Ephebeia*." In *The Black Hunter: Forms of Thought and Forms of Society in the Greek World.* Translated by Andrew Szegedy-Maszak, pp. 106-28. Baltimore: Johns Hopkins University Press, 1986.

Walbank, F. W. "Monarchies and Monarchic Ideas." In *The Cambridge Ancient History,* vol. 7, part 1: *The Hellenistic World,* edited by A. E. Astin, F. W. Walbank, M. W. Fredriksen, and R. M. Ogilvie, pp. 62-100. Cambridge: Cambridge University Press, 1984.

Walraven, Klaas van, and Jon Abbink. "Rethinking Resistance in African History: An Introduction." In *Rethinking Resistance: Revolt and Violence in African History,* edited by Jon Abbink, Mirjam de Bruijn, and Klaas van Walraven, pp. 1-40. Leiden: Brill, 2003.

Walter, Eugene Victor. *Terror and Resistance: A Study of Political Violence.* New York: Oxford University Press, 1969.

Weber, Max. *Economy and Society.* Edited by Guenther Roth and Claus Wittich. Translated by Ephraim Fischoff. Berkeley: University of California Press, 1978. Translation of *Wirtschaft und Gesellschaft: Grundriss der verstehenden Soziologie,* 4th ed. Edited by Johannes Winckelmann. Tübingen: J. C. B. Mohr (Siebeck), 1956.

Weitzman, Steven. *Surviving Sacrilege: Cultural Persistence in Jewish Antiquity.* Cambridge, MA: Harvard University Press, 2005.

Welburn, Andrew J. *From a Virgin Womb: The Apocalypse of Adam and the Virgin Birth.* Leiden: Brill, 2008.

Werbner, Pnina. "The Dialectics of Cultural Hybridity." Introduction to *Debating Cultural Hybridity: Multi-Cultural Identities and the Politics of Anti-Racism.* Edited by Pnina Werbner and Tariq Modood. London: Zed Books, 1997.

Werline, Rodney A. "Prayer, Politics, and Social Vision in Daniel 9." In *The Development of Penitential Prayer in Second Temple Judaism,* edited by Mark J. Boda, Daniel K. Falk, and Rodney A. Werline, pp. 17-32. Vol. 2 of *Seeking the Favor of God.* Leiden: Brill, 2007.

West, Gerald O. "And the Dumb Do Speak: Articulating Incipient Readings of the Bible in Marginalized Communities." In *The Bible in Ethics: The Second Sheffield Colloquium,* edited by John William Rogerson, Margaret Davies, and M. Daniel Carroll R., pp. 174-92. London: Continuum, 1995.

———. "Gauging the Grain in a More Nuanced and Literary Manner: A Cautionary Tale Concerning the Contribution of the Social Sciences to Biblical Interpretation." In *Re-*

thinking Contexts, Rereading Texts: Contributions from the Social Sciences to Biblical Interpretation, edited by M. Daniel Carroll R., pp. 75-105. London: Continuum, 2000.

Westermann, William Linn. "Enslaved Persons Who Are Free," *American Journal of Philology* 59, no. 1 (1938): 1-30.

———. *The Slave Systems of Greek and Roman Antiquity.* Memoirs of the American Philosophical Society 40. Philadelphia: American Philosophical Society, 1955.

Wheelock, Wade T. "The Problem of Ritual Language: From Information to Situation," *Journal of the American Academy of Religion* 50, no. 1 (1982): 49-71.

Whiston, William, ed. and trans. *The Works of Flavius Josephus.* Edinburgh: Thomas Nelson & Peter Brown, 1828.

Whitfield, Peter. *New Found Lands: Maps in the History of Exploration.* London: Routledge, 1998.

Wiesehöfer, Josef. "Vom 'oberen Asien' zur 'gesamten bewohnten Welt': Die hellenistischrömische Weltreiche-Theorie." In *Europa, Tausendjähriges Reich und Neue Welt: Zwei Jahrtausende Geschichte und Utopie in der Rezeption des Danielbuches,* edited by Mariano Delgado, Klaus Koch, and Edgar Marsch, pp. 66-81. Stuttgart: Universitätsverlag Freiburg Schweiz, 2003.

Will, Édouard. "The Succession to Alexander." In *The Cambridge Ancient History,* vol. 7, part 1: *The Hellenistic World,* edited by A. E. Astin, F. W. Walbank, M. W. Fredriksen, and R. M. Ogilvie, pp. 23-61. Cambridge: Cambridge University Press, 1984.

Will, Édouard, and Claude Orrieux. *Ioudaïsmos-hellènismos: essai sur le judaïsme judéen à l'époque hellénistique.* Nancy: Presses universitaires de Nancy, 1986.

Williams, Raymond. *Marxism and Literature.* Oxford: Oxford University Press, 1977.

Wills, Lawrence M. *The Jewish Novel in the Ancient World.* Ithaca, NY: Cornell University Press, 1995.

Wilson, Gerald H. "The Prayer of Daniel 9: Reflection on Jeremiah 29," *Journal for the Study of the Old Testament* 15, no. 48 (1990): 91-99.

Wolf, Eric R. *Europe and the People without History.* Berkeley: University of California Press, 1982.

Wolff, Hans Walter. "The Kerygma of the Deuteronomic Historical Work." Translated by Frederick C. Prussner. In *The Vitality of Old Testament Traditions,* 2nd ed., edited by Walter Brueggemann and Hans Walter Wolff, pp. 83-100, 157-59. Atlanta: John Knox, 1975.

Woude, A. S. van der, ed. *The Book of Daniel in the Light of New Findings.* Leuven: Leuven University Press, 1993.

Wright, Benjamin, III. "1 Enoch and Ben Sira: Wisdom and Apocalypticism in Relationship." In *The Early Enoch Literature,* edited by Gabriele Boccaccini and John J. Collins, pp. 159-76. Leiden: Brill, 2007.

———. "Ben Sira and the Book of the Watchers on the Legitimate Priesthood." In *Intertextual Studies in Ben Sira and Tobit: Studies in Honor of Alexander A. Di Lella,* edited by Jeremy Corley and Vincent Skemp, pp. 241-54. Washington, DC: Catholic Biblical Association of America, 2005.

Wrigley, Richard. "Censorship and Anonymity in Eighteenth-Century French Art Criticism," *Oxford Art Journal* 6, no. 2 (1983): 7-28.

Wyrick, Jed. *The Ascension of Authorship: Attribution and Canon Formation in Jewish, Hellenistic, and Christian Traditions.* Cambridge, MA: Harvard University Press, 2004.

Young, James E. "Memory and Counter-Memory: The End of Monument in Germany," *Harvard Design Magazine* 9 (1999): 6-13.

Yuge, Toru, and Masaoki Doi, eds. *Forms of Control and Subordination in Antiquity.* Leiden: Brill, 1988.

Zahle, Jan. "Religious Motifs on Seleucid Coins." In *Religion and Religious Practice in the Seleucid Kingdom,* edited by Per Bilde, Troels Engberg-Pedersen, Lise Hannestad, and Jan Zahle, pp. 125-35. Aarhus: Aarhus University Press, 1990.

Zanker, Paul. *The Power of Images in the Age of Augustus.* Translated by Alan Shapiro. Ann Arbor: University of Michigan Press, 1990.

Zerbe, Gordon. *Non-Retaliation in Early Jewish and New Testament Texts.* Sheffield: JSOT Press, 1993.

―――. "'Pacifism' and 'Passive Resistance' in Apocalyptic Writings: A Critical Evaluation." In *The Pseudepigrapha and Early Biblical Interpretation,* edited by James H. Charlesworth and Craig Evans, pp. 65-95. Sheffield: JSOT Press, 1993.

Zerubavel, Eviatar. *Hidden Rhythms: Schedules and Calendars in Social Life.* Chicago: University of Chicago Press, 1981.

Index of Modern Authors

Index of Subjects

Abduction, 142, 144, 146-51, 160n.75, 174, 386. *See also* Slavery

Abraham, 194, 282n.8, 301, 321-23, 326-27, 338, 340-45

Achaemenid Dynasty. *See* Persia, Persian Empire

Aemilius Paullus, 147n.27, 160n.75, 163, 165-67

Akra, 55, 64, 66, 105n.111, 122-26, 129, 141-42, 161, 174, 187, 190-91, 195, 213, 319, 345, 383, 386

Alexander the Great: 17n.53, 203-4, 289-90; and conquest of Judea, 4, 382; and defeat of the Persian Empire, 30; and Hellenistic culture, identity, and power, 104-6, 110n.136, 113-14, 203-4; and ideology of conquest, 49-54; in Sibylline oracles, 19n.62

Amphipolis, parade and games at, 163n.86, 166, 167n.102

Ancestral customs, laws, and religion, 56, 58, 72-77, 244, 334, 379; abrogation of, 185, 189, 191-213, 383, 386; and authority, 62, 307; and collaboration, 112, 235; and Hellenism, 88, 94-103, 114; and power, 73, 83; concerning worship, 58, 61, 83; faithfulness to, 88, 114, 193, 276; and ordering of life, 97, 103; self-governance according to, 72-77, 94, 185-89, 191, 215, 383

Angels, Angelic figures: and battle, 115-16,

219, 237, 242, 260; and eternal life, 260, 275; and heavenly worship, 155; and imagination, 266, 382, 384; and intercession, 269, 380; and judgment, 331, 336, 338, 340, 359; and power, 13, 346-47, 355, 382, 386; angelophany, 239-40; as deliverers, 7-8, 260; as scribe, 376; 'Asa'el, 15-16, 21; fallen watchers, 15-17, 19-22, 289-93, 314-15, 321, 331, 340, 353-56, 359-61, 366, 380, 387; Gabriel, 20, 124, 136, 183-85, 253-57, 263, 271-74; imparting strength, 234, 238-41, 250; in Enochic traditions, 21-23, 280, 288-93, 314-15, 345, 380, 387; interpreting and revealing, 17, 135-36, 174, 179, 183, 220, 229, 234-35, 237, 241, 248-58, 262-63, 266, 274-78, 345, 387, 391-94; Michael, 237, 354; Moses, 301; prayer of, 360-63, 376; Sariel, 353

Animals, 290; birds, 170, 350, 373-74, 377-78; bulls, 53-54, 170; elephants, 53, 65, 78, 118, 167n.102, 385; horses, 53, 61, 264, 365; lambs, 13, 347, 351-52, 355, 363, 365-74, 379-81, 389; permitted/forbidden, 58-61, 191, 207-8; pigs, 184, 205; rams, 352, 370-76, 389; sacrifice of, 24-25, 54, 56-62, 152, 184, 191, 205; sheep, 170, 300-301, 346-47, 350-51, 355, 363-75, 378-79, 389; symbolism of, 170-71, 346-48, 389, 398; *venationes*, 165

Anonymity, 33-40

Index of Ancient Sources

3 Maccabees
4:11	167n.102
5:1–6:21	167n.102

Sibylline Oracles
3.383	19n.62

Testament of Moses
1:4-10	169
1:7	393
1:11-12	392
1:14	393
1:16	394
1:16-17	38
1:17	394
3:11	393n.9
9:6-7	169
10:1	39, 168n.104
10:3	168n.104
10:7	168n.104
10:11-12	28
11:10-11	393
11:14	393

DEAD SEA SCROLLS
1QIs	275n.199

1QS
8.6	327n.54, 336n.96
7.12–15	98n.80
4Q212	280n.2

4QEng
1 iv 13-26	313n.1

1Qap Genar
20–22	340n.113
20.14	334n.83

HELLENISTIC JEWISH AUTHORS

Josephus
Antiquitates Judaicae — 55, 57
12	67n.94
12.20-33	68n.100
12.129	67
12.138-44	56
12.142	56
12.143	57, 83
12.144	57
12.145	150
12.147	56n.44
12.151-53	123n.33
12.159	123n.33
12.229	126
12.238	121n.21
12.239	128
12.240	73n.125, 126
12.253	184
12.299	68n.100
13.288	141
15.326	141
16.86	94n.60
16.192	94n.60
16.280	94n.60
16.295	94n.60
16.305	94n.60

Bellum Judaicum
1.209	94n.60

Philo
In Flaccum
96	208n.119

Pseudo-Philo
Biblical Antiquities 300n.80

RABBINIC, TARGUMIC, AND CHRISTIAN SOURCES
Exodus Rabbah	300n.80
Targum Isaiah	330n.66

Jerome
In Danielem
11.13-14	69n.105

CLASSICAL SOURCES

Aeschylus
Prometheus Vinctus
11	15n.49
231-36	16
454-58	17n.52
465-66	17n.52
478-83	17n.52
484-99	17n.52
500-503	17n.52
890	16n.49
897	16n.49

Appian
Illyriaca
9–10	160n.75

Macedonian Affairs — 188

Syriaca
9.57	54

Aristophanes
Acharnians — 201

Aristotle
Politica
1313b	203

Arrian
Anabasis
1.17.3-8	203

Dio Chrysostom
Orationes
11.93	53n.29
48.9	160

Diodorus
15.38.2	122
18.59	119n.9
18.63.6	119n.9
19.58.2	119n.9
28.3	80n.9
29.15	80n.9
31.2	135n.78
31.16.2	162